Authorized Self-Study Guide

Cisco Voice over IP (CVOICE),
Third Edition

Kevin Wallace, CCIE No. 7945

Cisco Press

800 East 96th Street

Indianapolis, IN 46240

Authorized Self-Study Guide
Cisco Voice over IP (CVOICE),
Third Edition

Kevin Wallace

Copyright© 2009 Cisco Systems, Inc.

Published by:
Cisco Press
800 East 96th Street
Indianapolis, IN 46240 USA

Printed in the United States of America

First Printing July 2008

Library of Congress Cataloging-in-Publication Data:
Wallace, Kevin, CCNP.
  Authorized self-study guide : Cisco Voice over IP (CVoice) / Kevin Wallace. — 3rd ed.
     p. cm.
  ISBN 978-1-58705-554-6 (hbk. : CD-ROM) 1. Internet telephony—Examinations—Study guides. 2. Electronic data processing personnel—Certification—Study guides. I. Title. II. Title: Cisco Voice over IP (CVoice).
  TK5105.8865.W3345 2008
  004.69'5—dc22

                              2008022672

ISBN-13: 978-1-58705-554-6

ISBN-10: 1-58705-554-6

Warning and Disclaimer

This book is designed to provide information about the Cisco Voice over IP (CVOICE) certification topics. Every effort has been made to make this book as complete and as accurate as possible, but no warranty or fitness is implied.

The information is provided on an "as is" basis. The authors, Cisco Press, and Cisco Systems, Inc., shall have neither liability nor responsibility to any person or entity with respect to any loss or damages arising from the information contained in this book or from the use of the discs or programs that may accompany it.

The opinions expressed in this book belong to the author and are not necessarily those of Cisco Systems, Inc.

Trademark Acknowledgments

All terms mentioned in this book that are known to be trademarks or service marks have been appropriately capitalized. Cisco Press or Cisco Systems, Inc., cannot attest to the accuracy of this information. Use of a term in this book should not be regarded as affecting the validity of any trademark or service mark.

Corporate and Government Sales

The publisher offers excellent discounts on this book when ordered in quantity for bulk purchases or special sales, which may include electronic versions and/or custom covers and content particular to your business, training goals, marketing focus, and branding interests. For more information, please contact: **U.S. Corporate and Government Sales**   1-800-382-3419   corpsales@pearsontechgroup.com

For sales outside the United States lease contact: **International Sales**   international@pearsoned.com

Feedback Information

At Cisco Press, our goal is to create in-depth technical books of the highest quality and value. Each book is crafted with care and precision, undergoing rigorous development that involves the unique expertise of members from the professional technical community.

Readers' feedback is a natural continuation of this process. If you have any comments regarding how we could improve the quality of this book, or otherwise alter it to better suit your needs, you can contact us through email at feedback@ciscopress.com. Please make sure to include the book title and ISBN in your message.

We greatly appreciate your assistance.

Publisher: Paul Boger

Associate Publisher: Dave Dusthimer

Cisco Press Program Manager: Jeff Brady

Executive Editor: Brett Bartow

Managing Editor: Patrick Kanouse

Development Editor: Andrew Cupp

Senior Project Editor: San Dee Phillips

Copy Editor: Barbara Hacha

Technical Editors: Michelle Plumb
Anthony Sequeira

Editorial Assistant: Vanessa Evans

Book and Cover Designer: Louisa Adair

Composition: Bronkella Publishing, LLC

Indexer: Tim Wright

Proofreader: Jovana San Nicholas-Shirley

Americas Headquarters	Asia Pacific Headquarters	Europe Headquarters
Cisco Systems, Inc.	Cisco Systems, Inc.	Cisco Systems International BV
170 West Tasman Drive	168 Robinson Road	Haarlerbergpark
San Jose, CA 95134-1706	#28-01 Capital Tower	Haarlerbergweg 13-19
USA	Singapore 068912	1101 CH Amsterdam
www.cisco.com	www.cisco.com	The Netherlands
Tel: 408 526-4000	Tel: +65 6317 7777	www-europe.cisco.com
800 553-NETS (6387)	Fax: +65 6317 7799	Tel: +31 0 800 020 0791
Fax: 408 527-0883		Fax: +31 0 20 357 1100

Cisco has more than 200 offices worldwide. Addresses, phone numbers, and fax numbers are listed on the Cisco Website at **www.cisco.com/go/offices.**

©2007 Cisco Systems, Inc. All rights reserved. CCVP, the Cisco logo, and the Cisco Square Bridge logo are trademarks of Cisco Systems, Inc.; Changing the Way We Work, Live, Play, and Learn is a service mark of Cisco Systems, Inc.; and Access Registrar, Aironet, BPX, Catalyst, CCDA, CCDP, CCIE, CCIP, CCNA, CCNP, CCSP, Cisco, the Cisco Certified Internetwork Expert logo, Cisco IOS, Cisco Press, Cisco Systems, Cisco Systems Capital, the Cisco Systems logo, Cisco Unity, Enterprise/Solver, EtherChannel, EtherFast, EtherSwitch, Fast Step, Follow Me Browsing, FormShare, GigaDrive, GigaStack, HomeLink, Internet Quotient, IOS, IP/TV, iQ Expertise, the iQ logo, iQ Net Readiness Scorecard, iQuick Study, LightStream, Linksys, MeetingPlace, MGX, Networking Academy, Network Registrar, Packet, PIX, ProConnect, RateMUX, ScriptShare, SlideCast, SMARTnet, StackWise, The Fastest Way to Increase Your Internet Quotient, and TransPath are registered trademarks of Cisco Systems, Inc. and/or its affiliates in the United States and certain other countries.

All other trademarks mentioned in this document or Website are the property of their respective owners. The use of the word partner does not imply a partnership relationship between Cisco and any other company. (0609R)

About the Author

Kevin Wallace, CCIE No. 7945, is a certified Cisco instructor, and he teaches courses in the Cisco CCSP, CCVP, and CCNP tracks. With 19 years of Cisco networking experience, Kevin has been a network design specialist for the Walt Disney World Resort and a network manager for Eastern Kentucky University. Kevin holds a bachelor of science degree in electrical engineering from the University of Kentucky. Kevin also is a CCVP, CCSP, CCNP, and CCDP with multiple Cisco security and IP communications specializations.

About the Technical Reviewers

Michelle Plumb is a full-time certified Cisco instructor for SkillSoft, focusing on the Cisco IP Telephony track. Michelle has more than 18 years in the field as an IT and telephony specialist and maintains a high level of Cisco and Microsoft certifications, including CCVP, CCSI, and MCSE NT 4.0/2000. Michelle has been a technical reviewer for numerous books related to the Cisco CCNP and Cisco IP Telephony course material track.

Anthony Sequeira, CCIE No. 15626, completed the CCIE in Routing and Switching in January 2006. He is currently pursuing the CCIE in Security. For the past 15 years, he has written and lectured to massive audiences about the latest in networking technologies. Anthony is currently a senior technical instructor and certified Cisco instructor for SkillSoft. Anthony lives with his wife and daughter in Florida. When he is not reading about the latest Cisco innovations, he is exploring the Florida skies in a Cessna.

Dedication

I dedicate this book to my two daughters, Stacie and Sabrina. You are growing up far too fast.

Acknowledgments

My thanks go out to my fellow instructors at SkillSoft and our manager, Tom Warrick. It is an honor to work side by side with you all. Also, thanks to Brett Bartow at Cisco Press for his faith in me and allowing me to simultaneously author two books.

On a personal note, I acknowledge and thank God for His blessings in my life. Also, my wife, Vivian, and my daughters, Stacie and Sabrina, have patiently awaited the completion of this book and the *CCNA Security Official Exam Certification Guide*. Thank you for your patience during these past few months.

This Book Is Safari Enabled

The Safari® Enabled icon on the cover of your favorite technology book means the book is available through Safari Bookshelf. When you buy this book, you get free access to the online edition for 45 days.

Safari Bookshelf is an electronic reference library that lets you easily search thousands of technical books, find code samples, download chapters, and access technical information whenever and wherever you need it.

To gain 45-day Safari Enabled access to this book:

- Go to http://www.informit.com/onlineedition.
- Complete the brief registration form.
- Enter the coupon code 89GJ-11QH-EDPS-48IP-AJ6C.

If you have difficulty registering on Safari Bookshelf or accessing the online edition, please e-mail customer-service@safaribooksonline.com.

Contents at a Glance

Contents

Icons Used in This Book

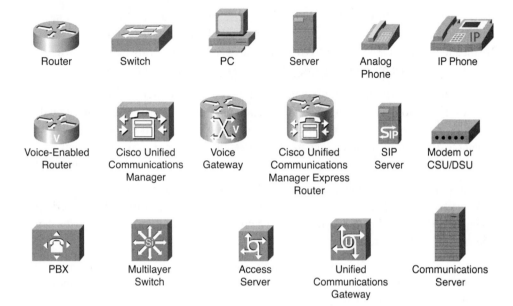

Command Syntax Conventions

The conventions used to present command syntax in this book are the same conventions used in the IOS Command Reference. The Command Reference describes these conventions as follows:

- **Boldface** indicates commands and keywords that are entered literally as shown. In actual configuration examples and output (not general command syntax), boldface indicates commands that are manually input by the user (such as a **show** command).

- *Italic* indicates arguments for which you supply actual values.

- Vertical bars (|) separate alternative, mutually exclusive elements.

- Square brackets ([ ]) indicate an optional element.

- Braces ({ }) indicate a required choice.

- Braces within brackets ([{ }]) indicate a required choice within an optional element.

Foreword

Cisco certification Self-Study Guides are excellent self-study resources for networking professionals to maintain and increase internetworking skills and to prepare for Cisco Career Certification exams. Cisco Career Certifications are recognized worldwide and provide valuable, measurable rewards to networking professionals and their employers.

Cisco Press exam certification guides and preparation materials offer exceptional—and flexible—access to the knowledge and information required to stay current in one's field of expertise or to gain new skills. Whether used to increase internetworking skills or as a supplement to a formal certification preparation course, these materials offer networking professionals the information and knowledge required to perform on-the-job tasks proficiently.

Developed in conjunction with the Cisco certifications and training team, Cisco Press books are the only self-study books authorized by Cisco, and they offer students a series of exam practice tools and resource materials to help ensure that learners fully grasp the concepts and information presented.

Additional authorized Cisco instructor-led courses, e-learning, labs, and simulations are available exclusively from Cisco Learning Solutions Partners worldwide. To learn more, visit http://www.cisco.com/go/training.

I hope you will find this guide to be an essential part of your exam preparation and professional development, as well as a valuable addition to your personal library.

Drew Rosen

Manager, Learning & Development

Learning@Cisco

June 2008

Introduction

With the rapid adoption of Voice over IP (VoIP), many telephony and data network technicians, engineers, and designers are now working to become proficient in VoIP. Professional certifications, such as the Cisco Certified Voice Professional (CCVP) certification, offer validation of an employee's or a consultant's competency in specific technical areas.

This book mirrors the level of detail found in the Cisco CVOICE Version 6.0 course, which many CCVP candidates select as their first course in the CCVP track. Version 6.0 represents a significant update over Version 5.0 of the CVOICE course, because Version 6.0 integrates much of the content previously found in the more advanced Implementing Cisco Voice Gateways and Gatekeepers (GWGK) course.

A fundamental understanding of traditional telephony, however, would certainly benefit a CVOICE student or a reader of this book. If you think you lack a fundamental understanding of traditional telephony, a recommended companion for this book is the Cisco Press *Voice over IP First-Step* book (ISBN: 978-1-58720-156-1), which is also written by this book's author. *Voice over IP First-Step* is written in a conversational tone and teaches concepts surrounding traditional telephony and how those concepts translate into a VoIP environment.

Additional Study Resources

This book contains a CD with approximately 90 minutes of video, where you will see the author demonstrate a variety of basic VoIP configurations. The videos were originally developed for NetMaster Class (http://www.netmasterclass.com), a company specializing in CCIE Lab training. These video-on-demand titles are as follows:

Analog Voice Port Configuration

Digital Voice Port Configuration

Dial Peer Configuration

H.323 Configuration

MGCP Configuration

SIP Configuration

As an additional reference for readers pursuing the CCVP certification, the author has created a website with recommended study resources (some free and some recommended for purchase) for all courses in the CCVP track. These recommendations can be found at the following URL: http://www.voipcertprep.com.

Goals and Methods

The primary objective of this book is to help the reader pass the 642-436 CVOICE exam, which is a required exam for the CCVP certification and for the Cisco Rich Media Communications Specialist specialization.

One key methodology used in this book is to help you discover the exam topics that you need to review in more depth, to help you fully understand and remember those details, and to help you prove to yourself that you have retained your knowledge of those topics. This book does not try to help you pass by memorization, but helps you truly learn and understand the topics by using the following methods:

- Helping you discover which test topics you have not mastered

- Providing explanations and information to fill in your knowledge gaps, including detailed illustrations and topologies as well as sample configurations

- Providing exam practice questions to confirm your understanding of core concepts

Who Should Read This Book?

This book is primarily targeted toward candidates of the CVOICE exam. However, because CVOICE is one of the Cisco foundational VoIP courses, this book also serves as a VoIP primer to noncertification readers.

Many Cisco resellers actively encourage their employees to attain Cisco certifications and seek new employees already possessing Cisco certifications, for deeper discounts when purchasing Cisco products. Additionally, having attained a certification communicates to your employer or customer that you are serious about your craft and have not simply "hung out a shingle" declaring yourself knowledgeable about VoIP. Rather, you have proven your competency through a rigorous series of exams.

How This Book Is Organized

Although the chapters in this book could be read sequentially, the organization allows you to focus your reading on specific topics of interest. For example, if you already possess a strong VoIP background, you could skim the first two chapters (which cover foundational VoIP topics, including an introduction to VoIP and elements of a VoIP network) and focus on the remaining seven chapters, which address more advanced VoIP concepts. Specifically, the chapters in this book cover the following topics:

Chapter 1, "Introducing Voice over IP Networks": This chapter describes VoIP, components of a VoIP network, the protocols used, and service considerations of integrating VoIP into an existing data network. Also, this chapter considers various types of voice gateways and how to use gateways in different IP telephony environments.

Chapter 2, "Considering VoIP Design Elements": This chapter describes the challenges of integrating a voice and data network and explains solutions for avoiding problems when designing a VoIP network for optimal voice quality. Also, you learn the characteristics of voice codecs and digital signal processors and how to perform bandwidth calculations for VoIP calls.

Chapter 3, "Routing Calls over Analog Voice Ports": This chapter describes the various call types in a VoIP network. You then learn how to configure analog voice interfaces as new devices are introduced into the voice path. Finally, you discover how to configure dial peers, in order to add call routing intelligence to a router.

Chapter 4, "Performing Call Signaling over Digital Voice Ports": This chapter describes various digital interfaces and how to configure them. Also, you are introduced to Q Signaling (QSIG) and learn how to enable QSIG support.

Chapter 5, "Examining VoIP Gateways and Gateway Control Protocols": This chapter details the H.323, MGCP, and SIP protocol stacks, and you learn how to implement each of these protocols on Cisco IOS gateways.

Chapter 6, "Identifying Dial Plan Characteristics": This chapter describes the components and requirements of a dial plan and discusses how to implement a numbering plan using Cisco IOS gateways.

Chapter 7, "Configuring Advanced Dial Plans": This chapter shows you how to configure various digit manipulation strategies using Cisco IOS gateways. Additionally, you learn how to influence path selection. This chapter then concludes with a discussion of the Class of Restriction (COR) feature, and you learn how to implement COR on Cisco IOS gateways to specify calling privileges.

Chapter 8, "Configuring H.323 Gatekeepers": This chapter describes the function of a Cisco IOS gatekeeper. Also, you learn how to configure a gatekeeper for functions such as registration, address resolution, call routing, and call admission control (CAC).

Chapter 9, "Establishing a Connection with an Internet Telephony Service Provider": This chapter describes Cisco Unified Border Element (Cisco UBE) functions and features. You learn how a Cisco UBE is used in current enterprise environments and how to implement a Cisco UBE router to provide protocol interworking.

After reading this chapter, you should be able to perform the following tasks:

■ Describe Voice over IP (VoIP), components of a VoIP network, the protocols used, and service considerations of integrating VoIP into an existing data network.

■ Describe various types of voice gateways and how to use gateways in different IP telephony environments.

CHAPTER 1

Introducing Voice over IP Networks

Voice over Internet Protocol (VoIP) allows a voice-enabled router to carry voice traffic, such as telephone calls and faxes, over an Internet Protocol (IP) network. This chapter introduces the fundamentals of VoIP, the various types of voice gateways, and how to use gateways in different IP telephony environments.

VoIP Fundamentals

Voice over IP is also known as VoIP. You might also hear VoIP referred to as *IP Telephony*. Both terms refer to sending voice across an IP network. However, the primary distinction revolves around the endpoints in use. For example, in a VoIP network, traditional analog or digital circuits connect into an IP network, typically through some sort of gateway. However, an IP telephony environment contains endpoints that natively communicate using IP. Be aware that much of the literature on the subject, including this book, might use these terms interchangeably.

VoIP routes voice conversations over IP-based networks, including the Internet. VoIP has made it possible for businesses to realize cost savings by utilizing their existing IP network to carry voice and data, especially where businesses have underutilized network capacity that can carry VoIP at no additional cost. This section introduces VoIP, the required components in VoIP networks, currently available VoIP signaling protocols, VoIP service issues, and media transmission protocols.

Cisco Unified Communications Architecture

The Cisco Unified Communications System fully integrates communications by enabling data, voice, and video to be transmitted over a single network infrastructure using standards-based IP. Leveraging the framework provided by Cisco IP hardware and software products, the Cisco Unified Communications System has the capability to address current and emerging communications needs in the enterprise environment. The Cisco Unified Communications family of products is designed to optimize feature functionality, reduce configuration and maintenance requirements, and provide interoperability with a variety of other applications. The Cisco Unified Communications System provides and maintains a high level of availability, quality of service (QoS), and security for the network.

The Cisco Unified Communications System incorporates and integrates the following communications technologies:

- **IP telephony:** IP telephony refers to technology that transmits voice communications over a network using IP standards. Cisco Unified Communications System includes hardware and software products such as call processing agents, IP phones (both wired and wireless), voice messaging systems, video devices, and other special applications.

- **Customer contact center:** Cisco IP Contact Center products combine strategy with architecture to enable efficient and effective customer communications across a global network. This allows organizations to draw from a broader range of resources to service customers. These resources include access to a large pool of customer service agents and multiple channels of communication as well as customer self-help tools.

- **Video telephony:** The Cisco Unified Video Advantage products enable real-time video communications and collaboration using the same IP network and call processing agent as Cisco Unified Communications. With Cisco Unified Video Advantage, making a video call is just as easy as dialing a phone number.

- **Rich-media conferencing:** Cisco Conference Connection and Cisco Unified MeetingPlace enhance the virtual meeting environment with an integrated set of IP-based tools for voice, video, and web conferencing.

- **Third-party applications:** Cisco works with other companies to provide a selection of third-party IP communications applications and products. This helps businesses focus on critical needs such as messaging, customer care, and workforce optimization.

VoIP Overview

VoIP is the family of technologies that allows IP networks to be used for voice applications, such as telephony, voice instant messaging, and teleconferencing. VoIP defines a way to carry voice calls over an IP network, including the digitization and packetization of the voice streams. IP Telephony VoIP standards create a telephony system where higher-level features such as advanced call routing, voice mail, and contact centers can be utilized.

VoIP services convert your voice into a digital signal that travels over an IP-based network. If you are calling a traditional phone number, the signal is converted to a traditional telephone signal before it reaches its destination. VoIP allows you to make a call directly from a computer, a VoIP phone, or a traditional analog phone connected to a special adapter. In addition, wireless "hot spots" in locations such as airports, parks, and cafes that allow you to connect to the Internet might enable you to use VoIP services.

Business Case for VoIP

The business advantages that drive the implementation of VoIP networks have changed over time. Starting with simple media convergence, these advantages evolved to include call-switching intelligence and the total user experience.

Originally, ROI calculations centered on toll-bypass and converged-network savings. Although these savings are still relevant today, advances in voice technologies allow organizations and service providers to differentiate their product offerings by providing the following:

- **Cost savings:** Traditional time-division multiplexing (TDM), which is used in the public switched telephone network (PSTN) environment, dedicates 64 kbps of bandwidth per voice channel. This approach results in bandwidth being unused when no voice traffic exists. VoIP shares bandwidth across multiple logical connections, which results in a more efficient use of the bandwidth, thereby reducing bandwidth requirements. A substantial amount of equipment is needed to combine 64-kbps channels into high-speed links for transport across a network. Packet telephony uses statistical analysis to multiplex voice traffic alongside data traffic. This consolidation results in substantial savings on capital equipment and operations costs.

- **Flexibility:** The sophisticated functionality of IP networks allows organizations to be flexible in the types of applications and services they provide to their customers and users. Service providers can easily segment customers. This helps them to provide different applications, custom services, and rates depending on traffic volume needs and other customer-specific factors.

- **Advanced features:** Following are some examples of the advanced features provided by current VoIP applications:

  - **Advanced call routing:** When multiple paths exist to connect a call to its destination, some of these paths might be preferred over others based on cost, distance, quality, partner handoffs, traffic load, or various other considerations. Least-cost routing and time-of-day routing are two examples of advanced call routing that can be implemented to determine the best possible route for each call.

  - **Unified messaging:** Unified messaging improves communications and productivity. It provides a single user interface for messages that have been delivered over a variety of mediums. For example, users can read their e-mail, hear their voice mail, and view fax messages by accessing a single inbox.

  - **Integrated information systems:** Organizations use VoIP to affect business process transformation. These processes include centralized call control, geographically dispersed virtual contact centers, and access to resources and self-help tools.

  - **Long-distance toll bypass:** Long-distance toll bypass is an attractive solution for organizations that place a significant number of calls between sites that are charged traditional long-distance fees. In this case, it might be more cost-effective to use VoIP to place those calls across an IP network. If the IP WAN becomes congested, calls can overflow into the PSTN, ensuring that no degradation occurs in voice quality.

- **Security:** Mechanisms in an IP network allow an administrator to ensure that IP conversations are secure. Encryption of sensitive signaling header fields and message bodies protect packets in case of unauthorized packet interception.

- **Customer relationships:** The capability to provide customer support through multiple mediums, such as telephone, chat, and e-mail, builds solid customer satisfaction and loyalty. A pervasive IP network allows organizations to provide contact center agents with consolidated and up-to-date customer records along with related customer communication. Access to this information allows quick problem solving, which builds strong customer relationships.

- **Telephony application services:** XML services on Cisco IP Phones give users another way to perform or access business applications. Some examples of XML-based services on Cisco IP Phones are user stock quotes, inventory checks, direct-dial directory, announcements, and advertisements. Some Cisco IP Phones are equipped with a pixel-based display that can display full graphics instead of just text in the window. The pixel-based display capabilities allow you to use sophisticated graphical presentations for applications on Cisco IP Phones and make them available at any desktop, counter, or location.

Components of a VoIP Network

Figure 1-1 depicts the basic components of a packet voice network.

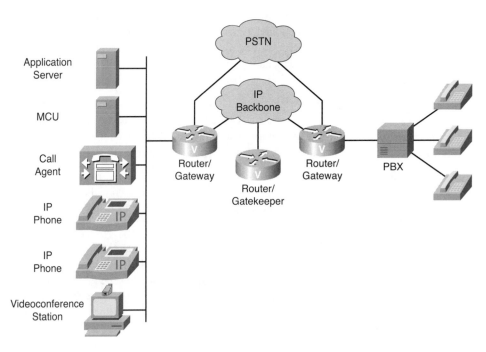

Figure 1-1   *Components of a VoIP Network*

The following is a description of these basic components:

- **IP Phones:** Cisco IP Phones provide IP endpoints for voice communication.

- **Gatekeeper:** A gatekeeper provides Call Admission Control (CAC), bandwidth control and management, and address translation.

- **Gateway:** The gateway provides translation between VoIP and non-VoIP networks, such as the PSTN. Gateways also provide physical access for local analog and digital voice devices, such as telephones, fax machines, key sets, and private branch exchanges (PBX).

- **Multipoint Control Unit (MCU):** An MCU provides real-time connectivity for participants in multiple locations to attend the same videoconference or meeting.

- **Call agent:** A call agent provides call control for IP phones, CAC, bandwidth control and management, and address translation. Unlike a gatekeeper, which in a Cisco environment typically runs on a router, a call agent typically runs on a server platform. Cisco Unified Communications Manager is an example of a call agent.

- **Application servers:** Application servers provide services such as voice mail, unified messaging, and Cisco Communications Manager Attendant Console.

- **Videoconference station:** A videoconference station provides access for end-user participation in videoconferencing. The videoconference station contains a video capture device for video input and a microphone for audio input. A user can view video streams and hear audio that originates at a remote user station.

Other components, such as software voice applications, interactive voice response (IVR) systems, and soft phones, provide additional services to meet the needs of an enterprise site.

VoIP Functions

In the traditional PSTN telephony network, all the elements required to complete a call are transparent to an end user. Migration to VoIP requires an awareness of these required elements and a thorough understanding of the protocols and components that provide the same functionality in an IP network.

Required VoIP functionality includes these functions:

- **Signaling:** Signaling is the capability to generate and exchange control information that will be used to establish, monitor, and release connections between two endpoints. Voice signaling requires the capability to provide supervisory, address, and alerting functionality between nodes. The PSTN network uses Signaling System 7 (SS7) to transport control messages. SS7 uses out-of-band signaling, which, in this case, is the exchange of call control information in a separate dedicated channel.

VoIP presents several options for signaling, including H.323, Session Initiation Protocol (SIP), H.248, Media Gateway Control Protocol (MGCP), and Skinny Client Control Protocol (SCCP). Some VoIP gateways are also capable of initiating SS7 signaling directly to the PSTN network. Signaling protocols are classified as either peer-to-peer or client/server protocols.

SIP and H.323 are examples of peer-to-peer signaling protocols where the end devices or gateways contain the intelligence to initiate and terminate calls and interpret call control messages. H.248, SCCP, and MGCP are examples of client/server protocols where the endpoints or gateways do not contain call control intelligence but send or receive event notifications to a server commonly referred to as a *call agent*. For example, when an MGCP gateway detects a telephone that has gone off hook, it does not know to automatically provide a dial tone. The gateway sends an event notification to the call agent, telling the agent that an off-hook condition has been detected. The call agent notifies the gateway to provide a dial tone.

- **Database services:** Access to services, such as toll-free numbers or caller ID, requires the capability to query a database to determine whether the call can be placed or information can be made available. Database services include access to billing information, caller name delivery (CNAM), toll-free database services, and calling-card services. VoIP service providers can differentiate their services by providing access to many unique database services. For example, to simplify fax access to mobile users, a provider can build a service that converts fax to e-mail. Another example is providing a call notification service that places outbound calls with prerecorded messages at specific times to notify users of such events as school closures, wake-up calls, or appointments.

- **Bearer control:** Bearer channels are the channels that carry voice calls. Proper supervision of these channels requires that appropriate call connect and call disconnect signaling be passed between end devices. Correct signaling ensures that the channel is allocated to the current voice call and that a channel is properly deallocated when either side terminates the call. Connect and disconnect messages are carried by SS7 in the PSTN network. Connect and disconnect message are carried by SIP, H.323, H.248, or MGCP within the IP network.

- **Codecs:** Codecs provide the coding and decoding translation between analog and digital facilities. Each codec type defines the method of voice coding and the compression mechanism that is used to convert the voice stream. The PSTN uses TDM to carry each voice call. Each voice channel reserves 64 kbps of bandwidth and uses the G.711 codec to convert an analog voice wave to a 64-kbps digitized voice stream. In VoIP design, codecs might compress voice beyond the 64-kbps voice stream to allow more efficient use of network resources. The most widely used codec in the WAN environment is G.729, which compresses the voice stream to 8 kbps.

VoIP Signaling Protocols

VoIP uses several control and call-signaling protocols. Among these are:

- **H.323:** H.323 is a standard that specifies the components, protocols, and procedures that provide multimedia communication services, real-time audio, video, and data communications over packet networks, including IP networks. H.323 is part of a family of International Telecommunication Union Telecommunication Standardization sector (ITU-T) recommendations called H.32x that provides multimedia communication services over a variety of networks. H.32x is an umbrella of standards that define all aspects of synchronized voice, video, and data transmission. It also defines end-to-end call signaling.

- **MGCP:** MGCP is a method for PSTN gateway control or thin device control. Specified in RFC 2705, MGCP defines a protocol that controls VoIP gateways that are connected to external call control devices, referred to as call agents. MGCP provides the signaling capability for less-expensive edge devices, such as gateways, that might not have implemented a full voice-signaling protocol such as H.323. For example, anytime an event, such as off-hook, occurs on a voice port of a gateway, the voice port reports that event to the call agent. The call agent then signals the voice port to provide a service, such as dial-tone signaling.

- **SIP:** SIP is a detailed protocol that specifies the commands and responses to set up and tear down calls. SIP also details features such as security, proxy, and transport control protocol (TCP) or User Datagram Protocol (UDP) services. SIP and its partner protocols, Session Announcement Protocol (SAP) and Session Description Protocol (SDP), provide announcements and information about multicast sessions to users on a network. SIP defines end-to-end call signaling between devices. SIP is a text-based protocol that borrows many elements of HTTP, using the same transaction request and response model and similar header and response codes. It also adopts a modified form of the URL addressing scheme used within e-mail that is based on Simple Mail Transfer Protocol (SMTP).

- **SCCP:** SCCP is a Cisco proprietary protocol used between Cisco Communications Manager and Cisco IP Phones. The end stations (telephones) that use SCCP are called Skinny clients, which consume less processing overhead. The client communicates with the Cisco Unified Communications Manager (often referred to as Call Manager, abbreviated UCM) using connection-oriented (TCP-based) communication to establish a call with another H.323-compliant end station.

The H.323 Umbrella

H.323 is a suite of protocols defined by the International Telecommunication Union (ITU) for multimedia conferences over LANs. The H.323 protocol was designed by the ITU-T and was initially approved in February 1996. It was developed as a protocol that provides IP networks with traditional telephony functionality. Today, H.323 is the most widely deployed standards-based voice and videoconferencing standard for packet-switched networks.

The protocols specified by H.323 include the following:

- **H.225 Call Signaling:** H.225 call signaling is used to establish a connection between two H.323 endpoints. This is achieved by exchanging H.225 protocol messages on the call-signaling channel. The call-signaling channel is opened between two H.323 endpoints or between an endpoint and an H.323 gatekeeper.

- **H.225 Registration, Admission, and Status:** Registration, admission, and status (RAS) is the protocol between endpoints (terminals and gateways) and gatekeepers. RAS is used to perform registration, admission control, bandwidth changes, status, and disengage procedures between endpoints and gatekeepers. A *RAS channel* is used to exchange RAS messages. This signaling channel is opened between an endpoint and a gatekeeper prior to the establishment of any other channels.

- **H.245 Control Signaling:** H.245 control signaling is used to exchange end-to-end control messages governing the operation of an H.323 endpoint. These control messages carry information related to the following:

  - Capabilities exchange

  - Opening and closing of logical channels used to carry media streams

  - Flow-control messages

  - General commands and indications

- **Audio codecs:** An audio codec encodes the audio signal from a microphone for transmission by the transmitting H.323 terminal and decodes the received audio code that is sent to the speaker on the receiving H.323 terminal. Because audio is the minimum service provided by the H.323 standard, all H.323 terminals must have at least one audio codec supported, as specified in the ITU–T G.711 recommendation (coding audio at 64 kbps). Additional audio codec recommendations such as G.722 (64, 56, and 48 kbps), G.723.1 (5.3 and 6.3 kbps), G.728 (16 kbps), and G.729 (8 kbps) might also be supported.

- **Video codecs:** A video codec encodes video from a camera for transmission by the transmitting H.323 terminal and decodes the received video code on a video display of the receiving H.323 terminal. Because H.323 specifies support of video as optional, the support of video codecs is optional as well. However, any H.323 terminal providing video communications must support video encoding and decoding as specified in the ITU–T H.261 recommendation.

In Cisco IP Communications environments, H.323 is widely used with gateways, gatekeepers, and third-party H.323 clients, such as video terminals. Connections are configured between devices using static destination IP addresses.

Note   Because H.323 is a peer-to-peer protocol, H.323 gateways are not registered with Cisco Unified Communications Manager as an endpoint is. An IP address is configured in the Cisco UCM to confirm that communication is possible.

MGCP

MGCP is a client/server call control protocol built on a centralized control architecture. MGCP offers the advantage of centralized gateway administration and provides for largely scalable IP telephony solutions. All dial plan information resides on a separate call agent. The call agent, which controls the ports on the gateway, performs call control. An MGCP gateway does media translation between the PSTN and VoIP networks for external calls. In a Cisco-based network, Communications Managers function as call agents.

MGCP is a plain-text protocol used by call-control devices to manage IP telephony gateways. MGCP was defined under RFC 2705, which was updated by RFC 3660, and superseded by RFC 3435, which was updated by RFC 3661.

With MGCP, Cisco UCM knows of and controls individual voice ports on an MGCP gateway. This approach allows complete control of a dial plan from Cisco UCM and gives Communications Manager per-port control of connections to the PSTN, legacy PBX, voice-mail systems, and POTS phones. MGCP is implemented with use of a series of plain-text commands sent via User Datagram Protocol (UDP) port 2427 between the Cisco UCM and a gateway.

It is important to note that for an MGCP interaction to take place with Cisco UCM, an MGCP gateway must have Cisco UCM support. If you are a registered customer of the Software Advisor, you can use this tool to make sure your platform and your Cisco IOS software or Cisco Catalyst operating system version are compatible with Cisco UCM for MGCP. Also, make sure your version of Cisco UCM supports the gateway.

PRI/BRI Backhaul

A Primary Rate Interface (PRI) and Basic Rate Interface (BRI) backhaul is an internal interface between the call agent (such as Cisco UCM) and Cisco gateways. It is a separate channel for backhauling signaling information. A PRI backhaul forwards PRI Layer 3 (Q.931) signaling information via a TCP connection.

An MGCP gateway is relatively easy to configure. Because the call agent has all the call-routing intelligence, you do not need to configure the gateway with all the dial peers it would otherwise need. A downside is that a call agent must always be available. Cisco MGCP gateways can use Survivable Remote Site Telephony (SRST) and MGCP fallback to allow the H.323 protocol to take over and provide local call routing in the absence of a Communications Manager (for example, during a WAN outage). In that case, you must configure dial peers on the gateway for use by H.323.

Session Initiation Protocol

SIP is a protocol developed by the Internet Engineering Task Force (IETF) Multiparty Multimedia Session Control (MMUSIC) Working Group as an alternative to H.323. SIP features are compliant with IETF RFC 2543, published in March 1999; RFC 3261, published in June 2002; and RFC 3665, published in December 2003. Because SIP is a common standard based on the logic of the World Wide Web and is very simple to implement, it is widely used with gateways and proxy servers within service provider networks for internal and end-customer signaling.

SIP is a peer-to-peer protocol where user agents (UAs) initiate sessions, similar to H.323. However, unlike H.323, SIP uses ASCII-text-based messages to communicate. Therefore, you can implement and troubleshoot SIP very easily.

Because SIP is a peer-to-peer protocol, the Cisco UCM does not control SIP devices, and SIP devices do not register with Cisco UCM. As with H.323 gateways, only the IP address is available on Cisco UCM to confirm that communication between a Cisco UCM and a SIP voice gateway is possible.

Skinny Client Control Protocol

SCCP is a Cisco proprietary protocol that is used for the communication between Cisco UCM and terminal endpoints. SCCP is a client-server protocol, meaning any event (such as on-hook, off-hook, or buttons pressed) causes a message to be sent to a Cisco UCM. Cisco UCM then sends specific instructions back to the device to tell it what to do about the event. Therefore, each press on a phone button causes data traffic between Cisco UCM and the terminal endpoint. SCCP is widely used with Cisco IP Phones. The major advantage of SCCP within Cisco UCM networks is its proprietary nature, which allows you to make quick changes to the protocol and add features and functionality.

SCCP is a simplified protocol used in VoIP networks. Cisco IP Phones that use SCCP can coexist in an H.323 environment. When used with Cisco Communications Manager, a SCCP client can interoperate with H.323-compliant terminals.

Comparing VoIP Signaling Protocols

The primary goal for all four of the previously mentioned VoIP signaling protocols is the same—to create a bidirectional Real-time Transport Protocol (RTP) stream between VoIP endpoints involved in a conversation. However, VoIP signaling protocols use different architectures and procedures to achieve this goal.

H.323

H.323 is considered a peer-to-peer protocol, although H.323 is not a single protocol. Rather, it is a suite of protocols. The necessary gateway configuration is relatively complex, because you need to define the dial plan and route patterns directly on the gateway. Examples of H.323-capable devices are the Cisco VG224 Analog Phone Gateway and the Cisco 2600XM Series, Cisco 2800 Series, 3700 Series, and 3800 Series routers.

The H.323 protocol is responsible for all the signaling between a Cisco UCM cluster and an H.323 gateway. The ISDN protocols, Q.921 and Q.931, are used only on the Integrated Services Digital Network (ISDN) link to the PSTN, as illustrated in Figure 1-2.

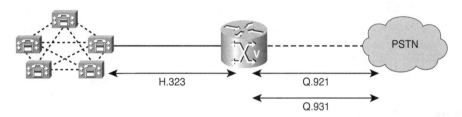

Figure 1-2   *H.323 Signaling*

MGCP

The MGCP protocol is based on a client/server architecture. That simplifies the configuration because the dial plan and route patterns are defined directly on a Cisco UCM server within a cluster. Examples of MGCP-capable devices are the Cisco VG224 Analog Phone Gateway and the Cisco 2600XM Series, 2800 Series, 3700 Series, and 3800 Series routers. Non-IOS MGCP gateways include the Cisco Catalyst 6608-E1 and Catalyst 6608-T1 module.

MGCP is used to manage a gateway. All ISDN Layer 3 information is backhauled to a Cisco UCM server. Only the ISDN Layer 2 information (Q.921) is terminated on the gateway, as depicted in Figure 1-3.

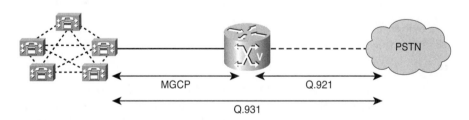

Figure 1-3   *MGCP Signaling*

SIP

Like the H.323 protocol, the SIP is a peer-to-peer protocol. The configuration necessary for the gateway is relatively complex because the dial plan and route patterns need to be defined directly on the gateway. Examples of SIP-capable devices are the Cisco 2800 Series and 3800 Series routers.

The SIP protocol is responsible for all the signaling between a Cisco UCM cluster and a gateway. The ISDN protocols, Q.921 and Q.931, are used only on an ISDN link to the PSTN, as illustrated in Figure 1-4.

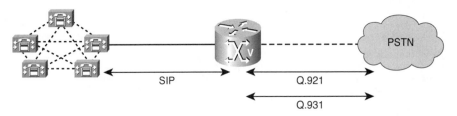

Figure 1-4   *SIP Signaling*

SCCP

SCCP works in a client/server architecture, as shown in Figure 1-5, which simplifies the configuration of SCCP devices such as Cisco IP Phones and Cisco ATA 180 Series and VG200 Series FXS gateways.

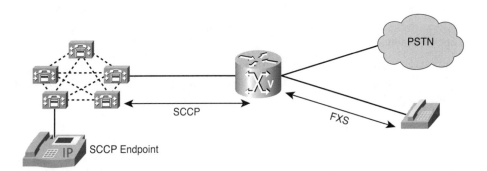

Figure 1-5   *SCCP Signaling*

SCCP is used on Cisco VG224 and VG248 analog phone gateways. ATAs enable communications between Cisco UCM and a gateway. The gateway then uses standard analog signaling to an analog device connected to the ATA's FXS port. Recent versions of Cisco IOS voice gateways—for example, the 2800 series—also support SCCP controlled Foreign Exchange Station (FXS) ports.

VoIP Service Considerations

In traditional telephony networks, dedicated bandwidth for each voice stream provides voice with a guaranteed delay across the network. Because bandwidth is guaranteed in a TDM environment, no variable delay exists (that is, *jitter*). Configuring voice in a data network requires network services with low delay, minimal jitter, and minimal packet loss. Bandwidth requirements must be properly calculated based on the codec used and the number of concurrent connections. QoS must be configured to minimize jitter and loss of voice packets. The PSTN provides 99.999 percent availability (that is, *the five nines of availability*). To match the availability of the PSTN, an IP network must be designed with redundancy and failover mechanisms. Security policies must be established to address both network stability and voice-stream security.

Table 1-1 lists issues associated with implementing VoIP in a converged network and solutions that address these issues.

Table 1-1   *Issues and Solutions for VoIP in a Converged Network*

Issue	Solutions
Latency	Increase bandwidth.
	Choose a different codec type.
	Fragment data packets.
	Prioritize voice packets.
Jitter	Use dejitter buffers.
	Prioritize voice packets.
Bandwidth	Calculate bandwidth requirements, including voice payload, overhead, and data.
Packet loss	Design the network to minimize congestion.
	Prioritize voice packets.
	Use codecs to minimize small amounts of packet loss.
Reliability	Provide redundancy for hardware, links, and power (uninterruptible power supply [UPS]).
	Perform proactive network management.
Security	Secure the following components: ■ Network infrastructure ■ Call-processing systems ■ Endpoints ■ Applications

Media Transmission Protocols

In a VoIP network, the actual voice data (conversations) are transported across the transmission media using RTP and RTP Control Protocol (RTCP). RTP defines a standardized packet format for delivering audio and video over the Internet. RTCP is a companion protocol to RTP as it provides for the delivery of control information for individual RTP streams. Compressed Real-time Transport Protocol (cRTP) and Secure Real-time Transport Protocol (sRTP) were developed to enhance the usage of RTP.

Datagram protocols, such as UDP, send a media stream as a series of small packets. This approach is simple and efficient. However, packets are liable to be lost or corrupted in transit. Depending on the protocol and the extent of the loss, a client might be able to recover lost data with error correction techniques, might interpolate over the missing data, or might suffer a data dropout. RTP and the RTCP were specifically designed to stream media over networks. They are both built on top of UDP.

Real-Time Transport Protocol

RTP defines a standardized packet format for delivering audio and video over the Internet. It was developed by the Audio-Video Transport Working Group of the IETF and was first published in 1996 as RFC 1889, which was made obsolete in 2003 by RFC 3550.

RTP provides end-to-end network transport functions intended for applications with real-time transmission requirements, such as audio and video. Those functions include payload-type identification, sequence numbering, time stamping, and delivery monitoring. Figure 1-6 shows a typical role played by RTP in a VoIP network. Specifically, notice RTP communicates directly between the voice endpoints, whereas the call setup protocols (that is, H.225 and H.245 in this example) are used to communicate with voice gateways.

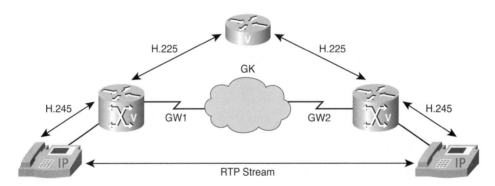

Figure 1-6   *Role of RTP*

RTP typically runs on top of UDP to use the multiplexing and checksum services of that protocol. RTP does not have a standard TCP or UDP port on which it communicates. The only standard it obeys is that UDP communications are done via an even port, and the next higher odd port is used for RTCP communications. Although no standards are assigned, in a Cisco environment RTP is generally configured to use UDP ports in the range 16,384–32,767.

RTP can carry any data with real-time characteristics, such as interactive audio or video. The fact that RTP uses a dynamic port range can make it difficult for it to traverse firewalls.

Although RTP is often used for unicast sessions, it is primarily designed for multicast sessions. In addition to the roles of sender and receiver, RTP defines the roles of translator and mixer to support multicast requirements.

RTP is frequently used in conjunction with Real-time Streaming Protocol (RTSP) in streaming media systems. RTP is also used in conjunction with H.323 or SIP in videoconferencing and push-to-talk systems. These two characteristics make RTP the technical foundation of the VoIP industry. Applications using RTP are less sensitive to packet loss, but typically very sensitive to delays, so UDP is a better choice than TCP for such applications.

RTP is a critical component of VoIP because it enables the destination device to reorder and retime the voice packets before they are played out to the user. An RTP header contains a time stamp and sequence number, which allow the receiving device to buffer and to remove jitter by synchronizing the packets to play back a continuous stream of sound. RTP uses sequence numbers only to order the packets. RTP does not request retransmission if a packet is lost.

RTP Control Protocol

RTCP is a sister protocol of RTP. It was first defined in RFC 1889 and was made obsolete by RFC 3550. RTP provides out-of-band control information for an RTP flow. It works alongside RTP in the delivery and packaging of multimedia data, but does not transport any data itself. Although RTCP is periodically used to transmit control packets to participants in a streaming multimedia session, the primary function of RTCP is to provide feedback on the quality of service being provided by RTP.

RTCP is used for QoS reporting. It gathers statistics on a media connection and information such as bytes sent, packets sent, lost packets, jitter, feedback, and round-trip delay. Applications use this information to increase the quality of service, perhaps using a low-compression codec instead of a high-compression codec.

There are several types of RTCP packets: Sender Report Packet, Receiver Report Packet, Source Description RTCP Packet, Goodbye RTCP Packet, and application-specific RTCP packets.

RTCP provides the following feedback on current network conditions:

- RTCP provides a mechanism for hosts involved in an RTP session to exchange information about monitoring and controlling the session. RTCP monitors the quality of elements such as packet count, packet loss, delay, and interarrival jitter. RTCP transmits packets as a percentage of session bandwidth, but at a specific rate of at least every five seconds.

- The RTP standard states that the Network Time Protocol (NTP) time stamp is based on synchronized clocks. The corresponding RTP time stamp is randomly generated and based on data packet sampling. Both NTP and RTP are included in RTCP packets by the sender of the data.

- RTCP provides a separate flow from RTP. When a voice stream is assigned UDP port numbers, RTP is typically assigned an even-numbered port and RTCP is assigned the next odd-numbered port. Each voice call has four ports assigned: RTP plus RTCP in the transmit direction and RTP plus RTCP in the receive direction.

Compressed RTP

RTP includes a data portion and a header portion. The data portion of RTP is a thin protocol that provides support for the real-time properties of applications, such as continuous media, including timing reconstruction, loss detection, and content identification. The header portion of RTP is considerably larger than the data portion. The header portion consists of the IP segment, the UDP segment, and the RTP segment. Given the size of the IP/UDP/RTP segment combinations, it is inefficient to send the IP/UDP/RTP header without compressing it. Figure 1-7 illustrates using RTP header cRTP over a relatively low-speed WAN link (such as a T1 link), which could benefit from the bandwidth freed up by compressing the IP/UDP/RTP header.

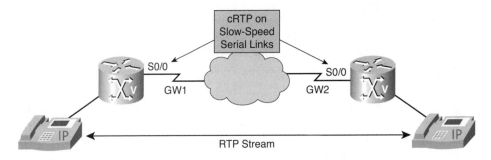

Figure 1-7   *RTP Header Compression*

The IP header portion consists of an IP segment, a UDP segment, and an RTP segment. The minimal 20 bytes of the IP segment, combined with the 8 bytes of the UDP segment and the 12 bytes of the RTP segment, create a 40-byte IP/UDP/RTP header. The RTP packet has a payload of approximately 20 to 150 bytes for audio applications that use compressed payloads.

The RTP header compression feature compresses the IP/UDP/RTP header in an RTP data packet from 40 bytes to approximately 2 to 4 bytes.

cRTP, specified in RFCs 2508, 2509, and 3545, was developed to decrease the size of the IP, UDP, and RTP headers.

- **RFC 2508:** Compressing IP/UDP/RTP Headers for Low-Speed Serial Links

- **RFC 2509:** IP Header Compression over PPP

- **RFC 3545:** Enhanced Compressed RTP (ECRTP) for Links with High Delay, Packet Loss and Reordering

RFC 2509 was designed to work with reliable and fast point-to-point links. In less than optimal circumstances, where there might be long delays, packet loss, and out-of-sequence packets, cRTP doesn't function well for VoIP applications. Another adaptation, ECRPT, was defined in a subsequent Internet draft document to overcome that problem.

RTP header compression is supported on serial lines using Frame Relay, HDLC, or PPP encapsulation. It is also supported over ISDN interfaces.

Why and When to Use cRTP

cRTP does not technically perform compression. Rather, cRTP leverages the fact that much of the header information in every packet in a VoIP stream contains redundant information, and cRTP then suppresses the sending of that redundant information. For example, after a VoIP call flow is established, every packet has the same source and destination IP addresses, the same source and destination UDP port numbers, and the same RTP payload type. By caching this redundant information in the gateways at each end of a link, sending reduced headers, and then reassembling the full header, cRTP can achieve significant bandwidth savings without any loss of information.

RTP header compression also reduces overhead for multimedia RTP traffic. The reduction in overhead for multimedia RTP traffic results in a corresponding reduction in delay. RTP header compression is especially beneficial when the RTP payload size is small; for example, for compressed audio payloads of 20 to 50 bytes.

Use RTP header compression on any WAN interface where you are concerned about bandwidth and where there is a high portion of RTP traffic. RTP header compression can be used for media-on-demand and interactive services such as Internet telephony. RTP header compression provides support for real-time conferencing of groups of any size within the Internet. This support includes source identification support for gateways such as audio and video bridges and support for multicast-to-unicast translators. RTP header compression can benefit both telephony voice and multicast backbone (MBONE) applications running over slow links.

Note Using RTP header compression on any high-speed interfaces (that is, anything over T1 speed) is not recommended. Any bandwidth savings achieved with RTP header compression might be offset by an increase in CPU utilization on the router.

Secure RTP

sRTP was first published by IETF in March 2004 as RFC 3711; it was designed to provide encryption, message authentication, and integrity, and replay protection to RTP data in both unicast and multicast applications.

sRTP also has a sister protocol, called Secure RTCP (sRTCP). sRTCP provides the same security-related features to RTCP as the ones provided by sRTP to RTP. sRTP can be used in conjunction with compressed RTP. Figure 1-8 demonstrates that an sRTP flow travels between devices (Cisco IP phones in Figure 1-8), which are capable of sending and receiving sRTP traffic.

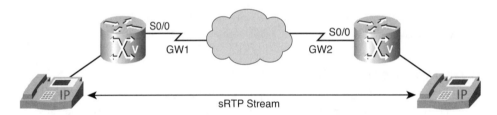

Figure 1-8 *Secure RTP Traffic Flow*

Flow Encryption

sRTP standardizes utilization of only a single cipher, Advanced Encryption Standard (AES), which can be used in two cipher modes, which turn the original block AES cipher into a stream cipher:

■ **Segmented Integer Counter Mode:** A counter mode that allows random access to any blocks and that is essential for RTP traffic running over unreliable networks with possible loss of packets. AES running in this mode is the default encryption algorithm, with a default encryption key length of 128 bits and a default session salt key length of 112 bits.

■ **f8-mode:** A variation of output feedback mode. The default values of the encryption key and salt key are the same as for AES in Counter Mode.

In addition to the AES cipher, sRTP gives the user the ability to disable encryption outright, using the so called NULL cipher. However, the NULL cipher does not perform any encryption. Rather, the encryption algorithm functions as though the key stream contains only zeroes, and it copies the input stream to the output stream without any changes.

Note   It is mandatory for the NULL cipher mode to be implemented in any sRTP-compatible system. As such, it can be used when the confidentiality guarantees ensured by sRTP are not required, and other sRTP features (such authentication and message integrity) might be used.

Because encryption algorithms do not secure message integrity themselves, allowing the attacker to either forge the data or at least to replay previously transmitted data, sRTP also provides the means to secure the integrity of data and safety from replay.

Authentication and Integrity

The HMAC-SHA1 algorithm (defined in RFC 2104) is used to authenticate a message and protect its integrity. This algorithm produces a 160-bit result, which is then truncated to 80 bits to become the authentication tag, which is then appended to a packet. The HMAC is calculated over the packet payload and material from the packet header, including the packet sequence number.

Replay Protection

To protect against replay attacks, a receiver must maintain the indices of previously received messages, comparing them with the index of each newly received message and admitting the new message only if it has not been played before. Such an approach heavily relies on integrity protection being enabled (to make it nearly impossible to spoof message indices).

Introducing VoIP Gateways

Gateways provide a number of ways to connect an IP telephony network to the PSTN, a legacy PBX, key systems, or other TDM systems. Gateways range from specialized, entry-level, and standalone voice gateways to high-end, integrated routers and Cisco IOS gateways. This section introduces voice gateways and deployment models in an IP telephony network.

Understanding Gateways

A voice gateway functions as a translator between different types of networks. Gateways allow terminals of one type, such as H.323, to communicate with terminals of another type, such as a PBX, by converting protocols. Gateways connect a company network to the PSTN, a PBX, or individual analog devices, such as a phone or fax.

Following are the two types of Cisco access gateways:

■ **Analog gateways:** There are two categories of Cisco analog access systems:

   ■ Analog station gateways connect an IP telephony network to POTS. They provide FXS ports to connect analog telephones, IVR systems, fax machines, PBX systems, and voice-mail systems.

   ■ Analog trunk gateways connect an IP telephony network to the PSTN central office (CO) or a PBX. They provide FXO ports for PSTN or PBX access and Ear and Mouth (E&M) ports for analog trunk connection to a legacy PBX. To minimize any answer and disconnect supervision issues, use digital gateways whenever possible. Analog direct-inward-dialing (DID) is also available for PSTN connectivity.

   ■ **Digital gateways:** Cisco access digital trunk gateways connect an IP telephony network to the PSTN or to a PBX via digital trunks, such as PRI or BRI common channel signaling (CCS) and T1 or E1 channel associated signaling (CAS). Digital T1 PRI trunks might also connect to certain legacy voice-mail systems.

IP telephony gateways should meet these core feature requirements:

■ **Gateway protocol support:** Cisco voice gateways support various signaling protocols, depending on the hardware platform. Cisco gateways support H.323, MGCP, SIP, and SCCP. H.323 and SIP gateways do not need a call control agent. Therefore, they can be deployed on networks in which call agents, such as Cisco UCM, are not present. MGCP and SCCP are streamlined protocols that work only on a network in which a call agent, such as Cisco UCM, is present. Cisco IP Phones use SCCP, which is a lighter-weight protocol. SCCP uses a client-server model, whereas H.323 is a peer-to-peer model. MGCP also follows a client-server model.

Note Protocol selection depends on site-specific requirements and the installed base of equipment. For example, many remote branch locations have Cisco 2600XM Series or 3700 Series multiservice routers installed. These routers support H.323 and MGCP 0.1, beginning with Cisco IOS Release 12.2(11)T and Cisco UCM Release 3.1 or later. You might prefer MGCP to H.323 because of simpler configuration. This option also works well with older IOS versions because of support for call survivability during a Cisco UCM failover from a primary to a secondary Cisco UCM server. On the other hand, you might prefer H.323 over MGCP because of the wider selection of interfaces supported.

The Simplified Message Desk Interface (SMDI) is a standard for integrating voice-mail systems with PBXs or Centrex systems. When connecting to a voice-mail system via SMDI and using either analog FXS or digital T1 PRI connections, you will use either the SCCP or MGCP protocol because H.323 devices do not identify the specific line being used from a group of ports. The use of H.323 gateways for this purpose means the Cisco Messaging Interface cannot correctly correlate the SMDI information with the actual port or channel being used for an incoming call.

- **Advanced gateway functionality:** The gateways should support the ability to transmit, without corruption, touch-tone digits (that is, Dual Tone Multifrequency [DTMF] tones) and also support a collection of other user services, as follows:

  - **DTMF relay capabilities:** Each digit dialed with tone dialing is assigned a unique pair of frequencies. Voice compression of these tones with a low bit-rate codec can cause DTMF signal loss or distortion. Therefore, DTMF tones can be separated from the voice bearer stream and sent as signaling indications through the gateway protocol (H.323, SCCP, or MGCP) signaling channel instead.

  - **Supplementary services support:** These services provide user functions such as hold, transfer, and conferencing, and are considered to be fundamental requirements of any voice installation.

- **Work with redundant Cisco UCM:** The gateways must support the capability to "rehome" to a secondary Cisco UCM in the event of a primary Cisco UCM failure.

- **Call survivability in Cisco UCM:** The voice gateway preserves the RTP bearer stream (the voice conversation) between two IP endpoints when a Cisco UCM server to which an endpoint is registered is no longer accessible.

- **Q Signaling (QSIG) support:** QSIG is becoming the standard for PBX interoperability in Europe and North America. With QSIG, the Cisco voice packet network appears to PBXs as a distributed transit PBX that can establish calls to any PBX or other telephony endpoint served by a Cisco gateway, including non-QSIG endpoints.

- **Fax and modem support:** Fax over IP enables interoperability of traditional analog fax machines with IP telephony networks. The fax image is converted from an analog signal and is transmitted as digital data over a packet network.

Gateways are deployed usually as edge devices on a network. Because gateways might interface with both the PSTN and a company WAN, they must have appropriate hardware and utilize an appropriate protocol for that network. Figure 1-9 represents a scenario where three types of gateways are deployed for VoIP and PSTN interconnections.

The scenario shown in Figure 1-9 displays the unified communications network of a company that was recently formed as a result of a merger of three individual companies. In the past, each company had its own strategy in terms of how it connected to the PSTN:

- The San Jose location used a Cisco UCM environment with a MGCP-controlled unified communications gateway to connect to the PSTN.

- The Chicago location used a Cisco UCM Express environment with an H.323-based unified communications gateway to connect to the PSTN.

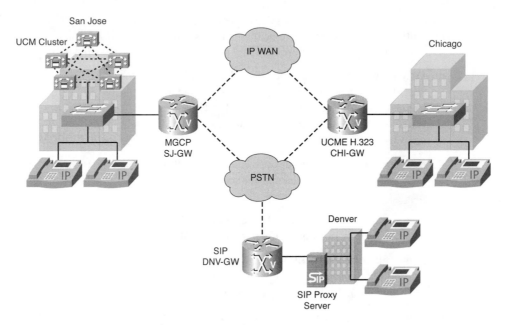

Figure 1-9   *Gateway Deployment Example*

■   The Denver location used a Cisco SIP proxy server and SIP IP phones as well as a
     SIP-based unified communications gateway to connect to the PSTN. Because the
     Denver location is only a small office, it does not use the WAN for IP telephony traf-
     fic to the other locations. Therefore, Denver's local VoIP network is connected only
     to the PSTN.

Modern Gateway Hardware Platforms

This section covers some of the current Cisco voice gateway models used in today's
enterprise environments.

Cisco 2800 Series Integrated Services Routers

The Cisco 2800 Series Integrated Services Routers, as pictured in Figure 1-10, comprise
four models (listed from top to bottom): Cisco 2801, Cisco 2811, Cisco 2821, and Cisco
2851. The 2800 Series provides increased security, voice, and overall performance,
embedded service options, and dramatically increased slot performance and density, as
compared to older 2600 Series models. It also maintains support for most of the more-
than-90 modules available for the Cisco 1700 Series Modular Access Routers, 2600
Series Multiservice Platforms, and 3700 Series Multiservice Access Routers.

Figure 1-10 *Cisco 2800 Series Integrated Services Routers*

The 2800 Series can deliver simultaneous, high-quality, wire-speed services up to multiple T1/E1/xDSL connections. The routers offer embedded encryption acceleration and, on the motherboard, voice digital-signal-processor (DSP) slots. They also offer intrusion prevention system (IPS) and firewall functions, optional integrated call processing and voice-mail support, high-density interfaces for a wide range of wired and wireless connectivity requirements, and sufficient performance and slot density for future network expansion requirements and advanced applications. Go to http://www.cisco.com/go/2800 to learn more about the Cisco 2800 Series routers.

Cisco 3800 Series Integrated Services Routers

The Cisco 3800 Series Integrated Services Routers, as shown in Figure 1-11, also feature embedded security processing, significant performance and memory enhancements, and new high-density interfaces that deliver the performance, availability, and reliability required to scale mission-critical security, IP telephony, business video, network analysis, and web applications in today's enterprise environments. The 3800 Series routers deliver multiple concurrent services at wire-speed T3/E3 rates.

The integrated services routing architecture of the 3800 Series is based on the 3700 Series. These routers are designed to embed and integrate security and voice processing with advanced wired and wireless services for rapid deployment of new applications, including application layer functions, intelligent network services, and converged communications. The 3800 Series supports the bandwidth requirements for multiple Fast Ethernet interfaces per slot, TDM interconnections, and fully integrated power distribution to modules supporting 802.3af Power over Ethernet (PoE). The Cisco 3800 Series also supports the existing portfolio of Cisco modular interfaces. This accommodates network expansion or changes in technology as new services and applications are deployed. By integrating the functions of multiple separate devices into a single compact unit, the 3800 Series reduces the cost and complexity of managing remote networks.

Figure 1-11 *Cisco 3800 Series Integrated Services Routers*

New 3800 Series models include the Cisco 3825 Integrated Services Router and the Cisco 3845 Integrated Services Router, available with three optional configurations for AC power, AC power with integrated inline power support, and DC power. Go to http://www.cisco.com/go/3800 to learn more about the 3800 Series routers.

Cisco Catalyst 6500 Series Switches

The Cisco Catalyst 6500 Series Switches, as shown in Figure 1-12, are high-performance and feature-rich platforms that can be used as voice gateways by installing a Cisco Communication Media Module (CMM).

Figure 1-12 *Cisco Catalyst 6500 Series Switches*

The CMM is a Cisco Catalyst 6500 Series line card that provides flexible and high-density VoIP gateway and media services. A Catalyst 6500 Series Switch can handle multiple digital trunk interfaces. For example, the Cisco Catalyst 6509 Switch supports up to 144 T1/E1 connections by using eight communications media modules with 18 ports each. These gateway and media services allow organizations to connect their existing TDM network to their IP communications network, provide connectivity to the PSTN, and enable conferencing and transcoding services. Go to http://www.cisco.com/go/catalyst6500 to learn more about the Catalyst 6500 Series Switches.

Well-Known and Widely Used Enterprise Models

Several Cisco modular access routers that might already be installed in enterprise networks have voice gateway capabilities. Although some of these models are well known and widely used, they have reached end of sale (EOS) status. However, because these routers were the leading voice gateway products for a long time, you should be familiar with and know how to support these models.

Cisco 1751-V Modular Access Router

The Cisco 1751-V modular access router, as pictured in Figure 1-13, supports multiservice integration of voice, video, data, and fax traffic. The router offers many WAN-access and voice-interface options, VoIP, high-performance routing with bandwidth management, inter-VLAN routing, and virtual private network (VPN) access with a firewall. Go to http://www.cisco.com/go/1700 to learn more about the Cisco 1700 Series Modular Access Routers.

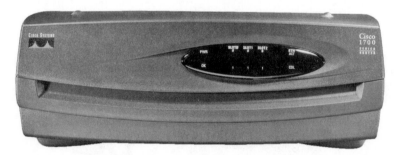

Figure 1-13   *Cisco 1751-V*

Cisco 1760-V Modular Access Router

The Cisco 1760-V Modular Access Router, as depicted in Figure 1-14, offers small-to-medium-sized businesses and small-enterprise branch offices a 19-inch rack-mount access solution designed to take advantage of the productivity of business applications. The router ensures the multiservice integration of voice, video, data, and fax traffic. It provides businesses with the complete functionality and flexibility to deliver secure Internet and intranet access. The router has many WAN access options, VoIP, high-performance routing with QoS, inter-VLAN routing, and VPN access with firewall options.

Figure 1-14   *Cisco 1760-V*

Cisco 2600XM Series Multiservice Routers

The modular architecture of the Cisco 2600XM Series multiservice routers, as shown in Figure 1-15, enables you to upgrade interfaces to accommodate network expansion or changes in technology as new services and applications are deployed. Modular interfaces are shared with the Cisco 1700 Series Modular Access Routers and the Cisco 3700 Series Multiservice Access Routers, providing investment protection and reducing the complexity of managing a remote network solution by integrating the functions of multiple, separate devices into a single, compact unit. Network modules available for the 2600XM Series and 3700 Series support many applications, including multiservice voice and data integration, integrated switching, analog and ISDN dial access, and serial device concentration. Go to http://www.cisco.com/go/2600 to learn more about the Cisco 2600XM Series multiservice routers.

Figure 1-15   *Cisco 2600XM Series*

Cisco 3600 Series Multiservice Access Routers

The Cisco 3600 Series, as shown in Figure 1-16, is a family of modular, multiservice access platforms for medium- and large-sized offices and smaller Internet service providers (ISPs). With more than 70 modular interface options, the Cisco 3600 Series provides solutions for data, voice, video, hybrid dial access, VPNs, and multiprotocol data routing. The high-performance, modular architecture protects customers' investments in network technology and integrates the functions of several devices within a single, manageable solution.

Figure 1-16   *Cisco 3600 Series*

Cisco extended the Cisco 3600 Series with the Cisco 3660 multiservice access platform. The Cisco 3660 platform provides higher densities, greater performance, and more expansion capabilities. The additional power and performance of the Cisco 3660 platform enables new applications, such as packetized voice aggregation and branch office Asynchronous Transfer Mode (ATM) access ranging from T1/E1 inverse multiplexing over ATM (IMA) to Optical Carrier 3 (OC-3). Go to http://www.cisco.com/go/3600 to learn more about the Cisco 3600 Series multiservice access routers.

Cisco 3700 Series Multiservice Access Routers

The Cisco 3700 Series Multiservice Access Routers, as illustrated in Figure 1-17, are modular routers that enable flexible and scalable deployment of e-business applications for the Cisco Full Service Branch (FSB) office. The 3700 Series Multiservice Access Routers optimize the branch office with high-performance routing, integrated low-density switching, security, voice, IP telephony, voice mail, video, and content networking in an integrated solution. This integrated design enables enterprise customers to adapt to evolving business needs by enhancing Cisco IOS services, such as QoS, IP multicast, VPN, firewall, and an intrusion prevention system (IPS). The 3700 Series Multiservice Access Routers are based on the same modular concepts as the 3600 Series, but they enable higher levels of performance and service integration for the branch office. Go to http://www.cisco.com/go/3700 to learn more about the Cisco 3700 Series Multiservice Access Routers.

Figure 1-17   *Cisco 3700 Series*

Standalone Voice Gateways

To fit special needs within a customer's unified messaging system, Cisco offers stand-alone voice gateways for specific purposes. Each of these voice gateways fulfills a different need, such as the integration of analog devices into a unified messaging system, enhanced performance, business-class functionality, adaptability, serviceability, and manageability.

Cisco VG224 and VG248 Analog Phone Gateways

Cisco VG200 Series Gateways, including Cisco VG224 Analog Phone Gateway and Cisco VG248 Analog Phone Gateway, provide support for traditional analog devices while taking advantage of the new capabilities that Cisco IP Communications affords.

Cisco VG200 Series Gateways include these features:

- VG200 Series Gateways are high-density gateways for using analog phones, fax machines, modems, voice-mail systems, and speakerphones.

- VG200 Series Gateways offer feature-rich functionality for enterprise voice systems based on Cisco Unified Communications Manager or Cisco Unified Communications Manager Express.

- The VG224 Analog Phone Gateway is based on a Cisco IOS software platform and offers 24 fully featured analog ports for use as extensions to Cisco Unified Communications Manager or Cisco Unified Communications Manager Express systems in a compact 19-inch rack-mount chassis.

- The VG248 Analog Phone Gateway, as shown in Figure 1-18, offers 48 fully featured analog ports for use as extensions to the Cisco UCM system in a compact 19-inch rack-mount chassis.

Figure 1-18   *Cisco VG248*

Cisco AS5300 Series Universal Gateways

The Cisco AS5300 Series, an example of which is provided in Figure 1-19, is a series of access servers that includes the Cisco AS5350 Universal Gateway and the Cisco AS5350XM Universal Gateway. The AS5350XM Universal Gateway doubles the performance of the Cisco AS5350 Universal Gateway, allowing the same applications to run faster and with lower CPU utilization levels. Go to http://www.cisco.com/go/as5300 to learn more about the Cisco AS5300 Series Universal Gateways.

Figure 1-19   *Cisco AS5300 Series*

Cisco AS5400 Series Universal Gateways

The Cisco AS5400 Series, which is another series of access servers, includes the Cisco AS5400HPX Universal Gateway, which enhances performance for processor-intensive voice and fax applications, and the Cisco AS5400XM Universal Gateway, shown in Figure 1-20. Go to http://www.cisco.com/go/as5400 to learn more about the Cisco AS5400 Series Universal Gateways.

Cisco AS5850 Universal Gateway

The Cisco AS5850 Universal Gateway, as illustrated in Figure 1-21, is a high-density, carrier-class gateway with high capacity and availability. The AS5850 Universal Gateway is specifically designed to meet the demands of large service providers by supporting up to five channelized T3s (CT3s), 96 T1s, or 86 E1s of data, voice, and fax services on any port at any time. It offers high-availability features such as hot swap on all cards, load-sharing and redundant hot-swappable power supplies, redundant route-processing cards, and CAC to ensure 99.999 percent availability. Go to http://www.cisco.com/go/as5850 to learn more about the Cisco AS5850 Universal Gateway.

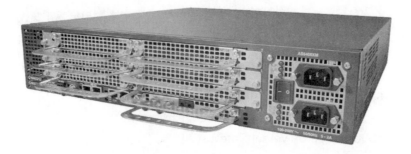

Figure 1-20 *Cisco AS5400XM Universal Gateway*

Figure 1-21 *Cisco AS5850 Universal Gateway*

Cisco 827-4V ADSL Router

The Cisco 827-4V ADSL Router, shown in Figure 1-22, provides business-class functionality for small businesses, small remote offices, and corporate teleworkers using Cisco IOS technology. It enables service providers and resellers to increase service revenue by supporting features for business-class security, integrated toll quality voice and data, differentiated service classes, and managed network access. These features, along with the manageability and reliability of Cisco IOS, provide mission-critical networking.

Figure 1-22   *Cisco 827-4V ADSL Router*

With the software upgradeable platform of the 827-4V ADSL Router, service providers and resellers can increase revenue by offering DSL services today and provide value-added services as their customers' technology needs grow. The Cisco 827-4V ADSL Router is a member of the Cisco 800 Series Routers. Go to http://www.cisco.com/go/800 to learn more about the Cisco 800 Series Routers.

Cisco ATA 186

The Cisco Analog Telephone Adaptor 186 (ATA 186), as depicted in Figure 1-23, is a handset-to-Ethernet adaptor that allows traditional telephony devices to function as VoIP devices. Customers can use IP telephony applications by connecting their analog devices to Cisco ATAs.

Figure 1-23   *Cisco ATA 186*

The ATA 186 supports two voice ports, which each have an independent telephone number and a single 10BASE-T Ethernet port. This adaptor can make use of existing Ethernet LANs, in addition to broadband pipes such as DSL, fixed wireless, and cable modem deployments.

The Cisco Analog Telephone Adaptor 180 Series products are standards-based IP communications devices that deliver VoIP terminations to businesses and residences. Go to http://www.cisco.com/go/ata186 to learn more about the Cisco ATA 186.

Cisco 7200 Series Routers

Cisco 7200 Series Routers, an example of which is shown in Figure 1-24, are service routers for Enterprise Edge and Service Provider Edge applications. These compact routers provide serviceability and manageability coupled with high-performance modular processors such as the Cisco 7200 Network Processing Engine NPE-G1 (NPE-G1). Go to http://www.cisco.com/go/7200 to learn more about the Cisco 7200 Series Routers.

Figure 1-24   *Cisco 7200 Series Router*

Summary of Voice Gateways

Table 1-2 summarizes the Cisco voice gateway platforms.

Table 1-2   *Gateway Hardware Platforms*

Platform	H.323	Cisco Unified Communications Manager MGCP	SIP	SCCP
Cisco 827-4V	Yes	No	No	No
Cisco 2800 Series	Yes	Yes	Yes	Yes
Cisco 3800 Series	Yes	Yes	Yes	Yes
Cisco 1751-V / 1760-V	Yes	Yes	No	Yes[1]
Cisco 2600XM Series	Yes	Yes	No	No[3]
Cisco 3600 Series	Yes	Yes	No	No[3]
Cisco 3700 Series	Yes	Yes	No	No[3]
Cisco VG224	Yes[2]	Yes[2]	No	Yes
Cisco VG248	No	No	No	Yes

Table 1-2 *Gateway Hardware Platforms*   *(continued)*

Platform	H.323	Cisco Unified Communications Manager MGCP	SIP	SCCP
Cisco AS53XX / AS5400 / AS5850	Yes	No	No	No
Communication Media Module	Yes	Yes	Yes	Yes
GW Module WS-X6608-x1 and FXS Module WS-X6624	No	Yes	No	Yes
Cisco ATA 180 Series	Yes[2]	Yes[2]	No	Yes[2]
Cisco 7200 Series	Yes	No	No	No

[1]Conferencing and transcoding only
[2]FXS only
[3]DSP farm

Table 1-3 offers insight into typical uses for the previously discussed voice gateways.

Table 1-3 *Gateway Model Uses*

Device/Series	Usage
Cisco 827-4V	Connect up to four analog devices via ADSL.
Cisco 2800 Series	Small- to medium-sized enterprise voice gateways.
Cisco 3800 Series	Large-sized enterprise voice gateways.
Cisco 1751-V and 1760-V	Small-sized enterprise voice gateways.
Cisco 2600XM Series	Medium-sized enterprise voice gateways.
Cisco 3600 Series	Medium-sized enterprise voice gateways.
Cisco 3700 Series	Large-sized enterprise voice gateways.
Cisco VG224	Connect up to 24 analog devices to the VoIP network.
Cisco VG248	Connect up to 48 analog devices to the VoIP network.
Cisco AS5350, AS5350XM, AS5400HPX, AS5400XM, and AS5850	Service provider voice gateway.
Communications Media Module	Provides T1/E1 and FXS interfaces and conferencing and transcoding resources on Cisco Catalyst 6500 Series Switches.
GW Module WS-X6608-x1 and FXS Module WS-X6624	Provides T1/E1 and FXS interfaces on Catalyst 6500 Series Switches.
Cisco ATA 186	Connect up to two analog devices to a VoIP network.
Cisco 7200 Series	Service provider voice gateway.

IP Telephony Deployment Models

Each IP Telephony deployment model differs in the type of traffic that is carried over the WAN, the location of the call-processing agent, and the size of the deployment. Cisco IP telephony supports these deployment models:

- Single site

- Multisite with centralized call processing

- Multisite with distributed call processing

- Clustering over the IP WAN

Single-Site Deployment

The single-site model for Cisco Unified Communications consists of a call-processing agent cluster located at a single site, or campus, with no telephony services provided over an IP WAN. Figure 1-25 illustrates a typical single-site deployment. All Cisco UCM servers, applications, and DSP resources are located in the same physical location. You can implement multiple clusters inside a LAN or a metropolitan-area network (MAN) and connect them through intercluster trunks if you need to deploy more IP phones in a single-site configuration.

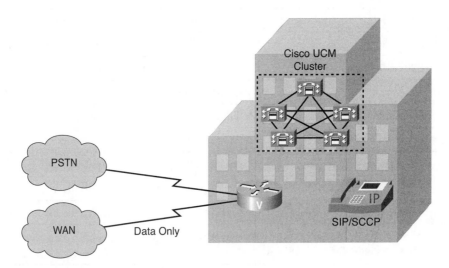

Figure 1-25   *Single-Site Deployment*

An enterprise typically deploys the single-site model over a LAN or MAN, which carries the voice traffic within the site. Gateway trunks that connect directly to the PSTN handle all external calls. If an IP WAN exists between sites, it is used to carry data traffic only; no telephony services are provided over the WAN.

Design Characteristics of Single-Site Deployment

The single-site model has the following design characteristics:

- Single Cisco UCM cluster.

- Maximum of 30,000 SCCP or SIP IP phones or SCCP video endpoints per cluster.

- Maximum of 1100 H.323 devices (gateways, MCUs, trunks, and clients) or MGCP gateways per UCM cluster.

- PSTN for all calls outside the site.

- DSP resources for conferencing, transcoding, and media termination point (MTP).

- Voicemail, unified messaging, Cisco Unified Presence, audio and video components.

- Capability to integrate with legacy PBX and voice-mail systems.

- H.323 clients, MCUs, and H.323/H.320 gateways that require a gatekeeper to place calls must register with a Cisco IOS Gatekeeper (Cisco IOS Release 12.3(8)T or greater). UCM then uses an H.323 trunk to integrate with a gatekeeper and provide call routing and bandwidth management services for H.323 devices registered to it. Multiple Cisco IOS Gatekeepers might be used to provide redundancy.

- MCU resources are required for multipoint video conferencing. Depending on conferencing requirements, these resources might be either SCCP or H.323, or both.

- H.323/H.320 video gateways are needed to communicate with H.320 videoconferencing devices on a public ISDN network.

- High-bandwidth audio (for example, G.711, G.722, or Cisco Wideband Audio) between devices within the site.

- High-bandwidth video (for example, 384 kbps or greater) between devices within the site. The Cisco Unified Video Advantage Wideband Codec, operating at 7 Mbps, is also supported.

Benefits of Single-Site Deployment

A single infrastructure for a converged network solution provides significant cost benefits and enables Cisco Unified Communications to take advantage of many IP-based applications in an enterprise. Single-site deployment also allows each site to be completely self-contained. There is no dependency for service in the event of an IP WAN failure or insufficient bandwidth, and there is no loss of call processing service or functionality.

The main benefits of the single-site model are the following:

- Ease of deployment.

- A common infrastructure for a converged solution.

- Simplified dial plan.

- No transcoding resources are required because of the use of a single high-bandwidth codec.

Design Guidelines for Single-Site Deployment

Single-site deployment is a subset of the distributed and centralized call-processing model. Future scalability requires you adhere to the recommended best practices specific to the distributed and centralized call-processing model. When you develop a stable, single site that is based on a common infrastructure philosophy, you can easily expand the IP telephony system applications, such as video streaming and videoconferencing, to remote sites.

Best Practices for Single-Site Deployment   Follow these guidelines and best practices when implementing the single-site model:

- Provide a highly available, fault-tolerant infrastructure based on a common infrastructure philosophy. A sound infrastructure is essential for easier migration to Cisco Unified Communications, integration with applications such as video streaming and video conferencing, and expansion of your Cisco Unified Communications deployment across the WAN or to multiple UCM clusters.

- Know the calling patterns for your enterprise. Use the single-site model if most of the calls from your enterprise are within the same site or to PSTN users outside your enterprise.

- Use G.711 codecs for all endpoints. This practice eliminates the consumption of DSP resources for transcoding, and those resources can be allocated to other functions such as conferencing and MTPs.

- Use SIP, SRST, and MGCP gateways for the PSTN. This practice simplifies dial plan configuration. H.323 might be required to support specific functionality, such as support for SS7 or Non-Facility Associated Signaling (NFAS), which allows a single channel on one digital circuit to carry signaling information for multiple digital circuits.

- Implement the recommended network infrastructure for high availability, connectivity options for phones (in-line power), QoS mechanisms, and security.

Multisite WAN with Centralized Call-Processing Deployment

The model for a multisite WAN deployment with centralized call processing consists of a single call-processing agent cluster that provides services for multiple remote sites and uses the IP WAN to transport Cisco Unified Communications traffic between sites. The IP WAN also carries call control signaling between central and remote sites. Figure 1-26 illustrates a typical centralized call processing deployment, with a UCM cluster as the call processing agent at the central site and an IP WAN with QoS enabled to connect all the sites. The remote sites rely on the centralized UCM cluster to handle their call processing. Applications such as voice mail and IVR systems are typically centralized as well to reduce the overall costs of administration and maintenance.

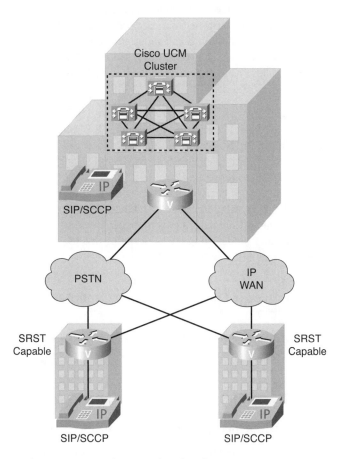

Figure 1-26 *Multisite WAN with Centralized Call Processing*

WAN connectivity options include the following:

- Leased lines

- Frame Relay

- ATM

- ATM and Frame Relay Service Inter-Working (SIW)

- Multiprotocol Label Switching (MPLS) VPN

- Voice and Video Enabled IP Security Protocol (IPsec) VPN (V3PN)

Routers that reside at WAN edges require QoS mechanisms, such as priority queuing and traffic shaping, to protect voice traffic from data traffic across the WAN, where bandwidth is typically scarce. In addition, a call admission control scheme is needed to avoid oversubscribing the WAN links with voice traffic and deteriorating the quality of established calls. For centralized call-processing deployments, the *locations* construct within UCM provides call admission control.

A variety of Cisco gateways can provide remote sites with PSTN access. When the IP WAN is down, or if all the available bandwidth on the IP WAN has been consumed, users at remote sites can dial a PSTN access code and place their calls through the PSTN. The Cisco Unified SRST feature, available for both SCCP and SIP phones, provides call processing at the branch offices for Cisco IP Phones if they lose their connection to the remote primary, secondary, or tertiary UCM server or if the WAN connection is down. Cisco Unified SRST functionality is available on Cisco IOS gateways running the SRST feature or on Cisco United Communications Manager Express (Unified CME) Release 4.0 and later running in SRST mode. Unified CME running in SRST mode provides more features for the phones than SRST on a Cisco IOS gateway.

Design Characteristics of Multisite WAN with Centralized Call-Processing Deployment

The multisite model with centralized call processing has the following design characteristics:

- Single UCM cluster.

- Maximum of 30,000 SCCP or SIP IP phones or SCCP video endpoints per cluster.

- Maximum of 1000 locations per UCM cluster.

- Maximum of 1100 H.323 devices (gateways, MCUs, trunks, and clients) or 1100 MGCP gateways per UCM cluster.

- PSTN for all external calls.

- DSP resources for conferencing, transcoding, and MTP.

- Voice mail, unified messaging, Cisco Unified Presence, audio and video components.

- Capability to integrate with legacy PBX and voicemail systems.

- H.323 clients, MCUs, and H.323/H.320 gateways that require a gatekeeper to place calls must register with a Cisco IOS Gatekeeper (Cisco IOS Release 12.3(8)T or later). UCM then uses an H.323 trunk to integrate with the gatekeeper and provide call routing and bandwidth management services for the H.323 devices registered to it. Multiple Cisco IOS Gatekeepers might be used to provide redundancy.

- MCU resources are required for multipoint video conferencing. Depending on conferencing requirements, these resources might be either SCCP or H.323, or both, and might all be located at a central site or might be distributed to the remote sites if local conferencing resources are required.

- H.323/H.320 video gateways are needed to communicate with H.320 videoconferencing devices on a public ISDN network. These gateways might all be located at the central site or distributed to the remote sites if local ISDN access is required.

- High-bandwidth audio (for example, G.711, G.722, or Cisco Wideband Audio) between devices in the same site and low-bandwidth audio (for example, G.729 or G.728) between devices in different sites.

- High-bandwidth video (for example, 384 kbps or greater) between devices in the same site and low-bandwidth video (for example, 128 kbps) between devices at different sites. The Cisco Unified Video Advantage Wideband Codec, operating at 7 Mbps, is recommended only for calls between devices at the same site.

- Minimum of 768 kbps or greater WAN link speeds. Video is not recommended on WAN connections that operate at speeds lower than 768 kbps.

- UCM locations provide call admission control, and automated alternate routing (AAR) is also supported for video calls, which allows calls to flow over the PSTN if a call across the WAN is rejected by the locations feature.

- SRST versions 4.0 and later support video. However, versions of SRST prior to 4.0 do not support video, and SCCP video endpoints located at remote sites become audio-only devices if the WAN connection fails.

- Cisco Unified CME versions 4.0 and later might be used for remote site survivability instead of an SRST router. Unified CME also provides more features than the SRST router during WAN outage.

- Cisco Unified Communications Manager Express (Unified CME) can be integrated with the Cisco Unity server in the branch office or remote site. The Cisco Unity server is registered to the UCM at the central site in normal mode and can fall back to Unified CME in SRST mode when the centralized UCM server is not reachable, or during a WAN outage, to provide the users at the branch offices with access to their voice mail with message waiting indicators (MWIs).

Design Guidelines for Multisite WAN with Centralized Call-Processing Deployment

Follow these guidelines when implementing the multisite WAN model with centralized call processing:

- Minimize delay between Cisco UCM and remote locations to reduce voice cut-through delays (also known as *clipping*). The ITU-T G.114 recommendation specifies a 150 ms maximum one way.

- Use HSRP for network resiliency.

- Use the locations mechanism in Cisco UCM to provide call admission control into and out of remote branches.

- The number of IP phones and line appearances supported in SRST mode at each remote site depends on the branch router platform, the amount of memory installed, and the Cisco IOS release. SRST on a Cisco IOS gateway supports up to 720 phones, whereas Unified CME running in SRST mode supports 240 phones. Generally speaking, however, the choice of whether to adopt a centralized call processing or distributed call processing approach for a given site depends on a number of factors, such as

    - IP WAN bandwidth or delay limitations

    - Criticality of the voice network

    - Feature set needs

    - Scalability

    - Ease of management

    - Cost

Note   If a distributed call-processing model is deemed more suitable for a customer's business needs, the choices include installing a UCM cluster at each site or running Unified CME at the remote sites.

- At the remote sites, use the following features to ensure call processing survivability in the event of a WAN failure:

    - For SCCP phones, use SRST on a Cisco IOS gateway or Unified CME running in SRST mode.

    - For SIP phones, use SIP SRST.

    - For MGCP phones, use MGCP Gateway Fallback.

SRST or Unified CME in SRST mode, SIP SRST, and MGCP Gateway Fallback can reside with each other on the same Cisco IOS gateway.

For specific sizing recommendations, refer to the Cisco Unified Communications SRND based on Cisco UCM 6.x at the following link:

http://www.cisco.com/en/US/products/sw/voicesw/ps556/products_implementation_design_guide_book09186a008085eb0d.html

Multisite WAN with Distributed Call-Processing Deployment

The model for a multisite WAN deployment with distributed call processing, as illustrated in Figure 1-27, consists of multiple independent sites, each with its own call-processing agent cluster connected to an IP WAN that carries voice traffic between the distributed sites.

An IP WAN interconnects all the distributed call processing sites. Typically, the PSTN serves as a backup connection between the sites in case the IP WAN connection fails or does not have anymore available bandwidth. A site connected only through the PSTN is a standalone site and is not covered by the distributed call processing model.

WAN connectivity options include the following:

- Leased lines

- Frame Relay

- ATM

- ATM and Frame Relay SIW

- MPLS VPN

- IPsec V3PN

Multisite distributed call processing allows each site to be completely self-contained. In the event of an IP WAN failure or insufficient bandwidth, a site does not lose call-processing service or functionality. Cisco UCM simply sends all calls between the sites across the PSTN.

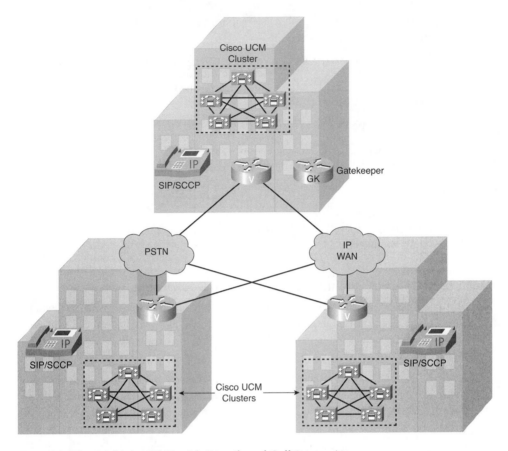

Figure 1-27 *Multisite WAN with Distributed Call Processing*

Design Characteristics of Multisite WAN with Distributed Call-Processing Deployment

The multisite model with distributed call processing has the following design characteristics:

■ Maximum of 30,000 SCCP or SIP IP phones or SCCP video endpoints per cluster.

■ Maximum of 1100 MGCP gateways or H.323 devices (gateways, MCUs, trunks, and clients) per UCM cluster.

■ PSTN for all external calls.

■ DSP resources for conferencing, transcoding, and MTP.

■ Voice mail, unified messaging, and Cisco Unified Presence components.

- Capability to integrate with legacy PBX and voice-mail systems.

- H.323 clients, MCUs, and H.323/H.320 gateways that require a gatekeeper to place calls must register with a Cisco IOS Gatekeeper (Cisco IOS Release 12.3(8)T or later). UCM then uses an H.323 trunk to integrate with the gatekeeper and provide call routing and bandwidth management services for the H.323 devices registered to it. Multiple Cisco IOS Gatekeepers might be used to provide redundancy. Cisco IOS Gatekeepers might also be used to provide call routing and bandwidth management between the distributed UCM clusters. In most situations, Cisco recommends that each UCM cluster have its own set of endpoint gatekeepers and that a separate set of gatekeepers be used to manage intercluster calls. It is possible in some circumstances to use the same set of gatekeepers for both functions, depending on the size of the network and complexity of the dial plan.

- MCU resources are required in each cluster for multipoint video conferencing. Depending on conferencing requirements, these resources might be either SCCP or H.323, or both, and might all be located at the regional sites or distributed to the remote sites of each cluster if local conferencing resources are required.

- H.323/H.320 video gateways are needed to communicate with H.320 videoconferencing devices on the public ISDN network. These gateways might all be located at the regional sites or distributed to the remote sites of each cluster if local ISDN access is required.

- High-bandwidth audio (for example, G.711, G.722, or Cisco Wideband Audio) between devices in the same site, but low-bandwidth audio (for example, G.729 or G.728) between devices in different sites.

- High-bandwidth video (for example, 384 kbps or greater) between devices in the same site, but low-bandwidth video (for example, 128 kbps) between devices at different sites. The Cisco Unified Video Advantage Wideband Codec, operating at 7 Mbps, is recommended only for calls between devices at the same site. Note that the Cisco VT Camera Wideband Video Codec is not supported over intercluster trunks.

- Minimum of 768 kbps or greater WAN link speeds. Video is not recommended on WAN connections that operate at speeds lower than 768 kbps.

- Call admission control is provided by UCM locations for calls between sites controlled by the same UCM cluster and by the Cisco IOS Gatekeeper for calls between UCM clusters (that is, intercluster trunks). AAR is also supported for both intracluster and intercluster video calls.

Benefits of Multisite WAN with Distributed Call-Processing Deployment

The main benefits of the multisite WAN with distributed call-processing deployment model are as follows:

- Cost savings when you use the IP WAN for calls between sites

- Use of the IP WAN to bypass toll charges by routing calls through remote site gateways, closer to the PSTN number dialed (that is, *tail-end hop-off* [TEHO])

- Maximum utilization of available bandwidth by allowing voice traffic to share an IP WAN with other types of traffic

- No loss of functionality during an IP WAN failure

- Scalability to hundreds of sites

Design Guidelines for Multisite WAN with Distributed Call-Processing Deployment

A multisite WAN deployment with distributed call processing has many of the same requirements as a single site or a multisite WAN deployment with centralized call processing. Follow the best practices from these other models in addition to the ones listed here for the distributed call processing model.

Gatekeeper or SIP proxy servers are among the key elements in the multisite WAN model with distributed call processing. They each provide dial plan resolution, with the gatekeeper also providing call admission control. A gatekeeper is an H.323 device that provides call admission control and E.164 dial plan resolution.

Best Practices for Multisite WAN with Distributed Call-Processing Deployment   The following best practices apply to the use of a gatekeeper:

- Use a Cisco IOS Gatekeeper to provide call admission control into and out of each site.

- To provide high availability of the gatekeeper, use HSRP gatekeeper pairs, gatekeeper clustering, and/or alternate gatekeeper support. In addition, use multiple gatekeepers to provide redundancy within the network.

- Size the platforms appropriately to ensure that performance and capacity requirements can be met.

- Use only one type of codec on the WAN because the H.323 specification does not allow for Layer 2, IP, UDP, or RTP header overhead in the bandwidth request.

- Using one type of codec on the WAN simplifies capacity planning by eliminating the need to over-provision the IP WAN to allow for a worst-case scenario.

- Gatekeeper networks can scale to hundreds of sites, and the design is limited only by the WAN topology.

SIP devices provide resolution of E.164 numbers as well as SIP uniform resource identifiers (URIs) to enable endpoints to place calls to each other. UCM supports the use of E.164 numbers only.

The following best practices apply to the use of SIP proxies:

- Provide adequate redundancy for the SIP proxies.

- Ensure that SIP proxies have the capacity for the call rate and number of calls required in the network.

Call-Processing Agents for the Distributed Call Processing Model   Your choice of call-processing agent will vary, based on many factors. The main factors, for the purpose of design, are the size of the site and the functionality required.

For a distributed call-processing deployment, each site has its own call-processing agent. The design of each site varies with the call-processing agent, the functionality required, and the fault tolerance required. For example, in a site with 500 phones, a UCM cluster containing two servers can provide one-to-one redundancy, with the backup server being used as a publisher and Trivial File Transfer Protocol (TFTP) server.

The requirement for IP-based applications also greatly affects the choice of call-processing agent because only UCM provides the required support for many Cisco IP applications.

Table 1-4 lists recommended call-processing agents for distributed call processing.

Table 1-4   *Recommended Call Processing Agents*

Call Processing Agent	Recommended Size	Comments
Cisco Unified Communications Manager Express (Unified CME)	Up to 240 phones	For small remote sites. Capacity depends on Cisco IOS platform.
Cisco UCM	50 to 30,000 phones	Small to large sites, depending on the size of the UCM cluster. Supports centralized or distributed call processing.
Legacy PBX with VoIP gateway	Depends on PBX	Number of IP WAN calls and functionality depend on the PBX-to-VoIP gateway protocol and the gateway platform.

Clustering over the IP WAN Deployment

Cisco supports Cisco UCM clusters over a WAN, as illustrated in Figure 1-28. Clustering over the WAN involves having the applications and UCM of the same cluster distributed across the IP WAN.

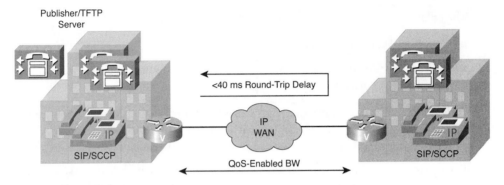

Figure 1-28   *Clustering over the IP WAN*

Clustering over the WAN can support two types of deployments:

- **Local Failover Deployment Model:** Local failover requires that you place UCM subscriber and backup servers at the same site, with no WAN between them. This deployment model is ideal for two to four sites with UCM.

- **Remote Failover Deployment Model:** Remote failover allows you to deploy the backup servers over the WAN. Using this deployment model, you might have up to eight sites with UCM subscribers being backed up by UCM subscribers at another site.

Note   The remote failover deployment model might need higher bandwidth because a large amount of intracluster traffic flows between the subscriber servers.

You can also use a combination of the two deployment models to satisfy specific site requirements. For example, two main sites might each have primary and backup subscribers, with another two sites containing only a primary server each and utilizing either shared backups or dedicated backups at the two main sites.

Benefits of the Clustering over the IP WAN Deployment

Although stringent requirements exist, the clustering over the IP WAN deployment design offers these advantages:

- Single point of administration for users for all sites within a cluster

- Feature transparency

- Shared line appearances

- Extension mobility within the cluster

- Unified dial plan

These features make this solution ideal as a disaster recovery plan for business continuance sites or as a single solution for as many as eight small or medium sites.

The cluster design is also useful for customers who require more functionality than the limited feature set offered by SRST. This network design also allows remote offices to support more Cisco IP Phones than SRST in the event that the connection to the primary Cisco UCM server is lost.

WAN Considerations

For clustering over the WAN to be successful, you must carefully plan, design, and implement various characteristics of the WAN itself. The Intra-Cluster Communication Signaling (ICCS) between UCM servers consists of many traffic types. The ICCS traffic types are classified as either priority or best effort. Priority ICCS traffic is marked with IP Precedence 3 (DSCP 24 or PHB CS3). Best-effort ICCS traffic is marked with IP Precedence 0 (DSCP 0 or PHB BE).

The following design guidelines apply to the indicated WAN characteristics:

- **Delay:** The maximum one-way delay between any UCM servers for all priority ICCS traffic should not exceed 20 ms, or 40 ms round-trip time (RTT). Delay for other ICCS traffic should be kept reasonable to provide timely database access. Propagation delay between two sites introduces 6 microseconds per kilometer without any other network delays being considered. This equates to a theoretical maximum distance of approximately 3000 km for 20 ms delay or approximately 1860 miles. These distances are provided only as relative guidelines and in reality will be shorter because of additional delay incurred within the network.

- **Jitter:** Jitter is the varying delay that packets incur through the network because of processing, queue, buffer, congestion, or path variation delay. Jitter for the IP Precedence 3 ICCS traffic must be minimized using QoS features.

- **Packet loss and errors:** The network should be engineered to provide sufficient prioritized bandwidth for all ICCS traffic, especially the priority ICCS traffic. Standard QoS mechanisms must be implemented to avoid congestion and packet loss. If packets are lost due to line errors or other "real world" conditions, an ICCS packet will be retransmitted because it uses the TCP protocol for reliable transmission. The retransmission might result in a call being delayed during setup, disconnect (teardown), or other supplementary services during the call. Some packet-loss conditions could result in a lost call, but this scenario should be no more likely than errors occurring on a T1 or E1, which affect calls via a trunk to the PSTN/ISDN.

■ **Bandwidth:** Provision the correct amount of bandwidth between each server for the expected call volume, type of devices, and number of devices. This bandwidth is in addition to any other bandwidth for other applications sharing the network, including voice and video traffic between the sites. The bandwidth provisioned must have QoS enabled to provide the prioritization and scheduling for the different classes of traffic. The general rule for bandwidth is to overprovision and undersubscribe.

■ **QoS:** The network infrastructure relies on QoS engineering to provide consistent and predictable end-to-end levels of service for traffic. Neither QoS nor bandwidth alone is a solution. Rather, QoS-enabled bandwidth must be engineered into the network infrastructure.

Summary

The main topics covered in this chapter are the following:

■ The Cisco Unified Communications System Architecture fully integrates communications by enabling data, voice, and video to be transmitted over a single network infrastructure using standards-based IP.

■ VoIP is the family of technologies that allows IP networks to be used for voice applications, such as telephony, voice instant messaging, and teleconferencing.

■ VoIP uses H.323, MGCP, SIP, and SCCP call signaling and call control protocols.

■ Signaling protocol models include peer-to-peer and client/server categories of protocols.

■ Configuring voice in a data network requires network services with low delay, minimal jitter, and minimal packet loss.

■ The actual voice conversations are transported across the transmission media using RTP and other RTP-related protocols.

■ Gateways connect IP Communications networks to traditional telephony networks.

■ Several types of voice gateways meet all kinds of customer needs, from small enterprises to large service provider networks.

■ Supported Cisco IP telephony deployment models are single site, multisite with centralized call processing, multisite with distributed call processing, and clustering over the IP WAN.

■ In the single-site deployment model, the Cisco UCM applications and the DSP resources are at the same physical location. The PSTN handles all external calls.

- The multisite centralized model has a single call-processing agent. Applications and DSP resources are centralized or distributed, and the IP WAN carries voice traffic and call control signaling between sites.

- The multisite distributed model has multiple independent sites, each with a call-processing agent, and the IP WAN carries voice traffic between sites but not call control signaling.

- Clustering over an IP WAN provides central administration, a unified dial plan, feature extension to all offices, and support for more remote phones during failover, but places strict delay and bandwidth requirements on the WAN.

Chapter Review Questions

The answers to these review questions are in the appendix.

1. Identify the VoIP network component that provides CAC, bandwidth control and management, and address translation.

   a. Gateway

   b. Gatekeeper

   c. MCU

   d. Call agent

2. Which two of the following signaling protocols are peer-to-peer protocols? (Choose 2.)

   a. H.323

   b. MGCP

   c. SIP

   d. SCCP

3. Which three headers are compressed by cRTP? (Choose 3.)

   a. Data link

   b. IP

   c. TCP

   d. UDP

   e. RTP

4. Which of the following best describes a function of RTCP?

   a. RTCP provides encryption, message authentication and integrity, and anti-replay service for voice streams.

   b. RTCP uses even-numbered UDP ports in the range 16,384–32,767 to transport voice payloads.

   c. RTCP provides out-of-band control information for an RTP flow.

   d. RTCP caches an RTP packet's Layer 3 and Layer 4 headers in the routers at each end of a link, resulting in lower bandwidth demand for subsequent RTP packets.

5. Which three of the following are appropriate solutions to address latency issues in a VoIP network? (Choose 3.)

   a. Use dejitter buffers.

   b. Increase bandwidth.

   c. Use SRTP instead of RTP.

   d. Fragment data packets.

   e. Prioritize voice packets.

6. Which two of the following VoIP gateway platforms are considered to be Integrated Services Routers (ISRs)? (Choose 2.)

   a. Cisco 2600XM Series

   b. Cisco 2800 Series

   c. Cisco Catalyst 6500 Series

   d. Cisco 3700 Series

   e. Cisco AS5850 Universal Gateway

   f. Cisco 3800 Series

7. In a Cisco UCM single-site deployment, what is the maximum number of IP phones that can register with a UCM cluster?

   a. 2500

   b. 7500

   c. 10,000

   d. 30,000

8. In a Cisco UCM multisite WAN with centralized call-processing deployment model, what redundancy feature should be configured on remote site routers to provide basic IP telephony services in the event of a WAN outage?

   a. AAR

   b. SRST

   c. CAC

   d. V3PN

9. Which four of the following are Cisco-supported IP telephony deployment models? (Choose 4.)

   a. Single site

   b. Single site with distributed call processing

   c. Multisite with centralized call processing

   d. Clustering over the IP WAN

   e. Multisite with distributed call processing

   f. Remote clustering with distributed call processing

10. Identify two gateway supplementary services. (Choose 2.)

   a. Hold

   b. DTMF relay

   c. Transfer

   d. Transcoding

After reading this chapter, you should be able to perform the following tasks:

- Describe the challenges of integrating a voice and data network and explain solutions for avoiding problems when designing a VoIP network for optimal voice quality.

- Describe the characteristics of voice codecs and digital signal processors and perform bandwidth calculations for VoIP calls.

CHAPTER 2

Considering VoIP Design Elements

Voice over IP (VoIP) introduces additional challenges into a network design. Some of these challenges stem from the necessity of providing a perceptible level of voice quality to end users, while efficiently using available bandwidth.

VoIP design also requires additional processing components not necessary in traditional data networks. Specifically, coder/decoders (that is, *codecs*) convert the spoken voice into a data stream. Some codecs compress voice to consume less bandwidth. However, compressing voice can degrade the quality of the voice. The loss of voice quality could cause issues when sending tones (for example, Dual Tone Multifrequency [DTMF] tones, modem tones, and fax tones) across a network.

Some voice processes require significant processor overhead. For example, if your voice network requires you to convert between a high-bandwidth codec and a low-bandwidth codec, you need to perform *transcoding*. The act of transcoding requires dedicated hardware called *digital signal processors* (DSPs). This chapter addresses voice quality issues, offers voice quality solutions, and describes VoIP hardware components (for example, codecs and DSPs).

VoIP Fundamentals

The inherent characteristics of a converged voice and data IP network cause network engineers and administrators to face certain challenges in delivering voice traffic correctly. This section describes the challenges of integrating a voice and data network and offers solutions for avoiding problems when designing a VoIP network for optimal voice quality.

IP Networking and Audio Clarity

Because of the nature of IP networking, voice packets sent via IP are subject to certain transmission problems. Conditions present in the network might introduce problems such as echo, jitter, or delay. These problems must be addressed with quality of service (QoS) mechanisms.

The clarity (that is, the "cleanliness" and "crispness") of the audio signal is of utmost importance. The listener must be able to recognize the identity and sense the mood of the speaker. The following factors can affect clarity:

- **Fidelity:** Fidelity is the degree to which a system, or a portion of a system, accurately reproduces at its output the essential characteristics of the signal impressed upon its input, or the result of a prescribed operation on the signal impressed upon its input (definition from the Alliance for Telecommunications Industry Solutions [ATIS]). The bandwidth of the transmission medium almost always limits the total bandwidth of the spoken voice. Human speech typically requires a bandwidth from 100 to 10,000 Hz, although 90 percent of speech intelligence is contained between 100 and 3000 Hz.

- **Echo:** Echo is a result of electrical impedance mismatches in the transmission path. Echo is always present, even in traditional telephony networks, but at a level that cannot be detected by the human ear. The two components that affect echo are amplitude (loudness of the echo) and delay (the time between the spoken voice and the echoed sound). You can control echo using suppressors or cancellers.

- **Jitter:** Jitter is variation in the arrival of coded speech packets at the far end of a VoIP network. The varying arrival time of the packets can cause gaps in the re-creation and playback of the voice signal. These gaps are undesirable and annoy the listener. Delay is induced in the network by variation in the routes of individual packets, contention, or congestion. You can resolve variable delay by using dejitter buffers.

- **Delay:** Delay is the time between the spoken voice and the arrival of the electronically delivered voice at the far end. Delay results from multiple factors, including distance (propagation delay), coding, compression, serialization, and buffers.

- **Packet Loss:** Voice packets might be dropped under various conditions such as an unstable network, network congestion, or too much variable delay in the network. Lost voice packets are not recoverable, resulting in gaps in the conversation that are perceptible to the user.

- **Side tone:** Side tone is the purposeful design of the telephone that allows the speakers to hear their spoken audio in the earpiece. Without side tone, the speaker is left with the impression that the telephone instrument is not working.

- **Background noise:** Background noise is the low-volume audio that is heard from the far-end connection. Certain bandwidth-saving technologies can eliminate background noise altogether, such as voice activity detection (VAD). When this technology is implemented, the speaker audio path is open to the listener, while the listener audio path is closed to the speaker. The effect of VAD is often that speakers think the connection is broken because they hear nothing from the other end. Therefore, VAD is often combined with comfort noise generation (CNG) to prevent the illusion that the call has been disconnected.

The following sections cover some of these in more detail.

Jitter

Jitter is defined as a variation in the arrival of received packets. On the sending side, packets are sent in a continuous stream with the packets spaced evenly. Because of network congestion, improper queuing, or configuration errors, this steady stream can become uneven because the delay between each packet varies instead of remaining constant, as displayed in Figure 2-1.

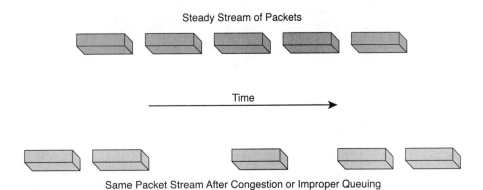

Steady Stream of Packets

Time

Same Packet Stream After Congestion or Improper Queuing

Figure 2-1   *Jitter in IP Networks*

When a router receives an audio stream for VoIP, it must compensate for the jitter that is encountered. The mechanism that handles this function is the play out delay buffer, or dejitter buffer. The play out delay buffer must buffer these packets and then play them out in a steady stream to the DSPs to be converted back to an analog audio stream. The play out delay buffer, however, affects overall absolute delay.

When a conversation is subjected to jitter, the results can be clearly heard. If the talker says, "Watson, come here. I want you," the listener might hear, "Wat....s...on.......come here, I......wa......nt........y......ou." The variable arrival of the packets at the receiving end causes the speech to be delayed and garbled.

Delay

Overall or absolute delay can affect VoIP. You might have experienced delay in a telephone conversation with someone on a different continent. The delays can cause entire words in the conversation to be cut off and can therefore be very frustrating. Figure 2-2 illustrates various areas in the network that can introduce delay.

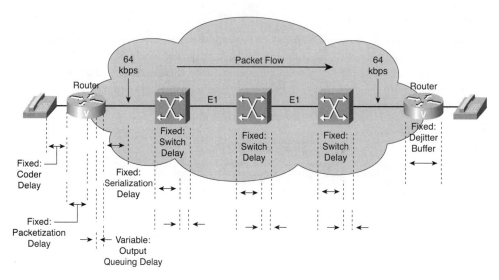

Figure 2-2   *Sources of Delay*

When you design a network that transports voice over packet, frame, or cell infrastructures, it is important to understand and account for the predictable delay components in the network. You must also correctly account for all potential delays to ensure overall network performance is acceptable. Overall voice quality is a function of many factors, including the compression algorithm, errors and frame loss, echo cancellation, and delay.

Following are the two distinct types of delay:

- **Fixed delay:** Fixed-delay components are predictable and add directly to overall delay on the connection. Fixed-delay components include the following:

  - **Coding:** The time it takes to translate the audio signal into a digital signal

  - **Packetization:** The time it takes to put digital voice information into packets and remove the information from packets

  - **Serialization:** The insertion of bits onto a link

  - **Propagation:** The time it takes a packet to traverse a link

- **Variable delay:** Variable delays arise from queuing delays in the egress trunk buffers that are located on the serial port connected to the WAN. These buffers create variable delays, called *jitter*, across the network.

Acceptable Delay

International Telecommunication Union Telecommunication Standardization Sector (ITU-T) specifies network delay for voice applications in Recommendation G.114. This recommendation defines three bands of one-way delay, as shown in Table 2-1.

Table 2-1   *Acceptable Delay: G.114*

Range in Milliseconds	Description
0 to 150	Acceptable for most user applications.
150 to 400	Acceptable, provided administrators are aware of the transmission time and its impact on the transmission quality of user applications.
Above 400	Unacceptable for general network planning purposes. (However, it is recognized that in some exceptional cases, this limit will be exceeded.)

Note   This recommendation is for connections with echo that are adequately controlled, implying that echo cancellers are used. Echo cancellers are required when one-way delay exceeds 25 ms (G.131).

The G.114 recommendation is oriented toward national telecommunications administrations and, therefore, is more stringent than recommendations that would normally be applied in private voice networks. When the location and business needs of end users are well known to a network designer, more delay might prove acceptable. For private networks, a 200 ms delay is a reasonable goal and a 250 ms delay is a limit. This goal is what Cisco Systems proposes as reasonable as long as excessive jitter does not affect voice quality. However, all networks must be engineered so the maximum expected voice connection delay is known and minimized.

Calculating Delay Budget

The G.114 recommendation is for one-way delay only and does not account for round-trip delay. Network design engineers must consider both variable and fixed delays. Variable delays include queuing and network delays, and fixed delays include coding, packetization, serialization, and dejitter buffer delays. Table 2-2 offers a sample delay budget calculation.

Table 2-2   *Delay Budget Calculations*

Delay Type	Fixed (ms)	Variable (ms)
Coder delay	18	
Packetization delay	30	
Queuing and buffering		8
Serialization (64 kbps)	5	

continues

Table 2-2   *Delay Budget Calculations   (continued)*

Delay Type	Fixed (ms)	Variable (ms)
Network delay (public frame)	40	25
Dejitter buffer	45	
Totals	138	33

Packet Loss

Lost data packets are recoverable if the endpoints can request retransmission. Lost voice packets, as depicted in Figure 2-3, are not recoverable, because the audio must be played out in real-time and retransmission is not an option.

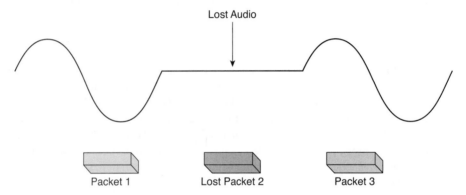

Figure 2-3   *Effect of Packet Loss*

Voice packets might be dropped under the following conditions:

■   The network is unstable (flapping links).

■   The network is congested.

■   Too much variable delay exists in the network, because packets might arrive too late to be admitted into an interface's dejitter buffer.

Packet loss causes voice clipping and skips. As a result, the listener hears gaps in the conversation, as shown in Figure 2-3. The industry standard codec algorithms that are used in Cisco DSPs correct for 20 ms to 50 ms of lost voice through the use of Packet Loss Concealment (PLC) algorithms. PLC intelligently analyzes missing packets and generates a reasonable replacement packet to improve the voice quality. Cisco VoIP technology uses 20 ms samples of voice payload per VoIP packet by default. Effective codec correction algorithms require that only a single packet can be lost at any given time. If more packets are lost, the listener experiences gaps.

If a conversation experiences packet loss, the effect is immediately heard. If the talker says, "Watson, come here. I want you," the listener might hear, "Wat——, come here, ———you."

Audio Quality Measurement

Several methods can be used to determine signal quality, including the following:

- Mean Opinion Score (MOS)

- Perceptual Speech Quality Measurement (PSQM)

- Perceptual Evaluation of Speech Quality (PESQ)

MOS

MOS is a scoring system for voice quality. A MOS score is generated when listeners evaluate prerecorded sentences that are subject to varying conditions, such as compression algorithms. Listeners then assign the sentences values, based on a scale from 1 through 5, where 1 is the worst and 5 is the best. The sentence used for English-language MOS testing is, "Nowadays, a chicken leg is a rare dish." This sentence is used, because it contains a wide range of sounds found in human speech, such as long vowels, short vowels, hard sounds, and soft sounds.

The test scores are then averaged to a composite score. The test results are subjective, because they are based on the opinions of the listeners. The tests are also relative because a score of 3.8 from one test cannot be directly compared to a score of 3.8 from another test. Therefore, you must establish a baseline for all tests, such as G.711, so the scores can be normalized and compared directly.

PSQM

PSQM is an automated method of measuring speech quality "in service," or as the speech happens. PSQM software usually resides with IP call management systems, which are sometimes integrated into Simple Network Management Protocol (SNMP) systems.

Equipment and software that can measure PSQM are available through third-party vendors; it is not implemented in Cisco equipment. The measurement is made by comparing the original transmitted speech to the resulting speech at the far end of the transmission channel. PSQM systems are deployed as in-service components. The PSQM measurements are made during real conversation on the network. This automated testing algorithm has over 90 percent accuracy compared to subjective listening tests, such as MOS. Scoring is based on a scale from 0 through 6.5, where 0 is the best and 6.5 is the worst. Because it was originally designed for circuit-switched voice, PSQM does not take into account the jitter or delay problems experienced in packet-switched voice systems.

PESQ

PESQ was specifically developed to be applicable to end-to-end voice-quality testing under real network conditions, like VoIP, Plain old telephone service (POTS), Integrated services digital network (ISDN), and Global System for Mobile Communication (GSM). PESQ was developed by KPN Research (now TNO Telecom), the Netherlands, and British Telecommunications (BT), by combining the two advanced speech quality measures PSQM+ and Perceptual Analysis Measurement System (PAMS).

PESQ, as demonstrated in Figure 2-4, has evolved into ITU-T Recommendation P.862, which is considered the current standard for voice-quality measurement. PESQ can take into account codec errors, filtering errors, jitter problems, and delay problems that are typical in a VoIP network. It combines the best of the PSQM method along with a method called PAMS. PESQ scores range from 1 (worst) through 4.5 (best), with 3.8 considered toll quality (acceptable quality in a traditional telephony network). PESQ is meant to measure only one aspect of voice quality. The effects of two-way communication, such as loudness loss, delay, echo, and side tone, are not reflected in PESQ scores.

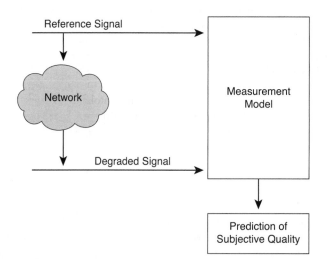

Figure 2-4   *PESQ Operation*

Voice-Quality Measurement Comparison

Early quality measurement methods, such as MOS and PSQM, were designed before widespread acceptance of VoIP technology. PESQ was designed to address the shortcomings of MOS and PSQM.

MOS uses subjective testing in which the average opinion of a group of test users is calculated to create the MOS score. This method is both time-consuming and expensive and might not provide consistent results between groups of testers.

PSQM and PESQ use objective testing in which an original reference file sent into the system is compared with the impaired signal that came out. This testing method provides an automated test mechanism that does not rely on human interpretation for result calculations. However, PSQM was originally designed for circuit-switched networks and does not take into account the effects of jitter and packet loss.

PESQ measures the effect of end-to-end network conditions, including codec processing, jitter, and packet loss. Therefore, PESQ is the preferred method of testing voice quality in an IP network. Table 2-3 offers a comparison of the features offered by MOS, PSQM, and PESQ.

Table 2-3   *Quality Measurement Comparison*

Feature	MOS	PSQM	PESQ
Test method	Subjective	Objective	Objective
End-to-end packet loss test	Inconsistent	No	Yes
End-to-end jitter test	Inconsistent	No	Yes

VoIP and QoS

Real-time applications, such as voice applications, have different characteristics and requirements from those of traditional data applications. Because they are real-time based, voice applications tolerate minimal variation in the amount of delay affecting delivery of their voice packets. Voice traffic is also intolerant of packet loss and jitter, both of which unacceptably degrade the quality of the voice transmission delivered to the recipient end user. To effectively transport voice traffic over IP, mechanisms are required that ensure reliable delivery of voice packets. Cisco IOS QoS features collectively embody these techniques, offering the means to provide priority service that meets the stringent requirements of voice packet delivery.

The QoS components for Cisco Unified Communications are provided through the IP traffic management, queuing, and shaping capabilities of a Cisco IP network infrastructure.

Following are a few of the Cisco IOS features that address the requirements of end-to-end QoS and service differentiation for voice packet delivery:

- **Header Compression:** Used in conjunction with Real-time Transport Protocol (RTP) and Transmission Control Protocol (TCP), it compresses the extensive RTP or TCP header, resulting in decreased consumption of available bandwidth for voice traffic. A corresponding reduction in delay is realized.

- **Frame Relay Traffic Shaping (FRTS):** Delays excess traffic using a buffer or queuing mechanism to hold packets and shape the flow when the data rate of the source is higher than expected.

- **FRF.12 (and Higher):** Ensures predictability for voice traffic, aiming to provide better throughput on low-speed Frame Relay links by interleaving delay-sensitive voice traffic on one virtual circuit (VC) with fragments of a long frame on another VC utilizing the same interface.

■ **Public Switched Telephone Network (PSTN) Fallback:** Provides a mechanism to monitor congestion in the IP network and either redirect calls to the PSTN or reject calls based on the network congestion.

■ **IP RTP Priority and Frame Relay IP RTP Priority:** Provides a strict priority queuing scheme that allows delay-sensitive data, such as voice, to be dequeued and sent before packets when other queues are dequeued. These features are especially useful on slow-speed WAN links, including Frame Relay, Multilink PPP [MLP], and T1 ATM links. It works with weighted fair queuing (WFQ) and Class-Based WFQ (CBWFQ).

■ **IP to ATM Class of Service (CoS):** Includes a feature suite that maps QoS characteristics between IP and ATM. Offers differential service classes across the entire WAN, not just the routed portion. Gives mission-critical applications exceptional service during periods of high network usage and congestion.

■ **Low Latency Queuing (LLQ):** Provides strict priority queuing on ATM VCs and serial interfaces. This feature enables you to configure the priority status for a class within CBWFQ and is not limited to User Datagram Protocol (UDP) port numbers, as is IP RTP Priority.

■ **MLP:** Allows large packets to be multilink encapsulated and fragmented so they are small enough to satisfy the delay requirements of real-time traffic. MLP also provides a special transmit queue for smaller, delay-sensitive packets, enabling them to be sent earlier than other flows.

■ **Resource Reservation Protocol (RSVP):** Supports the reservation of resources across an IP network, allowing end systems to request QoS guarantees from the network. For networks supporting VoIP, RSVP (in conjunction with features that provide queuing, traffic shaping, and voice call signaling) can provide call admission control (CAC) for voice traffic. Cisco also provides RSVP support for LLQ and Frame Relay.

Objectives of QoS

To ensure VoIP is an acceptable replacement for standard PSTN telephony services, customers must receive the same consistently high quality of voice transmission they receive with basic telephone services. Like other real-time applications, VoIP is extremely sensitive to issues related to bandwidth and delay. To ensure VoIP transmissions are intelligible to the receiver, voice packets cannot be dropped, excessively delayed, or be subject to variations in delay (jitter). A successful VoIP deployment must provide an acceptable level of voice quality by meeting VoIP traffic requirements for issues related to bandwidth, latency, and jitter.

QoS refers to the ability of a network to provide improved service to selected network traffic over various underlying technologies including Frame Relay, ATM, Ethernet and 802.1 networks, SONET, and IP-routed networks. VoIP guarantees high-quality voice transmission only if the signaling and audio channel packets have priority over other kinds of network traffic.

In particular, QoS features provide improved and more predictable network service by implementing the following services:

- **Support guaranteed bandwidth:** Designing the network so the necessary bandwidth is always available to support voice and data traffic

- **Improve loss characteristics:** Designing the Frame Relay network, for example, so discard eligibility is not a factor for frames containing voice, keeping voice below the committed information rate (CIR)

- **Avoid and manage network congestion:** Ensuring the LAN and WAN infrastructure can support the volume of data traffic and voice calls

- **Shape network traffic:** Using Cisco traffic-shaping tools to ensure smooth and consistent delivery of frames to the WAN

- **Set traffic priorities across the network:** Marking voice traffic as priority and queuing it first

Using QoS to Improve Voice Quality

Voice features that provide QoS are deployed at different points in the network and designed for use with other QoS features to achieve specific goals, such as minimization of jitter and delay.

Cisco IOS Software includes a complete set of features for delivering QoS throughout the network. Although a complete survey of QoS features is beyond the scope of this book, Cisco's recommended QoS mechanism for VoIP queuing, in a router's output interface, is LLQ.

LLQ provides strict priority queuing (PQ) in conjunction with CBWFQ. LLQ configures the priority status for a class within CBWFQ, in which voice packets receive priority over all other traffic.

For example, consider Figure 2-5. Whereas web traffic receives at least 128 kbps of bandwidth (if the web traffic needs that much bandwidth), voice traffic receives 256 kbps of "priority" bandwidth (if the voice traffic needs that much bandwidth), meaning the voice traffic is transmitted first, ahead of the web traffic. However, the voice traffic will not starve out the other traffic types, because the voice traffic is also limited to consuming no more than 256 kbps.

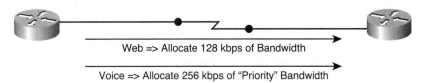

Figure 2-5 *Low Latency Queuing Example*

Transporting Modulated Data over IP Networks

An IP, or packet-switched, network enables data to be sent in packets to remote locations. The data is assembled by a packet assembler/disassembler (PAD) into individual packets of data, involving a process of segmentation or subdivision of larger sets of data as specified by the native protocol of the sending device. Each packet has a unique identifier that makes it independent and has its own destination address. Because the packet is unique and independent, it can traverse the network in a stream of packets and use different routes. This has some implications for fax transmissions that use data packets rather than using an analog signal over a circuit-switched network.

Differences from Fax Transmission in the PSTN

In IP networks, individual packets that are part of the same data transmission might follow different physical paths of varying lengths. They can also experience varying levels of propagation delay and delay that is caused by being held in packet buffers awaiting the availability of a subsequent circuit. The packets can also arrive in an order different from the order in which they entered the network. The destination node of the network uses the identifiers and addresses in the packet sequencing information to reassemble the packets into the correct sequence.

Fax transmissions are designed to operate across a 64 kbps pulse code modulation (PCM) encoded voice circuit, but in packet networks, the 64 kbps stream is often compressed into a much smaller data rate by passing it through a DSP. The codecs normally used to compress a voice stream in a DSP are designed to compress and decompress human speech, not fax or modem tones. For this reason, faxes and modems are rarely used in a VoIP network without some kind of relay or pass-through mechanism in place.

Fax Services over IP Networks

There are three conceptual methods of carrying fax-machine-to-fax-machine communications across packet networks:

- **Fax relay:** The T.30 fax from the PSTN is demodulated at the sending gateway. The demodulated fax content is enveloped into packets, sent over the network, and remodulated into T.30 fax at the receiving end.

Note   Cisco IOS supports two types of fax relay: T.38 fax relay and Cisco Fax Relay (which is proprietary).

- **Fax pass-through:** Modulated fax information from the PSTN is passed in-band end-to-end over a voice speech path in an IP network. There are two pass-through techniques:

    - The configured voice codec is used for the fax transmission. This technique works only when the configured codec is G.711 with no VAD and no echo cancellation (EC) or when the configured codec is a clear-channel codec or G.726/32. Low bit-rate codecs cannot be used for fax transmissions.

■ The gateway dynamically changes the codec from the codec configured for voice to G.711 with no VAD and no EC for the duration of the fax session. This method is specifically referred to as "codec up speed" or "fax pass-through with up speed."

■ **Store-and-forward fax:** Breaks the fax process into distinct sending and receiving processes and allows fax messages to be stored between those processes. Store-and-forward fax is based on the ITU-T T.37 standard, and it also enables fax transmissions to be received from or delivered to computers rather than fax machines.

Understanding Fax/Modem Pass-Through, Relay, and Store and Forward

Several features are available to overcome the issues involved with carrying fax and modem signals across an IP network including

■ Fax and Modem Pass-Through

■ Fax and Modem Relay

■ Fax Store and Forward

Fax Pass-Through

Fax pass-through, as illustrated in Figure 2-6, is the simplest technique for sending fax over IP networks, but it is not the default, nor is it the most desirable method of supporting fax over IP. T.38 fax relay provides a more reliable and error-free method of sending faxes over an IP network, but some third-party H.323 and Session Initiation Protocol (SIP) implementations do not support T.38 fax relay. These same implementations often support fax pass-through.

Fax pass-through is the state of the channel after the fax up-speed process has occurred. In fax pass-through mode, gateways do not distinguish a fax call from a voice call. Fax communication between the two fax machines is carried in its entirety in-band over a voice call. When using fax pass-through with up speed, the gateways are to some extent aware of the fax call. Although relay mechanisms are not employed, with up speed, the gateways recognize a called terminal identification fax tone, automatically change the voice codec to G.711 if necessary (thus the designation *up speed*), and turn off echo cancellation and VAD for the duration of the call.

Fax pass-through is also known as *voice band data* by the ITU. Voice band data refers to the transport of fax or modem signals over a voice channel through a packet network with an encoding appropriate for fax or modem signals. The minimum set of coders for voice band data mode is G.711 mu-law and a-law with VAD disabled.

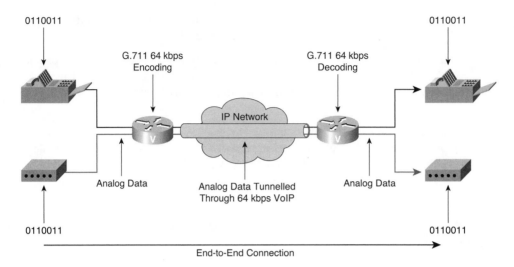

Figure 2-6   *Fax and Modem Pass-Through Topology*

Fax pass-through takes place when incoming T.30 fax data is not demodulated or compressed for its transit through the packet network. The two endpoints (fax machines or modems) communicate directly to each other over a transparent IP connection. The gateway does not distinguish fax calls from voice calls.

With pass-through, the fax traffic is carried between the two gateways in RTP packets using an uncompressed format resembling the G.711 codec. This method of transporting fax traffic takes a constant 64 kbps (payload) stream plus its IP overhead end-to-end for the duration of the call. IP overhead is 16 kbps for normal voice traffic, but when switching to pass-through, the packetization period is reduced from 20 ms to 10 ms. Table 2-4 compares a G.711 VoIP call that uses 20 ms packetization with a G.711 fax pass-through call that uses 10 ms packetization.

Table 2-4   *G.711 Packetization Periods*

Packetization	G.711 Payload	Overhead for Layers 3 and 4	Packet Size	Bit Rate
10 ms	80 byte	40 byte	120 byte	96 kbps
20 ms	160 byte	40 byte	200 byte	80 kbps

Packet redundancy might be used to mitigate the effects of packet loss in the IP network. Even so, fax pass-through remains susceptible to packet loss, jitter, and latency in the IP network. The two endpoints must be clocked synchronously for this type of transport to work predictably.

Performance might become an issue. To attempt to mitigate packet loss in the network, redundant encoding (1X or one repeat of the original packet) is used, which doubles the amount of data transferred in each packet. The doubling of packets imposes a limitation on the total number of ports that can run fax pass-through at one time. One fax pass-through session with redundancy needs as much bandwidth as two G.711 calls without VAD.

Fax pass-through does not support the switch from G.Clear to G.711. If fax pass-through and the G.Clear codec are both configured, the gateway cannot detect the fax tone.

Fax pass-through is supported under these call-control protocols:

■ H.323

■ SIP

■ Media Gateway Control Protocol (MGCP)

Modem Pass-Through

Modem pass-through over VoIP provides the transport of modem signals through a packet network by using PCM-encoded packets. It is based on the same logic as fax pass-through: An analog voice stream is encoded into G.711, passed through the network, and decoded back to analog signals at the far end.

The following factors need to be considered when determining whether to use modem pass-through:

■ Modem pass-through does not support the switch from G.Clear to G.711.

■ VAD and echo cancellation need to be disabled.

■ Modem pass-through over VoIP performs these functions:

   ■ Represses processing functions like compression, echo cancellation, high-pass filter, and VAD

   ■ Issues redundant packets to protect against random packet drops

   ■ Provides static jitter buffers of 200 ms to protect against clock skew

   ■ Discriminates modem signals from voice and fax signals, indicating the detection of the modem signal across the connection, and placing the connection in a state that transports the signal across the network with the least amount of distortion

   ■ Reliably maintains a modem connection across the packet network for a long duration under normal network conditions

Fax Relay

Cisco Fax Relay is the oldest method of supporting fax on Cisco IOS gateways and has been supported since Cisco IOS Release 11.3. Cisco Fax Relay uses RTP as the method of transport. In Cisco Fax Relay mode, gateways terminate T.30 fax signaling by spoofing a virtual fax machine to the locally attached fax machine. The gateways use a Cisco-proprietary fax relay RTP-based protocol to communicate between themselves.

Unlike fax pass-through, fax relay, as depicted in Figure 2-7, demodulates the fax bits at the local gateway, sends the information across the voice network using the fax relay protocol, and then remodulates the bits back into tones at the far gateway. The fax machines on either end are sending and receiving tones and are not aware that a demodulation/modulation fax relay process is occurring.

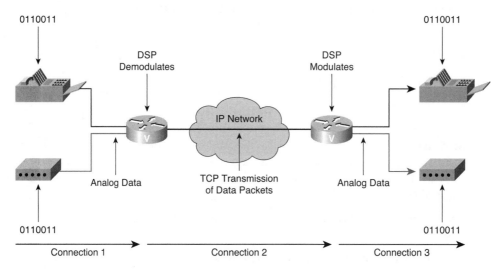

Figure 2-7   *Fax and Modem Relay Topology*

The default method for fax transmission on Cisco IOS gateways is Cisco Fax Relay. This is an RTP-based transmission method that uses proprietary signaling and encoding mechanisms. The mechanism for Cisco Fax Relay is the same for calls that are controlled by SIP, MGCP, and H.323 call control protocols.

Note   Before T.38 standards-based fax relay was introduced, configuration was required to enable Cisco Fax Relay.

Cisco provides two methods for fax relay:

- **Cisco Fax Relay:** A Cisco-proprietary method, and the default on most platforms if a fax method is not explicitly configured.

- **T.38 fax relay:** A method based on the ITU-T T.38 standard. It is real-time fax transmission (that is, two fax machines communicating with each other as if there were a direct phone line between them). T.38 fax relay is configured by using a few additional commands on gateway dial peers that have already been defined and configured for VoIP calls.

The T.38 fax relay feature can be configured for H.323, SIP, and MGCP call control protocols. For H.323 and SIP networks, the only configuration tasks that differ are those involving the configuration of VoIP dial peers.

T.38 is an ITU-T standards-based method and protocol for fax relay. Data is packetized and encapsulated according to the T.38 standard. T.38 fax relay has the following features:

- Fax relay PLC

- MGCP-based fax (T.38) and DTMF relay

- SIP T.38 fax relay

- T.38 fax relay for the T.37/T.38 fax gateway

- T.38 fax relay for VoIP H.323

Modem Relay

Cisco modem relay provides support for modem connections across traditional time-division multiplexing (TDM) networks. Modem relay demodulates a modem signal at one voice gateway and passes it as packet data to another voice gateway, where the signal is remodulated and sent to a receiving modem. On detection of the modem answer tone, the gateways switch into modem pass-through mode and then, if the call menu (CM) signal is detected, the two gateways switch into modem relay mode.

There are two ways to transport modem traffic over VoIP networks:

- **Modem pass-through:** The modem traffic is carried between the two gateways in RTP packets, using an uncompressed voice codec, G.711 mu-law or a-law. Although modem pass-through remains susceptible to packet loss, jitter, and latency in the IP network, packet redundancy can be used to mitigate the effects of packet loss in the IP network.

- **Modem relay:** The modem signals are demodulated at one gateway, converted to digital form, and carried in the Simple Packet Relay Transport (SPRT) protocol. SPRT is a protocol running over UDP packets to the other gateway, where the modem signal is re-created, remodulated, and passed to the receiving modem.

In this implementation, the call starts out as a voice call, switches into modem pass-through mode, and then into modem relay mode.

Modem relay significantly reduces the effects that dropped packets, latency, and jitter have on the modem session. Compared to modem pass-through, it also reduces the amount of bandwidth used.

Modem relay includes these features:

- Modem tone detection and signaling

- Relay switchover

- Controlled redundancy

- Packet size

- Clock slip buffer management

Consider the modem relay characteristics in the following sections.

Modem Tone Detection and Signaling

Modem relay supports V.34 modulation and the V.42 error correction and link layer protocol with maximum transfer rates of up to 33.6 kbps. It forces higher-rate modems to train down to the supported rates. Signaling support includes the SIP, MGCP, and H.323:

- For MGCP and SIP, during the call setup, gateways negotiate these items:

  - To use or not use the modem relay mode

  - To use or not use the gateway exchange identification (XID)

  - The value of the payload type for Named Signaling Event (NSE) packets

- For H.323, the gateways negotiate these items:

  - To use or not use the modem relay mode

  - To use or not use the gateway XID

Relay Switchover

When the gateways detect a data modem, both the originating gateway and the terminating gateway switch to modem pass-through mode by performing these actions:

- Switching to the G.711 codec

- Disabling the high-pass filter

- Disabling VAD

- Using special jitter buffer management algorithms

- Disabling the echo canceller upon detection of a modem phase reversal tone

At the end of the modem call, the voice ports revert to the previous configuration, and the DSPs switch back to the state they were in before the switchover. You can configure the codec by using the **g711alaw** or **g711ulaw** option of the **codec** command.

Payload Redundancy

You can enable payload redundancy so the modem pass-through over VoIP switchover causes the gateway to send redundant packets. Redundancy can be enabled in one or both of the gateways. When only a single gateway is configured for redundancy, the other gateway receives the packets correctly, but does not produce redundant packets. When redundancy is enabled, 10 ms sample-sized packets are sent. When redundancy is disabled, 20 ms sample-sized packets are sent.

Note   By default, the modem relay over VoIP capability and redundancy are disabled.

Dynamic and Static Jitter Buffers

When gateways detect a data modem, both the originating gateway and the terminating gateway switch from dynamic jitter buffers to static jitter buffers of 200 ms depth. The switch from dynamic to static is designed to compensate for PSTN clocking differences at the originating and terminating gateways. When the modem call is concluded, the voice ports revert to dynamic jitter buffers.

Gateway-Controlled Modem Relay

Beginning with Cisco IOS Release 12.4(4)T, Cisco supports gateway-controlled negotiation parameters for modem relay. This new feature is a non-negotiated, bearer-switched mode for modem transport that does not involve call-agent-assisted negotiation during the call setup. Instead, the negotiation parameters are configured directly on the gateway. These gateway-controlled negotiation parameters use NSEs to indicate the switchover from voice to voice band data to modem relay.

Upon detecting a 2100 Hz tone, the terminating gateway sends an NSE 192 to the originating gateway and switches over to modem pass-through. The terminating gateway also sends an NSE 199 to indicate modem relay. If this event is recognized by the originating gateway, the call occurs as modem relay. If the event is not recognized, the call occurs as modem pass-through.

Because Cisco modem relay uses configured parameters, it removes the signaling dependency from the call agent and allows modem relay support independent of call control. Cisco modem relay can be deployed over any call agent that is capable of setting up a voice connection between gateways, including Cisco Unified Communications Manager, Cisco Unified Communications Manager Express, and the Cisco BTS and PGW soft switches.

The gateway-controlled modem relay parameters are enabled by default when Cisco modem relay is configured. Interestingly, when Cisco modem relay is configured, gateway XID parameter negotiation is always enabled. Gateway XID parameters are negotiated using the SPRT protocol.

Store-and-Forward Fax

The transmitting gateway is referred to as an "on-ramp gateway," and the terminating gateway is referred to as an "off-ramp gateway." Figure 2-8 illustrates the operation of on-ramp and off-ramp gateways.

On-ramp receives faxes that are delivered as e-mail attachments.

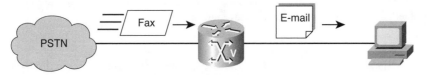

Off-ramp sends standard e-mail messages that are delivered as faxes.

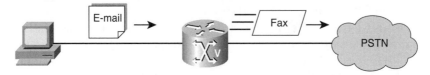

Figure 2-8   *Store-and-Forward Fax Topology*

The following are some of the basic characteristics of on- and off-ramp faxing:

- **On-ramp faxing:** A voice gateway that handles incoming calls from a standard fax machine or the PSTN converts a traditional G3 fax to an e-mail message with a Tagged Image File Format (TIFF) attachment. The fax e-mail message and attachment are handled by an e-mail server while traversing the packet network and can be stored for later delivery or delivered immediately to a PC or to an off-ramp gateway.

- **Off-ramp faxing:** A voice gateway that handles calls going out from the network to a fax machine or the PSTN converts a fax e-mail with a TIFF attachment into a traditional fax format that can be delivered to a standard fax machine or the PSTN.

On-ramp and off-ramp faxing processes can be combined on a single gateway, or they can occur on separate gateways. Store-and-forward fax uses two different interactive voice response (IVR) applications for on-ramp and off-ramp functionality. The applications are implemented in two Toolkit Command Language (TCL) scripts that you can download from Cisco.com.

The basic functionality of store-and-forward fax is facilitated through Simple Mail Transfer Protocol (SMTP), with additional functionality that provides confirmation of delivery using existing SMTP mechanisms, such as Extended Simple Mail Transfer Protocol (ESMTP).

Gateway Signaling Protocols and Fax Pass-Through and Relay

Figure 2-9 illustrates a fax pass-through operation. When a terminating gateway (TGW) detects a called terminal identification (CED) tone from a called fax machine, the TGW exchanges the voice codec that was negotiated during the voice call setup for a G.711 codec and turns off echo cancellation and VAD. This switchover is communicated to the originating gateway (OGW), which allows the fax machines to transfer modem signals as though they were traversing the PSTN. If the voice codec that was configured and negotiated for the VoIP call is G.711 when the CED tone is detected, there is no need to make any changes to the session other than turning off echo cancellation and VAD.

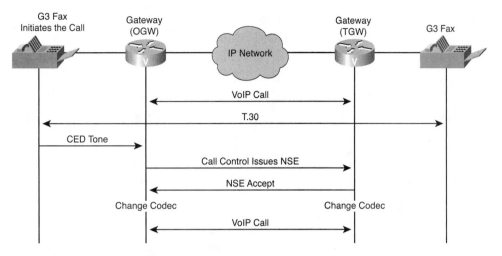

Figure 2-9   *Fax Pass-Through Operation*

If pass-through is supported, these events occur:

1. For the duration of the call, the DSP listens for the 2100-Hz CED tone to detect a fax or modem on the line.

2. If the CED tone is heard, an internal event is generated to alert the call control stack that a fax or modem changeover is required.

3. The call control stack on the OGW instructs the DSP to send an NSE to the TGW, informing the TGW of the request to carry out a codec change.

4. If the TGW supports NSEs, it responds to the OGW instruction and loads the new codec. The fax machines are able to communicate on an end-to-end basis with no further intervention by the voice gateways.

Control of fax pass-through is achieved through NSEs that are sent in the RTP stream. NSEs are a Cisco-proprietary version of IETF-standard named telephony events (NTEs), which are specially marked data packets used to digitally convey telephony signaling tones and events. NSEs use different event values than NTEs and are generally sent with RTP payload type 100, whereas NTEs use RTP payload type 101. NSEs and NTEs provide a more reliable way to communicate tones and events using a single packet rather than a series of in-band packets that can be corrupted or partially lost.

Fax pass-through and fax pass-through with up speed use peer-to-peer NSEs within the RTP stream or bearer stream to coordinate codec switchover and the disabling of echo cancellation and VAD. Redundant packets can be sent to improve reliability when the probability of packet loss is high.

When a DSP is put into voice mode at the beginning of a VoIP call, the DSP is informed by the call control stack whether or not the control protocol can support pass-through.

Cisco Fax Relay

Figure 2-10 illustrates the operation of Cisco Fax Relay.

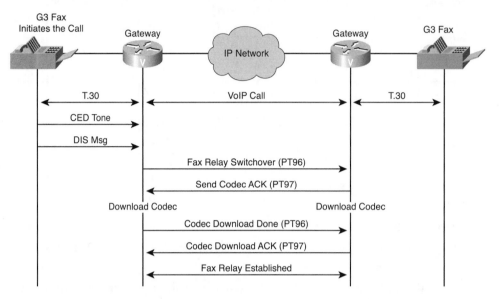

Figure 2-10 *Cisco Fax Relay Operation*

When a DSP is put into voice mode at the beginning of a VoIP call, the DSP is informed by the call control stack whether fax relay is supported and if it is supported, whether it is Cisco Fax Relay or T.38 fax relay. If Cisco Fax Relay is supported, the following events occur:

1. Initially, a VoIP call is established as if it were a normal speech call. Call control procedures are followed, and the DSP is put into voice mode, after which human speech is expected to be received and processed.

2. At anytime during the life of the call, if a fax answer or calling tone (ANSam [modified ANSwer tone] or CED) is heard, the DSP does not interfere with the speech processing. The ANSam or CED tone causes a switch to modem pass-through, if enabled, to allow the tone to pass cleanly to the remote fax.

3. A normal fax machine, after generating a CED or hearing a CNG (CalliNG) tone, sends a DIS (digital identification signal) message with the capabilities of the fax machine. The DSP in the Cisco IOS gateway attached to the fax machine that generated the DIS message (normally the TGW) detects the High-Level Data Link Control (HDLC) flag sequence at the start of the DIS message and initiates fax relay switchover. The DSP also triggers an internal event to notify the call control stack that fax switchover is required. The call control stack then instructs the DSP to change the RTP payload type to 96 and to send this payload type to the OGW.

4. When the DSP on the OGW receives an RTP packet with the payload type set to 96, it triggers an event to inform its own call control stack that a fax changeover has been requested by the remote gateway. The OGW then sends an RTP packet to the TGW with payload type 97 to indicate that the OGW has started the fax changeover. When the TGW receives the payload type 97 packet, the packet serves as an acknowledgement. The TGW starts the fax codec download and is ready for fax relay.

5. After the OGW has completed the codec download, it sends RTP packets with payload type 96 to the TGW. The TGW responds with an RTP packet with payload type 97, and fax relay can begin between the two gateways. As part of the fax codec download, other parameters such as VAD, jitter buffers, and echo cancellation are changed to suit the different characteristics of a fax call.

During fax relay operation, the T.30 analog fax signals are received from the PSTN or from a directly attached fax machine. The T.30 fax signals are demodulated by a DSP on the gateway and then packetized and sent across the VoIP network as data. The TGW decodes the data stream and remodulates the T.30 analog fax signals to be sent to the PSTN or to a destination fax machine.

The messages that are demodulated and remodulated are predominantly the phase B, phase D, and phase E messages of a T.30 transaction. Most of the messages are passed across without any interference, but certain messages are modified according to the constraints of the VoIP network.

During phase B, fax machines interrogate each other's capabilities. They expect to communicate with each other across a 64 kbps PSTN circuit, and they attempt to make best use of the available bandwidth and circuit quality of a 64 kbps voice path. However, in a VoIP network, the fax machines do not have a 64 kbps PSTN circuit available. The bandwidth per call is probably less than 64 kbps, and the circuit is not considered a clear circuit.

Because transmission paths in VoIP networks are more limited than in the PSTN, Cisco IOS CLI is used to adjust fax settings on the VoIP dial peer. The adjusted fax settings restrict the facilities that are available to fax machines across the VoIP call leg and are also used to modify values in DIS and NSF messages that are received from fax machines.

H.323 T.38 Fax Relay

Figure 2-11 illustrates an H.323 T.38 relay operation. The T.38 fax relay feature provides an ITU-T standards-based method and protocols for fax relay.

Data is packetized and encapsulated according to the T.38 standard. The encoding of the packet headers and the mechanism to switch from VoIP mode to fax relay mode are clearly defined in the specification. Annexes to the basic specification include details for operation under SIP and H.323 call control protocols.

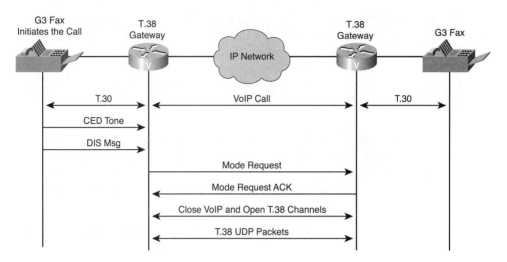

Figure 2-11   *H.323 Fax Relay Operation*

Figure 2-11 shows the H.245 message flow:

1. Initially, a VoIP call is established as if it were a normal speech call. Call control pro-
    cedures are followed, and the DSP is put into voice mode, after which human speech
    is expected to be received and processed.

2. At anytime during the life of the call, if a fax answer or calling tone (ANSam or
    CED) is heard, the DSP does not interfere with the speech processing. The ANSam
    or CED tone causes a switch to modem pass-through, if enabled, to allow the tone to
    pass cleanly to the remote fax.

3. A normal fax machine, after generating a CED or hearing a CNG, sends a DIS mes-
    sage with the capabilities of the fax machine. The DSP in the Cisco IOS gateway
    attached to the fax machine that generated the DIS message (normally the TGW)
    detects the HDLC flag sequence at the start of the DIS message and initiates fax
    relay switchover. The DSP also triggers an internal event to notify the call control
    stack that fax switchover is required. The call control stack then instructs the DSP to
    change the RTP payload type to 96 and to send this payload type to the OGW.

4. The detecting TGW sends a ModeRequest message to the OGW, and the OGW
    responds with a ModeRequestAck.

5. The OGW sends a closeLogicalChannel message to close its VoIP UDP port, and the
    TGW responds with a closeLogicalChannelAck message while it closes the VoIP
    port.

6. The OGW sends an openLogicalChannel message that indicates to which port to
    send the T.38 UDP information on the OGW, and the TGW responds with an
    openLogicalChannelAck message.

7. The TGW sends a closeLogicalChannel message to close its VoIP UDP port, and the
    OGW responds with a closeLogicalChannelAck message.

8. The TGW sends an openLogicalChannel message that indicates to which port to send the T.38 UDP stream, and the OGW responds with an openLogicalChannelAck message.

9. T.38-encoded UDP packets flow back and forth. At the end of the fax transmission, either gateway can initiate another ModeRequest message to return to VoIP mode.

T.38 fax relay uses data redundancy to accommodate packet loss. During T.38 call establishment, voice gateways indicate the level of packet redundancy they incorporate in their transmission of fax UDP transport layer packets. The level of redundancy (the number of times the packet is repeated) can be configured on Cisco IOS gateways.

The T.38 Annex B standard defines the mechanism that is used to switch over from voice mode to T.38 fax mode during a call. The capability to support T.38 must be indicated during the initial VoIP call setup. If the DSP on the gateway is capable of supporting T.38 mode, this information is indicated during the H.245 negotiation procedures as part of the regular H.323 VoIP call setup.

After the VoIP call setup is completed, the DSP continues to listen for a fax tone. When a fax tone is heard, the DSP signals the receipt of the fax tone to the call control layer, which then initiates fax changeover as specified in the T.38 Annex B procedures.

SIP T.38 Fax Relay

Figure 2-12 illustrates a SIP T.38 relay operation. When the call control protocol is SIP, T.38 Annex D procedures are used for the changeover from VoIP to fax mode during a call.

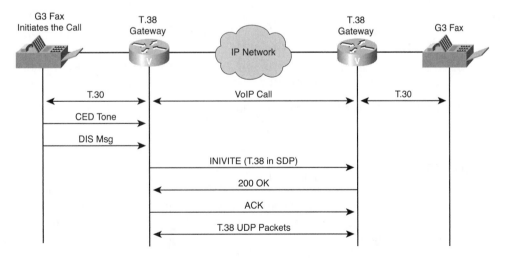

Figure 2-12 *SIP T.38 Fax Relay Operation*

Initially, a normal VoIP call is established using SIP INVITE messages. The DSP needs to be informed that it can support T.38 mode while it is put into voice mode. Then, during the call, when the DSP detects fax HDLC flags, it signals the detection of the flags to the call control layer, and the call control layer initiates a SIP INVITE message mid-call to signal the desire to change the media stream.

The SIP T.38 fax relay call flow is as follows:

1. Initially, a VoIP call is established as if it were a normal speech call. Call control procedures are followed, and the DSP is put into voice mode, after which human speech is expected to be received and processed.

2. At anytime during the life of the call, if a fax answer or calling tone (ANSam or CED) is heard, the DSP does not interfere with the speech processing. The ANSam or CED tone causes a switch to modem pass-through, if enabled, to allow the tone to pass cleanly to the remote fax.

3. A normal fax machine, after generating a CED or hearing a CNG, sends a DIS message with the capabilities of the fax machine. The DSP in the Cisco IOS gateway attached to the fax machine that generated the DIS message (normally the TGW) detects the HDLC flag sequence at the start of the DIS message and initiates fax relay switchover. The DSP also triggers an internal event to notify the call control stack that fax switchover is required. The call control stack then instructs the DSP to change the RTP payload type to 96 and to send this payload type to the OGW.

4. The TGW detects a fax V.21 flag sequence and sends an INVITE message with T.38 details in the SDP field to the OGW or to the SIP proxy server, depending on the network topology.

5. The OGW receives the INVITE message and sends back a 200 OK message.

6. The TGW acknowledges the 200 OK message and sends an ACK message directly to the OGW.

7. The OGW starts sending T.38 UDP packets instead of VoIP UDP packets across the same ports.

8. At the end of the fax transmission, another INVITE message can be sent to return to VoIP mode.

MGCP T.38 Fax Relay

The MGCP T.38 fax relay feature conforms to ITU-T T.38, "Procedures for real-time Group 3 (G3) facsimile communication over IP networks," which determines procedures for real-time facsimile communication in various External Gateway Control Protocol (XGCP) applications.

MGCP T.38 fax relay provides two modes of implementation:

■   **Gateway-controlled mode:** Gateways negotiate fax relay transmission by exchanging capability information in SDP messages. Transmission of SDP messages is transparent to the call agent. Gateway-controlled mode allows the use of a MGCP-based T.38 fax without the necessity of upgrading the call agent software to support the feature.

■   **Call agent-controlled mode:** Call agents use MGCP messaging to instruct gateways to process fax traffic. For MGCP T.38 fax relay, call agents can also instruct gateways to revert to gateway-controlled mode if the call agent is unable to handle the fax control messaging traffic, as is the case in overloaded or congested networks.

MGCP-based T.38 fax relay enables interworking between the T.38 application that already exists on Cisco gateways and the MGCP applications on call agents.

Following is the call flow for an MGCP-based T.38 fax relay:

1.   A call is initially established as a voice call.

2.   The gateways advertise capabilities in an SDP exchange during connection establishment.

3.   If both gateways do not support T.38 fax relay, fax pass-through is used for fax transmission. If both gateways support T.38, they attempt to switch to T.38 upon fax tone detection. The existing audio channel is used for T.38 fax relay, and the existing connection port is reused to minimize delay. If failure occurs at some point during the switch to T.38, the call reverts to the original settings it had as a voice call. If this failure occurs, a fallback to fax pass-through is not supported.

4.   Upon completion of the fax image transfer, the connection remains established and reverts to a voice call using the previously designated codec, unless the call agent instructs the gateways to do otherwise.

A fax relay MGCP event allows the gateway to notify the call agent of the status (start, stop, or failure) of T.38 processing for the connection. This event is sent in both call agent-controlled and gateway-controlled mode.

Gateway-Controlled MGCP T.38 Fax Relay

In gateway-controlled mode, a call agent uses the *fx:* extension of the local connection option (LCO) to instruct a gateway how to process a call. Gateways do not need instruction from the call agent to switch to T.38 mode. This mode is used if the call agent has not been upgraded to support T.38 and MGCP interworking, or if the call agent does not want to manage fax calls. Gateway-controlled mode can also be used to bypass the message delay overhead caused by call agent handling (for example, to meet time requirements for switchover to T.38 mode). If the call agent does not specify the mode to the gateway, the gateway defaults to gateway-controlled mode.

In gateway-controlled mode, the gateways exchange NSEs by performing these steps:

1.   Instruct the peer gateway to switch to T.38 for a fax transmission.

2.   Either acknowledge the switch and the readiness of the gateway to accept T.38 packets or indicate that the gateway cannot accept T.38 packets.

CA-Controlled MGCP T.38 Fax Relay

In call-agent-controlled mode, the call agent can instruct the gateway to switch to T.38 for a call. In Cisco IOS Release 12.3(1) and later releases, call-agent-controlled mode enables T.38 fax relay interworking between H.323 gateways and MGCP gateways and between two MGCP gateways under the control of a call agent. This feature supersedes previous methods for call-agent-controlled fax relay and introduces these gateway capabilities:

■ The capability to accept the MGCP FXR package, to receive the fxr prefix in commands from the call agent, and to send the fxr prefix in notifications to the call agent.

■ The capability to accept a new port when switching from voice to fax transmission during a call. This new capability allows successful T.38 call-agent-controlled fax communications between H.323 and MGCP gateways in those situations in which the H.323 gateway assigns a new port when changing a call from voice to fax. New ports are assigned in H.323 gateways using images from Cisco IOS Release 12.2(2)T through Cisco IOS Release 12.2(7.5)T. MGCP gateways in MGCP-to-MGCP fax calls reuse the same port, but call-agent-controlled T.38 fax relay enables MGCP gateways to handle both situations, either switching to a new port or reusing the same port, as directed by the call agent.

DTMF Support

DTMF is the tone generated on a touchtone phone when keypad digits are pressed. Gateways send these tones in the RTP stream by default. This default behavior is fine when the voice stream is sent uncompressed, but problems arise when sending voice across slower WAN links using compression algorithms, as illustrated in Figure 2-13.

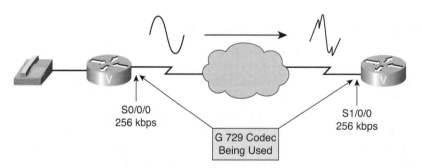

Figure 2-13   *The Need for DTMF Support*

During a call, DTMF digits might be entered to access IVR systems, such as voice mail or automated banking services. Although DTMF is usually transported accurately when using high-bit-rate voice codecs such as G.711, low-bit-rate codecs such as G.729 and

G.723.1 are highly optimized for voice patterns and tend to distort DTMF tones. As a result, IVR systems might not correctly recognize the tones.

DTMF relay solves the problem of DTMF distortion by transporting DTMF tones "out of band," or separate from the RTP voice stream.

H.323 DTMF Support

Cisco gateways currently support four methods of DTMF relay using H.323:

- **Cisco-proprietary:** DTMF tones are sent in the same RTP channel as voice data. However, the DTMF tones are encoded differently from the voice samples and are identified as payload type 121, which enables the receiver to identify them as DTMF tones. This method requires the use of Cisco gateways at both the originating and terminating endpoints of the H.323 call.

- **H.245 Alphanumeric:** Separates the DTMF digits from the voice stream and sends them through the H.245 signaling channel instead of through the RTP channel. The tones are transported in H.245 User Input Indication messages. The H.245 signaling channel is a reliable channel, so the packets that transport the DTMF tones are guaranteed to be delivered. This method does not send tone length information.

- **H.245 Signal:** This method does pass along tone length information, thereby addressing a potential problem with the alphanumeric method. This method is optional on H.323 gateways.

Note   All H.323 Version 2 compliant systems are required to support the "h245-alphanumeric" method, whereas support of the "h245-signal" method is optional.

- **NTEs:** Transports DTMF tones in RTP packets according to section 3 of RFC 2833. RFC 2833 defines formats of NTE RTP packets used to transport DTMF digits, hook flash, and other telephony events between two peer endpoints. With the NTE method, the endpoints perform per-call negotiation of the DTMF relay method. They also negotiate to determine the payload type value for the NTE RTP packets. As a result, DTMF tones are communicated via RTP packets, using an RTP payload type that prevents the tones from being compressed via the codec being used to encode the voice traffic.

MGCP DTMF Support

The four current implementations of MGCP-based DTMF relay include

- **Cisco proprietary:** DSPs on the gateways send and receive DTMF digits in-band in the voice RTP stream but code them differently so they can be identified by the receiver as DTMF tones.

- **NSE:** Conforms to RFC 2833 to provide a standardized method of DTMF transport using NTEs in RTP packets. RFC 2833 support is standards-based and allows greater interoperability with other gateways and call agents.

- **NTE:** Provides for two modes of implementation:

  - **Gateway-controlled mode:** In gateway-controlled mode, the gateways negotiate DTMF transmission by exchanging capability information in SDP messages. That transmission is transparent to the call agent. Gateway-controlled mode allows the use of the DTMF relay feature without upgrading the call agent software to support the feature.

  - **Call agent-controlled mode:** In call-agent-controlled mode, call agents use MGCP messaging to instruct gateways to process DTMF traffic.

- **Out-of-band:** Sends the tones as signals to Cisco Unified Communications Manager out-of-band over the control channel. Cisco Unified Communications Manager interprets the signals and passes them on.

SIP DTMF Support

SIP gateways can use Cisco proprietary NOTIFY-based out-of-band DTMF relay. In addition, NOTIFY-based out-of-band DTMF relay can also be used by analog phones attached to analog voice ports on the router.

NOTIFY-based out-of-band DTMF relay sends messages bidirectionally between the originating and terminating gateways for a DTMF event during a call. If multiple DTMF relay mechanisms are enabled on a SIP dial peer and are negotiated successfully, NOTIFY-based out-of-band DTMF relay takes precedence.

The originating gateway sends an Invite message with SIP Call-Info header to indicate the use of the NOTIFY-based out-of-band DTMF relay. The terminating gateway acknowledges the message with an 18x or 200 Response message, also using the Call-Info header. Whenever a DTMF event occurs, the gateway sends a SIP NOTIFY message for that event after the SIP Invite and 18x or 200 Response messages negotiate the NOTIFY-based out-of-band DTMF relay mechanism. In response, the gateway expects to receive a 200 OK message. The NOTIFY-based out-of-band DTMF relay mechanism is similar to the DTMF message format described in RFC 2833.

Processing Voice Packets with Codecs and DSPs

Because WAN bandwidth is probably the most expensive component of an enterprise network, network administrators must know how to calculate the total bandwidth required for voice traffic and how to reduce overall bandwidth consumption. This section describes in detail codecs, DSPs, codec complexity, and the bandwidth requirements for VoIP calls. Several variables affecting total bandwidth are explained, as well as how to calculate and reduce total bandwidth consumption.

Codecs

A codec is a device or program capable of performing encoding and decoding on a digital data stream or signal. Various types of codecs are used to encode and decode or compress and decompress data that would otherwise use large amounts of bandwidth on WAN links. Codecs are especially important on lower-speed serial links where every bit of bandwidth is needed and utilized to ensure network reliability.

One of the most important factors for a network administrator to consider while building voice networks is proper capacity planning. Network administrators must understand how much bandwidth is used for each VoIP call. To understand bandwidth, the administrator must know which codec is being utilized across the WAN link. With a thorough understanding of VoIP bandwidth and codecs, the network administrator can apply capacity planning tools.

Coding techniques are standardized by the ITU. The ITU G-series codecs are among the most popular standards for VoIP applications.

Following is a list of codecs supported by Cisco IOS gateways:

- **G.711:** The international standard for encoding telephone audio on a 64 kbps channel. It is a PCM scheme operating at an 8 kHz sample rate, with 8 bits per sample. With G.711, the encoded voice is already in the correct format for digital voice delivery in the PSTN or through PBXs. It is widely used in the telecommunications field because it improves the signal-to-noise ratio without increasing the amount of data.

  There are two subsets of the G.711 codec:

  - **mu-law:** mu-law is used in North American and Japanese phone networks.

  - **a-law:** a-law is used in Europe and elsewhere around the world.

  Both mu-law and a-law subsets use digitized speech carried in 8-bit samples. They use an 8 kHz sampling rate with 64 kbps of bandwidth demand.

- **G.726:** An ITU-T Adaptive Differential Pulse Code Modulation (ADPCM) coding at 40, 32, 24, and 16 kbps. ADPCM-encoded voice can be interchanged between packet voice, PSTN, and PBX networks if the PBX networks are configured to support ADPCM. The four bit rates associated with G.726 are often referred to by the bit size of a sample, which are 2-bits, 3-bits, 4-bits, and 5-bits, respectively.

- **G.728:** Describes a 16 kbps Low-Delay Code Excited Linear Prediction (LDCELP) variation of CELP voice compression. CELP voice coding must be translated into a public telephony format for delivery to or through the PSTN.

- **G.729:** Uses Conjugate Structure Algebraic Code Excited Linear Prediction (CS-ACELP) compression to code voice into 8 kbps streams. G.729a (that is, G.729 Annex A) requires less computation, but the lower complexity is not without a trade-off because speech quality is marginally worsened. Also, G.729b (that is, G.729 Annex B) adds support for VAD and CNG, to cause G.729 to be more efficient in its bandwidth usage. The features of G.729a and G.729b can be combined into G.729ab. Standard G.729 operates at 8 kbps, but there are extensions that provide 6.4 kbps (Annex D) and 11.8 kbps (Annex E) rates for marginally worse and better speech quality, respectively.

- **G.723:** Describes a dual-rate speech coder for multimedia communications. This compression technique can be used for compressing speech or audio signal components at a very low bit rate as part of the H.324 family of standards. This codec has two bit rates associated with it:

  - **r63:** 6.3 kbps; using 24-byte frames and the MPC-MLQ (Multipulse LPC with Maximum Likelihood Quantization) algorithm

  - **r53:** 5.3 kbps; using 20-byte frames and the ACELP algorithm

  The higher bit rate is based on ML-MLQ technology and provides a somewhat higher quality of sound. The lower bit rate is based on CELP and provides system designers with additional flexibility.

- **GSM Full Rate Codec (GSMFR):** Introduced in 1987, the GSMFR speech coder has a frame size of 20 ms and operates at a bit rate of 13 kbps. GSMFR is a RPE-LTP (Regular Pulse Excited—Linear Predictive) coder. To write VoiceXML scripts that can function as the user interface for a simple voice-mail system, the network must support GSMFR codecs. The network messaging must be capable of recording a voice message and depositing the message to an external server for later retrieval. This codec supports the Cisco infrastructure and application partner components required for service providers to deploy unified messaging applications.

- **Internet Low Bit Rate Codec (iLBC):** Designed for narrow band speech, it results in a payload bit rate of 13.33 kbps for 30-ms frames and 15.20 kbps for 20-ms frames. The algorithm is a version of Block-Independent Linear Predictive Coding, with the choice of data frame lengths of 20 and 30 milliseconds. The encoded blocks have to be encapsulated in a suitable protocol for transport, such as RTP. This codec enables graceful speech quality degradation in the case of lost frames, which occurs in connection with lost or delayed IP packets.

Note   iLBC is supported on Cisco AS5350XM and Cisco AS5400XM Universal Gateways with Voice Feature Cards (VFCs) and IP-to-IP gateways with no transcoding and conferencing.

The network administrator should balance the need for voice quality against the cost of bandwidth in the network when choosing codecs. The higher the codec bandwidth, the higher the cost of each call across the network.

Impact of Voice Samples and Packet Size on Bandwidth

Voice sample size is a variable that can affect total bandwidth used. A voice sample is defined as the digital output from a codec's DSP encapsulated into a protocol data unit (PDU). Cisco uses DSPs that output samples based on digitization of 10 ms worth of audio. Cisco voice equipment encapsulates 20 ms of audio in each PDU by default, regardless of the codec used. You can apply an optional configuration command to vary the number of samples encapsulated. When you encapsulate more samples per PDU, the total bandwidth is reduced. However, encapsulating more samples per PDU comes at the risk of larger PDUs, which can cause variable delay and severe gaps if PDUs are dropped. Table 2-5 demonstrates how the number of packets required to transmit one second of audio varies with voice sample sizes.

Table 2-5   *Impact of Voice Samples*

Codec	Bandwidth (bps)	Sample Size (Bytes)	Packets
G.711	64,000	240	33
G.711	64,000	160	50
G.726r32	32,000	120	33
G.726r32	32,000	80	50
G.726r24	24,000	80	25
G.726r24	24,000	60	33
G.726r16	16,000	80	25
G.726r16	16,000	40	50
G.728	16,000	80	13
G.728	16,000	40	25
G.729	8000	40	25
G.729	8000	20	50
G.723r63	6300	48	16
G.723r63	6300	24	33
G.723r53	5300	40	17
G.723r53	5300	20	33

Using a simple formula, it is possible for you to determine the number of bytes encapsulated in a PDU based on the codec bandwidth and the sample size (20 ms is the default):

Bytes_per_Sample = (Sample_Size * codec_Bandwidth) / 8

If you apply G.711 numbers, the formula reveals the following:

Bytes_per_Sample = (.020 * 64000) / 8

Bytes_per_Sample = 160

Notice from Table 2-5 that the larger the sample size, the larger the packet, and the fewer the encapsulated samples that have to be sent (which reduces bandwidth).

Data Link Overhead

Another contributing factor to bandwidth is the Layer 2 protocol used to transport VoIP. VoIP alone carries a 40 byte IP/UDP/RTP header, assuming uncompressed RTP. Depending on the Layer 2 protocol used, the overhead could grow substantially. More bandwidth is required to transport VoIP frames with larger Layer 2 overhead. The following illustrates the Layer 2 overhead for various protocols:

- **Ethernet II:** Carries 18 bytes of overhead—6 bytes for source MAC, 6 bytes for destination MAC, 2 bytes for type, and 4 bytes for cyclic redundancy check (CRC)

- **MLP:** Carries 6 bytes of overhead—1 byte for flag, 1 byte for address, 2 bytes for control (or type), and 2 bytes for CRC

- **Frame Relay Forum Standard 12 (FRF.12):** Carries 6 bytes of overhead—2 bytes for data-link connection identifier (DLCI) header, 2 bytes for FRF.12 header, and 2 bytes for CRC

Security and Tunneling Overhead

Certain security and tunneling encapsulations also add overhead to voice packets and should be considered when calculating bandwidth requirements. When using a virtual private network (VPN), IP Security (IPsec) will add 50 to 57 bytes of overhead, a significant amount when considering the relatively small voice-packet size. Layer 2 Tunneling Protocol/generic routing encapsulation (L2TP/GRE) adds 24 bytes. When using MLP, 6 bytes will be added to each packet. Multiprotocol Label Switching (MPLS) adds a 4-byte label to every packet. All these specialized tunneling and security protocols must be considered when planning for bandwidth demands.

For example, many companies have their employees telecommute from home. These employees often initiate a VPN connection into their enterprise for secure Internet transmission. When deploying a remote telephone at the employee's home using a router and a PBX Off-Premises eXtension (OPX), the voice packets experience additional overhead associated with the VPN.

Calculating the Total Bandwidth for a VoIP Call

Codec choice, data-link overhead, sample size, and RTP header compression have positive and negative impacts on total bandwidth, as demonstrated in Table 2-6.

Table 2-6   *Total Bandwidth Required*

Codec	Codec Speed (bps)	Sample Size (Bytes)	Frame Relay (bps)	Frame Relay with cRTP (bps)	Ethernet (bps)
G.711	64,000	240	76,267	66,133	79,467
G.711	64,000	160	82,400	67,200	87,200
G.726r32	32,000	120	44,267	34,133	47,467
G.726r32	32,000	80	50,400	35,200	55,200
G.726r24	24,000	80	37,800	26,400	41,400
G.726r24	24,000	60	42,400	27,200	47,200
G.726r16	16,000	80	25,200	17,600	27,600
G.726r16	16,000	40	34,400	19,200	39,200
G.728	16,000	80	25,200	17,600	27,600
G.728	16,000	40	34,400	19,200	39,200
G.729	8000	40	17,200	9600	19,600
G.729	8000	20	26,400	11,200	31,200
G.723r63	6300	48	12,338	7350	13,913
G.723r63	6300	24	18,375	8400	21,525
G.723r53	5300	40	11,395	6360	12,985
G.723r53	5300	20	17,490	7420	20,670

To perform the calculations, you must consider these contributing factors as part of the equation:

■   More bandwidth required for the codec requires more total bandwidth.

■   More overhead associated with the data link requires more total bandwidth.

■   Larger sample size requires less total bandwidth.

■   RTP header compression requires significantly less total bandwidth.

Consider a sample total bandwidth calculation. A company is implementing VoIP to carry voice calls between all sites. WAN connections between sites will carry both data and voice. To use bandwidth efficiently and keep costs to a minimum, voice traffic traversing the WAN will be compressed using the G.729 codec with 20-byte voice samples. WAN connectivity will be through a Frame Relay provider.

The following calculation is used to calculate total bandwidth required per call:

Total_Bandwidth = ([Layer_2_Overhead + IP_UDP_RTP Overhead + Sample_Size] / Sample_Size) * codec_Speed

Calculation for the G.729 codec, 20-byte sample size, using Frame Relay without Compressed RTP (cRTP) is as follows:

Total_Bandwidth = ([6 + 40 + 20] / 20) * 8000

Total_Bandwidth = 26,400 bps

Calculation for G.729 codec, 20-byte sample size, using Frame Relay with cRTP is as follows:

Total_Bandwidth = ([6 + 2 + 20] / 20) * 8000

Total_Bandwidth = 11,200 bps

Effects of Voice Activity Detection on Bandwidth

Statistically, an aggregate of 24 calls or more might contain 35 percent silence. With traditional telephony voice networks, all G.711 voice calls use 64 kbps fixed-bandwidth links regardless of how much of the conversation is speech and how much is silence. In Cisco VoIP networks, all conversations and silences are packetized. VAD can suppress packets containing silence. Instead of sending VoIP packets of silence, VoIP gateways interleave data traffic with VoIP conversations to more effectively use network bandwidth. Table 2-7 illustrates the type of bandwidth savings VAD offers.

Table 2-7   *Impact of VAD on Required Bandwidth*

Codec	Codec Speed (bps)	Sample Size (Bytes)	Frame Relay (bps)	Frame Relay with VAD (bps)
G.711	64,000	240	76,267	49,573
G.711	64,000	160	82,400	53,560
G.726r32	32,000	120	44,267	28,773
G.726r32	32,000	80	50,400	32,760
G.726r24	24,000	80	37,800	24,570
G.726r24	24,000	60	42,400	27,560
G.726r16	16,000	80	25,200	16,380
G.726r16	16,000	40	34,400	22,360
G.728	16,000	80	25,200	16,380
G.728	16,000	40	34,400	22,360
G.729	8000	40	17,200	11,180
G.729	8000	20	26,400	17,160

Table 2-7   *Impact of VAD on Required Bandwidth   (continued)*

Codec	Codec Speed (bps)	Sample Size (Bytes)	Frame Relay (bps)	Frame Relay with VAD (bps)
G.723r63	6300	48	12,338	8019
G.723r63	6300	24	18,375	11,944
G.723r53	5300	40	11,395	7407
G.723r53	5300	20	17,490	11,369

Note   Bandwidth savings of 35 percent is an average figure and does not take into account loud background sounds, differences in languages, and other factors.

Note   For the purposes of network design and bandwidth engineering, VAD should not be taken into account, especially on links that carry fewer than 24 voice calls simultaneously.

Various features, such as music on hold (MOH) and fax, render VAD ineffective. When the network is engineered for the full voice-call bandwidth, all savings provided by VAD are available to data applications.

VAD is enabled by default for all VoIP calls. Not only does VAD reduce the silence in VoIP conversations, but it also provides CNG. In some cases, silence might be mistaken for a disconnected call. CNG provides locally generated *white noise* to make the call appear normally connected to both parties.

For example, a company is assessing the effect of VAD in a Frame Relay VoIP environment. The company plans to use G.729 for all voice calls crossing the WAN. Previously, it was determined that each voice call compressed with G.729 uses 26,400 bps. VAD can reduce the bandwidth utilization to approximately 17,160 bps, which constitutes a bandwidth savings of 35 percent.

DSP

DSP is a specialized microprocessor designed specifically for digital signal processing. DSPs enable Cisco platforms to efficiently process digital voice traffic. DSPs on a router provide stream-to-packet signal processing functionality that includes voice compression, echo cancellation, and tone- and voice-activity detection.

A media resource is a software-based or hardware-based entity that performs media-processing functions on the data streams to which it is connected. A few examples are media-processing functions that include mixing multiple streams to create one output stream (conferencing), passing the stream from one connection to another (media termination point), converting the data stream from one compression type to another (transcoding), echo cancellation, signaling, termination of a voice stream from a TDM circuit (coding/decoding), packetization of a stream, and streaming audio (annunciation).

The terms "DSP" and "media resource" are often used interchangeably in some documentation.

The four major functions of DSPs in a voice gateway are as follows:

- **Transcoding:** Transcoding is the direct digital-to-digital conversion from one codec to another. Transcoding compresses and decompresses voice streams to match endpoint-device capabilities. Transcoding is required when an incoming voice stream is digitized and compressed (by means of a codec) to save bandwidth, but the local device does not support that type of compression. Ideally, all IP telephony devices would support the same codecs, but this is not the case. Rather, different devices support different codecs.

   Transcoding is processed by DSPs on the DSP farm. Sessions are initiated and managed by Cisco Unified Communications Manager. Cisco Unified Communications Manager also refers to transcoders as *hardware MTPs*.

   If an application or service can handle only one specific codec type, which is usually G.711, a G.729 call from a remote site must be transcoded to G.711. This can be done only via DSP resources. Because applications and services are often hosted in main sites, DSP transcoding resources are most common in central sites.

- **Voice termination:** Voice termination applies to a call that has two call legs, one leg on a TDM interface and the second leg on a VoIP connection. The TDM leg must be terminated by hardware that performs coding/decoding and packetization of the stream. DSPs perform this termination function. The DSP also provides echo cancellation, voice activity detection, and jitter management at the same time it performs voice termination.

- **Media Termination Point (MTP):** An MTP is an entity that accepts two full-duplex voice streams using the same codec. It bridges the media streams and allows them to be set up and torn down independently. The streaming data received from the input stream on one connection is passed to the output stream on the other connection, and vice versa. In addition, the MTP can be used to transcode a-law to mu-law and vice versa, or it can be used to bridge two connections that utilize different packetization periods. MTPs are also used to provide further processing of a call, such as RFC 2833 support.

- **Audio Conferencing:** In a traditional circuit-switched voice network, all voice traffic goes through a central device (such as a PBX system), which provides audio conferencing services as well. Because IP phones transmit voice traffic directly between phones, a network-based conference bridge is required to facilitate multiparty conferences.

A conference bridge is a resource that joins multiple participants into a single call. It can accept any number of connections for a given conference, up to the maximum number of streams allowed for a single conference on that device. A one-to-one correspondence exists between media streams connected to a conference and participants connected to the conference. The conference bridge mixes the streams together and creates a unique output stream for each connected party. The output stream for a given party is the composite of the streams from all connected parties minus their own input stream. Some conference bridges mix only the three loudest talkers on the conference and distribute that composite stream to each participant (minus their own input stream if they are one of the talkers).

Hardware conference bridges are used in two environments. They can be used to increase the conferencing capacity in a central site without putting an additional load on Cisco Unified Communications Manager servers, which can host software-based conference bridges. More important is the use of hardware conference bridges in remote sites. If no remote-site conference resources are deployed, every conference will be routed to central resources, resulting in sometimes-excessive WAN usage.

In addition, DSP-based conference bridges can mix G.711 and G.729 calls, thus supporting any call-type scenario in multisite environments. In contrast, software-based conference bridges deployed on Cisco Unified Communications Manager servers can mix only G.711 calls.

Other possible uses for MTPs include the following:

- **Repacketization:** An MTP can be used to transcode a-law to mu-law and vice versa, or it can be used to bridge two connections that utilize different packetization periods.

- **H.323 Supplementary Services:** MTPs can be used to extend supplementary services to H.323 endpoints that do not support the H.323v2 OpenLogicalChannel and CloseLogicalChannel request features of the Empty Capabilities Set (ECS). This requirement occurs infrequently. Cisco H.323 endpoints support ECS, and most third-party endpoints have support as well. When needed, an MTP is allocated and connected into a call on behalf of an H.323 endpoint. After insertion, the media streams are connected between the MTP and the H.323 device, and these connections are present for the duration of the call. The media streams connected to the other side of the MTP can be connected and disconnected as needed to implement features such as hold and transfer.

When an MTP is required on an H.323 call and none is available, the call will proceed but will not be able to invoke supplementary services.

Note   Implementations prior to Cisco Unified Communications Manager Release 3.2 required MTPs to provide supplementary services for H.323 endpoints, but Cisco Unified Communications Manager Release 3.2 and later no longer require MTP resources to provide this functionality.

MTP Types

Two types of MTPs are supported on Cisco VoIP equipment (for example, Cisco IOS routers and Cisco Unified Communications servers): software MTPs and hardware MTPs.

Software MTP

A software MTP is a resource that can be implemented by installing the Cisco IP Voice Media Streaming Application on a Cisco Unified Communications Manager server or by using a Cisco IOS gateway without using DSP resources. A software MTP device supports G.711 to G.711 and G.729 to G.729 streams. A Cisco IOS-enhanced software device can be implemented on a Cisco IOS router by configuring a software-only MTP under a DSP farm. This DSP farm can be used only as a pure MTP and does not require any hardware DSPs on the router. Examples are as follows:

■ **Cisco IP Voice Media Streaming Application:** This software MTP is a device that is implemented by installing the Cisco IP Voice Media Streaming Application on a server. When the installed application is configured as an MTP application, it registers with a Cisco Unified Communications Manager node and informs Cisco Unified Communications Manager of how many MTP resources it supports. The IP Voice Media Streaming Application is a resource that might also be used for several functions, and proper design must consider all functions together.

■ **Cisco IOS based:** This MTP allows configuration of any of the following codecs, but only one might be configured at a given time: G.711 mu-law and a-law, G.729a, G.729, G.729ab, G.729b, GSM, and pass-through. However, some of these are not pertinent to a Cisco Unified Communications Manager implementation.

The router configuration permits up to 500 individual streams, which support 250 transcoded sessions. This number of G.711 streams generates 5 Mbps of traffic.

Hardware MTP

A hardware MTP is a resource that uses gateway-based DSPs to interconnect two G.711 streams. This is done without using the gateway CPU. This hardware-only implementation uses a DSP resource for endpoints using the same G.711 codec but a different packetization time. The repacketization requires a DSP resource, so it cannot be done by software only. Examples are as follows:

■ Cisco NM-HDV2, NM-HD-1V/2V/2VE, 2800 and 3800 Series Routers

  ■ This hardware uses the PVDM-2 modules for providing DSPs.

  ■ Each DSP can provide 16 G.711 mu-law or a-law MTP sessions or 6 G.729, G.729b, or GSM MTP sessions.

■ Cisco WS-SVC-CMM-ACT

  ■ This module has four DSPs that can be configured individually.

- Each DSP can support 128 G.729, G.729b, or GSM MTP sessions or 256 G.711 mu-law or a-law MTP sessions.

■ Catalyst WS-X6608-T1 and WS-X6608-E1

- Codec support is G.711 mu-law or a-law, G.729, G.720b, or GSM.

- Configuration is done at the port level. Eight ports are available per module.

- Each port configured as an MTP resource provides 24 sessions.

Hardware Conferencing and Transcoding Resources

Figure 2-14 shows a multisite environment with deployed DSP resources. Router2 in Chicago is offering DSP-based conferencing services to support mixed codec environments and optimal WAN usage.

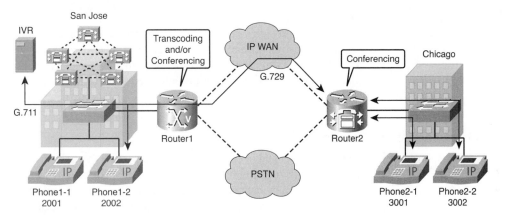

Figure 2-14 *Media Resource Deployment Example*

The central gateway, Router1, offers transcoding and conferencing services. The transcoding resources can be used to transcode G.729 to G.711 and then connect to an application server or even a software-based Cisco Unified Communications Manager conference bridge.

Codec Complexity

Codec complexity refers to the amount of processing required to perform voice compression. Codec complexity affects call density (that is, the number of calls reconciled on the DSPs). With higher codec complexity, fewer calls can be handled. Select a higher codec complexity when that is required to support a particular codec or combination of codecs. Select a lower codec complexity to support the greatest number of voice channels, provided the lower complexity is compatible with the particular codecs in use. Cisco DSP resources use one of two types of chipsets, the older C549 DSPs and the newer C5510 DSPs. Table 2-8 illustrates the complexity modes the C549 chipset needs to run to support a variety of codecs.

Table 2-8 *C549 Codec Complexity*

Medium Complexity (4 calls/DSP)	High Complexity (2 calls/DSP)
G.711 (a-law and mu-law)	G.728
G.726 (all versions)	G.723 (all versions)
G.729a, G.729ab (G.729a Annex B)	G.729, G.729b (G.729-Annex B)
Fax relay	Fax relay

Some codec compression techniques require more processing power than others. For example,

- Medium complexity allows the C549 DSPs to process up to four voice/fax relay calls per DSP and the C5510 DSPs to process up to eight voice/fax relay calls per DSP.

- High complexity allows the C549 DSPs to process up to two voice/fax relay calls per DSP and the C5510 DSPs to process up to six voice/fax relay calls per DSP.

The difference between medium and high complexity codecs is the amount of CPU utilization necessary to process the codec algorithm, and therefore, the number of voice channels that can be supported by a single DSP. For this reason, all the medium complexity codecs can also be run in high complexity mode, but fewer (usually about half) of the channels are available per DSP.

Configuring Codec Complexity

On platforms that support the C549 DSP technology, the codec complexity is configured on the voice card (for example, the 2600/3600/VG-200 High Density Voice Network Module). Some platforms support only high complexity because they have enough DSPs onboard to support all T1/E1 channels that use the high complexity mode. To specify call density and codec complexity according to the codec standard that is used, use the **codec complexity** command in voice-card configuration mode.

Consider Examples 2-1 and 2-2, which show the supported codec complexity modes for the C549 and C5510 DSPs, using context-sensitive help. Notice the C5510 DSPs support a *flex* complexity mode, which allows the DSPs to automatically switch into the optimal complexity mode for a given call, unlike the C549 DSPs, which require you to use the high complexity mode (which supports the fewest number of calls) if the DSPs *ever* need to run in high complexity mode.

Example 2-1 *Configuring Codec Complexity on C549 DSPs*

```
Router(config)#voice-card 1
Router(config-voicecard)#codec complexity ?
  high   Set codec complexity high. High complexity, lower call density.
  medium Set codec complexity medium. Mid range complexity and call density.
  <cr>
Router(config-voicecard)#codec complexity high
Router(config-voicecard)#
```

Example 2-2   *Configuring Codec Complexity on C5510 DSPs*

```
router(config)#voice-card 1
router(config-voicecard)#codec complexity ?
  flex    Set codec complexity Flex.  Flex complexity, higher call density.
  high    Set codec complexity high.  High complexity, lower call density.
  medium  Set codec complexity medium.  Mid range complexity and call density.
  secure  Set codec complexity secure.
Router(config-voicecard)#codec complexity flex
Router(config-voicecard)#
```

When you use flex complexity, up to 16 calls can be completed per DSP. The number of supported calls varies from 6 to 16 and is based on the codec used for a call. Also notice the **secure** option, which supports Secure RTP (SRTP). SRTP secures voice streams by providing authentication and encryption services to RTP.

The **show voice dsp** command, as demonstrated in Example 2-3, can be used to verify codec complexity configurations.

Example 2-3   *Verifying Codec Complexity*

```
HQ-1#show voice dsp

DSP  DSP              DSPWARE CURR  BOOT                        PAK    TX/RX
TYPE NUM CH CODEC     VERSION STATE STATE   RST AI VOICEPORT TS ABORT PACK COUNT
==== === == ======== ======= ===== ======= === == ========= == ===== ===========


--------------------------FLEX VOICE CARD 0 -----------------------------
                    *DSP VOICE CHANNELS*


CURR STATE : (busy)inuse (b-out)busy out (bpend)busyout pending
LEGEND     : (bad)bad    (shut)shutdown  (dpend)download pending

DSP   DSP            DSPWARE CURR  BOOT                        PAK    TX/RX
TYPE  NUM CH CODEC   VERSION STATE STATE   RST AI VOICEPORT TS ABRT PACK COUNT
===== === == ========= ======= ===== ======= === == ========= == ==== ===========
                    *DSP SIGNALING CHANNELS*
DSP   DSP            DSPWARE CURR  BOOT                        PAK    TX/RX
TYPE  NUM CH CODEC   VERSION STATE STATE   RST AI VOICEPORT TS ABRT PACK COUNT
===== === == ========= ======= ===== ======= === == ========= == ==== ===========
C5510 002 01 {flex}    8.2.0 alloc idle    0  0 0/2/0     02    0        0/0
C5510 002 02 {flex}    8.2.0 alloc idle    0  0 0/2/1     02    0        0/0
----------------------END OF FLEX VOICE CARD 0 -------------------------
```

DSP Requirements for Media Resources

The number of DSPs required is a key factor when deploying media resources using DSPs. This mainly depends on two factors: DSP type and the codec being used. In general, the old packet voice/data modules (PVDMs) support fewer sessions than the new packet voice DSP modules, generation 2 (PVDM2s), and G.711-only media resources require less resources than mixed-codec or G.729 resources.

Resource Allocation on the NM-HDV (C549-Based Hardware)

You configure each DSP individually, and each DSP functions independently of the others. The conferencing and transcoding MTP resources must be allocated to different DSPs, and a single DSP can support only one of these functions at a time. The configuration specifies which function each DSP will perform.

A High-Density Voice Network Module (NM-HDV) can be associated with only a single Cisco Unified Communications Manager.

Resource Allocation on the NM-HDV2, NM-HD-xx, and PVDM2 (C5510-Based Hardware)

Hardware resources based on the C5510 chipset are allocated using DSP profiles that define the resource type within the profile. Multiple profiles can be defined on a single gateway. These profiles can then be registered to different Cisco Unified Communications Manager clusters.

A PVDM2 is a module that can carry up to four C5510 DSPs. Table 2-9 lists the DSP per PVDM2 allocation.

Table 2-9 *DSPs per PVDM2*

PVDM2	Number of C5510 DSPs
PVDM2-8	1/2
PVDM2-16	1
PVDM2-32	2
PVDM2-48	3
PVDM2-64	4

Note Both the PVDM2-8 and the PVDM2-16 have a single DSP. The DSP on the PVDM2-8 has one-half the capacity of the DSP used on other PVDM2 modules. A PVDM2-8 can be used for conferencing, but with lower performance numbers than the other DSPs.

Conferencing resources can either be G.711-only or mixed mode (that is, at least one party with G.729). Mixed-mode conferences require more DSP resources because the DSP will perform transcoding and mixing operations.

Note   For PVDM and PVDM2-based conferencing, the maximum number of conference participants is independent from the maximum number of conferences. This means that whether a conference has three, five, or eight participants, it counts the same against the number of simultaneous conferences supported on a DSP.

Table 2-10 shows the various DSP resources for conferencing and their performance.

Table 2-10   *Conferencing DSP Resources*

Hardware Module or Chassis	DSP Configuration	Conferences	
		All Participants Use G.711 (a-law, mu-law)	**One or More Participants Use G.729 or G.729a**
NM-HDV2	1 to 4 of:	Conferences/PVDM2:	Conferences/PVDM2:
(8 participants	PVDM2-8 (1/2 DSP)	4	1
per conference)	PVDM2-16 (1 DSP)	8	2
	PVDM2-32 (2 DSPs)	16	4
	PVDM2-48 (3 DSPs)	24	6
	PVDM2-64 (4 DSPs)	32	8
		Maximum of 50 conferences per NM	
NM-HD-1V (8 participants per conference)	Fixed at 1 DSP	8 conferences per NM	2 conferences per NM
NM-HD-2V (8 participants per conference)	Fixed at 1 DSP	8 conferences per NM	2 conferences per NM
NM-HD-2VE (8 participants per conference)	Fixed at 3 DSPs	24 conferences per NM	6 conferences per NM

continues

Table 2-10   *Conferencing DSP Resources   (continued)*

Hardware Module or Chassis	DSP Configuration	Conferences All Participants Use G.711 (a-law, mu-law)	One or More Participants Use G.729 or G.729a
NM-HDV NM-HDV-FARM (6 participants per conference)	1 to 5 of PVDM-12 (3 DSPs per PVDM-12)	3, 6, 9, 12, or 15 conferences per NM	3, 6, 9, 12, or 15 conferences per NM
1751 (6 participants per conference)	1 to 2 of: PVDM-256K-4 (1 DSP) PVDM-256K-8 (2 DSPs) PVDM-256K-12 (3 DSPs) PVDM-256K-16HD (4 DSPs) PVDM-256K-20HD (5 DSPs)	1 conference per DSP Maximum of 5 conferences per chassis	1 conference per DSP Maximum of 5 conferences per chassis
1760 (6 participants per conference)	1 to 2 of: PVDM-256K-4 (1 DSP) PVDM-256K-8 (2 DSPs) PVDM-256K-12 (3 DSPs) PVDM-256K-16HD (4 DSPs) PVDM-256K-20HD (5 DSPs)	1 conference per DSP Maximum of 20 conferences per chassis	1 conference per DSP Maximum of 20 conferences per chassis
WS-6608-T1 and WS-6608-E1 (3 to 32 participants per conference)	Fixed at 64 of C549 (8 DSPs per port)	32 participants per port	32 participants per port G.729a and G.711 only
WS-SVC-CMM-ACT I (64 participants per conference)	Fixed at 4 of Broadcom 1500	128 conferences per module	128 conferences per module

The number of required DSPs for transcoding depends on the DSP type used and the codecs that need to be transcoded. C549 support up to four transcoding sessions for any codec combination. The C5510 supports 16 G.711 sessions; eight G.729a, ab, and GSM-FR sessions; and six G729, G729b, and GSM-E FR sessions.

Table 2-11 shows the various DSP resources that can be used for transcoding and their performance.

Table 2-11   *Transcoding DSP Resources*

Hardware Module or Chassis	DSP Configuration	Conferences	
		All Participants Use G.711 (a-law, mu-law)	One or More Participants Use G.729 or G.729a
NM-HDV2	1 to 4 of:	Sessions/PVDM2	Sessions/PVDM2
	PVDM2-8 (1/2 DSP)	8	4
	PVDM2-16 (1 DSP)	16	8
	PVDM2-32 (2 DSPs)	32	16
	PVDM2-48 (3 DSPs)	48	24
	PVDM2-64 (4 DSPs)	64	32
NM-HD-1V	Fixed at 1 DSP	16 sessions per NM	8 sessions per NM
NM-HD-2V	Fixed at 1 DSP	16 sessions per NM	8 sessions per NM
NM-HD-2VE	Fixed at 3 DSPs	48 sessions per NM	24 sessions per NM
NM-HDV NM-HDV-FARM	1 to 5 of PVDM-12 (3 DSPs per PVDM-12)	12, 24, 36, 48, or 60 sessions per NM	12, 24, 36, 48, or 60 sessions per NM
1751	1 to 2 of:	2 sessions per DSP	2 sessions per DSP
	PVDM-256K-4 (1 DSP)	Maximum of 16 sessions per chassis	Maximum of 16 sessions per chassis
	PVDM-256K-8 (2 DSPs)		
	PVDM-256K-12 (3 DSPs)		
	PVDM-256K-16HD (4 DSPs)		
	PVDM-256K-20HD (5 DSPs)		

continues

Table 2-11   *Transcoding DSP Resources   (continued)*

Hardware Module or Chassis	DSP Configuration	Conferences All Participants Use G.711 (a-law, mu-law)	One or More Participants Use G.729 or G.729a
1760	1 to 2 of:	2 sessions per DSP	2 sessions per DSP
	PVDM-256K-4 (1 DSP)	Maximum of 20 sessions per chassis	Maximum of 20 sessions per chassis
	PVDM-256K-8 (2 DSPs)		
	PVDM-256K-12 (3 DSPs)		
	PVDM-256K-16HD (4 DSPs)		
	PVDM-256K-20HD (5 DSPs)		
WS-6608-T1 and WS-6608-E1	Fixed at 64 of C549 (8 DSPs per port)	24 sessions per port	24 sessions per port
WS-SVC-CMM-ACT	Fixed at 4 of Broadcom 1500	128 sessions per module	128 sessions per module

In addition to transcoding, DSPs can also be used as hardware MTPs. Table 2-12 shows the various DSPs that can be used as MTPs and their performance.

Table 2-12   *MTP DSP Resources for Enhanced Cisco IOS Media Resources*

Hardware Module or Chassis	DSP Configuration	MTP G.711 (a-law, mu-law)
NM-HDV2	1 to 4 of:	Sessions per PVDM:
	PVDM2-81 (1/2 DSP)	8
	PVDM2-16 (1 DSP)	16
	PVDM2-32 (2 DSPs)	32
	PVDM2-48 (3 DSPs)	48
	PVDM2-64 (4 DSPs)	64
NM-HD-1V	Fixed at 1 DSP	4 sessions per NM

Table 2-12 *MTP DSP Resources for Enhanced Cisco IOS Media Resources*   *(continued)*

Hardware Module or Chassis	DSP Configuration	MTP G.711 (a-law, mu-law)
NM-HD-2V	Fixed at 1 DSP	16 sessions per NM
NM-HD-2VE	Fixed at 3 DSPs	48 sessions per NM
WS-SVC-CMM-ACT	Fixed at 4 of Broadcom 1500	256 sessions per module

DSP Calculator

For easier DSP calculation, a DSP calculator tool is available at the following URL (and requires appropriate login credentials for the Cisco website):

> http://www.cisco.com/cgi-bin/Support/DSP/dsp-calc.pl

The following example shows how to calculate the required DSPs to deploy the following media resources on a single gateway:

Router model: Cisco 2811

Cisco IOS release: 12.4(6)T

Installed voice interface cards (VICs): Onboard slot 0, VWIC2-1MFT-T1/E1 used as a PRI T1 with 23 voice bearer channels

Number of G.711 calls: 23

Number of transcoding sessions: 8 G.711 to G.729a

Number of conferences: 4 mixed-mode conferences

Follow these steps to perform the calculation:

Step 1.   Select the correct router model, in this case **Cisco 2811.**

Step 2.   Select the correct Cisco IOS release: mainline release, T train release, or special release, as shown in Figure 2-15. In this case, **12.4(6)T** is selected. Different Cisco IOS releases might lead to different DSP calculations because the firmware of a DSP depends on the Cisco IOS version used.

Step 3.   Select the appropriate VIC configuration. In this case, **VWIC2-1MFT-T1/E1 (T1 voice)** is selected. The T1 voice option is necessary because the VWIC2 supports both E1 and T1.

Step 4.   Specify the maximum number of calls for a specific codec or fax configuration. In this case, a full T1 is configured for PRI—that is, 23 G.711 calls, as illustrated in Figure 2-16.

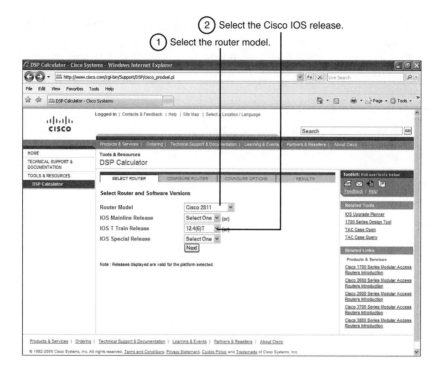

Figure 2-15 *DSP Calculator (Steps 1 and 2)*

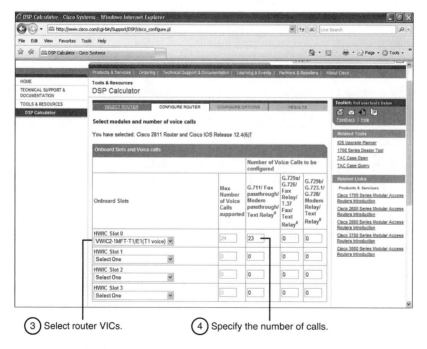

Figure 2-16 *DSP Calculator (Steps 3 and 4)*

Note   A full T1 PRI supports only 23 voice channels. A T1 channel associated signaling (CAS) or a T1 configured for Nonfacility Associated Signaling (NFAS) can support as many as 24 voice channels.

Step 5.   Specify the number of transcoding sessions with the appropriate codec. In this example, 8 G.711 to G.729a sessions are required.

Step 6.   Specify the number of conferences required on the gateway, either single-mode G.711 or mixed-mode conferences, as demonstrated in Figure 2-17.

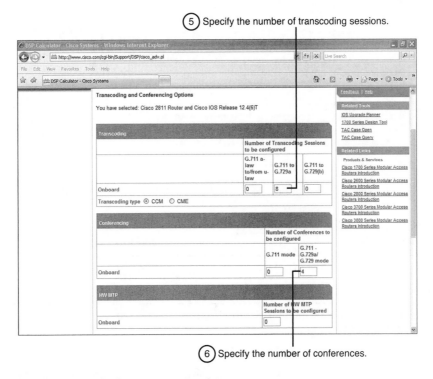

Figure 2-17   *DSP Calculator (Steps 5 and 6)*

Step 7.   After entering all parameters, you can calculate the required DSP resources. For our example, five C5510 DSPs need to be deployed, as shown in Figure 2-18.

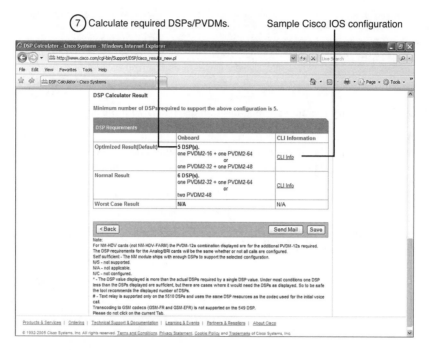

Figure 2-18   *DSP Calculator (Step 7)*

Table 2-13 summarizes the DSP requirements for the specified media resources.

Table 2-13   *DSP Requirements*

Media Resource	Number of DSPs
Voice termination for up to 23 G.711 calls	2 C5510
Transcoding for up to 8 G.729a sessions	1 C5510
4 conference bridges, each with up to 8 participants	2 C5510

Note   The calculator displays two results: Optimized Result and Normal Result. The optimized result uses the C5510s in flex mode, and the normal result uses either medium or high complexity mode, depending on the used codecs. You should use flex-mode because of higher performance and fewer required DSP resources. In rare cases, this might lead to oversubscribed DSP resources.

Also, notice the CLI Info link in Figure 2-18. Clicking this link provides a template of the Cisco IOS configuration to be applied to the router to support the DSP media resources.

Configuring Conferencing and Transcoding on Voice Gateways

The configuration of transcoding and conferencing on a voice gateway involves DSP resource requirements, Skinny Client Control Protocol (SCCP) configuration, DSP farm and DSP farm profile configuration, and hardware configurations.

The basic steps for configuring conferencing and transcoding on voice gateway routers are as follows:

Step 1.   Determine DSP Resource Requirements: DSPs reside either directly on a voice network module (such as the NM-HD-2VE), on PVDM2s that are installed in a voice network module (such as the NM-HDV2), or on PVDM2s that are installed directly onto the motherboard (such as on the Cisco 2800 and 3800 Series voice gateway routers). You must determine the number of PVDM2s or network modules required to support your conferencing and transcoding services and install the modules on your router.

Step 2.   Enable SCCP: The Cisco IOS router containing DSP resources communications with Cisco Unified Communications Manager using the SCCP. Therefore, SCCP needs to be enabled and configured on the router.

Step 3.   Configure Enhanced Conferencing and Transcoding: Configuring conferencing and transcoding on the voice gateway includes the following substeps:

  ■ Enable DSP farm services.

  ■ Configure a DSP farm profile.

  ■ Associate a DSP Farm Profile to a Cisco Unified Communications Manager Group.

  ■ Verify DSP Farm configuration.

The remainder of this section explores DSP farm configuration tasks, including both Cisco IOS configuration and Cisco Unified Communications Manager configuration. Examples are provided for each configuration task.

DSP Farms

A DSP farm is the collection of DSP resources available for conferencing, transcoding, and MTP services. DSP farms are configured on the voice gateway and managed by Cisco Unified Communications Manager through SCCP.

The DSP farm can support a combination of transcoding sessions, MTP sessions, and conferences simultaneously. The DSP farm maintains the DSP resource details locally. Cisco Unified Communications Manager requests conferencing or transcoding services from the gateway, which either grants or denies these requests, depending on resource availability. The details of whether DSP resources are used, and which DSP resources are used, are transparent to Cisco Unified Communications Manager.

The DSP farm uses the DSP resources in network modules on Cisco routers to provide voice conferencing, transcoding, and hardware MTP services.

Consider the topology in Figure 2-19. Prior to actual media resource configuration, the DSPs need to be enabled for DSP farm usage. The **dsp services dspfarm** voice card configuration mode command allocates the DSPs to the DSP farm.

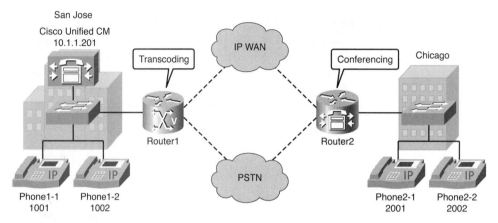

Figure 2-19 *DSP Farm Configuration Topology Example*

These commands are issued on both gateways, Router1 and Router2, as illustrated in Examples 2-4 and 2-5.

Example 2-4 *Allocating DSPs to a DSP Farm on Router1*

```
Router1(config)#voice-card 0
Router1(config-voicecard)#dsp services dspfarm
```

Example 2-5 *Allocating DSPs to a DSP Farm on Router2*

```
Router2(config)#voice-card 0
Router2(config-voicecard)#dsp services dspfarm
```

DSP Profiles

DSP-farm profiles are created to allocate DSP-farm resources. Under the profile, you select the service type (conference, transcode, MTP), associate an application, and specify service-specific parameters such as codecs and the maximum number of sessions. A DSP-farm profile allows you to group DSP resources based on the service type. Applications associated with the profile, such as SCCP, can use the resources allocated under the profile. You can configure multiple profiles for the same service, each of which can register with one Cisco Unified Communications Manager group. The profile ID and service type uniquely identify a profile, allowing the profile to uniquely map to a Cisco

Unified Communications Manager group that contains a single pool of Cisco Unified Communications Manager servers.

When the DSPs are ready, the DSP profile is configured using the **dspfarm profile** command. In this example, because transcoding is required on Router1, the **dspfarm profile 1 transcoding** command is used. On Router2, the **dspfarm profile 1 conferencing** command creates a profile for conferencing.

Because both G.711 and G.729 are used in this deployment, multiple codecs are enabled in both the transcoding and conferencing profiles using the **codec** *codec-type* command. Configurations for Router1 and Router2 are provided in Examples 2-6 and 2-7.

Example 2-6 *Creating a DSP Profile on Router1*

```
Router1(config)#dspfarm profile 1 transcode
Router1(config-dspfarm-profile)#codec g711ulaw
Router1(config-dspfarm-profile)#codec g711alaw
Router1(config-dspfarm-profile)#codec g729ar8
Router1(config-dspfarm-profile)#codec g729abr8
Router1(config-dspfarm-profile)#codec g729r8
Router1(config-dspfarm-profile)#maximum sessions 6
Router1(config-dspfarm-profile)#associate application SCCP
Router1(config-dspfarm-profile)#no shutdown
```

Example 2-7 *Creating a DSP Profile on Router2*

```
Router2(config)#dspfarm profile 1 conference
Router2(config-dspfarm-profile)#codec g711ulaw
Router2(config-dspfarm-profile)#codec g711alaw
Router2(config-dspfarm-profile)#codec g729ar8
Router2(config-dspfarm-profile)#codec g729abr8
Router2(config-dspfarm-profile)#codec g729br8
Router2(config-dspfarm-profile)#maximum sessions 2
Router2(config-dspfarm-profile)#associate application SCCP
Router2(config-dspfarm-profile)#no shutdown
```

Note Because mixed-mode conferencing is configured, the two configured conferences require a full DSP. If only G.711 would be allowed, a single DSP on a PVDM2 would allow up to eight conferences.

SCCP Configuration

After the profiles are set up, both routers should be configured for SCCP. As a reminder, the SCCP protocol is used for signaling between Cisco Unified Communications Manager and the router containing the DSP resources.

Both routers use their Fast Ethernet 0/1 interface as the SCCP source interface, and the primary Cisco Unified Communication Manager should be 10.1.1.201. Because Cisco Unified Communications Manager 4.1 is deployed, this is also specified in the SCCP configuration on each router to ensure full interoperability between the router and Cisco Unified Communications Manager.

After the Cisco Unified Communications Manager servers have been defined, the SCCP groups can be configured. Again, Fast Ethernet 0/1 is used as the source interface for the group, and the previously defined Cisco Unified Communications Manager is associated using the **associate ccm 1 priority 1** command. Note that the San Jose Cisco Unified Communications Manager server references the **identifier** option previously specified.

Then, the DSP farm profile is associated with the SCCP group using the **associate profile** command. The **register XCODERouter1** option used on Router1 assigns the name XCODERouter1 to the profile. This name will be used when registering with Cisco Unified Communications Manager and will be required when configuring the Cisco Unified Communications Manager to point back to the DSP resource. On Router2, the **register CFBRouter2** option is used, because this profile is a conference bridge.

These commands are issued on both gateways, Router1 and Router2, as illustrated in Examples 2-8 and 2-9.

Example 2-8   *Configuring SCCP on Router1*

```
Router1(config)#sccp local FastEthernet 0/1
Router1(config)#sccp ccm 10.1.1.201 identifier 1 priority 1 version 4.1
Router1(config)#sccp
Router1(config)#sccp ccm group 1
Router1(config-sccp-ccm)#bind interface FastEthernet0/1
Router1(config-sccp-ccm)#associate ccm 1 priority 1
Router1(config-sccp-ccm)#associate profile 1
Router1(config-sccp-ccm)#register XCODERouter1
```

Example 2-9   *Configuring SCCP on Router2*

```
Router2(config)#sccp local FastEthernet 0/1
Router2(config)#sccp ccm 10.1.1.201 identifier 1 priority 1 version 4.1
Router2(config)#sccp
Router2(config)#sccp ccm group 1
Router2(config-sccp-ccm)#bind interface FastEthernet0/1
Router2(config-sccp-ccm)#associate ccm 1 priority 1
Router2(config-sccp-ccm)#associate profile 1
Router2(config-sccp-ccm)#register CFBRouter2
```

Unified Communications Manager Configuration

After the Cisco IOS configuration is complete, the media resources need to be added to Cisco Unified Communications Manager.

Continuing with the current example, a conference bridge is defined in the **Service, Media Resource, Conference Bridge** menu, as shown in Figure 2-20.

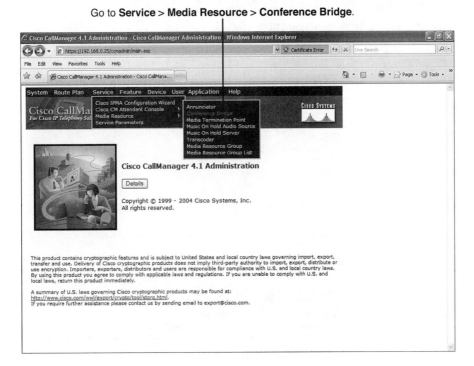

Figure 2-20   *Navigating to the Conference Bridge Configuration Screen*

The newly added conference bridge now needs to be set up. Because the conference bridge is using a PVDM2 deployed on an ISR, the **Conference Bridge Type** needs to be **Cisco IOS Enhanced Conference Bridge**, as illustrated in Figure 2-21.

After you select the correct type, specify the parameters described in Table 2-14 and illustrated in Figure 2-22.

Select **Cisco IOS Enhanced Conference Bridge** for PVDM2-based deployments.

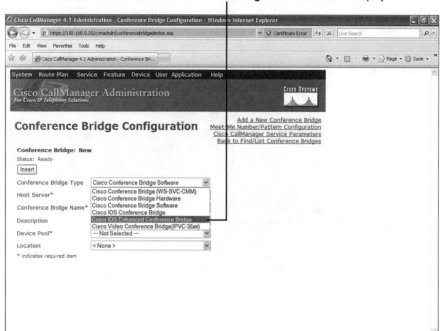

Figure 2-21   *Defining a Conference Bridge Type*

Table 2-14   *Conference Bridge Configuration*

Parameter	Value	Description
Conference Bridge Name	CFBRouter2	This needs to match the name previously configured in the **associate profile** command on the gateway.
Description	CFBRouter2	Choose a meaningful description.
Device Pool	Default	Select the correct device pool.
Location	< None >	Select the correct location.

Note   For simplicity, the device pool and location are left at their defaults.

Bridge name needs to match the name used in the SCCP group configuration.

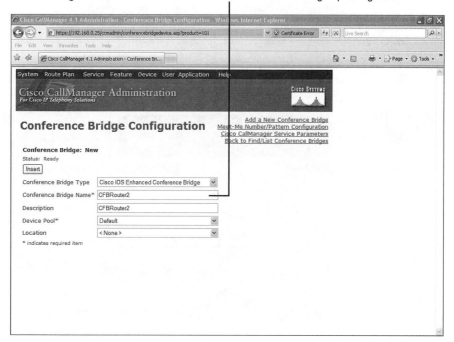

Figure 2-22   *Specifying Conference Bridge Parameters*

To add a transcoding resource, navigate to the **Service, Media Resource, Transcoder** menu option. Because PVDM2s are also used for transcoding, select **Cisco IOS Enhanced Media Termination Point** as the **Transcoder Type**. After you select the correct type, specify the parameters as described in Table 2-15 and illustrated in Figure 2-23.

Table 2-15   *Transcoder Configuration*

Parameter	Value	Description
Transcoder Name	XCODERouter1	This needs to match the name previously configured in the **associate profile** command on the Router1 gateway.
Description	XCODERouter1	Choose a meaningful description.
Device Pool	Default	Select the correct device pool.
Location	< None >	Select the correct location.
Special Load Information	N/A	This should be left blank.

Note   For simplicity, the device pool and location are left at their defaults.

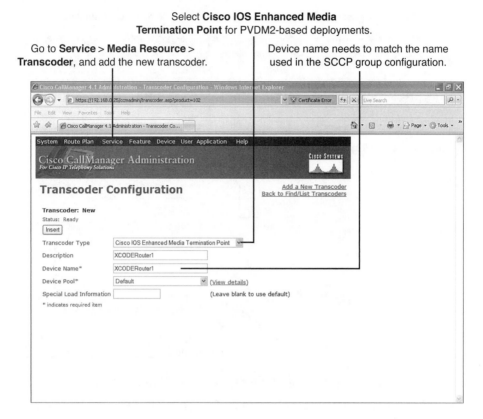

Figure 2-23   *Specifying Transcoder Parameters*

Cisco IOS Configuration Commands for Enhanced Media Resources

As previously demonstrated, you need to configure DSP-based media resources both on the hardware platform (for example, a Cisco IOS router) and on Cisco Unified Communications Manager. For reference, the following discussion details the Cisco IOS configuration commands for making router-based DSP resources available to Cisco Unified Communications Manager.

DSP Farm Configuration Commands for Enhanced Media Resources

Prior to creating a DSP farm profile, you need to enable the DSPs for DSP services. You do this in the respective voice card configuration mode. After you have enabled DSPs for media resources, you can configure a DSP farm profile for conferencing, transcoding, or as an MTP. The commands required to perform this initial DSP farm configuration are provided in Table 2-16.

Table 2-16   *DSP Farm Configuration Commands*

Command	Description
voice-card *slot*	To enter voice card configuration mode and configure a voice card, use the **voice-card** command in global configuration mode.
dsp services dspfarm	The router must be equipped with one or more voice network modules that provide DSP resources. DSP resources are used only if this command is configured for the particular voice card.
dspfarm profile *profile-identifier* {conference | mtp | transcode}	To enter DSP farm profile configuration mode and define a profile for DSP farm services, use the **dspfarm profile** command in global configuration mode. To delete a disabled profile, use the **no** form of this command.
	If the profile is successfully created, the user enters the DSP farm profile configuration mode. Multiple profiles can be configured for the same service. If a profile is active, the user will not be allowed to delete the profile.
	The profile identifier uniquely identifies a profile. If the service type and profile identifier are not unique, a message is displayed that asks the user to choose a different profile identifier.
	You can choose the profile type by using one of these options:
	■ To create a conference bridge, use the **conference** option.
	■ To create a transcoder, use the **transcode** option.
	■ To create a media termination point, use the **MTP** option.

Within the DSP farm configuration, you need to specify the supported codecs and maximum number of sessions. This configuration directly affects the number of required DSPs, so ensure that the configuration matches the design specifications.

You also need to associate the DSP farm profile with SCCP. This is done using the **associate application sccp** command. The DSP farm configuration mode commands are provided in Table 2-17.

Table 2-17   *DSP Farm Configuration Mode Commands*

Command	Description
codec {*codec-type* | **pass-through**}	To specify the codecs supported by a DSP farm profile, use the codec command in DSP farm profile configuration mode. To remove the codec, use the **no** form of this command.
	Depending on the media resource, multiple codecs can be configured. Using higher complexity codecs, such as G.729, might decrease the number of sessions per DSP.
	The **pass-through** option is available only for MTPs and is typically used for Cisco Unified Communications Manager 5.0 controlled RSVP-based call admission control.
maximum sessions *number*	To specify the maximum number of sessions supported by a profile, use the **maximum sessions** command in DSP farm profile configuration mode. To reset to the default, use the **no** form of the command.
	For conferencing, the number specifies the number of conferences, not participants.
associate profile sccp	To associate the SCCP to the DSP farm profile, use the **associate application** command in DSP farm profile configuration mode. To remove the protocol, use the **no** form of this command.
	This also requires a correct **sccp group** configuration to work correctly.

SCCP Configuration Commands for Enhanced Media Resources

Configuring enhanced media resources includes the SCCP configuration that will be used to register with Cisco Unified Communications Manager. Global configuration includes the configuration of the individual Cisco Unified Communications Managers, the local SCCP interface used for signaling, and activating SCCP.

The SCCP configuration commands are shown in Table 2-18.

Table 2-18   *SCCP Configuration Commands*

Command	Description
sccp ccm {*ip-address* | *dns*} identifier *identifier-number* [priority *priority*] [port *port-number*] [version *version_number*]	To add a Cisco Unified Communications Manager server to the list of available servers and set various parameters, including the IP address or Domain Name System (DNS) name, port number, and version number, use the **sccp ccm** command in global configuration mode. To remove a particular server from the list, use the **no** form of this command.
	You can configure up to four Cisco Unified Communications Manager servers, a primary and up to three backups, to support DSP farm services. To do this, use the priority option, with 1 being the highest priority and 4 being the lowest.
	To add the Cisco Unified Communications Manager server to a Cisco Unified Communications Manager group, use the **associate ccm** command.
sccp local *interface-type interface-number* [port *port-number*]	To select the local interface that SCCP applications (transcoding and conferencing) use to register with Cisco Unified Communications Manager, use the **sccp local** command in global configuration mode. To deselect the interface, use the no form of this command. This should be either a LAN interface or a loopback interface and needs to be reachable from Cisco Unified Communications Manager. WAN interfaces should be avoided. The **port** option should be used only if the default port 2000 has been changed on Cisco Unified Communications Manager.
sccp	To enable the SCCP protocol and its related applications (transcoding and conferencing), use the **sccp** command in global configuration mode. To disable the protocol, use the **no** form of this command.
	SCCP and its related applications (transcoding and conferencing) become enabled only if DSP resources for these applications are configured, DSP-farm service is enabled, and the Cisco Unified Communications Manager registration process is completed.
	The **no** form of this command disables SCCP and its applications by unregistering from the active Cisco Unified Communications Manager, dropping existing connections, and freeing allocated resources.

After globally configuring SCCP, you need to create an SCCP group. An SCCP group references previously configured Cisco Unified Communications Managers and then associates a DSP profile with the group. To bind an SCCP group to a local interface, use the **bind interface** command. Table 2-19 describes these SCCP group configuration commands.

Table 2-19   *SCCP Group Configuration Commands*

Command	Description
sccp ccm group *group_number*	To create a Cisco Communications Manager group and enter SCCP Cisco Unified Communications Manager configuration mode, use the **sccp ccm group** command in global configuration mode. To remove a particular Cisco Unified Communications Manager group, use the **no** form of this command.
	Use this command to group Cisco Unified Communications Manager servers that are defined with the **sccp ccm** command. You can use the **associate profile** command to associate designated DSP farm profiles so that the DSP services are controlled by the Cisco Unified Communications Manager servers in the group.
associate ccm *identifier-number* priority *priority*	To associate a Cisco Unified Communications Manager with a Cisco Communications Manager group and establish its priority within the group, use the **associate ccm** command in the SCCP Cisco Unified Communications Manager configuration mode. To disassociate a Cisco Unified Communications Manager from a Cisco Unified Communications Manager group, use the **no** form of this command.
	The identifier-number references the Cisco Unified Communications Managers that were previously configured using the **sccp ccm** command.
	You can configure up to four Cisco Unified Communications Manager servers, a primary and up to three backups, to support DSP farm services. To do this, use the priority option, with 1 being the highest priority and 4 being the lowest.

Table 2-19   *SCCP Group Configuration Commands   (continued)*

Command	Description
associate profile *profile-identifier* **register** *device-name*	To associate a DSP farm profile with a Cisco Unified Communications Manager group, use the **associate profile** command in SCCP Cisco Unified Communications Manager configuration mode. To disassociate a DSP farm profile from a Cisco Unified Communications Manager, use the **no** form of this command. The **profile** option references the identifier of a DSP farm profile configured using the **dspfarm profile** command.
	The device name must match the name configured in Cisco Unified Communications Manager. Otherwise, the profile is not registered to Cisco Unified Communications Manager.
	Each profile can be associated to only one Cisco Unified Communications Manager group.
bind interface *interface-type interface-number*	To bind an interface to a Cisco Communications Manager group, use the **bind interface** command in SCCP Cisco Unified Communications Manager configuration mode. To unbind the selected interface, use the **no** form of this command.
	The selected interface is used for all calls that belong to the profiles associated to this Cisco Unified Communications Manager group. If the interface is not selected, it uses the best interface's Cisco IP address in the gateway. Interfaces are selected according to user requirements. If only one group interface exists, configuration is not needed.

Verifying Media Resources

To verify the configuration of a DSP farm profile, use the **show dspfarm profile** command. Example 2-10 shows the DSP farm profile with ID 1 used for conferencing. Also note the "Number of Resource Configured : 2" line, which is set by the **maximum session 2** command.

Example 2-10   *The* show dspfarm profile *Command*

```
Router2#show dspfarm profile 1
Dspfarm Profile Configuration

 Profile ID = 1, Service = CONFERENCING, Resource ID = 1
```

continues

Example 2-10   *The* show dspfarm profile *Command*   *continued*

```
Profile Description :
 Profile Admin State : UP
 Profile Operation State : ACTIVE
 Application : SCCP   Status : ASSOCIATED
 Resource Provider : FLEX_DSPRM   Status : UP
 Number of Resource Configured : 2
 Number of Resource Available : 2
 Codec Configuration
 Codec : g711ulaw, Maximum Packetization Period : 30 , Transcoder: Not Required
 Codec : g711alaw, Maximum Packetization Period : 30 , Transcoder: Not Required
 Codec : g729ar8, Maximum Packetization Period : 60 , Transcoder: Not Required
 Codec : g729abr8, Maximum Packetization Period : 60 , Transcoder: Not Required
 Codec : g729r8, Maximum Packetization Period : 60 , Transcoder: Not Required
 Codec : g729br8, Maximum Packetization Period : 60 , Transcoder: Not Required
```

To check the DSP status used for DSP farm profiles, use the **show dspfarm dsp all** command. Example 2-11 shows two available DSPs configured for conferencing.

Example 2-11   *The* show dspfarm dsp all *Command*

```
Router2#show dspfarm dsp all
SLOT DSP VERSION  STATUS  CHNL USE    TYPE   RSC_ID BRIDGE_ID PKTS_TXED PKTS_RXED

0    5   1.0.6    UP      N/A  FREE   conf   1      -         -         -
0    5   1.0.6    UP      N/A  FREE   conf   1      -         -         -

Total number of DSPFARM DSP channel(s) 2
```

Summary

The main topics covered in this chapter are the following:

- Because of the nature of IP networking, voice packets sent via IP are subject to certain transmission problems.

- Several methods can be used to determine audio quality in a VoIP network.

- QoS is used to help meet the strict requirements concerning packet loss, delay, and delay variation in a VoIP network.

- Some challenges exist to transporting modulated data, including fax and modem calls, over IP networks.

- Features to support fax and modem traffic include

  - Fax and Modem Pass-Through

  - Fax and Modem Relay

  - Store-and-Forward Fax

- T.38, pass-through, and relay use special protocol enhancements available in the H.323, SIP, and MGCP call signaling protocols.

- DTMF support is provided by Cisco IOS gateways.

- Codecs are used to compress and decompress various types of data that would otherwise use up large amounts of bandwidth.

- Voice sample size is a variable that can affect the total bandwidth used.

- Several factors must be included in calculating the overhead of a VoIP call.

- Codec choice, data-link overhead, sample size, and compressed RTP have positive and negative impacts on total bandwidth.

- Codec complexity affects the call density.

- DSPs enable Cisco platforms to efficiently process digital voice traffic.

- The number of DSPs required is a key factor when deploying media resources using DSPs.

- The configuration of transcoding and conferencing on a voice gateway involves several components.

- DSP farm services are enabled on the voice card, and DSP profiles create the actual media resource.

- You can verify DSP media resources using **show dspfarm** commands.

Chapter Review Questions

The answers to these review questions are in the appendix.

1. According to the G.114 recommendation, the maximum one-way delay for voice should ideally not exceed how much delay?

   a. 100 ms

   b. 150 ms

   c. 200 ms

   d. 250 ms

2. Identify the preferred voice quality measurement approach for VoIP networks.

    a. MOS

    b. PESQ

    c. QRT

    d. PSQM

3. Which method of fax relay uses a store-and-forward approach?

    a. T.30

    b. T.37

    c. T.38

    d. Cisco Fax Relay

4. What codec is required for fax pass-through and/or modem pass-through?

    a. G.711

    b. G.723

    c. G.729

    d. G.729ab

5. Identify three quality issues that can result because of a lack of network bandwidth. (Choose 3.)

    a. Jitter

    b. Impedance

    c. Delay

    d. Packet loss

6. What protocol is used to communicate between a DSP farm configured on an IOS router and a Cisco Unified Communications Manager server?

    a. H.323

    b. MGCP

    c. SIP

    d. SCCP

7. What is the Layer 2 overhead (in bytes) for Frame Relay traffic?

    a. 3 bytes

    b. 5 bytes

    c. 6 bytes

    d. 18 bytes

8. Which three factors must be considered when calculating the total bandwidth of a VoIP call? (Choose 3.)

    a. Codec size

    b. CRC usage

    c. Data-link overhead

    d. Sample size

    e. Capacity of network links

9. The acronym CNG was used to refer to two different concepts in this chapter. One was the calling tone used when sending a fax, used to identify a call as a fax call. What is the other purpose of CNG (that is, not dealing with fax calls)?

    a. It provides features such as MOH.

    b. It provides white noise to make the call sound connected.

    c. It provides full voice call bandwidth.

    d. It reduces the delay in VoIP connections.

10. Which of the following media resources require DSPs (that is, the resource cannot be performed by Cisco Unified Communications Manager)?

    a. MTP

    b. MOH

    c. Transcoding

    d. Conferencing

After reading this chapter, you should be able to perform the following tasks:

- Describe the various call types in a VoIP network.

- Configure analog voice interfaces as new devices are introduced into the voice path.

- Configure dial peers so you can add call routing intelligence to a router.

CHAPTER 3

Routing Calls over Analog Voice Ports

Voice gateways bridge the gap between the VoIP world and the traditional telephony world (for example, a private branch exchange [PBX], the public switched telephone network {PSTN], or an analog phone). Cisco voice gateways connect to traditional telephony devices via voice ports. This chapter introduces basic configuration of analog and digital voice ports and demonstrates how to fine-tune voice ports with port-specific configurations. Upon completing this chapter, you will be able to configure voice interfaces on Cisco voice-enabled equipment for connection to traditional, nonpacketized telephony equipment.

Introducing Analog Voice Applications on Cisco IOS Routers

Before delving into the specific syntax of configuring voice ports, this section considers several examples of voice applications. The applications discussed help illustrate the function of the voice ports, whose configuration is addressed in the next section.

Different types of applications require specific types of ports. In many instances, the type of port is dependent on the voice device connected to the network. Different types of voice applications include the following:

- Local calls

- On-net calls

- Off-net calls

- Private line, automatic ringdown (PLAR) calls

- PBX-to-PBX calls

- Intercluster trunk calls

- On-net to off-net calls

The following sections discuss each in detail and provide an example.

Local Calls

Local calls, as illustrated in Figure 3-1, occur between two telephones connected to one Cisco voice-enabled router. This type of call is handled entirely by the router and does not travel over an external network. Both telephones are directly connected to Foreign Exchange Station (FXS) ports on the router.

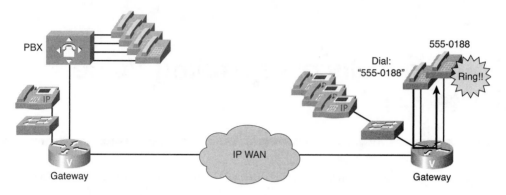

Figure 3-1   *Local Calls*

An example of a local call is one staff member calling another staff member at the same office. This call is switched between two ports on the same voice-enabled router.

On-Net Calls

On-net calls occur between two telephones on the same data network, as shown in Figure 3-2. The calls can be routed through one or more Cisco voice-enabled routers, but the calls remain on the same data network. The edge telephones attach to the network through FXS ports or through a PBX, which typically connects to the network via a T1 connection. IP phones that connect to the network via switches place on-net calls through Cisco Unified Communications Manager. The connection across the data network can be a LAN connection, as in a campus environment, or a WAN connection, as in an enterprise environment.

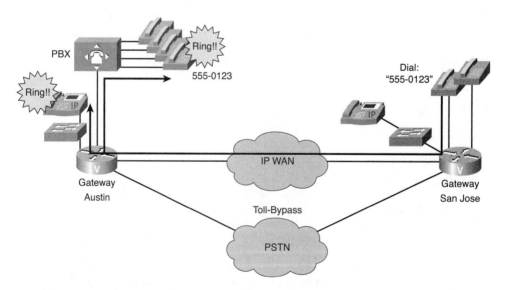

Figure 3-2   *On-Net Calls*

> **Note**   The act of routing voice data across the WAN instead of the PSTN is known as
> *toll-bypass*. Originally, companies saved significant amounts of money using this strategy,
> which was one of the first major business benefits of a VoIP-enabled network.

An example of an on-net call is one staff member calling another staff member at a remote
office. The call is sent from the local voice-enabled router, across the IP network, and terminated on the remote office voice-enabled router.

Off-Net Calls

Figure 3-3 shows an example of an off-net call. To gain access to the PSTN, the user dials
an access code, such as 9, from a telephone directly connected to a Cisco voice-enabled
router or PBX. The connection to the PSTN is typically a single analog connection via a
Foreign Exchange Office (FXO) port or a digital T1 or E1 connection.

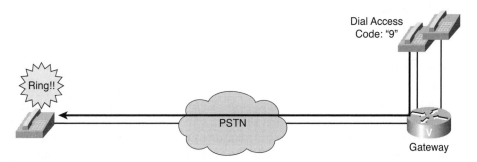

Figure 3-3   *Off-Net Calls*

An example of an off-net call is a staff member calling a client who is located in the same
city. The call is sent from the local voice-enabled router that is acting as a gateway to the
PSTN. The call is then sent to the PSTN for call termination.

PLAR Calls

PLAR calls automatically connect a telephone to a second telephone when the first telephone goes off hook, as depicted in Figure 3-4. When this connection occurs, the user
does not get a dial tone, because the voice-enabled port that the telephone is connected
to is preconfigured with a specific number to dial. A PLAR connection can work
between any type of signaling, including E&M, FXO, FXS, or any combination of analog and digital interfaces. For example, you might have encountered a PLAR connection
at an airline ticket counter where you pick up a handset and are immediately connected
with an airline representative.

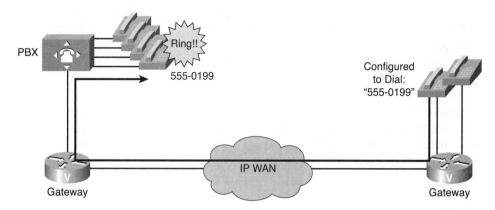

Figure 3-4   *PLAR Calls*

An example of a PLAR call is a client picking up a customer service telephone located in the lobby of the office and being automatically connected to a customer service representative without dialing any digits. The call is automatically dialed based on the PLAR configuration of the voice port. In this case, as soon as the handset goes off hook, the voice-enabled router generates the preconfigured digits to place the call.

PBX-to-PBX Calls

PBX-to-PBX calls, as shown in Figure 3-5, originate at a PBX at one site and terminate at a PBX at another site while using the network as the transport between the two locations. Many business environments connect sites with private tie trunks. When migrating to a converged voice and data network, this same tie-trunk connection can be emulated across an IP network. Modern PBX connections to a network are typically digital T1 or E1 with channel associated signaling (CAS) or Primary Rate Interface (PRI) signaling, although PBX connections can also be analog.

> **Note**   PBX-to-PBX calls are another form of toll-bypass.

An example of a PBX-to-PBX call is one staff member calling another staff member at a remote office. The call is sent from the local PBX, through a voice-enabled router, across the IP network, through the remote voice-enabled router, and terminated on the remote office PBX.

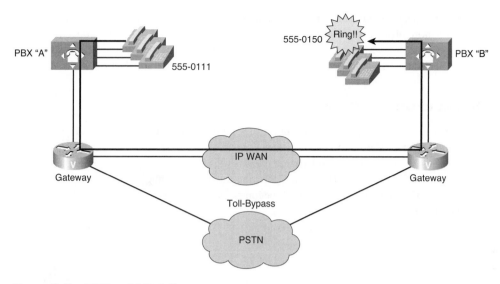

Figure 3-5   *PBX-to-PBX Calls*

Intercluster Trunk Calls

As part of an overall migration strategy, a business might replace PBXs with Cisco Unified Communications Managers. This includes IP phones connected to the IP network. Cisco Unified Communications Manager performs the call-routing functions formerly provided by the PBX. When an IP phone call is placed using a configured Cisco Unified Communications Manager, the call is assessed to see if the call is destined for another IP phone under its control or if the call must be routed to a remote Cisco Unified Communications Manager for call completion. Intercluster trunk calls, as depicted in Figure 3-6, are routed between Cisco Unified Communications Manager clusters using a trunk.

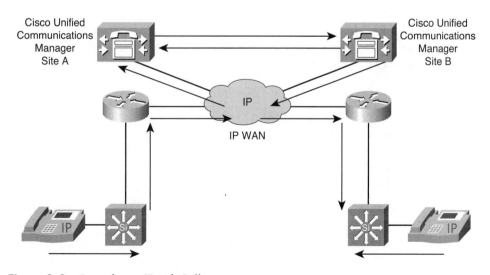

Figure 3-6   *Intercluster Trunk Calls*

An example of an intercluster trunk call is one staff member calling another staff member at a remote office using an IP phone. The call setup is handled by the Cisco Unified Communications Managers at each location. After the call is set up, the IP phones generate Real-time Transport Protocol (RTP) segments that carry voice data between sites.

On-Net to Off-Net Calls

When planning a resilient call-routing strategy, you might need to reroute calls through a secondary path should the primary path fail. An on-net to off-net call, as illustrated in Figure 3-7, originates on an internal network and is routed to an external network, usually to the PSTN. On-net to off-net call-switching functionality might be necessary when a network link is down or if a network becomes overloaded and unable to handle all calls presented.

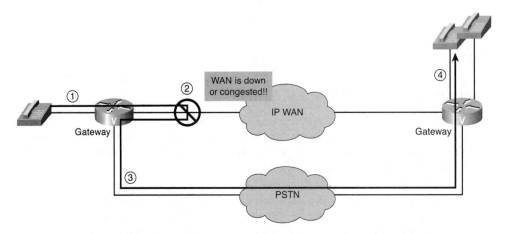

Figure 3-7   *On-Net to Off-Net Calls*

Note   On-net to off-net calls might occur as a result of dial plan configuration, or they might be redirected by Call Admission Control (CAC).

An example of an on-net to off-net call is one staff member calling another staff member at a remote office while the WAN link is congested. When the originating voice-enabled router determines it cannot complete the call across the WAN link, it sends the call to the PSTN with the appropriate dialed digits to terminate the call at the remote office via the PSTN network.

The following steps, numbered in Figure 3-7, summarize the call flow of an on-net to off-net call:

Step 1.   A user on the network initiates a call to a remote site.

Step 2.   The output of the WAN gateway is either down or congested, so the call is rerouted.

Step 3.   The call connects to the PSTN.

Step 4.   The PSTN completes the call to the remote site.

Summarizing Examples of Voice Port Applications

Table 3-1 lists application examples for each type of call.

Table 3-1   *Voice Port Call Types*

Type of Call	Example
Local call	One staff member calls another staff member at the same office. The call is switched between two ports on the same voice-enabled router.
On-net call	One staff member calls another staff member at a remote office. The call is sent from the local voice-enabled router, across the IP network, and is terminated on the remote office voice-enabled router.
Off-net call	A staff member calls a client who is located in the same city. The call is sent from the local voice-enabled router, which acts as a gateway, to the PSTN. The call is then sent to the PSTN for call termination.
PLAR call	A client picks up a customer service telephone located in the lobby of an office and is automatically connected to a customer service representative without dialing any digits. The call is automatically dialed based on the PLAR configuration of the voice port. In this case, as soon as the handset goes off hook, the voice-enabled router generates the prespecified digits to place the call.
PBX-to-PBX call	One staff member calls another staff member at a remote office. The call is sent from the local PBX, through a voice-enabled router, across the IP network, through the remote voice-enabled router, and terminated on the remote office PBX.
Intercluster trunk call	One staff member calls another staff member at a remote office using IP phones. The call setup is handled by a Cisco Unified Communications Manager server at each location. After the call is set up, the IP phones generate IP packets carrying voice between sites.
On-net to off-net call	One staff member calls another staff member at a remote office while the IP network is congested. When the originating voice-enabled router determines that it cannot complete the call across the IP network, it sends the call to the PSTN with the appropriate dialed digits to terminate the call at the remote office via the PSTN network.

Introducing Analog Voice Ports on Cisco IOS Routers

Connecting voice devices to a network infrastructure requires an in-depth understanding of the signaling and electrical characteristics specific to each type of interface. Improperly matched electrical components can cause echo and create poor audio quality. Configuring devices for international implementation requires knowledge of country-specific settings. This section examines analog voice ports, analog signaling, and configuration parameters for analog voice ports.

Voice Ports

Voice ports on routers and access servers emulate physical telephony switch connections so that voice calls and their associated signaling can be transferred intact between a packet network and a circuit-switched network or device. For a voice call to occur, certain information must be passed between the telephony devices at either end of the call, such as the on-hook status of the devices, the availability of the line, and whether an incoming call is trying to reach a device. This information is referred to as signaling, and to process it properly, the devices at both ends of the call segment, which are directly connected to each other, must use the same type of signaling.

The devices in the packet network must be configured to convey signaling information in a way that a circuit-switched network can understand. They must also be able to understand signaling information that is received from the circuit-switched network. This is accomplished by installing appropriate voice hardware in a router or access server and by configuring the voice ports that connect to telephony devices or the circuit-switched network. Figure 3-8 shows typical examples of how voice ports are used.

Signaling Interfaces

Voice ports on routers and access servers physically connect the router, access server, or call control device to telephony devices such as telephones, fax machines, PBXs, and PSTN central office (CO) switches through signaling interfaces.

These signaling interfaces generate information about things such as

- On-hook status

- Ringing

- Line seizure

The voice port hardware and software of the router need to be configured to transmit and receive the same type of signaling being used by the device they are interfacing with so calls can be exchanged smoothly between a packet network and a circuit-switched network.

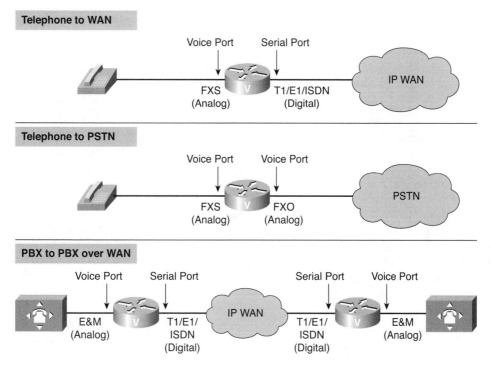

Figure 3-8   *Voice Ports*

The signaling interfaces discussed in the next sections include FXO, FXS, and E&M, which are types of analog interfaces. Digital signaling interfaces include T1, E1, and ISDN. Some digital connections emulate FXO, FXS, and E&M interfaces. It is important to know which signaling method the telephony side of the connection is using and to match the router configuration and voice interface hardware to that signaling method.

Analog Voice Ports

Analog voice port interfaces connect routers in packet-based networks to analog two-wire or four-wire circuits in telephony networks. Two-wire circuits connect to analog telephone or fax devices, and four-wire circuits connect to PBXs. Connections to the PSTN CO are typically made with digital interfaces. Three types of analog voice interfaces are supported by Cisco gateways, as illustrated in Figure 3-9.

The following is a detailed explanation of each of the three types of analog voice interfaces:

- **FXS:** An FXS interface connects the router or access server to end-user equipment such as telephones, fax machines, or modems. The FXS interface supplies ring, voltage, and dial tone to the station and includes an RJ-11 connector for basic telephone equipment, key sets, and PBXs.

- FXS
  - Connects directly to end-user equipment such as telephones, fax machines, or modems

___

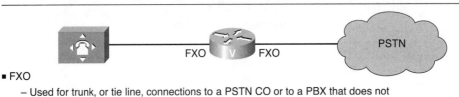

- FXO
  - Used for trunk, or tie line, connections to a PSTN CO or to a PBX that does not support E&M signaling

___

- E&M
  - Most common form of analog trunk circuit

Figure 3-9   *Analog Voice Ports*

■   **FXO:** An FXO interface is used for trunk, or tie-line, connections to a PSTN CO or to a PBX that does not support E&M signaling (when the local telecommunications authority permits). This interface is of value for off-premises station applications. A standard RJ-11 modular telephone cable connects the FXO voice interface card to the PSTN or PBX through a telephone wall outlet.

■   **E&M:** Trunk circuits connect telephone switches to one another. They do not connect end-user equipment to the network. The most common form of analog trunk circuit is the E&M interface, which uses special signaling paths that are separate from the trunk audio path to convey information about the calls. The signaling paths are known as the E-lead and the M-lead. E&M connections from routers to telephone switches or to PBXs are preferable to FXS and FXO connections because E&M provides better answer and disconnect supervision.

The name E&M is thought to derive from the phrase Ear and Mouth or rEceive and transMit, although it could also come from Earth and Magneto. The history of these names dates back to the early days of telephony, when the CO side had a key that grounded the E circuit, and the other side had a sounder with an electromagnet attached to a battery. Descriptions such as Ear and Mouth were adopted to help field personnel understanding and determine the direction of a signal in a wire.

Like a serial port, an E&M interface has a DTE/DCE type of reference. In the telecommunications world, the trunking side is similar to the DCE and is usually associated with CO functionality. The router acts as this side of the interface. The other side is referred to as the signaling side, like a DTE, and is usually a device such as a PBX.

> **Note**   Depending on how the router is connected to the PSTN, the voice gateway might provide clocking to an attached key system or PBX, because the PSTN has more accurate clocks, and the voice gateway can pass this capability to downstream devices.

Analog Signaling

The human voice generates sound waves, and the telephone converts the sound waves into electrical signals, analogous to sound. Analog signaling is not robust because of line noise. Analog transmissions are boosted by amplifiers because the signal diminishes the farther it travels from the CO. As the signal is boosted, the noise is also boosted, which often causes an unusable connection.

In digital networks, signals are transmitted over great distances and coded, regenerated, and decoded without degradation of quality. Repeaters amplify the signal and clean it to its original condition. Repeaters then determine the original sequence of the signal levels and send the clean signal to the next network destination.

Voice ports on routers and access servers physically connect the router or access server to telephony devices such as telephones, fax machines, PBXs, and PSTN CO switches. These devices might use any of several types of signaling interfaces to generate information about on-hook status, ringing, and line seizure.

Signaling techniques can be placed into one of three categories:

- **Supervisory:** Involves the detection of changes to the status of a loop or trunk. When these changes are detected, the supervisory circuit generates a predetermined response. A circuit (loop) can close to connect a call, for example.

- **Addressing:** Involves passing dialed digits (pulsed or tone) to a PBX or CO. These dialed digits provide the switch with a connection path to another phone or customer premises equipment (CPE).

- **Informational:** Provides audible tones to the user, which indicates certain conditions such as an incoming call or a busy phone.

FXS and FXO Supervisory Signaling

FXS and FXO interfaces indicate on-hook or off-hook status and the seizure of telephone lines by one of two access signaling methods: loop-start or ground-start. The type of access signaling is determined by the type of service from the telephone company's CO. Standard home telephone lines use loop-start, but business telephones can order ground-start lines instead.

Loop-Start

Loop-start, as shown in Figure 3-10, is the more common of the access signaling techniques. When a handset is picked up (the telephone goes off-hook), this action closes the 48V circuit that draws current from the telephone company CO and indicates a change in status, which signals the CO to provide a dial tone. An incoming call is signaled from the CO to the called handset by sending a signal in a standard on/off pattern, which causes the telephone to ring. When the called subscriber answers the call, the 48V circuit is closed and the CO turns off the ring voltage. At this point, the two circuits are tied together at the CO.

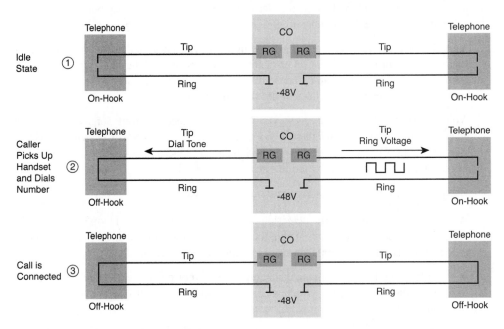

Figure 3-10   *Loop-Start Signaling*

The loop-start signaling process is as follows:

Step 1.   In the idle state, the telephone, PBX, or FXO module has an open two-wire loop (tip and ring lines open). It could be a telephone set with the handset on-hook or a PBX or FXO module that generates an open between the tip and ring lines. The CO or FXS waits for a closed loop that generates a current flow. The CO or FXS have a ring generator connected to the tip line and −48VDC on the ring line.

Step 2.   A telephone set, PBX, or FXO module closes the loop between the tip and ring lines. The telephone takes its handset off-hook or the PBX or FXO module closes a circuit connection. The CO or FXS module detects current flow and then generates a dial tone, which is sent to the telephone set, PBX, or FXO module. This indicates that the customer can start to dial. At the same time, the CO or FXS module seizes the ring line of the telephone, PBX, or FXO module called by superimposing a 20 Hz, 90 VAC signal over the -48VDC ring line. This procedure rings the called party telephone set or signals the PBX or FXS module that there is an incoming call. The CO or FXS module removes this ring after the telephone set, PBX, or FXO module closes the circuit between the tip and ring lines.

Step 3.   The telephone set closes the circuit when the called party picks up the handset. The PBX or FXS module closes the circuit when it has an available resource to connect to the called party.

Loop-start has two disadvantages:

■   There is no way to prevent the CO and the subscriber from seizing the same line at the same time, a condition known as *glare*. It takes about four seconds for the CO switch to cycle through all the lines it must ring. This delay in ringing a phone causes the glare problem because the CO switch and the telephone set seize a line simultaneously. When this happens, the person who initiated the call is connected to the called party almost instantaneously, with no ring-back tone.

> **Note**   The best way to prevent glare is to use ground-start signaling.

■   It does not provide switch-side disconnect supervision for FXO calls. The telephony switch is the connection in the PSTN, another PBX, or key system. This switch expects the FXO interface of the router, which looks like a telephone to the switch, to hang up the calls it receives through its FXO port. However, this function is not built in to the router for received calls. It operates only for calls originating from the FXO port.

These disadvantages are usually not a problem on residential telephones, but they become significant with the higher call volume experienced on business telephones.

Ground-Start

Ground-start signaling, as shown in Figure 3-11, is another supervisory signaling technique, like loop-start, that provides a way to indicate on-hook and off-hook conditions in a voice network. Ground-start signaling is used primarily in switch-to-switch connections. The main difference between ground-start and loop-start signaling is that ground-start requires ground detection to occur in both ends of a connection before the tip and ring loop can be closed.

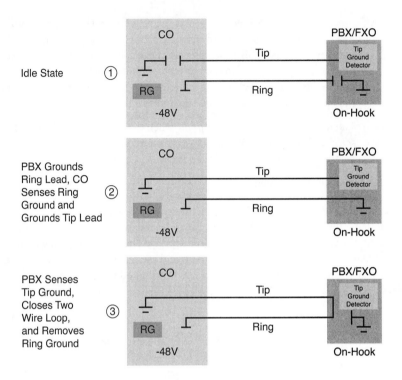

Figure 3-11   *Ground-Start Signaling*

Ground-start signaling works by using ground and current detectors that allow the network to indicate off-hook or seizure of an incoming call independent of the ringing signal and allow for positive recognition of connects and disconnects. Because ground-start signaling uses a request and/or confirm switch at both ends of the interface, it is preferable over FXOs and other signaling methods on high-usage trunks. For this reason, ground-start signaling is typically used on trunk lines between PBXs and in businesses where call volume on loop-start lines can result in glare.

The ground-start signaling process is as follows:

Step 1.   In the idle state, both the tip and ring lines are disconnected from ground. The PBX and FXO constantly monitor the tip line for ground, and the CO and FXS constantly monitor the ring line for ground. Battery (–48 VDC) is still connected to the ring line just as in loop-start signaling.

Step 2.   A PBX or FXO grounds the ring line to indicate to the CO or FXS that there is an incoming call. The CO or FXS senses the ring ground and then grounds the tip lead to let the PBX or FXO know that it is ready to receive the incoming call.

Step 3.   The PBX or FXO senses the tip ground and closes the loop between the tip and ring lines in response. It also removes the ring ground.

Analog Address Signaling

The dialing phase allows the subscriber to enter a phone number (address) of a telephone at another location. The customer enters this number with either a rotary phone that generates pulses or a touch-tone (push-button) phone that generates tones. Table 3-2 shows the frequency tones generated by dual tone multifrequency (DTMF) dialing.

Table 3-2 *DTMF Frequencies*

Frequencies	1209	1336	1477
697	1	2	3
770	4	5	6
852	7	8	9
941	*	0	#

Telephones use two different types of address signaling to notify the telephone company where a subscriber calls:

- Pulse dialing

- DTMF dialing

These pulses or tones are transmitted to the CO switch across a two-wire twisted-pair cable (tip and ring lines). On the voice gateway, the FXO port sends address signaling to the FXS port. This address indicates the final destination of a call.

Pulsed tones were used by the old rotary phones. These phones had a disk that was rotated to dial a number. As the disk rotated, it opened and closed the circuit a specified number of times based on how far the disk was turned. The exchange equipment counted those circuit interruptions to determine the called number. The duration of open-to-closed times had to be within specifications according to the country you were in.

These days, analog circuits use DTMF tones to indicate the destination address. DTMF assigns a specific frequency (consisting of two separate tones) to each key on the touch-tone telephone dial pad. The combination of these two tones notifies the receiving subscriber of the digits dialed.

Informational Signaling

The FXS port provides informational signaling using *call progress* (CP) *tones*, as detailed in Table 3-3. These CP tones are audible and are used by the FXS connected device to indicate the status of calls.

Table 3-3   *Network Call Progress Tones*

Tone	Frequency (Hz)	On Time (sec)	Off Time (sec)
Dial	350 + 440	Continuous	Continuous
Busy	480 + 620	0.5	0.5
Ringback, line	440 + 480	2	4
Ringback, PBX	440 + 480	1	3
Congestion (toll)	480 + 620	0.2	0.3
Reorder (local)	480 + 620	0.3	0.2
Receiver off-hook	1400 + 2060 + 2450 + 2600	0.1	0.1
No such number	200 to 400	Continuous	Continuous

The progress tones listed in Table 3-3 are for North American phone systems. International phone systems can have a totally different set of progress tones. Users should be familiar with most of the following call progress tones:

- **Dial tone:** Indicates that the telephone company is ready to receive digits from the user telephone.

- **Busy tone:** Indicates that a call cannot be completed because the telephone at the remote end is already in use.

- **Ring-Back (normal or PBX):** Tone indicates that the telephone company is attempting to complete a call on behalf of a subscriber.

- **Congestion:** Progress tone is used between switches to indicate that congestion in the long-distance telephone network currently prevents a telephone call from being processed.

- **Reorder:** Tone indicates that all the local telephone circuits are busy and thus prevents a telephone call from being processed.

- **Receiver off-hook:** Tone is the loud ringing that indicates the receiver of a phone is left off-hook for an extended period of time.

- **No such number:** Tone indicates that the number dialed cannot be found in the routing table of a switch.

E&M Signaling

E&M is another signaling technique used mainly between PBXs or other network-to-network telephony switches (Lucent 5 Electronic Switching System [5ESS], Nortel DMS-100, and so on). E&M signaling supports tie-line type facilities or signals between voice switches. Instead of superimposing both voice and signaling on the same wire, E&M uses separate paths, or leads, for each.

There are six distinct physical configurations for the signaling part of the interface. They are Types I–V and Signaling System Direct Current No.5 (SSDC5). They use different methods to signal on-hook or off-hook status, as shown Table 3-4. Cisco voice implementation supports E&M Types I, II, III, and V.

Table 3-4   *E&M Signaling Types*

Type	M-Lead Off-Hook	M-Lead On-Hook	E-Lead Off-Hook	E-Lead On-Hook
I	Battery	Ground	Ground	Open
II	Battery	Open	Ground	Open
III	Loop Current	Ground	Ground	Open
IV	Ground	Open	Ground	Open
V	Ground	Open	Ground	Open
SSDC5	Earth On	Earth Off	Earth On	Earth Off

The following list details the characteristics of each E&M signaling type introduced in Table 3-4:

- **Type I:** Type I signaling is the most common E&M signaling method used in North America. One wire is the E lead. The second wire is the M lead, and the remaining two pairs of wires serve as the audio path. In this arrangement, the PBX supplies power, or battery, for both E and M leads. In the idle (on-hook) state, both the E and M leads are open. The PBX indicates an off-hook by connecting the M lead to the battery. The line side indicates an off-hook by connecting the E lead to ground.

- **Type II:** Type II signaling is typically used in sensitive environments because it produces very little interference. This type uses four wires for signaling. One wire is the E lead. Another wire is the M lead, and the two other wires are signal ground (SG) and signal battery (SB). In Type II, SG and SB are the return paths for the E lead and M lead, respectively. The PBX side indicates an off-hook by connecting the M lead to the SB lead. The line side indicates an off-hook by connecting the E lead to SG lead.

- **Type III:** Type III signaling is not commonly used. Type III also uses four wires for signaling. In the idle state (on-hook), the E lead is open and the M lead is connected to the SG lead, which is grounded. The PBX side indicates an off-hook by moving the M lead from the SG lead to the SB lead. The line side indicates an off-hook by grounding the E lead.

- **Type IV:** Type IV also uses four wires for signaling. In the idle state (on-hook), the E and M leads are both open. The PBX side indicates an off-hook by connecting the M lead to the SB lead, which is grounded on the line side. The line side indicates an off-hook by connecting the E lead to the SG lead, which is grounded on the PBX side.

Note   E&M Type IV is not supported on Cisco voice gateways. However, Type IV operates similarly to Type II except for the M-lead operation. On Type IV, the M-lead states are open/ground, compared to Type II, which is open/battery. Type IV can interface with Type II. To use Type IV you can set the E&M voice port to Type II and perform the necessary M-lead rewiring.

- **Type V:** Type V is the most common E&M signaling form used outside of North America. Type V is similar to Type I because two wires are used for signaling (one wire is the E lead and the other wire is the M lead). In the idle (on-hook) state, both the E and M leads are open as in the preceding diagram. The PBX indicates an off-hook by grounding the M lead. The line side indicates an off-hook by grounding the E lead.

- **SSDC5:** Similar to Type V, SSDC5 differs in that on- and off-hook states are backward to allow for fail-safe operation. If the line breaks, the interface defaults to off-hook (busy). SSDC5 is most often found in England.

E&M Physical Interface

The physical E&M interface is an RJ-48 connector that connects to PBX trunk lines, which are classified as either two-wire or four-wire.

Note   Two-wire and four-wire refer to the voice wires. A connection might be called a four-wire E&M circuit although it actually has six to eight physical wires.

Two or four wires are used for signaling, and the remaining two pairs of wires serve as the audio path. This refers to whether the audio path is full duplex on one pair of wires (two-wire) or on two pairs of wires (four-wire).

E&M Address Signaling

PBXs built by different manufacturers can indicate on-hook/off-hook status and telephone line seizure on the E&M interface by using any of three types of access signaling:

- **Immediate-start:** Immediate-start, as illustrated in Figure 3-12, is the simplest method of E&M access signaling. The calling side seizes the line by going off-hook on its E lead, waits for a minimum of 150 ms and then sends address information as DTMF digits or as dialed pulses. This signaling approach is used for E&M tie trunk interfaces.

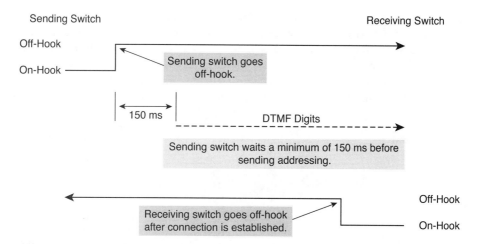

Figure 3-12   *Immediate-Start Signaling*

■ **Wink-start:** Wink-start, as shown in Figure 3-13, is the most commonly used method for E&M access signaling and is the default for E&M voice ports. Wink-start was developed to minimize glare, a condition found in immediate-start E&M, in which both ends attempt to seize a trunk at the same time. In wink-start, the calling side seizes the line by going off-hook on its E lead; it then waits for a short temporary off-hook pulse, or "wink," from the other end on its M lead before sending address information as DTMF digits. The switch interprets the pulse as an indication to proceed and then sends the dialed digits as DTMF or dialed pulses. This signaling is used for E&M tie trunk interfaces. This is the default setting for E&M voice ports.

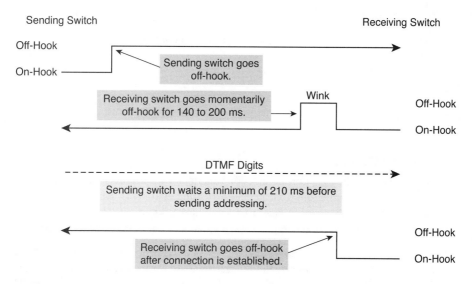

Figure 3-13   *Wink-Start Signaling*

■ **Delay-start:** With delay-start signaling, as depicted in Figure 3-14, the calling station seizes the line by going off-hook on its E lead. After a timed interval, the calling side looks at the status of the called side. If the called side is on-hook, the calling side starts sending information as DTMF digits. Otherwise, the calling side waits until the called side goes on-hook and then starts sending address information. This signaling approach is used for E&M tie trunk interfaces.

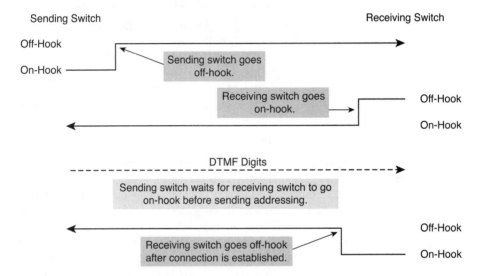

Figure 3-14   *Delay-Start Signaling*

Configuring Analog Voice Ports

The three types of analog ports that you will learn to configure are

■ FXS

■ FXO

■ E&M

FXS Voice Port Configuration

In North America, the FXS port connection functions with default settings most of the time. The same cannot be said for other countries and continents. Remember, FXS ports look like switches to the edge devices that are connected to them. Therefore, the configuration of the FXS port should emulate the switch configuration of the local PSTN.

For example, consider an international company that has offices in the United States and England. Each PSTN provides signaling that is standard for its own country. In the United States, the PSTN provides a dial tone that is different from the dial tone in England. The signals that ring incoming calls are different in England. Another instance where the default configuration might be changed is when the connection is a trunk to a PBX or key system. In each of these cases, the FXS port must be configured to match the settings of the device to which it is connected.

In this example, you have been assigned to configure a voice gateway to route calls to a plain old telephone service (POTS) phone connected to a FXS port on a remote router in Great Britain. Figure 3-15 shows how the British office is configured to enable ground-start signaling on FXS voice port 0/2/0. The call-progress tones are set for Great Britain, and the ring cadence is set for pattern 1.

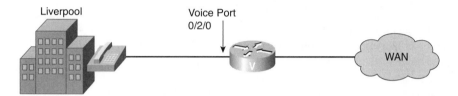

Figure 3-15   *FXS Configuration Topology*

The requirements for your configuration are the following:

■   Configure the voice port to use ground-start signaling.

■   Configure the call-progress tones for Great Britain.

You would then complete the following steps to accomplish the stated objectives:

Step 1.   Enter voice-port configuration mode.

```
Router(config)#voice-port slot/port
```

Step 2.   Select the access signaling type to match the telephony connection you are making.

```
Router(config-voiceport)#signal {loopstart | groundstart}
```

Note   If you change signal type, you must execute a **shutdown** and **no shutdown** command on the voice port.

Step 3.   Select the two-letter locale for the voice call progress tones and other locale-specific parameters to be used on this voice port.

```
Router(config-voiceport)#cptone locale
```

Step 4.   Specify a ring pattern. Each pattern specifies a ring-pulse time and a ring-interval time.

```
Router(config-voiceport)#ring cadence {pattern-number | define
pulse interval}
```

> **Note**   The **patternXX** keyword provides preset ring-cadence patterns for use on any plat-
> form. The **define** keyword allows you to create a custom ring cadence.

Step 5.   Activate the voice port.

```
Router(config-voiceport)#no shutdown
```

Example 3-1 shows the complete FXS voice port configuration.

Example 3-1   *FXS Voice Port Configuration*

```
Router(config)#voice-port 0/2/0
Router(config-voiceport)#signal groundstart
Router(config-voiceport)#cptone GB
Router(config-voiceport)#ring cadence pattern01
Router(config-voiceport)#no shutdown
```

FXO Voice Port Configuration

An FXO trunk is one of the simplest analog trunks available. Because Dialed Number
Information Service (DNIS) information can only be sent out to the PSTN, no direct
inward dialing (DID) is possible. ANI is supported for inbound calls. Two signaling types
exist, loopstart and groundstart, with groundstart being the preferred method.

For example, consider the topology shown in Figure 3-16. Imagine you have been
assigned to configure a voice gateway to route calls to and from the PSTN through an
FXO port on the router.

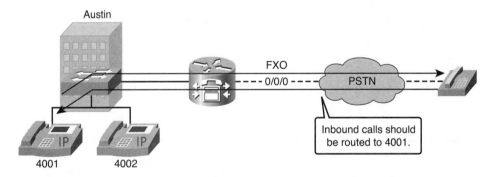

Figure 3-16   *FXO Configuration Topology*

In this scenario, you must set up a PLAR connection using an FXO port connected to
the PSTN.

The configuration requirements are the following:

■ Configure the voice port to use ground-start signaling.

■ Configure a PLAR connection from a remote location to extension 4001 in Austin.

■ Configure a standard dial peer for inbound and outbound PSTN calls.

Because an FXO trunk does not support DID, two-stage dialing is required for all inbound calls. If all inbound calls should be routed to a specific extension, (for example, a front desk), you can use the **connection plar opx** command. In this example, all inbound calls are routed to extension 4001.

You could then complete the following steps to configure the FXO voice port:

Step 1.   Enter voice-port configuration mode.

```
Router(config)#voice-port 0/0/0
```

Step 2.   Select the access signaling type to match the telephony connection you are making.

```
Router(config-voiceport)#signal ground-start
```

Step 3.   Specify a PLAR off-premises extension (OPX) connection.

```
Router(config-voiceport)#connection plar opx 4001
```

Note   PLAR is an autodialing mechanism that permanently associates a voice interface with a far-end voice interface, allowing call completion to a specific telephone number or PBX without dialing. When the calling telephone goes off-hook, a predefined network dial peer is automatically matched. This sets up a call to the destination telephone or PBX.

Using the **opx** option, the local voice port provides a local response before the remote voice port receives an answer. On FXO interfaces, the voice port does not answer until the remote side has answered.

Step 4.   Activate the voice port.

```
Router(config-voiceport)#no shutdown
```

Step 5.   Exit voice port configuration mode.

```
Router(config-voiceport)#exit
```

Step 6.   Create a standard dial peer for inbound and outbound PSTN calls.

```
Router(config)#dial-peer voice 90 pots
```

Step 7.   Specify the destination pattern.

```
Router(config-dialpeer)#destination-pattern 9T
```

> **Note** The **T** control character indicates that the destination-pattern value is a variable-length dial string. Using this control character enables the router to wait until all digits are received before routing the call.
>
> Dial-peer configuration is covered in the section, "Introducing Dial Peers."

Step 8. Specify the voice port associated with this dial peer.

```
Router(config-dialpeer)#port 0/0/0
```

Example 3-2 shows the complete FXO voice port configuration.

Example 3-2 *FXO Voice Port Configuration*

```
Router(config)#voice-port 0/0/0
Router(config-voiceport)#signal groundstart
Router(config-voiceport)#connection plar opx 4001
Router(config)#dial-peer voice 90 pots
Router(config-dialpeer)#destination-pattern 9T
Router(config-dialpeer)#port 0/0/0
```

E&M Voice Port Configuration

Configuring an E&M analog trunk is straightforward. Three key options have to be set:

- The signaling E&M signaling type

- Two- or four-wire operation

- The E&M type

As an example, consider the topology shown in Figure 3-17.

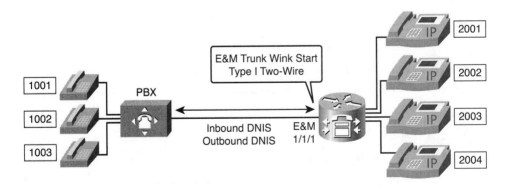

Figure 3-17 *E&M Configuration Topology*

In this example, you have been assigned to configure a voice gateway to work with an existing PBX system according to network requirements. You must set up a voice gateway to interface with a PBX to allow the IP phones to call the POTS phones using a four-digit extension.

The configuration requirements are the following:

■   Configure the voice port to use wink-start signaling.

■   Configure the voice port to use 2-wire operation mode.

■   Configure the voice port to use Type I E&M signaling.

■   Configure a standard dial peer for the POTS phones behind the PBX.

Both sides of the trunk need to have a matching configuration. The following example configuration shows an E&M trunk using wink-start signaling, E&M Type I, and two-wire operation. Because E&M supports inbound and outbound DNIS, DID support is also configured on the corresponding dial peer.

You could then complete the following steps to configure the E&M voice port:

Step 1.   Enter voice-port configuration mode.

Step 2.   Select the access signaling type to match the telephony connection you are making.

```
Router(config-voiceport)#signal wink-start
```

Step 3.   Select a specific cabling scheme for the E&M port.

```
Router(config-voiceport)#operation 2-wire
```

Note   This command affects only voice traffic. If the wrong cable scheme is specified, the user might get voice traffic in only one direction.

Also, using this command on a voice port changes the operation of both voice ports on a voice port module (VPM) card. The voice port must be shut down and then opened again for the new value to take effect.

Step 4.   Specify the type of E&M interface.

```
Router(config-voiceport)#type 1
```

Step 5.   Activate the voice port.

```
Router(config-voiceport)#no shutdown
```

Step 6.   Exit voice port configuration mode.

```
Router(config-voiceport)#exit
```

Step 7.   Create a dial peer for the POTS phones.

```
Router(config)#dial-peer voice 10 pots
```

Step 8.   Specify the destination pattern for the POTS phones.

```
Router(config-dialpeer)#destination-pattern 1...
```

Step 9.   Specify direct inward dial.

```
Router(config-dialpeer)#direct-inward-dial
```

> **Note**   DID is needed when POTS phones call IP Phones. In this case we match the POTS dial peer. This same dial peer is also used to call out to POTS phones.

Step 10.   Specify digit forwarding all, so that no digits will be stripped as they are forwarded out of the voice port. By default, only digits matched by wildcard characters in the **destination-pattern** command are forwarded.

```
Router(config-dialpeer)#forward-digits all
```

Step 11.   Specify the voice port associated with this dial peer.

```
Router(config-dialpeer)#port 1/1/1
```

Example 3-3 shows the complete E&M voice port configuration.

Example 3-3   *E&M Voice Port Configuration*

```
Router(config)#voice-port 1/1/1
Router(config-voiceport)#signal wink-start
Router(config-voiceport)#operation 2-wire
Router(config-voiceport)#type 1
Router(config-voiceport)#no shutdown
Router(config-voiceport)#exit
Router(config)#dial-peer voice 10 pots
Router(config-dialpeer)#destination-pattern 1...
Router(config-dialpeer)#direct-inward-dial
Router(config-dialpeer)#forward-digits all
Router(config-dialpeer)#port 1/1/1
```

Trunks

Trunks are used to interconnect gateways or PBX systems to other gateways, PBX systems, or the PSTN. A trunk is a single physical or logical interface that contains several physical interfaces and connects to a single destination. This could be a single FXO port that provides a single line connection between a Cisco gateway and a FXS port of small PBX system, a POTS device, or several T1 interfaces with 24 lines each in a Cisco gateway providing PSTN lines to several hundred subscribers.

Trunk ports can be analog or digital and use a variety of signaling protocols. Signaling can be done using either the voice channel (in-band) or an extra dedicated channel (out-of-band). The available features depend on the signaling protocol in use between the devices.

Figure 3-18 illustrates a variety of possible trunk connections.

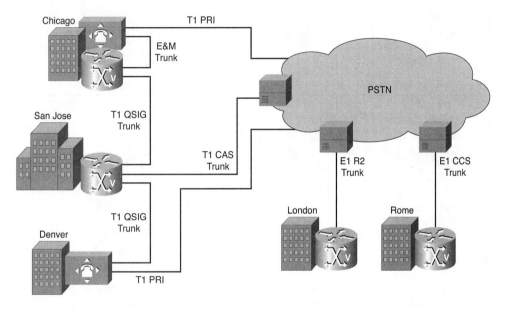

Figure 3-18   *E&M Trunks*

Consider the following characteristics of the trunks depicted in Figure 3-18:

- If a subscriber at the London site places a call to the PSTN, the gateway uses one voice channel of the E1 R2 trunk interface.

- If a subscriber of the legacy PBX system at the Chicago site needs to place a call to a subscriber with an IP phone connected to the Chicago gateway, the call will go via the E&M trunk between the legacy PBX and the gateway.

- The Denver and the Chicago sites are connected to San Jose via Q Signaling (QSIG) to build up a common private numbering plan between those sites. Because Denver's Cisco IP telephony rollout has not started yet, the QSIG trunk is established directly between San Jose's gateway and Denver's legacy PBX.

Analog Trunks

Because many organizations continue to use analog devices, a requirement to integrate analog circuits with VoIP or IP telephony networks still exists. To implement a Cisco voice gateway into an analog trunk environment, the FXS, FXO, DID, and E&M interfaces are commonly used, as illustrated in Figure 3-19.

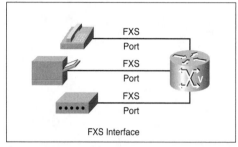
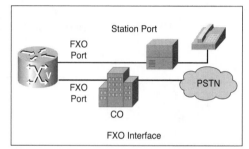
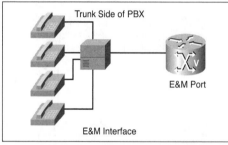
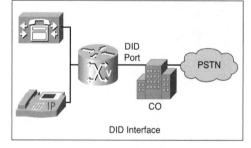

Figure 3-19   *Analog Trunks*

PSTN carriers typically offer analog trunk features that can be supported on home phones. Table 3-5 presents a description of the common analog trunk features.

Table 3-5   *Analog Trunk Features*

Feature	Description
Caller ID	Caller ID allows users to see the calling number before answering the phone.
Message waiting	Two methods activate an analog message indicator: ■ High-DC voltage message-waiting indicator (MWI) light and frequency-shift keying (FSK) messaging. ■ Stuttered dial tone for phones without a visual indicator.
Call waiting	When a user is on a call and a new call comes in, the user hears an audible tone and can "click over" to the new caller.
Caller ID on call waiting	When a user is on a call, the name of the second caller is announced or the caller ID is shown.

Table 3-5   *Analog Trunk Features   (continued)*

Feature	Description
Transfer	This feature includes both blind and supervised transfers using the standard established by Bellcore laboratories. The flash hook method is common with analog trunks.
Conference	Conference calls are initiated from an analog phone using flash hook or feature access codes.
Speed dial	A user can set up keys for commonly dialed numbers and dial these numbers directly from an analog phone.
Call forward all	Calls can be forwarded to a number within the dial plan.
Redial	A simple last-number redial can be activated from analog phones.
DID	Supported on E&M and FXS DID ports.

Figure 3-20 shows small business voice networks connected through a gateway to the PSTN. The voice network supports both analog phones and IP phones. The connection to the PSTN is through an FXO port, and the analog phone is connected to the small business network through an FXS port. The issue in this scenario is how the caller ID is passed to call destinations.

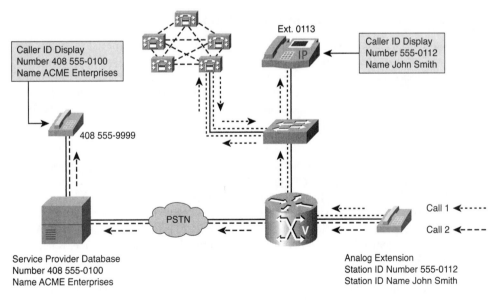

Figure 3-20   *Analog Trunks - Example*

This example describes two calls; the first call is to an on-premises destination, and the second call is to an off-premises destination:

- **Call 1:** Call 1 is from the analog phone to another phone on the premises. The FXS port is configured with a station ID name and station ID number. The name is John Smith, and the number is 555-0212. When a call is placed from the analog phone to another phone on the premises, an IP phone in this case, the caller name and number are displayed on the screen of the IP phone.

- **Call 2:** Call 2 is placed from the same analog phone, but the destination is off the premises on the PSTN. The FXO port forwards the station-ID name and station-ID number to the CO switch. The CO switch discards the station ID name and station ID number and replaces them with information it has configured for this connection.

For inbound calls, the caller ID feature is supported on the FXO port in the gateway. If the gateway is configured for H.323, the caller ID is displayed on the IP phones and on the analog phones (if supported).

Note   Although the gateway supports the caller ID feature, Cisco Unified Communications Manager does not support this feature on FXO ports if the gateway is configured for Media Gateway Control Protocol (MGCP).

Centralized Automated Message Accounting

A Centralized Automated Message Accounting (CAMA) trunk is a special analog trunk type originally developed for long-distance billing but now mainly used for emergency call services (911 and E911 services). You can use CAMA ports to connect to a Public Safety Answering Point (PSAP) for emergency calls. A CAMA trunk can send only out-bound automatic number identification (ANI) information, which is required by the local public safety answering point (PSAP).

CAMA interface cards and software configurations are targeted at corporate enterprise networks and at service providers and carriers who are creating new or supplementing existing networks with Enhanced 911 (E911) services. CAMA carries both calling and called numbers by using in-band signaling. This method of carrying identifying informa-tion enables the telephone system to send a station identification number to the PSAP via multifrequency (MF) signaling through the telephone company E911 equipment. CAMA trunks are currently used in 80 percent of E911 networks. The calling number is needed at the PSAP for two reasons:

- The calling number is used to reference the Automatic Location Identification (ALI) database to find the exact location of the caller and any extra information about the caller that might have been stored in the database.

■ The calling number is used as a callback number in case the call is disconnected. A number of U.S. states have initiated legislation that requires enterprises to connect directly to the E911 network. The U.S. Federal Communications Commission (FCC) has announced model legislation that extends this requirement to all U.S. states. Enterprises in areas where the PSTN accepts 911 calls on ISDN trunks can use existing Cisco ISDN voice-gateway products because the calling number is an inherent part of ISDN.

Note   You must check local legal requirements when using CAMA.

Calls to emergency services are routed based on the calling number, not the called number. The calling number is checked against a database of emergency service providers that cross-references the service providers for the caller location. When this information is determined, the call is then routed to the proper PSAP, which dispatches services to the caller location.

During the setup of an E911 call, before the audio channel is connected, the calling number is transmitted to each switching point, known as a selective router, via CAMA.

The VIC2-2FXO and VIC2-4FXO cards support CAMA via software configuration. CAMA support is also available for the Cisco 2800 Series and 3800 Series ISRs. It is common for E911 service providers to require CAMA interfaces to their network.

Figure 3-21 shows a site that has a T1 PRI circuit for normal inbound and outbound PSTN calls. Because the local PSAP requires a dedicated CAMA trunk for emergency (911) calls, all emergency calls are routed using a dial peer pointing to the CAMA trunk.

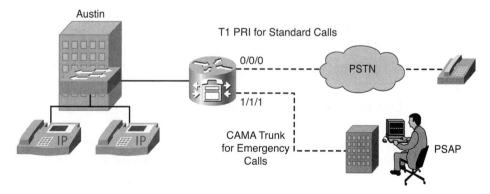

Figure 3-21   *Configuring a CAMA Trunk*

The voice port 1/1/1 is the CAMA trunk. The actual configuration depends on the PSAP requirements. In this case, the digit 1 is used to signal the area code 312. The voice port is then configured for CAMA signaling using the **signal cama** command. Five options exist:

■   **KP-0-NXX-XXXX-ST**: 7-digit ANI transmission. The Numbering Plan Area (NPA), or area code, is implied by the trunk group and is not transmitted.

■   **KP-0-NPA-NXX-XXXX-ST**: 10-digit transmission. The E.164 number is fully transmitted.

■   **KP-0-NPA-NXX-XXXX-ST-KP-YYY-YYY-YYYY-ST**: Supports CAMA signaling with ANI/Pseudo ANI (PANI).

■   **KP-2-ST**: Default transmission when the CAMA trunk cannot get a corresponding Numbering Plan Digit (NPD) in the look-up table or when the calling number is fewer than 10 digits. (NPA digits are not available.)

■   **KP-NPD-NXX-XXXX-ST**: 8-digit ANI transmission, where the NPD is a single MF digit that is expanded into the NPA. The NPD table is preprogrammed in the sending and receiving equipment (on each end of the MF trunk). For example: 0=415, 1=510, 2=650, 3=916

    05551234 = (415) 555-1234, 15551234 = (510) 555-1234

    The NPD value range is 0–3.

When you use the NPD format, the area code needs to be associated with a single digit. You can preprogram the NPA into a single MF digit using the **ani mapping** voice port command. The number of NPDs programmed is determined by local policy as well as by the number of NPAs the PSAP serves. Repeat this command until all NPDs are configured or until the NPD maximum range is reached.

In this example, the PSAP expects NPD signaling, with the area code 312 being represented by the digit 1.

You could then complete the following steps to configure the voice port for CAMA operation:

Step 1.   Configure a voice port for 911 calls.

```
Router(config)#voice-port 1/1/1
Router(config-voiceport)#ani mapping 1 312
Router(config-voiceport)#signal cama kp-npd-nxx-xxxx-st
```

Step 2.   Configure a dedicated dial peer to route emergency calls using the CAMA trunk when a user dials "911."

```
Router(config)#dial-peer voice 911 pots
Router(config-dialpeer)#destination-pattern 911
Router(config-dialpeer)#prefix 911
Router(config-dialpeer)#port 1/1/1
```

Step 3.   Configure a dedicated "9911" dial peer to route all emergency calls using the CAMA trunk when a user dials "9911."

```
Router(config)#dial-peer voice 9911 pots
Router(config-dialpeer)#destination-pattern 9911
Router(config-dialpeer)#prefix 911
Router(config-dialpeer)#port 1/1/1
```

Step 4.   Configure a standard PSTN dial peer for all other inbound and outbound PSTN calls.

```
Router(config)#dial-peer voice 910 pots
Router(config-dialpeer)#destination-pattern 9[2-8].........
Router(config-dialpeer)#port 0/0/0:23
```

Example 3-4 shows the complete CAMA trunk configuration.

Example 3-4   *CAMA Trunk Configuration*

```
Router(config)#voice-port 1/1/1
Router(config-voiceport)#ani mapping 1 312
Router(config-voiceport)#signal cama KP-NPD-NXX-XXXX-ST
Router(config)#dial-peer voice 911 pots
Router(config-dialpeer)#destination-pattern 911
Router(config-dialpeer)#prefix 911
Router(config-dialpeer)#port 1/1/1
Router(config)#dial-peer voice 9911 pots
Router(config-dialpeer)#destination-pattern 9911
Router(config-dialpeer)#prefix 911
Router(config-dialpeer)#port 1/1/1
Router(config)#dial-peer voice 910 pots
Router(config-dialpeer)#destination-pattern 9[2-8].........
Router(config-dialpeer)#port 0/0/0:23
```

Direct Inward Dial

Typically, FXS ports connect to analog phones, but some carriers offer FXS trunks that support DID. The DID service is offered by telephone companies, and it enables callers to dial an extension directly on a PBX or a VoIP system (for example, Cisco Unified

Communications Manager and Cisco IOS routers and gateways) without the assistance of an operator or automated call attendant. This service makes use of DID trunks, which forward only the last three to five digits of a phone number to the PBX, router, or gateway. For example, a company has phone extensions 555-1000 to 555-1999. A caller dials 555-1234, and the local CO forwards 234 to the PBX or VoIP system. The PBX or VoIP system then rings extension 234. This entire process is transparent to the caller.

An FXS DID trunk can receive only inbound calls, thus a combination of FXS, DID, and FXO ports is required for inbound and outbound calls. Two signaling types exist, loop-start and groundstart, with groundstart being the preferred method.

Figure 3-22 shows an analog trunk using an FXS DID trunk for inbound calls and a standard FXO trunk for outbound calls.

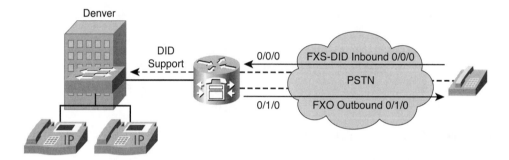

Figure 3-22 *Configuring DID Trunks*

You could then complete the following steps to enable DID signaling on the FXS port:

Step 1.   Configure the FXS port for DID and wink-start.

```
Router(config)#voice-port 0/0/0
Router(config-voiceport)#signal did wink-start
```

Step 2.   Configure the FXO port for groundstart signaling.

```
Router(config)#voice-port 0/1/0
Router(config-voiceport)#signal groundstart
```

Step 3.   Create an inbound dial peer using the FXS DID port. Note that direct inward dial is enabled.

```
Router(config)#dial-peer voice 1 pots
Router(config-dialpeer)#incoming called-number .
Router(config-dialpeer)#direct-inward-dial
Router(config-dialpeer)#port 0/0/0
```

Step 4.   Create a standard outbound dial peer using the FXO port.

```
Router(config)#dial-peer voice 910 pots
Router(config-dialpeer)#destination-pattern 9[2-8].........
Router(config-dialpeer)#port 0/1/0
```

Example 3-5 shows the complete DID trunk configuration.

Example 3-5 *DID Trunk Configuration*

```
Router(config)#voice-port 0/0/0
Router(config-voiceport)#signal did wink-start
Router(config)#voice-port 0/1/0
Router(config-voiceport)#signal groundstart
Router(config)#dial-peer voice 1 pots
Router(config-dialpeer)#incoming called-number .
Router(config-dialpeer)#direct-inward-dial
Router(config-dialpeer)#port 0/0/0
Router(config)#dial-peer voice 910 pots
Router(config-dialpeer)#destination-pattern 9[2-8].........
Router(config-dialpeer)#port 0/1/0
```

Timers and Timing

You can set a number of timers and timing parameters for fine-tuning a voice port. Following are voice-port configuration mode commands you can use to a set variety of timing parameters:

- **timeouts initial** *seconds*: Configures the initial digit timeout value in seconds. This value controls how long the dial tone is presented before the first digit is expected. This timer value typically does not need to be changed.

- **timeouts interdigit** *seconds*: Configures the number of seconds for which the system will wait between caller-entered digits before sending the input to be assessed. If the digits are coming from an automated device, and the dial plan is a variable-length dial plan, you can shorten this timer so the call proceeds without having to wait the full default of 10 seconds for the interdigit timer to expire.

- **timeouts ringing** {*seconds* | **infinity**}: Configures the length of time a caller can continue to let the telephone ring when there is no answer. You can configure this setting to be less than the default of 180 seconds so that you do not tie up a voice port when it is evident the call is not going to be answered.

- **timing digit** *milliseconds*: Configures the DTMF digit signal duration for a specified voice port. You can use this setting to fine-tune a connection to a device that might have trouble recognizing dialed digits. If a user or device dials too quickly, the digit might not be recognized. By changing the timing on the digit timer, you can provide for a shorter or longer DTMF duration.

- **timing interdigit** *milliseconds*: Configures the DTMF interdigit duration for a specified voice port. You can change this setting to accommodate faster or slower dialing characteristics.

- **timing hookflash-input** *milliseconds* and **hookflash-output** *milliseconds*:
  Configures the maximum duration (in milliseconds) of a hookflash indication.
  Hookflash is an indication by a caller that wants to do something specific with the
  call, such as transfer the call or place the call on hold. For the **hookflash-input** command, if the hookflash lasts longer than the specified limit, the FXS interface
  processes the indication as on-hook. If you set the value too low, the hookflash
  might be interpreted as a hang-up. If you set the value too high, the handset has to
  be left hung up for a longer period to clear the call. For the **hookflash-output** command, the setting specifies the duration (in milliseconds) of the hookflash indication
  that the gateway generates outbound. You can configure this to match the requirements of the connected device.

Under normal use, these timers do not need to be adjusted. In two instances, these timers
can be configured to allow more or less time for a specific function:

- When ports are connected to a device that does not properly respond to dialed digits or hookflash

- When the connected device provides automated dialing

Example 3-6 shows a configuration for a home for someone with a disability that might
require more time to dial digits. Notice the requirement to allow the telephone to ring,
unanswered, for 4 minutes. The configuration enables several timing parameters on a
Cisco voice-enabled router voice port 0/1/0. The initial timeout is lengthened to 15 seconds; the interdigit timeout is lengthened to 15 seconds; the ringing timeout is set to 240
seconds; and the **hookflash-in** is set to 500 ms.

Example 3-6   *Timers and Timing Configuration*

```
Router(config)#voice-port 0/1/0
Router(config-voiceport)#timeouts initial 15
Router(config-voiceport)#timeouts interdigit 15
Router(config-voiceport)#timeouts ringing 240
Router(config-voiceport)#timing hookflash-in 500
```

Verifying Voice Ports

After physically connecting analog or digital devices to a Cisco voice-enabled router, you
might need to issue **show**, **test**, or **debug** commands to verify or troubleshoot your configuration. For example, the following list enumerates six steps to monitor and troubleshoot voice ports:

Step 1.   Pick up the handset of an attached telephony device and check for a dial
tone. If there is no dial tone, check the following:

- Is the plug firmly seated?

- Is the voice port enabled?

- Is the voice port recognized by the Cisco IOS?

- Is the router running the correct version of Cisco IOS in order to recognize the module?

- Is a dial peer configured for that port?

Step 2.   If you have a dial tone, check for DTMF voice band tones, such as touch-tone detection. If the dial tone stops when you dial a digit, the voice port is probably configured properly.

Step 3.   Use the **show voice port** command to verify that the data configured is correct. If you have trouble connecting a call, and you suspect that the problem is associated with voice-port configuration, you can try to resolve the problem by performing steps 4 through 6.

Step 4.   Use the **show voice port** command to make sure the port is enabled. If the port is administratively down, use the **no shutdown** command. If the port was working previously and is not working now, it is possible the port is in a hung state. Use the **shutdown/no shutdown** command sequence to reinitialize the port.

Step 5.   If you have configured E&M interfaces, make sure the values associated with your specific PBX setup are correct. Specifically, check for two-wire or four-wire wink-start, immediate-start, or delay-start signaling types, and the E&M interface type. These parameters need to match those set on the PBX for the interface to communicate properly.

Step 6.   You must confirm that the voice network module (VNM) (that is, the module in the router that contains the voice ports) is correctly installed. With the device powered down, remove the VNM and reinsert it to verify the installation. If the device has other slots available, try inserting the VNM into another slot to isolate the problem. Similarly, you must move the voice interface card (VIC) to another VIC slot to determine whether the problem is with the VIC card or with the module slot.

For your reference, Table 3-6 lists six **show** commands for verifying the voice-port configuration.

Table 3-6   *Commands to Verify Voice Ports*

Command	Description
show voice port	Shows all voice-port configurations in detail
show voice port *slot/subunit/port*	Shows one voice-port configuration in detail
show voice port summary	Shows all voice-port configurations in brief
show voice busyout	Shows all ports configured as busyout
show voice dsp	Shows status of all DSPs
show controller T1 | E1	Shows the operational status of a controller

Example 3-7 provides sample output for the **show voice port** command.

Example 3-7   show voice port *Command*

```
Router#show voice port

Foreign Exchange Station 0/0/0 Slot is 0, Sub-unit is 0, Port is 0
 Type of VoicePort is FXS  VIC2-2FXS
 Operation State is DORMANT
 Administrative State is UP
 No Interface Down Failure
 Description is not set
 Noise Regeneration is enabled
 Non Linear Processing is enabled
 Non Linear Mute is disabled
 Non Linear Threshold is -21 dB
 Music On Hold Threshold is Set to -38 dBm
 In Gain is Set to 0 dB
 Out Attenuation is Set to 3 dB
 Echo Cancellation is enabled
 Echo Cancellation NLP mute is disabled
 Echo Cancellation NLP threshold is -21 dB
 Echo Cancel Coverage is set to 64 ms
 Echo Cancel worst case ERL is set to 6 dB
 Playout-delay Mode is set to adaptive
 Playout-delay Nominal is set to 60 ms
```

Example 3-8 provides sample output for the **show voice port summary** command.

Example 3-8   show voice port summary *Command*

```
router#show voice port summary
                                  IN       OUT
PORT       CH  SIG-TYPE   ADMIN OPER STATUS   STATUS   EC
=========  ==  ========== ===== ==== ======== ======== ==
0/0/0      —   fxs-ls     up    dorm on-hook  idle     y
0/0/1      —   fxs-ls     up    dorm on-hook  idle     y
50/0/11    1   efxs       up    dorm on-hook  idle     y
50/0/11    2   efxs       up    dorm on-hook  idle     y
50/0/12    1   efxs       up    dorm on-hook  idle     y
50/0/12    2   efxs       up    dorm on-hook  idle     y
```

For your further reference, Table 3-7 provides a series of commands used to test Cisco voice ports. The **test** commands provide the capability to analyze and troubleshoot voice ports on voice-enabled routers. As Table 3-7 shows, you can use five **test** commands to force voice ports into specific states to test the voice port configuration. The **csim start** *dial-string* command simulates a call to any end station for testing purposes.

Table 3-7   test *Commands*

Command	Description
test voice port *port_or_DS0-group_identifier* detector {m-lead | battery-reversal | ring | tip-ground | ring-ground | ring-trip} {on | off | disable}	Forces a detector into specific states for testing.
test voice port *port_or_DS0-group_identifier* inject-tone {local | network} {1000hz | 2000hz | 200hz | 3000hz | 300hz | 3200hz | 3400hz | 500hz | quiet | disable}	Injects a test tone into a voice port. A call must be established on the voice port under test. When you are finished testing, be sure to use the **disable** option to end the test tone.
test voice port *port_or_DS0-group_identifier* loopback {local | network | disable}	Performs loopback testing on a voice port. A call must be established on the voice port under test. When you finish the loopback testing, be sure to use the **disable** option to end the forced loopback.
test voice port *port_or_DS0-group_identifier* relay {e-lead | loop | ring-ground | battery-reversal | power-denial | ring | tip-ground} {on | off | disable}	Tests relay-related functions on a voice port.
test voice port *port_or_DS0-group_identifier* switch {fax | disable}	Forces a voice port into fax or voice mode for testing. If the voice port does not detect fax data, the voice port remains in fax mode for 30 seconds and then reverts automatically to voice mode. After you enter the **test voice port switch fax** command, you can use the **show voice call** command to check whether the voice port is able to operate in fax mode.
csim start *dial-string*	Simulates a call to the specified dial string. This command is most useful when testing dial plans.

Introducing Dial Peers

As a call is set up across the network, the existence of various parameters is checked and negotiated. A mismatch in parameters can cause call failure. Therefore, it is important to understand how routers interpret call legs and how call legs relate to inbound and outbound dial peers. Successful implementation of a VoIP network relies heavily on the proper application of dial peers, the digits they match, and the services they specify. A network designer needs in-depth knowledge of dial-peer configuration options and their uses. This section discusses the proper use of digit manipulation and the configuration of dial peers.

Understanding Call Legs

Call legs are logical connections between any two telephony devices, such as gateways, routers, Cisco Unified Communication Managers, or telephony endpoint devices. Additionally, call legs are router-centric. When an inbound call arrives, it is processed separately until the destination is determined. Then a second outbound call leg is established, and the inbound call leg is switched to the outbound voice port. The topology shown in Figure 3-23 illustrates the four call legs involved in an end-to-end call between two voice-enabled routers.

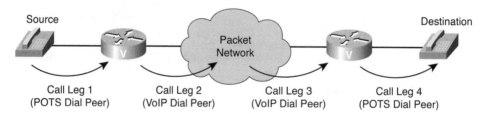

| Call Leg 1 | Call Leg 2 | Call Leg 3 | Call Leg 4 |
| (POTS Dial Peer) | (VoIP Dial Peer) | (VoIP Dial Peer) | (POTS Dial Peer) |

Figure 3-23 *Dial Peers and Call Legs*

An end-to-end call consists of four call legs: two from the source router's perspective and two from the destination router's perspective. To complete an end-to-end call from either side and send voice packets back and forth, you must configure all four dial peers. Dial peers are used only to set up calls. After the call is established, dial peers are no longer employed.

An inbound call leg occurs when an incoming call comes *into* the router or gateway. An outbound call leg occurs when a call is placed *from* the router or gateway, as depicted in Figure 3-24.

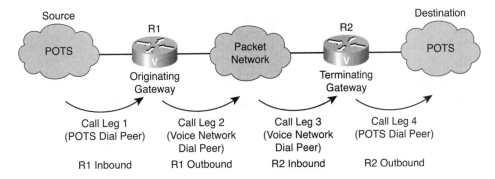

Figure 3-24 *End-to-End Calls*

A call is segmented into call legs, and a dial peer is associated with each call leg. The process for call setup, as diagrammed in Figure 3-24, is the following:

- The POTS call arrives at R1, and an inbound POTS dial peer is matched.

- After associating the incoming call to an inbound POTS dial peer, R1 creates an inbound POTS call leg and assigns it a call ID (call leg 1).

- R1 uses the dialed string to match an outbound VoIP dial peer.

- After associating the dialed string to an outbound voice network dial peer, R1 creates an outbound voice network call leg and assigns it a call ID (call leg 2).

- The voice network call request arrives at R2, and an inbound VoIP dial peer is matched.

- After R2 associates the incoming call to an inbound VoIP dial peer, R2 creates the inbound voice network call leg and assigns it a call ID (call leg 3). At this point, both R1 and R2 negotiate voice network capabilities and applications, if required. The originating router or gateway might request nondefault capabilities or applications. When this is the case, the terminating router or gateway must match an inbound VoIP dial peer that is configured for such capabilities or applications.

- R2 uses the dialed string to match an outbound POTS dial peer.

- After associating the incoming call setup with an outbound POTS dial peer, R2 creates an outbound POTS call leg, assigns it a call ID, and completes the call (call leg 4).

Understanding Dial Peers

When a call is placed, an edge device generates dialed digits as a way of signaling where the call should terminate. When these digits enter a router voice port, the router must decide whether the call can be routed and where the call can be sent. The router does this by searching a list of dial peers.

A *dial peer* is an addressable call endpoint. The address is called a *destination pattern* and is configured in every dial peer. Destination patterns use both explicit digits and wildcard variables to define one telephone number or range of numbers.

Dial peers define the parameters for the calls they match. For example, if a call is originating and terminating at the same site and is not crossing through slow-speed WAN links, the call can cross the local network uncompressed and without special priority. A call that originates locally and crosses the WAN link to a remote site might require compression with a specific coder-decoder (codec). In addition, this call might require that voice activity detection (VAD) be turned on and will need to receive preferential treatment by specifying a higher priority level.

Cisco voice-enabled routers support five types of dial peers, including POTS, VoIP, Voice over Frame Relay (VoFR), Voice over ATM (VoATM), and Multimedia Mail over IP (MMoIP). However, this book focuses on POTS and VoIP dial peers, which are the fundamental dial peers used in constructing a VoIP network:

- **POTS dial peers:** Connect to a traditional telephony network, such as the PSTN or a PBX, or to a telephony edge device such as a telephone or fax machine. POTS dial peers perform these functions:

    - Provide an address (telephone number or range of numbers) for the edge network or device.

    - Point to the specific voice port that connects the edge network or device.

- **VoIP dial peers:** Connect over an IP network. VoIP dial peers perform these functions:

    - Provide a destination address (telephone number or range of numbers) for the edge device located across the network.

    - Associate the destination address with the next-hop router or destination router, depending on the technology used.

In Figure 3-25, the telephony device connects to the Cisco voice-enabled router. The POTS dial-peer configuration includes the telephone number of the telephony device and the voice port to which it is attached. The router determines where to forward incoming calls for that telephone number.

The Cisco voice-enabled router VoIP dial peer is connected to the packet network. The VoIP dial-peer configuration includes the destination telephone number (or range of numbers) and the next-hop or destination voice-enabled router network address.

Follow these steps to enable a router to complete a VoIP call:

- Configure a compatible dial peer on the source router that specifies the recipient destination address.

- Configure a POTS dial peer on the recipient router that specifies which voice port the router uses to forward the voice call.

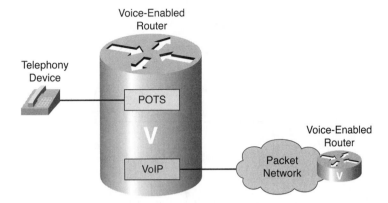

Figure 3-25 *Dial Peers*

Configuring POTS Dial Peers

Before the configuration of Cisco IOS dial peers can begin, you must have a good understanding of where the edge devices reside, what type of connections need to be made
between these devices, and what telephone numbering scheme is applied to the devices.

Follow these steps to configure POTS dial peers:

Step 1.   Configure a POTS dial peer at each router or gateway where edge telephony
                devices connect to the network.

Step 2.   Use the **destination-pattern** command in dial-peer configuration mode to
                configure the telephone number.

Step 3.   Use the **port** command in dial-peer configuration mode to specify the physi-
                cal voice port that the POTS telephone is connected to.

The dial-peer type will be specified as POTS because the edge device is directly connected to a voice port, and the signaling must be sent from this port to reach the device. Two
basic parameters need to be specified for the device: the telephone number and the voice
port. When a PBX is connecting to the voice port, a range of telephone numbers can be
specified.

Figure 3-26 shows a POTS dial peer. Example 3-9 illustrates proper POTS dial-peer configuration on the Cisco voice-enabled router shown in Figure 3-26. The **dial-peer voice 1
pots** command notifies the router that dial peer 1 is a POTS dial peer with a tag of 1. The
tag is a number that is locally significant to the router. Although the tag does not need to
match the phone number specified by the **destination-pattern** command, many administrators recommend configuring a tag that does match a dial-peer's phone number to help
make the configuration more intuitive. The **destination-pattern 7777** command notifies
the router that the attached telephony device terminates calls destined for telephone number 7777. The **port 1/0/0** command notifies the router that the telephony device is
plugged into module 1, VIC slot 0, and voice port 0.

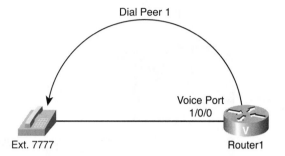

Figure 3-26   *POTS Dial Peer*

Example 3-9   *Configuration for Dial Peer 1 on Router 1*

```
Router1#configure terminal
Router1(config)#dial-peer voice 1 pots
Router1(config-dialpeer)#destination-pattern 7777
Router1(config-dialpeer)#port 1/0/0
Router1(config-dialpeer)#end
```

Practice Scenario 1: POTS Dial Peer Configuration

To practice the configuration of a POTS dial peer, consider a scenario. In this scenario, assume that a data center exists at the R1 site and executive offices at the R2 site. Using the diagram shown in Figure 3-27, create POTS dial peers for the four telephones shown.

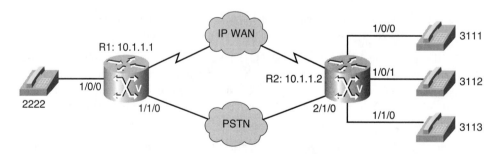

Figure 3-27   *Practice Scenario 1*

Note that three configuration commands are required for R1, and nine configuration commands are required for R2. You can write the commands in the space provided here or use a separate sheet of paper. The suggested solution follows.

R1:

_____

_____

_____

R2:

_____

_____

_____

_____

_____

_____

_____

_____

_____

Practice Scenario 1 Suggested Solution

Although your choice of dial-peer tags might vary, the following offers a suggested solution to Practice Scenario 1:

R1:

```
dial-peer voice 2222 pots
      destination-pattern 2222
      port 1/0/0
```

R2:

```
dial-peer voice 3111 pots
      destination-pattern 3111
      port 1/0/0
dial-peer voice 3112 pots
      destination-pattern 3112
      port 1/0/1
dial-peer voice 3113 pots
      destination-pattern 3113
      port 1/1/0
```

Configuring VoIP Dial Peers

The administrator must know how to identify the far-end voice-enabled device that will terminate the call. In a small network environment, the device might be the IP address of the remote device. In a large environment, identifying the device might mean pointing to a Cisco Unified Communications Manager or gatekeeper for address resolution and CAC to complete the call.

Follow these steps to configure VoIP dial peers:

Step 1. Configure the path across the network for voice data.

Step 2. Specify the dial peer as a VoIP dial peer.

Step 3. Use the **destination-pattern** command to configure a range of numbers reachable by the remote router or gateway.

Step 4. Use the **session target** command to specify the IP address of the terminating router or gateway.

Step 5. (Optional) As a best practice, use the remote device loopback address as the IP address.

The dial peer specified as a VoIP dial peer alerts the router that it must process a call according to the various dial-peer parameters. The dial peer must then send the call setup information in IP packets for transport across the network. Specified parameters might include the codec used for compression (for example, VAD) or marking the packet for priority service.

The **destination-pattern** parameter configured for this dial peer is typically a range of numbers reachable via the remote router or gateway.

Because this dial peer points to a device across the network, the router needs a destination IP address to put in the IP packet. The **session target** parameter allows the administrator to specify either an IP address of the terminating router or gateway or another device. For example, a gatekeeper or Cisco Unified Communications Manager might return an IP address of that remote terminating device.

To determine which IP address a dial peer should point to, Cisco recommends that you use a loopback address. The loopback address is always up on a router as long as the router is powered on and the interface is not administratively shut down. The reason an interface IP address is not recommended is that if the interface goes down, the call will fail, even if an alternate path to the router exists.

Figure 3-28 shows a topology needing a VoIP dial peer configured on Router1. Example 3-10 lists the proper VoIP dial-peer configuration on Router 1, which is a Cisco voice-enabled router. The **dial-peer voice 2 voip** command notifies the router that dial peer 2 is a VoIP dial peer with a tag of 2. The **destination-pattern 8888** command notifies the router that this dial peer defines an IP voice path across the network for telephone number 8888. The **session target ipv4:10.18.0.1** command defines the IP address of the router connected to the remote telephony device.

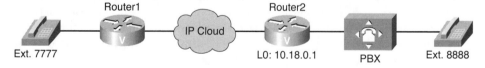

Ext 7777 is Calling 8888

Figure 3-28 *VoIP Dial Peers*

Example 3-10   *Configuration for Dial Peer 2 on Router 1*

```
Router1#configure terminal
Router1(config)#dial-peer voice 2 voip
Router1(config-dialpeer)#destination-pattern 8888
Router1(config-dialpeer)#session target ipv4:10.18.0.1
Router1(config-dialpeer)#end
```

Practice Scenario 2: VoIP Dial Peer Configuration

Create VoIP dial peers for each of the R1 and R2 sites based on the diagram presented in
Figure 3-29.

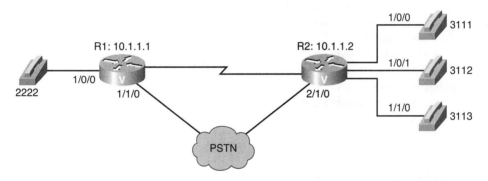

Figure 3-29   *Practice Scenario 2*

R1:

_____

_____

_____

_____

_____

_____

_____

_____

_____

R2:

_____

_____

_____

Practice Scenario 2 Suggested Solution

Although your choice of dial-peer tags might vary, the following offers a suggested solution to Practice Scenario 2:

R1:

```
dial-peer voice 3111 voip
      destination-pattern 3111
      Session target ipv4:10.1.1.2
dial-peer voice 3112 voip
      destination-pattern 3112
      Session target ipv4:10.1.1.2
dial-peer voice 3113 voip
      destination-pattern 3113
      Session target ipv4:10.1.1.2
```

R2:

```
dial-peer voice 2222 voip
      destination-pattern 2222
      Session target ipv4:10.1.1.1
```

From this practice scenario, notice how configuration intensive it would be for an administrator to configure a dial peer for each phone number in a VoIP network. Next, consider how wildcards can be used with the **destination-pattern** command to allow a single dial peer to point to multiple phone numbers.

Configuring Destination Pattern Options

The destination pattern you configure is used to match dialed digits to a dial peer. The dial peer is then used to complete the call.

When a router receives voice data, it compares the called number (the full E.164 telephone number) in the packet header with the number configured as the destination pattern for the voice-telephony peer. It also determines the dialed digits the router collects and forwards to the remote telephony interface, such as a PBX, Cisco Unified Communications Manager, or the PSTN.

Note   In the case of POTS dial peers, the router strips out the left-justified numbers that explicitly match the destination pattern. If you have configured a prefix (using the **prefix** *digits* command), the prefix is appended to the front of the remaining numbers, creating a dial string, which the router then dials. If all numbers in the destination pattern are stripped out, the user receives a dial tone.

To specify either the prefix or the full E.164 telephone number to be used for a dial peer, use the **destination-pattern** command in dial peer configuration mode, which has the following syntax:

```
destination-pattern [+] string [T]
```

Destination-pattern options include the following:

- **Plus sign (+)**: An optional character that indicates an E.164 standard number. E.164 is the International Telecommunication Union Telecommunication Standardization sector (ITU-T) recommendation for the international public telecommunication numbering plan. The plus sign in front of a destination-pattern string specifies that the string must conform to E.164.

- *string*: A series of digits specifying the E.164 or private dial-plan telephone number. The following examples show the use of special characters often found in destination pattern strings:

  - **Asterisk (*) and pound sign (#)**: An asterisk (*) and pound sign (#) appear on standard touch-tone dial pads. These characters might need to be used when passing a call to an automated application that requires these characters to signal the use of a special feature. For example, when calling an interactive voice response (IVR) system that requires a code for access, the number dialed might be 5551212888#, which would initially dial the telephone number 5551212 and input a code of 888 followed by the pound key to terminate the IVR input query.

  - **Comma (,)**: A comma (,) inserts a one-second pause between digits. The comma can be used, for example, where a 9 is dialed to signal a PBX that the call should be processed by the PSTN. The 9 is followed by a comma to give the PBX time to open a call path to the PSTN, after which the remaining digits are played out. An example of this string is 9,5551212.

  - **Period (.)**: A period (.) matches any single entered digit from 0 to 9 and is used as a wildcard. The wildcard can be used to specify a group of numbers that might be accessible via a single destination router, gateway, PBX, or Cisco Unified Communications Manager. A pattern of **200.** allows for ten uniquely addressed devices, whereas a pattern of **20..** can point to 100 devices. If one site has the numbers 2000 through 2049 and another site has the numbers 2050 through 2099, a bracket notation would be more efficient, as described next.

- **Brackets ([ ]):** Brackets ([ ]) indicate a range. A range is a sequence of characters enclosed in the brackets. Only single numeric characters from 0 through 9 are allowed in the range. In the previous example, the bracket notation could be used to specify exactly which range of numbers is accessible through each dial peer. For example, the pattern of **20[0–4].** would be used for the first site, and a pattern of **20[5–9].** would be used for the second site. Note that in both cases, a dot is used in the last digit position to represent any single digit from 0 through 9. The bracket notation offers much more flexibility in how numbers can be assigned.

- **T:** An optional control character indicating that the **destination-pattern** value is a variable-length dial string. In cases where callers might be dialing local, national, or international numbers, the destination pattern must provide for a variable-length dial plan. If a particular voice gateway has access to the PSTN for local calls and access to a transatlantic connection for international calls, calls being routed to that gateway have a varying number of dialed digits. A single dial peer with a destination pattern of .T could support the different call types. The **interdigit timeout** determines when a string of dialed digits is complete. The router continues to collect digits until there is an interdigit pause longer than the configured value, which by default is 10 seconds.

- However, the calling party can immediately terminate the interdigit timeout by entering the pound character (#), which is the default termination character. Because the default interdigit timer is set to 10 seconds, users might experience a long call-setup delay.

Note   Cisco IOS Software does not check the validity of the E.164 telephone number. It accepts any series of digits as a valid number.

Table 3-8 demonstrates the use of various destination pattern wildcards, including the period, brackets, and the .T wildcards.

Table 3-8   *Destination Pattern Options*

Destination Pattern	Matching Telephone Numbers
5550124	Matches one telephone number exactly, 5550124.
	This is typically used when a single device, such as a telephone or fax, is connected to a voice port.

Table 3-8 *Destination Pattern Options*   *(continued)*

Destination Pattern	Matching Telephone Numbers
55501[1-3].	Matches a seven-digit telephone number where the first five digits are 55501. The sixth digit can be a 1, 2, or 3, and the last digit can be any valid digit.

This type of destination pattern is used when telephone number ranges are assigned to specific sites. In this example, the destination pattern is used in a small site that does not need more than 30 numbers assigned. |
| .T | Matches any telephone number that has at least one digit and can vary in length from 1 through 32 digits total.

This destination pattern is used for a dial peer that services a variable-length dial plan, such as local, national, and international calls. It can also be used as a default destination pattern so any calls that do not match a more specific pattern will match this pattern and can be directed to an operator. |

Matching Inbound Dial Peers

When determining how inbound dial peers are matched on a router, it is important to note whether the inbound call leg is matched to a POTS or VoIP dial peer. Matching occurs in the following manner:

- Inbound POTS dial peers are associated with the incoming POTS call legs of the originating router or gateway.

- Inbound VoIP dial peers are associated with the incoming VoIP call legs of the terminating router or gateway.

Three information elements sent in the call setup message are matched against four configurable **dial-peer** command attributes. Table 3-9 describes the three call setup information elements.

Table 3-9 *Call Setup Information Elements*

Call Setup Element	Description
Called number dialed number identification service	This is the call-destination dial string, and it is derived from the ISDN setup message or channel associated signaling (CAS) DNIS.
Calling number automatic number identification	This is a number string that represents the origin, and it is derived from the ISDN setup message or CAS ANI. The ANI is also referred to as the calling line ID (CLID).
Voice port	This represents the POTS physical voice port.

The four configurable **dial-peer** command attributes are detailed in Table 3-10.

Table 3-10 *Command Attributes for the* **dial-peer** *Command*

dial-peer Command Attribute	Description
incoming called-number	Defines the called number or DNIS string.
answer-address	Defines the originating calling number or ANI string.
destination-pattern	Uses the calling number (originating or ANI string) to match the incoming call leg to an inbound dial peer.
Port	Attempts to match the configured dial peer port to the voice port associated with the incoming call (POTS dial peers only).

When the Cisco IOS router or gateway receives a call setup request, it looks for a dial-peer match for the incoming call. This is not digit-by-digit matching. Instead, the router uses the full digit string received in the setup request for matching against the configured dial peers.

The router or gateway matches call setup element parameters in the following order:

1. The router or gateway attempts to match the called number of the call setup request with the configured **incoming called-number** of each dial peer.

2. If a match is not found, the router or gateway attempts to match the calling number of the call setup request with the **answer-address** of each dial peer.

3. If a match is not found, the router or gateway attempts to match the calling number of the call setup request to the **destination-pattern** of each dial peer.

4. The voice port uses the voice port number associated with the incoming call setup request to match the inbound call leg to the configured dial peer **port** parameter.

5. If multiple dial peers have the same port configured, the router or gateway matches the first dial peer added to the configuration.

6. If a match is not found in the previous steps, dial peer 0 is matched.

Because call setups always include DNIS information, you should use the **incoming called-number** command for inbound dial peer matching. Configuring **incoming called-number** is useful for a company that has a central call center providing support for a number of different products. Purchasers of each product get a unique toll-free number to call for support. All support calls are routed to the same trunk group destined for the call center. When a call comes in, the computer telephony system uses the DNIS to flash the appropriate message on the computer screen of the agent to whom the call is routed. The agent will then know how to customize the greeting when answering the call.

The calling number ANI with **answer-address** is useful when you want to match calls based on the originating calling number. For example, when a company has international customers who require foreign-language-speaking agents to answer the call, the call can be routed to the appropriate agent based on the country of call origin.

You must use the calling number ANI with **destination-pattern** when the dial peers are set up for two-way calling. In a corporate environment, the head office and remote sites must be connected. As long as each site has a VoIP dial peer configured to point to each site, inbound calls from each remote site will match against that dial peer.

Characteristics of the Default Dial Peer

When a matching inbound dial peer is not found, the router resorts to a virtual dial peer called the *default dial peer*. The default dial peer is often referred to as *dial peer 0*.

Note   Default dial peers are used for inbound matches only. They are not used to match outbound calls that do not have a dial peer configured.

Dial peer 0 for inbound VoIP peers has the following characteristics:

- Any codec
- IP precedence 0
- VAD enabled
- No RSVP support
- **fax-rate** service

For inbound POTS peers, dial peer 0 is configured with the **no ivr application** command.

You cannot change the default configuration for dial peer 0. Default dial peer 0 fails to negotiate nondefault capabilities or services. When the default dial peer is matched on a

VoIP call, the call leg that is set up in the inbound direction uses any supported codec for voice compression that is based on the requested codec capability coming from the source router. When a default dial peer is matched, the voice path in one direction might have different parameters from the voice path in the return direction. This might cause one side of the connection to report good quality voice while the other side reports poor quality voice. For example, the outbound dial peer has VAD disabled, but the inbound call leg is matched against the default dial peer, which has VAD enabled. VAD would be on in one direction and off in the return direction.

When the default dial peer is matched on an inbound POTS call leg, there is no default IVR application with the port. As a result, the user gets a dial tone and proceeds with dialed digits. Interestingly, the default dial peer cannot be viewed using **show** commands.

In Figure 3-30, only one-way dialing is configured. Example 3-11 and Example 3-12 illustrate the configuration for this topology. The caller at extension 7777 can call extension 8888 because a VoIP dial peer is configured on Router 1 to route the call across the network. However, no VoIP dial peer is configured on Router 2 to point calls across the network toward Router 1. Therefore, no dial peer exists on Router 2 that will match the calling number of extension 7777 on the inbound call leg. If no incoming dial peer matches the calling number, the inbound call leg automatically matches to a default dial peer (POTS or VoIP).

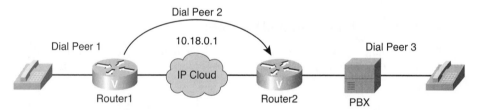

Figure 3-30 *Default Dial Peer 0*

Example 3-11 *Router 1 Configuration*

```
Router1(config)#dial-peer voice 1 pots
Router1(config-dial-peer)#destination-pattern 7777
Router1(config-dial-peer)#port 1/0/0
Router1(config-dial-peer)#exit
Router1(config)#dial-peer voice 2 voip
Router1(config-dial-peer)#destination-pattern 8888
Router1(config-dial-peer)#session target ipv4:10.18.0.1
```

Example 3-12 *Router 2 Configuration*

```
Router2(config)#dial-peer voice 3 pots
Router2(config-dial-peer)#destination-pattern 8888
Router2(config-dial-peer)#port 1/1/0
```

Matching Outbound Dial Peers

Outbound dial-peer matching is completed on a digit-by-digit basis. Therefore, the router or gateway checks for dial-peer matches after receiving each digit and then routes the call when a full match is made.

The router or gateway matches outbound dial peers in the following order:

Step 1.   The router or gateway uses the dial peer **destination-pattern** command to determine how to route the call.

Step 2.   The **destination-pattern** command routes the call in the following manner:

- On POTS dial peers, the **port** command forwards the call.

- On VoIP dial peers, the **session target** command forwards the call.

Step 3.   Use the **show dialplan number** *string* command to determine which dial peer is matched to a specific dialed string. This command displays all matching dial peers in the order that they are used.

In Example 3-13, dial peer 1 matches any digit string that does not match the other dial peers more specifically. Dial peer 2 matches any seven-digit number in the 30 and 40 range of numbers starting with 55501. Dial peer 3 matches any seven-digit number in the 20 range of numbers starting with 55501. Dial peer 4 matches the specific number 5550124 only. When the number 5550124 is dialed, dial peers 1, 3, and 4 all match that number, but dial peer 4 places that call because it contains the most specific destination pattern.

Example 3-13   *Matching Outbound Dial Peers*

```
Router(config)#dial-peer voice 1 voip
Router(config-dial-peer)#destination-pattern .T
Router(config-dial-peer)#session target ipv4:10.1.1.1

Router(config)#dial-peer voice 2 voip
Router(config-dial-peer)#destination-pattern 55501[3-4].
Router(config-dial-peer)#session target ipv4:10.2.2.2

Router(config)#dial-peer voice 3 voip
Router(config-dial-peer)#destination-pattern 555012.
Router(config-dial-peer)#session target ipv4:10.3.3.3

Router(config)#dial-peer voice 4 voip
Router(config-dial-peer)#destination-pattern 5550124
Router(config-dial-peer)#session target ipv4:10.4.4.4
```

Summary

The main topics covered in this chapter are the following:

- A VoIP network has seven typical call types.

- A local call is handled entirely by the router and does not travel over an external network.

- On-net calls can be routed through one or more voice-enabled routers, but the calls remain on the same network.

- An off-net call occurs when a user dials an access code (such as 9) from a telephone directly connected to a voice-enabled router or PBX to gain access to the PSTN.

- Voice port call types include local, on-net, off-net, PLAR, PBX to PBX, intercluster trunk, and on-net to off-net calls.

- Voice ports on routers and access servers emulate physical telephony switch connections.

- Analog voice port interfaces connect routers in packet-based networks to analog two-wire or four-wire analog circuits in telephony networks.

- FXS, FXO, and E&M ports have several configuration parameters.

- CAMA is used for 911 and E911 services.

- DID service enables callers to dial an extension directly on a PBX or packet voice system.

- You can set a number of timers and timing parameters for fine-tuning a voice port.

- The **show**, **debug**, and **test** commands are used for monitoring and troubleshooting voice functions in the network.

- Dial peers are used to identify call source and destination endpoints and to define the characteristics applied to each call leg in the call connection.

- An end-to-end voice call consists of four call legs.

- A dial peer is an addressable call endpoint.

- POTS dial peers retain the characteristics of a traditional telephony network connection.

- When a matching inbound dial peer is not found, the router resorts to the default dial peer.

- The destination pattern associates a telephone number with a given dial peer.

- When determining how inbound dial peers are matched on a router, it is important to note whether the inbound call leg is matched to a POTS or VoIP dial peer.

- Outbound dial-peer matching is completed on a digit-by-digit basis.

Chapter Review Questions

The answers to these review questions are in the appendix.

1. If a client picked up a customer service handset and was automatically connected to a customer service representative without dialing any digits, what kind of call would it be?

    a. Intercluster trunk call

    b. PBX-to-PBX call

    c. On-net call

    d. PLAR call

2. Which configuration parameter would you change to set the dial tone, busy tone, and ringback tone on an FXS port?

    a. Cptone

    b. Ring frequency

    c. Ring cadence

    d. Description

    e. Signal

    f. PSQM

3. What is the default (and most commonly used) method of access signaling used on E&M voice ports?

    a. Immediate-start

    b. Wink-start

    c. Delay-start

    d. Loop-start

4. Which situation most likely requires changes to the FXS port default settings?

    a. The caller and the called party are in different parts of the country.

    b. The caller and the called party are in different countries.

    c. The connection is a trunk to a PBX.

    d. The FXS port configuration does not match the local PSTN switch configuration.

5. Which two conditions can be checked by using the **show voice port** *port* command for an FXS port? (Choose 2.)

   a. Whether the port is using ground-start or loop-start signaling

   b. The ring frequency configured for the port

   c. The E&M signaling type configured for the port

   d. The number of rings after which the port will answer

6. When an end-to-end call is established across a VoIP network, how many inbound call legs are associated with the call?

   a. One

   b. Two

   c. Three

   d. Four

7. A POTS dial peer performs which of the following two functions? (Choose 2.)

   a. Provides a phone number for the edge network or device

   b. Provides a destination address for the edge device located across the network

   c. Routes a call across a network

   d. Identifies the specific voice port that connects the edge network or device

8. When configuring a VoIP dial peer, which command is used to specify the address of the terminating router or gateway?

   a. destination-port

   b. destination-pattern

   c. session target

   d. destination address

   e. dial-peer terminal

9. What happens if there is no matching dial peer for an outbound call?

   a. The default dial peer is used.

   b. Dial peer 0 is used.

   c. The POTS dial peer is used.

   d. The call is dropped.

10. Which dial-peer configuration command attempts to match the calling number (that is, the ANI string)?

    a. destination-pattern

    b. port

    c. answer-address

    d. incoming called-number

After reading this chapter, you should be able to perform the following tasks:

■   Describe the various digital interfaces and how to configure them.

■   Describe QSIG and how to enable QSIG support.

CHAPTER 4

Performing Call Signaling over Digital Voice Ports

Enterprise networks often use digital circuits, in contrast to analog circuits, when interconnecting their Voice over IP (VoIP) network to traditional telephony environments, such as the public switched telephone network (PSTN) or a private branch exchange (PBX). One major advantage of using digital circuits is the economies of scale made possible by transporting multiple conversations over a single circuit. For example, a digital T1 circuit using Channel Associated Signaling (CAS) (which is described in this chapter) can carry 24 simultaneous voice conversations on a single circuit.

Many enterprises also have the need to interconnect PBX systems, and these PBXs might be from different manufacturers. In many cases, two PBXs from different manufacturers can be interconnected via a digital circuit. However, a common signaling language needs to be spoken between the PBXs to communicate various call state information. Fortunately, if both PBXs support the Q Signaling (QSIG) protocol, they can use QSIG as their common signaling protocol. This chapter explores QSIG theory and configuration.

Introducing Digital Voice Ports

Digital trunks are used to connect to the PSTN, to a PBX, or to the WAN and are widely available worldwide. In some areas, CAS trunks are the only connections available. Basic rate interface (BRI) and primary rate interface (PRI) trunks are very common when connecting a voice gateway to the PSTN. This section maps out the various digital interfaces and explains how to implement and verify digital trunks.

Digital voice ports are found at the intersection of a packet voice network and a digital, circuit-switched telephone network. The digital voice port interfaces that connect the router or access server to T1 or E1 lines pass voice data and signaling between the packet network and the circuit-switched network.

Three types of digital voice circuits are supported on Cisco voice gateways:

- **T1:** Uses Time Division Multiplexing (TDM) to transmit digital data over 24 voice channels using CAS.

- **E1:** Uses TDM to transmit digital data over 30 voice channels using either CAS or Common Channel Signaling (CCS).

- **ISDN:** A circuit-switched telephone network system using CCS. Variations of Integrated Services Digital Network (ISDN) circuits include the following:

  - **BRI:** 2 B (Bearer) channels and 1 D (Delta) channel

  - **T1 PRI:** 23 B channels and 1 D channel

  - **E1 PRI:** 30 B channels and 1 D channel

Digital Trunks

Digital voice ports are used to interconnect gateways or PBX systems to other gateways, PBX systems, or the PSTN. A trunk is a single physical or logical interface that contains several logical interfaces and connects to a single destination.

There are two aspects to consider when signaling on digital lines. One aspect is the actual information about line and device states that is transmitted, and the second aspect is the method that is used to transmit the information on the digital lines.

The actual information about line and device states is communicated over digital lines using signaling methods that emulate the methods used in analog circuit-switched networks: Foreign Exchange Station (FXS), Foreign Exchange Office (FXO), and RecEive and TransMit (E&M).

For signaling to pass between a packet network and a circuit-switched network, both networks must use the same type of signaling. The voice ports on Cisco routers and access servers can be configured to match the signaling of most central offices (CO) and PBXs. Table 4-1 lists some of the common digital circuit options.

Table 4-1   *Digital Trunks*

Type	Circuit Option		Comments
Digital	T1/E1 CAS		Analog signaling over digital T1/E1
	E1 R2		Can provide Automatic Number Identification (ANI)
	ISDN	T1 PRI	More services than CAS
		E1 PRI	Separate data channel (D channel)
			Common on modern PBXs
		PRI NFAS	Multiple ISDN PRI interfaces controlled by a single D channel
			Backup D channel can be configured
		BRI	Mostly for Europe, Middle East, and Africa
		QSIG	Created for interoperation of PBXs from different vendors
			Rich in supplementary services

The T1, E1, or ISDN lines that connect a telephony network to the digital voice ports on a router or access server contain channels for voice calls. A T1 or ISDN PRI line contains 24 full-duplex channels or timeslots, and an E1 line contains 30. The signal on each channel is transmitted at 64 kbps, a standard known as digital signal level 0 (DS0). The channels are known as DS0 channels. The **ds0-group** command creates a logical voice port (a DS0 group) from some or all of the DS0 channels, which allows you to address those channels easily, as a group, using voice-port configuration commands.

The method used to transmit the information describes the way that the emulated analog signaling is transmitted over digital lines.

Digital lines use two types of signaling:

- **CAS:** Takes place within the voice channel itself.

- **CCS:** Sends signaling information over a dedicated channel.

Two main types of digital trunks with channel associated signaling exist, as illustrated in Figure 4-1:

- **T1 CAS trunk:** This type of circuit allows analog signaling via a digital T1 circuit. Many CAS variants operate over analog and digital interfaces. A common digital interface is used where each grouping of T1 frames (known as a *super frame* or an *extended super frame*) includes two or four dedicated signaling bits. The type of signaling most commonly used with T1 CAS is E&M signaling. In addition to setting up and tearing down calls, CAS provides the receipt and capture of dialed number identification (DNIS) and ANI information, which are used to support authentication and other functions. The main disadvantage of CAS signaling is its use of user bandwidth to perform these signaling functions.

- **E1 R2 trunk:** R2 signaling is a CAS system developed in the 1960s that is still in use today in Europe, Latin America, Australia, and Asia. R2 signaling exists in several country versions or variants in an international version called Consultative Committee for International Telegraph and Telephone (CCITT-R2). The R2 signaling specifications are contained in International Telecommunication Union Telecommunication Standardization sector (ITU-T) Recommendations Q.400 through Q.490. R2 also provides ANI.

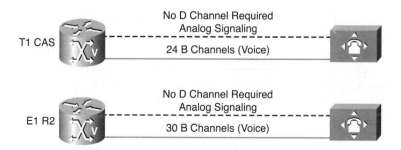

Figure 4-1   *Voice Ports*

T1 CAS

T1s have been around since early voice networks. They were developed as a means of carrying multiple calls across one copper loop. Because the copper loop could carry much more bandwidth than the 4000 Hz required for voice transmission, they first used frequency-division multiplexing (FDM) to transmit 24 calls across a single copper loop. Currently, T1 circuits use TDM to transmit digital data (1s and 0s) instead of the old analog signals.

A single digital voice channel requires 64 kbps of bandwidth. This is calculated using the following formula:

$$64 \text{ kbps} = 8000 \text{ samples/sec} \times 8 \text{ bits/sample} = 64{,}000 \text{ bits/sec}$$

This 64 kbps voice channel is also known as DS-0. With 24 voice channels at 64 kbps per channel, a T1 represents 1.536 Mbps of data. Add an additional 8 kbps for framing, and the total speed of a T1 circuit comes to 1.544 Mbps.

T1 CAS uses a digital T1 circuit together with in-band CAS. This is done by using bits in the actual voice channel to transmit signaling information. CAS is sometimes called robbed-bit signaling because user bandwidth is robbed by the network for signaling. A bit is taken from every sixth frame of voice data to communicate on- or off-hook status, wink, ground start, dialed digits, and other information about the call.

T1 CAS uses the same signaling types available for analog trunks: loop start, ground start, and E&M variants such as wink-start, delay-start, and immediate-start. There are also various feature groups available when you use E&M. Here are some common feature groups:

- **E&M FG-B:** Inbound and outbound DNIS, inbound ANI (only on Cisco AS5x00)

- **E&M FG-D:** Inbound and outbound DNIS, inbound ANI

- **E&M FG-D EANA:** Inbound and outbound DNIS, outbound ANI

Figure 4-2 shows CAS with the T1 Super Frame (SF) format. The top row of boxes represents a single T1 frame with 24 time slots of 8 bits each. An additional bit is added at the end of each frame that is used to synchronize the SF. A sequence of 12 T1 frames makes up one SF. CAS is implemented by bit-robbing in frames 6 and 12 in this sequence. The bottom row of boxes represents T1 frames 6 and 12. The least significant bit of each voice channel is robbed, leaving 7 bits for voice data.

Extended Super Frame (ESF) format, as depicted in Figure 4-3, was developed as an upgrade to SF and is now dominant in public and private networks. Both formats retain the basic frame structure of one framing bit followed by 192 data bits. However, ESF repurposes the use of the F bit. In ESF, of the total 8000 F bits used in T1, 2000 are used for framing, 2000 are used for cyclic redundancy check (CRC) for error checking only, and 4000 are used as an intelligent supervisory channel to control functions end to end (such as loopback and error reporting).

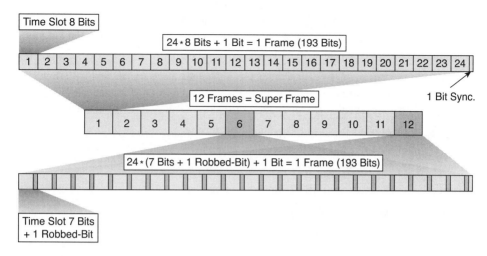

Figure 4-2 *T1 CAS Super Frame Format*

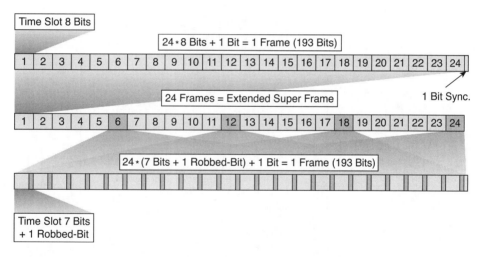

Figure 4-3 *T1 CAS Extended Super Frame Format*

E1 R2 CAS

An E1 circuit is similar to a T1 circuit. It is a TDM circuit that carries several DS-0s in one connection. E1 circuits are widely used in Europe, Asia, and Central and South America.

One big difference between an E1 and a T1 is that an E1 bundles 32 time slots instead of 24. This results in a bandwidth of 2.048 Mbps. With an E1, one time slot is used for framing and one is used for signaling. This leaves 30 time slots available for user data.

E1 digital circuits can be deployed using R2 signaling. These trunks are called E1 R2 trunks. To understand how E1 R2 signaling works, you need to understand the E1 multiframe format, which is used with E1 R2.

A multiframe consists of 16 consecutive 256-bit frames. Each frame carries 32 time slots. The first time slot is used exclusively for frame synchronization. Time slots 2 to 16 and 18 to 32 carry the actual voice traffic, and time slot 17 is used for R2 signaling.

The first frame in an E1 multiframe includes the multiframe format information in time slot 17. Frames 2 to 16 include the signaling information, each frame containing the signaling for two voice time slots.

Using this signaling method, E1R2 supports inbound and outbound DNIS and ANI.

Figure 4-4 shows the signaling concept used by E1 R2.

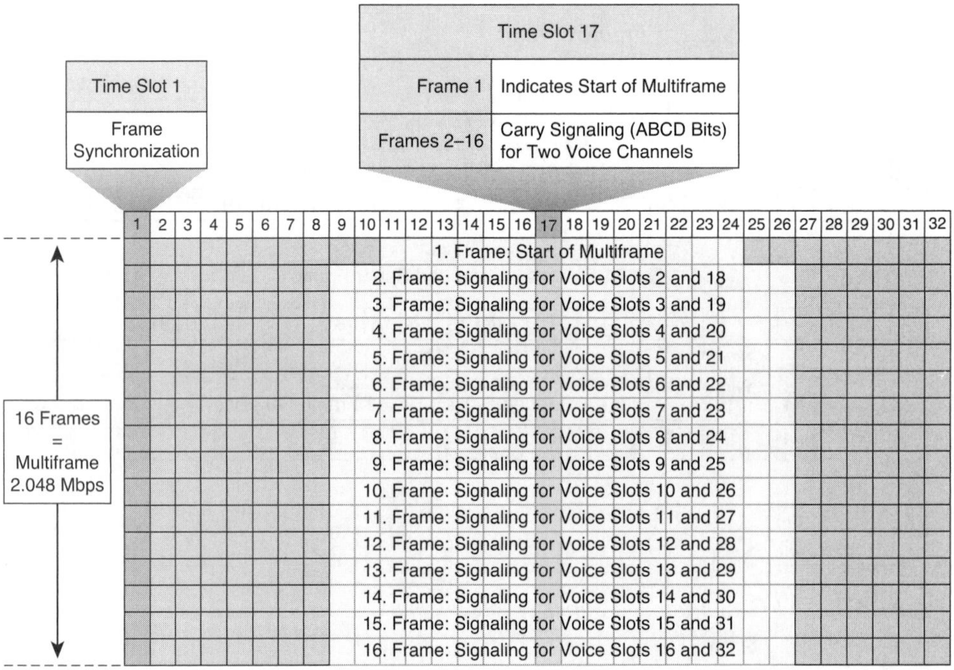

Figure 4-4   *E1 R2 CAS*

Time slot 17 is used for signaling, and each of its frames carries information for two voice time slots. This results in the following frame allocation for signaling:

- **1. Frame, Time slot 17:** Declares the multiframe

- **2. Frame, Time slot 17:** Signaling for time slots 2 and 18

- **3. Frame, Time slot 17:** Signaling for time slots 3 and 19

- **4. Frame, Time slot 17:** Signaling for time slots 4 and 20
- **5. Frame, Time slot 17:** Signaling for time slots 5 and 21
- **6. Frame, Time slot 17:** Signaling for time slots 6 and 22
- **7. Frame, Time slot 17:** Signaling for time slots 7 and 23
- **8. Frame, Time slot 17:** Signaling for time slots 8 and 24
- **9. Frame, Time slot 17:** Signaling for time slots 9 and 25
- **10. Frame, Time slot 17:** Signaling for time slots 10 and 26
- **11. Frame, Time slot 17:** Signaling for time slots 11 and 27
- **12. Frame, Time slot 17:** Signaling for time slots 12 and 28
- **13. Frame, Time slot 17:** Signaling for time slots 13 and 29
- **14. Frame, Time slot 17:** Signaling for time slots 14 and 30
- **15. Frame, Time slot 17:** Signaling for time slots 15 and 31
- **16. Frame, Time slot 17:** Signaling for time slots 16 and 32

ISDN

Another protocol used for digital trunks is ISDN. ISDN is a circuit-switched telephone network system designed to allow digital transmission of voice and data over ordinary telephone copper wires, resulting in better quality and higher speeds than is available with the PSTN system.

ISDN comprises digital telephony and data-transport services offered by regional telephone carriers. ISDN involves the digitization of the telephone network, which permits voice, data, text, graphics, music, video, and other source material to be transmitted over existing telephone wires. The emergence of ISDN represents an effort to standardize subscriber services, user/network interfaces, and network and internetwork capabilities.

ISDN Services

In contrast to the CAS and R2 signaling, which provide only DNIS, ISDN offers additional supplementary services such as Call Waiting and Do Not Disturb (DND). ISDN applications include high-speed image applications (such as Group IV facsimile), additional telephone lines in homes to serve the telecommuting industry, high-speed file transfer, and video conferencing. Voice service is also an application for ISDN.

ISDN Media Types

Cisco routing devices support ISDN BRI and ISDN PRI. Both media types use B channels and D channels. The B channels carry user data. The D channel, in its role as signal carrier for the B channels, directs the CO switch to send incoming calls to particular timeslots on the Cisco access server or router. It also identifies the call as a circuit-switched digital call or an analog modem call. Circuit-switched digital calls are relayed directly to the ISDN processor in the router. Analog modem calls are decoded and then sent to the onboard modems. Figure 4-5 illustrates three sample ISDN installation options.

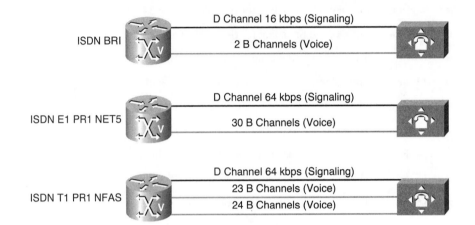

Figure 4-5   *ISDN Installation Options*

ISDN BRI, referred to as "2 B + D," has the following characteristics:

- Two 64-kbps B channels carry voice or data for a maximum transmission speed of 128 kbps.

- One 16-kbps D channel carries signaling traffic—that is, instructions about how to handle each of the B channels, although it can support user data transmission under certain circumstances.

The D channel signaling protocol comprises Layers 1 through 3 of the Open Systems Interconnection (OSI) reference model. BRI also provides for framing control and other overhead, bringing its total bit rate to 192 kbps.

The BRI physical layer specification is ITU-T I.430. BRI is very common in Europe and is also available in North America. BRI allows up to two simultaneous calls.

ISDN PRI, referred to as "23 B + D" or "30 B + D," has the following characteristics:

- 23 B channels (in North America and Japan) or 30 B channels (in the rest of the world) carry voice or data, yielding a total bit rate of 1.544 Mbps and 2.048 Mbps, respectively.

- One 64-kbps D channel carries signaling traffic.

The PRI physical layer specification is ITU-T Standards Section I.431.

Note The PRI interface is economically preferable to BRI because an interface card supporting PRI is usually already in place on modern PBXs.

Following are worldwide standards for PRI:

- **T1-PRI:** Use this interface to designate North American ISDN PRI with 23 B channels and one CCS channel.

- **E1-PRI:** Use this interface to designate European ISDN PRI with 30 B channels, one CCS channel, and one framing channel.

- **ISDN-PRI Nonfacility Associated Signaling (NFAS):** ISDN NFAS enables a single D channel to control multiple ISDN PRIs on a chassis. This D channel functions as the primary channel with the option of having another D channel in the group as a backup. After you have configured the channelized controllers for ISDN NFAS, you need to configure only the NFAS primary D channel. Its configuration is distributed to all the members of the associated NFAS group. The benefit of PRI NFAS is it frees the B channel by using a single D channel to control multiple PRI interfaces. One B channel on each additional interface is free to carry other traffic.

- **Fractional PRI:** The term fractional PRI has different meanings in different parts of the world. One meaning indicates multiple PRI groups (bearer channels [B channel] and associated D channel) on the same T1/E1 interface. Because the NM-HDV supports only a single D channel per T1/E1, the PRI feature does not support this definition of fractional PRI. However, the other version of the term indicates the capability to define a single D channel for each interface with less than 23/31 B channels associated with it. This definition of fractional PRI is supported on Cisco voice gateways.

BRI and PRI Interfaces

Table 4-2 compares the capabilities of BRI and PRI interfaces.

Table 4-2 *BRI and PRI Interfaces*

Capability	BRI	T1 PRI	E1 PRI
B-Channels	2×64 kbps	23×64 kbps	30×64 kbps
D-Channels	1×16 kbps	1×64 kbps	1×64 kbps
Framing	16 kbps	8 kbps	64 kbps
Total Data Rate	160 kbps	1.544 Mbps	2.048 Mbps
Framing	NT, TE Frame	SF, ESF	Multiframe
Line Coding	2B1Q or 4B3T	AMI or B8ZS	HDB3
Country	World	North America, Japan	Europe, Australia

Using ISDN for voice traffic has these benefits:

■ ISDN is perfect for G.711 pulse code modulation (PCM) because each B channel is a full 64 kbps with no robbed bits.

■ ISDN has a built-in call control protocol known as ITU-T Q.931.

■ ISDN can convey standards-based voice features, such as speed dialing, automated operator services, call waiting, call forwarding, and geographic analysis of customer databases.

■ ISDN supports standards-based enhanced dial-up capabilities, such as Group 4 (G4) fax and audio channels.

With ISDN, user data is separated from signaling data. User data, such as the payload from a digitized phone call, goes to a 64-kbps B channel, and signaling data, such as a call setup message, goes to a D channel. A single D channel supports multiple B channels, which is why ISDN service is known as CCS.

The *drop and insert* capability allows for dynamic multiplexing of B channels between different interfaces. This feature is available only if all interfaces use a common clock source, as is the case with Integrated Service Routers (ISRs).

Figure 4-6 shows an example of the drop and insert feature. The channels of an ISDN PRI connection from an Internet service provider (ISP) are split up. Twenty-one channels are routed to another PRI interface of the router connected to a PBX, and two channels are routed to a BRI interface connected to an access server.

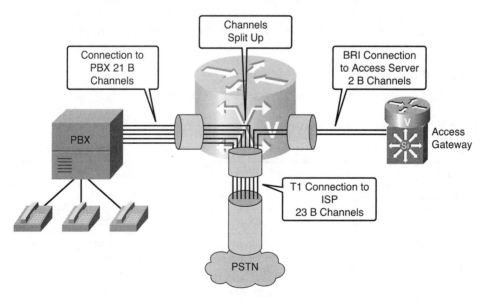

Figure 4-6   *Drop and Insert*

ISDN Signaling

ISDN uses Q.921 as its Layer 2 signaling protocol and Q.931 as its Layer 3 signaling protocol.

Q.921

Layer 2 of the ISDN signaling protocol is Link Access Procedure, D channel (LAPD). LAPD is similar to High-Level Data Link Control (HDLC) and Link Access Procedure, Balanced (LAPB). As the expansion of the LAPD acronym indicates, this layer is used across the D channel to ensure that control and signaling information flows and is received properly. The LAPD frame format is very similar to that of HDLC. Like HDLC, LAPD uses supervisory information and unnumbered frames. The LAPD protocol is formally specified in ITU-T Q.920 and ITU-T Q.921. The Terminal Endpoint Identifier (TEI) field identifies either a single terminal or multiple terminals. A TEI of all 1s indicates a broadcast.

Q.931

Two Layer 3 specifications are used for ISDN signaling: ITU-T I.450 (also known as ITU-T Q.930) and ITU-T I.451 (also known as ITU-T Q.931). Together, these protocols support user-to-user, circuit-switched (the B channels), and packet-switched (the D channel) connections. A variety of call-establishment, call-termination, information, and miscellaneous messages are specified, including SETUP, CONNECT, RELEASE, USER INFORMATION, CANCEL, STATUS, and DISCONNECT. These messages are functionally similar to those provided by the X.25 protocol.

Because ISDN message types might influence the function of a BRI or PRI trunk configuration, you should examine the messages that are part of the Q.931 packet structure and see how ISDN carries out the signaling function. Figure 4-7 illustrates the format of an ISDN frame.

8 n	7	6	5	4	3	2	1
Protocol Discriminator							
0	0	0	0	Length of Reference Call Value			
Flag	Call Reference Value						
0	Message Type						
IEs as Required							

Figure 4-7   *ISDN Frame Format*

ISDN signaling takes place in the D channel and uses a message-oriented protocol that supports call control signaling and packet data. In its role as signal carrier for the B channels, the D channel directs the CO switch to send incoming calls to particular time slots on the Cisco access server or router.

Following are the components of the ISDN frame that transmit these instructions:

■ **Protocol discriminator:** This is the protocol used to encode the remainder of the layer.

■ **Length of call reference value:** This defines the length of the next field. The call reference might be one or two bytes (octet) long, depending on the size of the value being encoded.

■ **Flag:** This is set to zero (0) for messages sent by the party that allocated the call reference value. Otherwise, it is set to one (1).

■ **Call reference value:** This is an arbitrary value that is allocated for the duration of the specific session. This value identifies the call between the device maintaining the call and the ISDN switch.

■ **Message type:** This identifies the message type (for example, SETUP) that determines what additional information is required and allowed. The message type might be one or more octets. When there is more than one octet, the first octet is coded as eight 0s.

■ **ISDN Information Element (IE):** Most D-channel messages include additional information needed for call processing, such as the calling party number, called party number, and CID. The additional information in a message is passed in information elements.

ISDN sends instructions in Layer 3 messages that are put into Layer 2 frames and are finally time-multiplexed onto a medium with either a BRI or a PRI Layer 1 line-coding specification.

A depiction of D-channel messages is shown in Figure 4-8. These messages allow complete control over call establishment and clearing, network maintenance, and the passing of other call-related information between switches.

The additional information required by an ISDN message is passed in IEs and varies depending on the message type, the action being performed, and the connected equipment. Mandatory and optional IEs for D-channel messages are defined in ITU-T Q.931.

An IE can be a single byte or several bytes, and by reading the message, the switch can determine this information. For example, in octet 1 of the IE, if bit 8, or the extension bit, is 0, the IE is of a variable length. If the bit is 1, the IE is a single byte.

The information contained in octet 3 is the coding standard and the location. Tables 4-3 and 4-4 provide the possible content of these fields.

The ISDN Protocol Stack

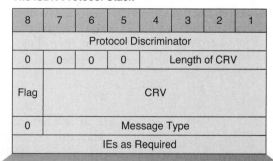

Typical Format of a Variable-Length IE:

Octet	8	7	6	5	4	3	2	1
1	0	IE Identifier						
2	Length of IEs							
3	1	Coding Standard		0	Location			
4	1	IEs (Multiple Bytes)						

Figure 4-8 *ISDN Protocol Stack*

Table 4-3 *Coding Standard*

Bit Sequence	Meaning
00	ITU standardized coding
11	Standard specific to the location field

Table 4-4 *Location*

Bit Sequence	Meaning
0000	User
0001	Private network serving the local user
0010	Public network serving the local user
0011	Transit network
0100	Public network serving the remote user
0101	Remote private network
0111	International network
1010	Network beyond the interworking point

A called number is passed to the PSTN by an IE. The IE contains bytes describing the numbering plan and the type of number. Typically, the numbering type is not changed. However, there might be times when a network administrator elects to have a specific gateway handle all international calls. If this connection to the PSTN is an ISDN PRI, the IE must tell the PSTN that the called number is in international format.

ISDN Messages

ISDN signaling is carried out by messages that are sent between endpoints on the D channel. The Message Type is a single byte (octet) that indicates what type of message is being sent or received. Four general categories of messages might be present: Call Establishment, Call Information, Call Clearing, and Miscellaneous. Generally, the most useful messages to understand are the Call Establishment and Call Clearing messages. The most common messages are listed in Table 4-5.

Table 4-5 *ISDN Messages*

Message Type	Binary Value	Message Name
000 Call Establishment	00001	ALERTing
	00010	CALL PROCeeding
	00011	PROGress
	00101	SETUP
	00111	CONNect
	01101	SETUP ACKnowledge
	01111	CONNect ACKnowledge
001 Call Information	00000	USER INFOrmation
	00001	SUSPend REJect
	00010	RESume REJect
	00101	SUSPend
	00110	RESume
	01101	SUSPend ACKnowledge
	01110	RESume ACKnowledge
010 Call Clearing	00101	DISConnect
	00110	Restart
	01101	RELease
	01110	Restart ACKnowledge
	11010	RELease COMplete

Table 4-5   *ISDN Messages*   *(continued)*

Message Type	Binary Value	Message Name
011 Miscellaneous	00000	SEGment
	00010	FACility
	01110	NOTIFY
	10101	STATUS ENQuiry
	11001	Congestion Control
	11011	INFOrmation
	11101	STATUS

Table 4-6 provides a list of message types and the IEs that can be associated with each message.

Table 4-6   *Most Common Message Types and Associated IEs*

Message Type	IEs Associated with Message
ALERTing	Bearer capability, CID, Progress indicator, Display, Signal, Higher layer compatibility
CALL PROCeeding	Bearer capability, CID, Progress indicator, Display, Higher layer compatibility
SETUP	Sending complete, Repeat indicator, Bearer capability, CID, Progress indicator, Network specific facilities, Display, Keypad facility, Signal, Calling party number, Calling party sub address, Called party number, Called party sub address, Transit network selection, Repeat indicator, Lower layer compatibility, Higher layer compatibility
CONNect	Bearer capability, CID, Progress indicator, Display, Date/time, Signal, Lower layer compatibility, Higher layer compatibility
SETUP ACKnowledge	CID, Progress indicator, Display, Signal
CONNect ACKnowledge	Display, Signal
DISConnect	Cause, Progress indicator, Display, Signal
RELease	Cause, Display, Signal
RELease COMplete	Cause, Display, Signal
STATUS ENQuiry	Display
STATUS	Cause, Call state, Display

ISDN Information Elements

Each type of message has Mandatory and Optional IEs associated with it. The Information Element is identified with a single octet. Although a few single octet IEs exist, most have multiple octets associated with them.

A study of all available IEs is beyond the scope of this book. However, commonly used IEs are listed in Table 4-7. For further details, many public references are available on the Internet. For this section, the cause, facility, progress, and display IEs are reviewed. They represent the information most in demand in telephony systems and, therefore, most important in the communications between the voice gateway and PBX or PSTN. Figure 4-9 illustrates the structure of common information elements.

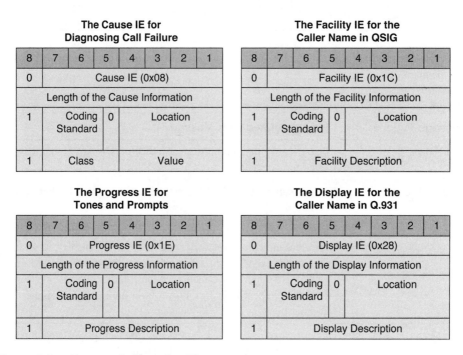

Figure 4-9   *Common Information Elements*

Cause IE

The cause IE provides one or more octets that might help in diagnosing network or customer premises equipment (CPE) problems. When a call is terminated, a cause ID indicates the reason for the termination. Both sides can generate a cause ID, and cause IDs are created for every call. When an ISDN problem occurs in the network, the cause value, shown in octet 4 in Figure 4-9, represents useful debug information in the ISDN protocol log. The telephone company equipment translates these values to associated phrases. Cause messages are classified as normal events, resource or service availability, message validity, protocol error, or interworking. The most common phrases are listed in Table 4-8.

Facility IE

Supplemental services are invoked by sending facility IEs in a facility message to an ISDN switching device such as a PBX.

Supplemental services are widely used by PBXs and in the PSTN. IP telephony systems that are connected to these types of switches must be able to send and receive these messages. The supplemental service and associated parameters that are invoked are PBX-specific and should be provided by the PBX manufacturer.

Progress IE

Progress tones such as ring back and busy tones, and announcements, such as "The number you have dialed is no longer in service," are required to successfully signal voice calls. Progress tones can be generated by the originating, terminating, or intermediate devices.

The indication of in-band tones and announcements is controlled by the progress IE in ISDN and H.323 networks. The progress IE signals those interworking situations where in-band tones and announcements must be used.

The indication that tones and announcements are available is signaled by an alerting, call proceeding, progress, connect, setup acknowledge, or disconnect message containing a progress indicator (PI) of PI = 1 or 8, which would be sent in the progress description field in octet 4. A SETUP message of PI = 3 means the switch is indicating to the originating gateway that in-band messages are expected.

Table 4-7 describes the meanings for various Progress Description field values.

Table 4-7   *ISDN Progress Description Field Values*

Hex Value	Decimal	Binary	Description
0x01	1	000 0001	Call is not end-to-end ISDN.
0x02	2	000 0010	Destination address is non-ISDN.
0x03	3	000 0011	Origination address is non-ISDN.
0x04	4	000 0100	Call has returned to the ISDN.
0x08	8	000 1000	In-band information or the appropriate pattern is now available.
0x0A	10	000 1010	Delay in response at the destination interface.

Display IE

The display IE sends text to do such things as provide output for an LCD display. This IE is commonly used to pass caller name information over a PRI, although PBXs and telecommunications service providers with NI3-type ISDN switches exist that only pass calling name information with the facility IE in QSIG. The display and facility IEs are used by Cisco Unified Communications Manager (UCM) to support caller name and number identification presentation. These services are based on the device control protocols that handle the call. Not all device protocols provide caller number and name information in the protocol messages.

Table 4-8 details common information elements.

Table 4-8   *Common IEs*

Value	Name	Description
0x04	Bearer	Specifies packet or circuit mode, data rate, and type of information content (voice).
0x08	Cause	Provides the reason a call was rejected or disconnected. Following is a sample of possible causes:
		0x01 Unassigned number
		0x03 No route to destination
		0x06 Channel unacceptable
		0x10 Normal call clearing
		0x11 User busy
		0x12 User not responding
		0x13 User alerting; no answer
		0x1B Destination out of order
		0x1C Invalid number format
		0x22 No circuit or channel available
		0x2A Switching equipment congestion
0x14	Call State	Current status of a call in terms of the standard Q.931 state machine.
0x18	CID	Defines the B channel being used.

Table 4-8   *Common IEs*   *(continued)*

Value	Name	Description
0x1C	Facility	Indicates the invocation and operation of supplemental services, identified by the corresponding operation value within the facility IE. Following are some examples of supplemental services: Called or calling party identification Sub addressing Hold or retrieve Call transfer Message waiting
0x1E	Progress Indication	Provides information about the call in progress. Following are some examples of progress indication: 0x01 Call is not end-to-end ISDN. 0x02 Destination address is non-ISDN. 0x03 Origination address is non-ISDN. 0x04 Call has returned to the ISDN. 0x08 In-band information or the appropriate pattern is now available. 0x0A Delay in response at the destination interface.
0x28	Display	Provides human-readable text that can be specified with almost any message (for example, to provide text for an LCD display).
0x2C	Keypad	Dialed digits.
0x34	Signal	Provides call status tones according to the following chart: 0x00 Dial tone 350 Hz + 440 Hz; continuous 0x01 Ringing 440 Hz + 480 Hz; 2 sec on/4 sec off 0x02 Intercept Alternating 440 Hz and 620 Hz; 250 ms 0x03 Network congestion (fast busy) 480 Hz + 620 Hz; 250 ms on/250 ms off 0x04 Busy 480 Hz + 620 Hz; 500 ms on/500 ms off 0x05 Confirm 350 Hz + 440 Hz; repeated three times: 100 ms on/100 ms off 0x06 Answer Not used 0x07 Call waiting 440 Hz; 300 ms burst 0x08 Off-hook warning 1400 Hz + 2060 Hz + 2450 Hz + 2600 Hz; 100 ms on/100 ms off 0x3F Tones Off

continues

Table 4-8   *Common IEs*   *(continued)*

Value	Name	Description
0x3A	SPID	Contains a service profile identifier (SPID).
0x4C	Connected Number	Indicates the remaining caller if a disconnect occurs during CONFERENCE.
0x6C	Calling Party Number	Origin phone number.
0x70	Called Party Number	Phone number being dialed.
0x7C	LLC	Lower layer compatibility.
0x7D	HLC	Higher layer compatibility.
0x7E	User-User	User-user information.

The **debug isdn q931** command can be used to view detailed Layer 3 signaling information (that is, Q.931 information). Example 4-1 provides sample output from a **debug isdn q931** command.

Example 4-1   debug isdn q931 *Command Output*

```
*Mar 27 15:11:40.472: ISDN Se0/0:23 Q931: TX -> SETUP pd = 8  callref = 0x0006
          Bearer Capability i = 0x8090
                Standard = CCITT
                Transfer Capability = Speech
                Transfer Mode = Circuit
                Transfer Rate = 64 kbit/s
        Channel ID i = 0xA98397
                Exclusive, Channel 23
        Calling Party Number i = 0x2181, 'XXXXXXXXXX'
                Plan:ISDN, Type:National
        Called Party Number i = 0x80, 'XXXXXXXXXX'
                Plan:Unknown, Type:Unknown
*Mar 27 15:11:40.556: ISDN Se0/0:23 Q931: RX <- CALL_PROC pd = 8 callref = 0x8006
        Channel ID i = 0xA98397
                Exclusive, Channel 23
*Mar 27 15:11:42.231: ISDN Se0/0:23 Q931: RX <- PROGRESS pd = 8 callref = 0x8006
        Progress Ind i = 0x8488 - In-band info or appropriate now available
*Mar 27 15:11:45.697: ISDN Se0/0:23 Q931: TX -> DISCONNECT pd = 8
    callref = 0x0006
        Cause i = 0x8090 - Normal call clearing
*Mar 27 15:11:45.733: ISDN Se0/0:23 Q931: RX <- RELEASE pd = 8  callref = 0x8006
*Mar 27 15:11:45.757: ISDN Se0/0:23 Q931: TX -> RELEASE_COMP pd = 8 callref =
```

Although at first glance the output seems somewhat complex to interpret, several sources are available on Cisco.com to help read the output from a **debug isdn q931** command. Refer to the following sources (which require appropriate login credentials for the Cisco website):

■ The "ISDN Codes" chapter in the *Cisco IOS Debug Command Reference, Release 12.4T:* http://www.cisco.com/en/US/partner/products/ps6441/products_command_reference_chapter09186a00804ab4b9.html.

■ The **debug isdn q931** command in the *Debug Command Reference* at http://www.cisco.com/en/US/partner/products/ps6441/products_command_reference_chapter09186a00804ab699.html#wp1012971.

Table 4-9, taken from the *Debug Command Reference*, provides an example of how to read the hexadecimal values with the ISDN bearer capability values.

Table 4-9   *ISDN Bearer Capability Values*

Field	Value Description
0x	Indication that the values that follow are in hexadecimal
88	ITU-T coding standard; unrestricted digital information
90	Circuit mode, 64 kbps
21	Layer 1, V.110/X.30
8F	Synchronous, no in-band negotiation, 56 kbps
0x8090A2	Voice call (mu-law)
0x9090A2	Voice call (mu-law), 3.1 kHz Audio
0x8090A3	Voice call (a-law)
0x9090A3	Voice call (a-law), 3.1 kHz Audio

0x8890 is for 64 kbps or 0x218F is for 56 kbps. In Example 4-1, the SETUP message in the example configuration indicates Bearer Capability i = 0x8090. Therefore, you know that you have a 64-kbps bearer stream.

ISDN cause codes use the following format: i = 0x $y1$ $y2$ $z1$ $z2$ [$a1$ $a2$], as detailed in Table 4-10.

Table 4-10   *ISDN Cause Code Fields*

Field	Value—Description
0x	The values that follow are in hexadecimal.
y1	8—ITU-T standard coding.
y2	0—User
	1—Private network serving local user
	2—Public network serving local user
	3—Transit network
	4—Public network serving remote user
	5—Private network serving remote user
	7—International network
	A—Network beyond internetworking point
z1	Class (the more significant hexadecimal number) of cause value.
z2	Value (the less significant hexadecimal number) of cause value.
a1	(Optional) Diagnostic field that is always 8.
a2	(Optional) Diagnostic field that is one of the following values:
	0—Unknown
	1—Permanent
	2—Transient

Table 4-11 lists some of the cause value fields of the cause information element.

Table 4-11   *ISDN Cause Values*

Decimal	Hexadecimal	Cause	Explanation
30	1E	Response to STATUS ENQUIRY	The status message was generated in direct response to the prior receipt of a status enquiry message.
31	1F	Normal, unspecified	Reports the occurrence of a normal event when no standard cause applies. No action required.
34	22	No circuit/channel available	The connection cannot be established because no appropriate channel is available to take the call.

Non-Facility Associated Signaling

ISDN NFAS, as illustrated in Figure 4-10, allows a single D channel to control multiple PRI interfaces. Use of a single D channel to control multiple PRI interfaces frees one B channel on all other interfaces to carry other traffic. A backup D channel can be configured for use when the primary NFAS D channel fails. When a backup D channel is configured, any hard system failure causes a switchover to the backup D channel, and currently connected calls remain connected.

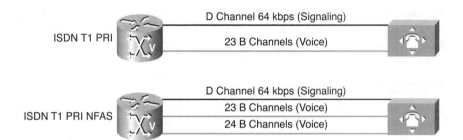

Figure 4-10 *NFAS*

NFAS is supported only with a channelized T1 controller and must be ISDN PRI-capable. After the channelized T1 controllers are configured for ISDN PRI, only the NFAS primary D channel must be configured. Its configuration is distributed to all members of the associated NFAS group. Any configuration changes made to the primary D channel will be propagated to all NFAS group members. The primary D-channel interface is the only interface shown after the configuration is written to memory.

The channelized T1 controllers on the router must also be configured for ISDN. The router must connect to either an AT&T 4ESS, Northern Telecom DMS-100 or DMS-250, or National ISDN switch type.

The ISDN switch must be provisioned for NFAS. The primary and backup D channels should be configured on separate T1 controllers. The primary, backup, and B-channel members on the respective controllers should be the same configuration as that configured on the router and ISDN switch. The interface ID assigned to the controllers must match that of the ISDN switch.

You can disable a specified channel or an entire PRI interface, thereby taking it out of service or placing it into one of the other states that is passed in to the switch using the **isdn service interface** configuration command.

In the event that a controller belonging to an NFAS group is shut down, all active calls on the controller that is shut down will be cleared (regardless of whether the controller is set to primary, backup, or none), and one of the following events will occur:

■   If the controller that is shut down is configured as the primary, and no backup is configured, all active calls on the group are cleared.

- If the controller that is shut down is configured as the primary, and the active (in service) D channel is the primary, and a backup is configured, the active D channel changes to the backup controller.

- If the controller that is shut down is configured as the primary, and the active D channel is the backup, the active D channel remains as backup controller.

- If the controller that is shut down is configured as the backup, and the active D channel is the backup, the active D channel changes to the primary controller.

The expected behavior in NFAS when an ISDN D channel (serial interface) is shut down is that ISDN Layer 2 should go down but keep ISDN Layer 1 up, and that the entire interface will go down after the amount of seconds specified for timer T309.

Configuring a T1 CAS Trunk

Configuring a T1 CAS trunk involves the configuration of controller settings as well as voice port parameters.

Controller Settings

Before configuring a T1 or E1 trunk, you must decide on a variety of parameters for the T1 or E1 digital controller. The following discussions explain the implications of these parameter selections.

Framing Formats

The framing format parameter describes the way bits are robbed from specific frames to be used for signaling purposes. The controller must be configured to use the same framing format as the line from the PBX or CO that connects to the voice port you are configuring.

Digital T1 lines use SF or ESF framing formats. SF provides two-state, continuous supervision signaling, in which bit values of 0 are used to represent on-hook, and bit values of 1 are used to represent off-hook. ESF robs four bits instead of two, yet has little impact on voice quality. ESF is required for 64 kbps operation on DS0 and is recommended for PRI configurations.

E1 lines can be configured for cyclic redundancy check (CRC4) or no cyclic redundancy check, with an optional argument for E1 lines in Australia.

Line Coding

Digital T1/E1 interfaces require line encoding be configured to match that of the PBX or CO that is being connected to the voice port. Line encoding defines the type of framing that is used on the line.

T1 line encoding methods include alternate mark inversion (AMI) and binary 8-zero sub-stitution (B8ZS). AMI is used on older T1 circuits and references signal transitions with a binary 1, or "mark." B8ZS, a more reliable method, is more popular and is recommended for PRI configurations. B8ZS encodes a sequence of eight zeros in a unique binary sequence, including two line-coding violations at specific bit positions, which are inter-preted as a byte containing all zeros.

Supported E1 line encoding methods are AMI and high-density bipolar 3 (HDB3), which is a form of zero-suppression line coding.

Clock Sources

Digital T1/E1 interfaces use timers called *clocks* to ensure voice packets are delivered and assembled properly. All interfaces handling the same packets must be configured to use the same source of timing so packets are not lost or delivered late. The timing source that is configured can be external (from the line) or internal to a router's digital interface.

If the timing source is internal, timing derives from the onboard phase lock loop (PLL) chip in the digital voice interface. If the timing source is line (external), timing derives from the PBX or PSTN CO to which the voice port is connected. It is generally preferable to derive timing from the PSTN because their clocks are maintained at an extremely accurate level. This is the default setting for the clocks. When two or more controllers are configured, one should be designated as the primary clock source. It will drive the other controllers.

Consider a couple of examples:

- **Single voice port providing clocking:** In this scenario, the digital voice hardware is the clock source for the connected device, as shown in Figure 4-11 and Example 4-2. The PLL generates the clock internally and drives the clocking on the line. Generally, this method is useful only when connecting to a PBX, key system, or channel bank. A Cisco VoIP gateway rarely provides clocking *to* the CO because CO clocking is much more reliable.

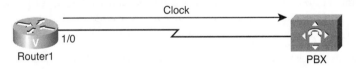

Figure 4-11   *Clock Source Example 1*

Example 4-2   *Clock Source Example 1*

```
Router1(config)#controller T1 1/0
Router1(config-controller)#framing crc4
Router1(config-controller)#linecoding hdb3
Router1(config-controller)#clock source internal
Router1(config-controller)#ds0-group timeslots 1-15 type e&m-wink-start
```

- **Single voice port receiving internal clocking:** In this scenario, the digital voice hardware receives clocking from the connected device (CO telephony switch or PBX), as illustrated in Figure 4-12 and Example 4-3. The PLL clocking is driven by the clock reference on the receive (Rx) side of the digital line connection.

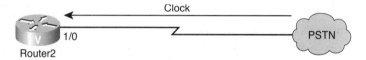

Figure 4-12   *Clock Source Example 2*

Example 4-3   *Clock Source Example 2*

```
Router2(config)#controller T1 1/0
Router2(config-controller)#framing esf
Router2(config-controller)#linecoding ami
Router2(config-controller)#clock source line
Router2(config-controller)#ds0-group timeslots 1-12 type e&m-wink-start
```

Network Clock Timing

Voice systems that pass digitized (PCM) speech rely on the clocking signal being embedded in the received bit stream. This reliance allows connected devices to recover the clock signal from the bit stream and then use this recovered clock signal to ensure data on different channels keeps the same timing relationship with other channels.

If a common clock source is not used between devices, the binary values in the bit streams might be misinterpreted because the device samples the signal at the wrong moment. For example, if the local timing of a receiving device is using a slightly shorter time period than the timing of the sending device, a string of eight continuous binary 1s might be interpreted as nine continuous 1s. If this data is then re-sent to further downstream devices that use varying timing references, the error could be compounded. By ensuring that each device in the network uses the same clocking signal, you can ensure the integrity of the traffic.

If timing between devices is not maintained, a condition known as *clock slip* can occur. Clock slip is the repetition or deletion of a block of bits in a synchronous bit stream because of a discrepancy in the read and write rates at a buffer.

Slips are caused by the inability of an equipment buffer store (or other mechanisms) to accommodate differences between the phases or frequencies of the incoming and outgoing signals in cases where the timing of the outgoing signal is not derived from that of the incoming signal.

A T1 or E1 interface sends traffic inside repeating bit patterns called *frames*. Each frame is a fixed number of bits, allowing a device to see the start and end of a frame. The receiving device also knows exactly when to expect the end of a frame simply by counting the appropriate number of bits that have come in. Therefore, if the timing between the sending and receiving device is not the same, the receiving device might sample the bit stream at the wrong moment, resulting in an incorrect value being returned.

Even though Cisco IOS Software can be used to control the clocking on these platforms, the default clocking mode is effectively free running, meaning that the received clock signal from an interface is not connected to the backplane of the router and used for internal synchronization between the rest of the router and its interfaces. The router will use its internal clock source to pass traffic across the backplane and other interfaces.

For data applications, this clocking generally does not present a problem because a packet is buffered in internal memory and is then copied to the transmit buffer of the destination interface. The reading and writing of packets to memory effectively removes the need for any clock synchronization between ports.

Digital voice ports have a different issue. It would appear that unless otherwise configured, Cisco IOS Software uses the backplane (or internal) clocking to control the reading and writing of data to the digital signal processors (DSPs). If a PCM stream comes in on a digital voice port, it will obviously be using the external clocking for the received bit stream. However, this bit stream will not necessarily be using the same reference as the router backplane, meaning the DSPs will possibly misinterpret the data coming in from the controller.

This clocking mismatch is seen on an E1 or T1 controller of the router as a clock slip. The router is using its internal clock source to send traffic out the interface, but the traffic coming into the interface is using a different clock reference. Eventually, the difference in the timing relationship between the transmit and receive signal becomes so great that the controller registers a slip in the received frame.

To eliminate the problem, change the default clocking behavior through Cisco IOS configuration commands. It is absolutely critical to set up the clocking commands properly.

Even though these commands are optional, Cisco strongly recommends you enter them as part of your configuration to ensure proper network clock synchronization:

```
network-clock-participate [slot slot-number | wic wic-slot | aim aim-slot-number]
network-clock-select priority {bri | t1 | e1} slot/port
```

The **network-clock-participate** command allows the router to use the clock from the line via the specified slot, WAN interface card (WIC), or Advanced Integration Module (AIM) and synchronize the onboard clock to the same reference.

If multiple voice WAN interface cards (VWICs) are installed, the commands must be repeated for each installed card. The system clocking can be confirmed using the **show network clocks** command.

Note   If you are configuring a Cisco 2600 XM voice gateway with an NM-HDV2 or NM-HD-2VE installed in slot 1, do not use the **network-clock-participate slot 1** command in the configuration. In this particular hardware scenario, the **network-clock-participate slot 1** command is not necessary. If the **network-clock-participate slot 1** command is configured, voice and data connectivity on interfaces terminating on the NM-HDV2 or NM-HD-2VE network module might fail to operate properly. Data connectivity to peer devices might not be possible at all, and even loopback plug tests to the serial interface spawned via a channel-group configured on the local T1/E1 controller will fail. Voice groups such as CAS ds0-groups and ISDN pri-groups might fail to signal properly. The T1/E1 controller might accumulate large amounts of timing slips as well as Path Code Violations (PCVs) and Line Code Violations (LCVs).

DS0 Groups

For digital voice ports, a single command, **ds0-group**, performs the following functions:

- Defines the T1/E1 channels for compressed voice calls

- Automatically creates a logical voice port

- Defines the emulated analog signaling method the router uses to connect to the PBX or PSTN

When you purchase a T1 or E1 connection, make sure your service provider gives you the appropriate settings.

VoIP Dial Peers

You must create a digital voice port on the T1 or controller to be able to configure voice port parameters. You must also assign time slots and signaling to the logical voice port through configuration. The first step is to create the T1 or E1 digital voice port with the **ds0-group** *ds0-group-no* **timeslots** *timeslot-list* **type** *signal-type* command.

Note   The **ds0-group** command automatically creates a logical voice port that is numbered as *slot/port:ds0-group-no*.

The *ds0-group-no* argument identifies the DS0 group (number from 0 to 23 for T1 and from 0 to 30 for E1). This group number is used as part of the logical voice port numbering scheme.

The **timeslots** command allows the user to specify which time slots are part of the DS0 group. The *timeslot-list* argument is a single time slot number, a single range of numbers, or multiple ranges of numbers separated by commas.

The **type** command defines the emulated analog signaling method the router uses to connect to the PBX or PSTN. The type depends on whether the interface is T1 or E1.

To delete a DS0 group, you must first shut down the logical voice port. When the port is in shutdown state, you can remove the DS0 group from the T1 or E1 controller with the **no ds0-group** *ds0-group-no* command.

Figure 4-13 and shows how a **ds0-group** command gathers some of the DS0 time slots from a T1 line into a group that becomes a single logical voice port, which can later be addressed as a single entity in voice port configurations. Other DS0 groups for voice can be created from the remaining time slots shown in Figure 4-13, or the time slots can be used for data or serial pass-through.

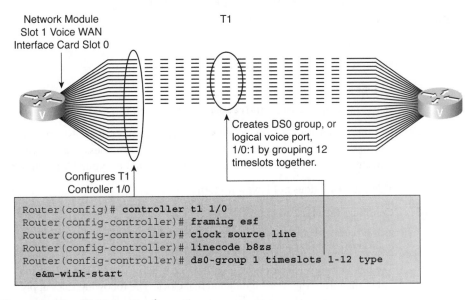

Figure 4-13   *T1 Voice Configuration*

T1 CAS Controller Configuration Example   In this example, you have been asked to configure a T1 controller for a voice gateway according to the following network requirements:

- T1

    - Framing = ESF

    - Line code = B8ZS

    - Clock source = PSTN

    - DS0 group = 1 will utilize 12 time slots with E&M wink-start signaling

- Voice Port

    - Call progress tones = US

    - Companding standard = u-law

To configure controller settings for digital T1/E1 voice ports, use the following steps:

Step 1.   Enter controller configuration mode.

```
Router(config)#controller {t1 | e1} slot/port
```

Step 2.   Select frame type for T1 or E1 line.

T1 Lines:

```
Router(config-controller)#framing {sf | esf}
```

E1 Lines:

```
Router(config-controller)#framing {crc4 | no-crc4} [Australia]
```

Use this command in configurations in which the router or access server is intended to communicate with T1 or E1 fractional data lines. The service provider determines the framing type that is required for your T1/E1 circuit.

This command does not have a **no** form.

Step 3.   Configure the clock source.

```
Router(config-controller)#clock source {line [primary | bits] |
   internal | free-running}
```

The **line** keyword specifies the clock source is derived from the active line rather than from the free-running internal clock. The following rules apply to clock sourcing on the controller ports:

- When both ports are set to line clocking with no primary specification, port 0 is the default primary clock source, and port 1 is the default secondary clock source.

- When both ports are set to line, and one port is set as the primary clock source, the other port is by default the backup or secondary source and is loop-timed.

- If one port is set to **clock source line** or **clock source line primary,** and the other is set to **clock source internal**, the internal port recovers clock from the clock source line port if the clock source line port is up. If it is down, the internal port generates its own clock.

- If both ports are set to **clock source internal**, only one clock source exists: internal.

Step 4.   Specify the line encoding to use.

T1 Lines:

```
Router(config-controller)#linecode {ami | b8zs}
```

E1 Lines:

```
Router(config-controller)#linecode {ami | hdb3}
```

Use this command in configurations in which the router or access server must communicate with T1 fractional data lines. The T1 service provider determines which line code type, either **ami** or **b8zs**, is required for your T1 circuit. Likewise, the E1 service provider determines which line code type, either **ami** or **hdb3**, is required for your E1 circuit.

Step 5.   Define the T1 channels for use by compressed voice calls and the signaling method the router uses to connect to the PBX or CO.

```
Router(config-controller)#ds0-group ds0-group-number timeslots
    timeslot-list [service service-type] type {e&m-fgb | e&m-fgd | e&m-
    immediate-start | fgd-eana | fgd-os | fxs-ground-start | fxs-loop-start
    | none | r1-itu | r1-modified | r1-turkey}
```

The **ds0-group** command automatically creates a logical voice port. The resulting logical voice port will be 1/0:1, where 1/0 is the module and slot number and :1 is the ds0-group-number argument you assign in this step.

Step 6.   Activate the controller.

```
Router(config-controller)#no shutdown
```

Digital Voice Port Parameters

After setting up the controller, you can configure voice port parameters for that digital voice port. When you specified a **ds0-group**, the system automatically created a logical voice port. You must then enter the voice-port configuration mode to configure port-specific parameters. Each voice port you set up in digital voice port configuration is one of the logical voice ports you created with the **ds0-group** command.

Follow these steps to configure basic parameters for digital T1/E1 voice ports:

Step 1.   Enter voice-port configuration mode.

```
Router(config)#voice-port slot/port:ds0-group-number
```

Step 2. Select a two-letter keyword for the voice call progress tones and other locale-specific parameters to be used on this voice port.

```
Router(config-voiceport)#cptone locale
```

Step 3. Specify the companding standard that is used to convert between analog and digital signals.

```
Router(config-voiceport)#compand-type {u-law | a-law}
```

> **Note** This command is used in cases when a DSP is not used, such as local cross-connects, and overwrites the **compand-type** value set by the **cptone** command.

Step 4. Activate the voice port.

```
Router(config-voiceport)#no shutdown
```

Figure 4-14 and Example 4-4 illustrate a complete digital voice port configuration that specifies US as the type of call progress tones to use and u-law as the companding type.

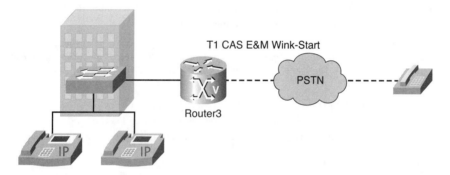

Figure 4-14 *Digital Voice Port Configuration Topology*

Example 4-4 *Digital Voice Port Configuration*

```
Router3(config)#voice-port 1/0:1
Router3(config-voiceport)#cptone US
Router3(config-voiceport)#compand-type u-law
Router3(config-voiceport)#no shutdown
```

Configuring T1 CAS Trunks: Inbound E&M FGD and Outbound FGD EANA

Because E&M FGD supports only inbound ANI, a deployment requiring both inbound and outbound ANI can combine an E&M FGD and FGD EANA trunk. The FGD trunk will be used for inbound calls, and the FGD EANA trunk will be used for outbound calls.

T1 CAS with E&M FGD and FGD EANA Trunk Configuration Example

In this example, you have been asked to configure an E1 controller for a voice gateway according to the following network requirements:

- E1
    - Framing = ESF
    - Line code = B8ZS
    - Time slots 1–12 should be the FGD trunk
    - Time slots 13–24 should be the FGD EANA trunk
- The voice gateway must support inbound and outbound ANI.

Follow this procedure to configure a T1 CAS digital voice port with inbound and outbound ANI:

Step 1. Enter controller configuration mode.

```
Router(config)#controller T1 0/0/0
```

Step 2. Specify the framing format.

```
Router(config-controller)#framing esf
```

Step 3. Specify line coding.

```
Router(config-controller)#linecode b8zs
```

Step 4. Configure one DS0 group to use time slots 1 to 12 and E&M feature group-D.

```
Router(config-controller)#ds0-group 0 timeslots 1-12 type e&m-fgd
```

Step 5. Configure another DS0 group to use time slots 13 through 24 and E&M feature group-D EANA.

```
Router(config-controller)#ds0-group 1 timeslots 13-24 type fgd-eana
```

Note   This creates two voice ports, 0/0/0:0 and 0/0/0:1.

Step 6. An inbound dial peer is configured using the 0/0/0:0 trunk, which supports inbound ANI:

```
Router(config)#dial-peer voice 1 pots
Router(config-dialpeer)#incoming called-number .
Router(config-dialpeer)#port 0/0/0:0
```

Step 7. An outbound dial peer is configured using the 0/0/0:1 trunk, which supports outbound ANI:

```
Router(config)#dial-peer voice 90 pots
Router(config-dialpeer)#destination-pattern 9T
Router(config-dialpeer)#port 0/0/0:1
```

Figure 4-15 and Example 4-5 illustrate the complete configuration that was previously described.

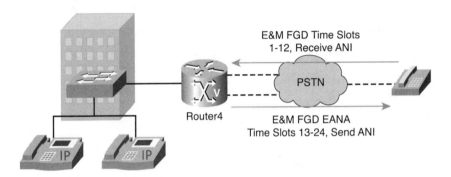

Figure 4-15 *Configuring a T1 CAS Trunk for Inbound and Outbound Calls*

Example 4-5 *T1 CAS Trunk Configuration Example*

```
Router4(config)#controller T1 0/0/0
Router4(config-controller)#framing esf
Router4(config-controller)#linecode b8zs
Router4(config-controller)#ds0-group 0 timeslots 1-12 type e&m-fgd
Router4(config-controller)#ds0-group 1 timeslots 13-24 type fgd-eana
Router4(config)#dial-peer voice 1 pots
Router4(config-dialpeer)#incoming called-number .
Router4(config-dialpeer)#direct-inward-dial
Router4(config)#dial-peer voice 90 pots
Router4(config-dialpeer)#destination-pattern 9T
Router4(config-dialpeer)#port 0/0/0:1
```

Configuring an E1 R2 Trunk

You use the **ds0-group** controller command to configure E1 R2 trunks as well. The Cisco implementation of R2 signaling has DNIS support enabled by default. If you enable the ANI option, DNIS information is still collected. Specification of the ANI option does not disable the DNIS collection.

T1 CAS with E&M FGD and EANA FGD Trunk Configuration Example

In this example, you have been asked to configure an E1 controller for a voice gateway according to the following network requirements:

- E1

  - Framing = ESF

  - Line code = B8ZS

  - Time slots 1–31 should use R2 digital signaling

- The voice gateway must support inbound and outbound DNIS and ANI.

Follow this procedure to configure a T1 CAS digital voice port with inbound and outbound ANI.

Step 1. Enter controller configuration mode.

```
Router(config)#controller e1 0/0/0
```

Step 2. Define DS0 groups.

```
Router(config-controller)#ds0-group 0 timeslots 1-31 type r2-digital
    r2-compelled ani
```

After the DS0 group has been created, you can tune additional parameters using the **cas custom** *ds0-id* command.

Step 3. Customize E1 R2 signaling parameters.

```
Router(config-controller)#cas-custom 0
```

Use the other **cas-custom** subcommands for further customization required to accommodate a certain PBX or switch.

```
Router(config-ctrl-cas)#country china use-defaults
```

Use this command to specify the local country, regional, and some corporation settings for R2 signaling. Replace the name variable with one of the supported country names. The default country setting is ITU.

Note Cisco strongly recommends you include the **use-defaults** option, which enables the default settings for a specific country.

Step 4. Create a dial peer.

```
Router(config)#dial-peer voice 90 pots
Router(config-dialpeer)#destination-pattern 9T
Router(config-dialpeer)#port 0/0/0:0
Router(config-dialpeer)#direct-inward-dial
```

Figure 4-16 and Example 4-6 illustrate the complete configuration that was previously described.

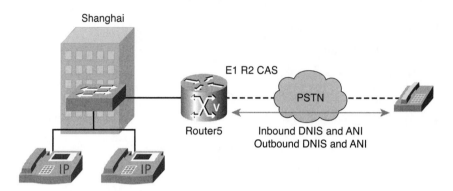

Figure 4-16   *E1 R2 Trunk Configuration Topology*

Example 4-6   *E1 R2 Trunk Configuration*

```
Router5(config)#controller E1 0/0/0
Router5(config-controller)#ds0-group 0 timeslots 1-31 type r2-digital
   r2-compelled ani
Router5(config-controller)#cas-custom 0
Router5(config-ctrl-cas)#country china use-defaults
Router5(config)#dial-peer voice 90 pots
Router5(config-dialpeer)#destination-pattern 9T
Router5(config-dialpeer)#direct-inward-dial
Router5(config-dialpeer)#port 0/0/0:0
```

Configuring an ISDN Trunk

Many PBX vendors support either T1/E1 PRI or BRI connections. In Europe, where ISDN is more popular, many PBX vendors support BRI connections. When designing how the PBX passes voice to the network, you must ensure the router supports the correct connection. The first step in provisioning ISDN capabilities for T1 or E1 PRI is to enter the basic configuration of the controllers. After the clock source, framing, and line code are configured, ISDN voice functionality requires these configuration commands:

- **isdn switch-type:** Configures the ISDN switch type. You can enter this parameter in global configuration mode or at the interface level. If you configure both, the interface switch type takes precedence over the global switch type. This parameter must match the provider ISDN switch. This setting is required for both BRI and PRI connections.

■ **pri-group:** Configures time slots for the ISDN PRI group. T1 allows for time slots 1 through 23 to be configured as B channels, with time slot 24 allocated to the data channel (D channel). E1 allows for time slots 1 through 31, with time slot 16 allocated to the D channel. You can configure the PRI group to include all available time slots, or you can configure only a select group of time slots.

■ **isdn incoming-voice:** Configures the interface to send all incoming calls to the DSP card for processing.

■ **isdn switch-type [primary-qsig | basic-qsig]:** Configures the use of QSIG signaling on the D channel. You typically use this setting when connecting via ISDN to a PBX. The command to enable QSIG signaling is **isdn switch-type primary-qsig** for PRI and **isdn switch-type basic-qsig** for BRI connections.

Figure 4-17 and Example 4-7 show the configuration for a PBX connection to the Cisco voice-enabled router. The connection is configured for QSIG signaling across all 23 time slots.

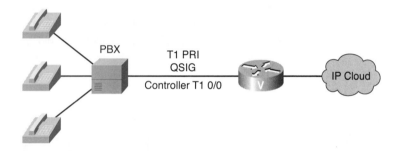

Figure 4-17   *ISDN Configuration Topology Example*

Example 4-7   *ISDN Configuration*

```
Router(config)#isdn switch-type primary-qsig
Router(config)#controller t1 0/0
Router(config-controller)#pri-group timeslots 1-24
Router(config-controller)#interface serial 0/0:23
Router(config-if)#isdn incoming-voice voice
```

The following steps detail the previous configuration:

Step 1.   Specify the CO switch type on the ISDN interface.

```
Router(config)#isdn switch-type primary-qsig
```

You have a choice of configuring the **isdn-switch-type** command to support QSIG at either the global configuration level or at the interface configuration level.

Step 2. Enter controller configuration mode.

`Router(config)#`**`controller t1 0/0`**

Step 3. Specify an ISDN PRI group.

`Router(config-controller)#`**`pri-group timeslots 1-24`**

Step 4. Enter voice port configuration mode for the D channel. Channel 23 is the D channel because the channel numbering begins at 0. Therefore, Channel 23 is the 24th channel.

`Router(config)#`**`interface serial 0/0:23`**

Step 5. Send incoming calls to DSPs.

`Router(config-if)#`**`isdn incoming-voice voice`**

Step 6. Activate the voice port.

`Router(config-if)#`**`no shutdown`**

Configuring a BRI Trunk Example

In this example, you have been asked to configure a BRI connection to the PSTN according to the following network requirements. Figure 4-18 presents the topology used in this example.

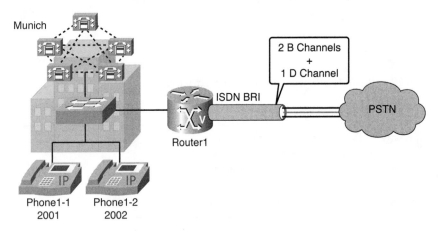

Figure 4-18 *ISDN BRI Configuration Topology Example*

The requirements are as follows:

■ Because the ISDN switch is located in Munich, you need to configure the **isdn switch-type** as **basic-net3** for Germany.

■ The DSP clocking will be synchronized with the WIC in slot 0.

- Because the possibility exists for the incoming number being sent digit by digit and not en bloc, you need to configure **isdn overlap-receiving.**

- To define incoming calls as voice-only, configure **isdn incoming-voice voice.** This will send incoming calls to the DSP resources.

- If the current configuration is set to the network-side, use the **isdn protocol-emulate user** command to switch to user-side ISDN. The user-side setting is the default, so it is not shown in the configuration.

Perform these steps to build the BRI trunk to the PSTN:

Step 1. Configure DSP clocking so it is synchronized with the PSTN clock.

Step 2. Configure the ISDN switch type according to the country's ISDN implementation.

Step 3. Configure ISDN overlap-receiving for countries with variable-length numbering plans.

Step 4. Configure incoming ISDN calls as voice. The calls will be directly passed to the DSPs.

Step 5. Configure BRI as user-side, if necessary. This is the default; so it does not need to be configured under most circumstances.

Step 6. Reset the interface if necessary, depending on the configuration.

Example 4-8 illustrates the completed configuration.

Example 4-8   *BRI Trunk*

```
Router1#clear interface bri0/0
Router1(config)#network-clock-participate wic 0
Router1(config)#interface bri 0/0
Router1(config-if)#isdn switch-type basic-net3
Router1(config-if)#isdn overlap-receiving
Router1(config-if)#isdn incoming-voice voice
Router1(config-if)#isdn protocol-emulate user
```

Configuring a PRI Trunk Example

In this example, you have been asked to configure a PRI connection to the PSTN according to the following network requirements. Figure 4-19 presents the topology used in this example.

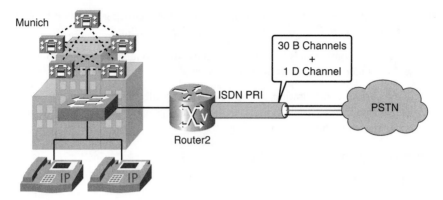

Figure 4-19   *ISDN PRI Configuration Topology Example*

The requirements are as follows:

■   The ISDN switch is located in Munich, Germany. According to the ISDN Switch Type BRI Parameters table, you need to configure the **isdn switch-type** as **primary-net5**.

■   The DSP clocking will be synchronized with the WIC in slot 0.

■   The line coding for the E1 controller will be linecoding ami. (This is not shown in Example 4-9 because this is the default configuration.)

■   The framing needs to be defined for the E1 controller. In this case, crc4 framing will be used. (This is not shown in Example 4-9 because this is the default configuration.)

■   The clock source will be set to the PSTN. (This is the default setting, so it is also not shown in the configuration.)

■   The logical voice ports need to be created. This is done with the **pri-group timeslots 1-31** command, which defines all 30 B channels as logical voice ports. (Again, this is the default configuration.)

■   A variable-length numbering plan needs to be configured. Although the users have a four-digit extension, the switchboard is available via a "0" extension. You therefore configure overlap-receiving.

■   To define incoming calls as voice-only, you configure **isdn incoming-voice voice**. This will send incoming calls to the DSP resources.

Perform these steps to build the PRI trunk to the PSTN:

Step 1.   Configure the ISDN switch type according to the country's ISDN implementation.

Step 2.   Configure DSP clocking so it is synchronized with the PSTN clock.

Step 3.   Configure the E1 line code. Refer to the local service provider for the correct setting.

Step 4.   Configure the E1 frame format. Refer to the local service provider for the correct setting.

Step 5.   Configure the clock source to define which side will provide clocking.

Step 6.   Configure a logical voice port to define which channels will be used for voice.

Step 7.   Configure ISDN overlap-receiving for countries with variable-length numbering plans.

Step 8.   Configure incoming ISDN calls as voice. The calls will be directly passed to the DSPs.

Step 9.   Reset the interface if necessary, depending on the configuration.

Example 4-9 illustrates the completed configuration.

Example 4-9   *PRI Trunk*

```
Router2(config)#network-clock-participate wic 0
Router2(config)#isdn switch-type primary-net5
Router2(config)#controller e1 0/0/0
Router2(config-controller)#pri-group timeslots 1-31
Router2(config)#interface Serial0/0/0:15
Router2(config-if)#isdn switch-type primary-net5 Router(config-if)# isdn overlap-
  receiving
Router2(config-if)#isdn incoming-voice voice
```

Verifying Digital Voice Ports

After configuring the voice ports on your router, perform the following steps to verify proper operation.

Step 1.   Pick up the handset of an attached telephony device, and check for a dial tone. Note that current versions of Cisco IOS require a POTS dial peer be configured for the voice port being tested before a dial tone will be heard.

Step 2.   If you have a dial tone, check for DTMF detection. If the dial tone stops when you dial a digit, the voice port is probably configured properly.

Step 3.   Use the **show voice port summary** command to identify the port numbers of voice interfaces installed in your router.

Step 4.   Use the **show voice port** command to verify voice-port parameter settings.

Step 5.   Use the **show running-config** command to verify the codec complexity setting for digital T1/E1 connections.

Step 6.   Use the **show controller** command to verify the digital T1/E1 controller is up and no alarms have been reported, and to display information about clock sources and other controller settings.

Step 7. Use the **show voice dsp** command to display voice-channel configuration information for all DSP channels.

Step 8. Use the **show voice call summary** command to verify the call status for all voice ports.

Step 9. Use the **show call active voice** command to display the contents of the active call table, which shows all the calls currently connected through the router or concentrator.

Step 10. Use the **show call history voice** command to display the contents of the call history table.

Following are some examples of commands used to verify digital port configurations. Example 4-10 shows the output of the **show voice port summary** command. For example, the highlighted portion of the output shows the status of an FXS port.

Example 4-10   show voice port summary *Command*

```
Router#show voice port summary


                              IN       OUT
PORT    CH SIG-TYPE    ADMIN OPER STATUS   STATUS   EC
======  == ========== ===== ==== ======== ======== ==
0:17    18 fxo-ls      down  down idle     on-hook  y
0:18    19 fxo-ls      up    dorm idle     on-hook  y
0:19    20 fxo-ls      up    dorm idle     on-hook  y
0:20    21 fxo-ls      up    dorm idle     on-hook  y
0:21    22 fxo-ls      up    dorm idle     on-hook  y
0:22    23 fxo-ls      up    dorm idle     on-hook  y
0:23    24 e&m-imd     up    dorm idle     idle     y
1/1     —  fxs-ls      up    dorm on-hook  idle     y
1/2     —  fxs-ls      up    dorm on-hook  idle     y
1/3     —  e&m-imd     up    dorm idle     idle     y
1/4     —  e&m-imd     up    dorm idle     idle     y
1/5     —  fxo-ls      up    dorm idle     on-hook  y
1/6     —  fxo-ls      up    dorm idle     on-hook  y
```

Example 4-11 shows the output of the **show voice port** command.

Example 4-11   show voice port *Command*

```
Router#show voice port
DS0 Group 1:0 - 1:0
 Type of VoicePort is CAS
 Operation State is DORMANT
 Administrative State is UP
 No Interface Down Failure
 Description is not set
 Noise Regeneration is enabled
 Non Linear Processing is enabled
 Music On Hold Threshold is Set to -38 dBm
 In Gain is Set to 0 dB
 Out Attenuation is Set to 0 dB
 Echo Cancellation is enabled
 Echo Cancel Coverage is set to 8 ms
 Playout-delay Mode is set to default
 Playout-delay Nominal is set to 60 ms
 Playout-delay Maximum is set to 200 ms
 Connection Mode is normal
 Connection Number is not set
 Initial Time Out is set to 10 s
 Interdigit Time Out is set to 10 s
 Call-Disconnect Time Out is set to 60 s
 Ringing Time Out is set to 180 s
 Companding Type is u-law
 Region Tone is set for US
 Wait Release Time Out is 30 s
 Station name None, Station number None

 Voice card specific Info Follows:
 DS0 channel specific status info:
                              IN      OUT
    PORT   CH SIG-TYPE  OPER STATUS  STATUS   TIP   RING
```

Example 4-12 shows the output of the **show controller T1** command. You can use this command to verify operation of the controller plus correct framing, line code, and clock source.

Example 4-12 show controller T1 *Command*

```
Router#show controller T1 1/0/0
T1 1/0/0 is up.
  Applique type is Channelized T1
  Cablelength is long gain36 0db
  No alarms detected.
  alarm-trigger is not set
  Framing is ESF, Line Code is B8ZS, Clock Source is Line.
  Data in current interval (180 seconds elapsed):
     0 Line Code Violations, 0 Path Code Violations
     0 Slip Secs, 0 Fr Loss Secs, 0 Line Err Secs, 0 Degraded Mins
     0 Errored Secs, 0 Bursty Err Secs, 0 Severely Err Secs, 0 Unavail Secs
```

Example 4-13 shows the output of the **show voice dsp** command.

Example 4-13 show voice dsp *Command*

```
Router#show voice dsp
TYPE DSP CH CODEC     VERS STATE STATE   RST AI PORT    TS ABORT  TX/RX-PAK-CNT
==== === == ======== ==== ===== ======= === == ======= == ===== ================
C549 007 00 {medium}  3.3 IDLE  idle     0  0 1/0:1    4   0               0/0
                      .13
C549 008 00 {medium}  3.3 IDLE  idle     0  0 1/0:1    5   0               0/0
                      .13
C549 009 00 {medium}  3.3 IDLE  idle     0  0 1/0:1    6   0               0/0
                      .13
C549 010 00 {medium}  3.3 IDLE  idle     0  0 1/0:1    7   0               0/0
                      .13
C549 011 00 {medium}  3.3 IDLE  idle     0  0 1/0:1    8   0               0/0
                      .13
C549 012 00 {medium}  3.3 IDLE  idle     0  0 1/0:1    9   0               0/0
                      .13
C542 001 01 g711ulaw  3.3 IDLE  idle     0  0 2/0/0        0           512/519
                      .13
C542 002 01 g711ulaw  3.3 IDLE  idle     0  0 2/0/1        0           505/502
                      .13
C542 003 01 g711alaw  3.3 IDLE  idle     0  0 2/1/0        0         28756/28966
                      .13
C542 004 01 g711ulaw  3.3 IDLE  idle     0  0 2/1/1        0             834/8
```

Example 4-14 shows the output of the **show voice call summary** command.

Example 4-14   show voice call summary *Command*

```
Router#show voice call summary

PORT      CODEC    VAD VTSP STATE          VPM STATE
========= ======== === ==================== ========================
1/015.1  g729r8    y  S_CONNECT            S_TSP_CONNECT
1/015.2  g729r8    y  S_CONNECT            S_TSP_CONNECT
1/015.3  g729r8    y  S_CONNECT            S_TSP_CONNECT
1/015.4  g729r8    y  S_CONNECT            S_TSP_CONNECT
1/015.5  g729r8    y  S_CONNECT            S_TSP_CONNECT
1/015.6  g729r8    y  S_CONNECT            S_TSP_CONNECT
1/015.7  g729r8    y  S_CONNECT            S_TSP_CONNECT
1/015.8  g729r8    y  S_CONNECT            S_TSP_CONNECT
1/015.9  g729r8    y  S_CONNECT            S_TSP_CONNECT
1/015.10 g729r8    y  S_CONNECT            S_TSP_CONNECT
1/015.11 g729r8    y  S_CONNECT            S_TSP_CONNECT
1/015.12 g729r8    y  S_CONNECT            S_TSP_CONNECT
```

Example 4-15 shows the output of the **show call active voice** command.

Example 4-15   show call active voice *Command*

```
Router#show call active voice
GENERIC:
SetupTime=94523746 ms
Index=448
PeerAddress=##73072

PeerSubAddress=
PeerId=70000

PeerIfIndex=37
LogicalIfIndex=0
ConnectTime=94524043
DisconnectTime=94546241
CallOrigin=1
ChargedUnits=0
InfoType=2
TransmitPackets=6251
TransmitBytes=125020
ReceivePackets=3300
ReceiveBytes=66000
```

continues

Example 4-15   show call active voice *Command*   *(continued)*

```
VOIP:
ConnectionId[0x142E62FB 0x5C6705AF 0x0 0x385722B0]
RemoteIPAddress=171.68.235.18

RemoteUDPPort=16580

RoundTripDelay=29 ms
SelectedQoS=best-effort
tx_DtmfRelay=inband-voice
SessionProtocol=cisco
SessionTarget=ipv4:171.68.235.18
OnTimeRvPlayout=63690
GapFillWithSilence=0 ms
GapFillWithPrediction=180 ms
GapFillWithInterpolation=0 ms
GapFillWithRedundancy=0 ms
HiWaterPlayoutDelay=70 ms
LoWaterPlayoutDelay=30 ms
ReceiveDelay=40 ms

LostPackets=0 ms
EarlyPackets=1 ms
LatePackets=18 ms

VAD = disabled

CoderTypeRate=g729r8
CodecBytes=20

cvVoIPCallHistoryIcpif=0

SignalingType=cas
```

Example 4-16 shows the output of the **show call history voice** command.

Example 4-16   show call history voice *Command*

```
Router#show call history voice

GENERIC:
SetupTime=94893250 ms
Index=450
PeerAddress=##52258
PeerSubAddress=
```

Example 4-16   show call history voice *Command*   *(continued)*

```
PeerId=50000
PeerIfIndex=35
LogicalIfIndex=0
DisconnectCause=10
DisconnectText=normal call clearing.

ConnectTime=94893780
DisconectTime=95015500
CallOrigin=1

ChargedUnits=0
InfoType=2
TransmitPackets=32258
TransmitBytes=645160
ReceivePackets=20061
ReceiveBytes=401220
VOIP:
ConnectionId[0x142E62FB 0x5C6705B3 0x0 0x388F851C]
RemoteIPAddress=171.68.235.18

RemoteUDPPort=16552

RoundTripDelay=23 ms
SelectedQoS=best-effort
tx_DtmfRelay=inband-voice
SessionProtocol=cisco
SessionTarget=ipv4:171.68.235.18
OnTimeRvPlayout=398000
GapFillWithSilence=0 ms

GapFillWithPrediction=1440 ms

GapFillWithInterpolation=0 ms
GapFillWithRedundancy=0 ms
HiWaterPlayoutDelay=97 ms
LoWaterPlayoutDelay=30 ms
ReceiveDelay=49 ms
LostPackets=1 ms
EarlyPackets=1 ms

LatePackets=132 ms

VAD = disabled
```

continues

Example 4-16   show call history voice *Command*   *(continued)*

```
CoderTypeRate=g729r8

CodecBytes=20
cvVoIPCallHistoryIcpif=0
```

Using QSIG for Digital Signaling

QSIG is an extension of ISDN and supports enterprise-class call features, such as signaling message-waiting indicators and call back. This section describes the characteristics of QSIG and how to implement QSIG trunks on a Cisco IOS gateway.

QSIG Overview

QSIG is a variant of ISDN Q.921 and Q.931 ISDN D-channel signaling for use in devices such as PBXs or key systems that are called Private Integrated-services Network-eXchange (PINX). Using QSIG signaling, a router can route incoming voice calls from a PINX across the WAN to a peer router, which can then transport the signaling and voice packets to another PINX. QSIG is becoming the standard for PBX interoperability in Europe and North America.

Cisco UCM nodes that support the QSIG protocol, or other equipment, perform these functions:

■ Telecommunications services within its own area

■ Telecommunications services from the public ISDN or PSTN

■ Telecommunications services between PINXs in a multisite private network

QSIG ensures the essential functions in Q.931 are carried from node to node. QSIG functions with these two sublayers:

■ **QSIG Basic Call:** This standard defines the signaling procedures and protocol for the purpose of circuit-switched Call Control. This standard is based on Q.931.

Note   See more QSIG Basic Call (ECMA-143) info at: http://www.ecma-international.org/publications/standards/Ecma-143.htm.

■ **QSIG Generic Function:** This standard defines the signaling protocol for the control of Supplementary Services and Additional Network Features (ANFs) at the Q reference point. The standard enables capabilities beyond a basic call capability.

Note   See more QSIG Generic Function (ECMA-165) info at
http://www.ecma-international.org/publications/standards/Ecma-165.htm

QSIG Features

QSIG includes these features:

- **Basic call:** QSIG basic call setup provides the dynamic establishment of voice connections from an originating PINX (PBX or Cisco UCM) across a private network or virtual private network (VPN) to another PINX. You must use digital T1 or E1 PRI trunks to support the QSIG protocol.

- **Call completion:** These call completion services rely on the facility selection and reservation feature and provide Cisco Call Back functionality over QSIG-enabled trunks:

  - **Completion of Calls to Busy Subscribers (CCBS):** When a calling party receives a busy tone, the caller can request that the call complete when the busy destination hangs up the phone and becomes available.

  - **Completion of Calls on No Reply (CCNR):** When a calling party receives no answer at the destination, the calling party can request that the call complete after activity occurs on the phone of the called party.

- **Call diversion:** When call diversion by rerouting occurs, the originating PINX receives a request from the receiver of the call to divert the call to another user. The system creates a new call between the originator and the diverted-to user, and an additional Call Detail Record (CDR) gets generated. QSIG diversion supplementary services provide call-forwarding capabilities that are similar to familiar Cisco UCM call-forwarding features:

  - Call Forward All (CFA) configuration supports Call Forwarding Unconditional (CFU).

  - Call Forward Busy (CFB) configuration supports Call Forwarding Busy (CFB).

  - Call Forward No Answer (CFNA) configuration supports Call Forwarding No Reply (CFNR).

  - To provide feature transparency with other PBXs in the network, the system passes information about a forwarded call during the call setup and connection over QSIG trunks. Phone displays can present calling name and/or number, original called name and/or number, and last redirecting name and/or number information to show the destination of the forwarded call.

- **Call transfer:** When a user transfers a call to another user, the QSIG identification service changes the connected name and number that displays on the transferred party phone. Call identification restrictions can impact what displays on the phone. The call transfer supplementary service interacts with the path replacement feature to optimize the trunk connections when a call transfers to a caller in another PINX.

■ **Identification services:** When a call alerts and connects to a PINX, identification services can display the caller name and/or ID on a phone in the terminating PINX, and likewise, the connected party name and/or ID on a phone in the originating PINX. QSIG identification restrictions enable you to control the presentation or display of this information between Cisco UCM and the connected PINX. Supported supplementary services apply on a per-call basis, and presentation settings for call identification information are set at both ends of the call.

■ **Message waiting indication service:** In a QSIG network, when a PINX has a connected voice-messaging system that services users in another PINX, the message-center PINX can send these Message Waiting Indicator (MWI) signals to the other PINX:

■ **MWI Activate:** Sends a signal to activate MWI on the served user's phone after the voice-messaging system receives a message for that phone.

■ **MWI De-activate:** Sends a signal to deactivate the MWI after the user listens to messages in the associated voice-messaging system.

■ **Do not disturb (DND) and Do not disturb override (DNDO):** When a user does not want to be disturbed, the Private Integrated Services Network (PISN) can reject calls. DND and DNDO are described separately because Supplementary-Services Do Not Disturb (SS-DND) is a service used by a called user, and SS-DNDO is a service used by a calling user.

■ **DND:** A supplementary service that enables a served user to cause the PISN to reject any calls, or just those associated with a specified basic service, addressed to the served user's PISN number. The calling user is given an appropriate indication. Incoming calls are rejected as long as the service is active. The served user's outgoing service is unaffected.

■ **DNDO:** A supplementary service that enables a served user to override SS-DND at a called user (that is, to allow the call to proceed as if the called user had not activated SS-DND).

Path Replacement

Path replacement allows for a potentially more efficient connection to be established between two parties in an active call. In Cisco UCM, this can occur after a QSIG transfer via a join or a diversion by forward switching.

In a QSIG network, after a call is transferred or forwarded to a phone in a third PINX, multiple connections through several PINX(s) can exist for the call. After the call connects, the path replacement feature drops the connection to the transit PINXs and creates a new call connection to the terminating PINX. Calls that involve multiple trunks (for example, conference calls) do not use path replacement. However, if you choose the QSIG option from the **Tunneled Protocol** drop-down list and check the **Path**

Replacement Support check box for gatekeeper-controlled or non-gatekeeper-controlled intercluster trunks (in the Cisco UCM Administration interface), path replacement occurs over the intercluster trunk and the other QSIG intercluster or PRI trunk that is used to transfer or divert the call.

It is important that you understand the new path established by path replacement is not guaranteed to be more efficient. Rather, it is only "likely." The network topology and route patterns in the network determine if and when the new path will be more optimal than the old path. Path replacement does not get invoked by the Cisco UCM in other situations, such as a conference call.

Figure 4-20 illustrates a path replacement example where path replacement replaces an existing TDM circuit between two parties on an active call with a new one in order to use the TDM resources more efficiently.

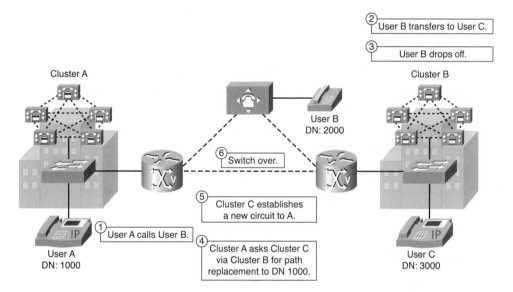

Figure 4-20   *QSIG Path Replacement*

The following steps describe the sequence of events depicted in Figure 4-20:

Step 1.   User A calls User B.

Step 2.   User B transfers the call to User C.

Step 3.   User B drops off the call by pressing **Transfer** again.

Step 4.   Cluster A sends a message via B to C proposing that Cluster C should call DN 1000 for a path replacement.

Step 5.   Cluster C establishes a new circuit to A.

Step 6.   Cluster C and Cluster A "switch over" the active call to use the new connection.

Configuring QSIG Support

Figure 4-21 depicts a QSIG deployment topology example.

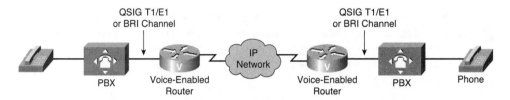

Figure 4-21 *Configuring Global QSIG Support Topology Example*

In this example, you have been asked to configure a T1 controller for a voice gateway with a connection type of PRI using time slots 1 through 24.

You can use the following steps to configure global QSIG support for BRI or PRI.

Step 1. Configure the global ISDN switch type to support QSIG signaling.

Step 2. Configure the DSP farm at the specified slot/port.

Step 3. Specify the card type (T1 or E1) at the specified slot so the router provides sufficient DSP resources.

Example 4-17 and Example 4-18 illustrate the global QSIG support configurations for both a BRI and a PRI connection, respectively.

Example 4-17 *Global QSIG Support Configuration for BRI*

```
Router(config)#isdn switch-type basic-qsig
```

Example 4-18 *Global QSIG Support Configuration for PRI*

```
Router(config)#isdn switch-type primary-qsig
Router(config)#card type t1 0
```

Configuring QSIG over PRI

Figure 4-22 depicts a QSIG over PRI interface configuration topology example.

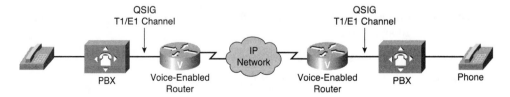

Figure 4-22 *QSIG over PRI Interface Configuration Example*

You can use the following steps to configure the T1 or E1 controller for QSIG over PRI:

Step 1. Enter T1 or E1 controller configuration mode for the specified controller.

Step 2. Specify PRI on the time slots that make up the PRI group. Maximum T1 range: 1–24. Maximum E1 range: 1–31. Separate low and high values with a hyphen.

Step 3. Enter interface configuration mode for the specified PRI slot/port and D-channel ISDN interface.

Note D-channel ISDN interface is (for T1) 23 and (for E1) 15.

Step 4. If you configured the global PRI ISDN switch type for QSIG support in global configuration mode, this command overrides that command and configures the interface ISDN switch type to support QSIG signaling.

Step 5. This step varies based on whether you are configuring the controller to act as a user side device or a network side device.

(User side only) Configure Layer 2 and Layer 3 port mode emulation and clock status for the user (that is, the Terminal Equipment (TE)). This is the default.

or

(Network side only) Configure Layer 2 and Layer 3 port mode emulation and clock status for the network (that is, the Network Termination (NT)).

Example 4-19 illustrates the configuration for a QSIG over a PRI interface. The example provides both a user side and a network side configuration.

Example 4-19   *QSIG over PRI Interface Configuration*

```
Router(config)#controller t1 0/1
Router(config-controller)#pri-group timeslots 1-24
Router(config)#interface serial 0/1:23
Router(config-if)#isdn switch-type primary-qsig
Router(config-if)#isdn protocol-emulate user


!                  OR


Router(config-if)#isdn protocol-emulate network
```

Configuring QSIG over BRI

Figure 4-23 depicts a QSIG over BRI interface configuration topology example.

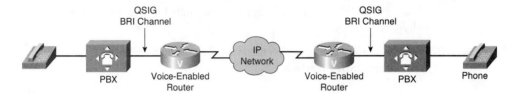

Figure 4-23   *QSIG over BRI Interface Configuration Example*

You can use the following steps to configure QSIG support for BRI:

Step 1.   Enter BRI interface configuration mode for the specified BRI interface.

Step 2.   Configure Layer 1 port mode emulation and clock status for the user—that is, the TE.

Step 3.   Enable routing of incoming voice calls.

Step 4.   This step varies based on whether you are configuring the BRI interface to act as a user side device or a network side device.

   (User side only) Configure Layer 2 and Layer 3 port mode emulation and clock status for the user—that is, the TE.

   or

   (Network side only) Configure Layer 2 and Layer 3 port mode emulation and clock status for the network—that is, the NT.

Example 4-20 illustrates the configuration for a QSIG over BRI.

Example 4-20   *QSIG over BRI Configuration*

```
Router(config)#interface bri 1/1
Router(config-if)#isdn layer1-emulate user


!                    OR


Router(config)#interface bri 1/1
Router(config-if)#isdn layer1-emulate network
Router(config-if)#isdn incoming-voice voice
Router(config-if)#isdn protocol-emulate user


!                    OR


Router(config)#interface bri 1/1
Router(config-if)#isdn protocol-emulate network
```

Verifying QSIG Trunks

To display information about the PRI interface controller, use the **show controllers** command, as demonstrated in Example 4-21.

Example 4-21   show controllers *Command*

```
Router#show controllers t1 0/1/0
T1 0/1/0 is up.
  Applique type is Channelized T1
  Cablelength is long gain36 0db
  No alarms detected.
  alarm-trigger is not set
  Soaking time: 3, Clearance time: 10
  AIS State:Clear  LOS State:Clear  LOF State:Clear
  Version info Firmware: 20051006, FPGA: 20, spm_count = 0
  Framing is ESF, Line Code is B8ZS, Clock Source is Line.
  CRC Threshold is 320. Reported from firmware  is 320.
  Data in current interval (601 seconds elapsed):
     2 Line Code Violations, 3 Path Code Violations
     601 Slip Secs, 0 Fr Loss Secs, 2 Line Err Secs, 1 Degraded Mins
     601 Errored Secs, 0 Bursty Err Secs, 0 Severely Err Secs, 0 Unavail Secs
```

Use the **show isdn status** command, as illustrated in Example 4-22, to verify the ISDN Layer 1 is ACTIVE and the Layer 2 state is MULTIPLE_FRAME_ESTABLISHED. If these conditions are satisfied, any problem you encounter with the QSIG trunk is probably not with ISDN Layer 1 or Layer 2, and troubleshooting should focus on ISDN Layer 3 using the **debug isdn q931** command. If a TEI_UNASSIGNED or AWAITING_ESTABLISHMENT state is reported, verify the configuration. For a back-to-back configuration, such as in a connection between a voice gateway and a PBX, one of the sides must be set to emulate the network.

Example 4-22   show isdn status *Command*

```
Router#show isdn status
Global ISDN Switchtype = primary-qsig
ISDN Serial0/1/1:23 interface
        dsl 0, interface ISDN Switchtype = primary-qsig
        **** Slave side configuration ****
    Layer 1 Status:
        ACTIVE
    Layer 2 Status:
        TEI = 0, Ces = 1, SAPI = 0, State = MULTIPLE_FRAME_ESTABLISHED
    Layer 3 Status:
        0 Active Layer 3 Call(s)
```

continues

Example 4-22   show isdn status *Command*   *(continued)*

```
Active dsl 0 CCBs = 0
The Free Channel Mask:  0x00000000
Number of L2 Discards = 0, L2 Session ID = 0
Total Allocated ISDN CCBs = 0
```

Note   Remember, if network emulation is not correctly set, Layer 2 will not come up.

There are a few commands you can use to debug a QSIG trunk.

The debug isdn q921 Command

The **debug isdn q921** command output is limited to commands and responses exchanged during peer-to-peer communication carried over the D channel. This debug information does not include data transmitted over the B channels that are also part of the router ISDN interface. The peers (data link layer entities and layer management entities on the routers) communicate with each other with an ISDN switch over the D channel.

Note   The ISDN switch provides the network interface defined by Q.921. This debug command does not display data link layer access procedures taking place within the ISDN network (that is, procedures taking place on the network side of the ISDN connection).

A router can be the calling or called party of the ISDN Q.921 data link layer access procedures. If the router is the calling party, the command displays information about an outgoing call. If the router is the called party, the command displays information about an incoming call and the keepalives.

You can use the **debug isdn q921** command simultaneously with the **debug isdn event, debug isdn q931, debug isdn q921 frame,** and **debug isdn q921 detail** commands. However, the output from these commands are intermingled.

The **debug isdn q931** Command

Use the **debug isdn q931** command to watch the Q931 signaling messages go back and forth while the router negotiates the ISDN connection.

Although the **debug isdn event** and the **debug isdn q931** commands provide similar debug information, the information is displayed in a different format. If you want to see the information in both formats, enable both commands at the same time. The displays will be intermingled:

■ The ISDN events that can be displayed are Q.931 events (call setup and teardown of ISDN network connections).

■ Use the **show dialer** command to retrieve information about the status and configuration of the ISDN interface on a router.

Example 4-23 shows an ISDN Q.931 debug in an E1 Euro PRI environment.

Example 4-23   *ISDN Q.931 Debugging in an E1 Euro PRI Environment*

```
Router#show debugging

The following ISDN debugs are enabled on all DSLs:

debug isdn error is          ON.
debug isdn event is          ON.
debug isdn q931 is           ON.    (filter is OFF)

[... output omitted ...]

*Mar  4 13:25:20.698: ISDN Se0/2:15 Q931: RX <- ALERTING pd = 8  callref = 0x8004
       Progress Ind i = 0x8088 - In-band info or appropriate now available
*Mar  4 13:25:22.336: ISDN Se0/2:15 Q931: RX <- CONNECT pd = 8  callref = 0x8004
*Mar  4 13:25:22.344: ISDN Se0/2:15 Q931: TX -> CONNECT_ACK pd = 8
   callref = 0x0004*Mar  4 13:25:24.408: ISDN Se0/2:15 Q931: RX
   <- DISCONNECT pd = 8  callref = 0x8004
       Cause i = 0x8090 - Normal call clearing
*Mar  4 13:25:24.436: ISDN Se0/2:15 Q931: TX -> RELEASE pd = 8  callref = 0x0004
*Mar  4 13:25:24.468: ISDN Se0/2:15 Q931: RX <- RELEASE_COMP pd = 8
   callref = 0x8004
```

Example 4-24 shows an ISDN Q.931 debug in an E1 QSIG environment. In contrast to the E1 Euro PRI, the QSIG connected number is presented in the output.

Example 4-24   *ISDN Q.931 Debugging in an E1 QSIG Environment*

```
Router#show debugging

The following ISDN debugs are enabled on all DSLs:

debug isdn error is         ON.
debug isdn q931 is          ON.   (filter is OFF)

[... output omitted ...]

*Mar  4 13:27:51.549: ISDN Se0/2:15 Q931: RX <- ALERTING pd = 8  callref = 0x8001
        Progress Ind i = 0x8088 - In-band info or appropriate now available
*Mar  4 13:27:55.528: ISDN Se0/2:15 Q931: RX <- CONNECT pd = 8  callref = 0x8001
        Connected Number i = 0x0081, '3000'
*Mar  4 13:27:55.540: ISDN Se0/2:15 Q931: TX -> CONNECT_ACK pd = 8
    callref = 0x0001*Mar  4 13:27:57.294: ISDN Se0/2:15 Q931: RX
    <- DISCONNECT pd = 8  callref = 0x8001
        Cause i = 0x8090 - Normal call clearing
*Mar  4 13:27:57.335: ISDN Se0/2:15 Q931: TX -> RELEASE pd = 8  callref = 0x0001
*Mar  4 13:27:57.363: ISDN Se0/2:15 Q931: RX <- RELEASE_COMP pd = 8
    callref = 0x8001
```

Summary

The main topics covered in this chapter are the following:

- Digital voice ports are found at the intersection of a packet voice network and a digital, circuit-switched telephone network.

- T1 CAS uses a digital T1 circuit together with in-band CAS.

- E1 digital circuits can be deployed using R2 signaling.

- ISDN is a circuit-switched telephone network system designed to allow digital transmission of voice and data over ordinary telephone copper wires.

- ISDN uses Q.921 and Q.931 for signaling.

- Before configuring a T1 or E1 trunk, you must gather information about the requirements for

    - Framing

    - Linecode

    - DS0 groups

- Configuring an E1 trunk is similar to configuring a T1.

- Many PBX vendors support either T1/E1 PRI or BRI connections.

- Various **show** commands are available to verify and monitor digital voice ports.

- QSIG allows feature transparency between different vendor PBXs.

- QSIG can be configured over PRI or BRI.

- Various **show** and **debug** commands are available to verify the QSIG connection.

Chapter Review Questions

The answers to these review questions are in the appendix.

1. T1 CAS uses _____ signaling.

   a. wink-start

   b. loop-start

   c. robbed-bit

   d. ground-start

2. What are three types of digital voice ports? (Choose 3.)

   a. ISDN

   b. PPP

   c. E1

   d. T1

3. The _____ command is used to configure a T1 controller for CAS.

   a. pri-group

   b. bri-group

   c. ds0-group

   d. ds1-group

4. ISDN uses _____ for Layer 2 signaling, which is defined in _____.

   a. LAPB, Q.931

   b. LAPD, Q.921

   c. LAPB, Q.921

   d. LAPD, Q.931

5. The two types of ISDN interfaces are _____ and _____.

    a. T1, E1

    b. PRI, BRI

    c. T1, PRI

    d. E1, BRI

6. Which two are QSIG supplemental services or additional network features? (Choose 2.)

    a. Path replacement

    b. Do not disturb

    c. Identification conversion

    d. Address translation

7. Which two sublayers does QSIG use? (Choose 2.)

    a. Supplementary Services

    b. Generic Function

    c. Basic Call

    d. Additional Network Features

8. Which command specifies the ISDN switch type as PRI?

    a. isdn switch-type qsig-primary

    b. isdn switch-type primary-qsig

    c. isdn switch-type basic-qsig

    d. isdn switch-type qsig-basic

9. Which command would you use to display information about the ISDN PRI interface?

    a. debug isdn events

    b. debug isdn q931

    c. show controllers

    d. show isdn status

10. Which command specifies the ISDN switch type as BRI?

    a. isdn switch-type qsig-primary

    b. isdn switch-type primary-qsig

    c. isdn switch-type basic-qsig

    d. isdn switch-type qsig-basic

After reading this chapter, you should be able to perform the following tasks:

- Describe the H.323 protocol stack and how to implement H.323 on gateways.

- Describe the MGCP stack and how to implement MGCP on gateways.

- Describe SIP enterprise features and how to implement SIP on gateways.

CHAPTER 5

Examining VoIP Gateways and Gateway Control Protocols

To provide voice communication over an IP network, Real-time Transport Protocol (RTP) sessions are created. These sessions are dynamically created and facilitated by one of several call control procedures. Typically, these procedures also embody mechanisms for signaling events during voice calls and for managing and collecting statistics about the voice calls. Several types of protocols exist within Cisco Unified Communications networks. Network engineers need to know all these protocols, how they can be used, and where the advantages and disadvantages are in order to select the best protocol for a specific environment.

This chapter focuses on protocols that are used in Cisco Unified Communications networks to implement gateways and offer call control support for VoIP: H.323, the Session Initiation Protocol (SIP), and the Media Gateway Control Protocol (MGCP).

Configuring H.323

H.323 gateways are among the most common Cisco IOS voice gateways within Cisco Unified Communications Manager environments. An H.323 gateway is an endpoint on a LAN that provides real-time, two-way communications between H.323 terminals on the LAN and other International Telecommunication Union Standardization Sector (ITU-T) terminals on the network. An H.323 gateway can also communicate with other H.323 gateways. Gateways enable H.323 terminals to communicate with non-H.323 terminals by converting protocols. The gateway is the point at which a circuit-switched call is encoded and repackaged into IP packets. Because gateways function as H.323 endpoints, they provide admission control, address lookup and translation, and accounting services.

H.323 Gateway Overview

ITU-T Recommendation H.323 pertains to the H.323 packet-based multimedia communications systems. It describes an infrastructure of terminals, common control components, services, and protocols that are used for multimedia (voice, video, and data) communications.

An H.323 gateway is an optional type of endpoint that provides interoperability between H.323 endpoints and endpoints located on a Switched Circuit Network (SCN), such as the public switched telephone network (PSTN) or an enterprise voice network. Ideally, the gateway is transparent to both the H.323 endpoint and the SCN-based endpoint.

H.323 and IP

Recommendation H.323 describes an infrastructure of terminals, common control components, services, and protocols that are used for multimedia (voice, video, and data) communications. Figure 5-1 illustrates the elements of an H.323 terminal and highlights the protocol infrastructure of an H.323 endpoint.

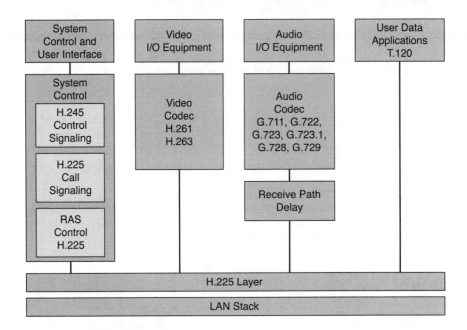

Figure 5-1   *H.323 Elements*

H.323 was originally created to provide a mechanism for transporting multimedia applications over LANs. Although numerous vendors still use H.323 for videoconferencing applications, it has rapidly evolved to address the growing needs of Voice over IP (VoIP) networks. H.323 is currently the most widely used VoIP signaling and call control protocol, with international and domestic carriers relying on it to handle billions of minutes of use each year.

H.323 is considered an "umbrella protocol" because it defines all aspects of call transmission, from call establishment to capabilities exchange to network resource availability. H.323 defines these protocols:

- **H.245** for capabilities exchange
- **H.225.0** for call setup
- **H.225.0** for registration, admission, and status (RAS) control for call routing

H.323 is based on the Integrated Services Digital Network (ISDN) Q.931 protocol, which allows H.323 to easily interoperate with legacy voice networks, such as the PSTN or Signaling System 7 (SS7). In addition to providing support for call setup, H.225.0 provides a message transport mechanism for the H.245 control function and the RAS signaling function. Following is a description of these functions:

■ **Call-signaling function:** The call-signaling function uses a call-signaling channel that allows an endpoint to create connections with other endpoints. The call-signaling function defines call setup procedures, based on the call setup procedures for ISDN (ITU-T Recommendation Q.931). The call-signaling function uses messages formatted according to H.225.0.

■ **H.245 control function:** The H.245 control function uses a control channel to transport control messages between endpoints or between an endpoint and a common control component, such as a gatekeeper or multipoint controller (MC). The control channel used by the H.245 control function is separate from the call-signaling channel.

The H.245 control function is responsible for these functions:

  ■ **Logical channel signaling:** Opens and closes a channel that carries the media stream

  ■ **Capabilities exchange:** Negotiates audio, video, and coder-decoder (codec) capability between endpoints

  ■ **Master or responder determination:** Determines which endpoint is master and which is responder; used to resolve conflicts during the call

  ■ **Mode request:** Requests a change in mode, or capability, of the media stream

  ■ **Timer and counter values:** Establishes values for timers and counters and agreement of those values by the endpoints

■ **RAS signaling function:** The RAS signaling function uses a separate signaling channel (RAS channel) to perform registration, admissions, bandwidth changes, status, and disengage procedures between endpoints and a gatekeeper. The RAS signaling function uses messages formatted according to H.225.0.

H.323 Adapted to IP Example

A typical implementation of H.323 goes beyond the original LAN context of H.323. Figure 5-2 illustrates a specific application of H.323 on an IP internetwork. Notice that real-time aspects of H.323 rely on User Datagram Protocol (UDP). Both the session-oriented control procedures and the data media type of H.323 use TCP.

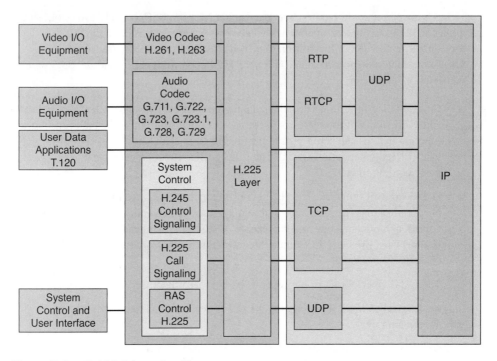

Figure 5-2   *H.323 Adapted to IP*

Why H.323

Several advantages exist to using H.323 gateways as voice gateways:

- **Dial plans can be configured directly on the gateway:** This makes it possible to handle special calls, such as calls to directly connected analog devices locally on the gateway without routing them to the Cisco Unified Communications Manager. Another option is to route calls that are directed to other sites directly on the gateway without sending them to the local Cisco Unified Communications Manager cluster.

- **Translations can be defined per gateway:** This makes it possible to meet regional requirements such as calling party transformations or special number formats. It also makes it possible to translate all incoming calls directly on the gateway to meet the internally used number format and then process only calls with those internal numbers on the Cisco Unified Communications Manager clusters within the network.

- **Call-routing configuration can be more specific than on Cisco Unified Communications Manager:** Cisco IOS gateways enable translating and matching to called number and calling number, which can improve call routing. (Cisco Unified Communications Manager matches only the called number.) This makes it possible to route calls from unwanted people to a special destination, for example.

■ **There is no need for extra Survivable Remote Site Telephony (SRST)-related call-routing configuration:** Because the call routing configuration is done directly on the gateway, you do not need to configure the routing twice. This is because SRST is using the same configuration parameters for call routing as the gateway does on the H.323 gateway.

■ **There is no dependency on the Cisco Unified Communications Manager version:** Because the configuration is performed on the gateway and the H.323 umbrella is a peer-to-peer protocol, Cisco Unified Communications Manager does not need to support a special Cisco IOS version, or vice versa.

■ **More voice interface types are supported:** Because Cisco Unified Communications Manager does not need to control the interface cards within H.323 environments, many more interface cards are supported when you use H.323 rather than MGCP or any other protocol based on the client/server mode.

■ **ISDN Nonfacility Associated Signaling (NFAS) is supported:** The H.323 gateway signaling protocol supports NFAS, which MGCP does not.

■ **Fax support is improved:** Fax support is better on H.323 gateways than on MGCP gateways because H.323 supports T.37 and T.38, and an H.323 gateway can route a fax direct-inward-dialing (DID) number directly to a Foreign Exchange Station (FXS) port on the gateway.

■ **Call preservation is enhanced:** H.323 VoIP call preservation enhancements for WAN link failures sustain connectivity for H.323 topologies where signaling is handled by an entity that is different from the other endpoint, such as Cisco Unified Communications Manager. Call preservation is useful when a gateway and the other endpoint (typically a Cisco Unified IP Phone) are collocated at the same site, and the call agent is remote and therefore more likely to experience connectivity failures.

Regional Requirements Example Using H.323 Gateways

This example, as shown in Figure 5-3, describes how you can meet regional dialing requirements when you use H.323 gateways.

In this scenario, the number 917216111 from Spain (Madrid) is calling the United States and to Germany. Because the International Direct Dialing (IDD) prefix for Spain is 34, the number that is sent out as the calling party by the Spanish provider is "34917216111" with "international" as the Type of Number (TON). The following procedure then allows number modification to make sure people are able to call back to Madrid from their Cisco IP Phone missed call list:

1. The calling party number of the Madrid phone is 34917216111 with an international TON.

2. Madrid is calling Mel in the United States.

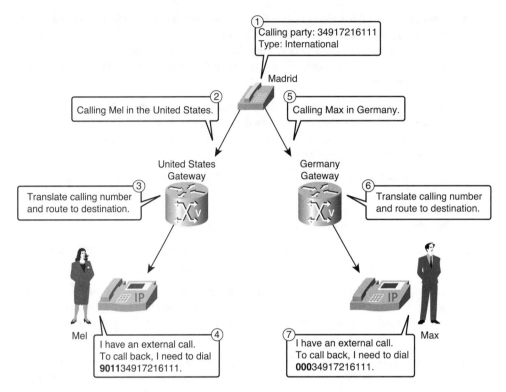

Figure 5-3 *Regional Requirements Example*

3. As the call is coming into the gateway within the United States, the calling party number (34917216111) is being translated to meet the common dialing regulations of the United States. This means the number uses these translation parameters:

   - A leading 9 as the access code for external calls from the company network

   - 011 as the international dialing prefix

4. Mel's missed calls list displays a call from 901134917216111, and she will be able to call back Madrid as soon as she returns.

5. Madrid is calling Max in Germany. The calling party number of the Madrid phone is 34917216111 with an international TON.

6. As the call is coming into the gateway in Germany, the calling party number (34917216111) is being translated to meet the common dialing regulations of Germany. This means the number uses these translation parameters:

   - A leading 0 as the access code for external calls from the company network

   - 00 as the international dialing prefix

7. Max's missed calls list displays a call from 00034917216111, and he will be able to call back Madrid as soon as he returns.

H.323 Network Components

Figure 5-4 shows some typical terminal devices in an H.323 network.

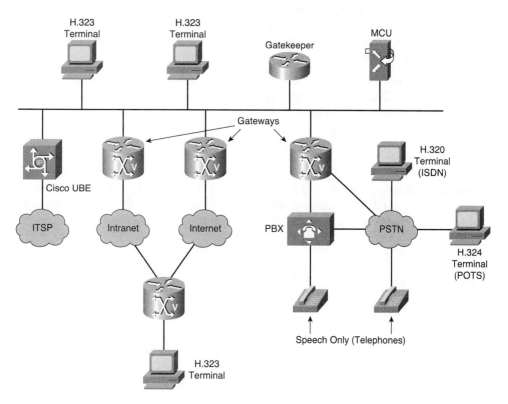

Figure 5-4   *H.323 Network Components*

Components of an H.323 network include the following:

- Terminals

    - H.323

    - H.324

- Gateways

- Cisco Unified Border Elements (Cisco UBEs), also known as session border controllers

- Gatekeepers

- MCUs

The following sections cover each in more detail.

H.323 Terminals

An H.323 terminal is an endpoint that provides real-time voice (and optionally, video and data) communications with another endpoint, such as an H.323 terminal, or multipoint control unit (MCU). The communications consist of control, indications, audio, moving color video pictures, or data between two terminals. A terminal might provide audio only; audio and data; audio and video; or audio, data, and video. The terminal can be a computer-based video conferencing system or other device.

An H.323 terminal must be capable of transmitting and receiving G.711 (a-law and Ì-law) 64 kbps Pulse Code Modulation (PCM)-encoded voice and might support other encoded voice formats, such as G.729 and G.723.1.

H.324 Terminals

ITU-T Recommendation H.324 defines the overall system structure and therefore the device commonly known as an H.324 terminal. H.324 is an ITU-T recommendation for voice, video, and data transmission over regular analog phone lines. It uses a regular 33,600 bps modem for transmission, H.263 codec for video encoding, and G.723 for audio.

H.323 Gateways

Figure 5-5 shows a gateway between an H.323 terminal and a non-H.323 terminal such as an analog telephone.

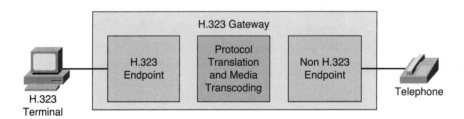

Figure 5-5   *H.323 Gateways*

An H.323 gateway is an endpoint on the LAN that provides real-time communications between H.323 terminals on the LAN and other ITU terminals on a WAN or to other H.323 gateways.

Gateways allow H.323 terminals to communicate with devices that are running other protocols. They provide protocol conversion between the devices that are running different types of protocols. Ideally, the gateway is transparent to both the H.323 endpoint and the non-H.323 endpoint.

An H.323 gateway performs these services:

■ Translation between audio, video, and data formats

■ Conversion between call setup signals and procedures

■ Conversion between communication control signals and procedures

Cisco Unified Border Elements

Figure 5-6 shows sample placement of Cisco UBEs in a service provider's network.

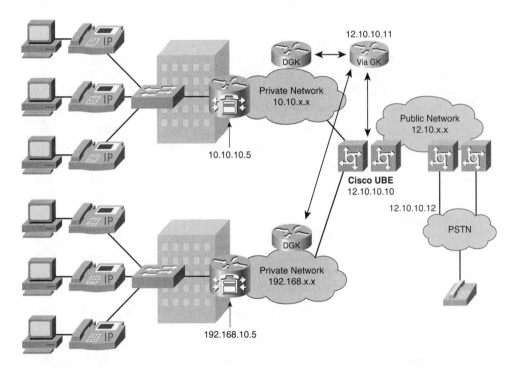

Figure 5-6 *Cisco Unified Border Element*

A Cisco UBE is an optional H.323 component. The Cisco UBE facilitates easy and cost-effective connectivity between independent VoIP service provider networks. Some in the industry refer to Cisco UBEs as "session border controllers." The Cisco UBE provides a network-to-network interface point for billing, security, Cisco Unified Communications Manager interconnectivity, Call Admission Control (CAC), and signaling interworking. It performs most of the same functions of a PSTN-to-IP gateway, but joins two VoIP call legs. Media packets can either flow through the gateway and hide the networks from each other, or flow around the Cisco UBE if network security is not of primary importance.

Figure 5-6 illustrates a basic Cisco UBE network. From the perspective of the private, or customer, networks, the Cisco UBE will appear as a single public address that must be routable on their private networks (in this case, a 12.x.x.x address routable on the 10.10.x.x and 192.168.x.x networks). Care must be taken at the Cisco UBE to ensure proper routing restrictions are in place to prevent communication directly between the private networks attached to it. Also note that this model works only if no overlapping address schemes are used on the customer networks. Finally, to the hop-off gateways on the public network, all calls will appear to originate from the 12.x.x.x address of the Cisco UBE and not the private addresses on the customer networks. Also note that the gatekeepers shown in Figure 5.6 control each zone independently, with the 12.10.10.11 gatekeeper acting as the control point for the public network, and therefore the Cisco UBE.

Codec-order preservation enables a gateway to pass codec preferences to the terminating leg of a VoIP call. This feature was developed primarily for Cisco UBEs, which are configured to use a transparent codec. The transparent codec enables a Cisco UBE to pass codecs from the originating endpoint to the terminating endpoint. However, previous versions of the Cisco UBE did not preserve the preferential order of the codecs.

With codec-order preservation, the Cisco UBE passes codecs transparently from the originating device, listed in order of preference, to the terminating device. It also enables gateways to pass user-configured codecs in their preferred order when the endpoints exchange capabilities, enabling endpoints to use the codec that best suits both devices.

H.323 Gatekeepers

An H.323 gatekeeper, as illustrated in Figure 5-7, is an H.323 entity on the LAN that provides address translation and that controls access to the LAN for H.323 terminals, gateways, and MCUs. Gatekeepers are optional nodes that manage endpoints in an H.323 network. The endpoints communicate with the gatekeeper using the RAS protocol.

Endpoints attempt to register with a gatekeeper on startup. When they want to communicate with another endpoint, they request admission to initiate a call using a symbolic alias for the endpoint, such as an E.164 address or an e-mail address. If the gatekeeper decides the call can proceed, it returns a destination IP address to the originating endpoint. This IP address might not be the actual address of the destination endpoint, but it might be an intermediate address, such as the address of a proxy or a gatekeeper that routes call signaling.

The Cisco gatekeeper provides H.323 call management, including admission control, bandwidth management, and routing services for calls in the network.

Note   Although the gatekeeper is an optional H.323 component, it must be included in the network if proxies are used.

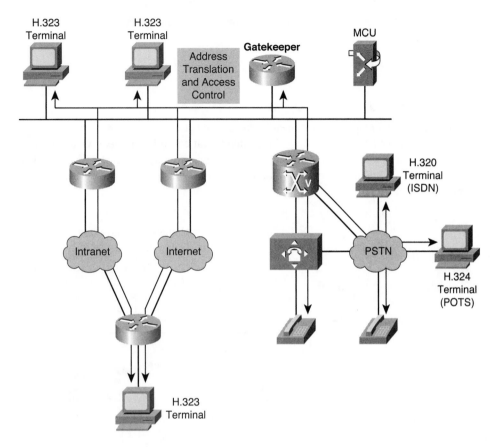

Figure 5-7   *H.323 Gatekeepers*

The scope of endpoints over which a gatekeeper exercises its authority is called a zone. H.323 defines a one-to-one relationship between a zone and a gatekeeper.

When a gatekeeper is included, it must perform these functions:

- **Address translation:** Converts an alias address to an IP address

- **Admission control:** Limits access to network resources based on call bandwidth restrictions

- **Bandwidth control:** Responds to bandwidth requests and modifications

- **Zone management:** Provides services to registered endpoints

The gatekeeper might also perform these functions:

- **Call control signaling:** Performs call signaling on behalf of the endpoint (gatekeeper-routed call signaling)

- **Call authorization:** Rejects calls based on authorization failure

- **Bandwidth management:** Limits the number of concurrent accesses to IP internetwork resources (CAC)

- **Call management:** Maintains a record of ongoing calls

Multipoint Control Units

MCU, as shown in Figure 5-8, is an endpoint on the network that allows three or more endpoints to participate in a multipoint conference. It controls and mixes video, audio, and data from endpoints to create a robust multimedia conference. An MCU might also connect two endpoints in a point-to-point conference, which might later develop into a multipoint conference.

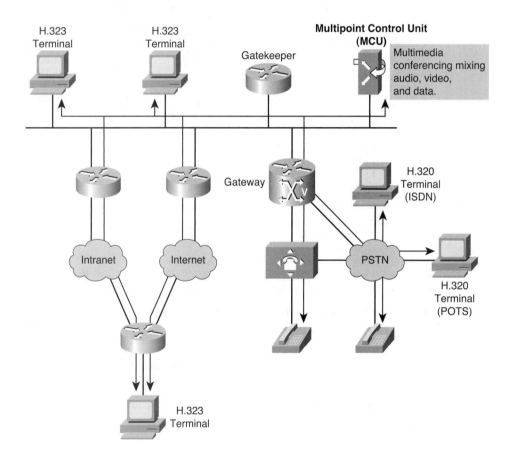

Figure 5-8   *Multipoint Control Unit*

H.323 Call Establishment and Maintenance

Although H.323 is based on the concepts of a distributed call control model, it often embodies centralized call control model concepts. Calls can be established between any of these components:

- **Endpoint to endpoint:** The intelligence of H.323 endpoints allows them to operate autonomously. In this mode of operation, endpoints locate other endpoints through nonstandard mechanisms and initiate direct communication between the endpoints.

- **Endpoint to gatekeeper:** When a gatekeeper is added to the network, endpoints interoperate with the gatekeeper using the RAS channel.

- **Gatekeeper to gatekeeper:** In the presence of multiple gatekeepers, gatekeepers communicate with each other on the RAS channel.

H.323 Call Flows

H.323 calls might occur with or without the use of a gatekeeper. Figure 5-9 shows an H.323 basic call setup exchange between two gateways. The optional gatekeeper is not present in this example. Although gateways are shown, the same procedure is used when one or both endpoints are H.323 terminals.

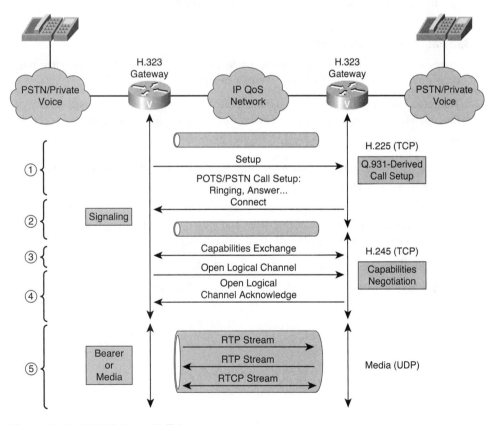

Figure 5-9 *H.323 Basic Call Setup*

H.323 Basic Call Setup

The flow procedure without a gatekeeper includes these steps:

1. The originating gateway initiates an H.225.0 session with the destination gateway on registered TCP port 1720. The gateway determines the IP address of the destination gateway internally. The gateway has the IP address of the destination endpoint in its configuration, or it knows a Domain Name System (DNS) resolvable domain name for the destination.

2. Call setup procedures based on Q.931 create a call-signaling channel between the endpoints.

3. The endpoints open another channel for the H.245 control function. The H.245 control function negotiates capabilities and exchanges logical channel descriptions.

4. The logical channel descriptions open RTP sessions.

5. The endpoints exchange multimedia over the RTP sessions, including exchanging call quality statistics using RTP Control Protocol (RTCP).

H.323 Fast Connect Call Setup

Figure 5-10 shows an H.323 setup exchange that uses the Fast Connect abbreviated procedure available in version 2 of ITU-T Recommendation H.323.

The Fast Connect procedure reduces the number of round-trip exchanges and achieves the capability exchange and logical channel assignments in one round trip.

The Fast Connect procedure includes these steps:

1. The originating gateway initiates an H.225.0 session with the destination gateway on registered TCP port 1720.

2. Call setup procedures based on Q.931 create a combined call-signaling channel and control channel for H.245. Capabilities and logical channel descriptions are exchanged within the Q.931 call setup procedure.

3. Logical channel descriptions open RTP sessions.

4. The endpoints exchange multimedia over the RTP sessions.

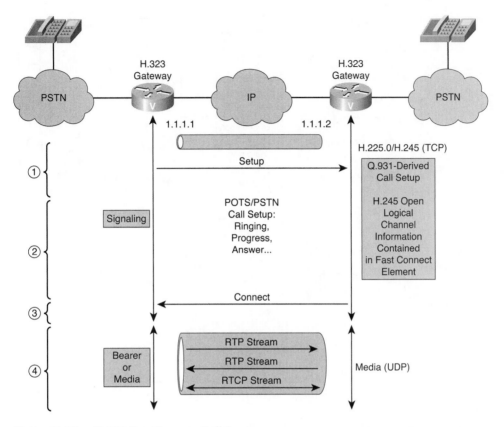

Figure 5-10   *H.323 Fast Connect Call Setup*

H.323 Multipoint Conferences

H.323 defines three types of multipoint conferences, as shown in Figure 5-11: central-ized, decentralized (or sometimes called distributed), and ad hoc. H.323 also defines a hybrid of the first two.

All types of multipoint conferences rely on a single MC to coordinate the membership of a conference. Each endpoint has an H.245 control channel connection to the MC. Either the MC or the endpoint initiates the control channel setup. H.323 defines the following three types of conferences:

■ **Centralized multipoint conference:** The endpoints must have their audio, video, or data channels connected to a multipoint processor (MP). The MP performs mixing and switching of the audio, video, and data, and if the MP supports the capability, each endpoint can operate in a different mode.

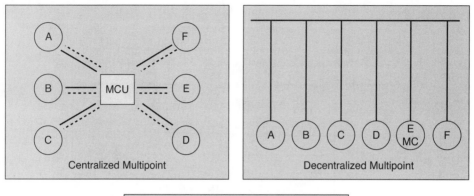

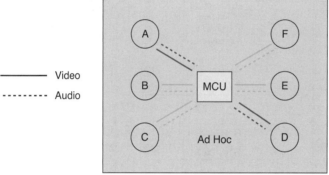

Figure 5-11 *Multipoint Conferences*

■   **Distributed multipoint conference:** The endpoints do not have a connection to an MP. Instead, endpoints multicast their audio, video, and data streams to all participants in the conference. Because an MP is not available for switching and mixing, any mixing of the conference streams is a function of the endpoint, and all endpoints must use the same communication parameters.

To accommodate situations in which two streams (audio and video) would be handled by the different multipoint conference models, H.323 defines a "hybrid." A hybrid describes a situation in which the audio and video streams are managed by a single H.245 control channel with the MC, but where one stream relies on multicast (according to the distributed model) and the other uses the MP (as in the centralized model).

■   **Ad hoc multipoint conference:** Any two endpoints in a call can convert their relationship into a point-to-point conference. If neither of the endpoints has a collocated MC, the services of a gatekeeper are used. When the point-to-point conference is created, other endpoints become part of the conference by accepting an invitation from a current participant, or the endpoint can request to join the conference.

Configuring H.323 Gateways

Options for setting up an H.323 gateway include the following:

■ Enable H.323 VoIP call services (required)

■ Configure an interface as an H.323 gateway interface (required)

■ Configure codecs (optional)

■ Configure Dual Tone Multifrequency (DTMF) and fax relay (optional)

■ Adjust H.225 settings (optional)

Depending on the deployment scenario, you might be configuring only the required features or many of the options available for an H.323 voice gateway.

H.323 Configuration Example

Figure 5-12 offers a sample topology that needs to be configured for H.323.

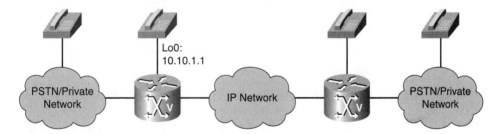

Figure 5-12   *H.323 Configuration Example Topology*

As a network administrator, you have been asked to deploy an H.323-based VoIP network between two corporate sites. Both sites are using a Cisco IOS H.323 capable gateway for the remote connection. You should deploy the network to meet network requirements:

■ Use H.323 as a signaling protocol.

■ The H.323 ID of the gateway should be **gw1**.

■ A loopback interface is to be used as the connection to the remote site.

■ Multiple codecs must be available for negotiation in this order:

■ G.711

■ G.729

■ E.164-Address Registration must be configured, because some phones are directly connected to the gateway.

■ H.323 timers need to be tuned.

A four-step procedure can then be followed to configure an H.323 gateway according to network requirements:

Step 1.   Enable H.323 VoIP services globally.

Step 2.   Configure an interface as an H.323 gateway.

Step 3.   Create a codec voice class and populate with a list of codecs in order of their preference.

Step 4.   Adjust H.225 timers.

These four steps are detailed as follows:

Step 1.   Enable H.323 VoIP services globally.

Enter voice-service configuration mode and specify a voice-encapsulation type.

```
Router(config)#voice service {pots | voatm | vofr | voip}
```

The following is a description of the syntax:

■ **pots:** Plain Old Telephone Service (POTS) voice service

■ **voatm:** Voice over ATM (VoATM) encapsulation

■ **vofr:** Voice over Frame Relay (VoFR) encapsulation

■ **voip:** Voice over IP (VoIP) encapsulation

Voice-service configuration mode is used for packet telephony service commands that affect the gateway globally.

Select H.323-call-processing submode and enable the H.323 voice service configuration commands.

```
Router(conf-voi-serv)#h323
```

Activate the service.

```
Router(conf-voi-serv)#no shutdown
```

Step 2.   Configure an interface as an H.323 gateway.

Enter interface configuration mode for the interface that is connected to the gatekeeper.

```
Router(config)#interface interface
```

Assign an IP address to the interface.

```
Router(config-if)#ip address ip-address network-mask
```

Identify the interface as a VoIP gateway interface.

```
Router(config-if)#h323-gateway voip interface
```

Define the H.323 name of the gateway.

```
Router(config-if)#h323-gateway voip h323-id name
```

> **Note**   Usually this step is the name of the gateway, with the gatekeeper domain name appended, for example: name@domainname.

Designate a source IP address for the voice gateway.

```
Router(config-if)#h323-gateway voip bind srcaddr ip-address
```

This command sets the source IP address to be used for this gateway. The IP address is used for outgoing H.323 traffic, which includes H.225, H.245, and RAS messages. You do not have to issue this command on the interface that you defined as the voice gateway interface (although it might be more convenient to do so). Use this command on the interface that contains the IP address to which you want to bind (for example, a loopback interface).

Configuring Codecs on an H.323 Gateway

Normally you configure only one codec when you configure a dial peer on a gateway. However, you can configure a prioritized list of codecs to increase the probability of establishing a connection between endpoints during the H.245 exchange phase.

Codec-order preservation is enabled by default in Cisco gateways running Cisco IOS Release 12.3(1) and later. No further configuration is needed.

Step 3.   To configure codec negotiation, you must first create a codec voice class and populate with a list of codecs in order of their preference.

Enter voice-class configuration mode and assign an identification tag number for this codec voice class.

```
Router(config)#voice class codec tag
```

This command only creates the voice class for codec selection preference and assigns an identification tag. Use the **codec preference** command to specify the parameters of the voice class, and use the **voice-class codec** dial-peer command to apply the voice class to a VoIP dial peer.

Specify a list of preferred codecs to use on a dial peer.

```
Router(config-class)#codec preference value codec-type [bytes payload-
    size]
```

Table 5-1 details the syntax options for this command.

Table 5-1   codec preference *Syntax Description*

Value	The order of preference, with 1 being the most preferred and 14 being the least preferred
codec-type	The codec preferred. Values are as follows:
	clear-channel: Clear Channel 64,000 bps
	g711alaw: G.711 a-law 64,000 bps
	g711ulaw: G.711 mu-law 64,000 bps
	g723ar53: G.723.1 ANNEX-A 5300 bps
	g723ar63: G.723.1 ANNEX-A 6300 bps
	g723r53: G.723.1 5300 bps
	g723r63: G.723.1 6300 bps
	g726r16: G.726 16,000 bps
	g726r24: G.726 24,000 bps
	g726r32: G.726 32,000 bps
	g728: G.728 16,000 bps
	g729abr8: G.729 ANNEX-A and B 8000 bps
	g729br8: G.729 ANNEX-B 8000 bps
	g729r8: G.729 8000 bps
	gsmamr-nb: Enables GSMAMR codec capability
	gsmefr: Global System for Mobile Communications Enhanced Full Rate (GSMEFR) 12,200 bps
	gsmfr: Global System for Mobile Communications (GSM) Full Rate (GSMFR) 13,200 bps
	ilbc: internet Low Bit rate Codec (iLBC) at 13,330 bps or 15,200 bps
	transparent: Enables codec capabilities to be passed transparently between endpoints (Note: The **transparent** keyword is not supported when the **call-start** command is configured.)
bytes payload-size	(Optional) Number of bytes you specify as the voice payload of each frame. Values depend on the codec type and the packet voice protocol.

Enter dial-peer configuration mode for the VoIP dial peer.

```
Router(config)#dial-peer voice tag voip
```

Specify a single codec or assign the previously configured codec selection preference list to the VoIP dial peer.

To specify a single codec

```
Router(config-dial-peer)#codec {clear-channel | g711alaw | g711ulaw |
    g723ar53 | g723ar63 | g723r53 | g723r63 | g726r16 | g726r24 | g726r32 |
    g726r53 | g726r63 | g728 | g729abr8 | g729ar8 | g729br8 | g729r8 |
    gsmefr | gsmfr} [bytes payload_size]
```

Tuning H.323 Timers

The last part of the scenario requires you to adjust some of the H.323 timers to meet network specifications.

Step 4.   Adjust H.225 timers.

Create an H.323 voice class and enter voice class configuration mode.

```
Router(config)#voice class h323 tag
```

To set the H.225 TCP establish timeout value for VoIP dial peers, configure the H.323 TCP establish timeout value.

```
Router(config-class)#h225 timeout tcp establish seconds
```

The number of seconds for the timeout range is 0 to 30. The default is 15. If you specify 0, the H.225 TCP timer is disabled.

Configure the SETUP Response Timeout value.

```
Router(config-class)#h225 timeout setup value
```

This command sets the timeout value, in seconds, for the response of the outgoing SETUP message. Range: 0 to 30. Default: 15.

Enter dial-peer configuration mode for the VoIP dial peer.

```
Router(config)#dial-peer voice tag voip
```

Assign the previously configured H.323 voice class to this VoIP dial peer.

```
Router(config-dial-peer)#voice-class h323 tag
```

Enter voice-service configuration mode and specify a voice-encapsulation type.

```
Router(config)#voice service {pots | voatm | vofr | voip}
```

Enable the H.323 voice service configuration commands.

```
Router(conf-voi-serv)#h323
```

To set a timer for an idle call connection, change the Idle Timer for concurrent calls.

```
Router(conf-serv-h323)#h225 timeout tcp call-idle {value value | never}
```

The following is a description of the syntax:

■ **value** *value*: The timeout value, in minutes. The range is 0 to 1440. The default is 10. If you specify 0, the timer is disabled, and the TCP connection is closed immediately after all the calls are cleared.

■ **never:** The connection is maintained permanently or until the other endpoint closes it.

This command specifies the time to maintain an established H.225 TCP connection when there are no calls on that connection. If the timer expires, the connection is closed. If the timer is running and any new call is made on that connection, the timer stops. When all the calls are cleared on that connection, the timer starts again.

H.323 Complete Configuration

Example 5-1 illustrates the complete H.323 configuration example previously described.

Example 5-1   *H.323 Configuration Example*

```
Router(config)#voice service voip
Router(conf-voi-serv)#h323
Router(conf-voi-serv)#no shutdown
Router(config)#interface loopback 0
Router(config-if)#ip address 10.10.1.1 255.255.255.0
Router(config-if)#h323-gateway voip interface
Router(config-if)#h323-gateway voip h323-id gw1
Router(config-if)#h323-gateway voip bind srcaddr 10.10.1.1
Router(config)#voice class codec 100
Router(config-class)#codec preference 1 g711alaw
Router(config-class)#codec preference 2 g729br8
Router(config)#dial-peer voice 500 voip
Router(config-dial-peer)#voice-class codec 100
                        Or
Router(config-dial-peer)#codec g711alaw
Router(config)#voice class h323 600
Router(config-class)#h225 timeout tcp establish 10
Router(config-class)#h225 timeout setup 10
Router(config)#dial-peer voice 500 voip
Router(config-dial-peer)#voice-class h323 600
Router(config)#voice service voip
Router(conf-voi-serv)#h323
Router(conf-serv-h323)#h225 timeout tcp call-idle never
```

Configuring H.323 Fax Pass-Through and Relay

Tones used by fax machines can be degraded by a codec (for example, G.729) to the point that they are unintelligible by a far-end fax machine. In an H.323 environment, two approaches for preserving fax tones across an IP WAN include fax relay and fax pass-through.

Fax Pass-Through Example

Figure 5-13 shows an example of a topology containing a voice gateway that is configured for H.323 and fax pass-through. Fax pass-through is configured to forward faxes
from a T1 (mu-law), and fax relay is disabled.

Figure 5-13   *H.323 Fax Pass-Through Configuration Example Topology*

This scenario requires a company's headquarters in San Jose to be able to fax to its
Austin office using fax pass-through. As a network administrator, your responsibility is
to configure the gateway to meet the requirements of the network.

Requirements dictate that you

- Create a dial peer to match a destination pattern for the Austin fax machine extension number.

- Specify the session target for the VoIP dial peer as the Austin fax.

- Configure Cisco fax pass-through to be used for fax support between the networks.

- Specify the codec that is to be used for fax pass-through operation.

- Specify the fax rate to be used for fax transmission to the Austin fax machine.

Complete the following steps to configure fax pass-through and relay with dial-peers.

Step 1.   Enter VoIP dial-peer configuration mode.

```
Router(config)#dial-peer voice id voip
```

Step 2.   Specify the destination pattern.

```
Router(config-dial-peer)#destination-pattern pattern
```

Step 3.   Specify the session target for VoIP dial peer.

```
Router(config-dial-peer)#session target ipv4:ip-address
```

Step 4.   Specify the fax protocol to be used for a specific VoIP dial peer.

```
Router(config-dial-peer)#fax protocol {cisco | none | system | pass-
   through {g711ulaw | g711alaw}}
```

Use the fax protocol command in dial-peer configuration mode to configure the type of fax relay capability for a specific dial peer. Note the following command behavior:

- **fax protocol none:** Disables all fax handling.

- **no fax protocol:** Sets the fax protocol for the dial peer to the default, which is **system**.

If the **fax protocol** (voice-service) command is used to set fax relay options for all dial peers and the **fax protocol** (dial peer) command is used on a specific dial peer, the dial peer configuration takes precedence over the global configuration for that dial peer.

Step 5.   Specify the rate at which a fax is sent to a specified dial peer.

```
Router(config-dial-peer)#fax rate {2400 | 4800 | 7200 | 9600 | 12000 |
   14400} {disable | voice} [bytes rate]
```

Use this command to specify the fax transmission rate to the specified dial peer.

The higher transmission speed values (for example, 14,400 bps) provide a faster transmission speed but monopolize a significantly large portion of the available bandwidth. The lower transmission speed values (for example, 2400 bps) provide a slower transmission speed and use a relatively smaller portion of the available bandwidth.

Note   The fax call is not compressed using the **ip rtp header-compression** command because UDP is being used and not RTP. For example, a 9600 bps fax call requires approximately 24 kbps.

If the fax rate transmission speed is set higher than the codec rate in the same dial peer, the data sent over the network for fax transmission is above the bandwidth reserved for Resource Reservation Protocol (RSVP).

The **voice** keyword specifies the highest possible transmission speed allowed by the voice rate. For example, if the voice codec is G.711, the fax transmission might occur at a rate up to 14,400 bps because 14,400 bps is less than the 64 kbps voice rate. If the voice codec is G.729 (8 kbps), the fax transmission speed is 7200 bps.

Example 5-2 illustrates the complete H.323 fax pass-through configuration example previously described.

Example 5-2   *H.323 Fax Pass-Through Configuration Example*

```
Router(config)#dial-peer voice 550 voip
Router(config-dial-peer)#destination-pattern 550
Router(config-dial-peer)#session target ipv4:10.1.1.50
Router(config-dial-peer)fax protocol pass-through g711ulaw
Router(config-dial-peer)#fax rate 14400
```

Fax Relay Example

Figure 5-14 shows a topology example for a voice service VoIP and dial-peer configuration of a voice gateway that is configured for fax relay.

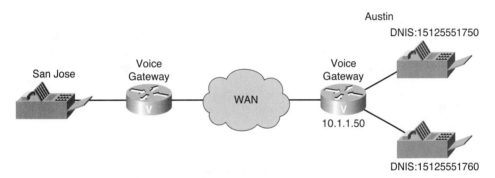

Figure 5-14   *H.323 Fax Relay Configuration Topology Example*

This scenario requires a company's headquarters in San Jose to be able to fax to its Austin office using T.38 and Cisco fax relay. As a network administrator, your responsibility is to configure the gateway to meet the requirements of the network.

Requirements dictate that you

■ Create two separate dial peers.

■ Configure T.38 fax relay for VoIP dial peers globally.

■ Configure Cisco Fax Relay for a single VoIP dial peer to override the global value.

■ Disable error-correction-mode for a specific dial peer.

■ Specify the fax transmission rate for a specific dial peer.

The default fax protocol is set to T.38 using the **fax protocol t38** command to the voice service VoIP configuration and then is overridden in dial peer 14152 to **cisco**. In addition, the fax relay is set to support G3 fax machines and allows a maximum transfer speed of 14.4 kbps for calls to 14151xx numbers.

You can use the following procedure to configure H.323 fax relay.

Step 1.   Enter voice-service configuration mode and specify a voice-encapsulation type.

```
Router(config)#voice service {pots | voatm | vofr | voip}
```

Voice-service configuration mode is used for packet telephony service commands that affect the gateway globally.

Step 2.   Specify the global default ITU-T T.38 standard fax protocol to be used for all VoIP dial peers.

```
Router(conf-voi-serv)#fax protocol t38 [nse [force]] [ls-redundancy
    value [hs-redundancy value]] [fallback {none | pass-through {g711ulaw
    | g711alaw}}]
```

Use the **fax protocol t38** command and the **voice service voip** command to configure T.38 fax relay capability for all VoIP dial peers. If the **fax protocol t38** (voice-service) command is used to set fax relay options for all dial peers, and the **fax protocol t38** (dial peer) command is used on a specific dial peer, the dial-peer configuration takes precedence over the global configuration for that dial peer.

Step 3.   Exit voice-service configuration mode.

```
Router(conf-voi-serv)#exit
```

Step 4.   Enter VoIP dial-peer configuration mode.

```
Router(config)#dial-peer voice id voip
```

Step 5.   Disable fax-relay Error Correction Mode (ECM).

```
Router(config-dial-peer)#fax-relay ecm disable
```

When this command is entered, the digital signal processor (DSP) fax-relay firmware disables ECM by modifying the Digital Information Signal (DIS) T.30 message. This is performed on DIS signals in both directions so that the ECM is disabled in both directions, even if only one gateway is configured with ECM disabled.

Note   This setting is provisioned when the DSP channel starts fax relay and cannot be changed during the fax relay session.

Step 6.   Enable the fax stream between two Super Group 3 (SG3) fax machines to negotiate down to G3 speeds.

```
Router(config-dial-peer)#fax-relay sg3-to-g3
```

Example 5-3 illustrates the complete H.323 fax-relay configuration example previously described.

Example 5-3   *H.323 Fax-Relay Configuration Example*

```
Router(config)#voice service voip
Router(conf-voi-serv)#fax protocol t38
Router(conf-voi-serv)#exit
Router(config)#dial-peer voice 14151 voip
Router(config-dial-peer)#destination-pattern 15125551750
Router(config-dial-peer)#session target ipv4:10.1.1.50
Router(config-dial-peer)#fax-relay ecm disable
Router(config-dial-peer)#fax-relay sg3-to-g3
Router(config-dial-peer)#fax rate 14400
Router(config-dial-peer)#exit
Router(config)#dial-peer voice 14152 voip
Router(config-dial-peer)#destination-pattern 15125551760
Router(config-dial-peer)#session target ipv4:10.1.1.50
Router(config-dial-peer)#fax protocol cisco
```

Configuring H.323 DTMF Relay

DTMF is the tone generated when you press a button on a touch-tone phone. This tone is compressed at one end of a call. When the tone is decompressed at the other end, it can become distorted, depending on the codec used. The DTMF relay feature transports DTMF tones generated after call establishment out-of-band using either a standard H.323 out-of-band method or a proprietary RTP-based mechanism. For SIP calls, the most appropriate method to transport DTMF tones is RTP-NTE or SIP-NOTIFY.

Although DTMF is usually transported accurately when using high-bit-rate voice codecs such as G.711, low-bit-rate codecs, such as G.729 and G.723.1 are highly optimized for voice patterns and tend to distort DTMF tones. As a result, interactive voice response (IVR) systems might not correctly recognize the tones.

To specify how an H.323 or a SIP gateway relays dual-tone multifrequency (DTMF) tones between telephony interfaces and an IP network, use the **dtmf-relay** command.

You can use the following procedure to configure DTMF relay on a Cisco IOS gateway.

Step 1.   Enter dial-peer configuration mode for the appropriate dial peer.

Step 2.   Enable DTMF tone forwarding.

```
Router(config-dial-peer)#dtmf-relay {[cisco-rtp] [h245-alphanumeric]
      [h245-signal] [rtp-nte [digit-drop]] [sip-notify]}
```

The principal advantage of the **dtmf-relay** command is that it sends DTMF tones with greater fidelity than is possible in-band for most low-bandwidth codecs, such as G.729 and G.723. Without the use of DTMF relay, calls established with low-bandwidth codecs might have trouble accessing automated DTMF-based systems, such as voice mail, menu-based Automatic Call Distributor (ACD) systems, and automated banking systems.

Figure 5-15 and Example 5-4 illustrate a complete H.323 DTMF relay configuration example.

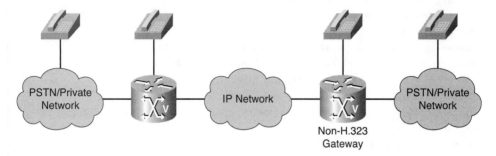

Figure 5-15   *H.323 DTMF Relay Configuration Topology Example*

Example 5-4   *H.323 DTMF Configuration Example*

```
Router(config)#dial-peer voice 500 voip
Router(config-dial-peer)#dtmf-relay h245-alphanumeric
```

Verifying an H.323 Gateway

Use the **show gateway** command to verify that an H.323 gateway is operational and to display the current status of the gateway.

Example 5-5 shows a sample report that appears when a gateway is not registered with a gatekeeper.

Example 5-5   show gateway *Command with an Unregistered Gateway*

```
Router#show gateway
H.323 ITU-T Version: 4.0   H323 Stack Version: 0.1

 H.323 service is up
 This gateway  is not registered to any gatekeeper

Alias list (CLI configured) is empty
Alias list (last RCF) is empty
```

Example 5-6 shows a sample report that indicates an E.164 address has been assigned to the gateway.

Example 5-6   show gateway *Command with a Registered Gateway*

```
Router#show gateway
Gateway gateway1 is registered to Gatekeeper gk1
Gateway alias list
H323-ID gateway1
H323 resource thresholding is Enabled and Active
H323 resource threshold values:
DSP: Low threshold 60, High threshold 70
DS0: Low threshold 60, High threshold 70
```

Implementing MGCP Gateways

The MGCP enables the remote control and management of voice and data communications devices at the edge of multiservice IP packet networks. Because of its centralized architecture, MGCP overcomes the distributed configuration and administration problems inherent in the use of protocols such as H.323. This section describes how to configure MGCP on a gateway and describes the features and functions of the MGCP environment.

MGCP Overview

MGCP is a protocol used within a distributed VoIP system. MGCP is defined in RFC 3435, which obsoletes an earlier definition in RFC 2705. Another protocol used for the same purpose is Megaco, a coproduction of Internet Engineering Task Force (IETF) (RFC 3525) and ITU (Recommendation H.248-1). Both protocols follow the guidelines of the *API Media Gateway Control Protocol Architecture and Requirements* at RFC 2805.

These IETF standards describe MGCP as a centralized device control protocol with simple endpoints. The MGCP protocol allows a central control component, or call agent, to remotely control various devices. This protocol is referred to as a stimulus protocol because the endpoints and gateways cannot function alone. MGCP incorporates the IETF Session Description Protocol (SDP) to describe the type of session to initiate.

MGCP is an extension of the earlier version of Simple Gateway Control Protocol (SGCP) and supports SGCP functionality in addition to several enhancements. Systems using SGCP can easily migrate to MGCP, and MGCP commands are available to enable SGCP capabilities.

MGCP is a plaintext protocol that uses a server-to-client relationship between the call agent and the gateway to fully control the gateway and its associated ports. The plaintext commands are sent to gateways from the call agent using UDP port 2427. Port 2727 is used to send messages from the gateways to the call agent.

An MGCP gateway handles translation between audio signals and a packet network. Gateways interact with a call agent (CA), also called a Media Gateway Controller (MGC), that performs signal and call processing on gateway calls. In the MGCP configurations that Cisco IOS supports, a gateway can be a Cisco router, access server, or cable modem, and the CA is a server from a third-party vendor.

Configuration commands for MGCP define the path between the call agent and the gateway, the type of gateway, and the type of calls handled by the gateway.

MGCP uses endpoints and connections to construct a call. Endpoints are sources or destinations for data and can be physical or logical locations in a device. Connections can be point-to-point or multipoint.

Similar to SGCP, MGCP uses UDP for establishing audio connections over IP networks. However, MGCP also uses "hairpinning" to return a call to the PSTN when the packet network is not available.

Why MGCP

There are several advantages to using MGCP controlled gateways as voice gateways:

■ **Alternative dial tone for VoIP environments:** Deregulation in the telecommunications industry gives Competitive Local-Exchange Carriers (CLECs) opportunities to provide toll-bypass from the Incumbent Local-Exchange Carriers (ILECs) by means of VoIP. MGCP enables a VoIP system to control call setup and teardown and Custom Local Area Subscriber Services (CLASS) features for less-sophisticated gateways.

■ **Simplified configuration for static VoIP network dial peers:** When you use MGCP as the call agent in a VoIP environment, you need not configure static VoIP network dial peers. The MGCP call agent provides functions similar to VoIP-network dial peers.

Note   POTS dial-peer configuration is still required.

■ **Migration paths:** Systems using earlier versions of the protocol can easily migrate to MGCP.

■ **Centralized dial plan configured on Cisco Unified Communications Manager:** A centralized dial plan configuration on Cisco UBE enables you to handle and manage the entire dial plan configuration on Cisco Unified Communications Manager cluster within a multisite network. This simplifies the management and troubleshooting of a company telephone network.

■ **Centralized gateway configuration on Cisco Unified Communications Manager:** As in the case of the dial plan, centralized gateway configurations for all gateways are managed via one central configuration page, which simplifies the management and troubleshooting of a company telephony network.

> **Note**   Some network management tools do not work correctly when performing the configuration via Cisco Unified Communications Manager. In such cases, you might need to manually configure the gateway for MGCP without using the config download functionality.

■ **Simple Cisco IOS gateway configuration:** Because the gateway configuration is mostly done on Cisco Unified Communications Manager, far fewer Cisco IOS router commands are necessary to bring up the gateway, as compared to any other gateway type.

■ **Supports Q Signaling (QSIG) supplementary services with Cisco Unified Communications Manager:** With the support of QSIG supplementary services, MGCP is a protocol you can use to interconnect a Cisco Unified Communications Manager environment with a traditional PBX.

MGCP Architecture

The distributed system is composed of a Call Agent (or Media Gateway Controller), at least one Media Gateway (MG) that performs the conversion of media signals between circuits and packets, and at least one Signaling Gateway (SG) when connected to the PSTN.

MGCP defines a number of components and concepts. You must understand the relationships between components and how the components use the concepts to implement a working MGCP environment.

Following are the components that are used in an MGCP environment:

■ **Endpoints:** Represent the point of interconnection between a packet network and a traditional telephone network.

■ **Gateways:** Handle the translation of audio between a SCN and a packet network. The media gateway uses MGCP to report events (such as off-hook or dialed digits) to a call agent.

■ **Call Agent:** Exercises control over the operation of a gateway. The call agent uses MGCP to tell the gateway

■ What events should be reported to the call agent

■ How endpoints should be connected

■ What signals should be implemented on endpoints

MGCP also allows the call agent to audit the current state of endpoints on a gateway.

Figure 5-16 shows an MGCP environment with all three components.

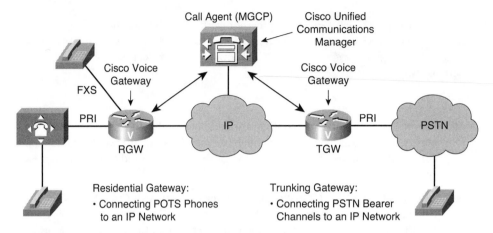

Figure 5-16 *MGCP Components*

Cisco voice gateways can act as MGCP gateways, and Cisco Unified Communications Manager acts as an MGCP call agent.

MGCP Gateways

Using Cisco IOS Software, voice gateways can be configured as MGCP gateways. Cisco Unified Communications Manager acts as an MGCP call agent, controlling the setting up and tearing down of connections between the endpoints in a VoIP network and endpoints in the PSTN, while managing all dial-plan related configuration elements.

In the case of MGCP, calls are routed via route patterns using Cisco Unified Communications Manager, not by dial peers on the gateway. The gateway voice ports must be configured for proper signaling. However, no dial peers exist for MGCP except when a router is using Cisco Unified SRST for fallback.

MGCP supports both residential and trunking gateways.

■ **Trunking gateway:** A trunking gateway (TGW) provides an interface between PSTN trunks and a VoIP network. A trunk can be a DS0, a T1, or an E1 line. Examples of TGWs include access servers and routers.

■ **Residential gateway:** A residential gateway (RGW) provides an interface between analog (RJ-11) calls from a telephone and a VoIP network. The interfaces on a residential gateway might terminate a POTS connection to a phone, a key system, or a PBX. Examples of RGWs include cable modems and Cisco 2600 Series routers.

MGCP gateway connections can be point-to-point or multipoint. A point-to-point connection is an association between two endpoints with the purpose of transmitting data between these endpoints. Data transfer between these endpoints can take place after this association is established for both endpoints. A multipoint connection is established by connecting the endpoint to a multipoint session. Connections can be established over several types of bearer networks:

- Transmission of audio packets using the RTP and UDP over an IP network.

- Transmission of audio packets using ATM adaptation Layer 2 (AAL2), or another adaptation layer, over an ATM network.

- Transmission of packets over an internal connection, such as a time-division multiplexing (TDM) backplane or the interconnection bus of a gateway. This method is used, in particular, for "hairpin" connections that are connections that terminate in a gateway but are immediately rerouted over the telephony network.

Note For point-to-point connections, the endpoints of a connection could be in separate gateways or in the same gateway.

Creating a call connection involves a series of *signals* and *events* that describe the connection process. Each event causes signal messages to be sent to the call agent, and associated commands are sent back. That information might include indicators such as the off-hook event that triggers a dial-tone signal. These events and signals are specific to the type of endpoint that is involved in the call. MGCP groups these events and signals into *packages*.

MGCP Call Agents

A call agent, or MGC, represents the central controller in an MGCP environment, as depicted in Figure 5-17.

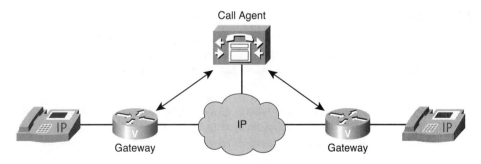

Figure 5-17 *MGCP Call Agent*

A call agent exercises control over the operation of a gateway and its associated endpoints by requesting that a gateway observe and report events. In response to the events, the call agent instructs the endpoint what signal, if any, the endpoint should send to the attached telephone equipment. This requires a call agent to recognize each endpoint type it supports and the signaling characteristics of each physical and logical interface that is attached to a gateway.

A call agent uses its directory of endpoints and the relationship each endpoint has with the dial plan to determine appropriate call routing. Call agents initiate all VoIP call legs.

Basic MGCP Concepts

The basic MGCP concepts are as follows:

- **MGCP calls and connections:** Allow end-to-end calls to be established by connecting two or more endpoints

- **MGCP control commands:** Fundamental MGCP concept that allows a call agent to provide instructions for a gateway

- **Package types:** Fundamental MGCP concept that allows a gateway to determine the call destination

MGCP Calls and Connections

End-to-end calls are established by connecting two or more endpoints. To establish a call, the call agent instructs the gateway that is associated with each endpoint to make a connection with a specific endpoint or an endpoint of a particular type. The gateway returns the session parameters of its connection to the call agent, which in turn sends these session parameters to the other gateway. With this method, each gateway acquires the necessary session parameters to establish RTP sessions between the endpoints. All connections that are associated with the same call will share a common Call ID and the same media stream. Figure 5-18 illustrates the setup and teardown of an MGCP call.

At the conclusion of a call, the call agent sends a DeleteConnection (DLCX) request to each gateway.

MGCP Control Commands

MGCP packets are unlike what you find in many other protocols. Usually wrapped in UDP port 2427, the MGCP datagrams are formatted with white space, much like you would expect to find in TCP protocols. An MGCP packet is either a command or a response.

A call agent uses control messages to direct its gateways and their operational behavior. Gateways use the control messages in responding to requests from a call agent and notifying the call agent of events and abnormal behavior.

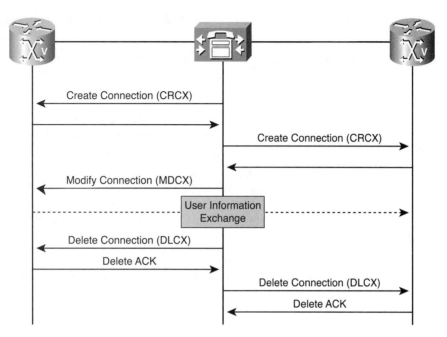

Figure 5-18   *Calls and Connections*

There are eight command verbs.

Two verbs are used by a call agent to query the state of a media gateway:

■   **AuditEndpoint (AUEP):** This message requests the status of an endpoint. The call agent issues the command.

■   **AuditConnection (AUCX):** This message requests the status of a connection. The call agent issues the command.

Three verbs are used by a call agent to manage an RTP connection on a media gateway. (A media gateway can also send a DLCX when it needs to delete a connection for its self-management.)

■   **CreateConnection (CRCX):** This message instructs the gateway to establish a connection with an endpoint. The call agent issues the command.

■   **DLCX:** This message informs the recipient to delete a connection. The call agent or the gateway can issue the command. The gateway or the call agent issues the command to advise that it no longer has the resources required to sustain the call.

■   **ModifyConnection (MDCX):** This message instructs the gateway to update its connection parameters for a previously established connection. The call agent issues the command.

One verb is used by a call agent to request notification of events on the media gateway and to request a media gateway to apply signals:

■   **NotificationRequest (RQNT):** This message instructs the gateway to watch for events on an endpoint and specifies the action to take when they occur. The call agent issues the command.

One verb is used by a media gateway to indicate to the call agent that it has detected an event for which the call agent had previously requested notification (via the RQNT command verb):

■   **Notify (NTFY):** This message informs the call agent of an event for which notification was requested. The gateway issues the command.

One verb is used by a media gateway to indicate to the call agent that it is in the process of restarting:

■   **RestartInProgress (RSIP):** This message notifies the call agent that the gateway and its endpoints are removed from service or are being placed back in service. The gateway issues the message.

Package Types

A call connection involves a series of events and signals, such as off-hook status, a ringing signal, or a signal to play an announcement, that are specific to the type of endpoint involved in the call.

MGCP groups these events and signals into packages. A trunk package, for example, is a group of events and signals relevant to a trunking gateway. An announcement package is a group of events and signals relevant to an announcement server. These packages are enabled by using the **mgcp package-capability** command. MGCP supports the following seven package types using the provided command example:

■   Trunk: **mgcp package-capability trunk-package**

■   Line: **mgcp package-capability line-package**

■   DTMF: **mgcp package-capability dtmf-package**

■   Generic media: **mgcp package-capability gm-package**

■   RTP: **mgcp package-capability rtp-package**

■   Announcement server: **mgcp package-capability as-package**

■   Script: **mgcp package-capability script-package**

The trunk package and line package are supported by default on certain types of gateways. Although configuring a gateway with additional endpoint package information is optional, you might want to specify packages for your endpoints to add to or override the defaults.

MGCP Call Flows

Figure 5-19 illustrates a dialog between a call agent and two gateways.

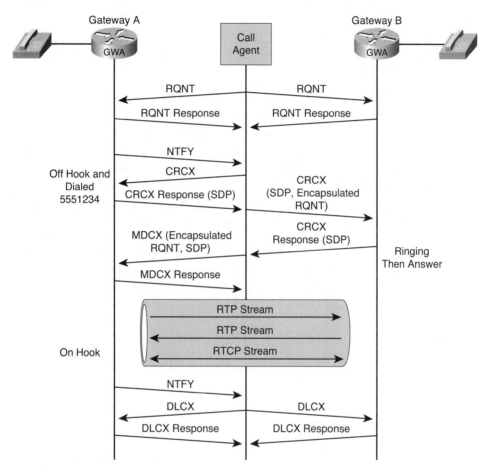

Figure 5-19 *Call Flows*

Although the gateways in this example are both residential gateways, the principles of operation listed here are the same for other gateway types:

1. The call agent sends a RQNT to each gateway. Because they are residential gateways, the request instructs the gateways to wait for an off-hook transition (event). When the off-hook transition event occurs, the call agent instructs the gateways to supply dial tone (signal). The call agent asks the gateway to monitor for other events as well. By providing a digit map in the request, the call agent can have the gateway collect digits before it notifies the call agent.

2. The gateways respond to the request. At this point, the gateways and the call agent wait for a triggering event.

3. A user on Gateway A goes off-hook. As instructed by the call agent in its earlier request, the gateway provides a dial tone. Because the gateway is provided with a digit map, it begins to collect digits (as they are dialed) until either a match is made or no match is possible. For the remainder of this example, assume that the digits match a digit map entry.

4. Gateway A sends a NTFY to the call agent to advise the call agent that a requested event was observed. The NTFY identifies the endpoint, the event, and in this case the dialed digits.

5. After confirming that a call is possible based on the dialed digits, the call agent instructs Gateway A to CRCX with its endpoint.

6. The gateway responds with a session description if it is able to accommodate the connection. The session description identifies at least the IP address and UDP port for use in a subsequent RTP session. The gateway does not have a session description for the remote side of the call, and the connection enters a wait state.

7. The call agent prepares and sends a connection request to Gateway B. In the request, the call agent provides the session description obtained from Gateway A. The connection request is targeted to a single endpoint, if only one endpoint is capable of handling the call, or to any one of a set of endpoints. The call agent also embeds a notification request that instructs the gateway about the signals and events it should now consider relevant. In this example, in which the gateway is residential, the signal requests ringing and the event is an off-hook transition.

Note   The interaction between Gateway B and its attached user has been simplified.

8. Gateway B responds to the request with its session description. Notice that Gateway B has both session descriptions and recognizes how to establish its RTP sessions.

9. The call agent relays the session description to Gateway A in an MDCX. This request might contain an encapsulated NTFY request that describes the relevant signals and events at this stage of the call setup. Now Gateway A and Gateway B have the required session descriptions to establish the RTP sessions over which the audio travels.

10. At the conclusion of the call, one of the endpoints recognizes an on-hook transition. In the example, the user on Gateway A hangs up. Because the call agent requested the gateways to notify in such an event, Gateway A notifies the call agent.

11. The call agent sends a DLCX request to each gateway.

12. The gateways delete the connections and respond.

Configuring MGCP Gateways

Configuring MGCP on a gateway depends on what type of gateway you are configuring. Residential gateway configuration is done in dial-peer configuration mode, whereas a trunking gateway is configured under the controller interface.

Note   After configuring the gateway, the gateway must be added to the call agent.

To configure MGCP on a gateway, perform the tasks in the following sections.

MGCP Residential Gateway Configuration Example

MGCP is invoked with the **mgcp** command. If the call agent expects the gateway to use the default port (UDP 2427), the **mgcp** command is used without any parameters. If the call agent requires a different port, the port must be configured as a parameter in the **mgcp** command; for example, **mgcp 5036** would tell the gateway to use port 5036 instead of the default port.

You can perform the following steps to configure a RGW:

Step 1.   Initiate the MGCP application.

Step 2.   Specify the call agent's IP address or domain name, port, and gateway control service type.

At least one **mgcp call-agent** command is required after the **mgcp** command. The command identifies the call agent by an IP address or a hostname. Using a hostname adds a measure of fault tolerance in a network that has multiple call agents. When the gateway asks the DNS for the IP address of the call agent, the DNS might provide more than one address, in which case the gateway can use either one. If multiple instances of the **mgcp call-agent** command are configured, the gateway uses the first call agent to respond.

Step 3.   Set up the dial peer for a voice port.

■ Specify the MGCP application to run on the voice port.

■ Specify the voice port to bind with MGCP.

When the parameters of the MGCP gateway are configured, the active voice ports (endpoints) are associated with MGCP. Dial peer 1, in Example 5-7, illustrates an **application mgcpapp** subcommand. This command binds the voice port (1/0/0 in this case) to MGCP. Also, notice that the dial peer does not have a destination pattern. A destination pattern is not used, because the relationship between the dial number and the port is maintained by the call agent.

Step 4. (Optional) Specify the event packages that are supported on the residential gateway. The default package is line-package.

The configuration example illustrated in Figure 5-20 and Example 5-7 illustrates the commands required to configure an MGCP residential gateway, including the commands to identify the packages that the gateway expects the call agent to use when it communicates with the gateway.

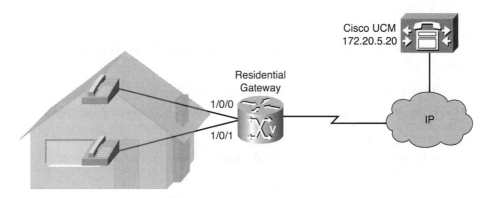

Figure 5-20 *MGCP Residential Gateway Topology*

Example 5-7 *MGCP Residential Gateway Configuration*

```
Router(config)#ccm-manager mgcp
Router(config)#mgcp
Router(config-mgcp)#mgcp call-agent 172.20.5.20 service-type mgcp
Router(config)#dial-peer voice 1 pots
Router(config-dialpeer)#application mgcpapp
Router(config-dialpeer)#port 1/0/0
Router(config)#dial-peer voice 2 pots
Router(config-dialpeer)#application mgcpapp
Router(config-dialpeer)#port 1/0/1
Router(config-dialpeer)#exit
Router(config)#mgcp package-capability dtmf-package
Router(config)#mgcp package-capability gm-package
Router(config)#mgcp package-capability line-package
Router(config)#mgcp package-capability rtp-package
Router(config)#mgcp default-package line-package
```

Configuring an MGCP Trunk Gateway Example

Figure 5-21 and Example 5-8 illustrate commands for configuring an MGCP trunk gateway.

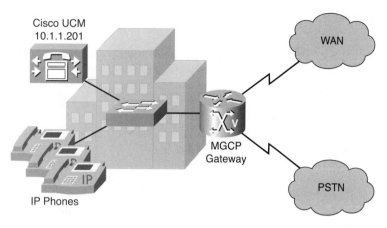

Figure 5-21   *MGCP Trunk Gateway Topology*

Example 5-8   *MGCP Trunk Gateway Configuration Example*

```
Router(config)#ccm-manager mgcp
Router(config)#mgcp 4000
Router(config)#mgcp call-agent 10.1.1.201 4000
Router(config)#controller t1 0/1/0
Router(config-controller)#framing esf
Router(config-controller)#clock source internal
Router(config-controller)#ds0-group 1 timeslots 1-24 type none service mgcp
Router(config)#controller t1 0/1/1
Router(config-controller)#framing esf
Router(config-controller)#clock source internal
Router(config-controller)#ds0-group 1 timeslots 1-24 type none service mgcp
```

Instead of using the **application mgcpapp** command in a dial peer, a trunk endpoint identifies its association with MGCP using the **service mgcp** parameter in the ds0-group controller subcommand. As always in MGCP, the call agent maintains the relationship between the endpoint (in this case, a digital trunk) and its address.

You can complete the following steps to configure a trunking gateway:

Step 1.   Initiate the MGCP application.

Note   The **ccm-manager mgcp** command is required only if the call agent is a Cisco Unified Communications Manager.

Step 2.   Specify the call agent's IP address or domain name, the port, and the gateway control service type.

Step 3.   Specify the controller number of the T1 trunk to be used for analog calls and enter controller configuration mode.

Step 4.   Configure the channelized T1 time slots to accept the analog calls and use the MGCP service.

Step 5.   (Optional) Specify the event packages that are supported on the trunking gateway. The default is **trunk-package**.

Configuring Fax Relay with MGCP Gateways

Figure 5-22 and Example 5-9 show an MGCP configuration of a voice gateway that is configured for T.38 fax support.

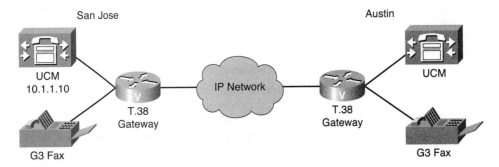

Figure 5-22   *Fax Pass-Through and Relay with MGCP Gateways Topology*

Example 5-9   *Fax Pass-Through and Relay with MGCP Gateways Example*

```
Router(config)#ccm-manager mgcp
Router(config)#no ccm-manager fax protocol cisco
Router(config)#mgcp
Router(config)#mgcp call-agent 10.1.1.10 service-type mgcp version 0.1
Router(config)#mgcp package-capability fxr-package
Router(config)#mgcp package-capability rtp-package
Router(config)#mgcp fax rate 14400
Router(config)#mgcp timer 300
Router(config)#mgcp fax-relay sg3-to-g3
```

This scenario requires a company's headquarters in San Jose to be able to fax to its Austin office using MGCP. As a network administrator, your responsibility is to configure the gateway to meet the requirements of the network.

Requirements dictate that you

- Configure a call agent to work with the gateway.

- Disable Cisco Fax Relay.

- Enable MGCP on the gateways.

- Specify additional MGCP package capabilities.

- Specify the maximum fax rate allowed for MGCP.

- Adjust the NSE timers for network conditions.

- Configure the fax machines to negotiate down to G3 speeds.

The following steps describe how to configure fax pass-through with MGCP gateways.

Step 1.   Enable the gateway to communicate with Cisco Unified Communications Manager through the MGCP.

```
Router(config)#ccm-manager mgcp
```

This command enables the gateway to communicate with Cisco Unified Communications Manager (UCM) through MGCP. This command also enables control agent redundancy when a backup UCM server is available.

Step 2.   Disable the Cisco Fax Relay protocol.

```
Router(config)#no ccm-manager fax protocol cisco
```

Step 3.   Allocate resources for the MGCP.

```
Router(config)#mgcp [port]
```

The port option specifies the UDP port for the MGCP gateway. The UDP port range is from 1025 through 65535. The default is UDP port 2427.

Step 4.   Specify the address and protocol of the call agent for MGCP.

```
Router(config)#mgcp call-agent {host-name | ip-address} [port]
  [service-type type [version protocol-version]]
```

Step 5.   Specify the FXR package for fax transmissions.

```
Router(config)#mgcp package-capability package
```

Events specified in the MGCP messages from the call agent must belong to one of the supported packages. Otherwise, connection requests are refused by the gateway.

By default, certain packages are configured as supported on each platform type. Using this command, you can configure additional package capability only for packages that are supported by your call agent. You can also disable support for a package with the **no** form of this command. Enter each package you want to add as a separate command.

Step 6.   Define the maximum fax rate for MGCP T.38 sessions.

```
Router(config)#mgcp fax rate [2400 | 4800 | 7200 | 9600 | 12000 | 14400
    | voice]
```

Step 7.   Define the timeout period for awaiting NSE responses from the dial peer.

```
Router(config)#mgcp timer {receive-rtcp timer | net-cont-test timer |
    nse-response t38 timer}
```

The **nse-response t38** option sets the timer for awaiting T.38 NSE responses. This timer is configured to tell the terminating gateway how long to wait for an NSE from a peer gateway. The NSE from the peer gateway can either acknowledge the switch and its readiness to accept packets or indicate that it cannot accept T.38 packets.

Step 8.   Allow SG3 fax machines to operate at G3 speeds in fax relay mode.

```
Router(config)#mgcp fax-relay sg3-to-g3
```

When this command is entered, the DSP fax-relay firmware suppresses the V.8 call menu (CM) tone, and the fax machines negotiate down to G3 speeds for the fax stream.

Verifying MGCP

Several **show** and **debug** commands provide support for verifying and troubleshooting MGCP. You should be familiar with the information provided from each command and how this information can help you.

Use the output of the **show mgcp** command, an example of which is provided in Example 5-10, to verify the status of a router's MGCP parameters. You should see the IP address of the UCM server that you use (10.1.1.101, in this example) and the port you are using to for MGCP. You should also see the administrative and operational states as ACTIVE. All other parameters are left at their default behavior in this example. Also highlighted in the example are the packages supported by the gateway.

Example 5-10   show mgcp *Command*

```
router#show mgcp
MGCP Admin State ACTIVE, Oper State ACTIVE - Cause Code NONE
MGCP call-agent: 10.1.1.101 4000 Initial protocol service is MGCP 0.1
MGCP validate call-agent source-ipaddr DISABLED
MGCP validate domain name DISABLED
MGCP block-newcalls DISABLED
MGCP send SGCP RSIP: forced/restart/graceful/disconnected DISABLED
MGCP quarantine mode discard/step
```

```
MGCP quarantine of persistent events is ENABLED
MGCP dtmf-relay for VoIP is SDP controlled
MGCP dtmf-relay for voAAL2 is SDP controlled
MGCP voip modem passthrough disabled
MGCP voaal2 modem passthrough disabled
MGCP voip tremolo modem relay: Disabled
MGCP T.38 Named Signalling Event (NSE) response timer: 200
MGCP Network (IP/AAL2) Continuity Test timer: 200
MGCP 'RTP stream loss' timer: 5
MGCP request timeout 500
MGCP maximum exponential request timeout 4000
MGCP gateway port: 4000, MGCP maximum waiting delay 3000
MGCP restart delay 0, MGCP vad DISABLED
MGCP rtrcac DISABLED
MGCP system resource check DISABLED
MGCP xpc-codec: DISABLED, MGCP persistent hookflash: DISABLED
MGCP persistent offhook: ENABLED, MGCP persistent onhook: DISABLED
MGCP piggyback msg ENABLED, MGCP endpoint offset DISABLED
MGCP simple-sdp DISABLED
MGCP undotted-notation DISABLED
MGCP codec type g711ulaw, MGCP packetization period 20
MGCP JB threshold lwm 30, MGCP JB threshold hwm 150
MGCP LAT threshold lwm 150, MGCP LAT threshold hwm 300
MGCP PL threshold lwm 1000, MGCP PL threshold hwm 10000
MGCP CL threshold lwm 1000, MGCP CL threshold hwm 10000
MGCP playout mode is adaptive 60, 40, 200 in msec
MGCP Fax Playout Buffer is 300 in msec
MGCP media (RTP) dscp: ef, MGCP signaling dscp: af31
MGCP default package: trunk-package
MGCP supported packages: gm-package dtmf-package trunk-package line-package
                         hs-package atm-package ms-package dt-package mo-package
                         res-package mt-package fxr-package md-package
MGCP Digit Map matching order: shortest match
SGCP Digit Map matching order: always left-to-right
MGCP VoAAL2 ignore-lco-codec DISABLED
```

The **show ccm-manager** command verifies the active and redundant configured Cisco
CallManager servers. It also indicates whether the gateway is currently registered with
Cisco Unified Communications Manager. Example 5-11 illustrates sample output from
the command.

Example 5-11   show ccm-manager *Command*

```
router#show ccm-manager
MGCP Domain Name: cisco-voice-01
Priority          Status                       Host
===============================================================
Primary           Registered                   10.89.129.211
First Backup      None
Second Backup     None


Current active Call Manager: 10.89.129.211
Backhaul/Redundant link port: 2428
Failover Interval: 30 seconds
Keepalive Interval: 15 seconds
Last keepalive sent: 5w1d (elapsed time: 00:00:04)
Last MGCP traffic time: 5w1d (elapsed time: 00:00:04)
Last failover time: None
Switchback mode: Graceful
MGCP Fallback mode: Not Selected
Last MGCP Fallback start time: 00:00:00
Last MGCP Fallback end time: 00:00:00


Configuration Error History:
```

The **show mgcp endpoint** command displays a list of the voice ports that are configured for MGCP. Example 5-12 illustrates sample output from the command.

Example 5-12   show mgcp endpoint *Command*

```
router#show mgcp endpoint

Interface T1 0/1/0

            ENDPOINT-NAME     V-PORT      SIG-TYPE    ADMIN
       S0/SU1/ds1-0/1@HQ-1    0/1/0:1        none      up
       S0/SU1/ds1-0/2@HQ-1    0/1/0:1        none      up
       S0/SU1/ds1-0/3@HQ-1    0/1/0:1        none      up
       S0/SU1/ds1-0/4@HQ-1    0/1/0:1        none      up
       S0/SU1/ds1-0/5@HQ-1    0/1/0:1        none      up
       S0/SU1/ds1-0/6@HQ-1    0/1/0:1        none      up
       S0/SU1/ds1-0/7@HQ-1    0/1/0:1        none      up
       S0/SU1/ds1-0/8@HQ-1    0/1/0:1        none      up
       S0/SU1/ds1-0/9@HQ-1    0/1/0:1        none      up
      S0/SU1/ds1-0/10@HQ-1    0/1/0:1        none      up
```

The **show mgcp statistics** command displays a count of the successful and unsuccessful control commands, as shown in Example 5-13. You should investigate a high unsuccessful count.

Example 5-13   show mgcp endpoint *Command*

```
router#show mgcp statistics

UDP pkts rx 8, tx 9
Unrecognized rx pkts 0, MGCP message parsing errors 0
Duplicate MGCP ack tx 0, Invalid versions count 0
CreateConn rx 4, successful 0, failed 0
DeleteConn rx 2, successful 2, failed 0
ModifyConn rx 4, successful 4, failed 0
DeleteConn tx 0, successful 0, failed 0
NotifyRequest rx 0, successful 4, failed 0
AuditConnection rx 0, successful 0, failed 0
AuditEndpoint rx 0, successful 0, failed 0
RestartInProgress tx 1, successful 1, failed 0
Notify tx 0, successful 0, failed 0
ACK tx 8, NACK tx 0
ACK rx 0, NACK rx 0
IP address based Call Agents statistics:
IP address 10.24.167.3, Total msg rx 8, successful 8, failed 0
```

Debug Commands

The following **debug** commands are useful for monitoring and troubleshooting MGCP:

- **debug voip ccapi inout:** This command shows every interaction with the call control application programming interface (API) on the telephone interface and the VoIP side. Watching the output allows users to follow the progress of a call from the inbound interface or VoIP peer to the outbound side of the call. This **debug** command is very active. Therefore, you should use it sparingly in a live network.

- **debug mgcp** [**all** | **errors** | **events** | **packets** | **parser**]: This command reports all **mgcp** command activity. You should use this **debug** command to trace the MGCP request and responses.

Implementing SIP Gateways

SIP is one of the most important voice-signaling protocols within service provider VoIP networks and is supported by most IP telephony system vendors. As such, it is an ideal protocol for interconnecting different VoIP systems and networks. An understanding of the features and functions of SIP components and the relationships the components establish with each other is important in implementing a scalable, resilient, and secure SIP environment. This section describes how to configure SIP and explores the features and functions of the SIP environment, including its components, how these components interact, and how to accommodate scalability and survivability.

SIP Overview

SIP is an ASCII text-based application layer control protocol that can be used to establish, maintain, and terminate calls between two or more endpoints. SIP is an alternative protocol developed by the IETF for multimedia conferencing over IP. Its features are compliant with IETF RFC 2543, *SIP: Session Initiation Protocol*, published in March 1999, and IETF RFC 3261, *SIP: Session Initiation Protocol*, published in June 2002.

Many applications of the Internet require the creation and management of a session, where a session is considered an exchange of data between an association of participants. The implementation of these applications is complicated by the practices of participants: users might move between endpoints; they might be addressable by multiple names; and they might communicate in several different media. Numerous protocols have been authored that carry various forms of real-time multimedia session data such as voice, video, or text messages.

SIP works in concert with these protocols by enabling Internet endpoints (called *user agents*) to discover one another and to agree on a characterization of a session they would like to share. For locating prospective session participants, and for other functions, SIP enables the creation of an infrastructure of network hosts (called *proxy servers*) to which user agents can send registrations, invitations to sessions, and other requests.

SIP is not a standalone communications system. Rather, SIP is a component that can be used with other IETF protocols to build a complete multimedia architecture. These architectures include protocols such as RTP for transporting real-time data and providing QoS feedback, Real-time Streaming Protocol (RTSP) for controlling delivery of streaming media, MGCP for controlling gateways to the PSTN, and Session Description Protocol (SDP) for describing multimedia sessions. Therefore, SIP should be used in conjunction with other protocols to provide complete services to the users. However, the basic functionality and operation of SIP does not depend on any of these protocols.

SIP operates on the principle of session invitations based on an HTTP-like request/response transaction model. Each transaction consists of a request that invokes a particular method or function on the server and at least one response. Through invitations, SIP initiates sessions or invites participants into established sessions. Descriptions of these sessions are advertised by any one of several means, including the Session Announcement Protocol (SAP) defined in RFC 2974, which incorporates a session description according to the SDP defined in RFC 2327.

SIP uses other IETF protocols to define other aspects of VoIP and multimedia sessions. For example, SIP uses URLs for addressing, DNS for service location, and Telephony Routing over IP (TRIP) for call routing.

Like other VoIP protocols, SIP is designed to address the functions of signaling and session management within a packet telephony network. Signaling allows call information to be carried across network boundaries. Session management provides the ability to control the attributes of an end-to-end call.

SIP supports five facets of establishing and terminating multimedia communications, resulting in the following capabilities:

- **Determines the location of the target endpoint:** SIP supports address resolution, name mapping, and call redirection.

- **Determines the media capabilities of the target endpoint:** SIP determines the lowest level of common services between the endpoints through SDP. Conferences are established using only the media capabilities that can be supported by all endpoints.

- **Determines the availability of the target endpoint:** If a call cannot be completed because the target endpoint is unavailable, SIP determines whether the called party is connected to a call already or did not answer in the allotted number of rings. SIP then returns a message indicating why the target endpoint was unavailable.

- **Establishes a session between the originating and target endpoints:** If the call can be completed, SIP establishes a session between the endpoints. SIP also supports midcall changes, such as the addition of another endpoint to the conference or the changing of a media characteristic or codec.

- **Handles the transfer and termination of calls:** SIP supports the transfer of calls from one endpoint to another. During a call transfer, SIP establishes a session between the transferee and a new endpoint (specified by the transferring party) and terminates the session between the transferee and the transferring party. At the end of a call, SIP terminates the sessions among all parties.

How SIP Works

SIP is a simple, ASCII-based protocol that uses requests and responses to establish communication among the various components in the network and to ultimately establish a conference between two or more endpoints.

Users in a SIP network are identified by unique SIP addresses. A SIP address is similar to an e-mail address and is in the format of sip:userID@gateway.com. The user ID can be either a username or an E.164 address. The gateway can be either a domain (with or without a hostname) or a specific IP address.

> **Note**   An E.164 address is a telephone number with a string of decimal digits that uniquely indicates the public network termination point. The number contains the information necessary to route the call to this termination point.

Users register with a registrar server using their assigned SIP addresses. The registrar server provides this information to a location server upon request.

When a user initiates a call, a SIP request is sent to a SIP server (either a proxy or a redirect server). The request includes the address of the caller (in the From header field) and the address of the intended called party (in the To header field).

Over time, a SIP end user might move between end systems. The location of the end user can be dynamically registered with the SIP server. The location server can use one or more protocols (including finger, rwhois, and LDAP) to locate the end user. Because the end user can be logged in at more than one station and because the location server can sometimes have inaccurate information, it might return more than one address for the end user. If the request is coming through a SIP proxy server, the proxy server tries each of the returned addresses until it locates the end user. If the request is coming through a SIP redirect server, the redirect server forwards all the addresses to the caller in the Contact header field of the invitation response.

Why SIP

Several advantages exist to using SIP gateways as voice gateways:

- **Dial plan configuration directly on the gateway:** This makes it possible, for example, to handle special calls, such as calls to directly connected analog devices, locally on the gateway without routing them to the Cisco Unified Communications Manager. Another scenario could be to route calls that are directed to other sites directly on the gateway without sending them to the local Cisco Unified Communications Manager cluster.

- **Translations defined per gateway:** This makes it possible to meet regional requirements such as calling party transformations or special number formats. This also allows you to translate all incoming calls directly on the gateway to meet the internally used number format and then process calls with only those internal numbers on the Cisco Unified CallManager clusters within the network.

- **Advanced support of third-party telephony systems:** Because SIP is the most widely used standard within VoIP systems of different vendors and has many features included as non-proprietary functions, using a SIP gateway enables you to integrate third-party telephony systems.

- **Interoperability with third-party voice gateways:** Most third-party voice gateways support SIP. Therefore, using SIP would be the most feasible way to connect a Cisco IOS voice gateway to a third-party voice gateway, rather then by using another VoIP signaling protocol.

SIP Architecture

SIP is a peer-to-peer protocol. Figure 5-23 offers an example of a SIP network.

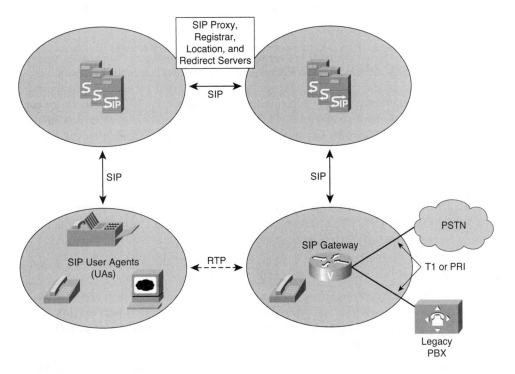

Figure 5-23 *SIP Architecture*

The peers in a session are called user agents (UA). A user agent can function in one of two roles:

- **User agent client (UAC):** A client application that initiates a SIP request

- **User agent server (UAS):** A server application that contacts the user when a SIP invitation is received and then returns a response on behalf of the user to the invitation originator

Typically, a SIP UA can function as a UAC or a UAS during a session, but not both in the same session. Whether the endpoint functions as a UAC or a UAS depends on the UA that initiated the request. The initiating UA uses a UAC, and the terminating UA uses a UAS.

From an architectural standpoint, the physical components of a SIP network are grouped into two categories:

- Clients (endpoints)

- Servers

Clients (endpoints) include the following:

- **Phone:** An IP telephone acts as a UAS or UAC on a session-by-session basis.

  - Software telephones and Cisco SIP IP Phones initiate SIP requests and respond to requests.

  - ephones are IP phones that are not configured on the gateway.

- **Gateway:** A gateway acts as a UAS or UAC and provides call control support. Gateways provide many services, the most common being a translation function between SIP conferencing endpoints and other terminal types. This function includes translation between transmission formats and between communications procedures. A gateway also translates between audio and video signals and performs call setup and clearing on both the IP side and the SCN side.

Servers include the following:

- **Proxy server:** An intermediate component that receives SIP requests from a client, and then forwards the requests on behalf of the client to the next SIP server in the network. The next server can be another proxy server or a UAS. Proxy servers can provide functions such as authentication, authorization, network access control, routing, reliable request transmissions, and security.

- **Redirect server:** Provides the client with information about the next hop or hops that a message should take, and then the client contacts the next-hop server or UAS directly. The UA redirects the invitation to the server identified by the redirect server. The server can be another network server or a UA.

- **Registrar server:** Receives requests from UACs for registration of their current location. Registrar servers are often located near or even collocated with other network servers, most often a location server.

- **Location server:** An abstraction of a service providing address resolution services to SIP proxy or redirect servers. A location server embodies mechanisms to resolve addresses. These mechanisms can include a database of registrations or access to commonly used resolution tools such as Finger protocol, RWhois, LDAP, or operating system-dependent mechanisms. A registrar server can be modeled as one subcomponent of a location server. The registrar server is partly responsible for populating a database associated with the location server.

Note In addition, the SIP servers can interact with other application services, such as LDAP servers, location servers, a database application, or an extensible markup language (XML) application. These application services provide back-end services, such as directory, authentication, and billing services.

SIP Call Flow

The call flows between SIP gateways can be direct or through a proxy or redirect server.

Direct Call Setup

When a UA recognizes the address of a terminating endpoint from cached information, or has the capacity to resolve it by some internal mechanism, the UAC might initiate direct (UAC-to-UAS) call setup procedures. If a UAC recognizes the destination UAS, the client communicates directly with the server, as illustrated in Figure 5-24. In situations in which the client is unable to establish a direct relationship, the client solicits the assistance of a network server.

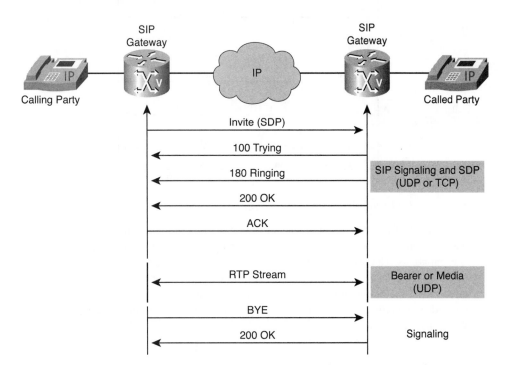

Figure 5-24   *Direct Call Setup*

Figure 5-24 illustrates the following steps of a direct call setup procedure:

1. The originating UAC sends an invitation (INVITE) to the UAS of the recipient. The message includes an endpoint description of the UAC and SDP.

2. If the UAS of the recipient determines that the call parameters are acceptable, it responds positively to the originator UAC.

3. The originating UAC issues an ACK.

At this point, the UAC and UAS have all the information that is required to establish RTP sessions between them.

Call Setup Using a Proxy Server

The proxy server procedure is transparent to a UA. The proxy server intercepts and forwards an invitation to the destination UA on behalf of the originator, as depicted in Figure 5-25.

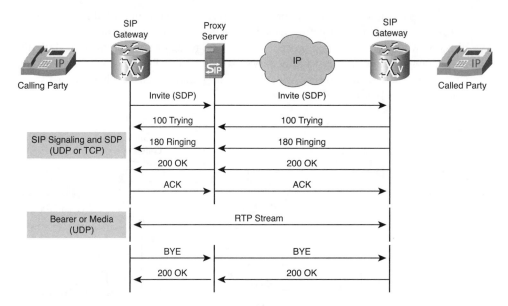

Figure 5-25   *Call Setup Using a Proxy Server*

A proxy server responds to the issues of the direct method by centralizing control and management of call setup and providing a more dynamic and up-to-date address resolution capability. The benefit to the UA is that it does not need to learn the coordinates of the destination UA, yet it can still communicate with the destination UA. The disadvantages of this method are that using a proxy server requires more messaging and creates a dependency on the proxy server. If the proxy server fails, the UA is incapable of establishing its own sessions.

Note   Although the proxy server acts on behalf of a UA for call setup, the UAs establish RTP sessions directly with each other.

When a proxy server is used, the call setup procedure, as illustrated in Figure 5-25, uses the following steps:

1.   The originating UAC sends an invitation (INVITE) to the proxy server.

2.   The proxy server, if required, consults the location server to determine the path to the recipient and its IP address.

3. The proxy server sends the INVITE to the UAS of the recipient.

4. If the UAS of the recipient determines that the call parameters are acceptable, it responds positively to the proxy server.

5. The proxy server responds to the originating UAC.

6. The originating UAC issues an ACK.

7. The proxy server forwards the ACK to the recipient UAS.

The UAC and UAS now have all the information that is required to establish RTP sessions between them.

Call Setup Using a Redirect Server

A redirect server is programmed to discover a path to the destination. Instead of forwarding the INVITE to the destination, the redirect server reports back to a UA with the destination coordinates the UA should try next, as indicated in Figure 5-26.

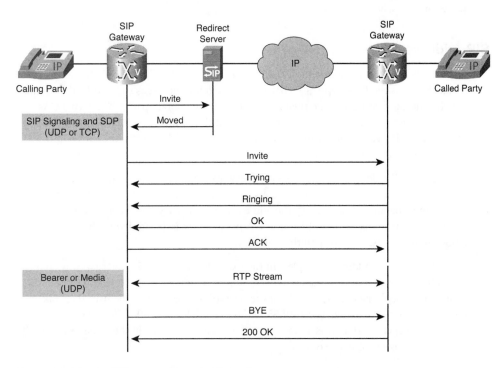

Figure 5-26   *Call Setup Using a Redirect Server*

A redirect server offers many of the advantages of the proxy server. However, the number of messages involved in redirection is fewer than with the proxy server procedure. The UA has a heavier workload because it must initiate the subsequent invitation.

When a redirect server is used, the call setup procedure, as illustrated in Figure 5-26, uses the following steps:

1. The originating UAC sends an invitation (INVITE) to the redirect server.

2. The redirect server, if required, consults the location server to determine the path to the recipient and its IP address.

3. The redirect server returns a "moved" response to the originating UAC with the IP address obtained from the location server.

4. The originating UAC acknowledges the redirection.

5. The originating UAC sends an INVITE to the remote UAS.

6. If the UAS of the recipient determines that the call parameters are acceptable, it responds positively to the UAC.

7. The originating UAC issues an ACK.

The UAC and UAS now have all the information that is required to establish RTP sessions between themselves.

SIP Addressing

An address in SIP is defined in the syntax for a URL with "sip:" or "sips:" (for secure SIP connections) as the URL type. SIP URLs are used in SIP messages to identify the originator, the current destination, the final recipient, and any contact party. When two UAs communicate directly with each other, the current destination and final recipient URLs are the same. However, the current destination and the final recipient are different if a proxy or redirect server is used.

To obtain the IP address of a SIP UAS or a network server, a UAC performs address resolution of a user identifier. An address consists of an optional user ID, a host description, and optional parameters to qualify the address more precisely. The host description might be a domain name or an IP address. A password is associated with the user ID, and a port number is associated with the host description.

Consider a few SIP address examples. In the example sip:14085551234@gateway.com; user=phone, the user=phone parameter is required to indicate that the user part of the address is a telephone number. Without the user=phone parameter, the user ID is taken literally as a numeric string. The 14085559876 in the URL sip:14085559876; password=chageme@10.1.1.1 is an example of a numeric user ID. In the same example, the password changeme is defined for the user.

A SIP address is acquired in several ways: by interacting with a user, by caching information from an earlier session, or by interacting with a network server. For a network server to assist, it must recognize the endpoints in the network. This knowledge is abstracted to reside in a location server and is dynamically acquired by its registrar server.

To contribute to this dynamic knowledge, an endpoint registers its user addresses with a registrar server. Figure 5-27 illustrates a voice REGISTER mode request to a registrar server.

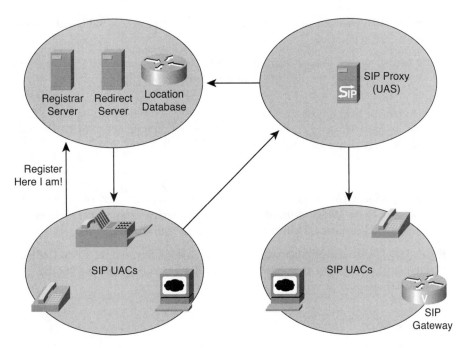

Figure 5-27 *Address Registration*

To resolve an address, a UA uses a variety of internal mechanisms such as a local host table, DNS lookup, Finger protocol, RWhois, or LDAP, or it leaves that responsibility to a network server, as shown in Figure 5-28. A network server uses any of the tools available to a UA or interacts with a location server.

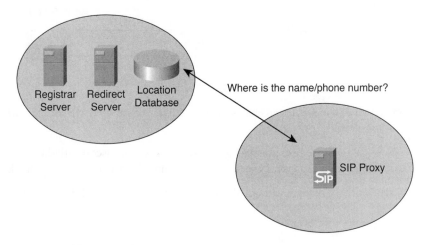

Figure 5-28 *Address Resolution*

SIP DTMF Considerations

The SIP DTMF relay method is needed in the following situations:

■ When SIP is used to connect a Cisco SRST system to a remote SIP-based IVR or voice-mail application

■ When SIP is used to connect a Cisco SRST system to a remote SIP PSTN voice gateway that goes through the PSTN to a voice-mail or IVR application

> **Note**   The need to use out-of-band DTMF relay conversion is limited to SCCP phones. SIP phones natively support in-band DTMF relay as specified in RFC 2833.

SIP usually sends DTMF in-band digits, whereas SCCP supports only out-of-band digits. The software-based Media Termination Point (MTP) device receives the DTMF out-of-band tones and generates DTMF in-band tones for the SIP client.

Figure 5-29 illustrates a call that begins with media streaming, and the Cisco Unified Communications Manager software-based MTP device has been informed of the dynamic DTMF payload type.

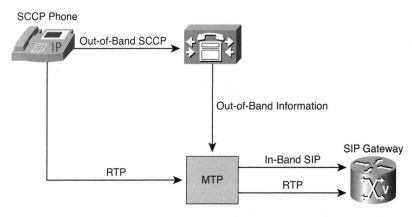

Figure 5-29   *SIP DTMF Configuration Considerations*

The procedure that makes it possible to send SCCP out-of-band DTMF tones to SIP networks is as follows:

1. The SCCP IP phone user presses buttons on the keypad. Cisco Unified Communications Manager collects the out-of-band digits from the SCCP IP phone.

2. Cisco Unified Communications Manager passes the out-of-band digits to the MTP device.

3. The MTP device converts the digits to RFC 2833-compliant in-band digits and forwards them to the SIP client.

> **Note**   Because the Cisco Unified Communications Manager software-based MTP can handle no more than 48 media streams in parallel, only 48 SCCP-to-SIP calls are available in older versions of Cisco Unified CallManager without a hardware MTP. In that case, it is necessary to configure the gateway to send DTMF out-of-band. (Cisco Unified Communications Manager Release 5.0 and later can handle SCCP-to-SIP calls without an MTP.)

As previously mentioned, SCCP IP phones are capable of sending only out-of-band DTMF digits. To support SCCP devices, originating and terminating SIP gateways can use Cisco proprietary NOTIFY-based out-of-band DTMF relay. In addition, NOTIFY-based out-of-band DTMF relay can also be used by analog phones attached to analog voice ports (known FXS) on the router.

NOTIFY-based out-of-band DTMF relay sends messages bidirectionally between the originating and terminating gateways for a DTMF event during a call. If multiple DTMF relay mechanisms are enabled on a SIP dial peer and are negotiated successfully, NOTIFY-based out-of-band DTMF relay takes precedence.

The originating gateway sends an INVITE message with SIP Call-Info header information to indicate the use of the NOTIFY-based out-of-band DTMF relay. The terminating gateway acknowledges the message with an 18x or 200 Response message, also using the Call-Info header. Whenever a DTMF event occurs, the gateway sends a SIP NOTIFY message for that event after the SIP Invite and 18x or 200 Response messages negotiate the NOTIFY-based out-of-band DTMF relay mechanism. In response, the gateway expects to receive a 200 OK message.

The NOTIFY-based out-of-band DTMF relay mechanism is similar to the DTMF message format described in RFC 2833.

Configuring SIP

A SIP configuration consists of two parts: the SIP UA and the VoIP dial peers that select SIP as the session protocol.

To integrate Cisco IOS gateways into a SIP service provider VoIP network, you can perform, at least, the following steps:

Step 1.   Enable the SIP voice service within Cisco IOS.

Step 2.   Specify the parameters for the SIP service.

Step 3.   Configure the SIP UA.

Step 4.   Configure the SIP-based VoIP dial peers to connect and route calls to the service provider's SIP network.

Configuring a SIP Gateway Example

Figure 5-30 shows a scenario where you connect Cisco Unified Communications Manager Express to a SIP service provider. The SIP voice service configuration is one part of the SIP configuration.

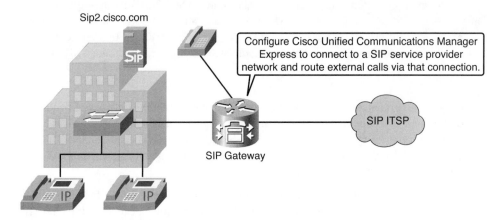

Figure 5-30 *Integrating IOS Gateways with a SIP ITSP*

SIP Gateway Configuration Scenario

As a network administrator, one of your duties is to configure a voice gateway to meet network requirements. Specifically, you have been asked to integrate SIP connectivity with your company's VoIP service provider.

The requirements are as follows:

- Use SIP as a signaling protocol.

- Set the transport protocol to UDP.

- Use interface Loopback 0 as the source interface for SIP.

- Modify the UA as follows:

    - Enable local authentication.

    - Enable E.164 address registration for directly attached analog phones.

    - Configure a SIP server to be used with dial peers.

    - Change the number of SIP INVITE, RESPONSE, BYE, and Cancel retries to 2.

SIP Gateway Configuration Procedure

The following procedure describes how to configure a SIP gateway as per network requirements:

Step 1.   Enter voice-service configuration mode and specify VoIP as the voice-encapsulation type.

```
Router(config)#voice service {pots | voatm | vofr | voip}
```

Step 2.   Enter SIP configuration mode.

```
Router(conf-voi-serv)#sip
```

Step 3.   Specify SIP parameters.

Specify the underlying transport layer protocol for SIP messages, and bind the source address for signaling and media packets to the IP address of a specific interface.

```
Router(conf-serv-sip)#session transport { tcp | udp }
Router(conf-serv-sip)#bind {control | media | all} source-interface
  interface-id
```

If the **bind** command is not enabled, the IP layer still provides the best local address.

Step 4.   Exit SIP configuration mode.

```
Router(conf-serv-sip)#exit
```

Step 5.   Activate the voice service.

```
Router(conf-voi-serv)#no shutdown
```

Step 6.   Enter SIP UA configuration mode.

```
Router(config)#sip-ua
```

Step 7.   Configure Digest Authentication.

```
Router(config-sip-ua)#authentication username name password password
  realm string
```

Step 8.   Enable the SIP gateway to register E.164 numbers on behalf of analog telephone voice ports (FXS), IP phone virtual voice ports (EFXS), and SCCP phones with an external SIP proxy or SIP registrar.

```
Router(config-sip-ua)#registrar name expires secs
```

Step 9.   Enter the hostname or IP address of the SIP server interface.

```
Router(config-sip-ua)#sip-server {dns:[hostname] | ipv4:ip_addr:[port-
  num]}
```

If you use this command, you can specify **session target sip-server** for each dial peer instead of repeatedly entering the SIP server interface address for each dial peer.

Step 10.   Adjust the SIP parameters per network requirements.

```
Router(config-sip-ua)#retry {invite number | response number | bye
  number | cancel number}
```

The complete configuration for these steps is presented in Example 5-14.

Example 5-14 *Integrating IOS Gateways with a SIP ITSP*

```
Router(config)#voice service voip
Router(conf-voi-serv)#sip
Router(conf-serv-sip)#session transport udp
Router(conf-serv-sip)#bind control source-interface Loopback 0
Router(conf-serv-sip)#bind media source-interface Loopback 0
Router(conf-serv-sip)#exit
Router(conf-voi-serv)#no shutdown
Router(config)#sip-ua
Router(config-sip-ua)#authentication username JDoe password secret
Router(config-sip-ua)#registrar dns:sip2.cisco.com expires 3600
Router(config-sip-ua)#sip-server dns:sip2.cisco.com
Router(config-sip-ua)#retry invite 2
Router(config-sip-ua)#retry response 2
Router(config-sip-ua)#retry bye 2
Router(config-sip-ua)#retry cancel 2
```

SIP Dial-Peer Example

SIP is selected as the call control protocol from inside a dial peer. SIP is requested by the **session protocol sipv2** dial-peer subcommand.

In this example, both dial peers include the **session protocol sipv2** subcommand, and SIP is used when the destination pattern matches either dial peer. The session target distinguishes one session from the other.

In dial-peer 999, the IP address of the server is provided as the session target. The address can be the address of a UA, proxy server, or redirect server.

In dial-peer 200, the session target is the **sip-server** *parameter*. When the **sip-server** parameter is the target, the IP address of the actual server is taken from the **sip-server** subcommand in the SIP UA configuration. This means that from global configuration mode, the network administrator has entered the **sip-ua** command and the **sip-server dns:server** subcommand. The address represents the location of a proxy server or redirect server. In this example, the name of the SIP server is "sip2.cisco.com." The dial peer must know how to deal with DTMF signals. The following example uses the **dtmf-relay sip-notify** command used for sending telephone-event notifications via SIP NOTIFY messages from a SIP gateway.

The topology and complete configuration for this scenario are presented in Figure 5-31 and in Example 5-15.

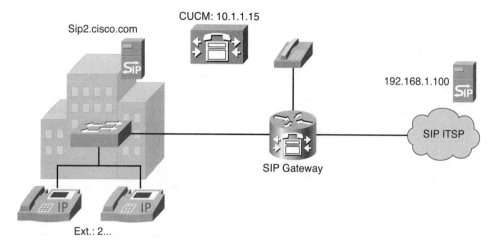

Figure 5-31   *SIP Dial-Peer Topology Example*

Example 5-15   *SIP Dial-Peer Configuration Example*

```
Router(config)#dial-peer voice 2000 pots
Router(config-dial-peer)#destination-pattern 2...
Router(config-dial-peer)#session protocol sipv2
Router(config-dial-peer)#session target sip-server
Router(config-dial-peer)#dtmf-relay rtp-nte
Router(config)#dial-peer voice 2001 pots
Router(config-dial-peer)#destination-pattern 2...
Router(config-dial-peer)#session protocol sipv2
Router(config-dial-peer)#session target ipv4:10.1.1.15
Router(config-dial-peer)#dtmf-relay sip-notify
Router(config-dial-peer)#preference 1
Router(config)#dial-peer voice 90 voip
Router(config-dial-peer)#destination-pattern 9T
Router(config-dial-peer)#session target ipv4:192.168.1.100
Router(config-dial-peer)#session protocol sipv2
Router(config-dial-peer)#dtmf-relay rtp-nte
```

Verifying SIP Gateways

The **show** commands listed in Table 5-2 are valuable when examining the status of SIP components and troubleshooting SIP environments.

Table 5-2   *SIP* show *Commands*

Command	Description
show sip service	Displays the status of the SIP VoIP service
show sip-ua status	Displays the status of the SIP UA
show sip-ua register status	Displays the status of E.164 numbers that a SIP gateway has registered with an external primary SIP registrar
show sip-ua timers	Displays SIP UA timers
show sip-ua connections	Displays active SIP UA connections
show sip-ua calls	Displays active SIP UA calls
show sip-ua statistics	Displays SIP traffic statistics

Use the **show sip service** command to display the status of SIP call service on a SIP gateway. Example 5-16 provides sample output from the **show sip service** command.

Example 5-16   show sip service *Command*

```
Router#show sip service
SIP Service is up
```

Use the **show sip-ua status** command to display the status for the SIP user agent, including whether call redirection is enabled or disabled. Example 5-17 provides sample output from the **show sip-ua status** command.

Example 5-17   show sip-ua status *Command*

```
Router#show sip-ua status
SIP User Agent Status
SIP User Agent for UDP : ENABLED
SIP User Agent for TCP : ENABLED
SIP User Agent bind status(signaling): DISABLED
SIP User Agent bind status(media): DISABLED
SIP max-forwards : 6
SIP DNS SRV version: 1 (rfc 2052)
Redirection (3xx) message handling: ENABLED
```

Use the **show sip-ua timers** command to display the current settings for the SIP user-agent timers. Example 5-18 provides sample output from the **show sip-ua timers** command.

Example 5-18   show sip-ua timers *Command*

```
Router#show sip-ua timers
SIP UA Timer Values (millisecs)
trying 500, expires 180000, connect 500, disconnect 500
comet 500, prack 500, rel1xx 500, notify 500
refer 500, register 500
```

Use the **show sip-ua register status** command to display the status of E.164 numbers that a SIP gateway has registered with an external primary SIP registrar. Example 5-19 provides sample output from the **show sip-ua register status** command.

Example 5-19   show sip-ua register status *Command*

```
Router#show sip-ua register status

Line peer expires(sec) registered
4001 20001 596          no
4002 20002 596          no
5100 1     596          no
9998 2     596          no
```

Example 5-20 shows the output of the **show sip-ua calls** command, which provides detailed information about current SIP calls.

Example 5-20   show sip-ua calls *Command*

```
router#show sip-ua calls
SIP UAC CALL INFO
   Number of SIP User Agent Client(UAC) calls: 0

SIP UAS CALL INFO
Call 1
SIP Call ID               : D215F304-7B5A11DC-8005EA1A-6A8F4AD@10.10.10.2
   State of the call      : STATE_ACTIVE (7)
   Substate of the call   : SUBSTATE_NONE (0)
   Calling Number         : 2818902001
   Called Number          : 1003
   Bit Flags              : 0x1212003A 0x100000 0x488
   CC Call ID             : 1
   Source IP Address (Sig ): 10.10.10.1
   Destn SIP Req Addr:Port : 10.10.10.2:5060
   Destn SIP Resp Addr:Port: 10.10.10.2:56884
   Destination Name       : 10.10.10.2
```

continues

Example 5-20 show sip-ua calls *Command   continued*

```
Number of Media Streams : 1
   Number of Active Streams: 1
   RTP Fork Object        : 0x0
   Media Stream 1
      State of the stream      : STREAM_ACTIVE
      Stream Call ID           : 1
      Stream Type              : voice-only (0)
      Negotiated Codec         : g729r8 (20 bytes)
      Codec Payload Type       : 18
      Negotiated Dtmf-relay    : inband-voice
      Dtmf-relay Payload Type  : 0
      Media Source IP Addr:Port: 10.10.10.1:18050
      Media Dest IP Addr:Port  : 10.10.10.2:16522
      Orig Media Dest IP Addr:Port : 0.0.0.0:0

Number of SIP User Agent Server(UAS) calls: 1
```

The following **debug** commands are valuable when examining the status of SIP components and troubleshooting SIP environments:

■ **debug asnl events:** Use this command to verify that the SIP subscription server is up. The output displays a pending message if, for example, the client is unsuccessful in communicating with the server.

■ **debug voip ccapi inout:** This command shows every interaction with the call control API on both the telephone interface and on the VoIP side. By monitoring the output, you can follow the progress of a call from the inbound interface or VoIP peer to the outbound side of the call. This **debug** command is very active. Therefore, you must use it sparingly in a live network.

■ **debug voip ccapi protoheaders:** This command displays messages sent between the originating and the terminating gateways. If no headers are being received by the terminating gateway, verify that the **header-passing** command is enabled on the originating gateway.

■ **debug ccsip all:** This command enables all ccsip-type debugging. This **debug** command is very active. Therefore, you should use it sparingly in a live network.

■ **debug ccsip calls:** This command displays all SIP call details as they are updated in the SIP call control block. You can use this **debug** command to monitor call records for suspicious clearing causes.

■ **debug ccsip errors:** This command traces all errors encountered by the SIP subsystem.

- **debug ccsip events:** This command traces events, such as call setups, connections, and disconnections. An events version of a **debug** command is often the best place to start because detailed debugs provide a great deal of useful information.

- **debug ccsip info:** This command enables tracing of general SIP Service Provider Interface (SPI) information, including verification that call redirection is disabled.

- **debug ccsip media:** This command enables tracing of SIP media streams.

- **debug ccsip messages:** This command shows the headers of SIP messages that are exchanged between a client and a server.

- **debug ccsip preauth:** This command enables diagnostic reporting of authentication, authorization, and accounting (AAA) for SIP calls.

- **debug ccsip states:** This command displays the SIP states and state changes for sessions within the SIP subsystem.

- **debug ccsip transport:** This command enables tracing of the SIP transport handler and the TCP or UDP process.

Examples 5-21, 5-22, and 5-23 show what a successful SIP session between two endpoints looks like in the output of the **debug ccsip messages** command. Example 5-21 shows a SIP INVITE message being sent from one phone to another.

Example 5-21   *INVITE Message*

```
HQ-1#debug ccsip messages

SIP Call messages tracing is enabled
HQ-1#
*Mar 6 14:19:14: Sent:
INVITE sip:3660210@166.34.245.231;user=phone;phone-context=unknown SIP/2.0
Via: SIP/2.0/UDP 166.34.245.230:55820
From: "3660110" <sip:3660110@166.34.245.230>
To: <sip:3660210@166.34.245.231;user=phone;phone-context=unknown>
Date: Sat, 06 Mar 1993 19:19:14 GMT
Call-ID: ABBAE7AF-823100E2-0-1CD274BC@172.18.192.194
Cisco-Guid: 2881152943-2184249568-0-483551624
User-Agent: Cisco VoIP Gateway/ IOS 12.x/ SIP enabled
CSeq: 101 INVITE
Max-Forwards: 6
Timestamp: 731427554
Contact: <sip:3660110@166.34.245.230:5060;user=phone>
Expires: 180
Content-Type: application/sdp
Content-Length: 138
```

Example 5-22 shows the other endpoint returning an OK. Notice the Contact information added to the output.

Example 5-22 *OK Message*

```
*Mar 6 14:19:16: Received:
SIP/2.0 200 OK
Via: SIP/2.0/UDP 166.34.245.230:55820
From: "3660110" <sip:3660110@166.34.245.230>
To: <sip:3660210@166.34.245.231;user=phone;phone-context=unknown>;tag=27DBC6D8-1357
Date: Mon, 08 Mar 1993 22:45:12 GMT
Call-ID: ABBAE7AF-823100E2-0-1CD274BC@172.18.192.194
Timestamp: 731427554
Server: Cisco VoIP Gateway/ IOS 12.x/ SIP enabled
Contact: <sip:3660210@166.34.245.231:5060;user=phone>
CSeq: 101 INVITE
Content-Type: application/sdp
Content-Length: 138


v=0
o=CiscoSystemsSIP-GW-UserAgent 1193 7927 IN IP4 166.34.245.231
s=SIP Call
t=0 0
c=IN IP4 166.34.245.231
m=audio 20224 RTP/AVP 0
```

Example 5-23 shows the other endpoint ending the session with a BYE message.

Example 5-23 *BYE Message*

```
*Mar 6 14:19:19: Received:
BYE sip:3660110@166.34.245.230:5060;user=phone SIP/2.0
Via: SIP/2.0/UDP 166.34.245.231:53600
From: <sip:3660210@166.34.245.231;user=phone;phone-context=unknown>;tag=27DBC6D8-
  1357
To: "3660110" <sip:3660110@166.34.245.230>
Date: Mon, 08 Mar 1993 22:45:14 GMT
Call-ID: ABBAE7AF-823100E2-0-1CD274BC@172.18.192.194
User-Agent: Cisco VoIP Gateway/ IOS 12.x/ SIP enabled
Max-Forwards: 6
Timestamp: 731612717
CSeq: 101 BYE
Content-Length: 0
```

Summary

The main topics covered in this chapter are the following:

- ITU-T Recommendation H.323 describes an infrastructure of terminals, common control components, services, and protocols that are used for multimedia communications.

- Functional components of H.323 include terminals, gateways, gatekeepers, Cisco UBEs, and MCUs.

- Calls can be established between endpoints, endpoints to gatekeepers, or gatekeepers to gatekeepers.

- H.323 calls can occur with or without the use of a gatekeeper.

- H.323 defines three types of multipoint conferences.

- When configuring codecs, you can specify one codec or set up codec negotiation.

- You might want to adjust some of the H.323 timers to meet network requirements.

- You can use several commands to configure fax features on H.323 gateways.

- DTMF relay solves the problem of DTMF distortion.

- Use the **show gateway** command to verify H.323 gateway status.

- MGCP defines an environment for controlling telephony gateways from a centralized call agent.

- MGCP components include endpoints, gateways, and call agents.

- Calls and connections are basic concepts in MGCP.

- MGCP call flow consists of an exchange of messages between a call agent and a gateway.

- The **mgcp** command can be used to configure residential and trunk gateways on a Cisco router.

- Several **show** and **debug** commands help to verify an MGCP configuration.

- SIP is defined by IETF RFCs 2543 and 3261 and allows integration with third-party VoIP networks.

- SIP is modeled on the interworking of UAs and network servers.

- A SIP call flow consists of signaling and transmission of bearer and media packets.

- Communication between SIP components uses a request and response message model.

- A SIP address consists of an optional user ID, a host description, and optional parameters to qualify the address more precisely.

- SIP call setup models include direct, proxy server, and redirection.

- You can use several commands on Cisco IOS to configure SIP on Cisco IOS routers.

- You can use several commands on Cisco IOS to verify and troubleshoot a SIP integration.

Chapter Review Questions

The answers to these review questions are in the appendix.

1. Which two tasks are performed by the RAS signaling function of H.225.0? (Choose 2.)

   a. Performs bandwidth changes

   b. Transports audio messages between endpoints

   c. Performs disengage procedures between endpoints and a gatekeeper

   d. Allows endpoints to create connections between call agents

   e. Defines call setup procedures based on ISDN call setup

2. What are the functions of an H.323 gateway?

   a. Converts an alias address to an IP address

   b. Responds to bandwidth requests and modifications

   c. Transmits and receives G.711 PCM-encoded voice

   d. Performs translation between audio, video, and data formats

   e. Receives and processes multiple streams of multimedia input

3. Which RAS message does a gateway use to request admission to a network and to also request phone number to IP address resolution?

   a. ARQ

   b. IRQ

   c. LRQ

   d. RRQ

   e. URQ

4. Use the _____ command to designate a source IP address for a voice gateway.

   a. h323-gateway voip interface

   b. h323-gateway voip h323-id

   c. h323-gateway voip bind srcaddr

   d. voice service

5. Which call control model does MGCP use?

   a. Distributed

   b. Centralized

   c. Ad hoc

   d. Hybrid

6. How do you configure a router to use MGCP on a digital port?

   a. Add the **application mgcpapp** subcommand to the dial peer.

   b. Add the **service mgcp** subcommand to the dial peer.

   c. Add the parameter **application mgcpapp** to the **ds0-group** controller subcommand.

   d. Add the **service mgcp** parameter to the **ds0-group** controller subcommand.

7. Which command displays a count of successful and unsuccessful control commands?

   a. **show mgcp calls**

   b. **show mgcp statistics**

   c. **show mgcp**

   d. **debug mgcp statistics**

8. Identify four SIP servers. (Choose 4.)

   a. Registrar

   b. Gateway

   c. Redirect

   d. Location

   e. Proxy

   f. Database

   g. Gatekeeper

9. In a SIP direct call setup, the originating UAC sends what message to the UAS of the recipient?

   a. INVITE

   b. RINGING

   c. ACK

   d. OK

10. Which command is required to enable a SIP user agent on a Cisco router?

   a.   **sip-ua** interface configuration mode subcommand

   b.   **sip-ua** dial-peer configuration mode subcommand

   c.   **sip-ua** global configuration mode command

   d.   No special command is required. SIP is on by default.

After reading this chapter, you should be able to perform the following tasks:

■ Describe the components and requirements of a dial plan.

■ Implement a numbering plan using Cisco IOS gateways.

CHAPTER 6

Identifying Dial Plan Characteristics

Dial plans are essential for any Cisco Unified Communications deployment. Whether implementing single-site or multisite deployments, having a thorough understanding of dial plans and the knowledge of how to implement them on Cisco gateways is essential for any voice implementation engineer. This chapter describes the characteristics of both dial plans and numbering plans.

Introducing Dial Plans

A dial plan is the central part of any telephony solution and defines how calls are routed and interconnected. A dial plan consists of various components that can be used in many combinations. This section describes the components of a dial plan and how they are used on Cisco IOS gateways.

Dial Plan Overview

Although most people are not acquainted with dial plans by name, they use them daily. A dial plan is a numbering plan for the voice-enabled network. It is the way you assign individual or blocks of telephone numbers (E.164 addresses) to physical lines or circuits. The North American telephone network is based on a 10-digit dial plan consisting of 3-digit area codes and 7-digit telephone numbers, as shown in Figure 6-1. For telephone numbers located within an area code, a 7-digit dial plan is used for the Public Switched Telephone Network (PSTN). Features within a telephone switch support a custom 5-digit dial plan for specific customers that subscribe to that service. PBXs also support variable-length dial plans, containing from 3 through 11 digits. The N in the NXX pattern used for the area code and the local exchange prefix refers to digits in the 2 to 9 range, whereas an X represents digits in the 0 to 9 range. Therefore, the first number of an area code or a local exchange prefix cannot be a 0 or a 1.

Dial plans in the H.323 network contain specific dialing patterns so users can reach a particular telephone number. Access codes, area codes, specialized codes, and combinations of the numbers of digits dialed are all part of any particular dial plan. Dial plans used with voice-capable routers essentially describe the process of determining which digits and how many to store in each of the configurations. If the dialed digits match the number and patterns, the call is processed for forwarding.

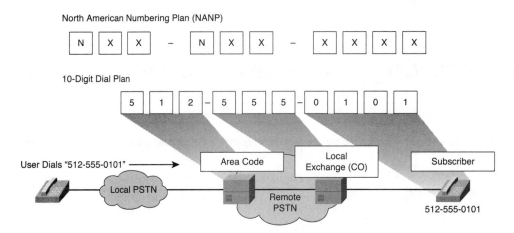

Figure 6-1   *North American Numbering Plan (NANP)*

Designing dial plans requires knowledge of the network topology, current telephone number dialing patterns, proposed router/gateway locations, and traffic routing requirements. No standard protocol is defined for the dynamic routing of E.164 telephony addresses. H.323 Voice over IP (VoIP) dial plans are statically configured and managed on gateway and gatekeeper platforms.

A dial plan consists of the following components:

- **Endpoint addressing (Numbering Plan):** Assigning directory numbers to all endpoints (such as IP phones, fax machines, and analog phones) and applications (such as voice-mail systems, auto attendants, and conferencing systems) enables you to access internal and external destinations.

- **Call routing and path selection:** Depending on the calling device, you can select different paths to reach the same destination. Moreover, you can use a secondary path when the primary path is not available. For example, a call can be transparently rerouted over the PSTN during an IP WAN failure.

- **Digit manipulation:** In some cases, you need to manipulate the dialed string before routing a call—for example, when a call originally dialed using the on-net access code is rerouted over the PSTN, or when an abbreviated code (such as 0 for the operator) is expanded to an extension. This can occur prior to or after a routing decision has been made.

- **Calling privileges:** You can assign different groups of devices to different classes of service by granting or denying access to certain destinations. For example, you might allow lobby phones to reach only internal and local PSTN destinations, whereas executive phones could have unrestricted PSTN access.

- **Call coverage:** You can create special groups of devices to handle incoming calls for a certain service according to different rules (top-down, circular hunt, longest idle, or broadcast). This also ensures that calls are not dropped without being answered.

Both Cisco Unified Communications Manager and Cisco IOS gateways, including Cisco Unified Communications Manager Express and Survivable Remote Site Telephony (SRST), support all dial plan components.

Table 6-1 compares the methods that Cisco Unified Communications Manager and Cisco IOS gateways use to implement dial plans.

Table 6-1 *Dial Plan Components on Cisco IOS Gateways and Cisco Unified Communications Manager*

Dial Plan Component	Cisco IOS Gateway	Cisco Unified Communications Manager
Endpoint addressing	POTS dial peers for FXS ports and ephone-dn if using UCME/SRST	Directory Number (DN)
Call routing and path selection	Dial peers	Route patterns, route groups, route lists, translation patterns, partitions, and calling search spaces
Digit manipulation	Voice translation profiles **prefix, digit-strip, forward-digits,** and **num-exp** commands	Translation patterns, route patterns, and route lists
Calling privileges	Class of Restriction (COR) and COR lists	Partitions, calling search spaces, and FACs
Call coverage	Dial peers, hunt groups, and call applications	Line groups, hunt lists, and hunt pilots

Figure 6-2 shows a typical dial plan scenario with various dial plan components being deployed. Calls can either be routed via an IP WAN link or a PSTN link, and routing should work for inbound and outbound PSTN calls, intrasite calls, and intersite calls.

Planning Considerations

The dial plan is the most fundamental attribute of a telephony system. It is at the very core of the user experience because it defines the rules that govern how a user reaches any destination. These rules include the following:

- **Extension dialing:** How many digits must be dialed to reach an extension on the system

- **Extension addressing:** How many digits are used to identify extensions

- **Dialing privileges:** Allowing or not allowing certain types of calls

- **Path selection:** For example, using the IP network for on-net calls or using one carrier for local PSTN calls and another for international calls

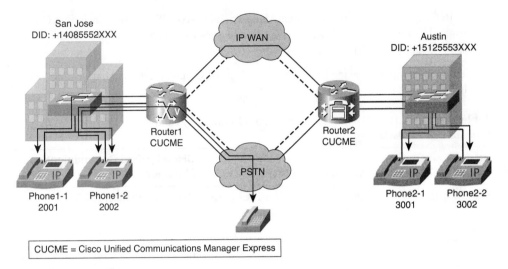

Figure 6-2 *Dial Plan Example*

- **Automated selection of alternate paths in case of network congestion:** For example, using the local carrier for international calls if the preferred international carrier cannot handle the call

- **Blocking certain numbers:** For example, pay-per-minute calls

- **Transformation of the called number:** For example, retaining only the last five digits of a call dialed as a ten-digit number

- **Transformation of the calling number:** For example, replacing a caller's extension with the office's main number when calling the PSTN

A dial plan suitable for an IP telephony system is not fundamentally different from a dial plan designed for a traditional Time Division Marketing (TDM) telephony system. However, an IP-based system presents the dial plan architect with some new possibilities. For example, because of the flexibility of IP-based technology, telephony users in separate sites who used to be served by different, independent TDM systems can now be included in one unified IP-based system. These new possibilities afforded by IP-based systems require some rethinking of the way we look at dial plans. This section examines some of the elements the system planner must consider to properly establish the requirements that drive the design of the dial plan.

Endpoint Addressing

Endpoint addressing is the dial plan component that is responsible for assigning directory numbers to endpoints such as telephones. This also includes the mapping of internal extensions to available direct-inward-dial (DID) ranges assigned by the PSTN. For non-DID numbers, an auto attendant can be used to route calls between the PSTN and the internal network.

One of the biggest challenges when you're creating an endpoint addressing scheme for a multisite installation is to come up with a design that allows for flexibility and scalability that has no impact on the end user. A typical issue to overcome in multisite design is existing overlapping directory numbers. This is where the same directory number exists in multiple sites.

Note   Endpoint addressing is primarily handled by a call agent, such as Cisco Unified Communications Manager or Cisco Unified Communications Manager Express. A pure gateway is usually configured to route inbound calls to the call agent, except gateways in SRST mode.

Call Routing and Path Selection

Call routing and path selection are the dial plan components that define where and how calls should be routed or interconnected. Call routing is usually dependent on the called number (that is, destination-based call routing is usually performed). This is very similar to IP routing, which also relies on destination-based routing. Multiple paths to the same destination might exist, especially in multisite environments—for example, a path using an IP connection or a path using a PSTN connection. Path selection helps you decide which of the available paths should be used.

A voice gateway might be involved with call routing and path selection, depending on the protocol used and the design. For example, an H.323 gateway will at least route the call between the call leg that points to the call handler and the call leg that points to the PSTN.

When a Cisco IOS gateway performs call routing and path selection, the key components used are dial peers. A Cisco Unified Communications Manager Express dial plan will need a high number of dial peers if the deployment is complex.

Digit Manipulation

Digit manipulation is closely connected with call routing and path selection. For inbound calls, the called number needs to be modified to match internally used patterns. For example, a call from the PSTN might use the DID number 4085552001, but the internal pattern is 2001. Thus, the leading 408555 needs to be removed to successfully route a call. Also, the inbound calling number should be dialable—for example, using the missed calls directory. This would include prefixing a 9 to the calling number of inbound PSTN calls.

For outbound calls, digit manipulation ensures that the calling and called party numbers match specific requirements. For example, the PSTN access code 9, which is typically used in telephony environments, needs to be stripped from the called number when sending a call to the PSTN.

Several commands and configurations are available on Cisco IOS gateways to perform digit manipulation depending on the scenario. In general, plain old telephone service (POTS) dial peers support a wider range of commands for simple digit stripping and pre-fixing, whereas VoIP dial peers are primarily dependent on voice translation profiles.

Calling Privileges

Calling privileges define the destinations a user is allowed to call. The primary use for this is to control telephony charges by limiting costly service numbers or international calls to a specific user range.

In PBX systems, this is often called class of service (CoS), which should not be confused with the networking CoS. CoS in data networks defines the priority of a Layer 2 frame, whereas CoS in telephony networks defines the dialable destinations.

Calling privileges are implemented on Cisco IOS gateways using COR and COR lists.

Call Coverage

The goal of call coverage is to lose as few calls as possible. Regardless of which destination is actually dialed, in the end, the call should be answered in the best way possible (the worst being an unanswered call ringing for minutes). Two different call coverage areas exist:

- Call coverage for individual users tries to forward a call to other users or to voice mail in case this user does not answer a call.

- Pilot numbers with associated user groups are typically used for help desks or operators. Incoming calls are distributed to assigned phones, and various algorithms can be used for distribution.

Scalable Dial Plans

Figure 6-3 shows a complex voice network that consists of the components discussed in this section. A comprehensive and scalable dial plan must be well planned and well implemented on networks such as this. The Centrex service requires 10-digit dialing between itself and site D. The IP network requires 10-digit dialing toward sites A, B, and C. Each of the PBXs requires four-digit dialing.

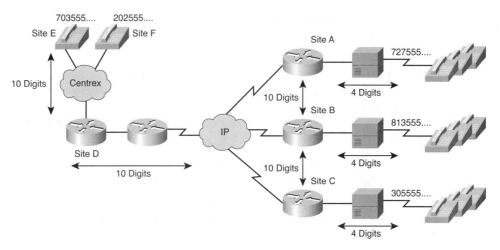

Figure 6-3   *Scalable Dial Plan Topology*

When designing a large-scale dial plan, you must adhere to these attributes:

- **Dial-plan logic distribution:** Good dial-plan architecture relies on the effective distribution of the dial-plan logic among the various components: call processing system, voice gateways, and gatekeepers (if used). Devices that are isolated to a specific portion of the dial plan reduce the complexity of the configuration. Each component focuses on a specific task accomplishment. Generally, the local switch or gateway handles details specific to the local point of presence (POP). Higher-level routing decisions are passed along to the gatekeepers and PBXs. For H.323 networks, a well-designed network places the majority of the dial-plan logic at the gatekeeper devices.

- **Hierarchical numbering plan:** You must strive to design a hierarchical numbering plan to scale the number of devices without introducing interdigit timeout or routing issues due to overlapping numbering ranges. Maintaining a hierarchical design makes the addition and deletion of number groups more manageable. A well-designed hierarchical numbering plan includes good route summarization.

- **Simplicity in provisioning:** Keep the dial plan simple and symmetrical when designing a network. Try to keep consistent dial plans on the network by using translation rules to manipulate the local digit dialing patterns. These number patterns are normalized into a standard format or pattern before the digits enter the VoIP core. Putting digits into a standard format simplifies provisioning and dial-peer management.

- **Post dial delay:** Consider the effects of post dial delay in the network when you design a large-scale dial plan. *Post dial delay* is the time between when the last digit is dialed and the phone rings at the receiving location. In the PSTN, people expect a short post dial delay and to hear ring back within seconds. The more translations, digit manipulations, and lookups that take place, the longer the post dial delay becomes. Overall network design, translation rules, and alternate paths affect post dial delay. Minimize the amount of dial peers and translations to reduce post dial delay. Other things to consider are processor-intensive functions the router might also be performing, such as VPNs and NAT. Anything that utilizes the processor to any degree might affect the capability of the gateway to process calls.

■ **Availability and fault tolerance:** Consider overall network availability and the call success rate when you design a dial plan. Fault tolerance and redundancy are some advantages of a VoIP network. Calls might be automatically routed over redundant IP paths or through the PSTN. Redundant gateways might be provided for mission-critical sites.

Cisco SRST is a gateway feature that allows an IP phone to register with the gateway if no Cisco Unified Communications Manager is available. SRST is beyond the scope of this course.

■ **Conformance to public standards:** Dial plans that interface to the PSTN need to conform to public standards where applicable.

PSTN Dial Plan Requirements

A PSTN dial plan has three key requirements:

■ **Inbound call routing:** Incoming calls from the PSTN need to be routed correctly to their final destination, which might be a directly attached phone, including endpoints that are handled by Cisco Unified Communications Manager or Cisco Unified Communications Manager Express. This inbound call routing also includes digit manipulation to ensure that the incoming Dialed Number Identification Service (DNIS), that is, the incoming called number, matches the pattern expected by the final destination.

■ **Outbound call routing:** Outgoing calls to the PSTN need to be routed to the voice interfaces of the gateway—for example, a T1/E1 or a Foreign Exchange Office (FXO) connection. As with inbound calls, outbound calls might also require digit manipulation to modify the DNIS according to the PSTN requirements. This outbound call routing usually includes stripping of any PSTN access code that might be included in the original called number.

■ **Correct PSTN Automatic Number Identification (ANI) presentation:** An often-neglected aspect is the correct ANI presentation for both inbound and outbound PSTN calls. The ANI for inbound PSTN calls is often left untouched, which might have a negative impact on the end user's experience. The calling number that is presented to the end user should include the PSTN access code and any other identifiers required by the PSTN to successfully place a call using that ANI—for example, using the missed calls directory.

Inbound PSTN Call Example

Figure 6-4 shows a call flow for an inbound call.

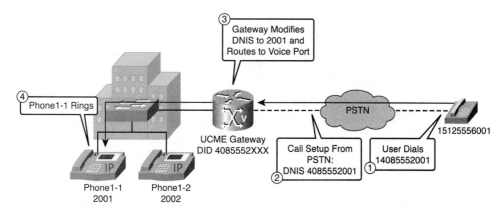

Figure 6-4   *Inbound PSTN Calls*

A site consists of an H.323 gateway that is controlled by Cisco Unified Communications Manager. The DID range of the PSTN trunk is 4085552XXX, and phones use the extension range 2XXX. Here is the process the inbound call goes through:

1. A PSTN user places a call to 14085552001; that is, to Phone1-1.

2. The call setup is received by the gateway with a DNIS of 4085552001.

3. The gateway modifies the DNIS to 2001, the extension of Phone1-1, and routes the call to the voice port created when the IP phone registered with UCME.

4. The phone rings.

Outbound PSTN Call Example

Figure 6-5 shows a call flow for an outbound call.

A site consists of an H.323 gateway and a Cisco Unified Communications Manager server. The DNIS that Cisco Unified Communications Manager sends to the gateway includes the PSTN access code 9, and the ANI is the 4-digit extension of the phone. The process of the outbound call is as follows:

1. Using Phone1-1 with the extension 0151, a user places a call to 9 1 512 555-0101.

2. The gateway accepts the call and modifies the DNIS to 1 512 555-0101, stripping off PSTN access code 9. The gateway also modifies the ANI to 408 555-0151 by prefixing the area code and local code to the 4-digit extension.

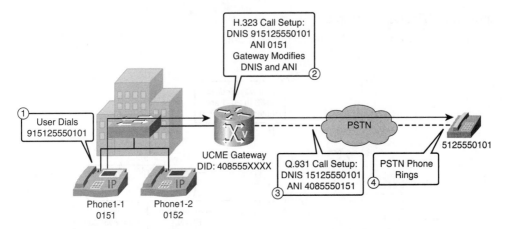

Figure 6-5   *Outbound PSTN Calls*

3. The gateway sends out a Q.931 setup message to the PSTN with an ANI of 4085550151.

4. The PSTN subscriber telephone at 512 555-0101 rings.

ISDN Dial Plan Requirements

When you are using ISDN trunks, additional requirements might exist:

■ **Correct PSTN inbound ANI presentation depending on TON:** Some ISDN networks present the inbound ANI as the shortest dialable number combined with the type of number (TON). This treatment of the ANI raises an issue because simply prefixing the PSTN access code might not result in an ANI that can be called back. The potential problem can be solved by proper digit manipulation on gateways.

■ **Correct PSTN outbound ANI presentation depending on TON:** Some ISDN networks and PBXs might expect a certain numbering plan and TON for both DNIS and ANI. Using wrong flags might result in incomplete calls or wrong DNIS and ANI presentation. Again, digit manipulation can be used to solve these issues.

Inbound ISDN Call Example

Figure 6-6 shows a call flow for an inbound ISDN call.

A site consists of an H.323 gateway that is controlled by Cisco Unified Communications Manager Express. The DID range of the PSTN trunk is 408555XXXXX, and phones use the extension range 01XX. The process of the inbound ISDN call is as follows:

1. A PSTN user in Chicago with the number 512 555-0101 dials 1 408 555-0101.

2. The gateway receives an ISDN setup message with the DNIS 4085550101 and the ANI 5125550101 TON National.

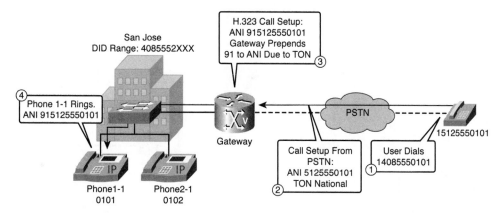

Figure 6-6   *Inbound ISDN Call*

3.   Based on the ANI TON, the gateway prefixes 91 to the ANI (9 as the PSTN access code and 1 as the national identifier).

4.   The call is routed to Phone 1-1, and the calling number is displayed: 915125550101. A user who misses the call can directly call back using the missed call directory without any modification.

Configuring PSTN Dial Plans

You can use the following steps to configure PSTN dial plans.

Step 1.   Configure digit manipulation for PSTN calls.

Step 2.   Configure digit manipulation for intersite calls.

Step 3.   Configure dial peer matching.

PSTN Dial Plan Example

In the example illustrated in Figure 6-7, you are required to develop and implement a dial plan for your company.

The dial plan must meet network requirements as specified. The configuration scenario that is represented in this figure will be used throughout this procedure.

Dial Plan Requirements

Dial plan requirements are as follows:

■   **San Jose site:**

Cisco Unified Communications Manager Express on Router1

DID range 4085552XXX

DN range 2XXX

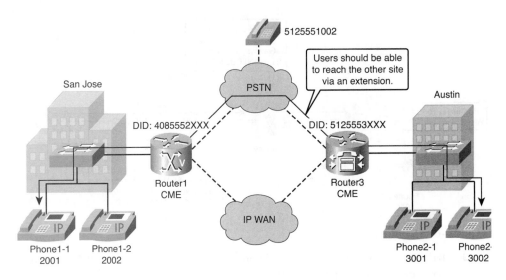

Figure 6-7   *PSTN Dial Plan Scenario*

■   Austin site:

Cisco Unified Communications Manager Express on Router3

DID range 5125553XXX

DN range 3XXX

■   Any intersite calls routed using the PSTN will require digit manipulation to change the dialed remote extension to a PSTN routable number (for example, 2001 to 14085552001).

Digit Manipulation for Inbound Calls

Examples 6-1 and 6-2 provide the configurations for Router1 and Router3, which perform digit manipulation for inbound calls.

Example 6-1   *Digit Manipulation for Inbound Calls on Router1*

```
Router1(config)#voice translation-rule 1
Router1(cfg-translation-rule)#rule 1 /^4085552/ /2/
Router1(cfg-translation-rule)#exit
Router1(config)#voice translation-profile pstn-in
Router1(cfg-translation-profile)#translate called 1
Router1(cfg-translation-profile)#exit
Router1(config)#voice-port 0/0/0:23
Router1(config-voiceport)#translation-profile incoming pstn-in
```

Example 6-2 *Digit Manipulation for Inbound Calls on Router3*

```
Router3(config)#voice translation-rule 1
Router3(cfg-translation-rule)#rule 1 /^5125553/ /3/
Router3(cfg-translation-rule)#exit
Router3(config)#voice translation-profile pstn-in
Router3(cfg-translation-profile)#translate called 1
Router3(cfg-translation-profile)#exit
Router3(config)#voice-port 0/0/0:23
Router3(config-voiceport)#translation-profile incoming pstn-in
```

The following describes the configuration applied to Router1 (which is similar to that of Router3):

Step 1.   Voice translation rule 1 is used to modify the inbound called number to the actual directory number:

```
Router1(config)#voice translation-rule 1
Router1(cfg-translation-rule)#rule 1 /^4085552/ /2/
```

Step 2.   The voice translation profile **pstn-in** is used to modify the incoming called and calling number:

```
Router1(config)#voice translation-profile pstn-in
Router1(cfg-translation-profile)#translate called 1
```

Step 3.   The voice translation profile **pstn-in** is bound to the voice port and will be used for any incoming call:

```
Router1(config)#voice-port 0/0/0:23
Router1(config-voiceport)#translation-profile incoming pstn-in
```

Digit Manipulation for Outbound Calls

Examples 6-3 and 6-4 show the digit manipulation configurations deployed on Router1 and Router3 for outbound calls.

Example 6-3 *Digit Manipulation for Outbound Calls on Router1*

```
Router1(config)#voice translation-rule 2
Router1(cfg-translation-rule)#rule 1 /^2/ /4085552/
Router1(cfg-translation-rule)#exit
Router1(config)#voice translation-profile pstn-out
Router1(cfg-translation-profile)#translate calling 2
Router1(cfg-translation-profile)#exit
Router1(config)#voice-port 0/0/0:23
Router1(config-voiceport)#translation-profile outgoing pstn-out
```

Example 6-4   *Digit Manipulation for Outbound Calls on Router3*

```
Router3(config)#voice translation-rule 2
Router3(cfg-translation-rule)#rule 1 /^3/ /5125553/
Router3(cfg-translation-rule)#exit
Router3(config)#voice translation-profile pstn-out
Router3(cfg-translation-profile)#translate calling 2
Router3(cfg-translation-profile)#exit
Router3(config)#voice-port 0/0/0:23
Router3(config-voiceport)#translation-profile outgoing pstn-out
```

The following describes the configuration applied to Router1 (which is very similar to that of Router3):

Step 1.   Voice translation rule 2 matches the four-digit 2XXX extenuation and expands it to DID number 4085552XXX:

```
Router1(config)#voice translation-rule 2
Router1(cfg-translation-rule)#rule 1 /^2/ /4085552/
```

Step 2.   The voice translation profile **pstn-out** uses this rule to translate the calling number:

```
Router1(config)#voice translation-profile pstn-out
Router1(cfg-translation-profile)#translate calling 2
```

Step 3.   The **pstn-out** profile is bound to voice port 0/0/0:23 as the outgoing voice translation profile:

```
Router1(config)#voice-port 0/0/0:23
Router1(config-voiceport)#translation-profile outgoing
    pstn-out
```

Digit Manipulation for Intersite Calls

The configuration deployed on Router1 to allow extension short-dialing to Austin is as follows:

```
Router1(config)#num-exp 3... 915125553...
```

The configuration deployed on Router3 to allow extension short-dialing to San Jose is as follows:

```
Router3(config)#num-exp 2... 914085552...
```

Outbound Dial Peer Matching

After the digit manipulation for inbound calls has been defined, the outbound dial peers need to be created. Both routers require a single dial peer that will be used to route calls to the PSTN.

The easiest configuration is a single dial peer with the destination pattern **9T**. The dial-peer configuration for both routers is identical. Example 6-5 shows the configuration for Router1.

Example 6-5   *Outbound Dial-Peer Matching on Router1*

```
Router1(config)#dial-peer voice 910 pots
Router1(config-dial-peer)#destination-pattern 9[2-9]..[2-9]......
Router1(config-dial-peer)#direct-inward-dial
Router1(config-dial-peer)#port 0/0/0:23
```

These dial peers will also be used for inbound call legs. Therefore, the **direct-inward-dial** command is configured to enable call routing using the received called-number information.

> **Note**   This example shows only the commands used for pure call routing and digit manipulation. Other settings—for example, H.323 timers—might be required as well, depending on the deployment scenario.

Inbound Dial Peer Matching

Next, the dial peers are tuned for dial-peer matching. Although call routing might work without any additional configuration, always configure appropriate inbound dial-peer matching using **incoming called-number** or **answer-address** to ensure that a call is actually routed as desired.

On Router1, dial peer 9 should be the inbound dial peer for PSTN calls. The most common approach is to match the incoming called number. In this case it is not the DID range 14085552XXX but the actual extension 2XXX. This is because of the voice-translation profile configured on the voice port, which emphasizes that it is important to know the order of digit manipulation and dial-peer matching.

Examples 6-6 and 6-7 show the inbound dial-peer matching configurations deployed on Router1 and Router3 for inbound calls, using the **incoming called-number** command.

Example 6-6   *Inbound Dial Peer Matching on Router1*

```
Router1(config)#dial-peer voice 910 pots
Router1(config-dial-peer)#destination-pattern 9[2-9]..[2-9]......
Router1(config-dial-peer)#direct-inward-dial
Router1(config-dial-peer)#incoming called-number 2...
Router1(config-dial-peer)#port 0/0/0:23
```

Example 6-7   *Inbound Dial Peer Matching on Router3*

```
Router3(config)#dial-peer voice 910 pots
Router3(config-dial-peer)#destination-pattern 9[2-9]..[2-9]......
Router3(config-dial-peer)#direct-inward-dial
Router3(config-dial-peer)#incoming called-number 3...
Router3(config-dial-peer)#port 0/0/0:23
```

Note   Wrong inbound dial-peer matching configuration is one of the biggest issues with Cisco IOS gateways. The default dial peer 0 will often mask an obvious misconfiguration, but this might often lead to unexpected results, such as wrong codec selection and wrong digit manipulation.

Complete Configurations

As a reference, Examples 6-8 and 6-9 show the complete configurations for both routers in this scenario.

Example 6-8   *Complete Configuration for Router1*

```
Router1#show run
... OUTPUT OMITTED ...
voice translation-rule 1
 rule 1 /^4085552/ /2/
voice translation-rule 2
 rule 1 /^2/ /4085552/
voice translation-profile pstn-out
 translate calling 2
voice translation-profile pstn-in
 translate called 1
voice-port 0/0/0:23
 translation-profile incoming pstn-in
 translation-profile outgoing pstn-out
dial-peer voice 910 pots
 destination-pattern 9[2-9]..[2-9]......
 incoming called-number 2...
 direct-inward-dial
 port 0/0/0:23
num-exp 3... 915125553...
... OUTPUT OMITTED ...
```

Example 6-9 *Complete Configuration for Router3*

```
Router3#show run
... OUTPUT OMITTED ...
voice translation-rule 1
 rule 1 /^3125553/ /3/
voice translation-rule 2
 rule 1 /^3/ /3125553/
voice translation-profile pstn-out
 translate calling 2
voice translation-profile pstn-in
 translate called 1
voice-port 0/0/0:23
 translation-profile incoming pstn-in
 translation-profile outgoing pstn-out
dial-peer voice 910 pots
 destination-pattern 9[2-9]..[2-9]......
 incoming called-number 3...
 direct-inward-dial
 port 0/0/0:23
num-exp 2... 914085552...
... OUTPUT OMITTED ...
```

Inbound PSTN Call Flow Example

Figure 6-8 illustrates an example of an inbound PSTN call flow.

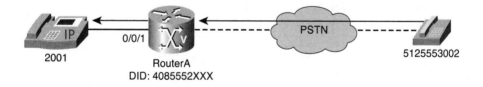

Figure 6-8 *Inbound PSTN Call Flow Example*

The following steps are involved in configuring this example:

Step 1. A user dials 14085552001 and RouterA receives an incoming call. Example 6-10 shows the configuration on RouterA, and Table 6-2 shows the resulting DNIS and ANI numbers.

- Outgoing DNIS: 2001

- Outgoing ANI: 915125553002

Example 6-10   *Inbound PSTN Call Flow Step 1*

```
RouterA(config)#voice translation-rule 1
RouterA(cfg-translation-rule)#rule 1 /^4085552/ /2/
RouterA(cfg-translation-rule)#exit
RouterA(config)#voice translation-profile pstn-in
RouterA(cfg-translation-profile)#translate called 1
RouterA(cfg-translation-profile)#exit
RouterA(config)#voice-port 0/0/0:23
RouterA(config-voiceport)#translation-profile incoming pstn-in
```

Table 6-2   *Inbound PSTN Call Flow Step 1—DNIS and ANI Matrix*

	Incoming	Outgoing
DNIS	4085552001	2001
ANI	5125553002	915125553002

Step 2.   The inbound dial peer is matched to dial peer 9 because of the **incoming called-number 2...** command, as shown in Example 6-11. Table 6-3 shows the resulting DNIS and ANI numbers.

Example 6-11   *Inbound PSTN Call Flow Step 2*

```
RouterA(config)#dial-peer voice 910 pots
RouterA(config-dial-peer)#destination-pattern 9[2-9].. [2-9]......
RouterA(config-dial-peer)#incoming called-number 2...
RouterA(config-dial-peer)#direct-inward-dial
RouterA(config-dial-peer)#port 0/0/0:23
```

Table 6-3   *Inbound PSTN Call Flow Step 2—DNIS and ANI Matrix*

	Incoming	Outgoing
DNIS	2001	2001
ANI	915125553002	915125553002

Step 3.   The outbound dial peer is matched to dial peer 2001 because of the **destination-pattern 2001** command, as shown in Example 6-12. Table 6-4 shows the resulting DNIS and ANI numbers.

Example 6-12   *Inbound PSTN Call Flow Step 3*

```
RouterA(config)#dial-peer voice 2001 pots
RouterA(config-dial-peer)#destination-pattern 2001
RouterA(config-dial-peer)#port 0/0/1
```

Table 6-4   *Inbound PSTN Call Flow Step 3—DNIS and ANI Matrix*

	Incoming	Outgoing
DNIS	2001	2001
ANI	915125553002	915125553002

Outbound PSTN Call Flow Example

Figure 6-9 illustrates an example of an outbound PSTN call flow.

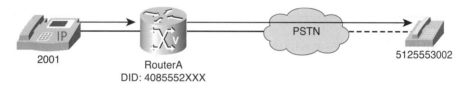

2001

RouterA
DID: 4085552XXX

PSTN

5125553002

Figure 6-9   *Outbound PSTN Call Flow Example*

The following steps are involved in configuring this example:

Step 1.   The inbound dial peer 2001 is matched because of the **destination-pattern 2001** command. Example 6-13 shows the configuration on RouterA, and Table 6-5 shows the resulting DNIS and ANI numbers.

Example 6-13   *Outbound PSTN Call Flow Step 1*

```
RouterA(config)#dial-peer voice 2001 pots
RouterA(config-dial-peer)#destination-pattern 2001
RouterA(config-dial-peer)#huntstop
RouterA(config-dial-peer)#port 0/0/1
```

Table 6-5   *Outbound PSTN Call Flow Step 1—DNIS and ANI Matrix*

	Incoming	Outgoing
DNIS	915125553002	915125553002
ANI	2001	2001

Step 2.   The outbound dial peer is matched to dial peer 9 because of the **destination-pattern 9T** command. The 9 is stripped from the DNIS by way of the default POTS dial-peer matching behavior, as shown in Example 6-14. Table 6-6 shows the resulting DNIS and ANI numbers.

Example 6-14   *Outbound PSTN Call Flow Step 2*

```
RouterA(config)#dial-peer voice 910 pots
RouterA(config-dial-peer)#destination-pattern 9[2-9].. [2-9]......
RouterA(config-dial-peer)#incoming called-number 2...
RouterA(config-dial-peer)#direct-inward-dial
RouterA(config-dial-peer)#port 0/0/0:23
```

Table 6-6   *Outbound PSTN Call Flow Step 2—DNIS and ANI Matrix*

	Incoming	Outgoing
DNIS	915125553002	15125553002
ANI	2001	2001

Step 3.   The outgoing voice translation profile on the voice port modifies the ANI to 4085552001, and the call is routed to the PSTN, as shown in Example 6-15. Table 6-7 shows the resulting DNIS and ANI numbers.

Example 6-15   *Outbound PSTN Call Flow Step 3*

```
RouterA(config)#voice translation-rule 2
RouterA(cfg-translation-rule)#rule 1 /^2/ /4085552/
RouterA(cfg-translation-rule)#exit
RouterA(config)#voice translation-profile pstn-out
RouterA(cfg-translation-profile)#translate calling 2
RouterA(cfg-translation-profile)#exit
RouterA(config)#voice-port 0/0/0:23
RouterA(config-voiceport)#translation-profile outgoing pstn-out
```

Table 6-7   *Outbound PSTN Call Flow Step 3—DNIS and ANI Matrix*

	Incoming	Outgoing
DNIS	15125553002	15125553002
ANI	2001	4085552001

Verifying PSTN Dial Plans

The **show dial-peer voice** and the **show dialplan number** commands are used to verify dial plans on a gateway, as detailed in Table 6-8.

Table 6-8 *Commands to Verify PSTN Dial Plans*

Command	Description
show dial-peer voice *number*	Displays information for a specific voice dial peer
show dial-peer voice summary	Displays a short summary of each voice dial peer
show dialplan number *dial-string* [**carrier** *identifier*] [**fax** | huntstop | **voice**] [**timeout**]	Displays which outgoing dial peer is reached when a particular telephone number is dialed

Example 6-16 provides sample output from the **show dial-peer voice summary** command. Notice the output shows the administrative and operational status of each dial peer, each dial-peer's destination pattern, dial-peer preference, session target (where applicable), and voice port (where applicable).

Example 6-16   show dial-peer voice summary *Command*

```
Router#show dial-peer voice summary
dial-peer hunt 0
              AD                           PRE PASS              OUT
  TAG    TYPE  MIN  OPER PREFIX DEST-PATTERN FER THRU SESS-TARGET  STAT PORT
  9      pots  up   up          9T           0                     up   1/0:23
  20     voip  up   up          2...         0   syst ipv4:192.168.1.1
  21     voip  up   up          2...         1   syst ipv4:192.168.1.2
```

Example 6-17 shows sample output from the **show dialplan number** command for a phone number of **1001**.

Example 6-17   show dialplan number 1001 *Command*

```
Router#show dialplan number 1001
VoiceEncapPeer20001
        peer type = voice, information type = voice,
        description = `',
        tag = 20001, destination-pattern = `1001$',
        answer-address = `', preference=0,
        CLID Restriction = None
        CLID Network Number = `'
        CLID Second Number sent
        CLID Override RDNIS = disabled,
```

continues

Example 6-17   show dialplan number 1001 *Command   continued*

```
           source carrier-id = `', target carrier-id = `',
           source trunk-group-label = `',  target trunk-group-label = `',
           numbering Type = `unknown'
           group = 20001, Admin state is up, Operation state is up,
           incoming called-number = `', connections/maximum = 0/unlimited,
           DTMF Relay = disabled,
           URI classes:
               Destination =
           huntstop = enabled,
           in bound application associated: 'DEFAULT'
           out bound application associated: ''
           dnis-map =
           permission :both
           incoming COR list:maximum capability
           outgoing COR list:minimum requirement
           Translation profile (Incoming):
           Translation profile (Outgoing):
           incoming call blocking:
           translation-profile = `'
           disconnect-cause = `no-service'
           advertise 0x40 capacity_update_timer 25 addrFamily 4 oldAddrFamily 4
           type = pots, prefix = `',
           forward-digits 0
           session-target = `', voice-port = `50/0/11',
           direct-inward-dial = disabled,
           digit_strip = enabled,
           register E.164 number with H323 GK and/or SIP Registrar = TRUE
           fax rate = system,   payload size =  20 bytes
           supported-language = ''

           Time elapsed since last clearing of voice call statistics never
           Connect Time = 0, Charged Units = 0,
           Successful Calls = 2, Failed Calls = 0, Incomplete Calls = 0
           Accepted Calls = 0, Refused Calls = 0,
               Last Disconnect Cause is "10  ", Last Disconnect Text is "normal
          call clearing (16)",
               Last Setup Time = 436050.
  Matched: 1001    Digits: 5
  Target:
```

Notice the previous output indicates the reason for the last disconnect. Specifically, in Example 6-17, the last disconnect cause code was 0x10, in hex (16 in decimal). The disconnect text was "normal call clearing." This is an example of a Q.850 cause code. As a reference, Table 6-9 lists standard Q.850 cause codes used for PRI and H.323.

Table 6-9 *Q.850 Cause Codes*

Cause Code		Definition
HEX	**DEC**	
0x1	1	Unallocated number
0x3	3	No route to destination
0x6	6	Channel unacceptable
0x7	7	Call awarded and being delivered in an established channel
0x10	16	Normal call clearing
0x11	17	User busy
0x12	18	No user responding
0x13	19	No answer from user
0x15	21	Call rejected
0x16	22	Number changed
0x1A	26	Nonselected user clearing
0x1B	27	Destination out of order
0x1C	28	Invalid number format
0x1D	29	Facility rejected
0x1E	30	Response to a status enquiry
0x1F	31	Normal, unspecified
0x22	34	No channel available
0x26	38	Network out of order
0x29	41	Temporary failure
0x2A	42	Switching equipment congestion
0x2B	43	Access information discarded
0x2C	44	Request channel not available
0x2F	47	Resource not available
0x31	49	Quality of service unavailable
0x32	50	Requested facility not subscribed
0x39	57	Bearer capability not authorized
0x3A	58	Bearer capability not presently available

continues

Table 6-9 *Q.850 Cause Codes* *(continued)*

Cause Code		Definition
HEX	DEC	
0x3F	63	Service or option not available
0x41	65	Bearer capability not implemented
0x42	66	Channel type not implemented
0x45	69	Request facility not implemented
0x46	70	Only restricted digital information bearer capability is available
0x4F	79	Service or option not implemented, unspecified
0x51	81	Invalid call reference value
0x52	82	Identified channel does not exist
0x53	83	Suspended call exists, but call identity does not
0x54	84	Call identity in use
0x55	85	No call suspended
0x56	86	Call with the specified call identity is cleared
0x58	88	Incompatible destination
0x5B	91	Invalid transit network selection
0x5F	95	Invalid message, unspecified
0x60	96	Mandatory information element is missing
0x61	97	Message type nonexistent or not implemented
0x62	98	Message not compatible with call state or message type nonexistent
0x63	99	Information element nonexistent or not implemented
0x64	100	Invalid information element contents
0x65	101	Message not compatible with call state
0x66	102	Recovery on timer expiry
0x6F	111	Protocol error, unspecified
0x7F	127	Internetworking, unspecified

Several **debug** commands are available for troubleshooting dial plans, as described in Table 6-10.

Table 6-10 *debug Commands for PSTN Dial Plans*

Command	Description
debug isdn q931	Debugs ISDN Layer 3 information, which includes DNIS and ANI information
debug voip dialpeer	Debugs dial-peer matching
debug voice translation	Debugs voice-translation-rule operation

Example 6-18 shows sample output from a **debug isdn q931** command from a call setup procedure for an incoming call.

Example 6-18   debug isdn q931 *Command–Part 1*

```
Router#debug isdn q931

RX <- SETUP pd = 8 callref = 0x06
Bearer Capability i = 0x8890
Channel ID i = 0x89
Calling Party Number i = 0x0083, `81012345678902'
TX -> CONNECT pd = 8 callref = 0x86
RX <- CONNECT_ACK pd = 8 callref = 0x06
```

Use the **debug isdn q931** command in privileged EXEC mode to display information about call setup and teardown of ISDN network connections (Layer 3) between the local router (user side) and the network. To disable debugging output, use the **no** form of this command.

The ISDN network layer interface that is provided by the router conforms to the user interface specification defined by ITU-T Recommendation Q.931, supplemented by other specifications such as for switch type VN4. The router tracks activities that occur only on the user side, not the network side, of the network connection. The **debug isdn q931** command output is limited to commands and responses that are exchanged during peer-to-peer communication and carried over the data channel (D channel). This debug information does not include data sent over the bearer channels (B channels), which are also part of the ISDN interface of the router. The peers (network layers) communicate with each other via an ISDN switch over the D channel.

A router can be the calling party or the called party of the ISDN Q.931 network-connection call setup and teardown procedures. If the router is the calling party, the command displays information about an outgoing call. If the router is the called party, the command displays information about an incoming call.

Example 6-19 shows sample output from the **debug isdn q931** command of a call setup procedure for an outgoing call.

Example 6-19   debug isdn q931 *Command—Part 2*

```
Router#debug isdn q931
TX -> SETUP pd = 8 callref = 0x04
 Bearer Capability i = 0x8890
 Channel ID i = 0x83
 Called Party Number i = 0x80, `4085552001'
RX <- CALL_PROC pd = 8 callref = 0x84
 Channel ID i = 0x89
RX <- CONNECT pd = 8 callref = 0x84
TX -> CONNECT_ACK pd = 8 callref = 0x04....
Success rate is 0 percent (0/5)
```

You can use the **debug isdn q931** command with the **debug isdn event** and **debug isdn q921** commands at the same time. The displays will be intermingled. Use the **service timestamps debug datetime msec** command in global configuration mode to include the time with each message.

To display information about the voice dial peers, use the **debug voip dialpeer** command in privileged EXEC mode. Example 6-20 shows an event that identifies the incoming dial peer and shows that it has been matched.

Example 6-20   debug voip dialpeer *Command*

```
Router#debug voip dialpeer
*Apr 18 21:07:35.291: //-1/xxxxxxxxxxxx/DPM/MatchNextPeer:
   Result=Success(0); Incoming Dial-peer=1 Is Matched
*Apr 18 21:07:35.291: //-1/xxxxxxxxxxxx/DPM/dpAssociateIncomingPeerCore:
   Match Rule=DP_MATCH_INCOMING_DNIS; Called Number=83103
*Apr 18 21:07:35.291: //-1/xxxxxxxxxxxx/DPM/dpMatchPeertype:
   Is Incoming=TRUE, Number Expansion=FALSE
*Apr 18 21:07:35.291: //-1/xxxxxxxxxxxx/DPM/dpMatchCore:
   Dial String=83103, Expanded String=83103, Calling Number=
   Timeout=TRUE, Is Incoming=TRUE, Peer Info Type=DIALPEER_INFO_FAX
*Apr 18 21:07:35.291: //-1/xxxxxxxxxxxx/DPM/dpMatchCore:
   Result=-1
*Apr 18 21:07:35.291: //-1/xxxxxxxxxxxx/DPM/dpAssociateIncomingPeerCore:
   Match Rule=DP_MATCH_ANSWER; Calling Number=4085550111
*Apr 18 21:07:35.291: //-1/xxxxxxxxxxxx/DPM/dpMatchPeertype:
   Is Incoming=TRUE, Number Expansion=FALSE
*Apr 18 21:07:35.291: //-1/xxxxxxxxxxxx/DPM/dpMatchCore:
   Dial String=, Expanded String=, Calling Number=4085550111T
   Timeout=TRUE, Is Incoming=TRUE, Peer Info Type=DIALPEER_INFO_FAX
```

```
*Apr 18 21:07:35.291: //-1/xxxxxxxxxxxx/DPM/dpMatchCore:
  Result=-1
*Apr 18 21:07:35.291: //-1/xxxxxxxxxxxx/DPM/dpAssociateIncomingPeerCore:
  Match Rule=DP_MATCH_ORIGINATE; Calling Number=4085550111
*Apr 18 21:07:35.291: //-1/xxxxxxxxxxxx/DPM/dpMatchPeertype:
  Is Incoming=TRUE, Number Expansion=FALSE
*Apr 18 21:07:35.291: //-1/xxxxxxxxxxxx/DPM/dpMatchCore:
  Dial String=, Expanded String=, Calling Number=4085550111T
  Timeout=TRUE, Is Incoming=TRUE, Peer Info Type=DIALPEER_INFO_FAX
*Apr 18 21:07:35.295: //-1/xxxxxxxxxxxx/DPM/dpMatchCore:
  Result=-1
```

To view voice translation rule information, use the **debug voice translation** command. Example 6-21 shows sample output from the **debug voice translation** command for the following translation rule:

```
voice translation-rule 1001
   rule 1 /^.*/ /5551212/
```

Example 6-21   debug voice translation *Command*

```
Router#debug voice translation
00:51:56:regxrule_get_profile_from_trunkgroup:Voice port 0x64143DA8
    does not belong to any trunk group
00:51:56:regxrule_get_profile_from_trunkgroup:Voice port 0x64143DA8
    does not belong to any trunk group
00:51:56:regxrule_stack_pop_RegXruleNumInfo:stack=0x63DECAF4; count=1
00:51:56:regxrule_stack_push_RegXruleNumInfo:stack=0x63DECAF4; count=0
This output shows the details of the original number following
    "regxrule_profile_translate".
00:51:56:regxrule_profile_translate:number=4088880101 type=unknown
    plan=unknown numbertype=calling
Following "regxrule_profile_match", the output shows that rule 1 in
    the translation rule 1001 was a match and the details of the SED
    substitution are shown.
00:51:56:regxrule_profile_match:Matched with rule 1 in ruleset 1001
00:51:56:regxrule_profile_match:Matched with rule 1 in ruleset 1001
00:51:56:sed_subst:Successful substitution; pattern=4088880101
    matchPattern=^.* replacePattern=5551212 replaced pattern=5551212
00:51:56:regxrule_subst_num_type:Match Type = none, Replace Type = none
    Input Type = unknown
00:51:56:regxrule_subst_num_plan:Match Plan = none, Replace Plan = none
    Input Plan = unknown
```

```
Then the output shows the details of the translated number following
    "regxrule_profile_translate".
00:51:56:regxrule_profile_translate:xlt_number=5551212 xlt_type=unknown
    xlt_plan=unknown
00:51:56:regxrule_profile_translate:number= type=UNKNOWN plan=UNKNOWN
numbertype=redirect-called
00:51:56:regxrule_get_RegXrule:Invalid translation ruleset tag=0
In this example, because there was no called number or redirect number
    translation that was configured on the translation profile, corresponding
    errors were generated with a message that no match was found.
00:51:56:regxrule_profile_match:Error:ruleset for redirect-called
    number not found
00:51:56:regxrule_profile_translate:No match:number= type=UNKNOWN plan=UNKNOWN
00:51:56:regxrule_profile_translate:number=5108880101 type=unknown
    plan=unknown numbertype=called
00:51:56:regxrule_get_RegXrule:Invalid translation ruleset tag=0
00:51:56:regxrule_profile_match:Error:ruleset for called number not found
00:51:56:regxrule_profile_translate:No match:number=5108880101 type=unknown
    plan=unknown
00:51:56:regxrule_stack_push_RegXruleNumInfo:stack=0x63DECAF4; count=1
Following "regxrule_dp_translate", the output indicates that there is no
    translation profile for outgoing direction, and then it prints the
    numbers sent to the outgoing service provider interface (SPI).
00:51:56:regxrule_dp_translate:No profile found in peer 5108888 for
    outgoing direction
00:51:56:regxrule_dp_translate:calling_number=5551212 calling_octet=0x0
        called_number=5108880101 called_octet=0x80
        redirect_number= redirect_type=4294967295        redirect_plan=4294967295
00:51:56:regxrule_stack_pop_RegXruleNumInfo:stack=0x63DECAF4; count=2
00:51:56:regxrule_stack_push_RegXruleNumInfo:stack=0x63DECAF4; count=1
```

Numbering Plan Fundamentals

To integrate VoIP networks into existing voice networks, network administrators must have the skills and knowledge to implement a scalable numbering plan to be used within a comprehensive, scalable, and logical dial plan. This section describes the attributes of numbering plans for voice networks, addresses the challenges of designing these plans, and identifies the methods of implementing numbering plans.

Numbering Plan Overview

A numbering plan describes the endpoint addressing scheme used in a VoIP network and is analogous to the IP addressing scheme used in an IP network. A numbering plan identifies each VoIP endpoint and application in the network with a unique telephone number.

A well-designed numbering plan should evaluate both current requirements and potential growth requirements to avoid the need to renumber as more users connect to the voice network.

Implementing a VoIP network involves designing a numbering plan for all endpoints or reviewing an existing numbering plan for scalability and completeness. A dial plan can be designed only after the numbering plan has been completed and after call patterns and connectivity to the PSTN are understood. All implementations of VoIP require both a numbering plan and a dial plan.

Numbering Plan Categories

Types of numbering plans include the following:

- **Private numbering plans:** Private numbering plans are used to address endpoints and applications within private networks. Private numbering plans are not required to adhere to any specific format and can be created to accommodate the needs of the network. Because most private telephone networks connect to the PSTN at some point in the design, it is good practice to plan the private numbering plan to coincide with publicly assigned number ranges. Number translation might be required when connecting private voice networks to the PSTN.

- **Public/PSTN numbering plans:** PSTN or public numbering plans are unique to the country in which they are implemented:

  - **The international public telecommunication numbering plan (E.164):** The E.164 standard is an international numbering plan for public telephone systems in which each assigned number contains a one-, two-, or three-digit country code (CC) followed by a national destination code (NDC) followed by a subscriber number (SN). There can be up to 15 digits in an E.164 number. The E.164 plan was originally developed by the International Telecommunication Union (ITU).

  - **National numbering plans:** A national numbering plan defines the numbering structure for a specific country or group of countries. One example is the NANP. It defines a 10-digit numbering plan. This number is represented as XXX XXX-XXXX. First is a three-digit Numbering Plan Area (NPA) code (commonly referred to as the area code). Next is a three-digit central office code. Last is a four-digit subscriber line number. The United States, Canada, and parts of the Caribbean all use the NANP for number assignment. Other countries have differing national numbering plans.

Private Numbering Plan Design Considerations

When designing a private numbering plan, the following issues must be addressed:

- **Number of addressable devices:** Try to use the fewest possible digits for internal dialing to make it easier for users to remember extensions.

- **Number of locations:** Use the fewest possible digits for calls within a location and site codes plus extensions for calls between locations.

- **Inbound call routing:** Some companies buy a block of numbers from a service provider and allow DID to all numbers. Other companies prefer to use a single number for external callers and then route all calls to a receptionist or an auto attendant who then forwards the call to the intended party.

- **PSTN access codes:** PSTN access codes differentiate internal from external calls. In the United States, we usually use 9 as a PSTN access code, although many other countries use 8. One effect of using PSTN access codes is that you cannot use the PSTN access code digit to begin an extension. In other words, if you use 9 as a PSTN access code, then you cannot have an extension range of 9XXX. The same thing goes for operator digits (for example, 0).

PSTN Numbering Plan Common Elements

Most countries' numbering plans share some common elements. They usually support the following types or classes of numbers:

- **Emergency services:** Some countries provide a single number for all emergency services, whereas other countries have separate numbers.

- **Information or directory services:** Most countries have a number for directory services. In the United States, it is typically 411.

- **Local calls:** Local calls are usually free and within a local geographic area.

- **Mobile calls:** Most countries bill a caller for calls to a mobile phone. The United States. is a notable exception. Billing the caller requires that the mobile phones be assigned a specific number range. In the United States, the caller is billed for incoming and outgoing calls, so mobile phones can be assigned numbers from the same pool as traditional phones.

- **Long distance or toll:** Long distance calls are calls outside of the local geographic area. These calls usually require an access code (when placed from behind a corporate telephony system) as well as an area code and subscriber number.

- **Toll free:** Toll-free calls are free to the person making the call. The call is billed to the recipient by the service provider.

- **Premium:** Premium calls incur per-minute or per-call charges. These calls are usually blocked by companies because they are frequently used for "entertainment" purposes, usually known in the United States as 900 numbers.

- **International:** International calls are placed to other countries using an access code, followed by the ITU E.164 country code, and then the full subscriber number including area code.

North American Numbering Plan Example

The example illustrated in Figure 6-10 shows the operation of the North American numbering plan.

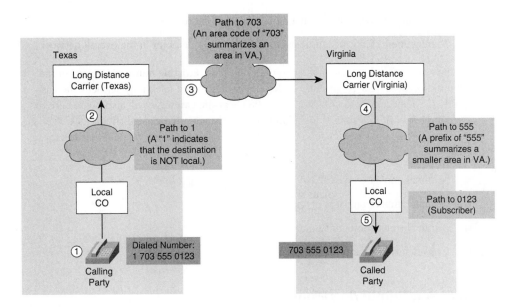

Figure 6-10   *North American Numbering Plan*

The call routing process is as follows:

1. A subscriber in Texas dials 1 703 555-0123.

2. The local CO in Texas recognizes that the 1 means this is not a local call and forwards the call to a long-distance carrier in Texas.

3. The long-distance carrier in Texas recognizes 703 as an area code in Virginia and forwards the call to a long-distance carrier in Virginia.

4. The long-distance carrier in Virginia forwards the call to the local CO.

5. The local CO delivers the call to the correct subscriber.

Scalable Numbering Plans

Scalable telephony networks require well-designed telephone numbering plans that are hierarchical. A hierarchical design has these advantages:

■ **Simplified provisioning:** Refers to the capability to easily add new groups and modify existing groups

- **Simplified routing:** Keeps local calls local and uses a specialized number key, such as an area code, for long-distance calls

- **Summarization:** Establishes groups of numbers in a specific geographical area or functional group

- **Scalability:** Provides additional high-level number groups

- **Management:** Controls number groups from a single point in the overall network

It is not easy to design a hierarchical numbering plan. Existing numbering plans in the network might include proprietary PBXs, key systems, and telephony services such as Centrex. The necessity to conform to the PSTN at the gateways will also contribute to the complexity of a design. Translation between these systems is a difficult task. If possible, avoid retraining system users. The goal is to design a numbering plan that has these attributes:

- Minimal impact on existing systems

- Minimal impact on users of the system

- Minimal translation configuration

- Consideration of anticipated growth

Overlapping Numbering Plans

In some cases, administrators must interconnect two or more voice networks with overlapping number ranges. Overlapping numbering plans occur when the DIDs assigned by a service provider have the same extension ranges at two or more locations. For example, when two companies merge, company X might have a user number range of 1xxx, and company Y might also use the number range of 1xxx. When dealing with overlapping number ranges, one solution is to assign a unique site code to each individual location. Users then dial an access code (indicating an intersite call), followed by a site code, followed by the extension number. The number of digits used for the access code depends on the total number of locations affected.

Figure 6-11 shows a multisite environment with two sites: San Jose and Austin. Both sites use the same directory number range, 2XXX. When you're interworking both sites, routing will be problematic because a user who dials 2001 might want to reach Phone1-1 in San Jose or Phone2-1 in Austin.

You can solve overlapping directory number problems in several ways:

- Redesign the directory number ranges to ensure nonoverlapping directory numbers.

- Use an intersite access code and a site code that will be prepended to directory numbers to create unique dialable numbers. For example, you could use an intersite access code of 8 and assign San Jose the site code 801 and Austin the site code 802.

- Do not assign DIDs. Instead, publish a single number, and use a receptionist or auto attendant.

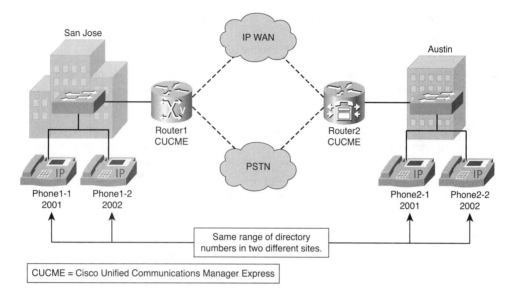

Figure 6-11 *Overlapping Directory Numbers*

Private and Public Numbering Plan Integration

Numbering plans vary throughout the world. Different countries use different number lengths and hierarchical plans within their borders. Also, telephony equipment manufacturers and service providers use nonstandard numbering. In an attempt to standardize numbering plans, the ITU developed the E.164 worldwide prefix scheme.

Numbering plan integration from an internal system, such as a VoIP and PBX system, to the PSTN requires careful planning. The hierarchical structure of the numbering plan and the problems associated with varying number lengths in different systems make numbering plan integration complex.

Following are some of the challenges you face with numbering plan integration:

■ **Varying number lengths:** Within the IP network, consideration is given to varying number lengths that exist outside the IP network. Local, long-distance, key system, and Centrex dialing from within the IP network might require digit manipulation.

■ **Specialized services:** Services such as Centrex and their equivalents typically have four-digit or five-digit numbers. Dialing from the PSTN into a private VoIP network and then out to a Centrex extension can also require extensive digit manipulation.

■ **Voice mail:** When a called party cannot be reached, the network might have to redirect the call to voice mail. Because the voice-mail system can require a different numbering plan than the endpoint telephones, translation is necessary.

- **Necessity of prefixes or area codes:** It can be necessary to strip or add area codes, or prepend or replace prefixes. For example, rerouting calls from the IP network to the PSTN for failure recovery can require extra digits.

- **International dialing consideration:** Country codes and numbering plans vary in length within countries. Dialing through an IP network to another country requires careful consideration.

- **End user training and "ease of use":** As the numbering plan is being implemented, time should be taken to train users on the new plan to minimize confusion as users are switched over to the new plan. The more training the users get, the easier it is for them to use the "new" system. Many VoIP implementations have received poor evaluations by users, because users weren't properly trained before the system switched over to a new numbering plan.

Integration of Internal and Public Numbering Plans Example

Figure 6-12 shows how a company integrates its internal numbering plan with the external public numbering plan.

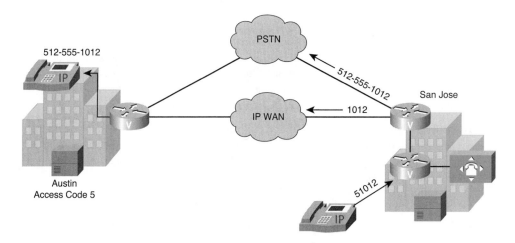

Figure 6-12   *Integration of Internal and Public Numbering Plans*

In this example, the PSTN will be used as a backup route for calls between San Jose and Austin. The following steps describe how the San Jose router performs digit manipulation based on the selected route.

1. The San Jose caller dials the site access code for Austin (5) followed by the four-digit extension number of the destination phone (1012).

2. The voice gateway determines whether the call can be completed using the IP WAN or whether it must be routed via the PSTN.

3. Digit manipulation occurs based on the path chosen:

- Strip the site access code and send four digits if completing the call across the IP WAN.

- Strip the site access code and prepend 1512 if completing the call across the PSTN.

Enhancing and Extending an Existing Plan to Accommodate VoIP

You can enhance and extend an existing numbering plan in many ways to accommodate a VoIP network. All require careful planning and consideration. In large-scale service provider designs, you might rely on the GW to perform digit manipulation, whereby the GW takes a calling (or called) number and strips or adds (prefixes) digits before sending the number to its destination. The process of formatting the number to a predefined pattern is called *number normalization*.

Number Normalization Example

Consider the topology example in Figure 6-13. When site E (703555....) dials 7275550199, the full 10-digit dial string is passed through the Frame Relay cloud to the router at site D. RouterD matches the destination pattern 7275550199 and forwards the 10-digit dial string to RouterA. RouterA matches the destination pattern 727555...., strips off the matching 727555, and forwards the remaining four-digit dial string to the PBX. The PBX matches the correct station and completes the call to the proper extension.

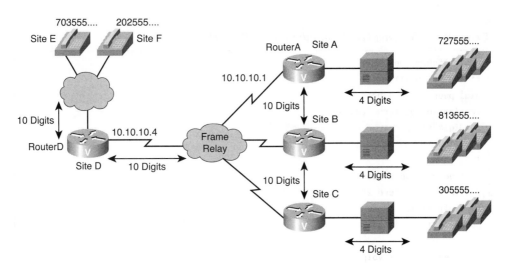

Figure 6-13   *Enhancing and Extending an Existing Dial Plan to Accommodate VoIP*

Calls in the reverse direction are handled similarly. However, because a Centrex service requires a full 10-digit dial string to complete calls, the POTS dial peer at RouterD is configured with digit stripping disabled. An alternative solution involves enabling digit stripping and configuring the dial peer with a six-digit prefix (in this case, 703555), which results in forwarding the full dial string to the Centrex service.

Examples 6-22 and 6-23 show the dial-peer configurations for the routers at Site A and at Site D.

Example 6-22 *Dial-Peer Configuration for RouterA*

```
RouterA#show run
*** OUTPUT OMITTED ***
dial-peer voice 1 pots
destination-pattern 727555….
port 1/0:1
!
dial-peer voice 4 voip
destination-pattern 703555….
session target ipv4:10.10.10.4
!
dial-peer voice 5 voip
destination-pattern 202555….
session target ipv4:10.10.10.4
*** OUTPUT OMITTED ***
```

Example 6-23 *Dial-Peer Configuration for RouterD*

```
RouterD#show run
*** OUTPUT OMITTED ***
dial-peer voice 4 pots
destination-pattern 703555….
no digit-strip
port 1/0:1
!
dial-peer voice 5 pots
destination-pattern 202555….
no digit-strip
port 1/0:1
!
dial-peer voice 1 voip
destination-pattern 727555….
session target ipv4:10.10.10.1
*** OUTPUT OMITTED ***
```

911 Services

To understand how VoIP networks can provide the location and telephone number for 911 services, you should understand the function of the basic components of 911 services, as follows:

- **Automatic Number Identification (ANI):** ANI is the calling-party number that is included with each call to identify where the call originated. Often, in a business environment, the original ANI might be changed by the service provider at the first switch to reflect the billing number of the company instead of reflecting the calling number of the original party. Discussions with the service provider need to ensure that the original ANI information is transmitted with all calls. Internal extensions or private numbering plans require mapping or translation for outbound ANI.

- **Automatic Location Identification (ALI):** The ALI database contains the records that map telephone numbers to geographic locations. The ALI database resides in the service provider network. Updates to the ALI database are submitted anytime a move, add, or change event occurs in a telephony network. Updates can take up to 48 hours to take effect, thereby making dynamic ALI updates unsuitable in a mobile environment.

- **Public Safety Answering Point (PSAP):** The PSAP is the answer point where an emergency call is terminated. Calls are directed to specific PSAPs based on the geographic location of the call origination point.

- **Emergency Response Location (ERL):** ERL is the location from which an emergency call is placed. In a network where VoIP mobility is common, the ANI of the calling telephone does not always identify the location of the emergency because the callers retain the same extension regardless of where they are actually located. The ERL is used in mobility environments by associating ports and devices to an ERL group. The recommendation is to define an ERL group for each floor in a building, each unit in a hotel or motel, or each tenant in a multitenant building.

- **Emergency Location Identification Number (ELIN):** An ELIN is a NANP telephone number that is used for routing an emergency call to the appropriate PSAP. In a mobile environment where the ANI is the mobile extension of the user, the ELIN is substituted for the ANI when the call is sent to the PSAP. This substitution enables the PSAP to record the calling number and be able to call the number back if the need arises. Each ERL has a unique ELIN associated with it. When a mobile caller logs in to a VoIP phone, the ELIN for the call is determined based on the ERL that the port is associated with.

- **Master Street Address Guide (MSAG):** MSAG is a database that is maintained by a government agency. This database maps geographic locations to the PSAPs that are responsible for handling emergency calls for those locations.

- **Selective router:** A selective router is a dedicated 911 switch in a service provider network that routes 911 calls to an appropriate PSAP based on the calling number. This approach is different from normal call routing, which routes based on the called number. When a call is routed to the selective router, the router looks at the ANI and determines which PSAP to send the call to.

- **Centralized Automated Message Accounting (CAMA):** CAMA is a type of analog trunk that connects a customer switch directly to the selective router in the service provider network. A CAMA trunk carries 911 calls only. It does not carry other user calls.

It is critical that network designers understand and adhere to local, municipal, state, and federal laws regarding compliance to 911 requirements.

911 Call Processing

To illustrate the call flow of a 911 call, examine Figure 6-14.

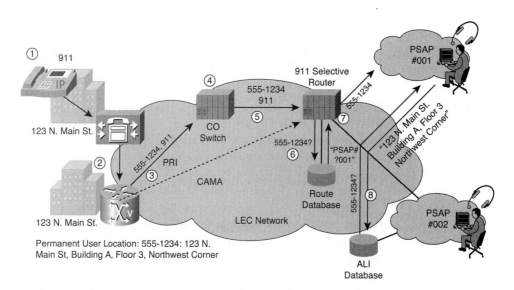

Figure 6-14   *911 Call Processing in a Nonmobile Environment*

The 911 call depicted in the figure is processed as follows:

1. The emergency call originates from the device with the ANI of 555-1234.

2. The call is routed via the main PSTN gateway at the headquarters.

3. The PSTN gateway either routes the call directly to the selective router via the CAMA trunk (if present) or routes the call via the normal PRI connection to the CO switch.

4. The CO switch retains the original ANI and does not replace it with the billing number.

5. The CO switch routes the call to the selective router.

6. The selective router queries the database to determine which PSAP is responsible for the location of the ANI.

7. The selective router routes the call to the PSAP.

8. The PSAP queries the ALI database to determine the exact location of the caller.

Implementing a Numbering Plan Example

In this example, as illustrated in Figure 6-15, your company has multiple locations and is currently evaluating the numbering plan associated with its Houston campuses and the Dallas location. The numbering plan design process includes enumerating the number of current users at each location and evaluating future growth requirements. The internal numbering plan will use the PSTN-assigned DID numbers that have been allocated at each site.

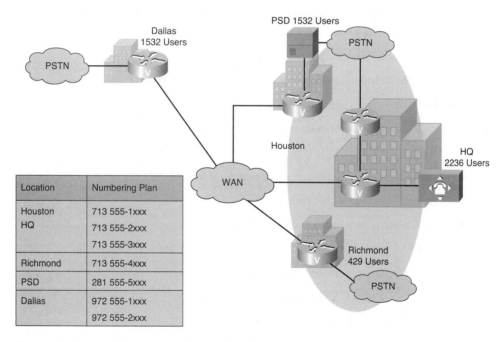

Location	Numbering Plan
Houston HQ	713 555-1xxx
	713 555-2xxx
	713 555-3xxx
Richmond	713 555-4xxx
PSD	281 555-5xxx
Dallas	972 555-1xxx
	972 555-2xxx

Figure 6-15   *Implementing a Numbering Plan*

Numbering Plan Scenario

The dial plan requirements are as follows:

- Single-digit (1–8) access code identifying each campus.

- Single-digit (9) access code that directs calls to the local PSTN.

- Intrasite dialing that is based on the four-digit extension.

- Intersite dialing that is based on the access code plus the four-digit extension.

- Local PSTN access that requires the access code 9 followed by the 10-digit number. It also requires that the 9 is stripped, and 10 digits are passed to the PSTN switch.

- Long-distance PSTN access that requires the access code 9 followed by the digit 1, followed by the 10-digit number. It also requires that the 9 is stripped, and 11 digits are passed to the PSTN switch.

Dial Plan Specifications

A list of specifications for your company's dial plan follows:

- The Houston HQ campus number ranges are 713 555-1xxx, 713 555-2xxx, and 713 555-3xxx.

- The Houston HQ campus site access code is 7.

- The Dallas campus number ranges are 972 555-1xxx and 972 555-2xxx.

- The Dallas campus site access code is 5.

- The PSD (airport location) number range is 281 555-5xxx.

- The PSD site access code is 6.

- The Richmond campus number range is 281 555-5xxx.

- The Richmond site access code is 4.

- The PSTN requires 10-digit dialing for local calls.

- The PSTN requires a "1" + 10 digits for long-distance calls.

- HQ to PSD is local through the PSTN.

- Houston to Dallas is long distance through the PSTN.

- Intrasite calls require a four-digit extension.

- Intersite calls require an access code and a four-digit extension.

Based on the dial plan specifications, the appropriate information is given in Table 6-11.

Table 6-11   *Dial Plan Example*

Call Information	Number Dialed	Number Sent to Remote Gateway Through WAN	Number Sent to PSTN
HQ caller calls Dallas extension 2312	52312	2312	1-972-555-2312
HQ caller calls PSD extension 5087	65087	5087	281-555-5087
Dallas caller calls HQ extension 3312	73312	3312	1-713-555-3312
Dallas caller calls Dallas extension 2887	2887	N/A	972-555-2887
HQ caller calls Richmond extension 4037	44037	4027	713-555-4037
Dallas caller calls PSD extension 5087	65087	5087	1-281-555-5087

Summary

The main topics covered in this chapter are the following:

- A dial plan defines how calls are interconnected and routed.

- Endpoint addressing assigns directory numbers to endpoints.

- Call routing and path selection define where a call is routed to and usually depends on the called party number.

- The digit manipulations feature ensures that numbers are presented in the correct format and is closely connected to call routing.

- Calling privileges define the destinations a user can dial.

- Call coverage ensures that incoming calls are not lost.

- Several factors must be considered when designing a scalable dial plan.

- Interworking with the PSTN requires appropriate call routing and digit manipulation.

- Digit manipulation based on a TON and numbering plan is required for ISDN networks.

- Configuring a PSTN dial plan includes configuration of digit manipulation, inbound dial peers, inbound dial-peer matching, and outbound dial-peer matching.

- Verify correct dial-peer matching and digit manipulation using **show** and **debug** commands.

- Numbering plans define telephone numbers for voice endpoints and applications, whereas dial plans define call routing and digit manipulation.

- Numbering plan types include private and public numbering plans.

- Scalable telephony networks require telephone numbering plans that are hierarchical.

- Overlapping number ranges are addressed through the use of site access codes.

- Varying number lengths, specialized services, voice mail, necessity of prefixes or area codes, and international dialing considerations are challenges associated with integrating a private numbering plan with a public numbering plan.

- Digit manipulation and number normalization are methods to extend and enhance VoIP numbering plans.

- Implementing a numbering plan requires that the design process includes enumerating current users at each location and evaluating future growth requirements.

Chapter Review Questions

The answers to these review questions are in the appendix.

1. Which dial plan component is responsible for selecting an appropriate path for a call?

   a. Endpoint addressing

   b. Call routing and path selection

   c. Call coverage

   d. Calling privileges

2. How are call routing and path selection implemented on Cisco IOS gateways?

   a. Call routing tables

   b. Dialer maps

   c. Dial peers

   d. Route patterns

3. What is one way to implement call coverage?

   a. COR

   b. Pilot numbers

   c. Digit manipulation

   d. Endpoint addressing

4. Which of the following are characteristics of a scalable dial plan? (Choose 3.)

   a. Fault tolerance

   b. Full-digit manipulation

   c. Hierarchical numbering plan

   d. Dial-plan logic distribution

5. What might some ISDN networks and PBXs expect along with a certain numbering plan for both DNIS and ANI?

    a. TOS

    b. TON

    c. QoS

    d. CoS

6. Which of the following best describes a numbering plan?

    a. It determines routes between source and destination devices.

    b. It defines a telephone number of a voice endpoint or application.

    c. It performs digit manipulation when sending calls to the PSTN.

    d. It performs least-cost routing for VoIP calls.

7. Which of the challenges associated with integration requires translations?

    a. Varying number lengths

    b. Specialized services

    c. Voice mail

    d. Necessity of prefixes or area codes

    e. International dialing

8. Which worldwide prefix scheme was developed by the ITU to standardize numbering plans?

    a. E.164

    b. G.114

    c. G.164

    d. E.114

9. What is the process of formatting a number to a predefined pattern called?

    a. Number translation

    b. Number conversion

    c. Number manipulation

    d. Number normalization

10. Which of the following best describes the ALI?

    a. A database that determines which PSAP services each geographic area

    b. An analog trunk that connects the gateway directly to the selective router and is used only for 911 calls

    c. A database that associates a telephone number to a specific location description

    d. A specialized telephony switch that routes calls based on the calling number rather than the called number

After reading this chapter, you should be able to perform the following tasks:

- Implement digit manipulation using Cisco IOS gateways.

- Describe path selection and how to manipulate it on Cisco IOS gateways.

- Implement calling privileges on Cisco IOS gateways.

CHAPTER 7

Configuring Advanced Dial Plans

Although a Cisco Unified Communications Manager (UCM) server can perform digit manipulation, perform path selection, and enforce calling privileges (for example, through the use of partitions and calling search spaces), voice-enabled Cisco IOS gateways can perform similar functions. In fact, IOS gateways have even more granular control of call routing, as compared to UCM (for example, being able to route based on caller ID information). This chapter demonstrates a variety of approaches to manipulate numbers on IOS gateways. Additionally, path selection is discussed, and you will learn how the Class of Restriction (COR) feature can be used to implement calling restrictions on dial peers.

Configuring Digit Manipulation

At times you might need to manipulate the digits of the telephone numbers that come into and go out of your voice gateway. You might need to remove site codes for intersite calls or add area codes and other digits for routing calls through the public switched telephone service (PSTN). This section covers digit manipulation and digit manipulation tools.

Digit Manipulation

Digit manipulation is the task of adding or subtracting digits from the original dialed number to accommodate user dialing habits (for example, the habit of prepending an area code to a seven-digit dial string) or gateway needs. Digit manipulation incorporates adding, subtracting, and changing telephone numbers. For example, you might need to add the area code to a call that will be routed out to the PSTN or remove a site code from an intersite call with the same company. You can manipulate called numbers, calling numbers, and redirected numbers, as well as the number type. You can apply digit manipulation to incoming or outgoing calls or to all calls globally. You can manipulate digits before or after matching a dial peer.

Because the call agent performs digit manipulation in a Media Gateway Control Protocol (MGCP) network, digit manipulation might be performed only on H.323 and Session Initiation Protocol (SIP) gateways.

Digit manipulation is an important aspect of any dial plan, and various tools exist on Cisco IOS gateways to perform this task, including the following:

- **Basic digit manipulation:** Digit manipulation covers a spectrum of possibilities, including prepending digits, stripping digits, or changing specific digits. Examples are

  - The **digit-strip** command is a dial-peer command that strips off the matched digits in a destination pattern of a dial peer. The digit-strip command is supported on plain old telephone service (POTS) dial peers only. Digit stripping occurs after the outbound dial peer is matched and before any digits are sent out. The called number is manipulated using digit stripping. Digit stripping is enabled by default on POTS dial peers.

  - The **forward-digits** {*num-digits* | **all** | **extra**} command is a dial-peer command that specifies how many matched digits should be forwarded. To specify which digits to forward for voice calls, use the **forward-digits** command in dial-peer configuration mode. To specify that any digits not matching the **destination-pattern** are not to be forwarded, use the **no** form of this command. This command applies only to POTS dial peers. Forwarded digits are always right-justified so that extra leading digits are stripped. The **destination-pattern** includes both explicit digits and wildcards if present. Digit forwarding occurs after the outbound dial peer is matched and before any digits are sent out. The called number is manipulated using digit forwarding.

  - The **prefix** command is a dial-peer command that prefixes the specified digits to the number forwarded by the dial peer. Use this command to specify a prefix for a specific dial peer. When an outgoing call is initiated to this dial peer, the prefix string value is sent to the telephony interface first, before the telephone number, associated with the dial peer. If you want to configure different prefixes for dialed numbers on the same interface, you need to configure different dial peers. This command is applicable only to POTS dial peers. This command also applies to off-ramp store-and-forward fax functions. Digit prefixing occurs after the outbound dial peer is matched and before any digits are sent out. The called number is manipulated using digit prefixing.

  - The **num-exp** command is a global command that applies to all calls and performs a match-and-replace operation to inflate or deflate numbers. This command is typically used for short dials and site codes. Number expansion occurs prior to matching a dial peer. The called number is manipulated using number expansion. For example, a four-digit number could be used by an employee to call a co-worker. That four-digit number could then be translated to that co-worker's home phone number and forwarded out to the PSTN.

  - The **clid** command can be used to modify the calling line ID (also known as Caller ID); for example, to restrict caller ID information. CLID manipulation occurs after the outbound dial peer is matched and before any digits are sent out. The calling number and name are manipulated using CLID manipulation.

■ **Voice translation rules and profiles:** Voice translation rules and profiles are the most powerful Cisco IOS tools you can use to perform digit manipulation. Using regular expressions, a numbering plan, and Type of Number (TON) matching, you can make nearly any possible modification. The only drawback is the complex syntax. Thus, voice translation rules are often combined with simpler mechanisms.

The order of operation in digit manipulation follows the call through the gateway, as shown in Figure 7-1. For inbound POTS calls, rules configured on the voice port are applied first, followed by the incoming dial peer, and then the outgoing dial peer. For inbound Voice over IP (VoIP) calls, global voice translation profiles are applied first, followed by the incoming dial peer, and then the outgoing dial peer. Note the **num-exp** command is applied globally before any dial-peer matching.

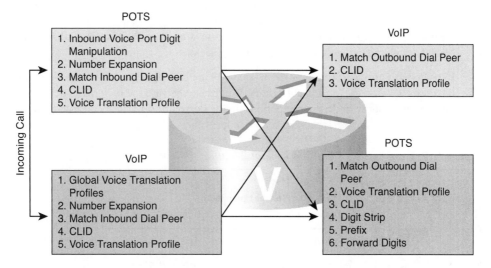

Figure 7-1 *Digit Manipulation Order of Operations*

When possible, you should use a single method of accomplishing the required digit manipulations. For example, do not use both the **forward-digits** and the **prefix** commands in a dial-peer configuration.

It is possible to use all the digit manipulation methods in a gateway. A single dial peer can be configured with prefixes, voice translation rules, and **clid** commands. A call can be modified by the voice port, number expansion, inbound dial-peer, and outbound dial-peer configuration commands in single or multiple gateways. Understanding the order of operation in digit manipulation is important not only for configuration and test purposes, but also for assisting in troubleshooting.

Digit Collection and Consumption

By default, when the terminating router matches a dial string to an outbound POTS dial peer, the router strips off the left-justified digits that explicitly match the destination pattern. The remaining digits are forwarded to the telephony interface, which connects devices such as a PBX or the PSTN.

Digit stripping is the desired action in some situations. You do not need to forward digits out of a POTS dial peer if it is pointing to a Foreign Exchange Station (FXS) port that connects a telephone or fax machine. When digit stripping is turned off on this type of port, the user will hear tones after answering the call, because any unconsumed and unmatched digits are passed through the voice path after the call is answered.

When a PBX or the PSTN is connected through the POTS dial peer, digit stripping is not desired because these devices need additional digits to further direct the call. In these situations, the administrator must assess the number of digits that need to be forwarded for the remote device to correctly process the call. With a VoIP dial peer, all digits are passed across the network to the terminating voice-enabled router.

Consider Example 7-1. When the digits 5550124 are dialed, using this configuration, only the digits 0124 are forwarded out port 0/1:1 because they are the only digits that were matched by wildcards (that is, the periods) in the **destination-pattern** command. The digits 555 are "consumed" rather than forwarded.

Example 7-1   *Digit Consumption Default Behavior*

```
Router(config)#dial-peer voice 1 pots
Router(config-dial-peer)#destination-pattern 555....
Router(config-dial-peer)#port 0/1:1
```

Next, consider Example 7-2. When the same digits (that is, 5550124) are dialed, all the digits are forwarded out of port 0/1:1 because the **no digit-strip** command was used to override the default digit consumption behavior of the dial peer and allowed all the dialed digits to be forwarded out of the port.

Example 7-2   *Digit Consumption with the* no digit-strip *Command*

```
Router(config)#dial-peer voice 1 pots
Router(config-dial-peer)#destination-pattern 555....
Router(config-dial-peer)#no digit-strip
Router(config-dial-peer)#port 0/1:1
```

When a voice call enters the network, the router collects digits as follows:

1. The originating router collects dialed digits until it matches an outbound dial peer.

2. The router immediately places the call and forwards the associated dial string.

3. The router collects no additional dialed digits.

Digit Collection Examples

In Example 7-3, the destination pattern (555) in dial-peer 1 is a subset of the destination pattern (555....) in dial-peer 2. The router matches one digit at a time against available dial peers. This means an exact match always occurs on dial-peer 1, and dial-peer 2 will never be matched.

Example 7-3   *Digit Collection Example with Dial Peer Improperly Configured*

```
Router(config)#dial-peer voice 1 voip
Router(config-dial-peer)#destination-pattern 555
Router(config-dial-peer)#session target ipv4:10.18.0.1
Router(config-dial-peer)#exit
Router(config)#dial-peer voice 2 voip
Router(config-dial-peer)#destination-pattern 5550124
Router(config-dial-peer)#session target ipv4:10.18.0.2
```

In Example 7-4, the length of the destination patterns in both dial peers is the same. Dial-peer 2 has a more specific value than dial-peer 1, so it will be matched first. If the path to IP address 10.18.0.2 is unavailable, dial-peer 1 will be used.

Example 7-4   *Digit Collection Example with Dial Peer Properly Configured*

```
Router(config)#dial-peer voice 1 pots
Router(config-dial-peer)#destination-pattern 555....
Router(config-dial-peer)#session target ipv4:10.18.0.1
Router(config-dial-peer)#exit
Router(config)#dial-peer voice 2 voip
Router(config-dial-peer)#destination-pattern 5550124
Router(config-dial-peer)#session target ipv4:10.18.0.2
```

Digit Stripping

Digit stripping strips any outbound digits that explicitly match the destination pattern of a particular dial peer. By default, POTS dial peers strip any outbound digits that explicitly match their destination pattern, whereas VoIP dial peers transmit all digits in the called number. For example, given a destination pattern of 5551... the number transmitted to the PSTN would contain the last three digits. The first four digits, 5551, would be stripped because they explicitly match the destination pattern.

In Figure 7-2, users dial a 9 to reach an outside number. If the configured destination pattern is 9T, the 9 is matched and stripped from the called number sent to the PSTN. On the other hand, you might have a dial peer for an emergency number such as 911 in the United States If the destination pattern is 911, you would not want the numbers stripped when they are explicitly matched. In this case you could use the **no digit-strip** command to disable the automatic digit-stripping function. This allows the router to match digits and pass them to the telephony interface. Figure 7-2 shows an example of this behavior.

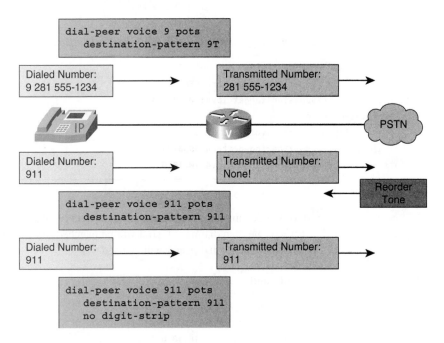

Figure 7-2 *Digit Stripping Example*

Digit Forwarding

If you need more control over the digits that are being transmitted to the PSTN, you can use digit forwarding.

Digit forwarding specifies the number of digits that must be forwarded to the telephony interface, regardless of whether they match explicitly or with wildcards. When a specific number of digits are configured for forwarding, the count is right-justified. For example, in Figure 7-3, the POTS dial peer has a destination pattern configured to match all extensions in the 1000 range. By default, only the last three digits are forwarded to the PBX that is connected to the specified voice port. If the PBX needs all four digits to route the call, you could use the commands **forward-digits 4** or **forward-digits all** so the appropriate number of digits are forwarded.

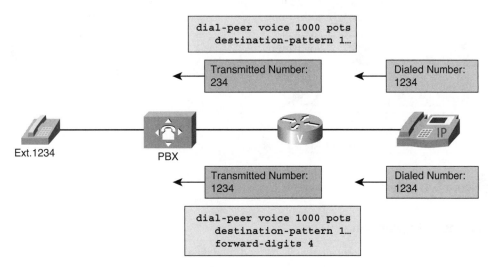

Figure 7-3 *Digit Forwarding Example*

> **Note**   Digit forwarding applies only to POTS dial peers.

Digit Prefixing

Digit prefixing adds digits to the front of a dial string before it is forwarded to a telephony interface. Use the **prefix** command when the dialed digits leaving the router must be changed from the dialed digits that had originally matched the dial peer. For example, consider Figure 7-4. A call is dialed using a four-digit extension, such as 2123, but the call needs to be routed to the PSTN, which requires 10-digit dialing. If the four-digit extension matches the last four digits of the actual PSTN number, you can use the **prefix 5125552** command to prepend the seven additional digits needed for the PSTN to route the call to 512 555-2123. After the POTS dial peer is matched with the destination pattern of 2123, the **prefix** command prepends the additional digits and the string "5125552123" is sent out of the voice port to the PSTN.

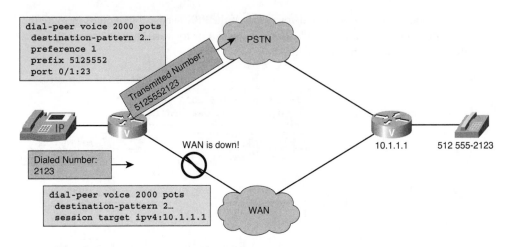

```
dial-peer voice 2000 pots
 destination-pattern 2…
 preference 1
 prefix 5125552
 port 0/1:23
```

Transmitted Number: 5125552123

PSTN

WAN is down!

10.1.1.1   512 555-2123

Dialed Number: 2123

```
dial-peer voice 2000 pots
 destination-pattern 2…
 session target ipv4:10.1.1.1
```

WAN

Figure 7-4 *Digit Prefixing Example*

Number Expansion

Number expansion is an alternative method of adding digits to outgoing calls. Whereas prefixing is applied to a single dial peer, number expansion is applied globally to all calls, not just to calls matching a single designated dial peer.

The **num-exp** global command expands a partial telephone number into a full telephone number or replaces one number with another. The number expansion table manipulates the called number. Because number expansion occurs before the outbound dial peer is matched, for the call to be successful you must configure the outbound dial peer with the expanded number in the destination pattern instead of the original number. The number expansion table becomes useful when the PSTN changes the dialing requirements from seven-digit dialing to ten-digit dialing. In this scenario, you can do one of the following:

- Make all the users dial all ten-digits to match the new POTS dial peer that is pointing to the PSTN.

- Allow the users to continue dialing the seven-digit number as they have before, but expand the number to include the area code before the ten-digit outbound dial peer is matched.

Consider Figure 7-5 and Example 7-5. Using the number expansion feature, a caller is using a seven-digit dial string. However, the number expansion feature configured in the router prepends the area code of 281 to the dial string. This ten-digit dial string is then passed to the PSTN.

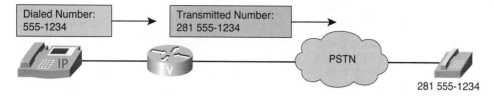

Figure 7-5   *Number Expansion Topology Example*

Example 7-5   *Number Expansion Configuration*

```
Router(config)#num-exp 5551... 2815551...
Router(config)#dial-peer voice 2000 pots
Router(config-dial-peer)#destination-pattern  2815551...
Router(config-dial-peer)#port 0/1:23
Router(config-dial-peer)#forward-digits all
```

Note   You can use the **show num-exp** command to view the configured number expansion table. You can use the **show dialplan number** *string* command to confirm the presence of a valid dial peer to match the newly expanded number.

Simple Digit Manipulation for POTS Dial-Peers Example

Figure 7-6 shows the operation of simple digit manipulation for POTS dial peers.

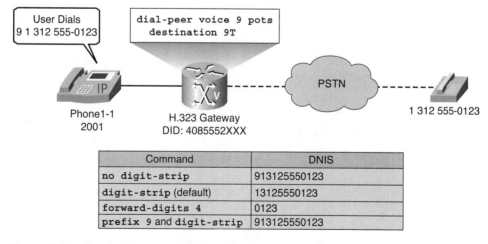

Command	DNIS
`no digit-strip`	913125550123
`digit-strip` (default)	13125550123
`forward-digits 4`	0123
`prefix` 9 and `digit-strip`	913125550123

Figure 7-6   *Simple Digit Manipulation for a POTS Dial Peer*

A user dials 9 1 312 555-0123, and the call is handled by the **dial-peer voice 9 pots** command on the H.323 gateway. Depending on the commands, the Dialed Number Information Service (DNIS) information will be modified differently:

- If the **no digit-strip** command is used, the DNIS will be 913125550123. No digits are modified.

- If the **digit-strip** command is used, which is the default on all POTS dial peers, the matched 9 will be stripped off, resulting in a DNIS of 13125550123.

- If the **forward-digits 4** command is used, only the last four digits will be forwarded, resulting in a DNIS of 0123.

- If the **prefix 9** and **digit-strip** commands are used in combination, the 9 is first stripped off and then prefixed again, resulting in a DNIS of 913125550123.

Number Expansion Example

Figure 7-7 and Example 7-6 show how the **num-exp** command defines short dials.

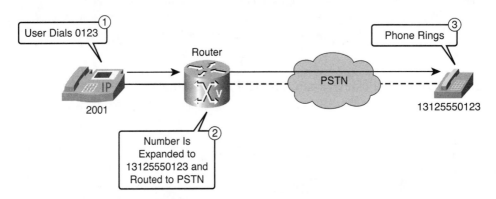

Figure 7-7 *Digit Manipulation with Number Expansion*

Example 7-6 *Digit Manipulation with Number Expansion Configuration*

```
Router(config)#num-exp 0... 913125550...
Router(config)#dial-peer voice 9 pots
Router(config-dial-peer)#destination 9T
```

If a user dials 0123, the call should be routed to DNIS 913125550123:

1. A user dials 0123.

2. Because the gateway has the configuration **num-exp 0... 913125550...**, DNIS 0123 is matched and modified to 913125550123. This DNIS matches dial-peer 9, which routes the call to the PSTN.

3. The PSTN phone rings.

> **Note**   This example shows how digit manipulation occurs prior to outbound dial-peer matching.

Caller ID Number Manipulation

You can use the **clid** command to modify caller ID information. The CLID message can include two calling numbers: one "user provided, unscreened" and one "network provided."

CLID Commands

Following are some of the **clid** commands:

- **clid network-number** *number*: Sets the network-provided number in the Information Element (IE) message and sets the presentation bit to allow the calling party number to be presented.

- **clid second-number strip:** Removes the user-provided number, or second number, from this IE message. You can also leave the existing network number unaltered while removing the user-provided number from the IE.

- **clid restrict:** Sets the presentation bit to prevent the display of the CLID information. This command does not remove the calling numbers from the IE message. It is possible to remove the numbers completely using the **clid strip** command. To remove both the calling number and the calling name, you must enter the **clid strip** command twice: once with the name option and once without.

Station ID Commands

You can use the **station-id** command to control the caller ID information sent by an FXS or FXO port. The information specified with this command shows up as the caller ID of the device connected to the FXS port. This command is often used on FXS ports connected to fax machines that make on-net calls, as illustrated in Figure 7-8 and Example 7-7.

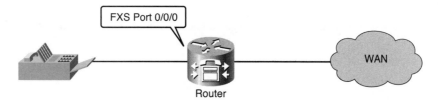

Figure 7-8   *Caller ID Number Manipulation*

Example 7-7   *Caller ID Number Manipulation Example*

```
Router(config)#voice-port 0/0/0
Router(config-voiceport)#station-id name HQ Fax
Router(config-voiceport)#station-id number 7135551003
```

Following are some of the **station-id** commands:

■ **station-id name** *string*: Specifies the name sent in CLID information

■ **station-id number** *number*: Specifies the number sent in the CLID information

Displaying Caller ID Information

Sometimes it is useful to display the CLID information that will be sent. Use the **show dialplan number** *number* command to determine what CLID information will be sent in an IE message. Example 7-8 shows the dial-plan information with no CLID commands applied.

Example 7-8   show dialplan number *Command—First Example*

```
Router#show dialplan number 914085551234
Macro Exp.: 914085551234
VoiceEncapPeer91
        peer type = voice, information type = voice,
        description = '',
        tag = 91, destination-pattern = '91..........',
        answer-address = '', preference=0,
        CLID Restriction = None
        CLID Network Number = ''
        CLID Second Number sent
        CLID Override RDNIS = disabled,
        source carrier-id = '', target carrier-id = '',
        source trunk-group-label = '',  target trunk-group-label = '', numbering
          Type = 'unknown'
```

Example 7-9 shows the result of adding a **clid network-number** command to the dial peer.

Example 7-9   show dialplan number *Command—Second Example*

```
Router(config-dial-peer)#clid network-number 5551234

Router#show dialplan number 914085551234
Macro Exp.: 914085551234


VoiceEncapPeer91
        peer type = voice, information type = voice,
        description = '',
        tag = 91, destination-pattern = '91..........',
        answer-address = '', preference=0,
        CLID Restriction = None
        CLID Network Number = '5551234'
        CLID Second Number sent
        CLID Override RDNIS = disabled,
        source carrier-id = '', target carrier-id = '',
        source trunk-group-label = '',  target trunk-group-label = '', numbering
          Type = 'unknown'
```

Example 7-10 shows the result of using the **clid strip** command.

Example 7-10   show dialplan number *Command—Third Example*

```
Router(config-dial-peer)#clid strip

Router#show dialplan number 914085551234
Macro Exp.: 914085551234


VoiceEncapPeer91
        peer type = voice, information type = voice,
        description = '',
        tag = 91, destination-pattern = '91..........',
        answer-address = '', preference=0,
        CLID Restriction = clid strip
        CLID Network Number = ''
        CLID Second Number sent
        CLID Override RDNIS = disabled,
        source carrier-id = '', target carrier-id = '',
        source trunk-group-label = '',  target trunk-group-label = '', numbering
          Type = 'unknown'
```

Voice Translation Rules and Profiles

Number translation occurs several times during the call routing process. In both the originating and terminating gateways, the incoming call is translated before an inbound dial peer is matched, before an outbound dial peer is matched, and before a call request is set up. Your dial plan should account for these translation steps when translation rules are defined.

Digit translation is a two-step configuration process. First, the translation rule is defined at the global level. Then, the rule is applied at the dial-peer level either as inbound or outbound translation on either the called or calling number. Translation rules also convert a telephone number into a different number before the call is matched to an inbound dial peer or before the outbound dial peer forwards the call. For example, an employee might dial a five-digit extension to reach another employee of the same company at another site. If the call is routed through the PSTN to reach the other site, the originating gateway might use translation rules to convert the five-digit extension into the ten-digit format that is recognized by the central office (CO) switch.

A translation rule might manipulate a calling party number (Automatic Number Identification (ANI)) or a called party number (DNIS) for incoming, outgoing, and redirected calls within voice-enabled gateways.

You can also use translation rules to change the numbering type for a call. For example, some gateways might tag a number with more than 11 digits as an international number, even when the user must dial 9 to reach an outside line. In this case, the number that is tagged as an international number needs to be translated into a national number, without the 9, before it is sent to the PSTN.

Voice-translation rules might define up to 15 rules that include Stream EDitor (SED)-like expressions (that is, similar to expressions used with the UNIX Stream EDitor utility) for processing the call translation. A maximum of 128 translation rules are supported. These translation rules are grouped into profiles that are referenced by trunk groups, dial peers, source IP groups, voice ports, and interfaces.

The voice translation rules are associated with a voice translation profile, which can reference up to three voice translation rules:

■ A voice translation rule that is used to manipulate the called number (that is, the DNIS)

■ A voice translation rule that is used to manipulate the calling number (that is, the ANI)

■ A voice translation rule that is used to manipulate the redirected called number (that is, the Redirected Dialed Number Identification Service (RDNIS))

The resulting voice-translation profile can be attached to these:

■ VoIP dial peers

■ Voice ports

- Any inbound VoIP call

- A specific range of source IP addresses in VoIP calls

- A trunk group

- A T1/E1 controller that is used for Nonfacility Associated Signaling (NFAS) trunks

- Survivable Remote Site Telephony (SRST)

Each of these can reference two voice translation profiles: one for incoming calls and one for outgoing calls. You can use the **voice translation-rule** command to create the definition of a translation rule.

Figure 7-9 illustrates the concept of voice translation profiles and rules. Each voice translation rule can have up to 15 individual subrules. The voice translation rule is then referenced by a voice translation profile for called, calling, and redirected called number. Note that the same voice translation rule can be referenced by multiple voice translation profiles. Up to 128 voice translation rules are supported in a Cisco IOS gateway.

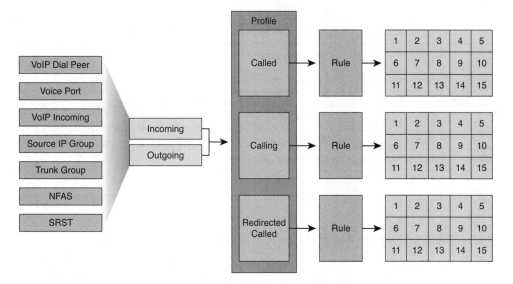

Figure 7-9   *Voice Translation Rules and Profiles*

Note   Although you can have up to 15 subrules within a voice translation rule, the first matching rule will be applied, and no further subrules will be considered.

Voice translation rules use regular expressions for match-and-replace operations. The syntax is very similar to the UNIX SED tool. Table 7-1 describes the most important regular expressions available.

Table 7-1   *Regular Expressions for Voice Translation Rules*

Voice Translation Rule Character	Description
^	Match the expression at the start of a line.
$	Match the expression at the end of the line.
/	Delimiter that marks the start and end of both the matching and replacement strings.
\	Escape the special meaning of the next character.
-	Indicates a range when not in the first/last position. Used with the "[" and "]" characters.
[list]	Match a single character in a list.
[^list]	Do not match a single character specified in the list.
.	Match any single character.
*	Repeat the previous regular expression (regex) zero or more times.
+	Repeat the previous regular expression one or more times.
?	Repeat the previous regular expression zero or one time (use CTRL-V to enter in Cisco IOS, because Cisco IOS interprets a "?" character as a request for context-sensitive help).
()	Groups regular expressions.

Understanding Regular Expressions in Translation Rules

It is important that you understand how regular expressions are used in translation rules. When the router evaluates a translation rule, it is really only performing a "match this" and "change to this" operation on the regex.

Consider the following example, as illustrated in Figure 7-10.

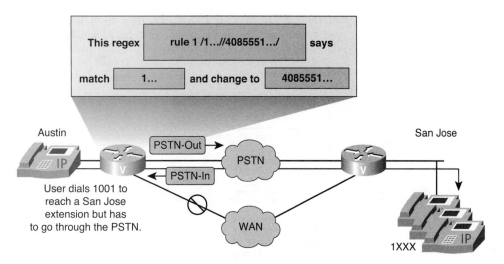

Figure 7-10 *Regular Expressions in Translation Rules*

To further illustrate the configuration of translation rules, consider the following:

■ This rule will be used to change the outgoing DNIS to a ten-digit number for routing across the PSTN. The rule will be applied outgoing on an interface, port, or dial peer.

```
Router(config)#voice translation-rule PSTN-out
Router(config)#rule 1 /1.../ /4085551.../
```

■ This rule will be used to change the incoming ANI to a four-digit number after routing across the PSTN. The rule will be applied incoming on an interface, port, or dial peer.

```
Router(config)#voice translation-rule PSTN-in
Router(config)#rule 1 /4085551... / /1.../
```

Table 7-2 illustrates the match and replace rules for these rules.

Table 7-2 *Match and Replace Table*

Rule	Match This	Change To
/1.../ /4085551.../	1...	4085551...
/408553.../ /1.../	/4085551.../	/1.../

What if you needed to prepend a 9 to all outgoing calls? It would not be feasible to use individual translation rules for each number because of the number of rules needed. For example:

```
rule 1 /4085550100/ /95125550100/
rule 2 /4085550101/ /95125550101/
rule 3 /4085550102/ /95125550102/
```

The solution would be using variables, as shown in Figure 7-11. Translation rule expressions can be divided into sections by using an escape character to create variables. The regex escape character is the "\" symbol.

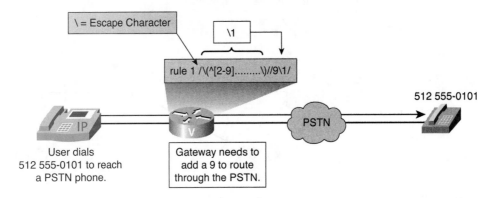

Figure 7-11   *Prepending Digits*

You might use the following translation rule to prepend a 9 to outgoing calls for routing through the PSTN:

> rule 1 /\(^[2-9]........\)/ /9\1/

This rule would prepend a 9 to whatever was matched in the first set of parenthesis (\1); in other words, replace \1 with ^[2-9]........ and add a 9 to the beginning.

Search and Replace with Voice Translation Rules Example

Table 7-3 shows how voice translation rules perform search-and-replace operations that use voice translation rules.

Table 7-3   *Examples of Voice Translation Rules*

Rule	Input String	Output String
/^9/ //	914085550123	14085550123
/^2001/ /3001/	2001	3001
/^[23].../ /4000/	2025 or 3051	4000
/^2.../ /801&/	2001	8012001
/^2.../ /801\0/	2001	8012001
/\(9\)\([^10].*\)/ /\11408\2/	95551234	914085551234
/.*/ /91&/ type national national	3125552001 type national	913125552001 type national

The example illustrated in Figure 7-12 shows a complex search-and-replace operation in which this rule is configured:

rule 1 /\(9\)\([^10].*\)/ /\11408\2/

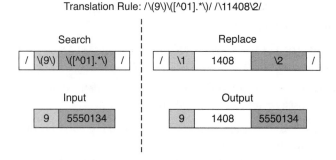

Figure 7-12   *Voice Translation Rule Search-and-Replace*

This example would be good for prepending a long distance 1 and an area code to a dialed number exiting the network via the PSTN and accessing a long-distance subscriber. The user would be dialing a 9 plus seven digits to access outside numbers.

This is how the operation proceeds if the input string 95550134 is used:

- The 9 is reinserted using the \1.

- It is followed by the digits 1408.

- Then 5550134 follows, which is referenced by the \2.

- The resulting string is 914085550134.

Note   The first set of parenthesis is referenced as **\1** and the second set as **\2**.

Voice Translation Profiles

Voice translation profiles introduce a new scheme to translate numbers. The older translation rules are to be gradually phased out of Cisco IOS. Cisco strongly recommends you use only one scheme of translation rules. If you mix the old and new schemes, you can have unforeseen results. Central to the new scheme is the capability to perform regular expression matches and replace substrings. The SED utility is used to translate numbers.

You can define these types of call numbers in a translation profile:

- **called:** Defines the translation profile rule for the called number

- **calling:** Defines the translation profile rule for the calling number

- **redirect-called:** Defines the translation profile rule for the redirect-called number

Each type of call number in the profile can have different translation rules.

After a translation profile is defined, it can be referenced by the following:

- **Trunk group:** Two different translation profiles can be defined in a trunk group to perform number translation for incoming and outgoing POTS calls. If an outgoing translation profile is defined in a trunk group, the number translation is done while the outgoing call is set up.

- **Source IP group:** A translation profile can be defined in a source IP group to perform number translation for incoming VoIP calls.

- **Dial peer:** Two different translation profiles can be defined in a dial peer to perform number translation for incoming and outgoing calls.

- **Voice port:** The translation profile can be defined in a voice port to perform number translation for incoming and outgoing POTS calls. If a voice port is also a trunk group member, the incoming translation profile of a voice port overrides the translation profile of a trunk group.

- **NFAS interface:** The translation profile can be defined for an NFAS interface through the **translation-profile** command from the global voice service pots configuration to perform the number translation for incoming and outgoing NFAS calls. This translation profile has a higher precedence than the translation profile of a voice port and trunk group in case a channel also belongs to a voice port and/or trunk group with the translation profile defined.

- **VoIP incoming:** The translation profile can be defined globally for all incoming VoIP (H.323/SIP) calls to perform number translation. If an incoming H.323/SIP call is associated with a source IP group with a translation profile defined, the translation profile of the source IP group overrides the global translation profile for incoming VoIP calls.

Translation Profile Processing

The order in which translation profiles are processed depends on where the profile is applied. Table 7-4 indicates the order in which voice translation profiles will be processed.

Table 7-4   *Translation Profile Order*

Applied	Processing Order	
	Inbound	Outbound
Voice port/NFAS	1	4
Trunk group/Source IP	2	3
Global	3	1
Dial peer	4	2

Voice Translation Profile Search-and-Replace Example

The example illustrated in Figure 7-13 shows a search-and-replace voice translation profile.

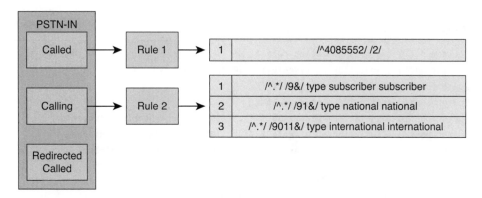

Figure 7-13   *Voice Translation Profile Search-and-Replace Example*

A voice translation profile is required to perform these manipulations:

■   The incoming DNIS 4085552XXX should be modified to 2XXX.

■   The incoming ANI should be prefixed with the appropriate PSTN access code and identifier:

  ■   **Local calls:** Prefix 9

  ■   **National calls:** Prefix 91

  ■   **International calls:** Prefix 9011

Following are the steps you take to configure the translation profile:

Step 1.   Create a translation rule to manipulate the called (DNIS) number.

```
Router(config)#voice translation-rule 1
Router(config-translation-rule)#rule 1 /^4085552/ /2/
```

Step 2.   Create a translation rule to manipulate the calling (ANI) number.

```
Router(config)#voice translation-rule 2
Router(config-translation-rule)#rule 1 /^.*/ /9&/ type subscriber
  subscriber
Router(config-translation-rule)#rule 2 /^.*/ /91&/ type national
  national
Router(config-translation-rule)#rule 3 /^.*/ /9011&/ type international
  international
```

Step 3.   Apply the rules to a translation profile.

```
Router(config)#voice translation-profile pstn-in
Router(cfg-translation-profile)#translate called 1
Router(cfg-translation-profile)#translate calling 2
```

Step 4. Include the translation profile within a dial-peer definition.

```
Router(config)#dial-peer voice 111 POTS
Router(config-dial-peer)#translation-profile incoming pstn-in
```

Example 7-11 shows the complete configuration, which was previously described.

Example 7-11 *Voice Profile Example*

```
Router(config)#voice translation-rule 1
Router(config-translation-rule)#rule 1 /^4085552/ /2/
Router(config-translation-rule)#exit
Router(config)#voice translation-rule 2
Router(config-translation-rule)#rule 1 /^.*/ /9&/ type subscriber subscriber
Router(config-translation-rule)#rule 2 /^.*/ /91&/ type national national
Router(config-translation-rule)#rule 3 /^.*/ /9011&/ type international
  international
Router(config-translation-rule)#exit
Router(config)#voice translation-profile pstn-in
Router(cfg-translation-profile)#translate called 1
Router(cfg-translation-profile)#translate calling 2
```

The following procedure describes an inbound PSTN call example:

1. A PSTN user dials 1 408 555-2001 from 312 555-0123.

2. The gateway accepts the call and modifies the DNIS and ANI. The rule /^4085552/ /2/ modifies the DNIS to 2001, and the rule /^.*/ /91&/ **type national national** modifies the ANI to 913125550123.

3. The phone rings.

Voice Translation Profile Call Blocking Example

The following example, as illustrated in Figure 7-14, shows a voice translation profile used for call blocking.

The only option for call blocking is in the incoming direction. From the perspective of the gateway, the incoming direction can be either of these:

- Incoming from a telephony device directly attached to a voice port on the gateway toward the gateway itself

- Incoming by way of an inbound VoIP call from a peer gateway

Following are the steps you take to configure call blocking:

Step 1. Define a translation rule with a **reject** keyword.

```
Router(config)#voice translation-rule 1
Router(config-translation-rule)#rule 1 reject /408555*/
```

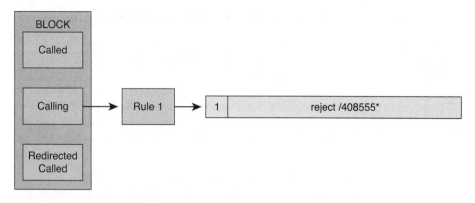

Figure 7-14   *Voice Translation Profile Call-Blocking Example*

Step 2.   Apply the rule to a translation profile for calling numbers.

```
Router(config)#voice translation profile block
Router(cfg-translation-profile)#translate calling 1
```

Step 3.   Include the translation profile within a dial-peer definition.

```
Router(config)#dial-peer voice 111 POTS
Router(config-dial-peer)#call-block translation-profile incoming block
Router(config-dial-peer)#call-block disconnect-cause incoming invalid-
number
```

In this call-blocking example, the gateway blocks any incoming call that successfully matches inbound dial-peer 111 and has a calling number that starts with 408555. A component of the **call block** command is the capability to return a disconnect cause. These values include **call-reject**, **invalid-number**, **unassigned-number**, and **user-busy**. When dial-peer 111 matches a dialed string starting with 408555, it will reject the call and return a disconnect cause of "invalid number" to the source of the call.

Example 7-12 shows the complete configuration, which was previously described.

Example 7-12   *Call Block Example*

```
Router(config)#voice translation-rule 1
Router(config-translation-rule)#rule 1 reject /408555*/
Router(config-translation-rule)#exit
Router(config)#voice translation profile block
Router(cfg-translation-profile)#translate calling 1
Router(cfg-translation-profile)#exit
Router(config)#dial-peer voice 111 pots
Router(config-dial-peer)#call-block translation-profile incoming block
Router(config-dial-peer)#call-block disconnect-cause incoming invalid-number
```

Voice Translation Profiles Versus the **dialplan-pattern** Command

You can use voice translation profiles to replace the Cisco Unified Survivable Remote Site Telephony (Cisco SRST) and Cisco UCM Express **dialplan-pattern** command. The **dialplan-pattern** command maps ephone-dns (that is, directory numbers assigned to IP phones in a Cisco UCM Express environment) to inbound direct-inward (DID) numbers. This mapping is done by dynamically creating a new dial peer that has the DID number of a phone as the destination pattern. This dial peer is also used for outbound calls to present the correct ANI and can be used to register the full DID number of an ephone with a gatekeeper.

Although this technique works for ephone-dns, other devices such as FXS ports and voice-mail pilots are not covered. At the same time, the **dialplan-pattern** command also increases the number of dial peers, which makes troubleshooting more complex.

To solve this problem, voice translation profiles can be used to fully replace the **dialplan-pattern** command, but other interactions need to be considered, such as gatekeeper registration issues.

Cisco Unified Communications Manager Express with **dialplan-pattern** Example

The topology shown in Figure 7-15 and the corresponding configuration in Example 7-13 show the caveats for the **dialplan-pattern** command.

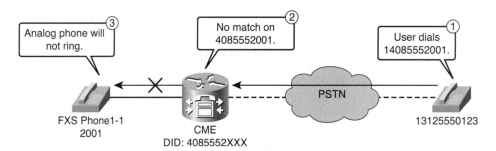

Figure 7-15 *Cisco UCM Express with* dialplan-pattern

Example 7-13 dialplan-pattern *Command Example*

```
Router(config)#telephony-service
Router(config-telephony)#dialplan-pattern 1 4085552... extension-length 4
Router(config-telephony)#exit
Router(config)#dial-peer voice 2001 pots
Router(config-dial-peer)#destination-pattern 2001
Router(config-dial-peer)#port 1/0/0
```

The **dialplan-pattern** command dynamically creates another dial peer for each ephone-dn. Other devices, such as analog phones that are connected to FXS ports, are not covered. Thus, the analog phone dial peer still has a pattern of 2001.

The call flow example in Figure 7-15 illustrates the problem:

1. A PSTN user dials 1 408 555-2001.

2. The call is routed to Cisco Unified Communications Manager Express, which has a DID range of 4085552XXX. No match is found for DNIS 4085552001 because the dial peer has the pattern 2001.

3. The analog phone will not ring.

Cisco Unified Communications Manager Express with Voice Translation Profiles Example

The topology shown in Figure 7-16 and the corresponding topology in Example 7-14 show how Cisco Unified Communications Manager Express is configured to use a voice translation profile instead of the **dialplan-pattern** command.

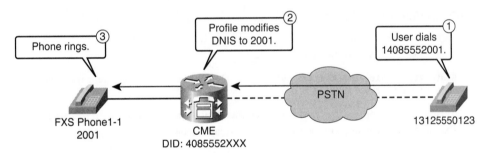

Figure 7-16 *Cisco Unified Communications Manager Express with Voice Translation Profiles*

Example 7-14 voice translation-profile *Command Example*

```
Router(config)#voice translation-rule 1
Router(config-translation-rule)#rule 1 /^4085552/ /2/
Router(config-translation-rule)#exit
Router(config)#voice translation-profile pstn-in
Router(cfg-translation-profile)#translate called 1
Router(config)#exit
Router(config-voice-port)#voice-port 0/0/0:23
Router(config-voice-port)#translation-profile incoming pstn-in
Router(config-voice-port)#dial-peer voice 2001 pots
Router(config-voice-port)#destination-pattern 2001
Router(config-voice-port)#port 1/0/0
```

Again, the hypothetical situation is repeated, but this time voice translation profiles are used.

Following are the steps in the successful call flow:

1. A PSTN user dials 1 408 555-2001.

2. The call is routed to Cisco Unified Communications Manager Express, which has a DID range of 4085552XXX. The voice translation profile modifies the DNIS to 2001, which matches the dial peer of Phone1-1.

3. The analog phone rings.

Note   Depending on the deployment, using voice translation profiles instead of the **dialplan-pattern** command might be the preferred solution. With gatekeepers, using the **dialplan-pattern** command often leads to less-complex configurations, and thus a configuration with voice translation profiles combined with the **dialplan-pattern** command might be a better solution.

Verifying Voice Translation Rules

To test the functionality of a translation rule, use the **test voice translation-rule** command. The syntax is as follows:

```
Router#test voice translation-rule number input-test-string [type match-type
  [plan match-type]]
```

This command applies the specified voice translation rule on the entered test string. Example 7-15 provides sample outputs from this command.

Example 7-15   test voice translation-rule *Command*

```
Router#test voice translation-rule 5 2015550101


Matched with rule 5
Original number:2015550101  Translated number:1025550101
Original number type: none    Translated number type: none
Original number plan: none    Translated number plan: none


Router#test voice translation-rule 6 2015550101


Error: Ruleset 6 not found
```

The **show voice translation-rule** and **show voice translation-profile** commands can also be useful. Example 7-16 shows how to verify configured translation rules and profiles.

Example 7-16 show voice translation-rule *and* show voice translation-profile
Commands

```
Router#show voice translation-rule 1
Translation-rule tag: 1


        Rule 1:
        Match pattern: ^555\(....\)
        Replace pattern: 444\1
        Match type: none              Replace type: none
        Match plan: none              Replace plan: none


        Rule 2:
        Match pattern: 777
        Replace pattern: 888
        Match type: national          Replace type: unknown
        Match plan: any               Replace plan: isdn


Router#show voice translation-profile
Translation Profile: mytranslation
        Rule for Calling number:
        Rule for Called number: 1
        Rule for Redirect number:
```

Configuring Digit Manipulation

The example illustrated in Figure 7-17 configures digit manipulation to meet the follow-ing network requirements.

■ Sites should be able to call a remote site using just the extensions for that site.

■ The PSTN should be used as a backup in case the WAN link is down or congested.

■ Users should be able to contact 911 emergency services.

The following procedure illustrates how to implement digit manipulation.

■ Configure the San Jose gateway to expand the dialed number when calling the 713
area code.

```
Router(config)#num-exp 4... 7135554...
Router(config)#dial-peer voice 4000 pots
Router(config-dial-peer)#destination-pattern 17135554...
Router(config-dial-peer)#port 0/1:23
```

Using the **num-exp** command in this example, the extension number 4... is expanded
to 7135554... before an outbound dial peer is matched. For example, the user dials
4001, but the outbound dial-peer 4000 is configured to match 7135554001.

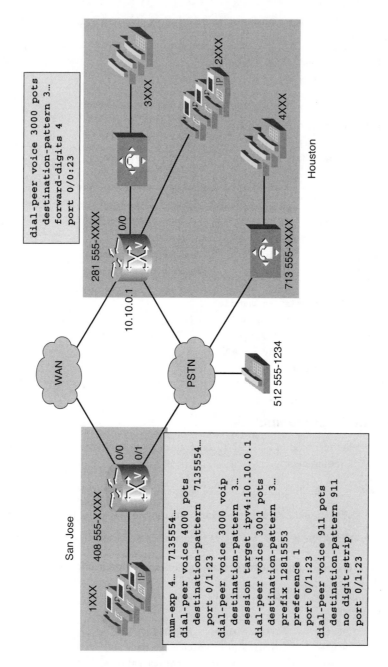

Figure 7-17 *Configuring Basic Digit Manipulation*

- Configure the San Jose gateway to send all digits when a user dials 911.

```
Router(config)#dial-peer voice 911 pots
Router(config-dial-peer)#destination-pattern 911
Router(config-dial-peer)#no digit-strip
Router(config-dial-peer)#port 0/1:23
```

In this example, all three digits are required to process the call through the PSTN. You can use the **no digit-strip** command to send the appropriate three digits to the PSTN.

- Configure a route to the 281 area code via the WAN.

```
Router(config)#dial-peer voice 3000 voip
Router(config-dial-peer)#destination pattern 3...
Router(config-dial-peer)#session target ipv4:10.10.0.1
```

- Configure a PSTN backup to the 281 area code.

```
Router(config)#dial-peer voice 3001 pots
Router(config-dial-peer)#destination pattern 3...
Router(config-dial-peer)#prefix 12815553
Router(config-dial-peer)#preference 1
Router(config-dial-peer)#port 0/1:23
```

In this example, all ten digits are required to process the call through the PSTN. Use the **prefix** command to send the prefix numbers 2815553 before forwarding the three wildcard-matched digits.

- Configure digit forwarding at the Houston gateway.

```
Router(config)#dial-peer voice 3000 pots
Router(config-dial-peer)#destination pattern 3...
Router(config-dial-peer)#forward-digits 4
Router(config-dial-peer)#port 0/0:23
```

In this example, using the **forward-digits** command allows the PBX to receive the proper number of digits to route the call to the appropriate extension.

Consider another example, as illustrated in Figure 7-18 and Example 7-17.

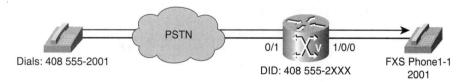

Figure 7-18   *Configuring Translation Rules*

Example 7-17   *Configuring Voice Translation Rules*

```
Router(config)#voice translation-rule 1
Router(config-translation-rule)#rule 1 /^4085552/ /2/
Router(config-translation-rule)#exit
Router(config)#voice translation-profile pstn-in
Router(cfg-translation-profile)#translate called 1
Router(cfg-translation-profile)#exit
Router(config)#voice-port 0/1:23
Router(config-voiceport)#translation-profile incoming pstn-in
Router(config-voiceport)#exit
Router(config)#dial-peer voice 2001 pots
Router(config-dial-peer)#destination-pattern 2001
Router(config-dial-peer)#port 1/0/0
```

This example shows how to configure digit manipulation using translation rules and profiles to allow an analog phone connected to an FXS port to be able to receive calls from the PSTN.

The following steps show how to configure digit manipulation to meet network requirements.

Step 1.   Configure a search-and-replace translation rule.

```
Router(config)#voice translation-rule 1
Router(config-translation-rule)#rule 1 /^4085552/ /2/
```

There are two types of rules:

Match and Replace Rule:

rule *precedence* */match-pattern/* */replace-pattern/* [**type** {*match-type replace-type*} [**plan** {*match-type replace-type*}]]

Reject Rule:

rule *precedence* **reject** */match-pattern/* [**type** *match-type* [**plan** *match-type*]]

Step 2.   Create a voice translation profile and bind the translation rule, created in Step 1, to it.

```
Router(config)#voice translation-profile pstn-in
Router(cfg-translation-profile)#translate called 1
```

Note   To specify a translation profile for all incoming VoIP calls, use the **voip-incoming translation-profile** command in global configuration mode. To delete the profile, use the **no** form of this command.

Step 3.   Bind the translation profile to a voice port.

```
Router(config)#voice-port 0/1:23
Router(config-voiceport)#translation-profile incoming pstn-in
```

Step 4.   Configure dial peer to match the appropriate extension of analog phone.

```
Router(config)#dial-peer voice 2001 pots
Router(config-dial-peer)#destination-pattern 2001
Router(config-dial-peer)#port 1/0/0
```

In the sample configuration using the **translation-rule** command, the rule is defined to translate 4085552 into 2. The translation profile "pstn-in" notifies the router to translate incoming called numbers. It is applied as an inbound translation to the voice port that connects to the PSTN. The sample configuration replaces the inbound DNIS number and covers inbound and outbound routing of any dial peers.

Configuring Path Selection

Path selection is one of the most important aspects of a well-designed VoIP system. High availability is desirable, so there is usually more than one path for a call to take to its final destination. Multiple paths provide several benefits, including redundancy in case of a link failure or insufficient resources on that link and a reduction in toll costs of a call. This section introduces you to path selection strategies and tools.

Call Routing and Path Selection

The call routing logic on Cisco IOS routers using the H.323 protocol relies on the dial-peer construct. Dial peers are similar to static routes. They define where calls originate and terminate and what path the calls take through the network. Dial peers are used to identify call source and destination endpoints and to define the characteristics applied to each call leg in a call connection. Attributes within the dial peer determine which dialed digits the router collects and forwards to telephony devices.

One of the keys to understanding call routing with dial peers is the concept of incoming versus outgoing call legs and, consequently, of incoming versus outgoing dial peers. Each call passing through a Cisco IOS router is considered to have two call legs, one entering the router and one exiting the router. The call leg entering the router is the *incoming call leg*, whereas the call leg exiting the router is the *outgoing call leg*.

Call legs can be of two main types:

- Traditional Time Division Multiplexing (TDM) telephony call legs that connect a router to the PSTN, analog phones, or PBXs

- IP call legs that connect a router to other gateways, gatekeepers, or Cisco UCM servers

Dial peers are also of two main types, according to the type of call leg with which they are associated:

- POTS dial peers, associated with traditional TDM telephony call legs

- VoIP dial peers, associated with IP call legs

Dial Peer Matching

Routers must match the correct inbound and outbound dial peers to successfully complete a call. For all calls going through the router, Cisco IOS associates one dial peer to each call leg.

Figure 7-19 shows the following examples of different types of calls going through a Cisco IOS router:

- Call 1 is from another H.323 gateway across an IP network to a traditional PBX connected to the router (for example, via a PRI interface). For this call, an incoming VoIP dial peer and an outgoing POTS dial peer are selected.

- Call 2 is from an analog phone connected to an FXS port on the router to a UCM cluster across an IP network. For this call, an incoming POTS dial peer and an outgoing VoIP dial peer are selected by the router.

- Call 3 is from an IP phone controlled by Cisco Unified CME or SRST to a PSTN interface on the router (for example, a PRI interface). For this call, an automatically generated POTS dial peer (corresponding to the [ephone] configured on the router) and an outgoing POTS dial peer are selected.

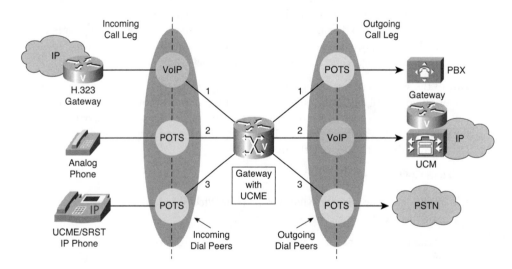

Figure 7-19 *Matching Dial Peers*

It is important to understand that a Cisco IOS gateway performs dial-peer matching every time it receives called-party information. For en bloc signaling, this is straightforward. Specifically, the called-party information is used to find the best dial peer.

For digit-by-digit signaling, such as PSTNs with overlap sending and receiving, Cisco Unified CME and SRST ephones, and FXS ports, the gateway performs dial-peer matching each time a digit is received.

For example, dial peers are configured on a gateway, as illustrated in Figure 7-20 and Example 7-18.

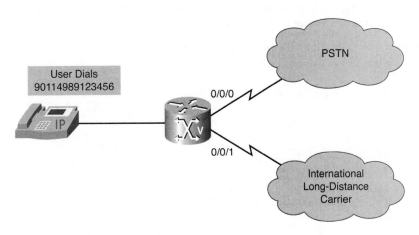

Figure 7-20 *Digit-by-Digit Signaling*

Example 7-18 *Digit-by-Digit Signaling Configuration*

```
Router(config)#dial-peer voice 90 pots
Router(config-dial-peer)#destination-pattern 9T
Router(config-dial-peer)#port 0/0/0:23
Router(config-dial-peer)#exit
Router(config)#dial-peer voice 90110 pots
Router(config-dial-peer)#destination-pattern 9011T
Router(config-dial-peer)#port 0/0/1:23
```

The following steps describe what occurs during the call in this example.

1. A user wants to call the international number 90114989123456 and starts to dial.

2. Because the first digit received is a 9, the gateway performs dial-peer matching.

3. Dial-peer 90 is matched, and any further digits are collected by the control character **T** that indicates the **destination-pattern** value is a variable-length dial string.

user finishes dialing, and the call is routed using dial-peer 90. Dial-peer 90110 never be considered.

c signaling, the DNIS is used, so the process is as follows:

1. A user wants to call the international number 90114989123456 and starts to dial.

2. Because en bloc signaling is enabled, the gateway continues to collect digits until the interdigit timeout value is exceeded.

3. The user finishes dialing, and the call is routed using dial-peer 90110.

When matching the destination pattern, the Cisco IOS gateway performs a left-aligned match (that is, the pattern is matched with the beginning of the received string).

In the scenario illustrated in Figure 7-21 and Example 7-19, both dial peers match three digits when 555-1234 is the called number.

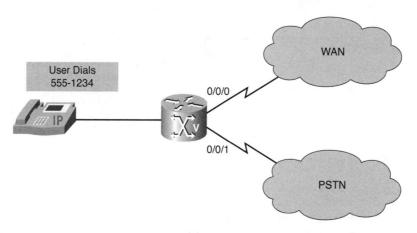

Figure 7-21   *Destination Pattern Matching*

Example 7-19   *Destination Pattern Matching Configuration*

```
Router(config)#dial-peer voice 1 pots
Router(config-dial-peer)#destination-pattern 555
Router(config-dial-peer)#port 0/0/0:23
Router(config-dial-peer)#exit
Router(config)#dial-peer voice 2 pots
Router(config-dial-peer)#destination-pattern 555....
Router(config-dial-peer)#port 0/0/1:23
```

If the first three digits of the called number are 555, dial-peer 1 will be matched because it explicitly matches the called number. The rest of the digits will not be processed.

Matching to Inbound and Outbound Dial Peers

When a Cisco IOS gateway routes a call, the inbound and outbound dial peers need to be matched. The gateway will search through all dial peers and apply matching criteria. After a dial peer has been matched, the gateway selects it as the inbound or outbound dial peer.

To match incoming call legs to incoming dial peers, the router selects a dial peer by matching the information elements in the setup message (called number/DNIS and calling number/ANI) with four configurable dial-peer attributes.

Inbound Dial-Peer Matching

Inbound dial-peer matching is prioritized as follows:

1. If the called number (that is, the DNIS) matches with the **incoming called-number** configuration on a dial peer, this dial peer will be selected as the inbound dial peer. No further matching is performed.

2. If no dial peer has been found, the calling number (that is, the ANI) is checked. If the **answer-address** configuration of a dial peer is matched, this dial peer will be selected, and no further matching is performed.

3. If the calling number (the ANI) matches with the **destination-pattern** configuration of a dial peer, this dial peer will be selected, and no further matching is performed.

4. If none of the previous attempts were successful and the call is inbound on a POTS port, a dial peer with a matching voice-port configuration is searched.

5. If still no match is found, the default dial-peer 0 is used.

Note   Default dial-peer matching is not desirable because default call characteristics might not be what you want.

The router needs to match only one of these conditions. It is not necessary for all the attributes to be configured in the dial peer or that every attribute match the call setup information. The router stops searching as soon as one dial peer is matched, and the call is routed according to the configured dial peer attributes. Even if other dial peers exist that would match, only the first match is used.

Note   A typical misconception about inbound dial-peer matching is that the session-target of a dial peer is used. This is not true. Instead, use the **incoming called-number** or **answer-address** command to ensure that the correct inbound dial peer is selected.

Outbound Dial-Peer Matching

How the router selects an outbound dial peer depends on whether DID is configured in the inbound POTS dial peer:

- If DID is not configured in the inbound POTS dial peer, the router collects the incoming dialed string digit-by-digit and compares these digits to configured destination patterns. After an inbound dial peer is matched, the gateway plays a second dial tone to the caller and waits for them to enter additional digits. This is referred to as *two-stage dialing*. As soon as a dial peer fully matches the destination pattern, the router immediately routes the call using the configured attributes in the matching dial peer.

- If DID is configured in the inbound POTS dial peer, the router uses the full incoming dial string to match the destination pattern in the outbound dial peer. This is known as *one-stage dialing*. With DID, the setup message contains all the digits necessary to route a call, so no additional digit collection is required. If more than one dial peer matches the dial string, all the matching dial peers are used to form a hunt group. The router attempts to place the outbound call leg using all of the dial peers in the hunt group until one is successful.

Outbound dial-peer matching is prioritized as follows by default:

1. The gateway searches through all dial peers and tries to match the called number (the DNIS) with the **destination-pattern** configuration. The dial peer with the closest match is selected.

2. If multiple equal matches are found, the dial peer with the lowest **preference** configuration wins.

3. If equal preferences are found, a random dial peer is selected.

Dial-Peer Call Routing and Path Selection Commands

Table 7-5 shows commands used to configure ANI and DNIS matching on dial peers.

Table 7-5   *ANI and DNIS Matching on Dial Peers*

Command	Description
destination-pattern [+]*string*[T]	Use this command in dial-peer configuration mode to specify either the prefix or the full E.164 telephone number to be used for a dial peer. To disable the configured prefix or telephone number, use the **no** form of this command. The following characters can be used: - The asterisk (*) and pound sign (#) that appear on standard touch-tone dial pads. - Comma (,), which inserts a pause between digits.

Table 7-5   *ANI and DNIS Matching on Dial Peers   (continued)*

Command	Description
	■ Period (.), which matches any entered digit. (This character is used as a wildcard.)
	■ Percent sign (%), which indicates that the preceding digit occurred zero or more times, similar to the wildcard usage.
	■ Plus sign (+), which indicates that the preceding digit occurred one or more times. **Note:** This plus sign has a different purpose than the plus sign in front of a digit string, which is used to indicate that the string is an E.164 standard number.
	■ Circumflex (^), which indicates a match to the beginning of the string.
	■ Dollar sign ($), which matches the null string at the end of the input string.
	■ Backslash symbol (\), which is followed by a single character and matches that character; can be used with a single character with no other significance (matching that character).
	■ Question mark (?), which indicates that the preceding digit occurred zero or one times.
	■ Brackets ([ ]), which indicate a range (a sequence of characters enclosed in the brackets); only numeric characters from 0 to 9 are allowed in the range.
	■ Parentheses (( )), which indicate a pattern and are the same as the regular expression rule.
incoming called-number [+]*string*[T]	Use this command in dial-peer configuration mode to specify a digit string that can be matched by an incoming call to associate the call with a dial peer. To reset to the default, use the **no** form of this command.
answer-address [+]*string*[T]	Use this command in dial-peer configuration mode to specify the full E.164 telephone number to be used to identify the dial peer of an incoming call. To disable the configured telephone number, use the **no** form of this command.

Table 7-6 shows commands used to configure direct-inward-dial, dial-peer preferences, and outbound status checks.

Table 7-6 *Direct-Inward-Dial and Dial-Peer Matching Commands*

Command	Description
direct-inward-dial	Use this command in dial-peer configuration mode to enable the DID call treatment for an incoming called number. When this feature is enabled, the incoming call is treated as if the digits were received from the DID trunk. The called number is used to select the outgoing dial peer. No dial tone is presented to the caller.
preference *value*	Use this command in dial-peer configuration mode to indicate the preferred order of a dial peer within a hunt group. The *value* variable can be a value in the range of 0 through 10. To remove the preference, use the **no** form of this command. The default is 0 and is not displayed in a configuration.
no dial-peer outbound status-check pots	Use this command in privileged EXEC mode to check the status of outbound POTS dial peers during call setup and to disallow, for that call, any dial peers whose status is down. This might be required on some ISDN links where the CO ISDN switch activates the ISDN layer only if activity is detected on the link.

Matching Dial Peers in a Hunt Group

By default, dial peers in a hunt group are selected according to the following criteria, in the order listed:

1. **Longest match in phone number:** This method selects the destination pattern that matches the greatest number of dialed digits. For example, if one dial peer is configured with a dial string of 345.... and a second dial peer is configured with 3456789, the router would first select 3456789 because it has the longest explicit match of the two dial peers.

2. **Explicit preference:** This method uses the priority configured with the **preference** dial-peer command. The lower the preference number, the higher the priority. The highest priority is given to the dial peer with preference order 0. If the same preference is defined in multiple dial peers with the same destination pattern, a dial peer is selected randomly.

3. **Random selection:** In this method, all destination patterns are weighted equally.

You can change this default selection order or choose different methods for hunting dial peers by using the **dial-peer hunt** global configuration command. Dial-peer hunt options include the following:

- **0:** Longest match in phone number, explicit preference, random selection. This is the default hunt order number.

- **1:** Longest match in phone number, explicit preference, least recent use.

- **2:** Explicit preference, longest match in phone number, random selection.

- **3:** Explicit preference, longest match in phone number, least recent use.

- **4:** Least recent use, longest match in phone number, explicit preference.

- **5:** Least recent use, explicit preference, longest match in phone number.

- **6:** Random selection.

- **7:** Least recent use.

H.323 Dial-Peer Configuration Best Practices

To illustrate best practice procedures when configuring H.323 dial peers on a Cisco IOS router, consider Figure 7-22 and the corresponding dial-peer configuration shown in Example 7-20. In the example, dial-peer 1 is used to route calls according to their DNIS, and dial peers 100 and 101 are used to route calls to the primary UCM server, unless it has lost connectivity, and then to use the backup, or secondary, UCM server.

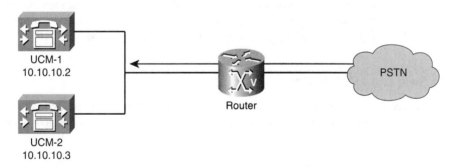

Figure 7-22   *Dial-Peer Best Practice Sample Topology*

Example 7-20   *Best Practice Dial-Peer Configuration*

```
Router(config)#dial-peer voice 1 pots
Router(config-dial-peer)#incoming called-number .
Router(config-dial-peer)#direct-inward-dial
Router(config-dial-peer)#exit
Router(config)#dial-peer voice 100 voip
```

continues

Example 7-20   *Best Practice Dial-Peer Configuration   continued*

```
Router(config-dial-peer)#preference 1
Router(config-dial-peer)#destination-pattern 1...
Router(config-dial-peer)#session target ipv4:10.10.10.2
Router(config-dial-peer)#exit
Router(config)#dial-peer voice 101 voip
Router(config-dial-peer)#preference 2
Router(config-dial-peer)#destination-pattern 1...
Router(config-dial-peer)#session target ipv4:10.10.10.3
```

The previous figure and example illustrate the following best practice procedures:

■ To ensure that incoming PSTN calls are directly routed to their destination based on the DNIS information, create a default POTS dial peer with the direct-inward-dial attribute.

Note   This should be the first POTS dial peer that you configure on the gateway. It should be the only dial peer that contains a "." for the destination pattern and direct inward dial. It should not contain a port number.

■ When using the router as an H.323 gateway connected to a Cisco UCM cluster, provide redundancy by configuring at least two VoIP dial peers with the same destination pattern pointing to two different UCM servers. Use the **preference** attribute to select the priority order between primary and secondary UCM servers.

Path Selection Strategies

When remote sites are involved, different path selection strategies are required. Multisite dial plans include all the requirements of a single-site dial plan, as well as the following requirements:

■ **Site-code dialing:** A typical requirement is the support of site-code dialing. Site-code dialing allows users to place an intersite call by dialing a site code that is typically three to four digits long followed by the actual extension of the remote site user. Call routing and path selection can support this by using digit manipulation to prefix and strip off site codes where necessary.

■ **Toll-bypass:** Toll-bypass uses the WAN link for call routing to avoid PSTN charges for intersite calls. This includes call routing and path selection for the actual call-routing process, including fallback PSTN routing in case the WAN link fails. Again, digit manipulation is also required to ensure proper number formatting.

- **TEHO:** Tail-End Hop-Off (TEHO) is similar to toll-bypass but extends the WAN usage for PSTN calls as well. The PSTN breakout should be as close as possible to the final PSTN destination to decrease phone charges. The same requirements exist as with toll-bypass.

Site-Code Dialing and Toll-Bypass

When you use site-code dialing, each site is assigned with a unique site code. For example, a network with three sites could have the site codes 801, 802, and 803. If a user wants to place a call to a remote site user, the dialed number would be the site code followed by the actual extension. This form of abbreviated dialing greatly improves the end-user experience because of shorter dialable numbers.

The calling-party number, also referred to as ANI, needs to include the appropriate site code. This allows called users to call back directly using their missed-calls and received-calls directory. You can use digit manipulation to support this as well.

You might also use site-code dialing to solve issues with overlapping numbering plans. Because all extensions of a site are prefixed with a unique site code, an overlapping numbering plan (where extensions in multiple sites overlap) can be turned into a unique numbering plan.

Toll-Bypass Example

The example illustrated in Figure 7-23 and Example 7-21 shows the concepts of call routing and path selection in a toll-bypass scenario.

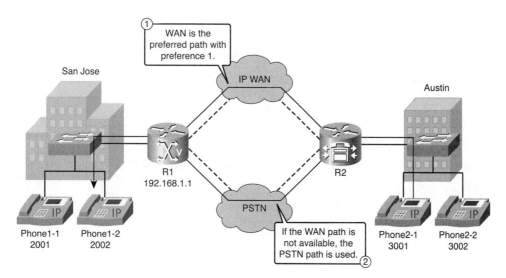

Figure 7-23 *Toll-Bypass Topology Example*

Example 7-21   *Toll-Bypass Configuration Example*

```
R2(config)#dial-peer voice 21 voip
R2(config-dial-peer)#destination-pattern 2...
R2(config-dial-peer)#preference 1
R2(config-dial-peer)#session-target ipv4:192.168.1.1
R2(config-dial-peer)#exit
R2(config)#dial-peer voice 22 pots
R2(config-dial-peer)#destination-pattern 2...
R2(config-dial-peer)#prefix 14085552
R2(config-dial-peer)#preference 2
R2(config-dial-peer)#port 0/0/0:23
```

Figure 7-23 shows a scenario with two sites, San Jose and Austin. The Austin Cisco Unified CME gateway is configured to route calls to San Jose primarily over the WAN, and if the WAN link fails, the PSTN link should be used.

The first dial-peer configuration is used to route calls that match **destination-pattern 2...** command to San Jose using the IP WAN. Because the dial peer is configured with a preference of 1, it is preferred over the PSTN dial peer with a preference of 2.

The second dial-peer configuration is used to route calls that match **destination-pattern 2...** command to San Jose using the PSTN. The preference of 2 makes this dial peer inferior to dial-peer 21 with a preference of 1.

Site-Code Dialing and Toll-Bypass Example

The example illustrated in Figure 7-24 and Examples 7-22 and 7-23 shows a scenario for site-code dialing and toll-bypass.

Example 7-22   *Site-Code Dialing and Toll-Bypass Example—R1's Configuration*

```
R1(config)#dial-peer voice 802 voip
R1(config-dial-peer)#destination-pattern 802....
R1(config-dial-peer)#session target ipv4:10.10.0.1
```

Example 7-23   *Site-Code Dialing and Toll-Bypass Example—R3's Configuration*

```
R3(config)#dial-peer voice 801 voip
R3(config-dial-peer)#destination-pattern 801....
R3(config-dial-peer)#session target ipv4:10.10.0.2
```

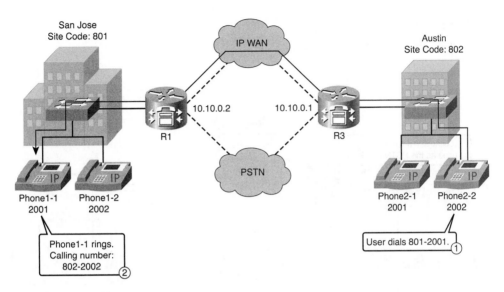

Figure 7-24   *Site-Code Dialing and Toll-Bypass Topology Example*

Figure 7-24 shows a sample scenario for site-code dialing combined with toll-bypass. San Jose has the site code 801, and Austin uses the site code 802. Also note that both sites use extensions in the range of 2XXX. This is a typical overlapping numbering plan. Following is the process the call goes through in this example:

1.   A user in Austin wants to place a call to Phone1-1. Because Phone1-1 resides in San Jose and has the site code 801, the user dials 801-2001 (that is, the site code 801 followed by the extension 2001).

2.   The call is routed over the IP WAN link to San Jose. Phone1-1 rings and displays the calling number 802-2002 (that is, the site code 802 of Austin followed by the extension of Phone2-2, which is 2002).

Tail-End Hop–Off (TEHO)

TEHO extends the concept of toll-bypass. Instead of only routing intersite calls over an IP WAN link, TEHO also uses the IP WAN link for PSTN calls. The goal is to route a call using the IP WAN as close to the final PSTN destination as possible. As with toll-bypass, PSTN fallback should always be possible in case the IP WAN link fails.

Note   Some countries do not allow TEHO. When implementing TEHO, ensure that the deployment complies with national legal requirements.

TEHO Example

Figure 7-25 shows the TEHO scenario for this example.

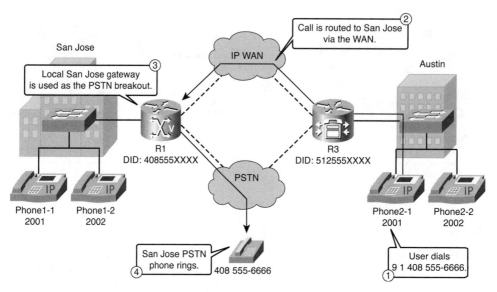

Figure 7-25 *Tail-End Hop-Off Scenario*

Here is the process the call goes through:

1. Phone2-1 dials 9 1 408 555-6666 (that is, it places a call to a PSTN phone located in San Jose).

2. The call is routed to San Jose using the IP WAN link.

3. The local San Jose voice gateway is used to route the call as a local call to the San Jose PSTN.

4. The San Jose PSTN phone rings.

Configuring Site-Code Dialing and Toll-Bypass

To demonstrate the configuration of site-code dialing and toll-bypass, the following example walks through a configuration that meets these requirements:

■ All calls from Austin to San Jose should be routed using the WAN link if possible. If the WAN link fails, the PSTN link should be used.

■ Site codes must be used for intersite dialing.

Follow these steps to configure site-code dialing and toll-bypass:

Step 1.   Configure voice translation rules and voice translation profiles for inbound and outbound VoIP intersite routing.

Step 2.   Define the dial peers for VoIP intersite routing that route the call using the WAN link.

Step 3.   Configure voice translation rules and voice translation profiles for inbound and outbound PSTN intersite routing.

Step 4.   Define the dial peers for PSTN intersite routing that route the call using the PSTN link in case the WAN link is not available.

The following configuration scenario, as illustrated in Figure 7-26, will be used throughout this example:

- San Jose:

    - DID range 408 555-2XXX

    - Directory number range 2XXX

    - Site code 801

- Austin:

    - DID range 312 555-2XXX

    - Directory number range 2XXX

    - Site code 802

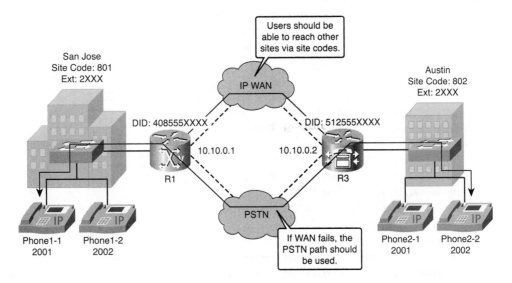

Figure 7-26   *Site-Code Dialing and Toll-Bypass Topology Example*

Step 1: Create Translation Rules and Profiles

To create translation rules and profiles for intersite routing and path selection via the WAN, you can use the following procedure.

For each site:

Step 1. Create a rule that prefixes the site code to the calling number.

Step 2. Create a rule that strips off the site code from the called number.

Step 3. Create a voice translation profile to prefix the site code to the outbound calling-party number.

Step 4. Create a voice translation profile to strip off the site code from the inbound called-party number.

Examples 7-24 and 7-25 provide the resulting configurations on the San Jose router (that is, R1) and the Austin router (that is, R3).

Example 7-24 *Step 1—R1*

```
R1(config)#voice translation-rule 1
R1(cfg-translation-rule)#rule 1 /^2/ /8012/
R1(cfg-translation-rule)#exit
R1(config)#voice translation-rule 2
R1(cfg-translation-rule)#rule 1 /^8012/ /2/
R1(cfg-translation-rule)#exit
R1(config)#voice translation-profile intersite-out
R1(cfg-translation-profile)#translate calling 1
R1(cfg-translation-profile)#exit
R1(config)#voice translation-profile intersite-in
R1(cfg-translation-profile)#translate called 2
```

Example 7-25 *Step 1—R3*

```
R3(config)#voice translation-rule 1
R3(cfg-translation-rule)#rule 1 /^2/ /8022/
R3(cfg-translation-rule)#exit
R3(config)#voice translation-rule 2
R3(cfg-translation-rule)#rule 1 /^8022/ /2/
R3(cfg-translation-rule)#exit
R3(config)#voice translation-profile intersite-out
R3(cfg-translation-profile)#translate calling 1
R3(cfg-translation-profile)#exit
R3(config)#voice translation-profile intersite-in
R3(cfg-translation-profile)#translate called 2
```

Step 2: Define VoIP Dial Peers

After you configure the voice translation profiles for VoIP routing, you need to define the VoIP dial peers for intersite routing via the WAN. Examples 7-26 and 7-27 provide the configurations for this example.

Example 7-26   *Step 2—R1*

```
R1(config)#dial-peer voice 8021 voip
R1(config-dial-peer)#destination-pattern 8022...
R1(config-dial-peer)#session-target ipv4:10.10.0.2
R1(config-dial-peer)#translation-profile incoming intersite-in
R1(config-dial-peer)#translation-profile outgoing  intersite-out
```

Example 7-27   *Step 2—R3*

```
R3(config)#dial-peer voice 8011 voip
R3(config-dial-peer)#destination-pattern 8012...
R3(config-dial-peer)#session-target ipv4:10.10.0.1
R3(config-dial-peer)#translation-profile incoming intersite-in
R3(config-dial-peer)#translation-profile outgoing intersite-out
```

Note   The same dial peer is used for both inbound and outbound call routing.

Step 3: Add Support for PSTN Fallback

To support PSTN fallback routing in case the WAN link fails, you need to configure an additional voice translation rule and profile:

■   This voice translation rule replaces the 801 site code with the PSTN dialable number, 1408555:

```
R3(config)#voice translation-rule 3
R3(cfg-translation-rule)#rule 1 /^8012/ /14085552/
```

■   To modify the called number for outbound calls to a PSTN routable format, use the following voice translation profile configuration:

```
R3(config)#voice translation-profile 801PSTN
R3(cfg-translation- profile)#translate called 3
```

Examples 7-28 and 7-29 show the resulting configurations for the San Jose and Austin routers in this example.

Example 7-28   *Step 3—R1*

```
R1(config)#voice translation-rule 3
R1(cfg-translation-rule)#rule 1 /^8022/ /15125552/
R1(cfg-translation-rule)#exit
R1(config)#voice translation-profile 802PSTN
R1(cfg-translation-profile)#translate called 3
```

Example 7-29   *Step 3—R3*

```
R3(config)#voice translation-rule 3
R3(cfg-translation-rule)#rule 1 /^8012/ /14085552/
R3(cfg-translation-rule)#exit
R3(config)#voice translation-profile 801PSTN
R3(cfg-translation-profile)#translate called 3
```

Step 4: Create a Dial Peer for PSTN Fallback

Finally, the PSTN fallback dial peer will be created. Examples 7-30 and 7-31 show these configurations for this example.

Example 7-30   *Step 4—R1*

```
R1(config)#dial-peer voice 8022 pots
R1(config-dial-peer)#destination-pattern 8022...
R1(config-dial-peer)#port 0/0/0:23
R1(config-dial-peer)#preference 1
R1(config-dial-peer)#translation-profile outgoing 802PSTN
```

Example 7-31   *Step 4—R3*

```
R3(config)#dial-peer voice 8012 pots
R3(config-dial-peer)#destination-pattern 8012...
R3(config-dial-peer)#port 0/0/0:23
R3(config-dial-peer)#preference 1
R3(config-dial-peer)#translation-profile outgoing 801PSTN
```

Note   The PSTN dial peer has a preference of 1; so it is the last dial peer that will be used when routing a call to San Jose. The called number will be translated into the PSTN routable format of 1408555XXXX after the dial peer has been matched.

Outbound Site-Code Dialing Example

To illustrate an outbound site code dialing call flow, consider the topology presented in Figure 7-27 and its corresponding configuration in Example 7-32.

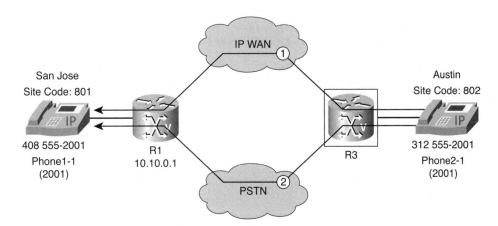

Figure 7-27   *Outbound Site-Code Dialing Topology Example*

Example 7-32   *Outbound Site-Code Dialing Configuration Example*

```
R3(config)#voice translation-rule 1
R3(cfg-translation-rule)#rule 1 /^2/ /8022/
R3(cfg-translation-rule)#exit
R3(config)#voice translation-profile intersite-out
R3(cfg-translation-profile)#translate calling 1
R3(cfg-translation-profile)#exit
R3(config)#dial-peer voice 8010 voip
R3(config-dial-peer)#destination-pattern 8012...
R3(config-dial-peer)#session-target ipv4:10.10.0.1
R3(config-dial-peer)#translation-profile outgoing intersite-out
R3(config-dial-peer)#exit
R3(config)#voice translation-rule 3
R3(cfg-translation-rule)#rule 1 /^8012/ /14085552/
R3(cfg-translation-rule)#exit
R3(config)#voice translation-profile 801PSTN
R3(cfg-translation-profile)#translate called 3
R3(cfg-translation-profile)#exit
R3(config)#dial-peer voice 8011 pots
R3(config-dial-peer)#destination-pattern 8012...
R3(config-dial-peer)#preference 1
R3(config-dial-peer)#port 0/0/0:23
R3(config-dial-peer)#translation-profile outgoing 801PSTN
```

Following are the specific steps that are involved in this example:

1. Phone2-1 in Austin dials 801-2001 (that is, it places a call to San Jose Phone1-1). The incoming called number, or DNIS, is 801-2001 and the calling number, or ANI, is 2001. The called number matches two dial peers: 8010 and 8011. Dial peer 8011 is matched because it has the best preference, and the **translation-profile outgoing intersite-out** command is applied because this is an outbound call. Thus, the call is routed to San Jose with DNIS 8012001 and ANI 8022001.

2. If the WAN fails, the call will be routed using dial-peer 8011 with preference 1 configured. The translation-profile 801 PSTN is used, which modifies the DNIS to 14085552001 (that is, the call can be routed by the PSTN to San Jose). Note that the ANI is modified using the global voice translation profiles configured on the voice port, which are used for all PSTN calls.

> **Note**   In addition to the digit manipulation used for site-code dialing, global voice translation profiles configured on the voice port are used.

Inbound Site-Code Dialing Example

To illustrate an inbound site code dialing call flow, consider the topology presented in Figure 7-28 and its corresponding configuration in Example 7-33.

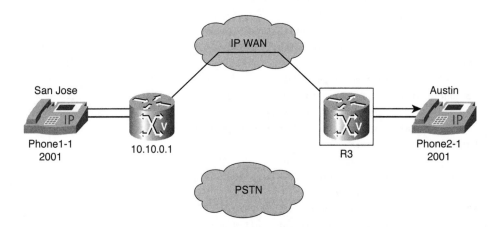

Figure 7-28   *Inbound Site-Code Dialing Example Topology*

Example 7-33   *Inbound Site-Code Dialing Configuration Example*

```
R3(config)#voice translation-rule 2
R3(cfg-translation-rule)#rule 1 /^8022/ /2/
R3(cfg-translation-rule)#exit
R3(config)#voice translation-profile intersite-in
R3(cfg-translation-profile)#translate called 2
R3(cfg-translation-profile)#exit
R3(config)#dial-peer voice 8010 voip
R3(config)#destination-pattern 8012...
R3(config)#session-target ipv4:10.10.0.1
R3(config)#translation-profile incoming intersite-in
```

Figure 7-28 shows how the same VoIP dial peers can be used for both inbound and outbound calls. Because the gateway in San Jose is also configured to prefix the site code to the calling number for calls to Austin, the inbound calling number to Austin matches the destination pattern of the San Jose dial peers. The inbound translation profile then strips off the Austin 802 site code from the inbound called number, and the call can be routed to Phone2-1 in Austin.

Configuring TEHO

You can complete the following tasks to configure TEHO:

Step 1.   Define the VoIP outbound digit manipulation.

Step 2.   Define the outbound VoIP dial peer.

Step 3.   Define the outbound POTS dial peer.

To illustrate the configuration of TEHO, consider a scenario whose topology is presented in Figure 7-29.

The design requirements for this scenario are as follows:

■ San Jose:

    ■ Local PSTN numbering range: 408XXXXXXX

■ Austin:

    ■ Local PSTN numbering range: 512XXXXXXX

All calls from Austin to the San Jose PSTN should be routed using the WAN link if possible. If the WAN link fails, the PSTN link should be used.

To ensure that the correct ANI is presented for TEHO calls, a SJC-TEHO-OUT voice translation profile should be configured and attached to both dial peers used for TEHO to the San Jose site.

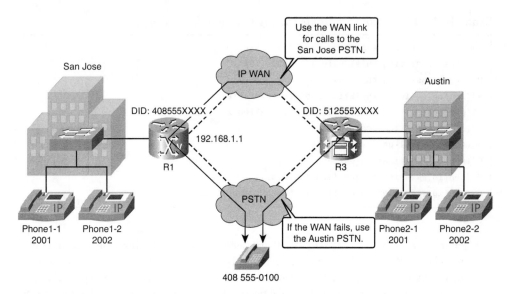

Figure 7-29   *TEHO Configuration Scenario Topology*

Step 1: Define VoIP Outbound Digit Manipulation for TEHO

Example 7-34 shows the configuration to define digit manipulation for TEHO on router R3 in this scenario.

Example 7-34   *Step 1—Defining VoIP Outbound Digit Manipulation for TEHO*

```
R3(config)#voice translation-rule 10
R3(cfg-translation-rule)#rule 1 /^2/ /15125552/
R3(cfg-translation-rule)#exit
R3(config)#voice translation-profile SJC-TEHO-OUT
R3(cfg-translation- profile)#translate calling 10
```

Step 2: Define Outbound VoIP TEHO Dial Peer

To ensure that the correct ANI is presented for TEHO calls, an **SJC-TEHO-OUT** voice translation profile is configured and attached to both VoIP dial peers used for TEHO to the San Jose site.

Example 7-35 defines an outbound dial peer on router R3 that routes calls to San Jose.

Example 7-35   *Step 2—Defining an Outbound VoIP TEHO Dial Peer*

```
R3(config)#dial-peer voice 914081 voip
R3(config-dial-peer)#destination-pattern 91408.......
R3(config-dial-peer)#session-target ipv4:192.168.1.1
R3(config-dial-peer)#translation-profile outgoing SJC-TEHO-OUT
```

Step 3: Define Outbound POTS TEHO Dial Peer

To support pure PSTN fallback routing in case the WAN link fails, an additional dial peer is configured. The **destination-pattern 91408** and the **prefix 1408** commands, as shown in Example 7-36, strip off the national identifier and the San Jose area code.

Example 7-36   *Step 3—Defining an Outbound POTS TEHO Dial Peer*

```
R3(config)#dial-peer voice 914083 pots
R3(config-dial-peer)#destination-pattern 91408.......
R3(config-dial-peer)#prefix 1408
R3(config-dial-peer)#preference 1
R3(config-dial-peer)#port 0/0/0:23
```

Note   The **prefix** command could also be replaced by the **forward-digits** command or a voice translation profile.

Complete TEHO Configuration

As a reference, Example 7-37 provides the full TEHO configuration on router R3.

Example 7-37   *TEHO Complete Configuration*

```
R3#show running-config
... OUTPUT OMITTED ...
voice translation-rule 10
 rule 1 /^2/ /13125552/
voice translation-profile SJC-TEHO-OUT
 translate calling 10
dial-peer voice 914081 voip
 destination-pattern 91408.......
 session-target ipv4:192.168.1.1
 translation-profile outgoing SJC-TEHO-OUT
dial-peer voice 914083 pots
 destination-pattern 91408.......
 prefix 1408
 preference 1
 port 0/0/0:23
... OUTPUT OMITTED ...
```

Implementing Calling Privileges on Cisco IOS Gateways

Calling privileges on Cisco IOS gateways are dial plan components, which define the types of calls that a phone, or group of phones, is able to place. This section describes the concept of calling privileges and how they can be implemented on Cisco IOS gateways using COR.

Calling Privileges

COR is a Cisco voice gateway feature that enables Class of Service (COS), or calling privileges, to be assigned. It is most commonly used with Cisco Unified SRST and Cisco Unified CME but can be applied to any dial peer.

The COR feature provides the capability to deny certain call attempts based on the incoming and outgoing CORs provisioned on the dial peers.

COR is used to specify which incoming dial-peer can use which outgoing dial-peer to make a call. Each dial-peer can be provisioned with an incoming and an outgoing corlist. COR functionality provides the capability to deny certain call attempts on the basis of the incoming and outgoing CORs that are provisioned on the dial peers. This functionality provides flexibility in network design, allows users to block calls (for example, calls to 900 numbers), and applies different restrictions to call attempts from different originators.

Figure 7-30 shows a route plan consisting of multiple PSTN dial peers, ready for COR.

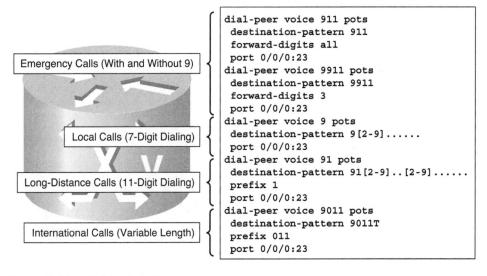

Figure 7-30   *Calling Privileges*

The 911 dial peer is used for emergency calls to the PSTN. Notice the **forward-digits all** command, which sends all matched digits (911 in this case) to the PSTN. Without this command, the dial peer would be matched, but no digits would be sent to the PSTN because of the default **digit-strip** command.

The 9911 dial peer is also used for emergency calls, but this time it also includes the PSTN access code 9. Note that only three digits are sent to the PSTN using the **forward-digits 3** command, because the PSTN access code 9 must not be included in the call setup.

The 9 dial peer is used for PSTN local calls for seven-digit dialing in the United States.

The 91 dial peer is used for PSTN national or long-distance calls for 11-digit dialing in the United States. Because the exactly matched digits are 91, the national identifier 1 needs to be prefixed. This is done using the **prefix 1** command.

The 9011 dial peer is used for PSTN variable length international calls from the United States. Because 9011 will be stripped because of the **digit-strip** setting, the **prefix 011** command is used to prefix the correct international identifier to the called number.

Understanding COR on Cisco IOS Gateways

The fundamental mechanism at the center of the COR functionality relies on the definition of incoming and outgoing corlists. Each corlist is defined to include a number of members, which are tags previously defined within Cisco IOS. Multiple CORs are defined, and corlists are configured that contain these CORs. Each corlist is then assigned to dial peers as an incoming or outgoing corlist.

When a call goes through the router, an incoming dial peer and an outgoing dial peer are selected based on the Cisco IOS dial-peer routing logic. If corlists are associated with the selected dial peers, the following additional check is performed before extending the call:

■   If the COR applied on an incoming dial-peer (for incoming calls) is a super set or equal to the COR applied to the outgoing dial-peer (for outgoing calls), the call goes through.

■   If the COR applied on an incoming dial-peer (for incoming calls) is NOT a super set or equal to the COR applied to the outgoing dial-peer (for outgoing calls), the call is rejected.

Note   *Incoming* and *outgoing* are terms used with respect to the voice ports. For example, if you hook up a phone to one of the FXS ports of a router and try to make a call from that phone, it is an incoming call for the router/voice port. Similarly, if you make a call to that FXS phone, it is an outgoing call.

If no corlist statements are applied to some dial peers, the following properties apply:

- When no incoming corlist is configured on a dial-peer, the default incoming corlist is used. The default incoming corlist has the highest possible priority, and it therefore allows this dial-peer to access all other dial-peers, regardless of their outgoing corlist.

- When no outgoing corlist is configured on a dial-peer, the default outgoing corlist is used. The default outgoing corlist has the lowest possible priority, and it therefore allows all other dial-peers to access this dial-peer, regardless of their incoming corlist.

COR Behavior Example

Figure 7-31 shows the behavior of COR.

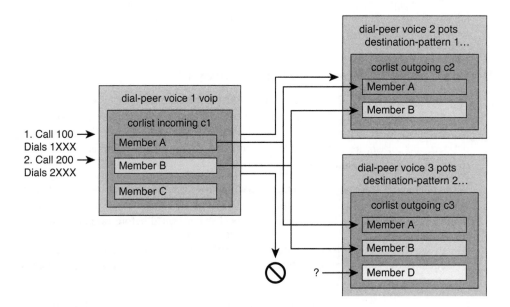

Figure 7-31   *COR Behavior*

The VoIP dial peer is associated with the c1 incoming corlist, with members A, B, and C. You can think of members of the incoming corlist as "keys."

The first POTS dial peer has a destination pattern of 1... and is associated with the c2 outgoing corlist, with members A and B. The second POTS dial peer has a destination pattern of 2.. and is associated with the c3 outgoing corlist, with members A, B, and D. You can think of members of the outgoing corlists as "locks."

For the call to succeed, the incoming corlist of the incoming dial peer must have all the "keys" needed to open all the "locks" of the outgoing corlist of the outgoing dial peer.

In the example shown in the Figure 7-31, a first VoIP call with destination 100 is received by the router. The Cisco IOS call-routing logic matches the incoming call leg with the VoIP dial peer and the outgoing call leg with the first POTS dial peer. The COR logic is then applied. Because the c1 incoming corlist has all the keys needed for the c2 outgoing corlist locks (A and B), the call succeeds.

A second VoIP call with destination 200 is then received by the router. The Cisco IOS call-routing logic matches the incoming call leg with the VoIP dial peer and the outgoing call leg with the second POTS dial peer. The COR logic is then applied. Because the c1 incoming corlist is missing one "key" for the c3 outgoing corlist (D), the call is rejected.

Calling privileges on Cisco IOS gateways use two components, as illustrated in Figure 7-32.

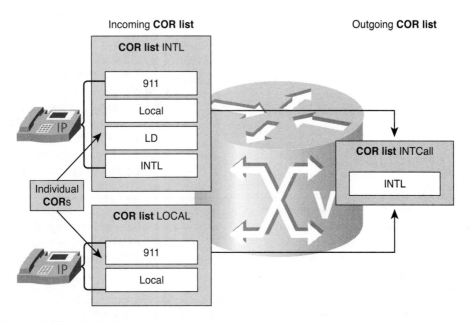

Figure 7-32   *COR Components*

The two components are

- **COR:** A COR is the building block of calling privileges.

- **corlist:** A corlist contains multiple CORs and is bound to dial peers.

When a call is routed, the gateway checks the corlist of the inbound and the corlist of the outbound dial peer. Table 7-7 reviews the various COR results, which depend on the corlists applied, or not applied, to incoming and/or outgoing dial peers.

Table 7-7   *Call Routing with Corlists*

Corlist on Incoming Dial Peer	Corlist on Outgoing Dial Peer	Result	Reason
No COR.	No COR.	Call succeeds.	COR is not involved.
No COR.	Corlist applied for outgoing calls.	Call succeeds.	The incoming dial peer, by default, has the highest COR priority when no COR is applied. Therefore, if you apply no COR for an incoming call leg to a dial peer, this dial peer can make calls out of any other dial peer, regardless of the COR configuration on the outgoing dial peer.
The corlist applied for incoming calls.	No COR.	Call succeeds.	The outgoing dial peer, by default, has the lowest priority. Because there are some COR configurations for incoming calls on the incoming, originating dial peer, it is a superset of the outgoing call COR configurations on the outgoing, terminating dial peer.
The corlist applied for incoming calls. (Superset of corlists applied for outgoing calls on the outgoing dial peer.)	The corlist applied for outgoing calls. (Subset of corlists applied for incoming calls on the incoming dial peer.)	Call succeeds.	The corlist for incoming calls on the incoming dial peer is a superset of corlists for outgoing calls on the outgoing dial peer.
The corlist applied for incoming calls. (Subset of corlists applied for outgoing calls on the outgoing dial peer.)	The corlist applied for outgoing calls. (Superset of corlists applied for incoming calls on the incoming dial peer.)	Call cannot be completed using this outgoing dial peer.	Corlists for incoming calls on the incoming dial peer are not a super set of corlists for outgoing calls on the outgoing dial peer.

COR Example

Figure 7-33 illustrates the concept of COR on Cisco IOS gateways.

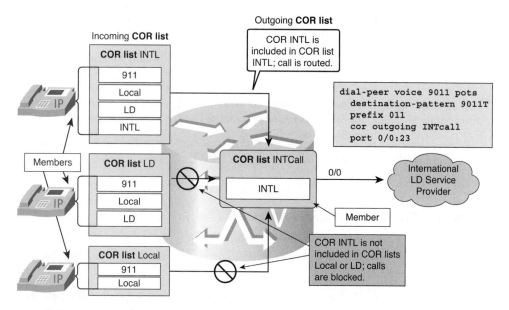

Figure 7-33   *COR Example*

A typical application of COR is to define a COR name for the number that an outgoing dial peer serves, then define a list that contains only that COR name, and assign that list as corlist outgoing for this outgoing dial peer. For example, the dial peer with destination pattern 9011T can have a corlist outgoing that contains COR INTL, as shown in Figure 7-33.

In this example, four CORs are defined:

■   911

■   Local

■   LD

■   INTL

The four CORs are used to create three incoming corlists that will be assigned to phones and users:

■   **Local:** This corlist contains the CORs 911 and Local. This list will allow users to place emergency calls and local PSTN calls.

■   **LD:** This corlist contains the CORs 911, Local, and LD. This corlist will allow users to place emergency calls, local calls, and long distance PSTN calls.

■   **INTL:** This corlist contains the CORs 911, Local, LD, and INTL. This corlist will allow users to place any PSTN call.

A corlist will be assigned to an outgoing POTS dial peer used to route international calls to the international long distance service provider:

■ **INTLCall:** This corlist contains the COR INTL and will be used for outbound INTL PSTN calls.

When a call is routed using the incoming corlist INTL and is matched against the outgoing corlist INTLCall, the call succeeds because COR INTL is included in the corlist INTL.

When a call is routed using the incoming corlist Local and is matched against the outgoing corlist INTLCall, the call is blocked because COR INTL is not included in the corlist Local.

Understanding COR for SRST and CME

When you use COR with SRST and Cisco Unified CME, a corlist cannot be simply bound to all dial peers, because one call leg will be represented by dynamic dial peers derived from ephones.

For Cisco Unified CME, the corlist is directly assigned to the appropriate ephone-dn and will then be included in the dynamic ephone dial peer. Both inbound and outbound corlists can be applied. An inbound corlist on an ephone restricts the destination to which a user can dial, whereas an outbound corlist defines who can call a user.

For standard SRST, ephones are not statically configured on the Cisco IOS gateway. Instead, the gateway pulls the configuration from the phone and dynamically creates corresponding ephones. To assign a corlist in SRST mode, a corlist is matched to a range of directory numbers in global SRST configuration mode.

Note   COR is not limited to Cisco Unified CME or SRST. COR can be applied to any inbound and outbound dial peer on a Cisco IOS gateway.

Figure 7-34 shows a sample configuration for Cisco Unified CME and SRST.

This Cisco Unified CME configuration assigns the incoming corlist INTL to ephone 1:

```
Router(config)#ephone-dn 1
Router(config-ephone-dn)#corlist incoming INTL
```

This SRST configuration assigns the incoming corlist INTL to all phones with the DN 2000 through 2010:

```
Router(config)#call-manager-fallback
Router(config-cm-fallback)#cor incoming INTL 1 2000 - 2010
```

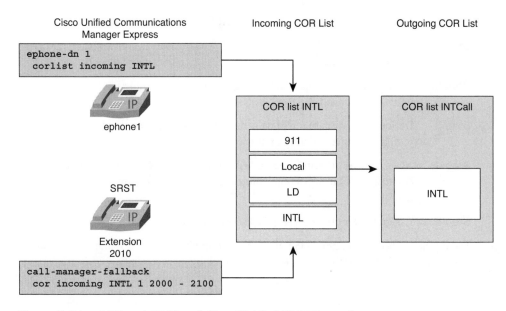

Figure 7-34 *COR and SRST and Cisco Unified CME Example*

> **Note** The number that precedes the directory number range in the SRST configuration is the corlist tag. Up to 20 tags can be configured (that is, up to 20 different corlists can be used for SRST ephones).

Configuring COR for Cisco Unified Communications Manager Express

In the following example, you are required to configure COR for Cisco Unified CME according to the following network requirements.

For this example, three calling privilege classes are required:

- **Local:** This class should allow emergency and local calls.

- **Long Distance:** This class should allow emergency, local, and long distance calls.

- **International:** This class should allow emergency, local, long distance, and international calls.

> **Note** No standard naming conventions exist for the privilege classes. Ensure that you choose a descriptive name.

You can use the following steps to configure COR for Cisco Unified CME:

Step 1. Define the four individual "tags" (CORs) to be used as corlist members with the command **dial-peer cor custom**.

Step 2. Define the corlists that will be assigned "outgoing" to the PSTN dial peers with the command **dial-peer cor list** *corlist-name*.

Step 3. Define the corlists that will be assigned "incoming" from the local dial peers with the command **dial-peer cor list** *corlist-name*.

Step 4. Associate corlists with existing VoIP or POTS PSTN dial-peers by using the command **corlist {incoming | outgoing}** *corlist-name* within the dial-peer configuration.

Step 5. Assign the corlists for user privileges to the corresponding ephone-dns.

The topology shown in Figure 7-35 will be used throughout the configuration steps in this scenario. Notice that the Chicago site is handled by a Cisco Unified CME router.

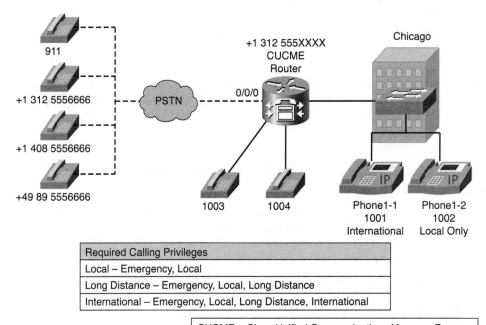

Figure 7-35 *COR Cisco UCME Scenario Topology*

Step 1: Define COR Labels

The first step is to define the individual CORs.

Four COR labels will be defined:

- **911:** Allows calls to emergency 911

- **Local:** Allows local calls only

- **LD:** Allows long distance calls

- **INTL:** Allows international calls

You can use the following procedure to configure these four CORs.

Step 1. Use the **dial-peer cor custom** command to enter COR configuration mode.

```
Router(config)#dial-peer cor custom
```

Step 2. Use the **name** command in COR configuration mode to create the named CORs.

```
Router(config-dp-cor)#name 911
Router(config-dp-cor)#name local
Router(config-dp-cor)#name ld
Router(config-dp-cor)#name intl
```

Step 2: Configure Outbound Corlists

After you define the CORs, you can configure the incoming and outgoing corlists.

Four outgoing corlists will be defined:

- **911call:** Allows calls to emergency 911

- **Localcall:** Allows local calls only

- **Ldcall:** Allows long distance calls

- **Intlcall:** Allows international calls

The following configuration defines the corlists used for the outbound PSTN dial peers. Note that each corlist contains a single COR member.

Step 1. Define a corlist name for 911 calls.

```
Router(config)#dial-peer cor list 911call
```

Step 2. Add members to dial-peer corlists. The member needs to reference a previously configured COR tag.

```
Router(config-dp-corlist)#member 911
```

Step 3.   Repeat Steps 1 and 2 for the other outgoing corlists.

```
Router(config)#dial-peer cor list localcall
Router(config-dp-corlist)#member local
Router(config)#dial-peer cor list ldcall
Router(config-dp-corlist)#member ld
Router(config)#dial-peer cor list intlcall
Router(config-dp-corlist)#member intl
```

Step 3: Configure Inbound Corlists

After the configuration of the outbound dial peers is complete, you can configure the inbound dial peer. The incoming corlists will later be assigned to the ephones and inbound dial peers used for attached phones.

Four incoming corlists will be defined:

- **911:** Allows 911 calls only

   Member is 911.

- **local:** Allows 911 and local calls only

   Members are 911 and local.

- **ld:** Allows 911, local, and long distance calls

   Members are 911, local, and ld.

- **intl:** Allows 911, local, long distance, and international calls

   Members are 911, local, ld, and intl.

The following steps define the four inbound corlists:

Step 1.   The following configuration creates a corlist that corresponds to the calling privilege allowing only emergency calls:

```
Router(config)#dial-peer cor list 911
Router(config-dp-corlist)#member 911
```

Step 2.   The following configuration creates a corlist that corresponds to the calling privilege allowing only emergency and local calls:

```
Router(config)#dial-peer cor list local
Router(config-dp-corlist)#member 911
Router(config-dp-corlist)#member local
```

Step 3.   The following configuration creates a corlist that corresponds to the calling privilege allowing emergency, local, and long distance calls:

```
Router(config)#dial-peer cor list ld
Router(config-dp-corlist)#member 911
Router(config-dp-corlist)#member local
Router(config-dp-corlist)#member ld
```

Step 4.   The following configuration defines the corlist that corresponds to the calling privilege allowing emergency, local, long distance, and international calls:

```
Router(config)#dial-peer cor list intl
Router(config-dp-corlist)#member 911
Router(config-dp-corlist)#member local
Router(config-dp-corlist)#member ld
Router(config-dp-corlist)#member intl
```

Step 4: Assign Corlists to PSTN Dial Peers

You can then define the corresponding outbound dial peers using the PSTN corlists. Note that each of the dial peers is configured with the corresponding outgoing corlist:

■   Dial-peer 911 has the outgoing 911call corlist.

■   Dial-peer 9911 has the outgoing 911call corlist.

■   Dial-peer 9 has the outgoing localcall corlist.

■   Dial-peer 91 has the outgoing ldcall corlist.

■   Dial-peer 9011 has the outgoing intlcall corlist.

The following configuration shows the complete dial-peer configuration, including correct destination patterns, digit prefixing, and corlist configuration:

Step 1.   Enter dial-peer configuration mode.

```
Router(config)#dial-peer voice 911 pots
Router(config-dial-peer)#destination-pattern 911
Router(config-dial-peer)#forward-digits all
```

Step 2.   Specify the corlist to be used when a specified dial peer acts as the incoming or outgoing dial peer. The corlist name needs to reference a previously configured corlist.

```
Router(config-dial-peer)#corlist outgoing 911call
Router(config-dial-peer)#port 0/0/0:23
```

Step 3.   Repeat Steps 1 and 2 for the remaining dial peers.

```
Router(config)#dial-peer voice 9911 pots
Router(config-dial-peer)#destination-pattern 9911
Router(config-dial-peer)#forward-digits 3
Router(config-dial-peer)#corlist outgoing 911call
Router(config-dial-peer)#port 0/0/0:23
Router(config)#dial-peer voice 9 pots
Router(config-dial-peer)#destination-pattern 9[2-9]......
Router(config-dial-peer)#corlist outgoing localcall
Router(config-dial-peer)#port 0/0/0:23
Router(config)#dial-peer voice 91 pots
Router(config-dial-peer)#destination-pattern 91[2-9]..[2-9]......
```

```
Router(config-dial-peer)#prefix 1
Router(config-dial-peer)#corlist outgoing ldcall
Router(config-dial-peer)#port 0/0/0:23
Router(config)#dial-peer voice 9011 pots
Router(config-dial-peer)#destination-pattern 9011T
Router(config-dial-peer)#prefix 011
Router(config-dial-peer)#corlist outgoing intlcall
Router(config-dial-peer)#port 0/0/0:23
```

Step 5: Assign Corlists to Incoming Dial Peers and Ephone-DNs

After the configuration of the outbound dial peers is complete, you can assign corlists to incoming dial peers and ephone-dns, as shown in Example 7-38.

Example 7-38 *Assign Corlists to Incoming Dial Peers and Ephone-DNs*

```
Router#show running-config
... OUTPUT OMMITTED ...
dial-peer voice 1003 pots
 destination-pattern 1003$
 port 1/0/0
 corlist incoming local
 corlist incoming 911
dial-peer voice 1004 pots
 destination-pattern 1004$
 port 1/0/1
 corlist incoming 911
 corlist incoming local
 corlist incoming ld
 corlist incoming intl
ephone-dn 1
 corlist incoming intl
ephone-dn 2
 corlist incoming local
... OUTPUT OMMITTED ...
```

This configuration is deployed for the ephones:

Step 1. Assign a corlist for each ephone-dn.

Step 2. Assign corlists to dial peers for the attached phones.

Configuring COR for SRST

The example illustrated in Figure 7-36 and Example 7-39 shows how to configure COR for SRST.

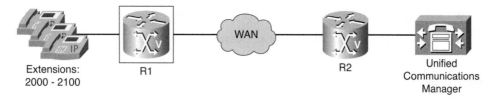

Figure 7-36   *COR SRST Scenario Topology*

Example 7-39   *SRST COR Configuration*

```
R1(config)#call-manager-fallback
R2(config-cm-fallback)#cor incoming INTL 1 2000 - 2100
```

To configure COR for SRST, use the **cor** command in SRST configuration mode.

You can have up to 20 corlists for each incoming and outgoing call. A default COR is assigned to directory numbers that do not match any corlist numbers or number ranges. An assigned COR is invoked for the dial peers and created for each directory number automatically during Communications Manager fallback registration.

When assigning an incoming or outgoing corlist to SRST ephones, corlists can be assigned to a specific directory number range (as the following syntax illustrates) or a default corlist can be applied.

```
Router(config)#call-manager-fallback
Router(config-cm-fallback)#cor incoming intl 1 2000 - 2100
```

The syntax of the **cor** command issued in call-manager-fallback configuration mode is

```
cor {incoming | outgoing} cor-list-name [cor-list-number starting-number -
   ending-number | default]
```

The following is an explanation of the syntax:

■ **incoming:** corlist to be used by incoming dial peers.

■ **outgoing:** corlist to be used by outgoing dial peers.

■ *cor-list-name*: corlist name.

- *cor-list-number*: corlist identifier. The maximum number of corlists that can be created is 20, comprising incoming or outgoing dial peers. The first six corlists are applied to a range of directory numbers. The directory numbers that do not have a COR configuration are assigned to the default corlist, provided a default corlist has been defined.

- *starting-number - ending-number*: Directory number range, such as 2000–2025.

- **default:** Instructs the router to use an existing default corlist.

Verifying COR

You can use the **show dial-peer cor** command to display corlists and members, as demonstrated in Example 7-40.

Example 7-40   show dial-peer cor *Command*

```
Router#show dial-peer cor

Class of Restriction
  name: 911
  name: local
  name: ld
  name: intl

COR list <911call>
  member: 911

COR list <localcall>
  member: local

COR list <ldcall>
  member: ld

COR list <intlcall>
  member: intl
```

Summary

The main topics covered in this chapter are the following:

- Digit manipulation is the task of adding or subtracting digits from the original dialed number to accommodate user dialing habits or gateway needs.

- Digit stripping strips any outbound digits that explicitly match the destination pattern of a particular dial peer.

- Digit forwarding specifies the number of digits that must be forwarded to a telephony interface.

- Digit prefixing adds digits to the front of the dial string before it is forwarded to a telephony interface.

- Number expansion is applied globally to all calls, not just to calls matching a single designated dial peer.

- By default, when a terminating router matches a dial string to an outbound POTS dial peer, the router strips off the left-justified digits that explicitly match the destination pattern.

- You can use the **clid** command to modify caller ID information.

- You can use voice translation profiles to replace the Cisco Unified CME **dialplan-pattern** command.

- Configuring digit manipulation might require the use of basic commands as well as translation rules and profiles.

- The call routing logic on Cisco IOS routers using the H.323 protocol relies on the dial peer construct.

- Routers must match the correct inbound and outbound dial peers to successfully complete a call.

- Dial peers in a hunt group are selected according to criteria such as longest match, explicit preference, or random selection.

- Best practices include a default POTS dial peer and redundant Cisco UCM.

- When remote sites are involved, different path selection strategies are required, including site-code dialing, toll-bypass, and TEHO.

- Site-code dialing uses the concept of prefixing a site code in front of the actual extension and can be combined with toll-bypass to route calls over a WAN link instead of a PSTN connection.

- TEHO extends the concept of toll-bypass by routing calls over a WAN to the closest PSTN breakout to avoid costly long-distance and international phone charges.

- Site-code configuration requires that each site be assigned a unique site code.

- TEHO configuration requires that all calls be routed over the WAN unless the WAN is down.

- Calling privileges are used within a dial plan to define the destination a user is allowed to call.

- Calling privileges are implemented on Cisco IOS gateways using the Class of Restriction (COR) feature.

- For Cisco Unified CME, a corlist is directly assigned to an appropriate ephone. To assign a corlist in SRST mode, a corlist is matched to a range of directory numbers in Communications Manager fallback configuration mode.

- Configuring COR includes configuring named CORs and corlists, and assigning corlists to dial peers, ephones, or SRST.

Chapter Review Questions

The answers to these review questions are in the appendix.

1. By default, _____ dial peers strip any outbound digits that explicitly match their destination pattern.

    a. PSTN

    b. WAN

    c. POTS

    d. VoIP

2. Which digit manipulation option is applied globally?

    a. Number expansion

    b. Digit prefixing

    c. Digit forwarding

    d. Digit stripping

3. Select a rule that would search and replace a ten-digit number with the internal 2XXX extension.

    a. rule 1 /^2/ /4085552/

    b. rule 1 /2/ /^4085552/

    c. rule 1 /4085552/ /^2/

    d. rule 1 /^4085552/ /2/

4. In Cisco IOS, which of the following is associated to each dial peer?

    a. Call leg

    b. Translation rule

    c. Translation profile

    d. Interface

5. One best practice is to create a default POTS dial peer with the direct-inward-dial attribute using the __ wildcard as the destination pattern.

   a.   *

   b.   #

   c.   ^

   d.   .

6. _____ is an easy way to overcome the problem of overlapping directory numbers.

   a.   Site-code dialing

   b.   Technology prefixes

   c.   TEHO

   d.   Toll-bypass

7. Instead of only routing intersite calls over an IP WAN link, _____ also uses the IP WAN link for PSTN calls.

   a.   site-code dialing

   b.   technology prefixes

   c.   TEHO

   d.   toll-bypass

8. Which of the following is defined to include a number of members that were previously defined?

   a.   Dial peer

   b.   cortags

   c.   Dial tags

   d.   corlist

9. In Unified CME, corlists are directly assigned to what?

   a.   ephone

   b.   ephone-dn

   c.   dial-peer

   d.   member

10. Which command is used to display corlists and members?

    a.   show cor

    b.   show dial-peer cor

    c.   show dial-peer

    d.   show corlist

After reading this chapter, you should be able to perform the following tasks:

- Describe Cisco gatekeeper functionality.

- Configure gatekeepers for device registration, address resolution, and call routing.

- Implement gatekeeper-based CAC.

CHAPTER 8

Configuring H.323 Gatekeepers

Gatekeepers are a major part of medium to large H.323 VoIP network solutions. When used, these components allow for dial-plan scalability and reduce the need to manage global dial plans locally. In this chapter, you will learn the functions of a gatekeeper and directory gatekeeper. Additionally, you will learn how to configure gatekeepers to inter-operate with gateways and how to provide gatekeeper redundancy in medium to large VoIP networks.

H.323 Gatekeeper Fundamentals

This section reviews the functions and roles of gatekeepers and directory gatekeepers. Also, this section discusses in depth the Registration, Admission, and Status (RAS) sig-naling sequencing between gateways and gatekeepers and discusses the use of the Gatekeeper Transaction Message Protocol (GKTMP).

Gatekeeper Overview

A gatekeeper is an H.323 entity on a network that provides services such as address translation and network access control for H.323 terminals, gateways, and MCUs. The primary functions of a gatekeeper are admission control, zone management, and E.164 address translation. Gatekeepers are logically separated from H.323 endpoints and optional devices in an H.323 network environment.

These optional gatekeepers can manage endpoints in an H.323 network. The endpoints communicate with the gatekeeper using the RAS protocol.

> **Note** The ITU-T specifies that although a gatekeeper is an optional device in H.323 net-works, if a network does include a gatekeeper, all H.323 endpoints should use it.

Gatekeepers have mandatory and optional responsibilities. The mandatory responsibili-ties include the following:

- **Address resolution:** Calls originating within an H.323 network might use an alias to address the destination terminal. Calls originating outside the H.323 network and received by a gateway can use an E.164 telephone number to address the destination terminal. The gatekeeper must be able to resolve the alias or the E.164 telephone number into the network address for the destination terminal. The destination endpoint can be reached using the network address on the H.323 network. The translation is done using a translation table that is updated with registration messages.

- **Admission control:** The gatekeeper can control the admission of the endpoints into the H.323 network. It uses these RAS messages to achieve this: Admission Request (ARQ), Admission Confirmation (ACF), and Admission Reject (ARJ). Admissions control might also be a null function that admits all requests.

- **Bandwidth control:** The gatekeeper manages endpoint bandwidth requirements. When registering with a gatekeeper, an endpoint will specify its preferred codec. During H.245 negotiation, a different codec might be required. These RAS messages are used to control this codec negotiation: Bandwidth Request (BRQ), Bandwidth Confirmation (BCF), and Bandwidth Reject (BRJ).

- **Zone management:** A gatekeeper is required to provide address translation, admission control, and bandwidth control for terminals, gateways, and Multipoint Control Units (MCUs) located within its zone of control.

All of these gatekeeper-required roles are configurable. The following are optional responsibilities a gatekeeper can provide:

- **Call authorization:** With this option, the gatekeeper can restrict access to certain endpoints or gateways based on policies, such as time of day.

- **Call management:** With this option, the gatekeeper maintains active call information and uses it to indicate busy endpoints or redirect calls.

- **Bandwidth management:** With this option, the gatekeeper can reject admission when the required bandwidth is not available.

Figure 8-1 provides a sample topology illustrating the interaction between gatekeepers and other H.323 network components.

Endpoints attempt to register with a gatekeeper on startup. When they want to communicate with another endpoint, they request admission to initiate a call using a symbolic alias for the destination endpoint, such as an E.164 address or an e-mail address. If the gatekeeper decides that the call can proceed, it returns a destination IP address to the originating endpoint. This IP address might not be the actual address of the destination endpoint, but it might be an intermediate address, such as the address of a proxy or a gatekeeper that routes call signaling. A Cisco gatekeeper provides H.323 call management, including admission control, bandwidth management, and routing services for calls in the network.

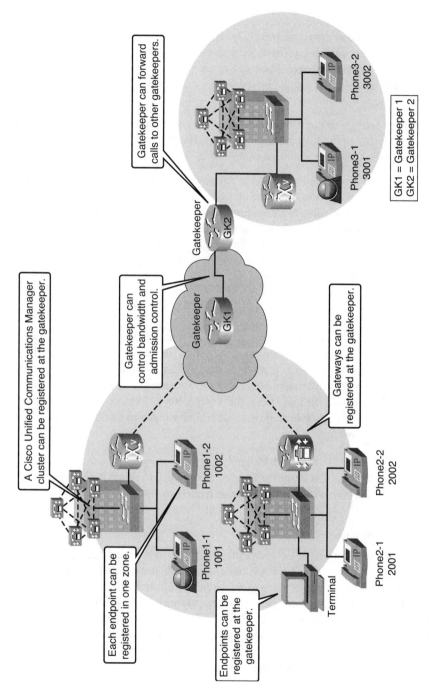

Figure 8-1 *Interaction of Gatekeepers with H.323 Network Components*

Zones

A zone is defined as the set of H.323 nodes controlled by a single logical gatekeeper. Gatekeepers that coexist on a network might be configured so that they register endpoints from different subnets. There can be only one active gatekeeper per zone. These zones can overlay subnets, and one gatekeeper can manage gateways in one or more of these subnets.

Endpoints attempt to discover a gatekeeper and consequently the zone of which they are members by using the RAS message protocol. The protocol supports a discovery message that might be sent using multicast or unicast.

If the message is sent via multicast, the endpoint registers nondeterministically with the first gatekeeper that responds to the message. To enforce predictable behavior, where endpoints on certain subnets are assigned to specific gatekeepers, the **zone subnet** command can be used to define the subnets that constitute a given gatekeeper zone. Any endpoint on a subnet that is not enabled for the gatekeeper is not accepted as a member of that gatekeeper zone. If the gatekeeper receives a discovery message from such an endpoint, it sends an explicit reject message.

Zone Prefixes

A zone prefix determines to which zone calls are sent. For a zone that is controlled by a gatekeeper, the zone prefixes help route the call to the appropriate endpoint. The zone prefixes (typically area codes) serve the same purpose as the domain names in the H.323-ID (such as gwy1@domain.com) address space. For example, if a local gatekeeper has been configured with the knowledge that zone prefix 212xxxxxxx (that is, any address beginning with 212 and followed by seven arbitrary digits) is handled by gatekeeper GK1, such as the following:

```
Router(config-gk)#zone prefix GK1 212.......
```

Then when the local gatekeeper is asked to admit a call to destination address 2125551111, it knows to send the location request to GK1.

Technology Prefixes

A network administrator selects technology prefixes to denote different types or classes of gateways. The gateways are then configured to register with their gatekeepers with these prefixes. For example, voice gateways might register with technology prefix 1#, H.320-gateways with 2#, and voice-mail gateways with 3#. More than one gateway can register with the same type prefix. When that happens, the gatekeeper makes a random selection among gateways of the same type. The caller, who knows the type of device he or she is trying to reach, can now prepend a technology prefix to the destination address to indicate the type of gateway to use to get to the destination.

Technology Prefix with Hop–Off

The other gateway-type feature is the capability to force a hop-off to a particular zone. Normally, when an endpoint or gateway makes a call admission request to its gatekeeper, the gatekeeper resolves the destination address by first looking for the technology prefix. When that is matched, the remaining string is compared against known zone prefixes. If the address resolves to a remote zone, the entire address, including both technology and zone prefixes, is sent to the remote gatekeeper in a Location Request (LRQ). That remote gatekeeper then uses the technology prefix to decide which of its gateways to hop off. The zone prefix determines the routing to a zone, and the technology prefix determines the gateway in that zone. This behavior can be overridden by associating a forced hop-off zone with a particular technology prefix. This forces the call to the specified zone, regardless of the zone prefix in the address.

Gatekeeper Hardware and Software Requirements

To determine the latest Cisco IOS Software version that is needed for the various router platforms, you will need to use the Feature Navigator tool to search for it. For example, you might want to search for which Cisco IOS version would be best to support a high-performance gatekeeper. You can find the platform and Cisco IOS version for the gate-keeper by using the Feature Navigator tool on Cisco.com at http://www.cisco.com/go/fn. To start the search, follow these steps:

Step 1.   Click the Search by Feature link.

Step 2.   Select High Performance Gatekeeper in the Available Features list.

Step 3.   Click the Add button to place the feature in the Selected Features box.

Step 4.   Click the Continue button.

The Feature Navigator returns all the versions of Cisco IOS that support this feature. This includes General Deployment (GD), Limited Deployment (LD), and Early Deployment (ED) releases as well as the release numbers, platform types, feature sets, image names, and DRAM and Flash requirements.

Gatekeeper Signaling

Cisco gatekeepers use H.323 RAS messages, the Gatekeeper Update Protocol (GUP), and the GKTMP as signaling methods when providing call services.

RAS is a subset of the H.225 signaling protocol. This signaling uses User Data Protocol (UDP). Signaling messages between gateways are H.225 call control, setup, or signaling messages.

H.225 call control signaling is used to set up connections between H.323 endpoints. The ITU H.225 recommendation specifies the use and support of Q.931 signaling messages. If no gatekeeper is present, H.225 messages are exchanged directly between endpoints.

As shown in Figure 8-2, after call signaling is set up between gateways, H.245 is negotiated. H.245, a control signaling protocol in the H.323 multimedia communication architecture, is for the exchange of end-to-end H.245 messages between communicating H.323 endpoints. The H.245 control messages are carried over H.245 control channels. The H.245 control channel is the logical channel 0 and is permanently open, unlike the media channels. The messages carried include messages to exchange capabilities of terminals and to open and close logical channels.

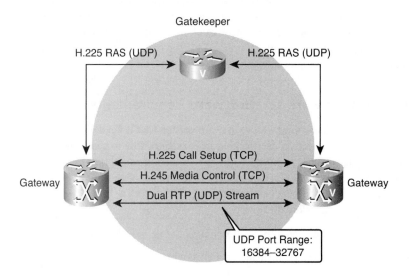

Figure 8-2   *Gatekeeper Signaling*

After a connection has been set up via the call signaling procedure, the H.245 call control protocol is used to resolve the call media type and establish the media flow before the call can be established. It also manages the call after it has been established.

As the call is set up between gateways, all other port assignments are dynamically negotiated, as in the following examples:

■   RTP ports are negotiated from the lowest number.

■   The H.245 TCP port is negotiated during H.225 signaling for a standard H.323 connection.

■   The RTP UDP port range is 16384–32767.

RAS Messages

Gatekeepers communicate through the RAS channel using different types of RAS messages. Table 8-1 shows common RAS signal messages, which are initiated by a gateway or gatekeeper.

Table 8-1   *H.225 RAS Messages*

Category of RAS Message	RAS Message
Gatekeeper Discovery	Gatekeeper Request (GRQ)
	Gatekeeper Confirmation (GCF)
	Gatekeeper Reject (GRJ)
Terminal and Gateway Registration	Registration Request (RRQ)
	Registration Confirmation (RCF)
	Registration Reject (RRJ)
Terminal and Gateway Unregistration	Unregistration Request (URQ)
	Unregistration Confirmation (UCF)
	Unregistration Reject (URJ)
Resource Availability	Resource Availability Indicator (RAI)
	Resource Availability Confirmation (RAC)
Bandwidth	Bandwidth Request (BRQ)
	Bandwidth Confirmation (BCF)
	Bandwidth Reject (BRJ)
Location	Location Request (LRQ)
	Location Confirmation (LCF)
	Location Reject (LRJ)
Call Admission	Admission Request (ARQ)
	Admission Confirmation (ACF)
	Admission Reject (ARJ)
Disengage	Disengage Request (DRQ)
	Disengage Confirmation (DCF)
	Disengage Rejection (DRJ)
Request in Progress	Request in Progress (RIP)
Status	Info Request (IRQ)
	Info Request Response (IRR)
	Info_Request_Acknowledge (IACK)
	(IRR) Information Request Response
	Info_Request_Neg_Acknowledge (INAK)
	Information Confirm (ICF)

RAS message types include those listed here:

- **Gatekeeper discovery messages:** An endpoint unicasts or multicasts a gatekeeper discovery request. The GRQ message requests that any gatekeeper receiving it respond with a GCF message granting it permission to register. The GRJ message is a rejection of this request, indicating the requesting endpoint should seek another gatekeeper.

  - **GRQ:** Message sent by an endpoint to a gatekeeper.

  - **GCF:** Reply from a gatekeeper to an endpoint indicating the transport address of the gatekeeper RAS channel.

  - **GRJ:** Reply from a gatekeeper to an endpoint rejecting the request from the end-point for registration. The GRJ message usually occurs because of a gateway or gatekeeper configuration error.

- **Terminal and Gateway registration messages:** The RRQ message is a request to register from a terminal to a gatekeeper. If the gatekeeper responds with a RCF message, the terminal will use the responding gatekeeper for future calls. If the gatekeeper responds with a RRJ message, the terminal must seek another gatekeeper with which to register.

  - **RRQ:** Sent from an endpoint to a gatekeeper RAS channel address. Included in this message is the technology prefix, if configured.

  - **RCF:** Reply from the gatekeeper confirming endpoint registration.

  - **RRJ:** Reply from the gatekeeper rejecting endpoint registration.

- **Terminal and Gateway unregistration messages:** The URQ message requests the association between a terminal and a gatekeeper be broken. Note the URQ request is bidirectional (that is, a gatekeeper can request a terminal to consider itself unregistered, and a terminal can inform a gatekeeper it is revoking a previous registration).

  - **Unregistration Request (URQ):** Sent from an endpoint or a gatekeeper to cancel registration.

  - **Unregistration Confirmation (UCF):** Sent from an endpoint or a gatekeeper to confirm an unregistration.

  - **Unregistration Reject (URJ):** Indicates that an endpoint was not preregistered with a gatekeeper.

- **Call Admission messages:** The ARQ message requests an endpoint be allowed access to a packet-based network by a gatekeeper. The request identifies the terminating endpoint and the bandwidth required. The gatekeeper either grants the request with an ACF message or denies it with an ARJ message.

- **Admission Request (ARQ):** An attempt by an endpoint to initiate a call.

- **Admission Confirmation (ACF):** An authorization by the gatekeeper to admit the call. This message contains the IP address of the terminating gateway or gatekeeper and enables the originating gateway to initiate call control signaling procedures.

- **Admission Reject (ARJ):** Denies the request from the endpoint to gain access to the network for this particular call if the endpoint is unknown or inadequate bandwidth is available.

- **Location messages:** These are commonly used between interzone gatekeepers to get the IP addresses of different zone endpoints.

  - **Location Request (LRQ):** Sent by a gatekeeper to the directory gatekeeper to request the contact information for one or more E.164 addresses. An LRQ is sent directly to a gatekeeper if one is known, or it is multicast to the gatekeeper discovery multicast address.

  - **Location Confirmation (LCF):** Sent by a responding gatekeeper, it contains the call signaling channel or RAS channel address (IP address) of itself or the requested endpoint. It uses the requested endpoint address when directed endpoint call signaling is used.

  - **Location Reject (LRJ):** Sent by gatekeepers that received an LRQ for a requested endpoint that is not registered or that has unavailable resources.

- **Status messages:** These are used to communicate gateway status information to the gatekeeper.

  - **Information Request (IRQ):** Sent from a gatekeeper to an endpoint requesting status.

  - **Information Confirm (ICF):** Sent from an endpoint to a gatekeeper to confirm the status.

  - **Information Request Response (IRR):** Sent from an endpoint to a gatekeeper in response to an IRQ. This message is also sent from an endpoint to a gatekeeper if the gatekeeper requests periodic status updates. Gateways use the IRR to inform the gatekeeper about active calls.

  - **Info_Request_Acknowledge (IACK):** Used by the gatekeeper to respond to IRR messages.

  - **Info_Request_Neg_Acknowledge (INAK):** Used by the gatekeeper to respond to IRR messages.

- **Bandwidth messages:** An endpoint sends a bandwidth change request (BRQ) to its gatekeeper to request an adjustment in call bandwidth. The gatekeeper either grants the request with a BCF message or denies it with a BRJ message.

  - **Bandwidth Request (BRQ):** Sent by an endpoint to a gatekeeper requesting an increase or decrease in call bandwidth.

- **Bandwidth Confirmation (BCF):** Sent by a gatekeeper confirming acceptance of a bandwidth request.

- **Bandwidth Reject (BRJ):** Sent by a gatekeeper rejecting a bandwidth request.

- **Resource availability messages:** RAI message is a notification from a gateway to a gatekeeper of its current call capacity for each H-series protocol and data rate for that protocol. Upon receiving an RAI message, a gatekeeper responds with a RAC message to acknowledge its reception.

  - **Resource Availability Indicator (RAI):** Used by gateways to inform the gatekeeper whether resources are available in the gateway to take on additional calls.

  - **Resource Availability Confirmation (RAC):** Notification from the gatekeeper to the gateway acknowledging receipt of an RAI message.

  - **Request in Progress (RIP) message:** The gatekeeper sends out an RIP message to an endpoint or gateway to prevent call failures because the RAS message timeouts during gatekeeper call processing. A gateway receiving a RIP message knows to continue to wait for a gatekeeper response.

- **Disengage messages:** When a call is disconnected, a variety of disconnect messages can be exchanged between an endpoint or gateway and a gatekeeper.

  - **Disengage Request (DRQ):** Notification sent from an endpoint or gateway to its gatekeeper, or vice versa.

  - **Disengage Confirmation (DCF):** A notification sent from a gatekeeper to a gateway or endpoint confirming a disconnect request, or vice versa.

  - **Disengage Rejection (DRJ):** A notification sent from a gatekeeper rejecting a disconnect request from an endpoint or gateway. Note that if a DRQ is sent from a gatekeeper to an endpoint, the DRQ message forces a call to be dropped. Such a request will not be refused.

Gatekeeper Discovery

Endpoints attempt to discover a gatekeeper, and consequently, the zone of which they are members, by using the RAS message protocol. The protocol supports a discovery message that can be sent via multicast or unicast, as depicted in Figure 8-3.

The initial signaling from a gateway to a gatekeeper is done through H.225 RAS. Gateways can discover their gatekeepers through one of these two processes:

- **Unicast discovery:**

  - Uses UDP port 1718.

  - In this process, endpoints are configured with the gatekeeper IP address and can attempt registration immediately.

  - The gatekeeper replies with a GCF or GRJ message.

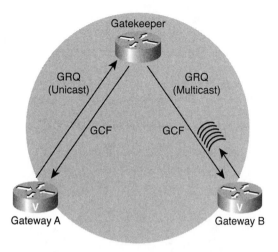

Figure 8-3   *Gatekeeper Discovery*

■ Multicast discovery:

    ■ Uses UDP multicast address 224.0.1.41.

    ■ Auto discovery enables an endpoint to discover its gatekeeper through a multicast message. Because endpoints do not have to be statically configured for gatekeepers, this method has less administrative overhead.

    ■ A gatekeeper replies with a GCF or GRJ message.

Note   A Cisco IOS gatekeeper always replies to a GRQ with a GCF or GRJ message. It never remains silent.

■ A gatekeeper can be configured to respond to specific subnets.

The GRQ message requests any gatekeeper receiving it to respond with a GCF message granting it permission to register. The GRJ message is a rejection of this request, indicating that the requesting endpoint should seek another gatekeeper.

If a gateway requests an explicit gatekeeper name, only that one will respond. If not, the first gatekeeper to respond will become the gatekeeper of that gateway. If a gatekeeper is not available, the gateway will periodically attempt to rediscover a gatekeeper. If the gateway-discovered gatekeeper has gone offline, it will stop accepting new calls, and the gateway will attempt to rediscover a gatekeeper. Active calls are not affected by this process because the RTP streams are directly between the phones.

Registration Request

The RRQ message is a request from a terminal or a gateway to a gatekeeper to register, as shown in Figure 8-4.

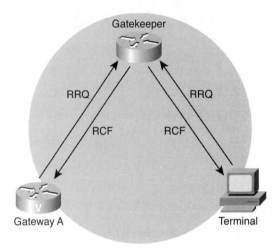

Figure 8-4   *Registration Request*

If the gatekeeper responds with an RCF message, the terminal will use the responding gatekeeper for future calls. If the gatekeeper responds with an RRJ message, the terminal must seek another gatekeeper with which to register.

An H.323 gateway learns of a gatekeeper by using a static configuration or dynamic discovery. Static configuration simply means configuring the gatekeeper's IP address on an interface used for H.323 signaling.

Following is an example of the information used to register an H.323 ID or an E.164 address:

■   **H323 ID:** gatewayname@domain.com

■   **E.164 address:** 4085551212

Lightweight Registration

Prior to H.323 version 2, Cisco gateways reregistered with the gatekeeper every 30 seconds. Each registration renewal used the same process as the initial registration, even though the gateway was already registered with the gatekeeper. This behavior generated considerable overhead at the gatekeeper. H.323 version 2 defines a lightweight registration procedure that still requires the full registration process for initial registration, but uses an abbreviated renewal procedure to update the gatekeeper and minimize overhead.

Lightweight registration, as illustrated in Figure 8-5, requires each endpoint to specify a Time to Live (TTL) value in its RRQ message. If the endpoint does not indicate a TTL, the gatekeeper assigns one and sends it to the gateway in the RCF message. When a gatekeeper receives an RRQ message with a TTL value, it returns an updated TTL timer value in an RCF message to the endpoint. Shortly before the TTL timer expires, the endpoint sends an RRQ message with the keepalive field set to True, which refreshes the existing registration. No configuration changes are permitted during a lightweight registration, so all fields are ignored other than the endpoint identifier, gatekeeper identifier, tokens, and TTL. With H.323 version 1, endpoints cannot process the TTL field in the RCF. The gatekeeper probes the endpoint with IRQs for a predetermined grace period to learn if the endpoint is still alive.

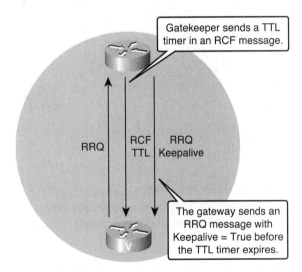

Figure 8-5 *Lightweight Registration*

Admission Request

Figure 8-6 shows an admission request. Before the call is set up, Gateway A sends an ARQ to the gatekeeper. The gatekeeper checks the status of called party and sends either an ACF message or an ARJ message. In this case the gatekeeper sends an ACF message. Typically, the H.225 call setup occurs directly between the two gateways.

Admission messages between endpoints and gatekeepers provide the basis for call admissions and bandwidth control. Gatekeepers authorize access to H.323 networks by confirming or rejecting an admission request.

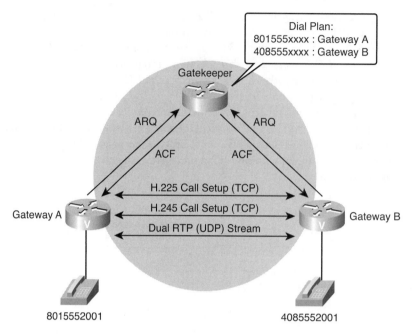

Figure 8-6   *Admission Request*

Admission Request Message Failures

It might not be clear from the RAS ARJ message why the message was rejected. Following are some basic ARJ messages that might be returned and the reasons why these messages occur:

- **calledPartyNotRegistered:** This message is returned because the called party either was never registered or has not renewed its registration with a keepalive RRQ.

- **invalidPermission:** The call violates some proprietary policy within the gatekeeper that is typically set by the administrator of the network or by the gatekeeper. For example, only certain categories of endpoints might be allowed to use gateway services.

- **requestDenied:** The gatekeeper performs zone bandwidth management, and the bandwidth required for this call would exceed the bandwidth limit of the zone.

- **undefinedReason:** This message is used only if none of the other reasons are appropriate.

- **callerNotRegistered:** The endpoint asking for permission to be admitted to the call is not registered with the gatekeeper from which it is asking permission.

- **routeCallToGatekeeper:** The registered endpoint has been sent a setup message from an unregistered endpoint, and the gatekeeper wants to route the call-signaling channel.

- **invalidEndpointIdentifier:** The endpoint identifier in the ARQ is not the one the gatekeeper assigned to this endpoint in the preceding RCF.

- **resourceUnavailable:** This message indicates that the gatekeeper does not have the resources, such as memory or administrated capacity, to permit the call. It could possibly also be used in reference to the remote endpoint, meaning the endpoint is unavailable. However, another reason might be more appropriate, such as the call capacity has been exceeded, which would return a callCapacityExceeded message.

- **securityDenial:** This message refers to the tokens or cryptoTokens fields. For example, failed authentication, lack of authorization (permission), failed integrity, or the received crypto parameters are not acceptable or understood. This message might also be used when the password or shared secret is invalid or not available, the endpoint is not allowed to use a service, a replay was detected, an integrity violation was detected, the digital signature was incorrect, or the certificate expired.

- **qosControlNotSupported:** The endpoint specified a transport quality of service (QoS) of gatekeeperControlled in its ARQ, but the gatekeeper cannot or will not provide QoS for this call.

- **incompleteAddress:** This is used for "overlapped sending." If there is insufficient addressing information in the ARQ, the gatekeeper responds with this message. This message indicates the endpoint should send another ARQ when more addressing information is available.

- **routeCallToSCN:** This message means the endpoint is to redirect the call to a specified telephone number on the Switched Circuit Network (SCN) or Public Switched Telephone Network (PSTN). This is used only if the ARQ was from an ingress gateway, where ARQ.terminalType.gateway was present and answerCall was FALSE.

- **aliasesInconsistent:** The ARQdestinationInfo contained multiple aliases that identify different registered endpoints. This is distinct from destinationInfo containing one or more aliases identifying the same endpoint plus additional aliases that the gatekeeper cannot resolve.

- **exceedsCallCapacity:** This message was formerly callCapacityExceeded. It signifies that the destination endpoint does not have the capacity to accept the call.

Information Request

A gatekeeper periodically sends an IRQ to each registered endpoint to verify it still exists, as illustrated in Figure 8-7. To limit traffic, the IRQ is sent only if the endpoint does not send some other RAS traffic within a certain interval. If an IRR is not received after an IRQ is sent, the registration is aged out of the system.

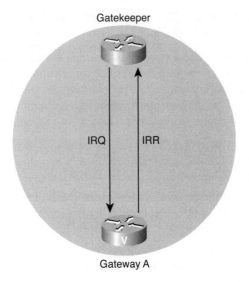

Figure 8-7 *Information Request*

> **Note**   In addition, during calls, endpoints are instructed to send periodic unsolicited
> IRRs to report their call state. Cisco endpoints (proxies and gateways) send IRRs whenever
> a state transition exists, so that accounting information is accurate.

Whenever an IRR is sent, the age tags on the registration information for the endpoint
are refreshed. In addition, if the IRR contains Cisco accounting information in its
nonStandardData field, this information is used to generate authentication, authorization,
and accounting (AAA) transactions.

To ensure that accounting is as accurate and simple as possible, the gatekeeper will confirm IRRs from Cisco gateways and proxies by sending an ICF. If the gateway or proxy
does not receive the ICF, the IRR should be resent.

The RAS status information messages include IRQ, IRR, IACK, and INAK.

Location Request

An H.323 LRQ message is sent by a gatekeeper to another gatekeeper to request information about a terminating endpoint, as shown in Figure 8-8.

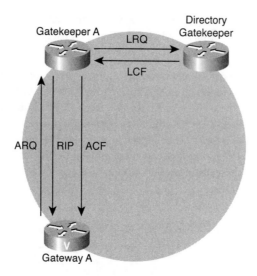

Figure 8-8   *Location Request*

The second gatekeeper determines the appropriate endpoint on the basis of the information contained in the LRQ message. However, sometimes all the terminating endpoints are busy servicing other calls, and none are available. If you configure the **lrq reject-resource-low** command, the second gatekeeper will reject the LRQ request if no terminating endpoints are available. If the command is not configured, the second gatekeeper will allocate and return a terminating endpoint address to the sending gatekeeper even if all the terminating endpoints are busy.

> **Note**   The gatekeeper sends out a RIP message to an endpoint or gateway to prevent call failures because the RAS message timeouts during gatekeeper call processing. A gateway receiving a RIP message knows to continue to wait for a gatekeeper response.

Gatekeeper Signaling: LRQ Sequential

For gatekeeper redundancy and load-sharing features, you can configure multiple gatekeepers to service the same zone or technology prefix by sending LRQs to two or more gatekeepers. Either the LRQs are sent sequentially to the gatekeepers or to all gatekeepers at the same time (blast).

Sequential forwarding of LRQs is the default forwarding mode. With sequential LRQ forwarding, the originating gatekeeper forwards an LRQ to the first gatekeeper in the matching list. The originating gatekeeper then waits for a response before sending an LRQ to the next gatekeeper on the list. If the originating gatekeeper receives an LCF while waiting, it will terminate the LRQ forwarding process.

If you have multiple matching prefix zones, you might want to consider using sequential LRQ forwarding instead of blast LRQ forwarding. With sequential forwarding, you can configure which routes are primary, secondary, and tertiary.

Figure 8-9 shows three gatekeepers to which Gatekeeper A can point. Gatekeeper A, whose configuration is provided in Example 8-1, will send an LRQ first to Gatekeeper B. Gatekeeper B will send a reply as either an LCF or an LRJ to Gatekeeper A. If Gatekeeper B returns an LCF to Gatekeeper A, the LRQ forwarding process will be terminated. If Gatekeeper B returns an LRJ to Gatekeeper A, then Gatekeeper A will send an LRQ to Gatekeeper C. Gatekeeper C will return either an LCF or LRJ to Gatekeeper A. Then Gatekeeper A will either terminate the LRQ forwarding process or start the LRQ process again with Gatekeeper D.

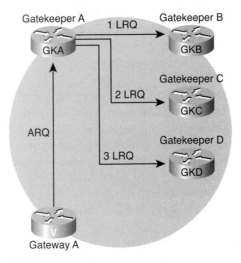

Figure 8-9   *Sequential LRQ*

Example 8-1   *Sequential LRQ Configuration*

```
GKA(config)#gatekeeper
GKA(config-gk)#zone local GKA cisco.com
GKA(config-gk)#zone remote GKB cisco.com
GKA(config-gk)#zone remote GKC cisco.com
GKA(config-gk)#zone remote GKD cisco.com
GKA(config-gk)#zone prefix GKB 1408555.... seq
GKA(config-gk)#zone prefix GKC 1408555.... seq
GKA(config-gk)#zone prefix GKD 1408555.... seq
```

Notice the zone prefix commands at the bottom of the router output. Because sequence is the default method for LRQ forwarding, the option **seq** can be included, and sequential LRQ forwarding will take place.

Note   With sequential LRQs, there is a fixed timer when LRQs are sent. Even if Gatekeeper A gets an LRJ back immediately from Gatekeeper B, it will wait a fixed amount of time before sending the next LRQ to Gatekeeper C and Gatekeeper D. You can speed up this process by using the **lrq lrj immediate-advance** command.

Gatekeeper Signaling: LRQ Blast

In Figure 8-10 and Example 8-2, when blast LRQ is used, Gatekeeper A will simultane-ously send LRQs to all three gatekeepers that match the zone prefix.

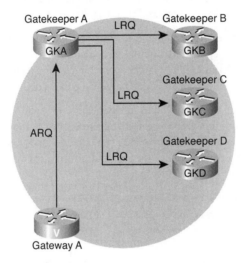

Figure 8-10   *Blast LRQ*

Example 8-2   *Blast LRQ Configuration*

```
GKA(config)#gatekeeper
GKA(config-gk)#zone local GKA cisco.com
GKA(config-gk)#zone remote GKB cisco.com
GKA(config-gk)#zone remote GKC cisco.com
GKA(config-gk)#zone remote GKD cisco.com
GKA(config-gk)#zone prefix GKB 1408555.... blast
GKA(config-gk)#zone prefix GKC 1408555.... blast
GKA(config-gk)#zone prefix GKD 1408555.... blast
```

If all three reply with a positive confirmation (that is, an LCF), Gatekeeper A chooses which one to use. Gatekeeper A can tailor the choice by using the **cost** and **priority** keywords at the end of the zone remote statement as follows:

```
GKA(config-gk)#zone remote GKB cisco.com cost 50 priority 50
GKA(config-gk)#zone remote GKC cisco.com cost 51 priority 49
GKA(config-gk)#zone remote GKD Cisco.com cost 52 priority 48
```

The **cost** and **priority** command options need to be examined carefully for correct operation. The default cost is 50, in the range 1–100. In the example, you see the three gatekeepers have costs of 50, 51, and 52. This means Gatekeeper B has a lower cost than Gatekeeper C, and Gatekeeper C has a lower cost than Gatekeeper D. Therefore, Gatekeeper B will be selected first, and then Gatekeeper C, and finally Gatekeeper D.

The priority can also be set. The default for this option is also 50 in the range 1–100. In the example, the gatekeepers with a higher cost also have a lower priority. When each of the gatekeepers returns an LCF to Gatekeeper A, a decision as to which gatekeeper the call should be forwarded to can be made based on either cost or priority.

You can assign cost and priority values independently of each other. You might choose to assign only a cost or a priority to a specific gatekeeper. If the values you assign to a specific gatekeeper are higher or lower than the default values, and there are other gatekeepers that are using default values for cost and priority, call routing might take these unexpected paths. In the following syntax,

```
GKA(config-gk)#zone prefix GKB 1408555.... blast
GKA(config-gk)#zone prefix GKC 1408555.... blast
GKA(config-gk)#zone prefix GKD 1408555.... blast
```

the **blast** option has been added to the **zone prefix** commands. This option is an important part of the configuration that is often overlooked. The **blast** option allows Gatekeeper A to simultaneously send LRQs to Gatekeeper B, Gatekeeper C, and Gatekeeper D. If the **blast** command option is omitted, the gatekeeper will use the default method, which is to choose the gatekeeper based on sequence.

To summarize, Gatekeeper A receives an ARQ from a gateway for 1408555xxxx. Gatekeeper A then blasts LRQs to all gatekeepers, which in this case are Gatekeeper B, Gatekeeper C, and Gatekeeper D. Gatekeeper A will use the **cost** and **priority** values to evaluate the received LCFs to determine where the call should be forwarded. In this case, if all the downstream gatekeepers respond with LCFs, Gatekeeper A will use the **priority** and **cost** values and choose Gatekeeper B as the gatekeeper to which to forward the call.

Intrazone Call Setup

Figure 8-11 shows the sequence of the signaling events and the basic signaling that takes place between a gateway and gatekeeper.

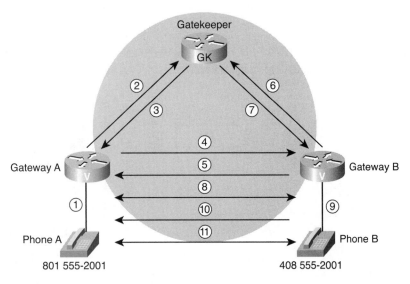

Figure 8-11 *Intrazone Call Setup*

The steps of this intrazone call setup are as follows:

1. Phone A dials the phone number 408 5555-2001 for Phone B.

2. Gateway A sends an ARQ to the gatekeeper, asking permission to call Phone B.

3. The gatekeeper does a lookup and finds Phone B registered to Gateway B and returns an ACF with the IP address of Gateway B.

4. Gateway A sends an H.225 call setup message to Gateway B with the phone number of Phone B.

5. Gateway B sends an H.255 call proceeding message to Gateway A.

6. Gateway B sends an ARQ to the gateway, asking permission to answer Gateway A's call.

7. The gateway returns an ACF with the IP address of Gateway A.

8. Gateway B and Gateway A initiate an H.245 capability exchange and open logical channels.

9. Gateway B sets up a plain old telephone service (POTS) call to Phone B at 408 555-2001.

10. When Phone B answers, Gateway B sends an H.245 call connect message to Gateway A.

11. Dual RTP streams flow between gateways.

Interzone Call Setup

Figure 8-12 shows how gatekeepers signal each other in a multizone gatekeeper network. It shows the sequence of RAS signaling events between gatekeepers, the LRQ RAS messages, and how an LRQ RAS message is used.

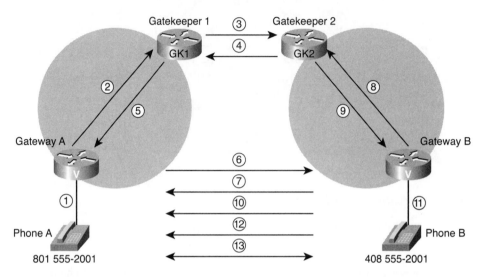

Figure 8-12   *Interzone Call Setup*

The basic gateway-to-gatekeeper signaling that occurs between zones is as follows:

1.   Phone A dials the phone number 408 555-2001 for Phone B.

2.   Gateway A sends Gatekeeper 1 an ARQ, asking permission to call Phone B.

3.   Gatekeeper 1 does a lookup and does not find Phone B registered. Gatekeeper 1 does a prefix lookup and finds a match with Gatekeeper 2. Gatekeeper 1 sends an LRQ to Gatekeeper 2 and a RIP to Gateway A.

4.   Gatekeeper 2 does a lookup, finds Phone B registered, and returns an LCF to Gatekeeper 1 with the IP address of Gateway B.

5.   Gatekeeper 1 returns an ACF with the IP address of Gateway B.

6.   Gateway A sends an H.225 call setup message to Gateway B with the phone number of Phone B.

7.   Gateway B sends an H.225 call proceeding message to Gateway A.

8.   Gateway B sends Gatekeeper 2 an ARQ, asking permission to answer the call from Gateway A.

9.   Gatekeeper 2 returns an ACF with the IP address of Gateway A.

10.   Gateway B and Gateway A initiate an H.245 capability exchange and open logical channels.

11. Gateway B sets up a POTS call to Phone B at 408 555-2001.

12. Gateway B sends a call connect to Gateway A.

13. Dual RTP streams flow between the gateways.

Call Disconnect

Figure 8-13 shows basic call-disconnect signaling between a gateway and a gatekeeper.

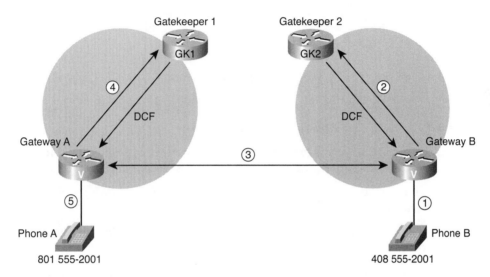

Figure 8-13 *Call Disconnect*

The RAS signaling messages used in this figure are DRQ and DCF.

Phones A and B are in a conversation, and RAS signaling occurs as follows:

1. Phone B hangs up.

2. Gateway B sends a DRQ to Gatekeeper 2, disconnecting the call between Phones A and B. A DCF is received some time later.

3. Gateway B sends a Q.931 release complete message to Gateway A.

4. Gateway A sends a DRQ to Gatekeeper 1, disconnecting the call between Phones A and B. A DCF is received some time later.

5. Gateway A signals a call disconnect to the voice network.

Call Flows with a Gatekeeper

Figure 8-14 illustrates how an endpoint locates and registers with a gatekeeper.

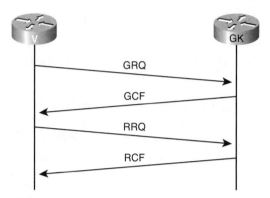

Figure 8-14 *Finding and Registering with a Gatekeeper*

A gatekeeper adds scalability to H.323. Without a gatekeeper, an endpoint must recognize or have the ability to resolve the IP address of a destination endpoint.

Before an endpoint can use a gatekeeper, it must register with the gatekeeper. To register, an endpoint must recognize the IP address of the gatekeeper.

As previously mentioned, one of the following two methods is used to determine the address of the gatekeeper:

■ An endpoint can be preconfigured to recognize the domain name or IP address of its gatekeeper. If configured to recognize the name, an endpoint must have a means to resolve the name to an IP address. A common address resolution technique is to use DNS.

■ An endpoint can issue a multicast GRQ to the gatekeeper discovery address (224.0.1.41) to discover the IP address of its gatekeeper. If the endpoint receives a GCF to the request, it uses the IP address to proceed with registration.

To initiate registration, an endpoint sends an RRQ to the gatekeeper. In the RRQ, the endpoint identifies itself with its ID and provides its IP address. Optionally, the endpoint lists the prefixes (for example, telephone numbers) that it supports. These prefixes are gleaned from the POTS dial-peer destination patterns associated with any Foreign Exchange Station (FXS) port.

With this procedure, a gatekeeper determines the location and identity of endpoints and the identities of SCN endpoints from gateway registrations.

In Figure 8-15, both endpoints have registered with the same gatekeeper.

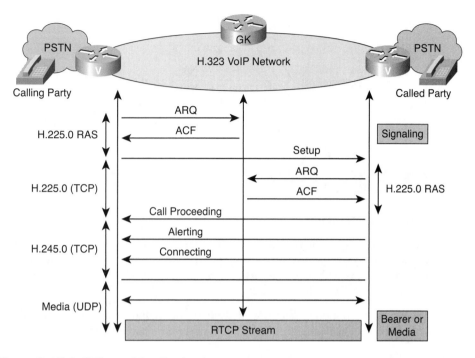

Figure 8-15 *Call Flow with a Gatekeeper*

Call flow with a gatekeeper proceeds as follows:

1. The gateway sends an ARQ to the gatekeeper to initiate the procedure. The gateway is configured with the domain or address of the gatekeeper.

2. The gatekeeper responds to the ARQ with an ACF. In the confirmation, the gatekeeper provides the IP address of the remote endpoint.

3. When the originating endpoint identifies the terminating endpoint, it initiates a basic call setup.

4. Before the terminating endpoint accepts the incoming call, it sends an ARQ to the gatekeeper to gain permission.

5. The gatekeeper responds affirmatively, and the terminating endpoint proceeds with the call setup procedure.

During this procedure, if the gatekeeper responds to either endpoint with an ARJ to the ARQ, the endpoint that receives the rejection terminates the procedure.

Figure 8-16 shows an example of gatekeeper-routed call signaling.

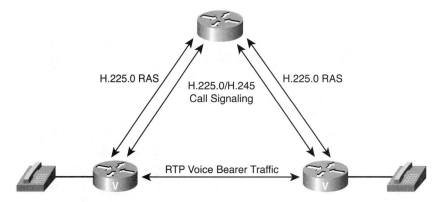

Figure 8-16 *Gatekeeper-Routed Call Signaling*

In the previous examples, the call-signaling channel is created from endpoint to endpoint. In some cases, it is desirable to have the gatekeeper represent the other endpoint for signaling purposes. This method is called *gatekeeper-routed call signaling*. The process for gatekeeper-routed call signaling is as follows:

1. The gatekeeper responds to an ARQ and advises the endpoint to perform the call setup procedure with the gatekeeper, not with the terminating endpoint.

2. The endpoint initiates the setup request with the gatekeeper.

3. The gatekeeper sends its own request to the terminating endpoint and incorporates some of the details acquired from the originating request.

4. When a connect message is received from the terminating endpoint, the gatekeeper sends a connect message to the originating endpoint.

5. The two endpoints establish an H.245 control channel between them. The call procedure continues normally from this point.

Call Flows with Multiple Gatekeepers

By simplifying configuration of the endpoints, gatekeepers aid in building large-scale VoIP networks, as shown in Figure 8-17. As a VoIP network grows, incorporating additional gatekeepers enhances the network's scalability.

Without a gatekeeper, endpoints must find each other by any means available. This limits the growth potential of a VoIP network. Through the registration and address resolution services of a gatekeeper, growth potential improves significantly.

A single gatekeeper design might not be appropriate for several reasons. A single gatekeeper can become overloaded, or it can have a suboptimal network location. Deploying multiple gatekeepers offers a more scalable and robust environment.

Figure 8-18 illustrates a call setup involving two gatekeepers.

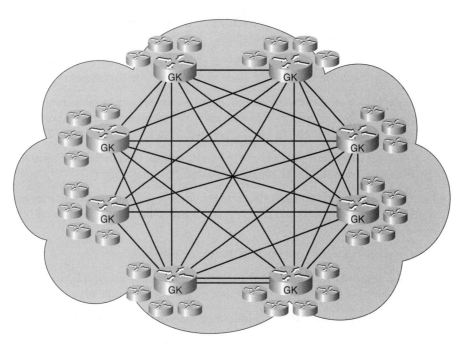

Figure 8-17   *Scalability with Multiple Gatekeepers*

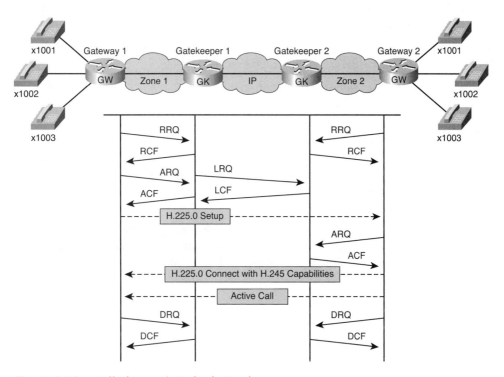

Figure 8-18   *Call Flow with Multiple Gatekeepers*

In this scenario, each endpoint is registered with a different gatekeeper. Notice the changes in the following call setup procedure:

1. The originating endpoint sends an ARQ to its gatekeeper requesting permission to proceed and asking for the session parameters for the terminating endpoint.

2. The gatekeeper for the originating endpoint (Gatekeeper 1) determines from its configuration or from a directory resource that the terminating endpoint is potentially associated with Gatekeeper 2. Gatekeeper 1 sends an LRQ to Gatekeeper 2.

3. Gatekeeper 2 recognizes the address and sends back an LCF. In the confirmation, Gatekeeper 2 provides the IP address of the terminating endpoint.

4. If Gatekeeper 1 considers the call acceptable for security and bandwidth reasons, it maps the LCF to an ARQ and sends the confirmation back to the originating endpoint.

5. The endpoint initiates a call setup to the remote endpoint.

6. Before accepting the incoming call, the remote endpoint sends an ARQ to Gatekeeper 2 requesting permission to accept the incoming call.

7. Gatekeeper 2 performs admission control on the request and responds with a confirmation.

8. The endpoint responds to the call setup request.

9. The call setup progresses through the H.225.0 call function and H.245 control function procedures until the RTP sessions are initiated.

10. At the conclusion of the call, each endpoint sends a disconnect request to its gatekeeper to advise the gatekeeper that the call is complete.

11. The gatekeeper responds with a confirmation.

Zone Prefixes

A zone prefix is the part of the called number that identifies the destination zone for a call. Zone prefixes are usually used to associate an area code to a configured zone, and they serve the same purpose as the domain names in the H.323-ID address space.

The Cisco gatekeeper determines whether a call is routed to a remote zone or handled locally. To illustrate, consider the example given in Figure 8-19 and Example 8-3. According to this configuration excerpt, gatekeeper Corp-GK forwards 408....... calls to the San Jose gateway. Calls to area code 281 are handled locally.

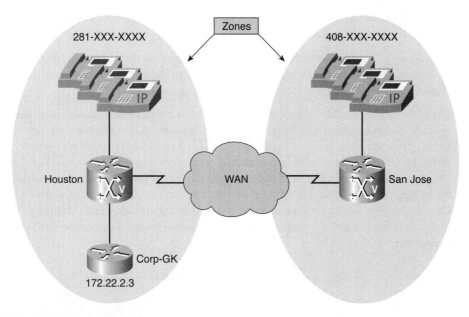

Figure 8-19   *Zone Prefix*

Example 8-3   *Zone Prefix Configuration*

```
GK-A(config)#gatekeeper
GK-A(config-gk)#zone local Houston cisco.com 172.22.2.3 1719
GK-A(config-gk)#zone local SanJose cisco.com
GK-A(config-gk)#zone prefix Houston 281.......
GK-A(config-gk)#zone prefix SanJose 408.......
```

When the San Jose gateway receives the request, the gatekeeper must resolve the address so the call can be sent to its final destination. An H.323 endpoint with that E.164 address might be registered with the San Jose gateway, in which case the San Jose gateway returns the IP address for that endpoint. However, it is possible the E.164 address belongs to a non-H.323 device (for example, a telephone or an H.320 terminal). Because non-H.323 devices do not register with gatekeepers, the San Jose gateway cannot resolve the address. The gatekeeper must be able to select a gateway that can be used to reach the non-H.323 device. This is where the technology prefixes (or "gateway-type") become useful.

Technology Prefixes

A technology prefix is an optional H.323 standards-based feature that is supported by Cisco gateways and gatekeepers and enables more flexibility in call routing within an

H.323 VoIP network. Technology prefixes are used to group gateways by type (such as voice or video) or class or define a pool of gateways.

Technology prefixes are used to separately identify gateways that support different types of services, such as video calls versus voice calls, where the gatekeeper can use this information to correspondingly route traffic to appropriate gateways.

The network administrator selects technology prefixes (tech-prefixes) to denote different types or classes of gateways. The gateways are then configured to register with their gatekeepers with these prefixes. For example, voice gateways can register with tech-prefix 1#, H.320 gateways with tech-prefix 2#, and voicemail gateways with tech-prefix 3#. More than one gateway can register with the same type prefix. When this happens, the gatekeeper makes a random selection among gateways of the same type. If the callers know the type of device they are trying to reach, they can include the technology prefix in the destination address to indicate the type of gateway to use to get to the destination, as illustrated in Figure 8-20.

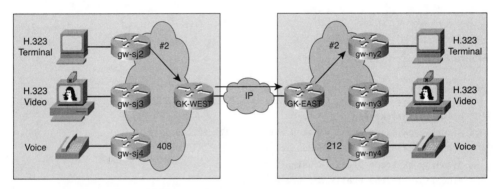

Figure 8-20   *Technology Prefixes*

For example, if a caller knows that address 2125551111 belongs to a regular telephone, the destination address of 1#2125551111 can be used, where 1# indicates that the address should be resolved by a voice gateway. When the voice gateway receives the call for 1#2125551111, it strips off the technology prefix and bridges the next leg of the call to the telephone at 2125551111.

Cisco gatekeepers use technology prefixes to route calls when no E.164 addresses registered (by a gateway) match the called number. In fact, this is a common scenario because most Cisco IOS gateways can either register their H.323 ID or destination patterns. Cisco Unified Communications Manager Express and Cisco Unified Survivable Remote Site Telephony (SRST) can register their Ethernet phone's directory numbers (ephone-dns) at the gatekeeper. Without E.164 addresses registered, the Cisco gatekeeper relies on these two options to make the call-routing decision:

■   With the technology prefix matches option, the Cisco gatekeeper uses the technology prefix appended in the called number to select the destination gateway or zone.

- With the default technology prefixes option, the Cisco gatekeeper assigns a default gateway or gateways for routing unresolved call addresses. This assignment is based on the registered technology prefix of the gateways.

The gatekeeper uses a default technology prefix for routing all calls that do not have a technology prefix or for gateways that do not have a technology prefix defined. That remote gatekeeper then matches the technology prefix to decide which of its gateways to hop off. The zone prefix determines the routing to a zone just as the technology prefix determines the gateway in that zone.

If the majority of calls hop off on a particular type of gateway, the gatekeeper can be configured to use that type of gateway as the default type so callers no longer have to prepend a technology prefix on the address. For example, if you use mostly voice gateways in your network, and you have configured all your voice gateways to register with technology prefix of 1#, you can configure your gatekeeper to use 1#* (that is, a 1# followed by zero or more characters) gateways as the default:

```
Router(config-gk)#gw-type-prefix 1#* default-technology
```

Gatekeeper Call Routing

When a gatekeeper receives an ARQ message from a gateway, it reacts as described by the flowchart shown in Figure 8-21.

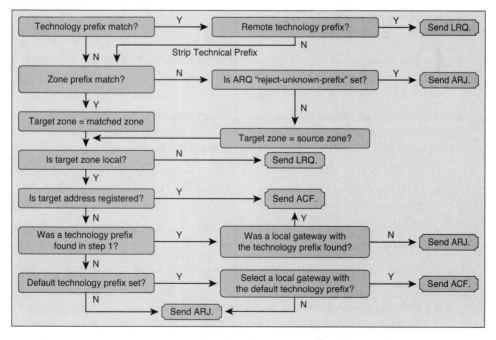

Figure 8-21   *Gatekeeper Address Resolution*

Examples of the flowchart logic are as follows:

■ If a technology prefix is specified in the admission request, and it is a hop-off technology prefix, the gatekeeper sends an LRQ message.

■ If no technology prefix exists, or the technology prefix is not a hop-off technology prefix, the gatekeeper uses the exact E.164 alias in the ARQ message, including the zone prefix, if any, to search its E.164 alias table. It then proceeds according to the result of the search and the configuration:

　　■ If no match is found, and the **arq reject-unknown prefix** command is set, the gatekeeper sends an ARJ message.

　　■ If a match is found, and the destination zone is not local, the gatekeeper sends an LRQ message to the remote zone.

　　■ If the destination zone is local, and the destination address is registered, the gatekeeper sends an ACF message.

　　■ If the destination zone is local, and the destination address is not registered, but the local gateway is found with the specified technology prefix or the default technology prefix, the gatekeeper sends an ACF. If no local gateway with the specified technology prefix is found, the gatekeeper sends an ARJ message.

■ If no matching technology prefix exists and no default technology prefix is set, the gatekeeper sends an ARJ message.

When a gatekeeper receives an LRQ message from a gateway, it performs one of these procedures:

■ If a hop-off technology prefix is specified in the admission request, the destination zone is not local, and the **lrq forward-queries** command is set, the gatekeeper sends an LRQ message.

■ If no technology prefix exists, or the technology prefix is not a hop-off technology prefix, the gatekeeper uses the exact E.164 alias in the LRQ message to search its E.164 alias table. Then, depending on the results of the search, it proceeds accordingly:

　　■ If no match is found, and the **lrq reject-unknown** prefix command is set, the gatekeeper sends an LRJ message.

　　■ If a match is found, and the destination zone is the matched zone, the gatekeeper sends an LRQ message to the destination zone.

　　■ If the destination zone is local, and the destination address is registered, the gatekeeper sends an LCF message.

　　■ If the destination zone is local, and the destination address is not registered, but the local gateway is found with the specified technology prefix or the default technology prefix, the gatekeeper sends an LCF message. If no local gateway with the specified technology prefix is found, the gatekeeper sends an LRJ message.

- If the destination zone is local, the destination address is not registered, no matching technology prefix exists, and no default technology prefix is set, the gatekeeper sends an LRJ message.

Gatekeeper Call Routing Examples

Figure 8-22 shows a gatekeeper call routing configuration with zone prefixes and default technology prefixes.

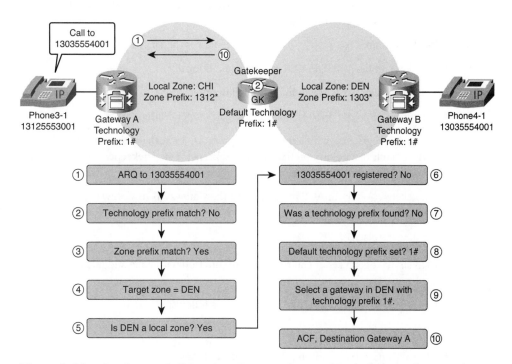

Figure 8-22 *Gatekeeper Call Routing: Zone Prefixes and Default Technology Prefixes*

Zone and technology prefixes in this example are as follows:

- Gatekeeper:
    - Local Zone: CHI (Chicago); Zone Prefix: 1312*
    - Local Zone: DEN (Denver); Zone Prefix: 1303*
    - Default technology prefix: 1#
- Gateway A technology prefix: 1#
- Gateway B technology prefix: 1#

The following steps describe the gatekeeper call routing process:

1. Phone3-1 dials 13035554001 to reach Phone4-1, and Gateway A sends an ARQ message to the gatekeeper.

2. The gatekeeper checks to see whether the dialed number includes a technology prefix, and in this example no technology prefix is specified in the dial string.

3. The zone prefix 1303 is matched.

4. Because of the zone prefix, the gatekeeper knows where to route the call. In this case, the call is routed to the DEN zone.

5. A local configured zone exists on the gatekeeper for the DEN zone.

6. The dialed number 13035554001 isn't registered locally.

7. No technology prefix is found in the dialed number.

8. A default technology prefix is found in the gatekeeper configuration.

9. Gateway B is registered with a technology prefix of 1# at the gatekeeper, which is also the default technology prefix on the gatekeeper. The gatekeeper selects the gateway in the DEN zone (Gateway B) with the technology prefix 1# for call routing.

10. The gatekeeper sends an ACF message with the Gateway B-to-Gateway A destination.

11. The call takes place.

Figure 8-23 shows a gatekeeper call routing configuration with zone and technology prefixes.

Zone and technology prefixes in this example are as follows:

- Gatekeeper:
  - Local Zone: CHI (Chicago); Zone Prefix: 1312*
  - Local Zone: DEN (Denver); Zone Prefix: 1303*
- Gateway A:
  - Technology prefix: 1#
  - Dial peer configured with a technology prefix: 1#
- Gateway B technology prefix: 1#

The following steps describe the gatekeeper call routing process:

1. Phone3-1 dials 13035554001 to reach Phone4-1. Gateway A prefixes 1# to the dialed number and sends an ARQ message to the gatekeeper.

2. The gatekeeper checks whether the dialed number includes a technology prefix. Technology prefix 1# is matching.

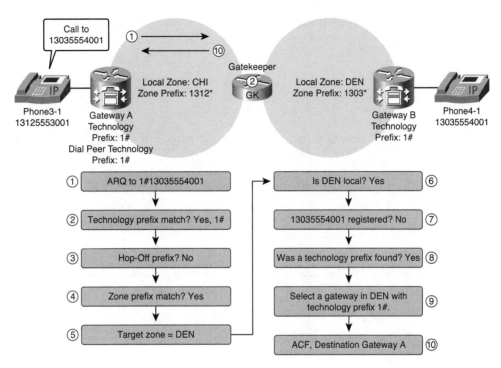

Figure 8-23 *Gatekeeper Call Routing: Zone Prefixes and Technology Prefixes*

3. The gatekeeper checks whether the technology prefix is a hop-off prefix. In this example, no hop off is configured.

4. The zone prefix 1303 is matched.

5. Because of the zone prefix, the gatekeeper knows where to route the call. In this case, the call is routed to the DEN zone.

6. For this configuration, the DEN zone is a locally configured zone on the gatekeeper, so the gatekeeper checks whether the number is registered at the gatekeeper.

7. The dialed number 13035554001 is not registered locally.

8. A default technology prefix is found in the gatekeeper configuration.

9. Gateway B is registered with a technology prefix of 1# at the gatekeeper, which is also the technology prefix for the called number 1#13035554001. The gatekeeper selects the gateway in the DEN zone (Gateway B) with the technology prefix 1# for call routing.

10. The gatekeeper sends an ACF message with the Gateway B-to-Gateway A destination.

11. The call takes place.

Figure 8-24 shows a gatekeeper call routing configuration with zone prefixes and registered numbers.

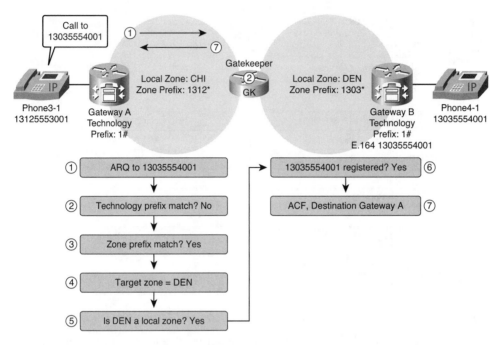

Figure 8-24   *Gatekeeper Call Routing: Zone Prefixes and Registered Numbers*

Zone and technology prefixes in this example are as follows:

- Gatekeeper:
    - Local Zone: CHI (Chicago); Zone Prefix: 1312*
    - Local Zone: DEN (Denver): Zone Prefix: 1303*
- Gateway A technology prefix 1#
- Gateway B:
    - Technology prefix: 1#
    - E.164 number registered at the gatekeeper: 13035554001

The following steps describe the gatekeeper call routing process:

1.   Phone3-1 dials 13035554001 to reach Phone4-1. Gateway A sends an ARQ message to the gatekeeper.

2.   The gatekeeper checks whether the dialed number includes a technology prefix. No technology prefix is matching.

3. The zone prefix 1303 is matched.

4. Because of the zone prefix, the gatekeeper decides where to route the call. In this case, the call is routed to the DEN zone.

5. For this configuration, the DEN zone is a locally configured zone on the gatekeeper, so the gatekeeper checks to see whether the number is registered at the gatekeeper. In the example, the number is registered locally on the gatekeeper.

6. The dialed number 13035554001 is registered locally.

7. The gatekeeper sends an ACF message with the Gateway B-to-Gateway A destination.

Figure 8-25 shows a gatekeeper call routing configuration with a remote zone.

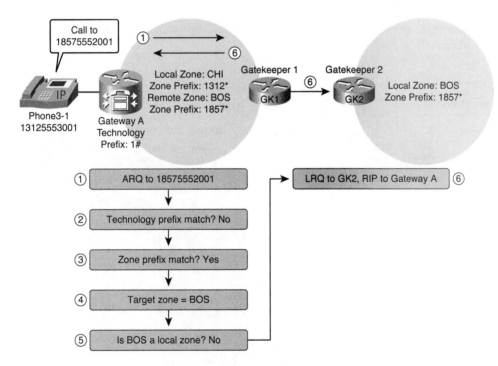

Figure 8-25   *Gatekeeper Call Routing: Remote Zone*

Zone and technology prefixes in this example are as follows:

- Gatekeeper 1:
    - Local Zone: CHI (Chicago); Zone Prefix: 1312*
    - Remote Zone: BOS (Boston); Zone Prefix: 1857*
- Gateway A technology prefix: 1#
- Gatekeeper 2 Local Zone: BOS; Zone Prefix: 1857*

The following steps describe the gatekeeper call routing process:

1. Phone3-1 dials 18575552001 to reach a phone in a remote zone. Gateway A sends an ARQ message to the gatekeeper.

2. The gatekeeper checks to see if the dialed number includes a technology prefix. No technology prefix is matching.

3. The zone prefix 1857 is matching.

4. Because of the zone prefix, the gatekeeper knows where to route the call. In this case, the call is routed to the BOS zone.

5. The BOS zone is configured as a remote zone on the gatekeeper.

6. The gatekeeper sends an LRQ message to Gatekeeper 2 and a RIP message to Gateway A.

Figure 8-26 shows a gatekeeper call routing configuration with a hop-off technology prefix.

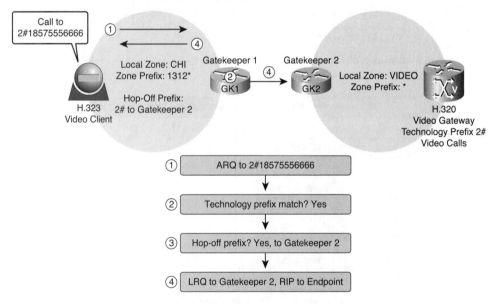

Figure 8-26 *Gatekeeper Call Routing: Hop-Off Technology Prefix*

Zone, hop-off, and technology prefixes in this example are as follows:

- Gatekeeper 1:

    - Local Zone: CHI (Chicago); Zone Prefix: 1312*

    - Hop-off prefix 2# to Gatekeeper 2

- Gatekeeper 2 Local Zone: Video; Zone Prefix: *

- H.320 video gateway technology prefix: 2#

The following steps describe the gatekeeper call routing process:

1. An H.323 video client dials 2#18575556666. The video client is registered at GK1, so it sends the ARQ message for the number 2#18575556666 to GK1.

2. GK1 checks whether the dialed number includes a technology prefix. Technology prefix 2# is matching.

3. The technology prefix is configured with a hop-off prefix, which is pointing to Gatekeeper 2.

4. GK1 sends an LRQ message to GK2 and a RIP message to the video endpoint.

Directory Gatekeepers

In a large network, configuring the prefixes of each zone on all of the gatekeepers can be time consuming. A directory gatekeeper can be used to reduce the configuration steps on nondirectory gatekeepers in a network. LRQ forwarding allows a gatekeeper to be appointed as a directory gatekeeper or super gatekeeper. With this feature, it is only necessary to configure each gatekeeper with its own local zones and zone prefixes, and a single match-all wildcard prefix for the zone of the directory gatekeeper. Only the directory gatekeeper has to be configured with the full set of all zones and zone prefixes within the network.

A directory gatekeeper is basically a gatekeeper that forwards LRQ messages to other gatekeepers, in search of E.164 resolution, as depicted in Figure 8-27. These LRQ messages are triggered by other gatekeepers that need to know how to locate an E.164 address to process a call.

When adding a directory gatekeeper to a network, consider these points:

- Using directory gatekeepers is a network design decision.

- Local zones and LRQ forwarding zones can be mixed.

- An LRQ from a non-Cisco gatekeeper cannot be forwarded.

Directory Gatekeeper Characteristics

Gatekeepers keep track of other H.323 zones and forward calls appropriately. When many H.323 zones are present, gatekeeper configuration can become intensive in administrative terms. In large VoIP installations, you can use a centralized directory gatekeeper that contains a registry of all the different zones and coordinates LRQ-forwarding processes. In the case of directory gatekeepers, you no longer need a full-mesh configuration between interzone gatekeepers.

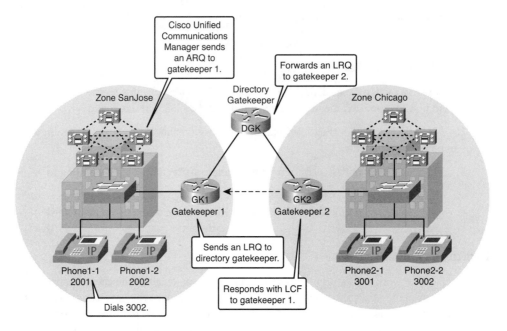

Figure 8-27   *Directory Gatekeepers*

A directory gatekeeper is essentially a super gatekeeper that forwards LRQ messages. LRQ messages are RAS messages triggered by an ARQ message from endpoints that are forwarded from gatekeeper to gatekeeper. There is a limit of five hops for an LRQ message, which allows up to a four-tier gatekeeper hierarchy.

By using a directory gatekeeper, you no longer need a full mesh between gatekeepers, which is a major advantage. Directory gatekeepers centralize a dial plan and also serve as a potential interface to other centralized applications. In a large-scale Voice over IP (VoIP) network, a centralized interface point is required. This interface can interact with other applications and protocol suites, such as the Advanced Intelligent Network (AIN) in Signaling System 7 (SS7), GKTMP route servers, and AAA.

Historically, directory gatekeepers were used only in large service provider wholesale deployments. Nowadays, directory gatekeepers are also used in large-scale enterprises. For example, banks with a large number of Cisco Unified Communications Manager Express sites can use a directory gatekeeper to interconnect the Cisco Unified Communications Manager Express sites with each other.

Using hierarchical gatekeepers provides a significant advantage in terms of scaling. Figure 8-28 shows four network deployments:

- **Small Network—Gateways Only:** In the case of an H.323 network without gatekeepers, a fully meshed dial plan is required for each gateway. This necessitates a significant amount of administrative work. One solution is to use a gatekeeper as shown in diagram 2.

- **Small Network—Simplified with a Gatekeeper:** Gatekeepers enable a connection with each gateway in the network, thus providing a central location for the dial plan and no longer requiring a full-mesh configuration.

- **Medium Network—Multiple Gatekeepers:** In a medium-sized network with multiple gatekeepers, a full mesh is required between the gatekeepers to share dial plan information. When a number of H.323 zones are present, gatekeeper configuration can become administratively intensive.

- **Medium to Large Network—Multiple Gatekeepers and a Directory Gatekeeper:** In large VoIP installations, a centralized directory gatekeeper that contains a registry of all zones and coordinates LRQ forwarding can be used. This eliminates the need for a full-mesh configuration.

For example, a large telephone company might use several gateways and might have one gatekeeper responsible for all the gateways in one city. Another level of centralization could use a centralized directory gatekeeper, sometimes called a *super gatekeeper*, to link multiple cities. This centralized gatekeeper could be an interface to intelligent route engines for dynamic route management, for instance.

Redundancy is always an important issue to consider, but it is more important when you are using a central device like a directory gatekeeper. If the directory gatekeeper shown in diagram 4 fails, the other gatekeepers no longer have access to the dial plan. The best solution is for full redundancy on all levels, including gateways, links, gatekeepers, directory gatekeepers, and all other correlating services.

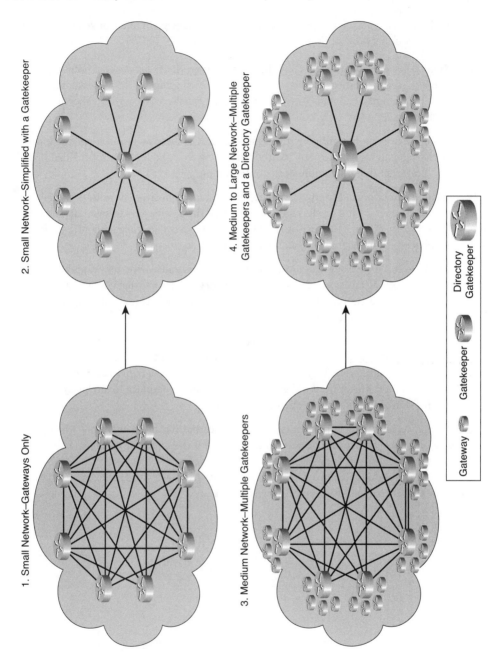

Figure 8-28 *Hierarchical Gatekeepers*

Figure 8-29 shows basic gateway and gatekeeper signaling between zones, but this time with a directory gatekeeper.

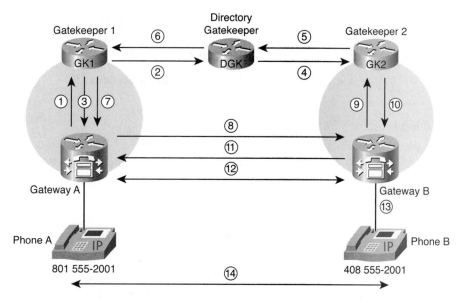

Figure 8-29   *Directory Gatekeeper Signaling*

Phone A places a call to phone number 408 555-2001 for Phone B. Then the following signaling process occurs:

1. Gateway A sends an ARQ to Gatekeeper 1, asking permission to call Phone B.

2. GK1 does a lookup and does not find Phone B registered. GK1 does a prefix lookup and finds a wildcard match with the directory gatekeeper. GK1 sends an LRQ to the DGK.

3. GK1 sends a RIP message to Gateway A.

4. The directory gatekeeper does a prefix lookup and finds GK2. It forwards the LRQ to GK2.

5. GK2 does a lookup and finds Phone B registered. It returns an LCF with the IP address of Gateway B to the directory gatekeeper.

6. The directory gatekeeper returns an LCF to GK1.

7. GK1 returns an ACF with the IP address of Gateway B.

8. Gateway A sends a H.225 call setup message to Gateway B with the phone number of Phone B.

9. Gateway B sends an ARQ to GK2, asking permission to answer the call from Gateway A.

10. GK2 returns an ACF with the IP address of Gateway A to Gateway B.

11. Gateway B sends an alert and a connect message to Gateway A.

12. Gateway B and Gateway A initiate an H.245 capability exchange and open logical channels.

13. Gateway B sets up a POTS call to Phone B at 408-555-2001.

14. Dual RTP streams are established between Gateway A and Gateway B.

Configuring Directory Gatekeepers

Configuration of a directory gatekeeper is fairly straightforward. Figure 8-30 and Examples 8-4, 8-5, 8-6, and 8-7 detail a typical directory gatekeeper configuration.

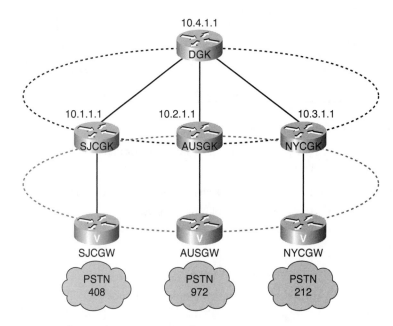

Figure 8-30   *Configuring Directory Gatekeepers*

Example 8-4 illustrates the configuration of the directory gatekeeper.

Example 8-4   *DGK Configuration*

```
DGK#show running-config
... OUTPUT OMITTED ...
gatekeeper
 zone local DGK cisco.com 10.4.1.1
 zone remote SJCGK cisco.com 10.1.1.1 1719
 zone remote AUSGK cisco.com 10.2.1.1 1719
 zone remote NYCGK cisco.com 10.3.1.1 1719
 zone prefix SJCGK 408*
 zone prefix DFWGK 972*
```

```
zone prefix NYCGK 212*
lrq forward-queries
lrq lrj immediate-advance
... OUTPUT OMITTED ...
```

Example 8-5 provides the configuration for the San Jose gatekeeper.

Example 8-5   *SJCGK Configuration*

```
SJCGK#show running-config
... OUTPUT OMITTED ...
gatekeeper
 zone local SJCGK cisco.com 10.1.1.1
 zone remote DGK cisco.com 10.4.1.1 1719
 zone prefix SJCGK 408* gw-priority 10 SJCGW
 zone prefix DGK *
... OUTPUT OMITTED ...
```

Example 8-6 shows the configuration for the Austin gatekeeper.

Example 8-6   *AUSGK Configuration*

```
AUSGK#show running-config
... OUTPUT OMITTED ...
gatekeeper
 zone local AUSGK cisco.com 10.2.1.1
 zone remote DGK cisco.com 10.4.1.1 1719
 zone prefix AUSGK 972* gw-priority 10 AUSGW
 zone prefix DGK *
... OUTPUT OMITTED ...
```

Example 8-7 demonstrates the configuration for the New York gatekeeper.

Example 8-7   *NYCGK Configuration*

```
NYCGK#show running-config
... OUTPUT OMITTED ...
gatekeeper
 zone local NYCGK cisco.com 10.3.1.1
 zone remote DGK cisco.com 10.4.1.1 1719
 zone prefix NYCGK 212* gw-priority 10 NYGW
 zone prefix DGK *
... OUTPUT OMITTED ...
```

Directory Gatekeeper Configuration

You can complete the following tasks to configure a directory gatekeeper:

Step 1. Create a single local zone on the directory gatekeeper with a local address.

Step 2. Create remote zones for each gatekeeper controlled by this directory gatekeeper with addresses of remote gatekeepers.

Step 3. Specify zone prefixes for the remote gatekeepers.

Step 4. Enable forwarding of location requests.

Individual Gatekeeper Configuration

You can complete the following tasks to configure an individual gatekeeper:

Step 1. Create a single local zone on the gatekeeper with a local address.

Step 2. Create a remote zone for the directory gatekeeper with the address of the directory gatekeeper.

Step 3. Specify a zone prefix to register with the directory gatekeeper.

Step 4. Specify the zone prefix of the directory gatekeeper.

Gatekeeper Transaction Message Protocol

GKTMP can extend the call control intelligence of a gatekeeper by providing an interface to a route application server where advanced routing decisions can be made. It converts incoming RAS messages to text messages and sends them to an external server. The server can override default gatekeeper behavior.

Gatekeeper Route Control Server (GKRCS) is an independent platform using GKTMP and can run on Solaris, Linux, or Microsoft Windows NT. An example of the use of GKTMP is where a service provider wants to control the call routing behavior of certain calls during a certain time of the day. The gatekeeper in this case will offload the routing instructions to the route application server and process the request from the server for altered call routing behavior.

GKTMP, as illustrated in Figure 8-31, notifies an external platform (Solaris, Linux, or Microsoft) when a gatekeeper receives RAS messages such as RRQ, URQ, and GRQ when performing endpoint authorization by an application server, or ARQ and LRQ messages for digit translation and call authorization.

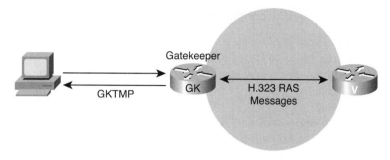

Figure 8-31 *Gatekeeper Transaction Message Protocol*

Verifying Gatekeepers

You can use the **show gatekeeper status** command to display overall gatekeeper status, including authorization and authentication status and zone status. Sample output from this command is shown in Example 8-8.

Example 8-8   show gatekeeper status *Command*

```
GK#show gatekeeper status
Gatekeeper State: UP
    Load Balancing:     DISABLED
    Flow Control:       ENABLED
    Zone Name:          Houston
    Accounting:         DISABLED
    Endpoint Throttling:        DISABLED
    Security:           DISABLED
    Maximum Remote Bandwidth:               unlimited
    Current Remote Bandwidth:           0 kbps
    Current Remote Bandwidth (w/ Alt GKs): 0 kbps
```

The **show gatekeeper endpoints** command shows the gateways that have registered to a gatekeeper. Sample output from this command is shown in Example 8-9.

Example 8-9   show gatekeeper endpoints *Command*

```
GK#show gatekeeper endpoints
                    GATEKEEPER ENDPOINT REGISTRATION
                    ================================
CallSignalAddr  Port  RASSignalAddr   Port  Zone Name      Type   Flags
--------------- ----- --------------- ----- ----------     ----   -----
10.100.100.100  1720  10.100.100.100  56937 SJ             VOIP-GW
    E164-ID: 4085551212
```

continues

Example 8-9   show gatekeeper endpoints *Command   continued*

```
   H323-ID: GW-SJ
   Voice Capacity Max.=  Avail.=  Current.= 0
10.100.100.101  1720  10.100.100.101  49521 SJ                VOIP-GW
   E164-ID: 4085551213
   H323-ID: GW-SJ2
   Voice Capacity Max.=  Avail.=  Current.= 0
Total number of active registrations = 2
```

The **show gatekeeper zone prefix** command displays the zone prefix table for the gatekeeper, as shown in Example 8-10.

Example 8-10   show gatekeeper zone prefix *Command*

```
GK#show gatekeeper zone prefix
     ZONE PREFIX TABLE
     =================
GK-NAME               E164-PREFIX
-------               -----------
gk2                   408*
gk2                   5551001*
gk2                   5551002*
gk2                   5553020*
gk2                   5553020*
gk1                   555....
gk2                   719*
gk2                   919*
```

You can use the **show gatekeeper zone status** command to display the status of zones related to a gatekeeper. Output from the **show gatekeeper zone status** command is provided in Example 8-11.

Example 8-11   show gatekeeper zone status *Command*

```
GK#show gatekeeper zone status
                  GATEKEEPER ZONES
                  ================
GK name     Domain Name   RAS Address    PORT  FLAGS MAX-BW  CUR-BW
                                                     (kbps)  (kbps)
-------     -----------   -----------    ----  ----- ------  ------
sj.xyz.com  xyz.com       10.0.0.0       1719  LS            0
```

Configuring H.323 Gatekeepers

In this section, you will learn how to configure basic gatekeeper functionality. You will learn how to configure gatekeepers and Cisco Unified Communications Manager to operate together. You will also learn how to configure gateways to register with a gatekeeper.

Gatekeeper Configuration Steps

Following are the basic steps necessary to configure a Cisco IOS gatekeeper and gateway:

Step 1.   Configure local and remote zones on the gatekeeper.

Step 2.   Configure zone prefixes for all zones where calls should be routed.

Step 3.   Configure technology prefixes to provide more flexibility in call routing.

Step 4.   Configure gateways to use H.323 gatekeepers.

Step 5.   Configure dial peers.

Figure 8-32 shows a common topology where a single device (which in this scenario is a gatekeeper) manages multiple zones. Only one gatekeeper can control a zone at any time. The San Jose gateway is registered with the gatekeeper in the San Jose zone, and the Houston gateway is registered in the Houston zone with the Houston gatekeeper. The gatekeeper is responsible for call resolution, Call Admission Control (CAC), and other features previously described in this chapter. After the call setup, the IP phones (which in this case are Phone1-1 and Phone2-2) are directly connected.

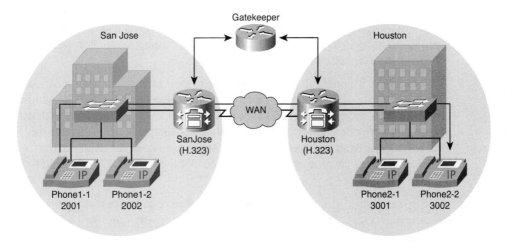

Figure 8-32   *Single Gatekeeper—Multizone Configuration Scenario*

Gateway Selection Process

The gatekeeper maintains a separate gateway list, ordered by priority, for each of its zone prefixes. If a gateway does not have an assigned priority for a zone prefix, it defaults to priority 5, which is the median. To explicitly bar the use of a gateway for a zone prefix, the gateway must be defined as having a priority 0 for that zone prefix.

When selecting gateways, the gatekeeper identifies a target pool of gateways by performing a longest zone prefix match. Then it selects from the target pool according to priorities and resource availability. If all high-priority gateways are busy, a low-priority gateway might be selected.

Cisco H.323 version 2 software improves the gateway selection process as follows:

- When more than one gateway is registered in a zone, the updated **zone prefix** command allows selection priorities to be assigned to these gateways on the basis of the dialed prefix.

- Gateway resource reporting allows the gateway to notify the gatekeeper when H.323 resources are getting low. The gatekeeper uses this information to determine which gateway to use to complete a call.

Configuration Considerations

When configuring a gatekeeper, keep the following in mind:

- Multiple local zones can be defined. The gatekeeper manages all configured local zones. Intrazone behavior is between the gatekeeper and the endpoints and gateways within a specific zone. A gatekeeper can support more than one zone. Even though there is a single gatekeeper per local zone, the communications between zones are considered to be interzone. So, the same gatekeeper can support both intrazone and interzone communications.

- Only one RAS IP argument can be defined for all local zones. You cannot configure each zone to use a different RAS IP address. If you define this IP address in the first zone definition, you can omit it for all subsequent zones that automatically pick up this address. If you set it in a subsequent zone local command, it also changes the RAS IP address of all previously configured local zones. After the IP address is defined, you can change it by reissuing any zone local command with a different RAS IP address.

- You cannot remove a local zone if there are endpoints or gateways registered in it. To remove the local zone, first shut down the gatekeeper, which forces the endpoints, gateways, and the local zone to unregister.

- Multiple logical gatekeepers control the multiple zones on the same Cisco IOS platform.

- The maximum number of local zones defined in a gatekeeper should not exceed 100.

Basic Gatekeeper Configuration Commands

Table 8-2 shows basic gatekeeper configuration commands.

Table 8-2 *Basic Gatekeeper Configuration Commands*

Command	Purpose
Gatekeeper	Enters gatekeeper configuration mode.
zone local *gatekeeper-name domain-name* [*ras-ip-address*] [invia *inbound_gatekeeper* | outvia *outbound_gatekeeper* [enable-intrazone]]	Specifies a zone controlled by a gatekeeper. ■ *gatekeeper-name*: Specifies the zone name. This is usually the fully qualified domain name of the gatekeeper. ■ *domain-name*: Specifies the domain name served by this gatekeeper. ■ *ras-ip-address*: (Optional) Specifies the IP address of one of the interfaces on the gatekeeper. When the gatekeeper responds to gatekeeper discovery messages, it signals the endpoint or gateway to use this address in future communications. ■ invia *inbound_gatekeeper*: Specifies the gatekeeper used for calls entering this zone. ■ outvia *outbound_gatekeeper*: Specifies the gatekeeper used for calls leaving this zone. ■ enable-intrazone: Forces all intrazone calls to use the via gatekeeper.
zone remote *other-gatekeeper-name other-domain-name other-gatekeeper-ip-address* [*port-number*] [cost *cost-value* [priority *priority-value*]] [*foreign-domain*] [invia *inbound_gatekeeper*] | [outvia *outbound_gatekeeper*]	Statically specifies a remote zone if domain name service (DNS) is unavailable or undesirable. ■ *other-gatekeeper-name*: Name of the remote gatekeeper. ■ *other-domain-name*: Domain name of the remote gatekeeper. ■ *other-gatekeeper-ip-address*: IP address of the remote gatekeeper. ■ *port-number*: (Optional) RAS signaling port number for the remote zone. The range is 1–65535. If the value is not set, the default is the well-known RAS port number of 1719. ■ cost *cost-value*: (Optional) Cost of the zone. The range is 1–100. The default is 50. ■ priority *priority-value*: (Optional) Priority of the zone. The range is 1–100. The default is 50. ■ *foreign-domain*: (Optional) The cluster is in a different administrative domain. ■ invia *inbound_gatekeeper*: Specifies the gatekeeper for calls entering this zone. ■ outvia *outbound_gatekeeper*: Specifies the gatekeeper for calls leaving this zone.

continues

Table 8-2 *Basic Gatekeeper Configuration Commands* *(continued)*

Command	Purpose
zone prefix *gatekeeper-name e164-prefix* [blast | seq] [gw-priority *priority gw-alias* [*gw-alias*, ...]]	Adds a prefix to the gatekeeper zone list. The optional **blast** and **seq** parameters are for fault tolerant gatekeeper networks. ■ *gatekeeper-name*: Name of a local or remote gatekeeper, which must have been defined by using the zone local or zone remote command. ■ *e164-prefix*: E.164 prefix in standard form followed by dots (.). Each dot represents a number in the E.164 address. ■ **blast**: (Optional) If you list multiple hop-offs, this indicates that the LRQs should be sent simultaneously to the gatekeepers based on the order in which they were listed. The default is seq. ■ **seq**: (Optional) If you list multiple hop-offs, this indicates that the LRQs should be sent sequentially to the gatekeepers based on the order in which they were listed. ■ **gw-priority** *priority gw-alias*: (Optional) Defines how the gatekeeper selects gateways in its local zone for calls to numbers beginning with the specified e164-prefix. The range is 0–10, where 0 prevents the gatekeeper from using the gateway's gw-alias for that prefix, and 10 places the highest priority on gateway's gw-alias. The default is 5.
gw-type-prefix *type-prefix* [[hopoff *gkid1*] [hopoff *gkid2*] [hopoff *gkidn*] [seq | blast]] [default-technology] [[gw ipaddr *ipaddr* [*port*]]]	Configures a technology prefix in the gatekeeper. Technology prefixes can be configured either on a gatekeeper or directly on a gateway. When using special flags (hop off or default-technology), configure the prefix on the gatekeeper and on the gateway. ■ *type-prefix*: A technology prefix is recognized and is stripped before checking for the zone prefix. ■ **hopoff** *gkid*: (Optional) Use this option to specify the gatekeeper where the call is to hop off, regardless of the zone prefix in the destination address. The gkid argument refers to a gatekeeper previously configured using the zone local and/or zone remote commands. ■ **seq | blast**: (Optional) If you list multiple hop offs, this indicates that the LRQs should be sent sequentially or simultaneously (blast) to the gatekeepers according to the order in which they were listed. ■ **default-technology**: (Optional) Gateways registering with this prefix option are used as the default for routing any addresses that are otherwise unresolved.

Table 8-2   *Basic Gatekeeper Configuration Commands   (continued)*

Command	Purpose
	■ **gw ipaddr** *ipaddr* [port]: (Optional) Use this option to indicate the gateway is incapable of registering technology prefixes. When it registers, it adds the gateway to the group for this type prefix, just as if it had sent the technology prefix in its registration.
no shutdown	Brings a gatekeeper online.

Configuring Gatekeeper Zones

The scenario presented in Figure 8-33 and Example 8-12 shows the basic steps to configure gatekeepers managing two local zones.

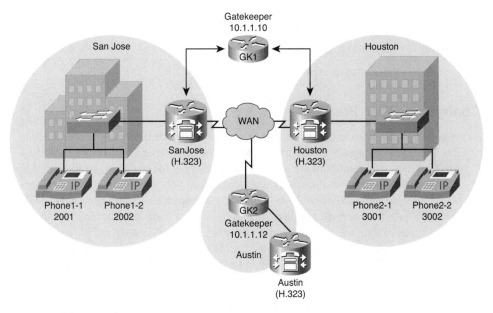

Figure 8-33   *Configuring Zones*

Example 8-12   *Zone Configuration Example*

```
GK1(config)#gatekeeper
GK1(config-gk)#zone local SanJose cisco.com 10.1.1.10
GK1(config-gk)#zone local Houston cisco.com enable-intrazone
GK1(config-gk)#zone remote Austin cisco.com 10.1.1.12
GK1(config-gk)#no shutdown
```

The gatekeeper is configured for the two zones: San Jose and Houston.

You can use the following procedure to configure zones on a gatekeeper:

Step 1.   Enter gatekeeper configuration mode.

```
GK1(config)#gatekeeper
```

Step 2.   Specify local zones to be controlled by the gatekeeper.

```
GK1(config-gk)#zone local SanJose cisco.com 10.1.1.10
GK1(config-gk)#zone local Houston cisco.com enable-intrazone
```

> **Note**   Setting the IP address for one local zone makes it the address used for all local zones.

Step 3.   Specify a remote gatekeeper to which the local gatekeeper can send location requests (LRQs).

```
GK1(config-gk)#zone remote Austin cisco.com 10.1.1.12
```

Step 4.   Activate the gatekeeper.

```
GK1(config-gk)#no shutdown
```

Configuring Zone Prefixes

A zone prefix is a string of numbers that is used to associate a gateway to a dialed number in a zone. In Figure 8-34 and Example 8-13, the gatekeeper supports the 2... and 3... zone prefixes. The four digits are used by the gatekeeper for resolving the addresses. The San Jose and Houston sites use these digits for dialing between the sites. The gateways in each zone register with either "2" or "3" at the gatekeeper. This allows the gatekeeper to route the calls for a specific number range to the correct zone and gateway. Instead of using 2... and 3... for the zone prefix configuration, you could use 2* and 3* for the prefixes. The *symbol defines an endless number of digits. For example, a call to 24, 22224444, 2123, or 299999999999 would be routed to the designated gateway.

Example 8-13   *Zone Prefix Configuration Example*

```
GK1(config)#gatekeeper
GK1(config)#zone local SanJose cisco.com 10.1.1.10
GK1(config)#zone local Houston cisco.com
GK1(config)#zone prefix SanJose1 2... gw-priority 5 SanJose
GK1(config)#zone prefix SanJose2 2... gw-priority 10 Houston
GK1(config)#no shutdown
```

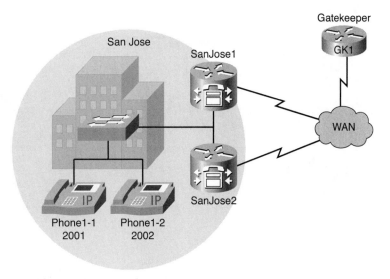

Figure 8-34 *Configuring Zone Prefixes*

You can complete the following steps to configure zone prefixes on a gatekeeper.

Step 1.   Enter gatekeeper configuration mode.

```
GK1(config)#gatekeeper
```

Step 2.   Add a prefix to the gatekeeper zone list.

```
GK1(config-gk)#zone prefix SanJose1 2... gw-priority 5 SanJose
GK1(config-gk)#zone prefix SanJose2 2... gw-priority 10 SanJose
```

Configuring Technology Prefixes

To enable the gatekeeper to select the appropriate hop-off gateway, use the **gw-type-prefix** command to configure technology or gateway-type prefixes. Select technology prefixes to denote different types or classes of gateways. The gateways are then configured to register with their gatekeepers using these technology prefixes.

As an example, Example 8-14 and Figure 8-35 illustrate a sample technology prefix configuration, with 99# being used as a voice gateway technology prefix and 1# being used as a default technology prefix.

Example 8-14 *Zone Prefix Configuration Example*

```
GK1(config)#gatekeeper
GK1(config-gk)#zone local SanJose cisco.com 10.1.1.10
GK1(config-gk)#zone local Houston cisco.com
GK1(config-gk)#zone prefix SanJose 2... gw-priority 10 SanJose
GK1(config-gk)#zone prefix Houston 3... gw-priority 10 Houston
GK1(config-gk)#gw-type-prefix 99#* gw ipaddr 192.168.1.1 1720
GK1(config-gk)#gw-type-prefix 1#* default-technology
GK1(config-gk)#no shutdown
```

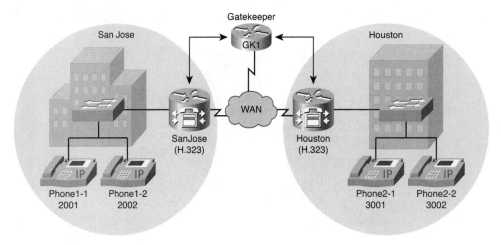

Figure 8-35   *Configuring Technology Prefixes*

As an additional example, voice gateways might register with a technology prefix of 1#, and H.320 gateways might register with a technology prefix of 2#. If several gateways of the same type exist, configure them to register with the same prefix type. By having them register with the same prefix type, the gatekeeper treats the gateways as a pool out of which a random selection is made whenever a call for that prefix type arrives.

Callers will need to know the technology prefixes that are defined and the type of device they are trying to reach. This enables them to prepend the appropriate technology prefix to the destination address for the type of gateway needed to reach the destination.

If the callers know the type of device they are trying to reach, they can include the technology prefix in the destination address to indicate the type of gateway to use to get to the destination. For example, if a caller knows that address 2125551111 belongs to a regular telephone, the destination address of 99#2125551111 can be used, where 99# indicates the address should be resolved by a voice gateway. When the voice gateway receives the call for 99#2125551111, it strips off the technology prefix and bridges the next leg of the call to the telephone at 2125551111.

Additionally, when you use the **gw-type-prefix** command, you can define a specific gateway-type prefix as the default gateway type to be used for addresses that cannot be resolved. This also forces a technology prefix to always hop off in a particular zone.

If the majority of calls hop off on a particular type of gateway, you can configure the gatekeeper to use that type of gateway as the default type so that callers no longer have to prepend a technology prefix on the address. For example, if voice gateways are mostly used in a network, and all voice gateways have been configured to register with technology prefix 1#, the gatekeeper can be configured to use 1# gateways as the default technology if this command is entered:

```
GK1(config-gk)#gw-type-prefix 1#* default-technology
```

Now a caller no longer needs to prepend 1# to use a voice gateway. Any address that does not contain an explicit technology prefix will be routed to one of the voice gateways that registered with 1#.

With this default technology definition, a caller could ask the gatekeeper for admission to 2125551111. If the local gatekeeper does not recognize the zone prefix as belonging to any remote zone, it will route the call to one of its local (1#) voice gateways so the call hops off locally. However, if it knows the San Jose gatekeeper handles the 212 area code, it can send a location request for 2125551111 to that gatekeeper. This requires the San Jose gatekeeper also be configured with some default gateway-type prefix and its voice gateways be registered with that prefix type.

> **Note**   You must use consistent technology prefixes throughout a gatekeeper deployment and have a consistent dial plan mapped out prior to implementation.

Configuring Gateways to Use H.323 Gatekeepers

Following are the configuration steps for registering a gateway on a gatekeeper:

Step 1.   Enable the gateway process on the router.

Step 2.   Configure interface commands for H.323 registration at the gatekeeper.

Step 3.   Configure the dial peers that are pointing to the gatekeeper.

Step 4.   If necessary, prevent ephone-dn and dial-peer registration at the gatekeeper.

Example 8-15 and Figure 8-36 show the configuration for a gateway registering with a gatekeeper.

Example 8-15   *H.323 Gateway Configuration*

```
SanJose#show running-config
gateway
!
interface Loopback 0
 ip address 192.168.1.3 255.255.255.0
 h323-gateway voip interface
 h323-gateway voip bind srcaddr 192.168.1.3
 h323-gateway voip id GK1 ipaddr 192.168.1.15 1719 priority 1
 h323-gateway voip h323-id Houston
 h323-gateway voip tech-prefix 1#
```

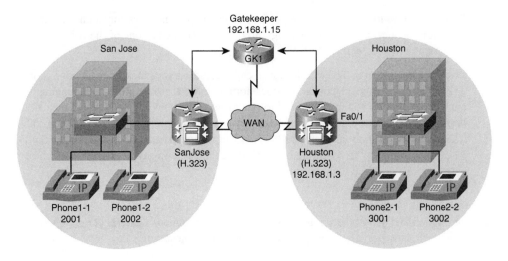

Figure 8-36   *Configuring Gateways to Use H.323 Gatekeepers*

You can use the following steps to configure gateways to use H.323 gatekeepers.

Step 1.   Enable the H.323 VoIP gateway to register with a gatekeeper.

```
Router(config)#gateway
```

Sometimes it is helpful to enable the gateway process at the end of your gateway configuration to avoid automatic gateway registration at the gatekeeper. For example, this is useful if you have multiple gatekeepers and want to make sure you are unicasting to a specific gatekeeper or using a specific H.323 ID. This allows all interface commands to be entered before the gateway attempts registration with the gatekeeper.

Step 2.   Enter interface configuration mode for the interface you intend to use for communication with the H.323 gatekeeper.

```
Router(config)#interface loopback 0
```

Step 3.   Give the interface an IP address.

```
Router(config-if)#ip-address 192.168.1.3 255.255.255.0
```

Step 4.   Configure the interface as an H.323 gateway interface.

```
Router(config-if)#h323-gateway voip interface
```

Step 5.   Define the IP address on the gateway to be used for H.323 communication.

```
Router(config-if)#h323-gateway voip bind srcaddr 192.168.1.3
```

Step 6.   Define the name and location of the gatekeeper.

```
Router(config-if)#h323-gateway voip id Houston ipaddr 192.168.1.15 1719
     priority 1
```

This command is used to specify the IP address of the gatekeeper and the zone the gateway should register with, in this case **Houston**. Without the **voip id** parameter, the gateway will use multicast for gatekeeper discovery. When using multicast, the gateway will register with the first available zone on the gatekeeper. The gatekeeper ID is the zone the gateway should register with.

Step 7. Specify the H.323 gateway name to identify it to its associated gatekeeper.

```
Router(config-if)#h323-gateway voip h323-id Houston
```

This is an optional command used to identify a gateway to its associated gatekeeper. In this case, the gateway will register with the name **Houston** at the gatekeeper.

Step 8. Specify the technology prefix the gateway registers with the gatekeeper.

```
Router(config-if)#h323-gateway voip tech-prefix 1#
```

The gateway will inform the gatekeeper it wants to register with a technology prefix of 1#. Each technology prefix can contain as many as 11 characters. Although not strictly necessary, a pound sign (#) is frequently used as the last digit in a technology prefix.

Table 8-3 provides a table of gateway interface configuration commands and explains their purpose.

Table 8-3 *Gateway Interface Configuration Commands*

Command	Purpose
h323-gateway voip interface	Identifies an interface as a VoIP gateway interface.
h323-gateway voip id *gatekeeper-id* {ipaddr *ip-address* [*port*]| multicast} [priority *priority*]	(Optional) Defines the name and location of the gatekeeper for this gateway. Following are the keywords and arguments: ■ *gatekeeper-id*: H.323 identification of the gatekeeper, which should match a zone configured on a gatekeeper. If no match is found, the gatekeeper will register the gateway with the first configured local zone. ■ **ipaddr** *ip-address*: IP address used to identify the gatekeeper. ■ *port*: UDP port number used for communicating with a gatekeeper. ■ **multicast**: Used by the gateway to locate a gatekeeper. ■ **priority** *priority*: This is the priority of this gatekeeper. The acceptable range is 1–127, and the default is 127.

continues

Table 8-3 *Gateway Interface Configuration Commands* *(continued)*

Command	Purpose
h323-gateway voip h323-id *interface-id*	(Optional) Defines the H.323 name of the gateway that identifies this gateway to its associated gatekeeper.
	Usually this ID is the name of the gateway, with the gatekeeper domain name appended to the end: name@domainname.
h323-gateway voip tech-prefix *prefix*	(Optional) Defines the numbers used as the technology prefix that the gateway uses to register with a gatekeeper.
	This command can contain up to 11 characters. Although it is not strictly necessary, a pound symbol (#) is frequently used as the last digit in a prefix. Valid characters are 0–9, #, and *.

Dial-Peer Configuration

The VoIP dial peer determines how to direct calls that originate from a local voice port into a VoIP cloud to the RAS session target. The session target indicates the address of the remote gateway where the call is terminated.

In the scenario presented in Figure 8-37 and Example 8-16, all calls designated for 2... will be routed from Houston to the gatekeeper.

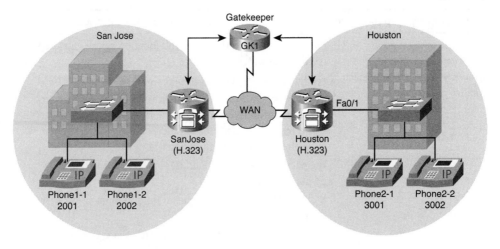

Figure 8-37 *Dial-Peer Configuration Topology*

Example 8-16   *Configuring a Dial Peer for Gatekeeper Operation*

```
GK1(config)#gateway
GK1(config)#dial-peer voice 1 voip
GK1(config-dial-peer)#destination pattern 2...
GK1(config-dial-peer)#tech-prefix 1#
GK1(config-dial-peer)#session target ras
```

You can use the following steps to create a dial peer to be used with a gatekeeper.

Step 1.   Enter dial-peer configuration mode.

```
Router(config)#dial-peer voice 1 voip
```

Step 2.   Specify the E.164 address associated with this dial peer.

```
Router(config-dial-peer)#destination pattern 2...
```

Step 3.   (Optional) Define the numbers used as the technology prefix that the gateway uses to register with the gatekeeper.

```
Router(config-dial-peer)#tech-prefix 1#
```

Note   In this example, no prepending of a technology prefix is necessary because of the default technology configuration on the gatekeeper.

Step 4.   Specify that the RAS protocol is being used to determine the IP address of the session target (meaning a gatekeeper translates the E.164 address to an IP address).

```
Router(config-dial-peer)#session target ras
```

Note   When dealing with services numbers, such as 911, make sure to include the **no e.164 register** command.

Example 8-17 shows the use of the **no e.164 register** command when configuring a dial peer for 911 operation.

Example 8-17   *911 Dial-Peer Configuration*

```
Router(config)#dial-peer voice 911 pots
Router(config-dial-peer)#destination pattern 911
Router(config-dial-peer)#prefix 911
Router(config-dial-peer)#no e.164 register
Router(config-dial-peer)#session target ras
```

Verifying Gatekeeper Functionality

Cisco IOS supports several commands for verifying and troubleshooting H.323 gateway and gatekeeper configuration, such as the following:

■ **show gatekeeper gw-type-prefix:** Displays the technology prefix of a gateway

■ **show gatekeeper status:** Displays the overall gatekeeper status, including zone status

■ **show gatekeeper zone prefix:** Displays the zone prefixes known to a gatekeeper

■ **show gatekeeper calls:** Displays current calls known to a gatekeeper

■ **show gatekeeper endpoints:** Displays endpoints currently registered with a gatekeeper

■ **show gatekeeper zone status:** Displays the status of zones registered with a gatekeeper

■ **debug h225 {asn1 | events}:** Displays H.225 activity in real-time

■ **debug h245 {asn1 | events}:** Displays H.245 activity in real-time

■ **debug ras:** Displays RAS messages, in real-time, to and from a gatekeeper

Note   The output from some of these commands is provided earlier in the "Verifying Gatekeepers" section of this chapter.

The following examples illustrate the output of a few of these commands. First, you can use the **show gatekeeper gw-type-prefix** command to display configured prefixes, as illustrated in Example 8-18.

Example 8-18   show gatekeeper gw-type-prefix *Command*

```
Router#show gatekeeper status
    Gatekeeper State: UP
    Load Balancing:    DISABLED
    Flow Control:      DISABLED
    Zone Name:         HQ
    Zone Name:         BR
    Accounting:        DISABLED
    Endpoint Throttling:        DISABLED
    Security:          DISABLED
    Maximum Remote Bandwidth:            unlimited
    Current Remote Bandwidth:            0 kbps
    Current Remote Bandwidth (w/ Alt GKs): 0 kbps
```

The **show gatekeeper status** command, as shown in Example 8-19, displays the status of the gatekeeper.

Example 8-19   show gatekeeper status *Command*

```
Router#show gatekeeper status
    Gatekeeper State: UP
    Load Balancing:    DISABLED
    Flow Control:      DISABLED
    Zone Name:         HQ
    Zone Name:         BR
    Accounting:        DISABLED
    Endpoint Throttling:        DISABLED
    Security:          DISABLED
    Maximum Remote Bandwidth:            unlimited
    Current Remote Bandwidth:            0 kbps
    Current Remote Bandwidth (w/ Alt GKs): 0 kbps
```

Additionally, you can use the **show gatekeeper zone prefix** command to display configured zone prefixes, as demonstrated in Example 8-20.

Example 8-20　show gatekeeper zone prefix *Command*

```
Router#show gatekeeper zone prefix
      ZONE PREFIX TABLE
      =================
GK-NAME               E164-PREFIX
-------               -----------
HQ                    1...
BR                    2...
```

You can use the **show gatekeeper endpoints** command to display registered endpoints of the gatekeeper, as shown in Example 8-21.

Example 8-21　show gatekeeper endpoints *Command*

```
Router#show gatekeeper endpoints
                    GATEKEEPER ENDPOINT REGISTRATION
                    ===================================
CallSignalAddr  Port  RASSignalAddr   Port  Zone Name        Type     Flags
--------------- ----- --------------- ----- ---------        ----     -----
10.1.250.101    1720  10.1.250.101    58963 HQ               H323-GW
   H323-ID: GW-A1
   E164-ID: 1101
   E164-ID: 1102
   Voice Capacity Max.= Avail.= Current.= 0
10.1.250.102    1720  10.1.250.102    58306 BR               VOIP-GW
   H323-ID: GW-A2
   Voice Capacity Max.= Avail.= Current.= 0
Total number of active registrations = 2
```

Providing Call Admission Control with H.323

In this section, you will learn how to implement gatekeeper-based CAC. You will also learn how CAC is working and how it is responsible for managing admission control and bandwidth for both voice and video calls. Further, you will learn the functions of the RAI mechanism and how it is configured in an H.323 network.

Gatekeeper Zone Bandwidth Operation

Consider the Cisco Unified IP Communications system shown in Figure 8-38. Because the IP network is based on a packet-switched network (PSN), no dedicated circuits are established to set up an IP communications call. Instead, the IP packets containing the voice samples are routed across the IP network together with other types of data packets.

QoS is used to differentiate the voice packets from the data packets, but bandwidth resources, especially on IP WAN links, are not infinite. Therefore, network administrators dedicate a certain amount of "priority" bandwidth to voice traffic on each IP WAN link. However, after the provisioned bandwidth has been fully utilized, the Cisco Unified IP Communications system must reject subsequent calls to avoid oversubscription of the priority queue on the IP WAN link, which would cause quality degradation for all voice calls.

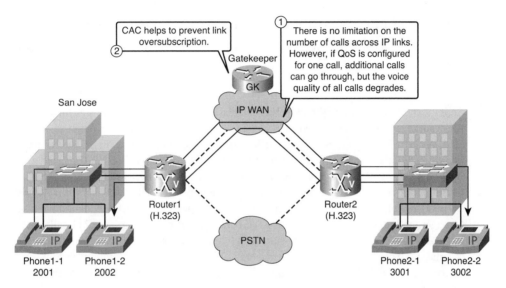

Figure 8-38   *Dial-Peer Configuration Topology*

This function is known as CAC and is essential to guarantee good voice quality in a multisite deployment. The gatekeeper maintains a record of all active calls so it can manage bandwidth in a zone.

You can use CAC to help maintain a desired level of voice quality over a WAN link. For example, you can use CAC to regulate the voice quality on a T1 line that connects your main campus to a remote site.

CAC regulates voice quality by limiting the number of calls that can be active on a particular link at the same time. CAC does not guarantee a particular level of audio quality on the link, but it does allow you to regulate the amount of bandwidth consumed by active calls on the link.

The Cisco IOS gatekeeper is the device in the IP communications network that is responsible for CAC between these devices:

■   Cisco Unified Communications Manager

■   Cisco Unified Communications Manager Express

■   H.323 gateways

The gatekeeper requires a static policy-based configuration of the available resources. The gatekeeper cannot assign variable resources like the Resource Reservation Protocol (RSVP) is able to do.

Zone Bandwidth Calculation

Zone bandwidth in a gatekeeper network can be calculated with this simple formula:

(Number of Calls) * (Codec Payload Bandwidth) * 2 = Zone Bandwidth

With this formula, the needed bandwidth in a gatekeeper network can be easily defined.

For example, following is a calculation for three simultaneous G.711 calls in a gatekeeper network:

3 * 64 kbps * 2 = 384 kbps

An important point for every bandwidth calculation is the number of devices for which you want to calculate the bandwidth. Gatekeepers and Cisco Unified Communications Manager servers have different bandwidth values for the same codecs. In a Cisco Unified Communications Manager environment, a G.711 call is assumed to use 80 kbps, and a G.729 call is assumed to use 24 kbps. However, in a gatekeeper environment, a G.711 call consumes 128 kbps, and a G.729 call consumes 16 kbps. If a call is signaled from a Cisco Unified Communications Manager server to a gatekeeper, Cisco Unified Communications Manager internally assumes that 80 kbps of bandwidth is required for a G.711 call, but will signal in its ARQ message to its gatekeeper a request for a G.711 call with 128 kbps of bandwidth required. Similarly, when using G.729, Cisco Unified Communications Manager will use 24 kbps for internal CAC calculations, but request 16 kbps from a gatekeeper.

Example 8-22 shows a gatekeeper with an active G.711 call requested by Cisco Unified Communications Manager. Note the 128 kbps in the "BW" column.

Example 8-22   *Viewing Active Gatekeeper Calls*

```
GK#show gatekeeper calls
Total number of active calls = 1.
                                    GATEKEEPER CALL INFO
                                    ====================
LocalCallID                         Age(secs)      BW
2-14476                             59             128(Kbps)
 Endpt(s): Alias                    E.164Addr
   src EP: CHI-CUCME                13125553001
               CallSignalAddr   Port   RASSignalAddr   Port
               192.168.3.254    1720   192.168.3.254   52668
 Endpt(s): Alias                    E.164Addr
   dst EP: ipipgw                   49895556666
               CallSignalAddr   Port   RASSignalAddr   Port
               192.168.1.3      1720   192.168.1.3     52060
```

The gatekeeper is the central device in the network. The bandwidth is configured for the network on the gatekeeper. The available bandwidth will be checked by the gatekeeper for every call, as illustrated in Figure 8-39.

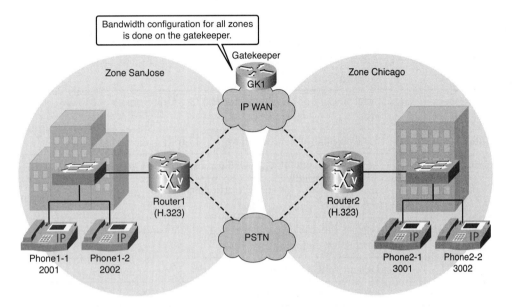

Figure 8-39 *Zone Bandwidth Sample Topology*

The **bandwidth** command allows the gatekeeper to manage the bandwidth limitations within a zone, across zones, and at a per-session level. By default, the maximum aggregate bandwidth is unlimited.

Example 8-23 configures the default maximum bandwidth for traffic between one zone and another zone to 128 kbps, the default maximum bandwidth for all zones to 5 Mbps, the default maximum bandwidth for a single session within any zone up to 384 kbps, and the default maximum bandwidth for a single session with zone "Denver" of up to 256 kbps.

Example 8-23 *Zone Bandwidth Command Example*

```
GK1(config)#gatekeeper
GK1(config-gk)#bandwidth interzone default 128
GK1(config-gk)#bandwidth total default 5000
GK1(config-gk)#bandwidth session default 384
GK1(config-gk)#bandwidth session zone denver 256
```

The **bandwidth** Command

The full command syntax for the **bandwidth** command is as follows:

```
bandwidth {interzone | total | session | remote | check-destination} {default |
    zone zone-name} bandwidth-size
```

Table 8-4 describes the parameters of the **bandwidth** command.

Table 8-4   *Bandwidth Command Parameters*

Parameter	Description
Interzone	Total amount of bandwidth for H.323 traffic from a zone to any other zone.
Total	Total amount of bandwidth for H.323 traffic allowed in a zone.
Session	Maximum bandwidth allowed for a session in a zone.
Remote	Total bandwidth for H.323 traffic between this gatekeeper and any other gatekeeper.
check-destination	Enables the gatekeeper to verify available bandwidth resources at a destination endpoint.
Default	Default value for all zones.
zone *zone-name*	Specifies a particular zone.
bandwidth-size	Maximum bandwidth, in kbps. For **interzone, remote** and **total**, the range is 1–10,000,000. For **session**, the range is 1–5000.

Following are Cisco-provided usage guidelines for the **bandwidth** command:

- To specify maximum bandwidth for traffic between one zone and any other zone, use the default keyword with the interzone keyword.

- To specify maximum bandwidth for traffic within one zone or for traffic between that zone and another zone (interzone or intrazone), use the default keyword with the total keyword.

- To specify maximum bandwidth for a single session within a specific zone, use the zone keyword with the session keyword.

- To specify maximum bandwidth for a single session within any zone, use the **default** keyword with the **session** keyword.

Zone Bandwidth Configuration Example

Figure 8-40 and Example 8-24 show a sample of a configuration for a gatekeeper.

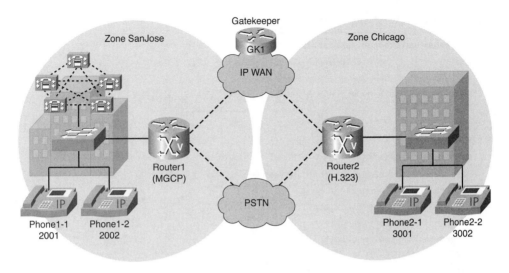

Figure 8-40 *Zone Bandwidth Configuration Topology*

Example 8-24 *Zone Bandwidth Configuration Example*

```
GK1(config)#gatekeeper
GK1(config-gk)#zone local SanJose cisco.com 192.168.1.15
GK1(config-gk)#zone local Chicago cisco.com
GK1(config-gk)#zone prefix SanJose 2... gw-priority 10 ICT_CM_1
GK1(config-gk)#zone prefix SanJose 2... gw-priority  9 ICT_CM_2
GK1(config-gk)#zone prefix Chicago 3... gw-priority 10 CME
GK1(config-gk)#gw-type-prefix 1#* default-technology
GK1(config-gk)#bandwidth interzone zone SanJose 384
GK1(config-gk)#bandwidth interzone zone Chicago 256
GK1(config-gk)#no shutdown
```

There are two local zones: SanJose and Chicago. Notice that the **bandwidth interzone** commands are highlighted. In the **bandwidth** command, the **interzone** option specifies the bandwidth from one zone to another zone. The first **bandwidth** command allocates 384 kbps of bandwidth for H.323 traffic between the SanJose zone and any other zone. The second **bandwidth** command allocates 256 kbps of bandwidth for H.323 traffic between the Chicago zone and any other zone.

Verifying Zone Bandwidth Operation

Example 8-25 shows the output of the **show gatekeeper zone status** command. In the bandwidth information output, you can see the maximum interzone bandwidth for all calls in the SanJose zone. In this scenario, a bandwidth of 384 kbps is configured.

Example 8-25 *Verifying Zone Bandwidth Operation*

```
Router#show gatekeeper zone status
                GATEKEEPER ZONES

                =================

GK name        Domain Name    RAS Address      PORT  FLAGS
-------        -----------    -----------      ----- -----


SanJose        cisco.com      192.168.1.15     1719  LS
  BANDWIDTH INFORMATION (kbps) :
    Maximum total bandwidth : unlimited
    Current total bandwidth : 0
    Maximum interzone bandwidth : 384
    Current interzone bandwidth : 0
    Maximum session bandwidth : unlimited
  SUBNET ATTRIBUTES :
    All Other Subnets : (Enabled)
```

RAI in Gatekeeper Networks

To enable gatekeepers to make intelligent call-routing decisions, the gateway can be configured to report the status of its resource availability to its gatekeeper. Resources that are monitored are digital service level 0 (DS0) and digital signal processor (DSP) channel resources.

The gateway reports its resource status to the gatekeeper with the use of RAI RAS messages. When a monitored resource falls below a configurable threshold, the gateway sends an RAI RAS message to the gatekeeper that indicates the gateway is almost out of resources. When the available resources then exceed another configurable threshold, the gateway sends an RAI that indicates the resource depletion condition no longer exists.

Resource reporting thresholds, as depicted in Figure 8-41, are configured by using the **resource threshold** command under the gateway command-line interface (CLI). The upper and lower thresholds are separately configurable to prevent the gateway from operating sporadically because of the availability or lack of resources.

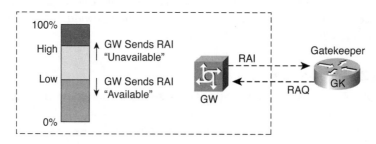

Figure 8-41 *Resource Availability Indicator Thresholds*

RAI Configuration

Following is the syntax of the **resource threshold** command, which is available in Cisco IOS to enable RAI on endpoints.

```
resource threshold [all] [high percentage-value] [low percentage-value]
```

Use the **resource threshold** command in gateway configuration mode to configure a gateway to report H.323 resource availability to its gatekeeper. You can specify **all** or specific **high** and **low** values. The default for high and low values is 90. Use the **no** form of this command to disable gateway resource-level reporting.

This command also includes an optional **report-policy** parameter to specify how resource utilization is calculated. Available resource types to be reported can be either of the following:

- **Idle-only:** Includes free and in-use channels only. This is the default calculation.

- **Addressable:** Includes free, in-use, and disabled channels.

RAI has to be configured on each endpoint that should send RAI information in your network. Figure 8-42 shows two gateways that send RAI information to a gatekeeper. The gatekeeper will check the RAI information to verify the load on each gateway in order to route the call.

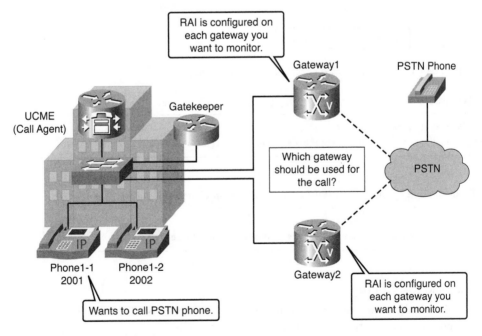

Figure 8-42   *RAI Configuration*

The RAI Feature

In Figure 8-43 and Examples 8-26 and 8-27, a **high** threshold of 70 is configured, which represents the high-resource utilization percentage. The default for the **high** threshold is 90 percent. After the gateway sends a high-utilization message, it waits to send the resource recovery message until the resource use drops below the value defined by the low parameter (which in this case is 50). The default for the **low** parameter is 90 percent.

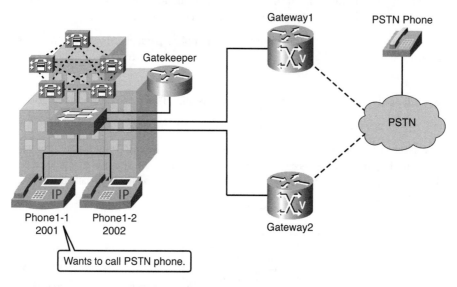

Figure 8-43   *RAI Threshold Configuration Technology*

Example 8-26   *RAI Threshold Configuration on Gateway1*

```
Gateway1(config)#gateway
Gateway1(config-gateway)#resource threshold high 70 low 50
```

Example 8-27   *RAI Threshold Configuration on Gateway2*

```
Gateway2(config)#gateway
Gateway2(config-gateway)#resource threshold high 70 low 50
```

Verifying RAI Operation

Various **show** commands are available to verify RAI operation. The following examples provide sample output from several of these commands.

First, the **show call resource voice threshold** command can be used from privileged EXEC mode to check the threshold state on a gateway, as illustrated in Example 8-28.

Example 8-28   show call resource voice threshold *Command*

```
Router#show call resource voice threshold
Resource Monitor -  Dial-up Resource Threshold Information:


        DS0 Threshold:


        Client Type: h323
        High Water Mark: 70
        Low Water Mark: 50
        Threshold State: low_threshold_hit


        DSP Threshold:


        Client Type: h323
        High Water Mark: 70
        Low Water Mark: 50
        Threshold State: low_threshold_hit
```

Use the **show call resource voice statistics** command to show the statistics of all the resources (DSPs and DS0s).

In output shown in Example 8-29, the DSP utilization is **54/112 = 48%**; the DS0 utilization is 67/96 = 70%; and the high threshold value configured in both cases (DSP and DS0 utilization) is not exceeded.

Example 8-29   show call resource voice statistics *Command*

```
Router#show call resource voice statistics
Resource Monitor -  Dial-up Resource Statistics Information:
DSP Statistics:
Utilization: 48 percent
Total channels: 112
Inuse channels: 54
Disabled channels: 0
Pending channels: 0
Free channels: 58
DS0 Statistics:
Utilization: 70 percent
Total channels: 96
Addressable channels: 96
Inuse channels: 67

Disabled channels: 0
Free channels: 29
```

The **show gateway** command, as demonstrated in Example 8-30, can be used to check the status of the H.323 resource threshold if it is enabled and active. This also gives you the configured low and high threshold values. In this output, you can see that the "resource threshold" is enabled and active. **Enabled** means configured, and **Active** means the H.323 RAS processes in the IOS are registered with the Resource Monitor.

Example 8-30   show gateway *Command*

```
Router#show gateway
Gateway  Router  is registered to Gatekeeper cisco_2
Alias list (CLI configured)
 H323-ID CUCME
Alias list (last RCF)
 H323-ID CUCME
 H323 resource thresholding is Enabled and Active
 H323 resource threshold values:
  DSP: Low threshold 60, High threshold 70
  DS0: Low threshold 60, High threshold 70
```

You can use the **show gatekeeper gw-type-prefix** and **show gatekeeper endpoint** commands to check the RAI status for each gateway on the gatekeeper. Example 8-31 shows sample output from the **show gatekeeper gw-type-prefix** command.

Example 8-31   show gatekeeper gw-type-prefix *Command*

```
GK#show gatekeeper gw-type-prefix
GATEWAY TYPE PREFIX TABLE
=========================
Prefix: 1#*    (Default gateway-technology)
  Zone SanJose master gateway list:
    192.168.1.1:1720 ICT_CM_1
    192.168.1.2:1720 ICT_CM_2
    192.168.1.3:1720 CUCME (out-of-resources)
  Zone SanJose prefix 2* priority gateway list(s):
  Priority 10:
    192.168.1.3:1720 CUCME (out-of-resources)
  Priority 9:
    192.168.1.1:1720 ICT_CM_1
  Priority 8:
    192.168.1.2:1720 ICT_CM_2
```

Also, notice the output of the **show gatekeeper endpoint** command in Example 8-32.

Example 8-32   show gatekeeper endpoint *Command*

```
GK#show gatekeeper endpoint
                    GATEKEEPER ENDPOINT REGISTRATION
                    ==================================
CallSignalAddr     Port  RASSignalAddr   Port   Zone Name   Type      F
--------------     -----  --------------  ------  ----------  -------   --
192.168.1.1        1720  192.168.1.1     4085   SanJose     VOIP-GW
   H323-ID: ICT_CM_1
192.168.1.2        1720  192.168.1.2     4085   SanJose     VOIP-GW
   H323-ID: ICT_CM_2
192.168.1.3        1720  192.168.1.3     53530  Chicago     VOIP-GW 0
   H323-ID: CUCME
Total number of active registrations = 3
```

In this output, the **0** flag in the output indicates that the gateway is out of resources.

Summary

The main topics covered in this chapter are the following:

- Gatekeepers are optional devices that are responsible for admission control, zone management, and E.164 address translation.

- The gatekeeper hardware and software requirements depend on the Cisco IOS version and feature set.

- Signaling between a gateway and a gatekeeper is done through H.225 RAS.

- Zone prefixes indicate the destination zone for a call.

- Technology prefixes are used by gatekeepers to be more flexible in call routing. Default technology prefixes are used as a gateway of last resort.

- A gatekeeper has a logical process for call routing that depends on technology prefix and zone prefix matching.

- Directory gatekeepers can intelligently forward LRQs to appropriate gatekeepers. These directory gatekeepers are used for eliminating the requirement for fully meshed gatekeeper networks.

- Gatekeeper Transaction Message Protocol (GKTMP) provides an interface for call control of a gatekeeper.

- A single gatekeeper can manage multiple local and remote zones.

- Gatekeeper configuration steps are done in gatekeeper configuration mode on Cisco IOS routers.

- A zone prefix is the part of a called number that identifies the zone to which a call hops off. Zone prefixes are often used to associate an area code to a configured zone.

- A technology prefix is an optional H.323 standards-based feature, supported by Cisco gateways and gatekeepers, that enables more flexibility in call routing within an H.323 VoIP network.

- Cisco IOS routers can be registered as gateways with gatekeepers.

- A VoIP dial peer determines how to direct calls that originate from a local voice port into a VoIP cloud to a RAS session target.

- Zone bandwidth management is used in an H.323 network to control bandwidth in or between zones.

- Cisco Unified Communications Manager can use a gatekeeper for CAC.

- Bandwidth calculation for a gatekeeper can be performed with an easy formula: (Number of Calls) * (Codec Payload Bandwidth) * 2 = Zone Bandwidth.

- Bandwidth commands are configured directly on the gatekeeper in the gatekeeper configuration mode.

- The **bandwidth** command is used to configure a specific bandwidth for interzone, total, session, or default zones.

- RAI is used in gatekeeper networks to inform the gatekeeper about the actual status of an end device.

- RAI is configured on the endpoint, not on the gatekeeper.

- RAI commands can be configured with fixed values or with default values.

Chapter Review Questions

The answers to these review questions are in the appendix.

1. Which of the following RAS messages can be sent using either unicast or multicast?

   a. RRQ

   b. ARQ

   c. GRQ

   d. RIP

2. Identify four mandatory features of an H.323 gatekeeper. (Choose 4.)

    a. Call authorization

    b. Admission control

    c. Address resolution

    d. Call management

    e. Bandwidth management

    f. Bandwidth control

    g. Zone management

3. What H.323 gatekeeper feature allows calls to be routed to a specific zone, regardless of the zone prefix in the address?

    a. Technology prefix with hop-off

    b. Default technology prefix

    c. E.164 registration

    d. Subnet scoping

4. Identify two methods of LRQ forwarding. (Choose 2.)

    a. LRQ init

    b. LRQ blast

    c. LRQ static

    d. LRQ sequential

5. Given the following configuration, what IP address will GK1 use to send and receive RAS messages?

```
GK1(config)#interface serial 0/0/0
GK1(config-if)#ip address 192.168.0.2 255.255.255.0
GK1(config-if)#exit
GK1(config)#interface serial 0/0/1
GK1(config-if)#ip address 172.16.0.2 255.255.255.0
GK1(config-if)#exit
GK1(config)#gatekeeper
GK1(config-gk)#zone local SanJose cisco.com 172.16.0.2
GK1(config-gk)#zone remote Austin cisco.com 192.168.0.1
GK1(config-gk)#zone prefix SanJose 2...
GK1(config-gk)#zone prefix Austin 3...
```

    a. 192.168.0.2

    b. 172.16.0.2

    c. 192.168.0.1

    d. RAS messages will be load balanced between 192.168.0.2 and 172.16.0.2

6. What VoIP dial-peer configuration mode command can be used to specify a technology prefix of 2#, indicating that when the dial peer is used as an outgoing dial peer, a 2# will be prepended to the dial string sent to the gatekeeper?

   a. technology-prefix 2#

   b. h323-gateway voip tech-prefix 2#

   c. gw-type-prefix 2#

   d. tech-prefix 2#

7. An H.323 gatekeeper maintains a separate gateway list, ordered by priority, for each of its zone prefixes. If a gateway does not have an assigned priority for a zone prefix, what priority does it use as a default?

   a. 0

   b. 5

   c. 10

   d. 32

8. How much bandwidth does an H.323 gatekeeper assume will be required by a G.729 call?

   a. 8 kbps

   b. 16 kbps

   c. 24 kbps

   d. 64 kbps

9. What parameter of the **bandwidth** command, used in gatekeeper configuration mode, specifies the maximum amount of bandwidth that can be allocated in a zone?

   a. interzone

   b. total

   c. session

   d. remote

10. Where should RAI be configured?

   a. On a gatekeeper

   b. On a gateway

   c. On both a gatekeeper and a gateway

   d. On a Cisco Unified Communications Manager server

After reading this chapter, you should be able to perform the following tasks:

- Describe Cisco Unified Border Element (Cisco UBE) functions and features and how a Cisco UBE is used in current enterprise environments.

- Implement a Cisco UBE router to provide protocol interworking.

CHAPTER 9

Establishing a Connection with an Internet Telephony Service Provider

A Cisco Unified Border Element (Cisco UBE) has the capability to interconnect voice and VoIP networks, offering protocol interworking, address hiding, and security services. This chapter gives an overview of Cisco UBE functionality and describes how to implement a Cisco UBE within an enterprise voice network.

Introducing the Cisco Unified Border Element Gateway

The Cisco UBE is similar to a traditional voice gateway, the main difference being the replacement of physical voice trunks with an IP connection. This section describes the concepts and features of a Cisco UBE in enterprise environments.

Cisco Unified Border Element Overview

The Cisco UBE is an intelligent unified communications network border element. A Cisco UBE, formerly known as the Cisco Multiservice IP-to-IP Gateway, terminates and reoriginates both signaling (H.323 and SIP) and media streams (Real-time Transport Protocol [RTP] and RTP Control Protocol [RTCP]) while performing border interconnection services between IP networks. Cisco UBE, in addition to other Cisco IOS Software features, includes session border controller (SBC) functions that help enable end-to-end IP-based transport of voice, video, and data between independent unified communications networks.

Originally, SBCs were used by service providers (SPs) to enable full billing capabilities within VoIP networks. But the functionality to interconnect VoIP networks is becoming more and more important for enterprise VoIP networks as well, because VoIP is becoming the new standard for any telephony solution.

Designed to meet enterprise and service-provider SBC device needs, the Cisco UBE is an integrated Cisco IOS Software application that runs on various Cisco router platforms. For a list of platforms, see the following link: http://www.cisco.com/en/US/products/sw/voicesw/ps5640/products_white_paper0900aecd8067937f.shtml.

Cisco UBE functionally is implemented on Cisco IOS gateways using a special Cisco IOS feature set. Using this feature set, a Cisco UBE can route a call from one Voice over IP (VoIP) dial peer to another VoIP dial peer.

VoIP dial peers can also be handled by either the Session Initiation Protocol (SIP) or H.323. As a result, the capability to interconnect VoIP dial peers also includes the capability to interconnect VoIP networks using different signaling protocols or VoIP networks using the same signaling protocols but facing interoperability issues.

Protocol interworking includes these combinations:

■   H.323-to-SIP interworking

■   H.323-to-H.323 interworking

■   SIP-to-SIP interworking

Figure 9-1 illustrates the capability of Cisco UBE to interconnect VoIP networks, including VoIP networks that use different signaling protocols. VoIP interworking is achieved by connecting an inbound VoIP dial peer with an outbound VoIP dial peer. A standard Cisco IOS gateway without the Cisco UBE functionality will not allow VoIP-to-VoIP connections.

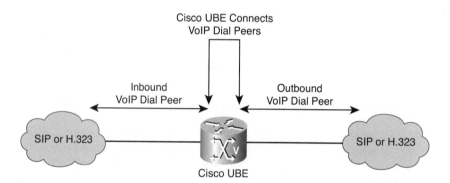

Figure 9-1   *Cisco UBE Functionality*

The Cisco UBE provides a network-to-network interface point for the following:

■   Signaling interworking (H.323, SIP)

■   Media interworking (dual-tone multifrequency [DTMF], fax, modem, and codec transcoding)

■   Address and port translations (privacy and topology hiding)

■   Billing and call detail record (CDR) normalization

■   Quality-of-service (QoS) and bandwidth management (QoS marking using differentiated services code point [DSCP] or IP precedence, bandwidth enforcement using Resource Reservation Protocol [RSVP], and codec filtering)

A Cisco UBE interoperates with several network elements, including voice gateways, IP phones, and call-control servers in many application environments, from advanced enterprise voice and/or video services with Cisco Unified Communications Manager or Cisco Unified Communications Manager Express, as well as simpler toll-bypass and VoIP transport applications.

The Cisco UBE provides organizations with all the border controller functions integrated into the network layer to interconnect unified communications voice and video enterprise-to-service-provider architectures. The Cisco UBE is used by enterprise and small- and medium-sized organizations to interconnect SIP public switched telephone network (PSTN) access with SIP and H.323 enterprise unified communications networks.

Cisco IOS Image Support for Cisco UBE Gateways

The Cisco UBE functionality is supported on most current Cisco IOS routers, including the Cisco 2800 and 3800 Series Integrated Services Routers (ISRs). The first Cisco IOS release supporting the Cisco UBE functionality was Cisco IOS Release 12.2(13)T. However, many of the newer features of the Cisco UBE were introduced with Cisco IOS Software Release 12.4T, so you should deploy this more current Cisco IOS release. Visit the following site for detailed information about features and version dependency:

http://www.cisco.com/en/US/products/sw/voicesw/ps5640/products_configuration_guide_book09186a0080409b6d.html

The Cisco UBE is supported in the following Cisco IOS feature sets:

■   INT VOICE/VIDEO, IPIPGW, TDMIP GW AES

■   INT VOICE/VIDEO, IPIPGW, TDMIP GW

Cisco UBE Gateways in Enterprise Environments

Cisco UBE in enterprise deployments serve two main purposes:

■   **External connections:** A Cisco UBE can be used as a demarcation point within a unified communications network and provides interconnectivity with external networks. This includes H.323 voice and video connections and SIP VoIP connections.

■   **Internal connections:** When used within a VoIP network, a Cisco UBE can be used to increase the flexibility and interoperability between different devices.

Following are some key features offered by Cisco UBE:

■   **Protocol interworking:** The Cisco UBE supports interworking of signaling protocols, including H.323-to-H.323, H.323-to-SIP, and SIP-to-SIP.

■   **Address hiding:** A Cisco UBE can hide or replace the endpoint IP addresses used for a media connection.

■ **Security:** A Cisco UBE can be placed in a demilitarized zone (DMZ) and provide outside connectivity to external networks.

■ **Video integration:** In addition to VoIP services, a Cisco UBE also supports H.323 video connections.

■ **Call Admission Control (CAC):** A Cisco UBE can use Cisco IOS-based CAC mechanisms, including the RSVP.

Table 9-1 lists key features and capabilities of the Cisco UBE. For detailed information about the Cisco UBE, visit the product page: http://www.cisco.com/en/US/products/sw/voicesw/ps5640/products_data_sheet09186a00801da698.html.

Table 9-1   *Key Features of the Cisco UBE Gateway*

Feature	Details
Protocols	H.323 and SIP
Network hiding	IP network privacy and topology hiding
	IP network security boundary
	Intelligent IP address translation for call media and signaling
	Back-to-back user agent, replacing all SIP-embedded IP addressing
CAC	RSVP
	Maximum number of calls per trunk
	CAC based on IP circuits
	CAC based on total calls, CPU usage, or memory usage thresholds
Protocol and signal interworking	H.323 to H.323 (including Cisco Unified Communications Manager)
	H.323 to SIP (including Cisco Unified Communications Manager)
	SIP to SIP (including Cisco Unified Communications Manager)
Media support	RTP and RTCP
Media modes	Media flow-through
	Media flow-around
Video codecs	H.261, H.263, and H.264
Transport mode	TCP
	User Datagram Protocol (UDP)
	TCP-to-UDP interworking

Table 9-1   *Key Features of the Cisco UBE Gateway   (continued)*

Feature	Details
DTMF	H.245 Alphanumeric
	H.245 Signal
	RFC 2833
	SIP Notify
	Key Press Markup Language (KPML)
	Interworking capabilities:
	■ H.323 to SIP
	■ RFC 2833 to G.711 in-band DTMF
Fax support	T.38 fax relay
	Fax passthrough
	Cisco fax relay
Modem support	Modem passthrough
	Cisco modem relay
Supplementary services	Call hold, call transfer, and call forward for H.323 networks using H.450 and transparent passing of Empty Capability Set (ECS)
	SIP-to-SIP supplementary services (holds and transfers) support using REFER
	H.323-to-SIP supplementary services for Cisco Unified Communications Manager with Media Termination Point (MTP) on the H.323 trunk
NAT Traversal	NAT traversal support for SIP phones deployed behind non-Application Line Gateway (ALG) data routers
	Stateful NAT traversal
QoS	IP precedence and DSCP marking
Voice-quality statistics	Packet loss, jitter, and round-trip time
Number translation	Number translation rules for VoIP numbers
	Electronic Numbering (ENUM) support for E.164 number mapping into Domain Name System (DNS)
Codecs	G711 mu-law and a-law
	G723ar53, G723ar63, G723r53, and G723r63
	G726r16, G726r24, and G726r32
	G728
	G729, G729A, G729B, and G729AB
	Internet Low Bitrate Codec (iLBC)

continues

Table 9-1   *Key Features of the Cisco UBE Gateway   (continued)*

Feature	Details
Transcoding	Transcoding between any two families of codecs from the following list: ■ G711 a-law and mu-law ■ G.729, G.729A, G.729B, and G.729AB ■ G.723 (5.3 and 6.3 kbps) ■ iLBC
Security	IP Security (IPsec) Secure RTP (SRTP) Transport Layer Security (TLS)
Authentication, authorization, and accounting (AAA)	AAA with RADIUS
Voice media applications	Tool Command Language (TCL) scripts support for application customization Voice Extensible Markup Language (VoiceXML 2.0) script support for application customization
Billing	Standard CDRs for accurate billing available through ■ AAA records ■ Syslog ■ Simple Network Management Protocol (SNMP)

Figure 9-2 shows the various deployment options for a Cisco UBE. Depending on the deployment scenario, multiple Cisco UBEs might be required. Whether the gateways are being deployed within a single VoIP network or used to interconnect to external VoIP networks, the same concepts apply.

Protocol Interworking on Cisco UBE Gateways

Cisco UBE can interwork signaling protocols, similar to a proxy. This feature can be used for two scenarios:

■ **Interworking between the same signaling protocol:** A Cisco UBE that is interworking between the same signaling protocol (for example H.323-to-H.323) can be used to solve interoperability issues between two devices having different capabilities. Because Cisco UBE builds two call legs to each peer, it can interwork between those two call legs. For example, Cisco Unified Communications Manager Express uses H.450, a subset of H.323, for call transfers and call forwarding. When connected directly to a Cisco Unified Communications Manager, which does not support H.450, call forwarding and transfers might lead to hair-pinned calls and suboptimal WAN usage. A Cisco UBE at the Cisco Unified Communications Manager site can be used to solve these issues.

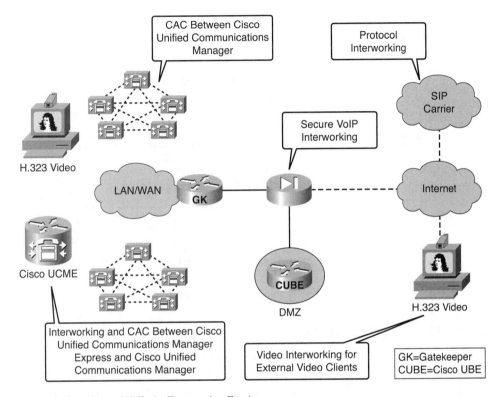

Figure 9-2 *Cisco UBEs in Enterprise Environments*

- **Interworking between different signaling protocols:** Cisco UBE can interconnect dial peers that use different signaling protocols, such as a SIP and an H.323 dial peer. This allows for greater flexibility when deploying an IP communications network.

Both H.323 and SIP support two methods of call setups. H.323 uses fast start and slow start, whereas SIP uses early offer and delayed offer. Both H.323 fast start and SIP early offer are used to set up the media channel faster than during standard call setup. Problems arise when one endpoint expects an H.323 slow start or SIP delayed offer and the other endpoint uses H.323 fast start or SIP early offer.

When interworking signaling protocols, a Cisco UBE supports the following combinations, as illustrated in Figure 9-3:

- **H.323-to-H.323:** An Cisco UBE fully supports fast start with slow start interworking in all directions.

- **H.323-to-SIP:** H.323 fast start to SIP early offer interworking is fully supported. An H.323 slow start to an SIP delayed offer is supported only for inbound H.323 to outbound SIP calls.

- **SIP-to-SIP:** Early offer and delayed offer are fully supported on Cisco UBE in all directions.

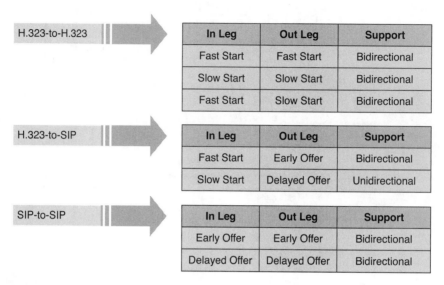

Figure 9-3 *Protocol Interworking Support on Cisco UBEs*

Media Flows on Cisco UBE Gateways

Because Cisco UBE is a signaling proxy, it also processes all signaling messages regarding the setup of media channels. This enables a Cisco UBE to affect the flow of media traffic. Two options exist: *media flow-through* and *media flow-around.*

When using media flow-through, Cisco UBE replaces the source IP address used for media connections with its own IP address. This operation can be utilized in different ways:

■ It solves IP interworking issues because Cisco UBE replaces potential duplicate IP addresses with a single, easy-to-control IP address.

■ It hides the original endpoint IP address from the remote endpoints.

This makes Cisco UBE with media flow-through ideal for interworking with external VoIP networks and enforcing a tighter security policy.

When using Cisco UBE internally, media flow-through might not be necessary or even desirable. One of the main drawbacks when using media flow-through is the higher load on a Cisco UBE router, which decreases the number of supported concurrent flows. In addition, media flow-through might result in suboptimal traffic flows because direct endpoint-to-endpoint communication is prohibited. Thus Cisco UBE can also be configured for media flow-around. When using media flow-around, Cisco UBE leaves the IP addresses used for the media connections untouched. Call signaling will still be processed by Cisco UBE, but after the call is set up, Cisco UBE is no longer involved with the traffic flow.

Figure 9-4 shows a Cisco UBE router configured for media flow-through. The signaling between the two Cisco Unified Communications Manager clusters is processed by Cisco UBE, and the source IP addresses of the endpoints are replaced by the Cisco UBE IP address. Both endpoints have the same IP address, but because Cisco UBE is involved, no interworking issues arise.

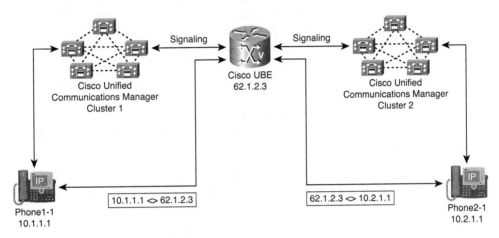

Figure 9-4   *Media Flow-Through Topology*

Figure 9-5 shows a Cisco UBE router configured for media flow-around. No duplicate IP address ranges exist, and IP address hiding is not required—so media flow-through is not required. Cisco UBE still processes all signaling traffic, but the endpoints have direct media channels. You might use media flow-around when you are not concerned with hiding your network addresses.

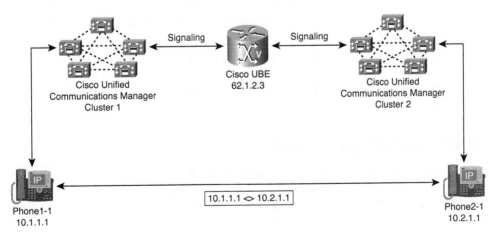

Figure 9-5   *Media Flow-Around Topology*

Codec Filtering on Cisco UBEs

VoIP networks usually support a large variety of codecs, and mechanisms exist to perform codec negotiations between devices. Regardless of which mechanisms are used, preferences determine which codecs will be selected over others.

Because a Cisco UBE router is essentially a Cisco IOS gateway with the capability to interconnect VoIP dial peers, the same codec selections mechanisms are available as on any other Cisco IOS gateway. A dial peer can be configured to allow a specific codec or to use a codec voice class to specify multiple codecs with a preference order. This enables Cisco UBE to perform codec filtering, because a dial peer will set up a call leg only if the desired codec criteria are satisfied. This adds to the Cisco UBE role of a demarcation point within a VoIP network.

If codec filtering is not required, Cisco UBE also supports transparent codec negotiations. This enables negotiations between endpoints with Cisco UBE leaving the codec information untouched.

Whether performing codec filtering or operating in transparent mode, Cisco UBE is required to support the codec used between endpoints. The following codecs are supported:

- **Audio codecs:** G.711u, G.711a, G.723, G.726, G.729r8, G.728, and AMR-NB

- **Video codecs (H.323 only):** H.261, H.263, and H.264

Figure 9-6 shows how codec negotiation is performed on a Cisco UBE router. Two VoIP clouds need to be interconnected. In this scenario, both VoIP 1 and VoIP 2 networks have G.711 a-law as the preferred codec.

In the first example, the Cisco UBE router is configured to use the G.729a codec. This can be done by using the appropriate **codec** command on both VoIP dial peers. When a call is set up, Cisco UBE will accept only G.729a calls, thus influencing the codec negotiation.

In the second example, the Cisco UBE is configured for a transparent codec and will leave the codec information contained within the call signaling untouched. Because both VoIP 1 and VoIP 2 have G.711 a-law as their first choice, the resulting call will be a G.711 a-law call.

RSVP-Based CAC on Cisco UBEs

Because a Cisco UBE router is a Cisco IOS gateway, it also supports RSVP-based CAC. Two Cisco Unified Communications Manager clusters can interconnect using Cisco UBE, thus enabling intercluster RSVP-based CAC. RSVP supports both voice and video calls.

Cisco UBE Codec Negotiation:

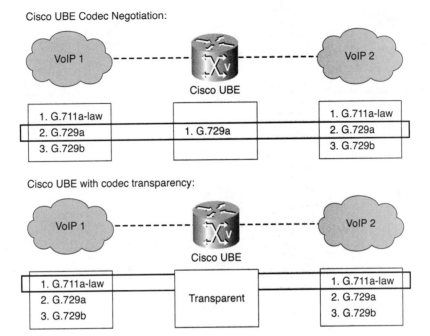

Figure 9-6 *Codec Filtering on Cisco UBEs*

RSVP requires at least two RSVP peers, so two Cisco UBE Gateways are required to enable RSVP-based CAC. When deploying Cisco UBE and RSVP-based CAC, ensure that the flows that should utilize RSVP are configured for media flow-through. Media flow-around is not supported with RSVP-based CAC.

Figure 9-7 shows a call setup combined with RSVP-based CAC example.

Following is the call flow:

1. The Cisco Unified Communications Manager Cluster 1 sends an H.225 setup to the Cisco UBE router.

2. Cisco UBE processes the call setup information and associates an outbound VoIP dial peer requiring an RSVP reservation. Cisco UBE sends out an RSVP request to the remote Cisco UBE router.

3. The remote Cisco UBE acknowledges the reservation and initiates the reservation for the return path, which is acknowledged by the local Cisco UBE router.

4. The H.225 setup message is routed to the remote Cisco UBE router, which then routes the call to the outbound VoIP dial peer pointing to Cisco Unified Communications Manager Cluster 2.

5. H.245 negotiation occurs with media flow-through enabled.

6. The call is established.

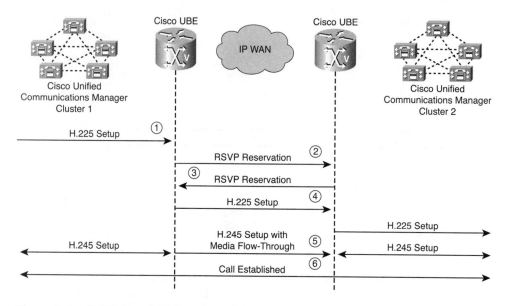

Figure 9-7 *RSVP-Based CAC on Cisco UBEs*

Cisco UBE Gateways and Gatekeeper Interworking

When you're interworking with gatekeepers, Cisco UBE can be used in two ways. First, it can register with the gatekeeper, similar to a standard Cisco IOS gateway.

Note Cisco UBE and a gatekeeper can be deployed on the same router, as long as CPU and memory requirements are met.

In addition, a gatekeeper can use a registered Cisco UBE router with via-zones. This means that when routing a call between two zones, a gatekeeper can be configured to route the call via a zone containing a Cisco UBE router. This enables interzone networking using a central Cisco UBE router without the need to deploy a Cisco UBE router at every site or redesign an already-deployed H.323 network.

Figure 9-8 shows how a Cisco UBE is integrated with gatekeeper deployments.

Consider the following design guidelines for Cisco UBE gateway and gatekeeper implementations:

- When a Cisco UBE router is used as an outbound voice gateway, the same concepts that apply when using traditional voice gateways with gatekeepers apply to Cisco UBE deployments.

- When routing calls between zones that require Cisco UBE functionality, via-zones should be used. Existing gatekeeper deployments can easily be modified to include Cisco UBE using this concept.

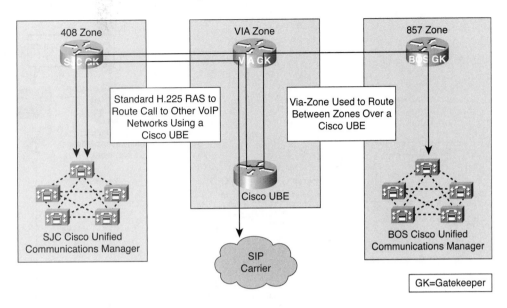

Figure 9-8   *Cisco UBEs and Gatekeeper Interworking*

Cisco UBE Gateway Call Flows

Cisco UBE call flow depends on network topology and features implemented. The following call-flow scenarios listed will be used to illustrate the concepts about Cisco UBE that have been discussed thus far:

- Cisco Unified Communications Manager—Cisco UBE—Cisco Unified Communications Manager Express

- Cisco Unified Communications Manager—Cisco UBE with RSVP—Cisco Unified Communications Manager

- Cisco Unified Communications Manager—Cisco UBE—SIP Carrier

- Cisco Unified Communications Manager—Gatekeeper—Cisco UBE—SIP Carrier

- Cisco Unified Communications Manager—Via-Zone Gatekeeper—Cisco UBE— Cisco Unified Communications Manager

Figure 9-9 shows a call flow between a Cisco Unified Communications Manager server and a Cisco Unified Communications Manager Express router using Cisco UBE.

Cisco Unified Communications Manager Express uses H.450 for optimized call transfers and call forwards without requiring hairpinning. Because Cisco Unified Communications Manager does not support H.450, a transfer involving H.323 VoIP connections might lead to suboptimal traffic flows.

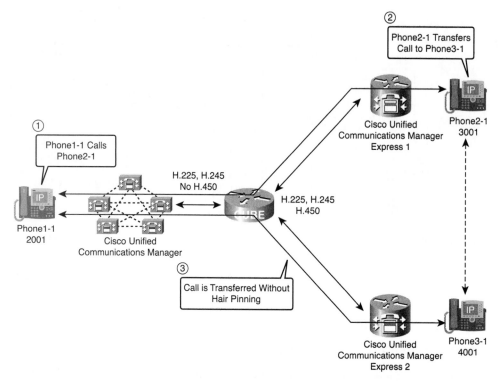

Figure 9-9 *Cisco UBE Call Flows: Cisco UCM to Cisco UCME*

Cisco UBE can be used to solve H.450 Cisco Unified Communications Manager and Cisco Unified Communications Manager Express interoperability issues. In this example, a call between Phone1-1 and Phone2-1 is transferred to Phone3-1. Because Cisco UBE supports H.450, the resulting traffic flow will be directly between the Cisco UBE router and Cisco Unified Communications Manager 2. Without Cisco UBE, the call transfer would be done using hairpinning on Cisco Unified Communications Manager 1.

RSVP-based intercluster CAC can be implemented using Cisco UBE. Figure 9-10 shows two Cisco Unified Communications Manager clusters interconnected by two Cisco UBE routers. Each Cisco Unified Communications Manager cluster has an H.323 call leg to the local Cisco UBE local. The two Cisco UBE routers perform RSVP-based CAC, and because RSVP-based CAC requires media flow-through, a call between the two clusters will flow through the two Cisco UBE routers. Note that phones still use the Skinny Client Control Protocol (SCCP) for signaling toward a Cisco Unified Communications Manager server.

Figure 9-11 shows a simple Cisco UBE deployment where Cisco UBE is used to translate a H.323 call leg with a Cisco Unified Communications Manager cluster to a SIP call leg point to a SIP carrier. Because this is a connection to an external VoIP network, media flow-through is required to hide internal IP addresses and overcome IP interworking issues, such as duplicate private IP addresses.

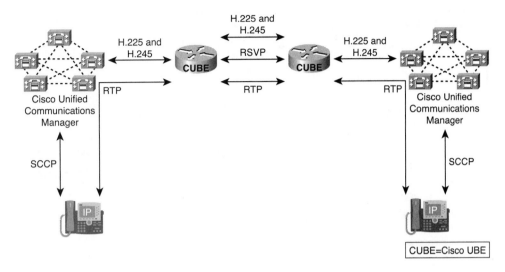

Figure 9-10 *Cisco UBE Call Flows: Cisco UCM to Cisco UCM*

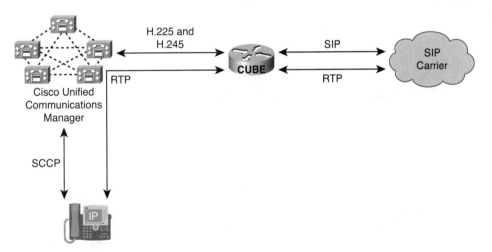

Figure 9-11 *Cisco UBE Call Flows: SIP Carrier Interworking*

Figure 9-12 shows an H.323 gatekeeper deployment that includes a Cisco UBE integrated with a gatekeeper and a SIP carrier. Calls from the Cisco Unified Communications Manager cluster are routed via H.225 RAS from the San Jose gatekeeper to the ITSP gatekeeper, which then routes the call to the Cisco UBE router. Cisco UBE then performs standard protocol interworking, allowing connections from the Cisco Unified Communications Manager H.323 network to the SIP carrier network.

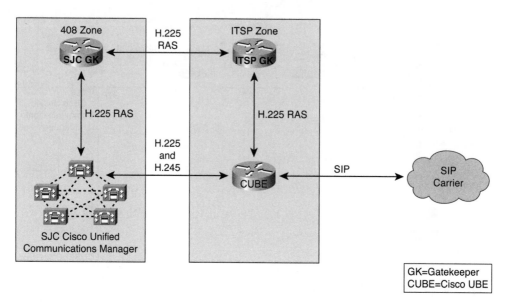

Figure 9-12   *Cisco UBE Call Flows: Gatekeeper and SIP Carrier Interworking*

Figure 9-13 shows the concept of via-zone enabled gatekeepers using Cisco UBE.

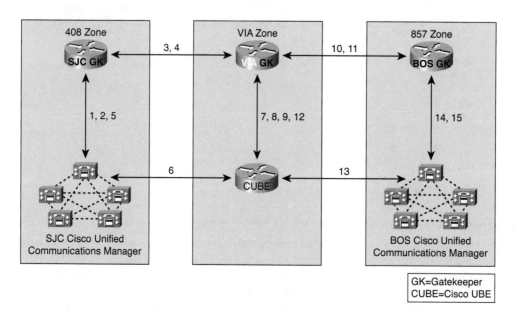

Figure 9-13   *Cisco UBE Call Flows: Cisco UBE and Via-Zone Gatekeeper*

Three gatekeepers are deployed:

- **San Jose gatekeeper:** This gatekeeper has a single zone called 408.

- **Boston gatekeeper:** This gatekeeper has a single zone called 857.

- **Via-zone gatekeeper:** This gatekeeper has a single zone called via-zone (VIA).

The San Jose (SJC) Cisco Unified Communications Manager cluster is registered at the San Jose gatekeeper; the Boston (BOS) Cisco Unified Communications Manager cluster is registered at the Boston gatekeeper; and the Cisco UBE router is registered at the via-zone gatekeeper.

The San Jose gatekeeper will route all calls made to the remote 857 zone to the via-zone gatekeeper, and the Boston gatekeeper will route all calls made to the remote 408 zone to the via-zone gatekeeper.

The via-zone gatekeepers will route the calls to the remote 408 and 857 zones, but not directly to the gatekeepers in San Jose and Boston. Instead, the routing will be done using the local VIA zone.

The following steps, numbered in Figure 9-13, describe an example call flow from the San Jose Cisco Unified Communications Manager cluster in zone 408 on the San Jose gatekeeper to the Boston Cisco Unified Communications Manager cluster located in zone 857 on the Boston gatekeeper:

1. A call is placed from the San Jose Cisco Unified Communications Manager to someone in area code 857.

2. The San Jose Cisco Unified Communications Manager sends an ARQ to the San Jose gatekeeper.

3. The San Jose gatekeeper resolves the 857 that belongs to the via-zone gatekeeper and sends a Location Request (LRQ).

4. The VIA gatekeeper receives an LRQ for 857 and resolves the 857 prefix to the Cisco UBE. The VIA gatekeeper sends a LCF to the San Jose gatekeeper.

5. The San Jose gatekeeper returns an ACF that specifies the Cisco UBE to the San Jose Cisco Unified Communications Manager.

6. The San Jose Cisco Unified Communications Manager sends a SETUP message to the Cisco UBE for the 857 number.

7. The Cisco UBE sends an ARQ to the VIA gatekeeper with the **answerCall=true** parameter set to admit the incoming call.

8. The VIA gatekeeper responds with an ACF to admit the call. From the perspective of the VIA gatekeeper, the first call leg is established.

9. The Cisco UBE gateway has a dial peer that specifies that RAS messages should be sent to the VIA gatekeeper for all prefixes. The Cisco UBE gateway initiates the process of resending the call by sending the ARQ message with **answerCall=false** to the VIA gatekeeper for 857.

10. The VIA gatekeeper knows that prefix 857 belongs to the Boston gatekeeper, and because the source zone is the via-zone, the VIA gatekeeper sends an LRQ to the Boston gatekeeper.

11. The Boston gatekeeper sees prefix 857 as a local zone and sends an LCF pointing to the Boston Cisco Unified Communications Manager.

12. The VIA gatekeeper returns an ACF to the Cisco UBE that specifies the Boston Cisco Unified Communications Manager.

13. The Cisco UBE gateway sends a SETUP message to the Boston Cisco Unified Communications Manager for the 857 call.

14. The Boston Cisco Unified Communications Manager sends an ARQ to the Boston gatekeeper to request admission for the call.

15. The Boston gatekeeper sends an ACF with the **answerCall=true** parameter.

Configuring Cisco Unified Border Elements

A Cisco Unified Border Element can be implemented in VoIP networks to enhance VoIP network interoperability. This section describes how to implement Cisco UBE routers to support protocol interworking between H.323 and SIP networks.

Protocol Interworking Command

To enable protocol interworking, use the **allow-connections** *from-type* **to** *to-type* command in voice service configuration mode. The *from-type* and *to-type* options specify the signaling protocols, as detailed in Table 9-2.

Table 9-2   **allow-connections** *Syntax Description*

Parameter	Description
from-type	Originating endpoint type. The following choices are valid: h323—H.323 sip—SIP
To	Indicates that the argument that follows is the connection target.
to-type	Terminating endpoint type. The following choices are valid: h323—H.323 sip—SIP

When interworking H.323 and SIP, the configuration is unidirectional; thus, if bidirectional interworking is required, you need to configure the mirroring statement as well. For example, if bidirectional H.323 to SIP interworking is required, you need to configure **allow connections h323 to sip** as well as **allow connections sip to h323**.

Figure 9-14 and Example 9-1 illustrate a sample protocol interworking configuration.

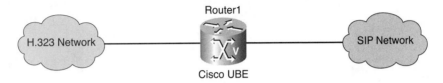

Figure 9-14 *Protocol Interworking Topology Example*

Example 9-1 *Protocol Interworking Configuration*

```
Router1(config)#voice service voip
Router1(config-voice-service)#allow-connections h323 to 323
Router1(config-voice-service)#allow-connections sip to sip
Router1(config-voice-service)#allow-connections h323 to sip
Router1(config-voice-service)#allow-connections sip to h323
```

Configuring H.323-to-H.323 Interworking

H.323-to-H.323 gateway configuration provides a network-to-network demarcation point between independent VoIP and video networks for billing, security, call-admission control, QoS, and signaling interworking. It performs most of the functions of a PSTN-to-IP gateway but joins two H.323 VoIP call legs.

Figure 9-15 shows a sample scenario used to configure H.323-to-H.323 interworking for a Cisco UBE router. The Cisco Unified Communications Manager cluster in San Jose is connected with the Cisco Unified Communications Manager Express router in Chicago using a Cisco UBE router.

To configure H.323-to-H.323 interworking between a Cisco Unified Communications Manager cluster and a Cisco Unified Communications Manager Express gateway, follow these steps:

Step 1.   Enable H.323-to-H.323 interworking.

Step 2.   Configure the H.323 dial peers on the Cisco UBE router to allow call routing between the Cisco Unified Communications Manager cluster and Cisco Unified Communications Manager Express router.

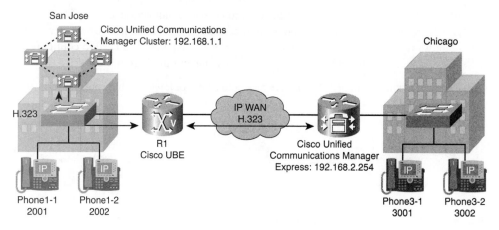

Figure 9-15   *H.323-to-H.323 Interworking Scenario*

Step 1: Enabling H.323-to-H.323 Interworking

By default, a Cisco IOS gateway will not allow connections between two VoIP dial peers. To change this behavior and allow H.323-to-H.323 connections, use the **allow-connections h323 to h323** command in voice service configuration mode, as shown in Example 9-2.

Example 9-2   *Enabling H.323 Protocol Interworking*

```
Router(config)#voice service voip
Router(config-voice-service)#allow-connections h323 to h323
```

Step 2: Configuring H.323 Dial Peers

After H323-to-H323 calls have been allowed, configure the appropriate dial peers to route between the Cisco Unified Communications Manager cluster and the Cisco Unified Communications Manager Express router. No special configuration on the dial peers is required. Example 9-3 illustrates this dial-peer configuration.

Example 9-3   *H.323 Dial Peers*

```
Router(config)#dial-peer voice 2001
Router(config-dial-peer)#description To Cisco Unified Communications Manager
Router(config-dial-peer)#destination-pattern 2...
Router(config-dial-peer)#session-target ipv4:192.168.1.1
Router(config-dial-peer)#exit
Router(config)#dial-peer voice 3000
Router(config-dial-peer)#description To Cisco Unified Communications Manager Express
Router(config-dial-peer)#destination-pattern 3...
Router(config-dial-peer)#session-target ipv4:192.168.2.254
```

Configuring H.323-to-SIP Interworking

Figure 9-16 shows a sample scenario used to configure H.323-to-SIP interworking with a Cisco UBE router. The Cisco Unified Communications Manager cluster in San Jose routes calls to the SIP carrier via a Cisco UBE router. The connection between the Cisco Unified Communications Manager and the Cisco UBE router is H.323 and the connection between the Cisco UBE router and the SIP carrier is SIP.

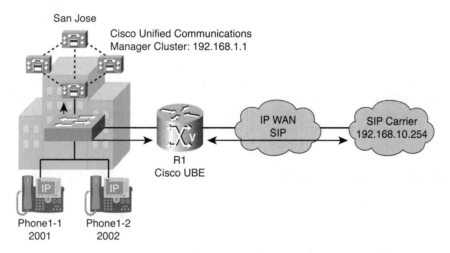

Figure 9-16   *H.323-to-SIP Interworking Scenario*

You can follow these steps to configure H.323-to-SIP interworking:

Step 1.   Enable H.323-to-SIP interworking.

Step 2.   Configure H.323 and SIP dial peers to route international calls between the Cisco Unified Communications Manager cluster and the SIP carrier.

Step 1: Enabling H.323-to-SIP Interworking

As with an H.323-to-H.323 connection, by default a Cisco IOS gateway will not allow connections between an H.323 and a SIP VoIP dial peer. To change this behavior and allow H.323-to-SIP connections, use the **allow-connections h323 to sip** command in voice service configuration mode. Then issue the **allow-connections sip to h323** command to enable SIP to H.323 calls, as demonstrated in Example 9-4.

Example 9-4   *H.323-to-SIP Interworking*

```
R1(config)#voice service voip
R1(config-voice-service)#allow-connections h323 to sip
R1(config-voice-service)#allow-connections sip to h323
```

Step 2: Configuring Dial Peers

For a SIP (**rtp-nte**)-to-H.323 (**h245-alphanumeric**) call via a Cisco UBE router, if any RTP named telephony event (NTE) packets are sent before the H.323 endpoint answers the call, the DTMF signal is not heard on a terminating gateway (TGW).

> **Note** **debug** output reveals that the H245 out-of-band messages are sent to the TGW. However, the digits are not heard on the phone.

To avoid sending both in-band and out-of-band tones to the outgoing leg when sending Cisco UBE calls in-band (**rtp-nte**) to out-of-band (**h245-alphanumeric**), configure the **dtmf-relay rtp-nte digit-drop** command on the incoming SIP dial peer. On the H.323 side, configure either **dtmf-relay h245-alphanumeric** or **dtmf-relay h245-signal**. This can also be used for H.323-to-SIP calls. Example 9-5 illustrates this dial-peer configuration.

Example 9-5 *Dial-Peer Configuration*

```
R1(config)#dial-peer voice 2000 voip
R1(config-dial-peer)#description To Cisco Unified Communications Manager
R1(config-dial-peer)#destination-pattern 2...
R1(config-dial-peer)#session target ipv4:192.168.1.1
R1(config-dial-peer)#dtmf-relay h245-alphanumeric
R1(config-dial-peer)#exit
R1(config)#dial-peer voice 9011 voip
R1(config-dial-peer)#description To International SIP Carrier
R1(config-dial-peer)#session protocol sipv2
R1(config-dial-peer)#destination-pattern 9011T
R1(config-dial-peer)#session target ipv4:192.168.10.254
R1(config-dial-peer)#dtmf-relay rtp-nte digit-drop h245-alphanumeric
```

Media Flow and Transparent Codec Commands

To configure media flow-through or media flow-around, use the following **media** command:

```
Router(config-dial-peer)#media [flow-around | flow-through]
```

Note that this command can be issued in dial-peer configuration mode or globally under the voice service configuration mode. The default is **media flow-through**.

To configure transparent codec pass-through, use the following **codec transparent** command:

```
Router(config-dial-peer)#codec transparent
```

Note that this command can be issued in dial-peer configuration mode or via a codec class.

Configuring Transparent Codec Pass-Through and Media Flow-Around

Figure 9-17 shows a sample scenario used to configure H.323-to-H.323 interworking, including transparent codec pass-through and media flow-around, using a Cisco UBE router. The Cisco Unified Communications Manager cluster in San Jose is connected with the Cisco Unified Communications Manager Express router in Chicago using a Cisco UBE router. Codec negotiation is performed directly between the Cisco Unified Communications Manager cluster and the Cisco Unified Communications Manager Express router, and RTP streams flow directly between the endpoints.

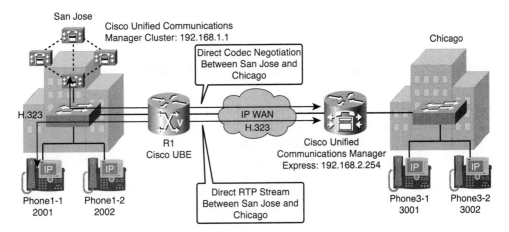

Figure 9-17   *Transparent Codec Pass-Through and Media Flow-Around Example Topology*

Codec transparency enables a Cisco UBE router to pass codec capabilities between endpoints. If you configure transparency, a Cisco UBE router uses the codec that was specified by the endpoints for setting up a call. To enable endpoint-to-endpoint codec negotiation without a Cisco UBE router, use the **codec transparent** command.

With the default configuration, a Cisco UBE router receives media packets from the inbound call leg, terminates them, and then reoriginates the media stream on an outbound call leg. Media flow-around enables media packets to be passed directly between the endpoints, without the intervention of a Cisco UBE router. The Cisco UBE router continues to handle routing and billing functions. Media flow-around for SIP-to-SIP calls is not supported. Use the **media flow-around** command to enable media flow-around. Example 9-6 illustrates the use of both the **codec transparent** and the **media flow-around** commands.

Example 9-6   *Transparent Codec Pass-Through and Media Flow-Around Configuration*

```
R1(config)#dial-peer voice 2000 voip
R1(config-dial-peer)#description To Cisco Unified Communications Manager
R1(config-dial-peer)#destination-pattern 2...
R1(config-dial-peer)#session target ipv4:192.168.1.1
R1(config-dial-peer)#dtmf-relay h245-alphanumeric
R1(config-dial-peer)#codec transparent
R1(config-dial-peer)#media flow-around
R1(config-dial-peer)#exit
R1(config)#dial-peer voice 9011 voip
R1(config-dial-peer)#description To Cisco Unified Communications Manager Express
R1(config-dial-peer)#destination-pattern 3...
R1(config-dial-peer)#session target ipv4:192.168.2.254
R1(config-dial-peer)#codec transparent
R1(config-dial-peer)#media flow-around
```

Configuring Cisco UBEs and Via-Zone Gatekeepers

Figure 9-18 shows a sample scenario used to configure a Cisco UBE router and a via-zone gatekeeper. A gatekeeper is configured with two standard local zones: San Jose (SJC) and Chicago (CHI). The Cisco Unified Communications Manager Express Router1 is registered in the SJC zone, and the Cisco Unified Communications Manager Express Router3 is registered in CHI zone. Calls between Chicago and San Jose should be routed by the gatekeeper. Instead of routing calls directly between the two zones, the gatekeeper should route the calls through the VIA, which includes a Cisco UBE router.

Note   The Cisco UBE function and the gatekeeper function are performed by the same router.

Configure the Gatekeeper

You can complete these steps to configure a gatekeeper:

Step 1.   Create a loopback interface to use for the gatekeeper.

Step 2.   Create local, remote, and VIA zones.

Two local zones, SJC and CHI, are configured, but instead of configuring a standard local zone, the **invia** and **outvia** options are used to route calls to and from the zones using the VIA zone.

In addition to the SJC and CHI local zones, another local via-zone is configured. This zone will contain the Cisco UBE router.

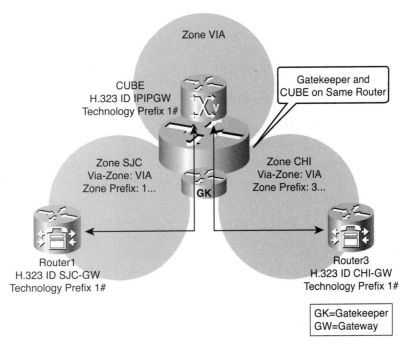

Figure 9-18 *Cisco UBEs and Via-Zone Gatekeepers Configuration Topology*

Step 3.   Specify zone and technology prefixes.

Standard zone prefix routing is set up, and the default technology 1# is configured. Example 9-7 illustrates a sample via-gatekeeper configuration.

Example 9-7 *Via-Zone Gatekeeper Configuration*

```
GK(config)#interface Loopback0
GK(config-if)#ip address 192.168.66.14 255.255.255.0
GK(config-if)#exit
GK(config)#gatekeeper
GK(config-gk)#zone local SJC cisco.com 192.168.66.14 invia VIA outvia VIA
GK(config-gk)#zone local CHI cisco.com invia VIA outvia VIA
GK(config-gk)#zone local VIA cisco.com
GK(config-gk)#zone prefix SJC 1*
GK(config-gk)#zone prefix CHI 3*
GK(config-gk)#gw-type-prefix 1#* default-technology
GK(config-gk)#no shutdown
```

Configure the Cisco UBE

After the gatekeeper configuration is done, the Cisco UBE configuration is performed on the same router.

You can complete these steps to configure the Cisco UBE feature:

Step 1. Enable H.323 interworking.

Step 2. Create a loopback interface to use as the source interface for Cisco UBE to register with the gatekeeper.

The Loopback1 interface is used as the H.323 gateway interface. The Cisco UBE router will register in zone VIA with the H.323 ID CUBE and the technology prefix 1#.

Step 3. Create two dial peers—one pointing to San Jose and the other to Chicago.

Step 4. Enable the gateway process.

Example 9-8 illustrates a sample Cisco UBE configuration.

Example 9-8 *Cisco UBE Configuration*

```
GK(config)#voice service voip
GK(config-voice-service)#allow-connections h323 to h323
GK(config-voice-service)#exit
GK(config)#interface loopback1
GK(config-if)#ip address 192.168.66.15 255.255.255.0
GK(config-if)#h323-gateway voip interface
GK(config-if)#h323-gateway voip id VIA ipaddr 192.168.66.14 1719
GK(config-if)#h323-gateway voip h323-id IPIPGW
GK(config-if)#h323-gateway voip tech-prefix 1#
GK(config-if)#exit
GK(config)#dial-peer voice 10 voip
GK(config-dial-peer)#destination-pattern 1...
GK(config-dial-peer)#session target ras
GK(config-dial-peer)#exit
GK(config)#dial-peer voice 30 voip
GK(config-dial-peer)#destination-pattern 3...
GK(config-dial-peer)#session target ras
GK(config-dial-peer)#exit
GK(config)#gateway
```

Verifying Cisco UBEs and Via-Zone Gatekeepers

When you use the **show gatekeeper endpoints** command on the gatekeeper, a Cisco UBE router will be displayed as an H323-GW type. In the output shown in Example 9-9, the Cisco UBE router is registered using the Loopback1 IP address 192.168.66.15.

Example 9-9 *Verifying Cisco UBEs and Via-Zone Gatekeepers with the* **show gatekeeper endpoints** *Command*

```
GKIPIPGW#show gatekeeper endpoints
                  GATEKEEPER ENDPOINT REGISTRATION
                  ==================================
CallSignalAddr  Port  RASSignalAddr   Port  Zone Name        Type    Flags
--------------  ----- ---------------  ----  ---------        ----    -----
192.168.66.15   1720  192.168.66.15   58083 VIA              H323-GW
   H323-ID: IPIPGW
   Voice Capacity Max.=  Avail.=  Current.= 0
192.168.1.254   1720  192.168.1.254   50220 SJC              VOIP-GW
   H323-ID: SJC-GW
   Voice Capacity Max.=  Avail.=  Current.= 0
192.168.3.254   1720  192.168.3.254   51105 CHI              VOIP-GW
   H323-ID: CHI-GW
   Voice Capacity Max.=  Avail.=  Current.= 0
Total number of active registrations = 3
```

When a call is active, the **show gatekeeper calls** command will display two call legs. The first call leg, as illustrated in Figure 9-19 and Example 9-10, is between the originating gateway (Router1 in this case) and the Cisco UBE router.

Router1 to Cisco UBE

Router1
H.323 ID SJC-GW
Technology Prefix 1#

Cisco UBE

Router3
H.323 ID CHI-GW
Technology Prefix 1#

Figure 9-19 *Verifying Cisco UBEs and Via-Zone Gatekeepers Topology—Call Leg 1*

Example 9-10 *Verifying Cisco UBEs and Via-Zone Gatekeepers with the* **show gatekeeper calls** *Command—Call Leg 1*

```
GKIPIPGW#show gatekeeper calls
... OUTPUT OMITTED ...
LocalCallID                        Age(secs)    BW
10-54685                           10           16(Kbps)
 Endpt(s): Alias                   E.164Addr
   src EP: SJC-GW
           CallSignalAddr  Port  RASSignalAddr   Port
           192.168.1.254   1720  192.168.1.254   50220
 Endpt(s): Alias                   E.164Addr
```

continues

Example 9-10 *Verifying Cisco UBEs and Via-Zone Gatekeepers with the* **show gatekeeper calls** *Command—Call Leg 1 continued*

```
 dst EP: IPIPGW              3001
        CallSignalAddr  Port  RASSignalAddr   Port
        192.168.66.15   1720  192.168.66.15   58083
... OUTPUT OMITTED ...
```

The second call leg, as illustrated in Figure 9-20 and Example 9-11, is between the Cisco UBE router and the terminating gateway (Router3 in this case).

Figure 9-20 *Verifying Cisco UBEs and Via-Zone Gatekeepers Topology—Call Leg 2*

Example 9-11 *Verifying Cisco UBEs and Via-Zone Gatekeepers with the* **show gatekeeper calls** *Command—Call Leg 2*

```
GKIPIPGW#show gatekeeper calls
... OUTPUT OMITTED ...
LocalCallID                     Age(secs)   BW
11-54685                        10          16(Kbps)
 Endpt(s): Alias                E.164Addr
   src EP: IPIPGW               4001
          CallSignalAddr  Port  RASSignalAddr   Port
          192.168.66.15   1720  192.168.66.15   58083
 Endpt(s): Alias                E.164Addr
   dst EP: CHI-GW               3001
          CallSignalAddr  Port  RASSignalAddr   Port
          192.168.3.254   1720  192.168.3.254   51105
... OUTPUT OMITTED ...
```

Summary

The main topics covered in this chapter are the following:

- Cisco UBE routers interconnect multiple VoIP networks by routing calls between two VoIP dial peers.

- Features include protocol interworking, address hiding, codec filtering, and video interworking.

- Protocol interworking interconnects VoIP networks, using the same or different signaling protocols.

- Media streams can flow through or bypass a Cisco UBE router.

- Cisco UBE routers use standard Cisco IOS codec negotiations to influence negotiations between VoIP networks.

- Cisco UBE routers can use RSVP to implement CAC, for example, between Cisco Unified Communications Manager clusters.

- Cisco UBE routers can register with gatekeepers and be used as a standard gateway or with via-zones.

- Cisco UBE call flow depends on network topology and features implemented.

- Protocol interworking is configured using the **allow-connection** command.

- H.323-to-H.323 interworking is configured using the **allow-connection h323 to h323** command.

- H.323-to-SIP interworking is configured using the **allow-connection h323 to sip** command.

- Media flow-through or flow-around can be configured globally or per dial peer.

- Ensure that the inbound and outbound dial peers have matching media and codec configurations.

- Cisco UBE routers can be used in conjunction with gatekeepers by registering them in a via-zone.

- A gatekeeper will show two call legs when using a Cisco UBE router.

Chapter Review Questions

The answers to these review questions are in the appendix.

1. Cisco UBE features include _____, _____, codec filtering, and video interworking. (Choose 2.)

    a. phone registration

    b. address hiding

    c. protocol interworking

    d. multiple gatekeeper registration

2. Protocol interworking interconnects VoIP networks, using the same or different _____ protocols.

    a. signaling

    b. compression

    c. codec

    d. transport

3. Media streams can _____ or _____ a Cisco UBE.

    a. bypass, flow-around

    b. flow-through, multiplex across

    c. flow-through, traverse

    d. flow-through, flow-around

4. If codec filtering is not required, a Cisco UBE router also supports _____ codec negotiations.

    a. multiple

    b. null

    c. dynamic

    d. transparent

5. When deploying Cisco UBE and RSVP-based CAC, ensure the flows that should utilize RSVP are configured for media _____.

    a. flow-around

    b. bypass

    c. flow-through

    d. parity

6. When interworking H.323 and SIP, the configuration applied with the **allow-connections** command is _____.

    a. unilateral

    b. bilateral

    c. unidirectional

    d. bidirectional

7. Choose the correct command to enable H.323 to H.323 interworking.

    a. allow-connections h323 to sip

    b. allow-connections sip to h323

    c. allow-connections sip to sip

    d. allow-connections h323 to h323

8. Use the _____ command to configure codec pass-through.

    a. transparent codec

    b. codec transparent

    c. codec auto

    d. codec preference

9. A gatekeeper should be configured to route calls between local zones via a Cisco UBE gateway. How can this be achieved?

    a. The gatekeeper should route calls directly via a Cisco UBE gateway.

    b. The gatekeeper should route calls via a local zone that contains a Cisco UBE gateway.

    c. The gateways should route calls to a Cisco UBE gateway instead of a gatekeeper.

    d. The gateway should register with a technology prefix that matches the technology prefix of a Cisco UBE gateway.

10. When you use the **show gatekeeper endpoints** command on the gatekeeper, a Cisco UBE router will be displayed as a(n) _____ type.

    a. VOIP-GW

    b. POTS-GW

    c. H323-GW

    d. TDM-GW

Answers to Chapter Review Questions

Chapter 1

1. B
2. A and C
3. B, D, and E
4. C
5. B, D, and E
6. B and F
7. D
8. B
9. A, C, D, and E
10. A and C

Chapter 2

1. B
2. B
3. B
4. A
5. A, C, and D
6. D
7. C
8. A, C, and D
9. B
10. C

Chapter 3

1. D
2. A
3. B
4. B
5. A and B
6. B
7. A and D
8. C
9. D
10. C

Chapter 4

1. C
2. A, C, and D
3. C
4. B
5. B
6. A and B
7. B and C
8. B
9. C
10. C

Chapter 5

1. A and C
2. D
3. A
4. C
5. B
6. D

7. B

8. A, C, D, and E

9. A

10. C

Chapter 6

1. B

2. C

3. B

4. A, C, and D

5. B

6. B

7. D

8. A

9. D

10. C

Chapter 7

1. C

2. A

3. D

4. A

5. D

6. A

7. C

8. D

9. B

10. B

Chapter 8

1.   C

2.   B, C, F, and G

3.   A

4.   B and D

5.   B

6.   D

7.   B

8.   B

9.   B

10. B

Chapter 9

1.   B and C

2.   A

3.   D

4.   D

5.   C

6.   C

7.   D

8.   B

9.   B

10. C

Index

Numerics

A

B

G

J-K-L

M

W-X-Y-Z

Safari®
BOOKS ONLINE
ENABLED

THIS BOOK IS SAFARI ENABLED

INCLUDES FREE 45-DAY ACCESS TO THE ONLINE EDITION

The Safari® Enabled icon on the cover of your favorite technology book means the book is available through Safari Bookshelf. When you buy this book, you get free access to the online edition for 45 days.

Safari Bookshelf is an electronic reference library that lets you easily search thousands of technical books, find code samples, download chapters, and access technical information whenever and wherever you need it.

TO GAIN 45-DAY SAFARI ENABLED ACCESS TO THIS BOOK:

- Go to **http://www.informit.com/onlineedition**
- Complete the brief registration form
- Enter the coupon code found in the front of this book before the "Contents at a Glance" page

If you have difficulty registering on Safari Bookshelf or accessing the online edition, please e-mail customer-service@safaribooksonline.com.

Safari Library
Subscribe Now!
http://safari.ciscopress.com/library

Safari's entire technology collection is now available with no restrictions. Imagine the value of being able to search and access thousands of books, videos, and articles from leading technology authors whenever you wish.

EXPLORE TOPICS MORE FULLY

Gain a more robust understanding of related issues by using Safari as your research tool. With Safari Library you can leverage the knowledge of the world's technology gurus. For one flat, monthly fee, you'll have unrestricted access to a reference collection offered nowhere else in the world—all at your fingertips.

With a Safari Library subscription, you'll get the following premium services:

●●> **Immediate access to the newest, cutting-edge books**—Approximately eighty new titles are added per month in conjunction with, or in advance of, their print publication.

●●> **Chapter downloads**—Download five chapters per month so you can work offline when you need to.

●●> **Rough Cuts**—A service that provides online access to prepublication information on advanced technologies. Content is updated as the author writes the book. You can also download Rough Cuts for offline reference

●●> **Videos**—Premier design and development videos from training and e-learning expert lynda.com and other publishers you trust.

●●> **Cut and paste code**—Cut and paste code directly from Safari. Save time. Eliminate errors.

●●> **Save up to 35% on print books**—Safari Subscribers receive a discount of up to 35% on publishers' print books.

Books Online

Addison Wesley

AdobePress

ALPHA

lynda.com

Cisco Press

FT Press
FINANCIAL TIMES

O'REILLY

Microsoft Press

New Riders

que

Peachpit Press

PRENTICE HALL

Wharton School Publishing

Redbooks

SAMS

IBM Press

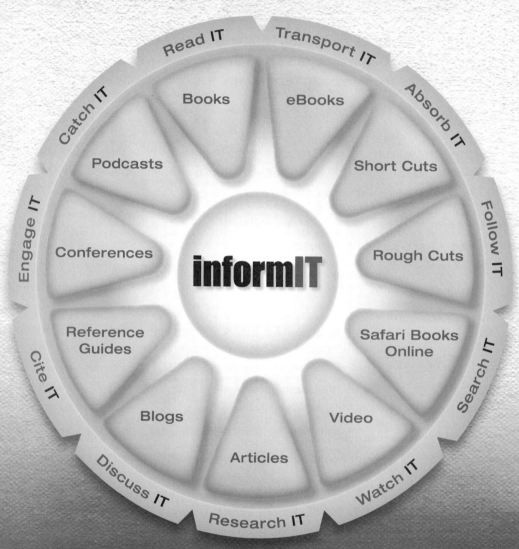